Beginning
Essentials
in Early Childhood Education

Join us on the web at
EarlyChildEd.delmar.com

Beginning
Essentials
in Early Childhood Education

Ann Miles Gordon • Kathryn Williams Browne

THOMSON

DELMAR LEARNING

Australia Canada Mexico Singapore Spain United Kingdom United States

THOMSON
DELMAR LEARNING

Beginning Essentials in Early Childhood Education
by Ann Miles Gordon and Kathryn Williams Browne

Vice President, Career Education SBU:
Dawn Gerrain

Director of Learning Solutions:
Sherry Dickinson

Managing Editor:
Robert L. Serenka, Jr.

Senior Acquisitions Editor:
Erin O'Connor

Editorial Assistant:
Stephanie Kelly

Director of Production:
Wendy A. Troeger

Production Manager:
J.P. Henkel

Production Editor:
Joy Kocsis

Production Assistant:
Angela Iula

Technology Project Manager:
Sandy Charette

Director of Marketing:
Wendy E. Mapstone

Channel Manager:
Kristin McNary

Cover Design:
Joseph Villanova

Composition:
Graphic World Inc.

Cover Image:
© Getty Images, Inc.

Any additional questions about permissions can be submitted by email to thomsonrights@thomson.com

Library of Congress Cataloging-in-Publication Data

Gordon, Ann Miles.
  Beginning essentials in early childhood education / Ann Miles Gordon, Kathryn Williams Browne.
     p. cm.
  Includes bibliographical references and index.
  ISBN-10: 1-4180-1133-9
  ISBN-13: 978-1-4180-1133-8
  1. Early childhood education. 2. Early childhood education—Curricula. 3. Child development.
  I. Browne, Kathryn Williams. II. Title.
  LB1139.23.G6627 2007
  372.21--dc22

                                        2005035606

NOTICE TO THE READER

Contents

Preface

What are "essentials"? They are the absolute, basic, and indispensable elements that create a foundation for learning. *Beginning Essentials in Early Childhood Education* is a brand new book that gives students that underlying basis for teaching young children. Although this book builds on the success of the authors' text, *Beginnings and Beyond: Foundations in Early Childhood Education,* there are significant differences. Most importantly, this book serves different needs for different users.

Some course descriptions for an introductory text include curriculum; some do not. Some instructors want more technology; some do not. Some courses are taught for a semester, some for a quarter, and some are shorter courses such as a summer or an intersession period. For these reasons, instructors and students are looking for a distilled version of early childhood education (ECE) fundamentals, one that is less comprehensive in scope but still focused on the essential components for use in an introductory course in early childhood education.

Beginning Essentials in Early Childhood Education addresses the five key elements in preparing students for an early childhood care: the history of ECE, current issues in the field, knowledge of the young child, the roles and responsibilities of the teachers, and the dynamics of environment and curriculum. Two core differences between *Beginning Essentials* and *Beginnings and Beyond* create a new approach for this book:

1. History and current issues are combined in one chapter to give the student a sense of progression and a feel for subjects that are being discussed today. Curriculum is seen as "development in action," rather than curriculum planning by subject or topic. The teacher's role, skills, and development will be supported by age group examples from birth through age eight. Students who are beginning to teach or who are at the early part of a major or certificate in child study will find these combinations helpful. The past and present are woven into a smooth story with four key themes: the importance of childhood, social reform, transmitting values, and professionalism.

2. The daily challenges of planning curriculum are described in a condensed and coherent fashion. Examples of infant/toddlers, preschoolers, kindergartners, and school-age children are included in every chapter so the student or teacher can connect with whatever age group interests him or her.

The primary audience for *Beginnings Essentials in Early Childhood Education* includes:

- ✪ beginning and continuing early childhood students
- ✪ students in introduction to early childhood education courses and core courses for the field of child care
- ✪ individuals in intersession courses, short courses, or high school courses

The authors began this collaboration 30 years ago, and their original purpose still stands in *Beginning Essentials in Early Childhood Education*—to promote the competence and effectiveness of new teachers through a presentation of basic knowledge, skills, attitudes, and philosophies, based on the premise that new teachers must have opportunities to learn fundamental skills as they begin their teaching experience. *Beginning* to teach and understand young children requires learning the *essentials*.

Recent trends in the field suggest the need for a basic foundational introductory text. There is a greater use of technology on the part of the student learner, and *Beginning Essentials in Early Childhood Education* reinforces that reality. Child care is "coming of age" as it develops a set of technical skills and knowledge base of its own as a profession. In addition, the impact of legislation such as *No Child Left Behind* and *Head Start/Grow Smart*, which call for greater accountability for young children's development of academic skills, further enhances the need for a text that addresses the most important basic concepts and issues.

The early childhood education field is always in flux and requires teaching materials that reflect current issues and changes:

- ✪ There continues to be a new appreciation for the implications of brain research on quality experiences for young children. *Beginning Essentials in Early Childhood Education* demonstrates the relationship between brain research and its classroom application.

- ✪ "Universal preschool" is on the agenda throughout the nation and creates a need for more early childhood professionals who are well trained and qualified to teach this age range. In some states, such as California, lead teachers will need a bachelor of arts degree by 2010 to work in programs that are run by the state. *Beginning Essentials in Early Childhood Education* provides the necessary foundation for training teachers.

- ✪ The acceptance of multiple intelligences (MI) theory has given further support for individualizing an early childhood program and has highlighted the importance for instructors to use MI with adult learners as well. *Beginning Essentials in Early Childhood Education* demonstrates this approach through a variety of pedagogic devices that involve the student learner.

- ✪ Assessment and accountability for children and for teachers are topics of current interest. Instructors are being challenged to organize and teach courses based on student learning outcomes. Teachers are being required to document children's learning and assess their skills. An outgrowth of assessment issues is a parallel concern that children's programs are becoming more academic, becoming more inappropriately imbalanced toward cognitive development. *Beginning Essentials in Early Childhood Education* provides a context of developmentally appropriate practices (DAP) and applications throughout the text.

- ✪ Developmentally appropriate principles and practices continue to need definition and interpretation. These become a frame of reference for defining developmentally appropriate programs that respond to children's interests as well as their needs. *Beginning Essentials in Early Childhood Education* emphasizes the importance of creating programs based on an understanding of the nature of the child and the factors affecting a child's growth.

✪ The ongoing influence of the schools of Reggio Emilia provides an opportunity for students to examine an exemplary early childhood program. In *Beginning Essentials in Early Childhood Education*, students will consider the applications of the Reggio model to their own teaching philosophy and practice.

The authors' conceptual approach to *Beginning Essentials in Early Childhood Education* is to embed the content with a multicultural approach to teaching and learning based on the belief that every child and every family are unique and deserve the respect and affirmation of their cultural identity. The aim is to help prospective teachers and caregivers increase their sensitivity to different cultural practices and values. Equally as important is to provide a text that demonstrates DAP in theory and practice. This emphasis is woven throughout the text and is highlighted for immediate recognition.

The authors believe in interactive education for adult learners as well as young children and offer ways to involve adult students throughout the text. Learning takes place when students are able to connect the written word and reflect on their own experiences.

The organization of *Beginning Essentials in Early Childhood Education* is user-friendly, with four sections reflecting the central themes:

Section 1 defines the field. The first chapter outlines past history and current issues. A second chapter describes the variety and diversity of early childhood programs.

Section 2 describes the nature of young children. One chapter is devoted to identifying various age levels and their characteristics, and the second chapter describes the various develop-mental and learning theories on which knowledge of children is based.

Section 3 defines and elaborates the teacher's role. A chapter on teaching as a professional commitment sets the stage for the next three chapters on observing and assessing children, guiding children's behavior, and the partnership between teachers and families.

Section 4 reflects on what is being taught. The intentional use of the environment as a teaching strategy is explored in the first chapter. The second chapter explores the basic elements of creating curriculum, and the final chapter outlines development in action, the result of curriculum planning and responsive teaching.

Special features of *Beginning Essentials in Early Childhood Education* include:

✪ *Key terms.* Key terminology is listed at the end of each chapter and bolded on first introduction, highlighting those terms that are most important for student retention.

✪ *Our Diverse World*, a footnote at the bottom of the page, provides additional information to enrich students' understanding of cultural pluralism and inclusion. A primary function of Our Diverse World is to help students learn that the children they teach will have to interact in new and different ways with others in a world grown small.

✪ *What Do You Think?* In each chapter students are invited to reflect on the topic, which is highlighted and boxed, and its relationship to their own life and learning.

✪ *Questions for Thought.* Each chapter opens with several of these questions to prompt the student about the chapter's content.

- *Developmentally appropriate practice.* Throughout the text a DAP icon is used to highlight the applications of DAP. This provides students with a variety of insights and examples in the application of DAP in their learning.

- *Teaching applications.* At the end of each chapter students are provided with several activities that promote a greater understanding between what they read and the actual classroom application.

- *The use of technology.* A unique feature of this text is the Video View Points section that allows students and instructors to relate important chapter content to video clips provided on the CD at the back of the book. Critical thinking questions that tie to both the concepts presented in the book and the clips on the CD provide students with ample opportunities for reflection and to promote their development as future early childhood professionals.

ANCILLARY MATERIALS

CDs

The CDs contained in the back of this text include video clips of infants and toddlers, preschoolers, and school-age children in a variety of early childhood settings and at different developmental stages. Disc one contains video clips of infants and toddlers and preschool-age children; disc two contains video clips of school-age children. Designed to integrate technology and early childhood education, this invaluable resource provides instructors and students with ample opportunities for reflection and personal and professional development. The Video View Points boxes found in each chapter can be used to connect the material presented in the text to the segments contained on the CDs. To view the video clips, place the appropriate CD in your computer, then select the age range (infants and toddlers, preschool, or school-age), then select the competency from the list that corresponds to the Video View Point for that chapter.

Online Companion™

The Online Companion™ to accompany *Beginning Essentials in Early Childhood Education* is your link to additional early childhood education resources on the Internet. This informative supplement is a Study Guide with chapter review questions, multiple choice quizzes with answers and rationales for correct and incorrect answers, relevant Web links, case studies with critical thinking questions, and additional student activities. The Online Companion™ can be found at www.earlychilded.delmar.com.

Instructor's Manual

An Instructor's Manual is available to accompany this text. It includes chapter outlines, review questions, key terms, additional readings, chapter summaries, teaching tips, and resource lists.

Computerized Test Bank

A computerized test bank on CD-ROM allows teachers to create student examinations composed of multiple choice, true/false, short answer, and completion questions for each chapter. The CD-ROM provides approximately 1,000 questions in addition to the following features:

- Multiple methods of question selection
- Multiple outputs (print ASCII and Rich Text Format)
- Graphic support
- Random questioning support
- Special character support

WebTutor™

The WebTutor™ to accompany *Beginning Essentials in Early Childhood Education* allows you to take learning beyond the classroom. This Online Courseware is designed to complement the text and benefits students in that it enables them to better manage their time, prepare for examinations, organize their notes, and more. Special features include:

- ✴ Chapter Learning Objectives correlated with textbook chapter objectives

- ✴ Online Course Preparation that lists what students should have read or done prior to using online content

- ✴ Study Sheets that outline the content of each chapter and contain notes. Study Sheets can be printed to help students learn and remember important points.

- ✴ A glossary that provides definitions for terms in each chapter or in the course as a whole

- ✴ Flash cards that allow students to test themselves on word definitions

- ✴ Discussion Topics posted to encourage use as a threaded bulletin board and as assignments to develop critical thinking skills

- ✴ FAQs that provide questions and answers that students may have about specific content

- ✴ Online Class Notes that provide additional information about the chapters

- ✴ Online Chapter Quizzes that are given in various formats including matching exercises, true/false quizzes, short-answer questions, and multiple-choice questions with immediate feedback for correct and incorrect answers. Multiple-choice questions also include rationales for right and wrong choices.

- ✴ Web links that provide students with practice searching the Web for information. Learners choose from a variety of Web links and report findings to their instructor through email.

A benefit for instructors as well as students, the WebTutor™ allows for online discussion with the instructor and other class members, real-time chat to enable virtual office hours and encourage collaborative learning environments, a calendar of syllabus information for easy reference, e-mail connections to facilitate communication among classmates and between students and instructors, and customization tools that help instructors tailor their course to fit their needs by adding or changing content.

WebTutor™ allows you to extend your reach beyond the classroom and is available on either WebCT or Blackboard platforms.

❋ ABOUT THE AUTHORS

Ann Gordon has been in the field of early childhood education for more than 40 years as a teacher of young children, a teacher of parents, and a teacher of college students. She has taught in laboratory schools, church-related centers, and private and public preschool and kindergarten programs. While at Stanford, Ann was a head teacher at the Bing Nursery School for 11 years and was a lecturer in the Psychology Department. For 10 years she also served as an adjunct faculty member in four colleges, teaching the full gamut of early childhood courses. Ann served as executive director of the National Association of Episcopal Schools for 14 years, where more than 1,100 early childhood programs were a part of her network. She is now consulting in the areas of early childhood curriculum governance and professional development. Ann is the mother of two grown children. As a doting grandmother, Ann now brings an enhanced perspective on infants and toddlers to *Beginning Essentials in Early Childhood Education* as well as up-to-date experience with center-based child care. She is delighted that her granddaughters were and are enrolled in an NAEYC-accredited center.

Kathryn Williams Browne has been a teacher most of her adult life: a teacher of young children for nearly 20 years, a guide for parents of the families she served, a parent educator since 1990, and, currently, an instructor of college students for more than 15 years. Her work with children includes nursery school, parent cooperatives, full-day child care, prekindergarten and bilingual preschools, and kindergarten and first grade. Kate's background in child development research led her to choose early childhood education, for to truly understand child development one needs to *be* with children. While a Head Teacher at Bing Nursery School and a lecturer with Stanford University, Kate developed a professional relationship with Ann, which blossomed into working together in teacher and parent education. Moreover, *Beginning Essentials in Early Childhood Education* has been influenced by Kate's role as a parent; her two children were born during the first two editions, so the book grew along with them. Recent work as a consultant and public elementary School Board Trustee offered Kate new perspectives into schools, reform, and collaboration. Perhaps most important, Kate has been teaching in community colleges for 15 years. Working closely with her students, she has been given constructive insights that inform this text in every revision. The balance of career and family, of work with children and for children, and of the special challenges of the early childhood profession guide her work.

Ann and Kate are also co-authors of *Beginnings and Beyond: Foundations in Early Childhood Education*, 6th Edition (2004), and *Guiding Young Children in a Diverse Society* (Allyn & Bacon, 1996).

ACKNOWLEDGMENTS

The authors wish to thank the usual suspects: their husbands and families for their support and patience. Muchas gracias to Campbell Browne and Felicity Gordon for superb computer/technical assistance. We are ever grateful to Kay Bishop for exceptional hospitality and provision of working space. How can you not be inspired when looking out at the Golden Gate Bridge? To our reviewers, whose valuable feedback and suggestions helped to shape the final text, we owe special thanks:

Audrey Beard, Ed.D.
   Albany State University
   Albany, GA

Mary Cordell, M.Ed.
   Navarro College
   Corsicana, TX

Leann Curry, Ph.D.
   Midwestern State University
   Wichita Falls, TX

Christina Howell, Ph.D.
   California State University-Bakersfield
   Bakersfield, CA

Sheri Leafgren, M.Ed.
   Kent State University
   Kent, OH

Patricia Weaver, M.Ed.
   Fayetteville Technical Community College
   Fayetteville, NC

Alan Weber, M.S.
   Suffolk County Community College
   Selden, NY

Section 1

What Is the Field of Early Childhood Education?

History and Current Issues of Early Childhood Education

QUESTIONS FOR THOUGHT

What is the field of early childhood education?

What are the basic themes in early childhood education?

What are the major historical influences?

What are the major issues facing early childhood educators today?

How do the themes of our field get expressed in our history and our present challenges?

INTRODUCTION TO THE FIELD

Early childhood education is a rich and exciting field. The story of its development is also the chronicle of courageous people who took steps toward improving children's lives. Critical events of the past have had a hand in shaping today's issues. As the conditions of childhood and early education have changed through the centuries, so have its educators adapted to those challenges.

Over the past 50 years, early childhood education has evolved from being an option for middle-class preschool children to a necessity for millions of families with children from infancy through the primary years, and is a reflection of the economic, social, and political climate of the time. Changes in education historically have been linked to societal reform and upheaval and have signaled a new level of **professionalism** and training for teachers and family child care providers.

Issues of today and trends for tomorrow grow out of the problems and solutions of the past. It is appropriate to discuss current questions in light of what we learn from the history of the early childhood profession. For all its diverse and varied roots, the field has had a consistent commitment to four basic themes:

- the ethic of social reform
- the importance of childhood
- transmitting values
- professionalism

These four themes are reflected in what has gone on before us and in the major issues facing early childhood educators today.

New models are forged through necessity and innovation, changing what we know about children and their care and education. The energies of many on behalf of children have produced bold ideas, creative models, even contrary beliefs and practices. Across the globe and through the centuries, the education of young children has evolved. In this chapter, you will learn about our profession, its history and the issues of today. Appendix A puts this history into a timeline.

Why History?

Most early childhood education students and many educators know little about the origins of their chosen profession. Although the names of Rousseau, Froebel, Montessori, and Dewey may not seem significant, being familiar with your professional history and using it to inform your teaching practice is important. The past links us to the present.

Support

There is a sense of support that comes from knowing that history. For instance, works of Socrates, Plato, and Aristotle are part of the philosophical foundation on which our educational practices are built. Schools in ancient Greece and Rome taught literature, the arts, and science. One can see how traditional early childhood practices reflect and reinforce the European values and beliefs.[1] Looking beyond the dominant culture, we find that both oral and written records exist describing education in Africa, particularly about those cultures found in the Nile Valley (Hilliard, 1997). Teachers must educate

[1] To honor diversity, all perspectives deserve a place in our history. Educators can focus on many cultures, thus broadening everyone's viewpoints.

themselves about the culturally diverse roots of early educational practices.

Inspiration

Knowing that early childhood education philosophy has deep roots can be an inspiration and helps teachers develop professional expression. The ideas expressed by past educators help develop better methods of teaching. Looking at history gives an overview of how various children and their learning were viewed based on the religious, political, and economic pressures of the time.

Identity and Commitment

"Doing history" renews our sense of identity and commitment to our profession. As early childhood educators, each of us accepts the mission that is central to our field: We are committed to enhancing the education, development, and well-being of young children. We also get in touch with our own early childhood and education, thus connecting us to the children of long ago—ourselves—and those we care for every day.

At the same time, in learning about our profession's history, we must recognize that it is a reflection of certain cultural norms. Remember that the voices you hear in these chapters aren't from on high. Learn to be particularly cautious of theories or opinions claimed to be "universal American practices"; often, cross-cultural research shows that such practices are a reflection of some, but not all, cultural norms. For instance, schools of the past were overwhelmingly created for boys and young men. The gender bias of past practices added to the underdevelopment of girls and women and prevails today in some parts of the world. Educational opportunity was denied to people of color or poverty; lower social and economic classes thus had restricted access to education. By understanding the concept of institutional

what do YOU think?

Do you currently work in a center or family child care setting? What is its history? Which people or ideas inform the school's approach? Who of the historical figures in this chapter influences you as you arrange the environment? plan the curriculum? interact with children and their families?

as well as individual oppression, teachers can begin to examine their own notions and become "critical consumers" of information, from both the past and the present.

A Broad Base

There is more than one right way to educate young children. Every culture has had and still does have the task of socializing and educating their young. The written record may document several educational philosophies, and there is no single monopoly on ideas about children. Moreover, other disciplines (medicine, elementary education, and psychology) also inform early childhood teaching.

Defining the Terms

We define *early childhood* as the period of life from infancy through age eight. The term *early childhood education* refers to group settings deliberately intended to effect developmental changes in young children. *Early childhood programs* include group settings for infants through the primary years of elementary school, kindergarten through grade three. *Early childhood educators* are those professionals who build bridges between a child's two worlds, school (or group experience) and home. It is during these years that the foundation for future learning is set; these are the building-block years, during which a child learns to walk, talk, establish an identity, print, and count. In later years, that same child builds on these skills to be able to climb mountains, speak a second language, learn to express and negotiate, write in cursive, and understand multiplication.

INFLUENCES FROM ABROAD

It is impossible to pinpoint the origins of humankind because there are few records from millions of years ago. Some preparation for adult life was done informally, mostly through imitation. As language developed, communication occurred. Children learned dances, rituals, and ceremonies, and both boys and girls were taught skills for their respective roles in the tribe. Ancient historical documents seem to indicate that child-rearing practices were somewhat crude; DeMause (1974) even suggests that the further one goes back in history, the more likely it is that one will find abandonment and brutality.

The definition of *childhood* has varied greatly throughout history. For example, in ancient times children were considered adults by age seven. A society's definition of childhood influences how it educates its children. In the Western world, teachings of the Bible and the church gave education a religious emphasis. During the Renaissance and Reformation, children were seen as pure and good, all worthy of basic education.[1]

The printing press made books more available to the common person. Martin Luther (1482–1546) urged parents to educate their children by teaching them morals and catechism. The call for a *universal education and literacy* began. Skilled craftsmen formed a kind of middle class, and by the 1500s, reading, writing, arithmetic, and bookkeeping were fairly common school subjects throughout Europe. A timeline for early childhood education can be found in Appendix A.

The pioneers of our field gave voice to both the predominant ideas about children and new views for the time period. Many died before realizing their impact on teaching and learning; all give us insight into childhood and education.

Comenius

John Amos Comenius (1592–1670), a Czech educator, wrote the first picture book for children. Called *Orbis Pictus* (*The World of Pictures,* 1658), it was a guide for teachers that included training of the senses and the study of nature. Comenius believed that "in all the operations of nature, development is from within," so children should be allowed to learn at their own pace. Teachers should work with children's own inclinations, for "what is natural takes place without compulsion." This idea was later reflected in Montessori's "sensitive periods" and Piaget's "stages of development." Today it is recognized as the issue of **school readiness.**

Comenius also stressed a basic concept that is now taken for granted: *learning by doing.* He encouraged parents to let their children play with other children of the same age. He also reflected the growing social reform that would educate the poor as well as the rich.

Summary: *Probably the three most significant contributions of Comenius are books with illustrations, an emphasis on education with the senses, and the social reform potential of education.*

[1] Keep in mind how much of the research and history in our field has a race, class, and gender bias (i.e., the tendency to be based on the experiences of, writings about, and research on white, middle- to upper-class males.)

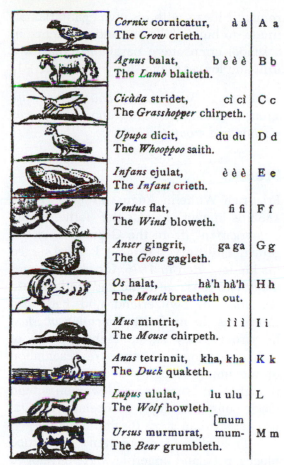

Cornix cornicatur, The *Crow* crieth.	à à	A a
Agnus balat, The *Lamb* blaiteth.	b è è è	B b
Cicàda stridet, The *Grasshopper* chirpeth.	cì cì	C c
Upupa dicit, The *Whooppoo* saith.	du du	D d
Infans ejulat, The *Infant* crieth.	è è è	E e
Ventus flat, The *Wind* bloweth.	fi fi	F f
Anser gingrit, The *Goose* gagleth.	ga ga	G g
Os halat, The *Mouth* breatheth out.	hà'h hà'h	H h
Mus mintrit, The *Mouse* chirpeth.	î î î	I i
Anas tetrinnit, The *Duck* quaketh.	kha, kha	K k
Lupus ululat, The *Wolf* howleth.	lu ulu	L
Ursus murmurat, The *Bear* grumbleth.	[mum mum-	M m

Orbis Pictus, by John Comenius, is considered the first picture book written for children.

Locke

An English philosopher, John Locke (1632–1714) is considered to be the founder of modern educational philosophy. He based his theory of education on the scientific method and the study of the mind and learning. Locke proposed the concept of **tabula rasa,** the belief that the child is born neutral, rather than good or evil, and is a "clean slate" on which the experiences of parents, society, education, and the world are written. He based his theory on the Scientific Method and was one of the first European educators to discuss the idea of individual differences gleaned from observing one child rather than simply teaching a group.

Because Locke believed that the purpose of education is to make man a reasoning creature, a working knowledge of the Bible and a counting ability sufficient to conduct business was fundamental. Locke suggested that instruction should be pleasant, with playful activities as well as drills. Today, teachers still emphasize a sensory approach to learning.

Summary: *Locke's contribution is felt most in our acceptance of individual differences, in giving children reasons for what they are being taught, and in the theory of a "clean slate," which emphasizes the effect of the environment on learning.*

Rousseau

Jean Jacques Rousseau (1712–1778), a writer and philosopher, believed that children were not inherently evil, but naturally good. He is best known for his book *Emile* (1761), in which he raised a hypothetical child to adulthood. Rousseau's ideas on education in and of themselves were nothing short of revolutionary for the times. They include the following:

- The true object of education should not be primarily vocational.

- Children really learn only from first-hand information.

- Children's view of the external world is quite different from that of adults.

- There are distinct phases of development of a child's mind and these should coincide with the various stages of education.

Rousseau thought that the school atmosphere should be very flexible to meet the needs of children and insisted on using concrete teaching materials, leaving the abstract and symbolic for later years. Pestalozzi, Froebel, and Montessori were greatly influenced by him. The theories of developmental stages, such as those of Jean

Piaget and Arnold Gesell (see Chapter 4), support Rousseau's idea of natural development.

Summary: *Free play, the child's inherent goodness, the ability to choose for oneself, and using concrete materials for young children are still cornerstones of developmentally appropriate curriculum in the early years.*

Pestalozzi

Johann Heinrich Pestalozzi (1746–1827) was a Swiss educator whose principles focused on how to teach basic skills and the idea of "caring" as well as "educating" the child. Pestalozzi stressed the idea of the **integrated curriculum** that would develop the whole child; education was to be of the hand, the head, and the heart. Teachers were to guide self-activity through intuition, exercise, and the senses. He differed from Rousseau in that he proposed teaching children in groups rather than using a tutor with an individual child. Pestalozzi's works *How Gertrude Teaches Her Children* and *Book for Mothers* detailed some procedures for mothers to use at home with their children. Probably his greatest contribution is the blending of Rousseau's strong romantic ideals with his own egalitarian attitude, to build skills and independence in a school atmosphere paralleling that of a firm and loving home.

Summary: *Pestalozzi's contributions are strongest around the integration of the curriculum and group teaching.*

Froebel

Friedrich Wilhelm August Froebel (1782–1852) is known to us as the "father of the kindergarten" (from the German *kinder + garten,* **"children's garden"**). Froebel started his kindergarten in 1836, for children ages about two to six, after he had studied with Pestalozzi in Switzerland and had read Comenius. In his book *Education of Man,* he wrote: "Play is the highest phase of child development—the representation of the inner necessity and impulse." He thought that both men and women should teach young children, as friendly facilitators rather than stern disciplinarians.

Froebel's kindergartens included blocks, pets, and fingerplays. He developed the first educational toys, which he termed "gifts," objects that demonstrate various attributes (such as color or size), and

Early kindergartens were patterned after Froebel's idea that early education should be pleasant. ©2002. Froebel Foundation.

arranged them in a special order that would assist the child's development. His theories influenced Montessori and were reflected in the educational materials she developed.

Summary: *Worldwide, teachers practice the Froebelian belief that a child's first educational experiences should be a garden: full of pleasant discoveries and delightful adventure, where the adults' role is to plant ideas and materials for children to use as they grow at their own pace.*

Montessori

At the turn of the 19th and 20th centuries, Maria Montessori (1870–1952) became the first female physician in Italy. She worked in the slums of Rome with poor children and with mentally retarded children. Sensing that what they lacked was proper motivation and environment, she opened a preschool, Casa di Bambini, in 1907. Her first class was composed of 50 children from two to five years of age. The children were at the center all day while their parents worked. They were fed two meals a day, given a bath, and provided medical attention. Montessori designed materials, classrooms, and a teaching procedure that proved her point to the astonishment of people all over Europe and America.

The Montessori concept is both a philosophy of child development and a plan for guiding growth. In the early years, Montessori held, children pass through "sensitive periods," in which their curiosity makes them ready for acquiring certain skills and knowledge. Montessori was an especially observant person and believed that a carefully **prepared environment** would help every child learn. By focusing on the *sequential steps of learning,* Montessori developed a set of learning materials still used widely today. Her procedures as well as her materials contain **self-correcting** features.

After Montessori was introduced in the United States in 1909, her methods received poor reception and were often misunderstood. Today, the majority of Montessori schools are private preschools and child care centers, serving three- to six-year-old children. But there are many that also serve elementary students, and a small (but growing) number of programs are for infants and toddlers.

Summary: *Montessori's contributions were substantial to all we do in early childhood programs today. A prepared environment, self-correcting and sequential materials, and a trust in children's innate drive to learn all stem from her work. For more information on Montessori programs, see Chapter 2.*

Steiner

Rudolf Steiner (1861–1925) was a German educator whose method is known today as the Waldorf School of Education. This system has influenced mainstream education in Europe, and its international reputation is being felt in American early childhood programs today. Steiner theorized that childhood is a phase of life important in its own right. It has three periods: that of the "will" (0–7 years), the "heart," or feelings (7–14 years), and the "head," or a fusion of the spirit and the body (14 years on). Early childhood is the period of the will, and the environment must be carefully planned to protect and nurture the child.

Steiner's philosophy emphasized children's spiritual development, imagination, and creative gifts. As did Froebel and Montessori, Steiner emphasized the whole child and believed that different areas of development and learning were connected into a kind of unity. Self-discipline emerges from the child's natural willingness to learn and initiate, so adult role-model experiences in early childhood must be carefully selected. For instance, fairy stories help children acquire time-honored wisdom; modern Waldorf followers insist that television be eliminated.

Summary: *For Steiner, the environment and people with whom the child interacts are of central importance. Waldorf schools are discussed in Chapter 2.*

Nontraditional Perspectives

Traditional early childhood educational practices reinforce European-American values and beliefs. But there have always been other influences on child-rearing and educational practices. There are many ways to care for and educate children and nontraditional perspectives that influenced early childhood education.[1]

Information about non-Western early childhood history is not easily accessible; Gonzalez-Mena (2001) summarizes some of these perspectives in this way:

- Historically, attitudes toward childhood in China and Japan were influenced by Confucius' writings (551–479 B.C.), which stressed harmony. Children were seen as good and worthy of respect, a view not held in Europe until more recently.

- Native American writings show close ties and interconnectedness, not only among families and within tribes but also between people and nature. Teaching children about relationships and interconnectedness are historical themes of early education among many indigenous peoples.

- Strong **kinship networks** are themes among both Africans and African-Americans; people bond together and pool resources for the common good. Whether these contemporary tendencies come from ancient roots, historic oppression, modern oppression, or all three remains unclear.

Summary: *As teachers and caregivers, we have an obligation to connect each child to the learning process in meaningful ways (see Chapter 2 and the National Association for the Education of Young Children Code of Ethics in Appendix B). To do this, we need to know the history of many nontraditional perspectives and gain a working knowledge of the variations in attitudes and child-rearing practices. Learning about nontraditional cultures and behaviors honors diversity (see Chapter 3).*

AMERICAN INFLUENCES

Colonial Days

The American educational system began in the colonies. The one-room schoolhouse was the mainstay of education in colonial New England. Children were sent to school primarily for religious reasons. The Bible was used in school, as was the New England Primer and Horn Book. In the South, it was a different story. Plantation owners imported tutors from England or opened small private schools to teach just their sons to read and write. By affirming fundamental principles of democratic liberty, the founders of the United States paved the way for a system of free, common, public school systems, the first the world had seen. However, after the Revolutionary War, there were no significant advances in education until the late 1800s. Although public schools were accepted in principle, in reality no tax basis was established to support them.

[1] We must be careful in our assumptions of what we think is good or right for young children. A wider view of history reveals that there are many "right" ways, and much that is "good" comes from sharing our diverse viewpoints.

Children in Enslavement

The first African-Americans were indentured servants, whose repayment of their debts by servitude would buy them their freedom. However, by 1620 Africans were being brought to the so-called New World as slaves. Prior to the Civil War, education was severely limited for African-Americans. Formal schools were scarce, and most education came through the establishment of "Sabbath schools."[1]

As part of religious instruction, slaves were often provided literary training. However, many plantation owners found these schools threatening and banned them by making laws prohibiting the teaching of slaves. Another facility then developed, that of the "midnight school." Because of its necessary secretive existence, few records are available, although it is reasonable to conclude that the curriculum was similar to that of the prohibited Sabbath schools.

After the Civil War, private and public schools were opened for African-Americans. Major colleges and universities were founded by the end of the 1800s. Booker T. Washington, born into slavery, founded the Tuskegee Normal and Industrial Institute in Alabama in 1881 and emphasized practical education and intercultural understanding between the races as a path to liberation. Many former slaves and graduates established schools for younger children. Hampton Institute established a laboratory kindergarten for African-Americans in Virginia in 1873, and by the turn of the century was offering a kindergarten training school and courses in child care.[2]

Summary: *Education for African-Americans was difficult and unevenly accessible. Generally, if the schools accepted African-Americans at all, it was on a strict quota. Thus, as the early childhood education movement began to grow and expand in the years following the Civil War, it grew along separate color lines.*

John Dewey and the Progressive Movement

By the end of the 1800s a nationwide reform movement had begun. The Progressive Movement (see section later in the chapter) received its direction primarily through one individual, John Dewey (1858–1952). Dewey was the first real native-born influence on education in the United States and had one of the greatest impacts on American education of all time. He believed that children were valuable and that childhood was an important part of their lives. Like Froebel, he felt that education should be integrated with life and should provide a training ground for cooperative living.

As did Pestalozzi and Rousseau, Dewey felt that schools should focus on the nature of the child. Until this time, childhood was considered of little consequence. Children as young as seven were a regular part of the workforce—on the farms, in the mines, and in the factories. To Dewey, children's interests were of the utmost importance. A teacher's responsibility was to build the subject matter around those interests. Dewey's beliefs about children and learning are summarized in Figure 1–1.

[1] Although great strides have been made in providing public education for all children in the United States, remember that inequities based on color, linguistic ability, and social class continue to exist.

[2] It would be worth investigating whether all the laboratory schools for African-Americans copied European models, as did those of most American universities, or reflected some African influences.

The Hampton Institute in Virginia established a laboratory school for nursery and kindergarten in the late 1800s. (Courtesy of Hampton University Archives.)

My Pedagogic Creed—John Dewey	What It Means Today
1. ". . . I believe that only true education comes through the stimulation of the child's powers by the demands of the social situations in which he finds himself."	This tells us that children learn to manage themselves in groups, to make and share friendship, to solve problems, and to cooperate.
2. ". . . The child's own instinct and powers furnish the material and give the starting point for all education."	We need to create a place that is child-centered, a place that values the skills and interests of each child and each group.
3. ". . . I believe that education, therefore, is a process of living and not a preparation for future living."	Prepare the child for what is to come by enriching and interpreting the present to him. Find educational implications in everyday experiences.
4. ". . . I believe that . . . the school life should grow gradually out of the home life . . . it is the business of the school to deepen and extend . . . the child's sense of the values bound up in his home life."	This sets the rationale for a relationship between teachers and parents. Values established and created in the home should be enhanced by teaching in the schools.
5. ". . . I believe, finally, that the teacher is engaged, not simply in the training of individuals, but in the formation of a proper social life. I believe that every teacher should realize the dignity of his calling."	This says that the work teachers do is important and valuable. They teach more than academic content; they teach how to live.

FIGURE 1–1 John Dewey expressed his ideas about education in an important document titled *My Pedagogic Creed* (Washington, DC: The Progressive Education Association, 1897).

Summary: *Dewey's child-centered schools are a model of child care centers and family child care homes, as learning and living are inseparable. As the following sections on kindergarten and nursery schools illustrate, John Dewey had a vision that is still alive today.*

✺ THE FIELD EXPANDS

Kindergarten

The word **kindergarten** is a delightful term, bringing to mind the image of young seedlings on the verge of blossoming. The first kindergarten was a German school started by Froebel in 1837. Nearly 20 years later, in 1856, Margaretha Schurz, a student of Froebel's, opened the first kindergarten in the United States and inspired Elizabeth Peabody (1804–1894) of Boston to open the first English-speaking kindergarten there in 1860. In 1873 Susan Blow (1843–1916) opened the first kindergarten in the United States that was associated with the public schools.

Looking at the kindergarten in historical perspective, it is interesting to trace its various purposes. During the initial period in this country (1856–1890), Froebel's philosophy remained the mainstay of kindergarten education. At the same time, kindergartens began to become an instrument of social reform. Called *charity kindergartens,* teachers conducted a morning class for about 15 children and made social (and welfare) calls on families during the afternoon. By early 1900 traditional kindergarten ideas had come under the scrutiny of G. Stanley Hall and others, who were interested in a scientific approach to education, and of Dewey, who also advocated a community-like (rather than garden-style) classroom. In an era of rising social conscience, helping the less fortunate became a "cause," much like the conditions that led to the creation of Head Start in the 1960s.

By the 1970s, a trend was developing for kindergarten to focus on the intellectual development of the child; thus, a programmatic shift placed more emphasis on academic goals for the five-year-old. In the 1990s, the concept of **developmentally appropriate practices** advocated a shift toward more holistic, broad planning for kindergarten, as well as cultural and family responsiveness. Currently, worksheets and teacher-directed instruction are again on the rise. Today, the kindergarten is found in some form in nearly every country of the world. Although the content of the program and the length of the day vary widely in the United States, kindergarten is available in every one of the states.

 Summary: *Kindergarten continues today to model its historical contrasting philosophies of Froebelian ideals (preferring teacher-directed free play) and of Dewey (advocating child-initiated projects). Moreover, as education for five-year-olds as they enter formal schooling, kindergarten is the stage for a clash between developmental play and academic preparation.*

Patty Smith Hill

Patty Smith Hill (1868–1946) of Teacher's College, Columbia University, was an outstanding innovator of the time and one of the Progressive Movement's most able leaders. It was she who wrote the song "Happy Birthday" and founded the National Association for Nursery Education, known today as the National Association for the Education of Young Children (NAEYC). Trained originally in the Froebelian tradition, she worked closely with G. Stanley Hall and later with John Dewey. She advocated free choice and a relevant curriculum. She expanded the Froebelian focus on small-motor work to include large-muscle equipment for climbing and construction. She also urged that kindergarten and first grade be merged so that both

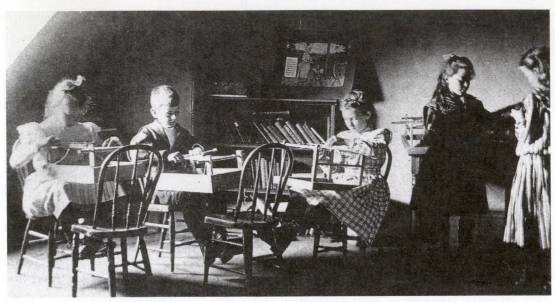

John Dewey's laboratory school involved children in activities of a practical, real-life nature, such as weaving small rugs to use in the classroom. (Special thanks to Sheila Roper of MacClintock Photo Collection, Special Collections, Morris Library, Southern Illinois University at Carbondale.)

groups would have independent, creative activity before formal academic instruction.

 Summary: *Patty Smith Hill helped merge several educational philosophies. Her ideas became the backbone of American kindergarten practice.*

Nursery Schools

Establishment in America

The very phrase *nursery school* conjures up images of a child's nursery, a gentle place of play and growing. In fact, the name was coined to describe a place in which children were nurtured (see the section on the McMillan sisters). Early childhood educators took Dewey's philosophy to heart. By the 1920s and 1930s, early childhood education had reached a professional status in the United States. Nursery schools and day nurseries went beyond custodial health care. They fostered the child's total development. Their schools reflected the principles of a **child-centered approach,** active learning, and social cooperation. The children were enrolled from middle- and upper-class homes as well as from working-class families. However, until the 1960s, nursery schools served few poor families.[1]

Parent education was acknowledged as a vital function and led to the establishment of **parent cooperative schools.** The first of these parent participation schools was developed in 1915 at the University of Chicago (see Chapter 2). Research centers and child development laboratories were started in many colleges and universities from about 1915 to 1930. The preschool movement from the beginning was integrated with the movement for child development research. "The purpose was to improve nursery schools, and, therefore,

[1] A challenge to our profession is to create funding mechanisms to provide an early childhood education experience for all children and families—regardless of income.

we brought in the people who were studying children, who were learning more about them, so we could do a better job" (Hymes, 1978–79).

Laboratory schools attempted a multidisciplinary approach, blending the voices from psychology and education with those of home economics, nursing, social work, and medicine. By 1950, when Katherine Read (Baker) first published *The Nursery School: A Human Relationships Laboratory* (in its ninth printing and in seven languages), the emphasis of the nursery school was first on understanding human behavior, then on building programs, guidance techniques, and relationships accordingly. In her estimation, the nursery school was for children to learn as they played and shared experiences with others. It was also where adults could learn about child development and human relationships by observing and participating. She saw learning and teaching as inseparable processes.

The history of early childhood education includes contributions from many ethnic groups. San Francisco's Golden Gate Kindergarten Association has provided nursery education for the city's various neighborhoods from the turn of the century to the present.

Summary: *Nursery schools have always been a place of "care," of physical needs, intellectual stimulation, and the socioemotional aspects of young children's lives. Whether parent participation, a laboratory school, or a private, part-day program, nursery school is for everyone to be learning and teaching.*

Lucy Sprague Mitchell

Early childhood education in the United States grew out of Dewey's progressive movement largely because of Lucy Sprague Mitchell (1878–1967) and her contemporaries. Raised in an environment of educational and social reform, Mitchell developed the idea of schools as community centers as well as places for children to learn to think. She gathered together many talented people to build a school to implement and experiment with progressive principles, a teachers' college to promote them, and a workshop for writers of children's literature. Mitchell became a major contributor to the idea of educational experiments, teacher-planned curriculum experiences that would then be observed and analyzed for children's reactions.

Summary: *By establishing Bank Street College of Education (and its laboratory school), Lucy Sprague Mitchell emphasized the link between theory and practice, i.e., the education of young children and the study of how children learn are intrinsically tied together.*

Abigail Eliot

Abigail Eliot (1892–1992) is generally credited with bringing the nursery school movement to the United States. She had worked with the McMillan sisters (see section in this chapter) in the slums of London. As a social worker in Boston, she had visited many day nurseries and recalled them as places with "dull green walls, no light colors, nothing pretty—spotlessly clean places, with rows of white-faced listless little children sitting, doing nothing" (Hymes, 1978–79). She founded the Ruggles Street Nursery School, teaching children and providing teacher training, and was the first director until it was incorporated into Tufts University to become the Eliot-Pearson Department of Child Study. Eliot became the first woman to receive a doctoral degree from Harvard University's Graduate School of Education, and after retiring from Tufts moved to California, where she helped establish Pacific Oaks College.

Summary: *Abigail Eliot integrated Froebel's gifts, Montessori's equipment, and the McMillan sisters' fresh air and added an organized program. In her new nursery school, the children were active and choosing.*

Midcentury Developments

While the economic crisis of the Depression and the political turmoil of World War II diverted attention from children's needs, both gave focus to adult needs for work. Out of this necessity came the nurseries run by the Works Progress Administration (WPA) in the 1930s and the Lanham Act nurseries of the 1940s. The most renowned program of midcentury was the Kaiser Child Care Centers.

Kaiser Child Care Centers

During World War II, many mothers worked in war-related industries. An excellent model for child care operated from 1943 to 1945 in Portland, Oregon. The Kaiser Child Care Centers became the world's largest children's facility and functioned around the clock all year long. The centers were operated by the shipyards, not by the public schools or community agencies, with the cost borne by the Kaiser Company and by parents using the service. The center was at the entrance to the two shipyards, and available on site were an infir-

Midcentury developments included a growing recognition of adult needs to work.

mary for both mothers and children and hot meals for mothers to take home when they picked up their children. These centers served 3,811 children. Once the war ended, though, child care was no longer needed, and the centers closed. The Kaiser experiment has never been equaled, either in its universal quality of care or in the variety of services it provided.

Chances to Learn

In the 1900s, gaining access to high-quality education for poor people and people of color was difficult. As Du Bois (1903 [1995]) wrote, "[T]he majority of Negro children in the United States, from 6 to 18, do not have the opportunity to read and write. . . . even in the towns and cities of the South, the Negro schools are so crowded and ill-equipped that no thorough teaching is possible." Only a legal challenge to segregation offered new focus, struggle, and ultimately improvement for African-American children. Midcentury marked a turning point in the history of black America. The movement for equality came under black leadership, embraced unprecedented numbers of African-Americans, and became national in scope. A persistent black initiative forced a reformulation of public policies in education. Finally, the historic case of *Brown v. Board of Education of Topeka* (1954) overturned the concept of "separate but equal." The Civil Rights Act of 1964 continued the struggle for equality of opportunity and education.

Head Start

After the war, few innovations took place until a small piece of metal made its worldwide debut. Sputnik, the Soviet satellite, was successfully launched in 1957 and caused an upheaval in educational circles. Two questions were uppermost in the minds of the mainstream in the United States: Why weren't we first in space? What is wrong with our schools? The emphasis in education quickly settled on engineering, science, and math in the hope of catching up with Soviet technology.

The Civil Rights struggle in the early 1960s soon followed. In pointing out the plight of the poor, education was highlighted as a major stumbling block toward equality of all people. It was time to act, and Project Head Start was conceived as education's place in the "war on poverty." Froebelian and Montessori goals formed the basis of Head Start, helping disadvantaged preschool children. This was a revolution in U.S. education, not seen since the short-lived child care programs during World War II. It was the first large-scale effort by the government to focus on children of poverty.

Project Head Start began in 1965 as a demonstration program aimed at providing educational, social, medical, dental, nutritional, and mental health services to preschool children from a diverse population of low-income families. In 1972, it was transformed into a predominantly part-day, full-year program. Over the years, Head Start has provided comprehensive developmental services to more than 10 million children and their families.

Head Start offered three major components: programs compensating for inadequate early life experiences **(compensatory education);** inclusion of parents in planning, teaching, and decision making (parent involvement); and local support and participation (community control). Thanks to Head Start, national attention turned to the

Head Start helped turn American attention to the need for providing child care and education for all young children.

need for providing good care and educational experiences for all young children.

The Head Start program is nationally recognized as an effective means of providing comprehensive services to children and families, serving as a model for the development of the ABC Child Care Act of 1990. Its huge influence today as the major federal program for young children is described at length in Chapter 2.

INTERDISCIPLINARY INFLUENCES

Several professions enrich the heritage of early childhood. This relationship has been apparent since the first nursery schools began, drawing from six different professions to create their practice: social work, home economics, nursing, psychology, education, and medicine. Three of the most consistent and influential of those disciplines are medicine, education, and psychology.

Medicine

The medical field has contributed to the study of child growth through the work of several physicians. These doctors became interested in child development and extended their knowledge to the areas of child-rearing and education.

Maria Montessori

Maria Montessori (1870–1952) was the first woman in Italy ever granted a medical degree. She began studying children's diseases; through her work with mentally defective children, she found education more appealing. Her philosophy is discussed earlier in this chapter and will be part of Chapter 2 on educational programs.

Sigmund Freud

Sigmund Freud (1856–1939) made important contributions to all modern thinking. The father of personality theory, he drastically changed how we look at childhood. Freud reinforced two specific ideas: (1) A person is influenced by his early life in fundamental and dramatic ways, and (2) early experiences shape the way people live and behave as adults. Though he was not involved directly in education, Freud and psychoanalytic theory influenced education greatly. Chapter 4 will expand on the theory and its application in early childhood education.

Arnold Gesell

Arnold Gesell (1880–1961) was a physician who was concerned with growth from a medical point of view. Gesell began studying child development when he was a student of G. Stanley Hall, an early advocate of child study. He later established the Clinic of Child Development at Yale University, where the data he collected with his colleagues became the basis of the recognized norms of how children grow and develop. He was also instrumental in encouraging Abigail Eliot to study with the McMillan sisters in England.

Gesell's greatest contribution was in the area of child growth. He saw maturation as innate, and developed what became known as the *maturation theory*. Through the Gesell Institute, guides were published with such experts as Dr. Frances Ilg and Dr. Louise Bates Ames. These guides describe the child's growth from birth to adolescence, but have been criticized for their overuse and inappropriate application to children of cultures other than those studied.[1] Still, the "ages and stages" material is

[1] This is another reminder of the importance of being able to notice the sociocultural bias in the research in our field, to keep the information that is supportive to sound practice, and to expand or disregard what does not support good practice with children in a multicultural society.

used widely as a yardstick of normal development (see Chapters 3 and 4).

Benjamin Spock

Benjamin Spock's book *Baby and Child Care* was a mainstay for parents in the 1940s and 1950s. In a detailed "how-to" format Dr. Spock (1903–1998) preached a common-sense approach, and the book has sold 50 million copies around the world in 42 languages. Spock saw himself as giving practical application to the theories of Dewey and Freud, particularly the idea that children can learn to direct themselves, rather than needing to be constantly disciplined. He suggested that parents "child proof" their homes—a radical thought at the time. Some people associated permissiveness (as it relates to child-rearing) with Spock's methods, although Spock himself described his advice as relaxed and sensible while still advocating firm parental leadership.

T. Berry Brazelton

Dr. T. Berry Brazelton (1918–) is a well-known pediatrician who supports and understands the development of infants and toddlers. He developed an evaluation tool called the Neonatal Behavior Assessment Scale (also known as "the Brazelton") to assess newborns. Cofounder of the Children's Hospital Unit in Boston, professor emeritus of pediatrics at Harvard Medical School, and founder of the Brazelton Touchpoints Center, he is well known for his pediatric guides for parents (Touchpoints). His writings speak to the parents' side of child-rearing, although he also reminds parents how teachers can help them. Brazelton has advocated a national parental-leave standard, is involved in a federal lobbying group known as Parent Action, and hosts the cable TV series *What Every Baby Knows*.

Education

Early childhood is one part of the larger professional field of education, which includes elementary, secondary, and college or post-secondary schools. Along with John Dewey and Abigail Eliot, several other influential figures from this field bear attention.

The McMillan Sisters

Nursery schools in Britain and the United States probably were developed because of the drive and dedication of the McMillan sisters. In the first three decades of the 20th century, these two sisters pioneered early education in England. Noticing the deplorable conditions in England for children under age five, Rachel and Margaret McMillan began a crusade for slum children. Health studies of the time showed that although 80% of London children were born in good health, by the time they entered school only 20% could be classified that way. In 1910 the sisters set up a clinic in Deptford, a London slum area, which became an open-air nursery a year later.

[Margaret] McMillan invented the name [nursery school]. She paid great attention to health: a daily inspection, the outdoor program, play, good food—what she called "nurture." But she saw that an educational problem was also involved and she set to work to establish her own method of education for young children. This was why she called it a "school" (Hymes, 1978–79).

The McMillan sisters' regimen for their nursery school children of fresh air, sleep, and bathing proved successful. While over 700 children between one and five died of measles in London in an approximately six-month period in 1914, there was not one fatal case at Deptford School.

Susan Isaacs

Susan Isaacs (1885–1948) was an educator of the early 20th century whose influence on nursery and progressive schools of the day was substantial. In 1929 she published *The Nursery Years,* interpreting Freudian theory for teachers and providing guidance for how schools could apply this new knowledge of the unconscious to the education of children. She wanted children to have the opportunity for free, unhindered imaginative play not only as a means to discover the world but also as a way to work through wishes, fears, and fantasies. The teacher's role was different from that of a therapist, she asserted, in that teachers were "to attract mainly the forces of love, to be the good but regulating parent, to give opportunity to express aggression but in modified form" (Biber, 1984).

The Progressive Education Movement

As indicated earlier in reference to John Dewey, it was the Progressive Movement of the late 1800s and first half of the 20th century that changed the course of education in both elementary and nursery schools in America. Coinciding with the political progressivism in this country, this philosophy emphasized a child-centered approach that gained advocates from both the scientific viewpoint, such as G. Stanley Hall and John Dewey, and a psychoanalytic bent, such as Susan Isaacs and Patty Smith Hill.

Some of the major features of the educational progressive philosophy were:

1. We must recognize individual needs and individual differences in children.

2. Teachers [must be] more attentive to the needs of children.

3. Children learn best when they are highly motivated and have a genuine interest in the material.

4. Learning via rote memory is useless to children.

5. The teacher should be aware of the child's total development—social, physical, intellectual, and emotional.

6. Children learn best when they have direct contact with the material (Osborn, 1991).

A new kind of school emerged from these ideals. Movable furniture replaced rows of benches. Children's projects, some still under construction, were found everywhere. The curriculum of the school began to focus on all of the basics, not just a few of the academics. If a group of six-year-olds decided to make a woodworking table, they would first have to learn to read to understand the directions. After calculating the cost, they would purchase the materials. In building the table, geometry, physics, and math were learned along the way. This was a group effort that encouraged children to work together in teams, so school became a society in miniature. Children's social skills were developed along with reading, science, and math. The teacher's role in the process was one of ongoing support, involvement, and encouragement.

The Waldorf School

The first Waldorf School was established in Stuttgart, Germany, in 1919, by Rudolf Steiner. It is the model of choice of eastern European school systems, and is one of the fastest-growing movements in America today. With its foundations in Froebelian tradition, and elements of Montessori and progressive education, the Waldorf School has a contribution to make to our knowledge of children and educational practices (see Chapter 2).

The Child Study Movement

The Child Study movement of the 1920s and 1930s gave education and psychology a common focus. Besides the Gesell Institute, many research centers and child development laboratories were established at colleges and universities around the country. Their inception reflects the interest of several disciplines in the growth of the young child. Schools of psychology looked for children to observe and study; schools of education wanted demonstration schools for their teachers-in-training and for student-teacher placement. Schools of home economics wanted their students to have firsthand experiences with children. These on-campus schools provided a place to gather information about child development and child psychology. This period of educational experimentation and child study led to an impressive collection of normative data by which we still measure ranges of ordinary development. It was the impetus in the United States that began the search for the most appropriate means of educating young children.

Reggio Emilia

Since the last part of the 20th century, an educational system in Italy has influenced early childhood thinking. Loris Malaguzzi (1920–1994) developed his theory of early childhood education from his work with infants, toddlers, and preschoolers as the founder and director of early education in the town of Reggio Emilia, Italy. His philosophy includes creating "an amiable school" (Malaguzzi, 1993) that welcomes families and the community and invites relationships among teachers, children, and parents to intensify and deepen to strengthen a child's sense of identity. Reggio Emilia has attracted the attention and interest of American educators because of its respect for children's work and creativity, its project approach, and its total community support. This curriculum model is discussed in Chapter 10.

Psychology

The roots of early childhood education are wonderfully diverse, but one tap root is especially deep: the connection with the field of psychology. In this century particularly, the study of people and their behavior is linked with the study of children and their growth. There is no one theory or name that encompasses all of developmental psychology. Many theories have affected how we see young children and early education: psychodynamic, behaviorist, cognitive, maturation, humanist, sociocultural, and multiple intelligences; most recently, brain-based research has expanded our knowledge of how children grow and learn. These will be discussed in Chapter 4.

See Appendix A for a historical timeline of early childhood education.

ISSUES OF TODAY

The themes of early childhood education continue to influence practices and policies of today. For instance, by the year 2000, 46% of the nation's schoolchildren were children of color (CDF, 2000a). Nearly one in 10 Americans was born elsewhere; 10% of residents in the United States are immigrants. The terrorist attacks of September 11, 2001, changed the way Americans viewed the world and in turn were seen by it. Events and circumstances are reflected in the major issues facing early childhood educators today:

1. Ethic of social reform: quality child care and educational reform
2. Importance of childhood: families under pressure and risking children's health
3. Transmission of values: the **media culture**, violence and disaster, and diversity
4. Professionalism: standards (for children's programs and teacher preparation) and the "trilemma"

Ethic of Social Reform

This first theme dictates that schooling for young children will lead to social change and improvement. Montessori, the McMillans, Patty Smith Hill, Abigail Eliot, and Head Start all tried to improve children's health and physical well-being by attending first to the physical and social welfare aspects of children's lives. Recent examples illustrate how important this theme is to our work.

Marian Wright Edelman is an outstanding children's advocate. Edelman began her career as a civil rights lawyer (the first African-American woman to be admitted to the Mississippi state bar). By the 1960s she had dedicated herself to the battle against poverty, founding a public interest law firm that eventually became the Children's Defense Fund (CDF). "[We] seek to ensure that no child is left behind and that every child has a Healthy Start, a Head Start, a Fair Start, a Safe Start, and a Moral Start in life with the support of caring parents and communities" (Edelman, 1998).

Louise Derman-Sparks, in collaboration with Elizabeth Jones and colleagues from Pacific Oaks College, published *Anti-Bias Curriculum: Tools for Empowering Young Children* (Derman-Sparks et al., 1989). This book outlined several areas in which children's behavior was influenced by biases in our society, and it suggested a host of ways that teachers (and parents) could begin addressing these issues.[1] These professionals have added an important dimension to the notion of social reform, for they focus our attention on ourselves, the school environment, children's interactions, and the community of parents and colleagues in educational settings.

Today, the ethic of social reform refers to an expectation that education has the potential for significant social change and improvement. This is dramatically demonstrated in two current issues: child care and educational reform.

Good early childhood programs do not distinguish between education and care but understand that both are vital for the growing child.

Quality Child Care

Child care in the United States used to be primarily custodial, providing basic health and physical care. But times have changed. Full-day care is part of an American way of life; each day, 20 million children spend time in early care and education settings as more than 67% of mothers are in the workforce (U.S. Census Bureau, 2002).

The key word is *quality*—the terms "good quality" and "high quality" identify specific features in early childhood programs (see Chapter 2). Quality early care and education contribute to the healthy cognitive, social, and emotional development of all children, but particularly those from low-income families.[1] Yet data from the CDF (2001) paint a bleak picture for those who might benefit the most. Child care costs are disproportionately high for poor parents and can equal as much as one-third of their income. Good, afford-

[1] It is critical that today's teachers learn to integrate cultural awareness and the effects of bias on children's behavior into their daily practices.

able, accessible child care that will meet the increasing needs of American families is one of today's most crucial issues.

The "quality" issue is underscored in three American studies:

1. The Carolina Abecedarian Project (1999), conducted by the Frank Porter Graham Child Development Center in Chapel Hill, North Carolina, is the first study to track participants from infancy to age 21. The children were considered at risk for potential school failure. The study showed the strong influence of high-quality child care when comparing those who were enrolled full time in a quality early childhood program from infancy to age five with those who did not attend a preschool program, although all attended comparable public schools from kindergarten on. Children enrolled in the preschool program were more likely to attend a four-year college and to delay parenthood until after high school. Moreover:

   ✪ At age 21, 65% of the child care graduates either had a good job or were in college, compared with 40% of the non–child care subjects.

   ✪ By age 15, twice as many of the children who had not received intervention services were placed in special education programs compared with those who had been in child care.

   ✪ Only 30% of the child care children had to repeat a grade in school compared with 56% of the non–child care subjects.

2. The Cost, Quality, and Child Outcomes Study (CQCOS, 1995) found that most child care centers provided mediocre services and that some were of such poor quality that they threatened chil-

dren's emotional and intellectual development.[1] Infants and toddlers were most likely to be at risk for poor care in these centers; nearly half of their settings failed to meet basic health and safety needs. A follow-up study, "The Children of the Cost, Quality, and Outcomes Study Go to School" (Peisner-Feinberg et al., 2000), tracked the children through second grade. The findings noted that:

   ✪ Children who receive good, quality child care had better social and cognitive skills in kindergarten and beyond.

   ✪ Children who were at risk gained the most from positive child care experiences and sustained these gains through second grade.

   ✪ Children who had closer relationships with their child care teachers had better behavior and social skills through second grade.

3. A study by the RAND Corporation (Karoly & Bigelow, 2005) for the first time reported the economic returns of one state's (California) investment in quality preschool for all four-year-old children. The study projected that for every dollar invested in a quality universal program, society would get between $2 and $4 back. The benefits include:

   ✪ major increases in lifetime earnings ($2.7 billion per class year of children served)

   ✪ improved K-12 schools (19% reduction in grade repetition per class year; 15% fewer special education years; 15% reduction in high school dropouts)

[1] Eliminating inequalities such as this requires a national agenda for children.

✪ significant reductions in violent juvenile offenses, arrests, and incarceration.

This study notes that to receive such benefits, preschool programs must be of high quality.

Quality is a function of group size, low teacher-child ratios, trained and experienced staff, adequate compensation, and safe and stimulating environments (see Chapter 2). Quality 2000: Advancing Early Child Care and Education is an initiative whose goal is to provide high-quality early care and education to all children from birth to age five by 2010 (Kagan & Neuman, 1997). Creating an early care and education system requires a comprehensive vision that includes factors about children and teachers such as:

✪ promoting cultural sensitivity and cultural pluralism

✪ increasing the number of accredited programs

✪ linking programs to support services and other community resources

✪ creating three separate types of licenses for early childhood care and education workers and developing national licensing guidelines

✪ focusing staff training and preparation on children and families, with respect to cultural and linguistic diversity

✪ funding that is commensurate with per-child levels for elementary school children

✪ establishing governance and accountability structures in every state and locality

These factors will help ensure that families have equal access to good programs in which consistent standards at a national and local level guarantee equality and excellence for all children. The most comprehensive description of quality implementation is that of developmentally appropriate practices (DAP) (Bredekamp, 1997; Gestwicki, 1999). These practices are described at length in Chapter 2, and their history is described in the next section.

Educational Reform

Turning ESEA into NCLB. One of the primary functions of the public school system in the United States is to prepare students for productive roles in society—to produce skilled workers who will enter the job market and contribute to a healthy, competitive economy worldwide. The Elementary and Secondary Education Act (ESEA) of 1965 was authorized to close the achievement gap between disadvantaged/minority students and their middle-class/white peers (U.S. Department of Education, 2001). Since then, a national education problem has been identified and a sense of urgency instilled in the public mind; at the federal level, it is known as the No Child Left Behind (NCLB) Act.

In the first wave of reform of the 1980s, virtually every state enacted reform measures of some kind. The focus was on higher standards of student performance through the upgrading of curricula, increased requirements for homework, and firmer disciplinary methods. Most notable was the move to standards-based instruction and the requirement that children be tested twice a year to measure progress.

In 1989, a national summit on the future of American education resulted in the creation of eight national goals (NEGP, 1991). It was the first time in history that we had a national consensus on a vision of public education. The first goal, "Ready to Learn," included the provision that all children would have equal access to high-quality and developmentally appropriate preschool programs that help prepare children for school.

In 2002, the ESEA was reauthorized with stronger goals. By 2005, it had become the NCLB Act. The major provisions of the act pertaining to early learning are:

- *Adequate yearly progress.* Children will be assessed in reading and math (and a third area by state choice) beginning in third grade. The trickle down of inappropriate testing or imbalanced curriculum to younger children is a valid concern of early educators.

- *Highly qualified teachers.* By the 2005–06 school year, all teachers in core academic subjects must have a B.A. degree, be fully certified, and be highly qualified (by state definition) in their areas of teaching assignment. The early learning field, plagued by high turnover and low pay, cannot meet these standards without significantly more funding.

- *Reading/literacy.* There are significantly increased funds aimed at having all children achieve reading proficiency by grade three. An early childhood concern is that other critical domains of childhood development will be undervalued or overlooked altogether.

It remains to be seen how this ambitious plan will fare over the coming years and how it will relate to the national child care crisis. If we want all our children to be ready for school, we must improve the quality of child care experiences available to all.

Developmentally Appropriate Practices.

The first definitive position on developmentally appropriate practices was adopted by the NAEYC in 1986. This was followed by expansions to include specifics for programs serving children from birth through age eight, outlining both appropriate and inappropriate practices (Bredekamp, 1987). Several key organizations followed suit: the Association for Childhood Education International (ACEI), the Association for Elementary School Principals, and the National Association for State Boards of Education (NASBE) elaborated on their own standards in 1988–91. The NASBE joined forces with NAEYC in 1992 to produce *Guidelines for Appropriate Curriculum Content and Assessment in Programs Serving Children Ages 3 to 8,* and the second volume, published in 1995, *Reaching Potentials.*

Meanwhile, DAP was being used and discussed throughout the broader early childhood education community. Derived from the changing knowledge base by way of research and extended conversations among professionals, the first major revision of NAEYC's position statement and guidelines was published in 1997, then next in 2005. It is likely that this document will need regular revision. The importance of the early years in brain research, the changing **demographics** and continuing diversity in cultural and linguistic backgrounds of the children served, and the inclusion of children with disabilities and developmental delays are just a few of the factors that demand a continuous look at what is developmentally appropriate (see Appendix C). Additionally, the movement toward national standards since the publication of Goals 2000 (NEGP, 1991) makes it critical that early childhood educators remind fellow educators and policymakers alike that knowledge about how children develop and learn is applied in program practice.

To meet the needs of working parents and ensure that children are ready to learn, education reform strategies should be enlarged to do the following:

1. *Link education and child care.* The dichotomy between care and education must be eliminated, as early childhood programs include both caregiving and educating aspects of teaching.

2. *Establish continuity between early childhood programs and kindergartens.* The perception that preschools are "only about play" and that primary schools are "all about academics" negates the whole child in both worlds.

3. *Address children's nonacademic needs.* Unless more is done to meet the early health and social needs of children, school reform is likely to fail.

4. *Promote developmental learning.* Get schools ready for young children, as opposed to having children be pressured and pushed to get ready for school.

5. *Initiate programs and policies that strengthen the family.* The family support for learning should be addressed by focusing on parental attitudes and involvement at home as well as at school and on the parents' responsibility for meeting the basic care and needs of their children.[1]

6. *Develop partnerships with the community and with businesses.* Coordinating with providers and collaborating with other community agencies make better use of public funds and improve the quality of all programs.

As indicated here, it is critical that the needs of the whole child and the knowledge of how children learn best need to be infused in all early childhood education programs.

Importance of Childhood

The second theme is the importance and uniqueness of childhood. In fact, the entire notion of the importance of childhood rests on the concept of the child as a special part of human existence and, therefore, a valuable part of the life cycle. Once families and society began to value children, they began to take responsibility for providing a quality life for them. "As the twig is bent, so grows the tree" applies to all children and their early childhood learning experiences. Two issues of today endanger childhood and demand our attention: families under pressure and risks to children's health.

Families Under Pressure

Who is today's family? The family of today has many shapes, sizes, and styles. A family can be formed by:

- dual-career parents, with two parents working outside the home and children in child care

- a single parent supporting children, often with little or no help—either financial or personal—from the absent parent

- older or elderly people raising their grandchildren

- teen parents living with or without family support

- an unmarried person living either alone or with others who do not have children

- a "blend" of family members—remarried adults with respective children living full- or part-time in residence

- extended relatives (or several families) living together

- a gay or lesbian couple raising children

Only a small percentage of U.S. households are traditional, nuclear families.[2]

[1] Children's programs should reflect the attitude that diversity is an opportunity for learning—not a problem.
[2] Some myths die hard. The early childhood educator must be aware of the demographics on family patterns.

The impact of social changes in the past three decades has been hardest felt by children. The increase in the divorce rate, poverty, and homelessness, and the dangerous effects of the media culture, drugs, and worldwide violence have thrust children into adult situations with adult troubles. Dual-career parents and single working parents, together with the lack of extended families, have meant that children's behavior is not as closely monitored as it once was.

Stress. Children and childhood have changed. Gone are the days when the majority of children arrived home from school to be greeted by a mother in the kitchen serving milk and homemade cookies. Today's child spends time in child care, at a center, or with a neighbor while the parent works. Many spend hours alone at home or caring for younger siblings. Parents and adult family members are often too busy or preoccupied to attend to children.

Some of the experiences that produce stress in young children are family related. Divorce and remarriage, a move to a new home, prolonged visits from a relative, and new siblings are classic stress situations for children. Yet there are less dramatic sources of stress, the simple everyday oc-

How do we help children cope with stress?

currences that children face: being told not to do something, not having a friend, being ignored by a parent, experiencing changes in the routine, not being able to read or zip a zipper or put a puzzle together. Stress may also occur in families in which both parents pursue careers and children feel the need to live up to exceptional standards in academic achievement or sports proficiency. Apathetic parents, parents who ignore their children or have no time for them, and parents who push children into frantic schedules of activity also cause stress in their children. Stress can result from happy occasions as well: holidays, vacation, or a new baby may be overanticipated, overstructured, and overstimulating to a child.

Children respond to stress in many ways. Signs of stress include sleeping problems (such as nightmares or sleepwalking), depression, regression to the behavior of an earlier stage, aches and pains, acting out, eating problems, and overreactions, as well as medical problems (such as headaches, upset stomach, and bleeding ulcers).

Stress is a natural part of life and is a factor in every child's development, but it must be managed by the adults who care for them. Brazelton and Greenspan (2000), in response to the overwhelmed, stressed-out life of children and parents today, defined seven irreducible needs of children:

1. The need for ongoing nurturing relationships
2. The need for physical protection, safety, and regulation
3. The need for experiences tailored to individual differences
4. The need for developmentally appropriate experiences
5. The need for limit setting, structure, and expectations
6. The need for stable, supportive communities and cultural continuity
7. The need to for the future to be protected on their behalf

By keeping these in mind in both child-rearing and education, we help reduce the unnecessary stress and take better care of all young children.

Divorce. Perhaps no one single change has affected children as much as the divorce rate. Nearly 50% of marriages end in divorce, and five of 10 children born in the 1990s will spend part of their growing years in a single-parent home (CDF, 2000a).[1]

One schoolchild in three has parents who are divorced—30% of these are children in stepfamilies, and the other 70% live with their mothers or fathers alone (Clarke-Stewart, 1989).

The effects of divorce are felt by children well before the event itself. Children exhibit "predivorce family stress" by increased impulsive or aggressive behavior, and parents show the stress with headaches, fatigue, mood swings, or depression. Children's initial reaction to their parents' separation is often traumatic. After divorce, many parents become overworked and overwhelmed. Children are often left with less than what both parents could provide, including emotional and financial support. Studies indicate that after a divorce, women suffer a drastic drop in income; because most children in divorced families live with their mothers, economic disaster is felt by most children of divorce: "Divorce is a cumulative experience for the child. Its impact increases over time" (Wallerstein, 1997).

Fortunately, children are amazingly resilient. The age and gender of the children involved seem to have some bearing on their adjustment. Very young children recover more easily than older ones, and boys react more intensely than girls to the loss of their fathers from the home (Carlisle, 1991). The parents' ability to be caring and available makes a difference, as does the parents' relationship with each other and the quality of the children's relationship with both parents.

Teachers and caregivers can help parents get access to outside help, such as a parent support group, community welfare services, or a parental stress hotline. Teachers can plan strategies for family involvement that take into account the work demands, resources, and expertise of parents themselves. Providing a place and time to heal makes a program or family child care home a safe haven to begin to heal and become whole again. Suggestions include:

- *Know your children.* Confer with families as often as possible and be aware of family stresses and crises.

- *Talk about feelings.* Anger and sadness are predominant, along with guilt, loss, helplessness, and loneliness; an understanding teacher can go a long way to help a child feel less alone and can offer appropriate opportunities—through intimate moments, puppets and dolls, unstructured drawings, role playing, and creative drawing—for expression.

- *Use bibliotherapy.* Books are powerful tools to connect with children, with understanding and kindness. They are also wonderful resources to families.

- *Keep aware of family diversity.* Be sure to include many family structures in the curriculum, during informal discussions, with any correspondence to home.

- *Communicate openly with parents and family members.* Divorce may compli-

[1] Consider the stories read to young children. Is this reality reflected in messages sent from program to home? when scheduling parent-program meetings?

cate communication between teachers and parents. Make adjustments in conferences, newsletters, and notes about the child so both parents are included as much as possible.

Working Parents.

Two-thirds of all preschool children younger than six have mothers in the workforce (CDF, 2000a), and the percentage rises when considering school-aged children as well. The implications for families are considerable. For women, the double roles of job/career and family nurturer can be overwhelming, creating great conflict and the stress of chronic fatigue. Many men are learning about greater involvement in child-rearing and how to adjust to a new financial role.[1]

For both parents, three issues loom large: the concern for good child care, the struggle to provide "quality time" with children and as a family unit, and the financial burden. Without parental leave, many parents are forced to return to work during the critical early months of infancy or lose income and even their jobs.

Working parents are less available for direct participation in a classroom or on a constant basis. Teachers can plan flexible opportunities for them to become involved in their children's education. Much stronger than in the United States are European models of family leave, which give parents several months of unpaid leave from their jobs to be at home and establish a bond and family setting, and of public programs for children and support services for parents.

We look toward a future trend of clearer U.S. policies that make it more attractive for adults to spend time with children.

Poverty.

There is a group of Americans who are destined for limited participation in the social, political, and economic mainstream of national life. The children who are at risk for academic failure are likely to be those who live in poverty, members of minority groups in racial isolation, children with various physical and mental disabilities, children with limited English proficiency, and children from single-parent families (Figure 1–2).

One in five children is poor in the United States (CDF, 2000a). Most poor children live in families with working parents whose wages are too low for them to earn their way out of poverty. In 1998, 74% of the poor children in America lived in a family in which someone worked. Even more startling, one of every three poor children lived in families where someone worked full time, year-round. This percentage is the highest in the 25 years these figures have been compiled.

There is a striking correlation between poverty and school failure. Children who start out at a disadvantage fall further behind in academic achievement throughout their school years.[2]

A study of 1,000 children in 10 cities (CDF, 2000b) examined maternal sensitivity, home environment, hours in child care, and quality of child care. Children were then given a school readiness test, and the data

[1] The sweeping changes in social behavior have resulted in changing attitudes about adults. However, there are vast differences among the various cultural groups and individual adults about the value of and care for children. Do not assume that a change in what you consider a "traditional" family pattern equals an inferior commitment to children.

[2] It is a paradox of the 21st century that nearly half of our school population is considered to be "at risk." As we learn more about what constitutes difficulty in achieving school success, and make assessments on more than a simple grade level academic performance, our concept of "at risk" diversifies and requires a stringer commitment to school reform.

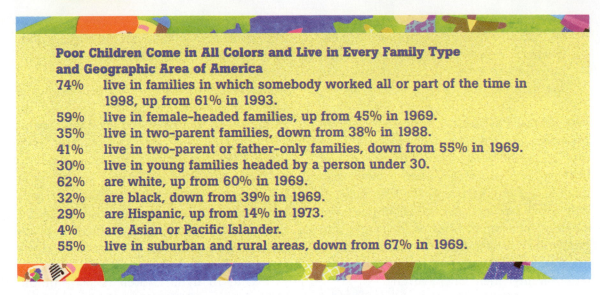

Poor Children Come in All Colors and Live in Every Family Type and Geographic Area of America

74%	live in families in which somebody worked all or part of the time in 1998, up from 61% in 1993.
59%	live in female-headed families, up from 45% in 1969.
35%	live in two-parent families, down from 38% in 1988.
41%	live in two-parent or father-only families, down from 55% in 1969.
30%	live in young families headed by a person under 30.
62%	are white, up from 60% in 1969.
32%	are black, down from 39% in 1969.
29%	are Hispanic, up from 14% in 1973.
4%	are Asian or Pacific Islander.
55%	live in suburban and rural areas, down from 67% in 1969.

FIGURE 1–2 Poverty affects all children in the United States. (Courtesy of CDF, 2000.)

were compared with those of children in similar settings. Researchers found that early maternal employment had negative effects on children's intellectual development. Children whose mothers worked by the time the babies were nine months old, had insensitive mothers, and poor-quality child care had scores significantly lower than those with sensitive mothers who were not employed by the ninth month and had good-quality child care. Although the study did not take into consideration such factors as father involvement or how much the mother wants to be employed, it certainly has serious implications for families at risk.

Risking Children's Health
Child Abuse and Neglect. Child abuse
and neglect are significant problems in this country. For instance, in 2000, 3 million cases of child abuse and neglect were reported to child protective services (U.S. Department of Health and Human Services, 2002).

✪ Two-thirds of the victims suffered neglect.

✪ Nearly 20% were physically abused.

✪ 10% were sexually abused.

✪ 8% were psychologically maltreated.

✪ An estimated 1,200 children died of abuse or neglect, and of those deaths, 44% were children younger than one year and 85% were under six years of age.

✪ More than 80% of the victims were abused by one or both parents.

A neglected child may be one whose waking hours are mostly unsupervised by adults, in front of the television or simply unconnected with—and unnoticed by—parents or an important caregiver. Child neglect takes more hazardous forms when the basic needs of adequate food, clothing, shelter, and health are unmet. Because families with children represent more than one-third of the homeless population (CDF, 2001), and the foster care system is strained, many "children on the move" are under great strain and pressure. Failure to exercise the care that children need shows an inattention to and lack of concern for children.

Child abuse is the most severe form of disrespect. Violence in the form of physical maltreatment and sexual abuse is improper, regardless of children's behavior. Abusive language and harsh physical aggression are other forms of child abuse that occur in families and, unfortunately, some settings for child care.

A national call to action is under way. Standardized licensing procedures, upgrading of the certification of child care workers, and national **accreditation** of all preschools are some of the most frequently mentioned solutions to the problem. Helping parents identify what qualities to look for when placing their children in someone else's care is another way to prevent child abuse in centers.

Reporting suspected child abuse is mandated by law in all states. Educators must assume the responsibility to inform the proper authorities if they suspect that a child in their care is being abused by adults (see Appendix B). Figure 1–3 lists the signs a teacher should look for if child abuse is

suspected and describes what to do if you suspect child abuse or if a child tells you that she/he has been abused.[1]

In 1996, NAEYC adopted a "Position Statement on the Prevention of Child Abuse in Early Childhood Programs and the Responsibilities of Early Childhood Professionals to Prevent Child Abuse," urging that early childhood programs in homes, centers, and schools adopt a set of policies based on guidelines such as:

- employing adequate staff
- adequately supervising staff
- reducing possible hiding or secluded places in the environment
- orienting and training personnel on child abuse detection, prevention, and reporting
- defining and articulating policies for a safe environment
- avoiding "no-touch" policies by the caregivers and staff

Perhaps most important, teachers must stay close to the parents of all their children so that they may be able to detect early signs of impending problems of both abuse and neglect. The perceptive teacher can then support parents through their difficulties, offering them help by informing them of parental stress hotlines, suggesting strategies to avoid stress and violence, and recommending professional help.

Children and AIDS. Acquired immunodeficiency syndrome (AIDS) is a communicable disease that breaks down the body's immune system, leaving it unable to fend off harmful bacteria and viruses. The AIDS virus may be

Video View Point 1-1

"Ethical Conduct: The exception to the Ethical Code guideline of confidentiality is when a child care provider is concerned about the welfare of the child."

Competency: Guidance

Age Group: Preschool

Critical Thinking Questions:

1. Do you know what a "mandated court reporter" is?
2. How might you address a concern about a child's welfare to your supervisor? to a family?

[1]A study of teachers' knowledge of the signs of child sexual abuse found that 15% could not recognize even the most obvious signs (Harvard Education Letter, 1995). Lung and Daro (1996) report that three children die each day because of parental abuse and credit the increase in poverty, substance abuse, and violence as causes.

32   SECTION 1   WHAT IS THE FIELD OF EARLY CHILDHOOD EDUCATION?

What to Do if You Suspect Child Abuse

- ✪ Make notes of child's appearance—any bruises, marks, or behaviors that cause you concern.

- ✪ Inform the director of the program and/or your immediate supervisor; plan together who will inform the proper authorities and how to contact the parent(s).

- ✪ Discuss ways to support the staff members who make the report, the parent(s), and the child.

- ✪ Call the locally designated agency for child abuse. A written report may be required within 24 to 48 hours.

- ✪ Support the parent(s) throughout the investigation. Be available to the parent(s) and the child as they deal with the other agencies that are trained and equipped to handle this problem.

- ✪ Follow through with assistance or support if requested to do so by the child protective services agency. Help the family by working with others who are counseling them and performing parent support services.

What to Do if a Child Tells You He or She Has Been Abused

- ✪ Believe the child; children rarely lie about sexual abuse.

- ✪ Commend the child for telling you what happened.

- ✪ Convey your support for the child. Children's greatest fear is that they are at fault and responsible for the incident. It is important to help children avoid blaming themselves.

- ✪ Temper your own reactions, recognizing that your perspective and acceptance are critical signals to the child. Do not convey your own feelings about the abuse.

- ✪ Report the suspected abuse to the child's parent(s), the designated social service agency, and/or the police.

- ✪ Find specialized agencies that evaluate sexual abuse victims and a physician with the experience and training to detect and recognize sexual abuse.

FIGURE 1–3 (Source: *Child sexual abuse prevention.* Washington, DC: U.S. Department of Health and Human Services, 1998)

present in the blood even though the full AIDS syndrome does not develop. Although the disease is prevalent among adults, children can contract it too. Although prenatal care and preventative treatment in the mid-1990s drastically reduced the number of babies born with AIDS, mother-to-child transmission of the disease accounts for more than 90% of all AIDS cases among U.S. children (CDC, 1999). Women of color and their children are disproportionately affected by the human immunodeficiency virus (HIV) epidemic. According to the Centers for Disease Control and Prevention (ibid.), 84% of the children with AIDS were African-American and Hispanic.

The greatest fears and misconceptions about AIDS involve how contagious the disease is and how it is transmitted. Sexual contacts and mingling of blood are the two known routes of infection. Not one case is known to have been transmitted any other way, even to close family members of AIDS patients. No children have contracted AIDS from ordinary contact with other children. None of the cases of pediatric AIDS in the United States were transmitted in a school or child care setting or through hugging, sharing a glass or a plate, sharing bathrooms, or in kissing that is not mouth to mouth (CDC, 1999).

Early childhood professionals clearly have a role to play regarding this disease:

- ✪ Be an informed resource to parents and other teachers. Keep abreast of current data and educate others about the facts of AIDS.

- ✪ Know how to answer the questions a preschooler will ask.

- ✪ Examine your own attitudes about sexually transmitted diseases, homosexuality, and drug usage.

- ✪ Keep up to date on research about AIDS; information changes rapidly and is released frequently.

- ✪ Take appropriate precautions—wash hands thoroughly and use plastic gloves when contact with blood may occur.

- ✪ Be prepared to counsel children and their families through long illness and death in the same way as with other fatal diseases.

- ✪ Develop school policies that reflect the current knowledge and recommendations of medical experts.

- ✪ Maintain confidentiality to protect the children and families involved.

Transmission of Values

The third recurrent theme in our educational heritage is that of transmitting values. Values—be they social, cultural, moral, or religious—have been the essence of education for centuries. Puritan fathers valued biblical theology; therefore, schools of their time taught children to read to learn the Bible. Rousseau and Froebel valued childhood, so they created special places for children to express their innate goodness and uniqueness. Montessori, Dewey, and Steiner believed in the worth and dignity of childhood, and these values are reflected in the educational practices we have inherited. Today the anti-bias movement reflects the priority of personal respect and an awareness and appreciation of ethnic heritage as an integral part of the early childhood curriculum.[1]

"People are so overwhelmed," write Brazelton and Greenspan (2000). "While they're whirling around, they don't have time to stop and think, 'What are my values? Do my children really come first? Am I making time for them in my life?'" Many families today are looking for spiritual and moral direction for themselves and their children. Both parents and teachers must acknowledge the many sources shaping children's values and behavior. Three issues of today are the influence of the media culture, violence and disaster, and diversity.

The Media Culture

Ninety-eight percent of the homes in the United States have televisions, and the average set is on for more than six hours each

---

[1] Informed early childhood educators really are leading the way in educational practice in terms of *celebrating* the diversity of the families!

day, replacing the adult supervision of the past. "The average American child watches about three and half hours of TV each day," reports Chen (1994). "That means by the time children graduate from high school, they've logged some 18,000 hours in front of a TV set—compared with about 13,000 hours in a classroom. Now consider what these kids are seeing: 20,000 commercials each year, and about 100,000 acts of TV violence—including 8,000 murders—by the time they reach sixth grade."

There are four basic concerns that parents and teachers express about children's viewing of television and videos:

1. Media violence can lead to aggression and desensitization to violence.

2. Television and computers promote passivity, slowing intellectual development and stifling imagination.

3. Media images promote racist and sexist attitudes.

4. Television promotes materialistic consumerism.

Video View Point 1-2

"Media: Much has been written on the effects of media on children."

Competency: Family Interactions

Age Group: School Age

Critical Thinking Questions:
1. How should programs for school-age children deal with children's interest in using media games and toys in their after-school program?
2. How would you respond when children talk about and act out television shows and movies that promote violence?

The Center for Media Literacy (1993) documents four effects of viewing media violence:

- increased aggressiveness and antisocial behavior
- increased fear of becoming a victim
- increased desensitization to violence and victims of violence
- increased appetite for more violence in entertainment and real life

Some research seems to indicate that children actually do many other activities while the set is on and that their attention to TV is variable. Preschool children seem to attend to minute details of a show that interests them; most parents report that very young children learn advertising jingles or details of slogans. Research about the cognitive effects of television viewing reveals that TV viewing seems to be a fairly complex cognitive activity. Still, there is little consistent evidence concerning television's influence on imagination and creativity. More research is critical, as well as an analysis of the content of the shows that children watch.

In the area of bias and stereotyping, a pattern of "boy dominance" extends beyond the networks into public and cable broadcasting. Networks generally assert that boys will not watch shows with female leads, but girls will watch shows with a male lead. Minority groups are also inadequately represented on TV. Thus, with children's television shows, the Euro-American and male attitudes and behaviors are reinforced.[1]

Television promotes consumerism. In 1990 the Children's Television Act required that stations submit an assessment of chil-

[1] An important task of early childhood educators is to actively counteract gender and ethnic group stereotypes.

Antidotes to the media culture.

dren's television offerings when they apply for license renewal with the Federal Communications Commission (FCC). The FCC adopted rules encouraging broadcasters to air more educational programming for children and limit the amount of advertising during children's shows.

The studies available today indicate clear modifiers of those effects, namely, parent co-viewing and teaching of critical televi-

sion viewing skills. Guidelines from NAEYC (1990) for dealing with the hazards of media culture (video games, computer games, assorted toys and games, etc.) include:

1. *Set limits.* Know how many hours of TV children watch and monitor it. The American Academy of Pediatrics suggests a maximum of one to two hours daily. Keep the TV turned off unless

someone is actively viewing. Involve children in discussions about video-game systems or computer games; consider establishing rules (for instance, "Game-playing counts as 'screen time'" and "I can't play when a friend comes over").

2. *Plan and participate.* Work together with children to decide what to watch. Help children choose shows with an age-appropriate viewing length, bias-free content, and peaceful action. Consider watching shows together, pointing out parts that are pro-social and asking about those parts you wonder about or disagree with. Use the "pause," "rewind," and "mute" buttons as part of the process. Watch carefully what children are doing with video and computer games.

3. *Resist commercials.* Young children do not distinguish easily between the sales-pitch commercial and the ordinary show. Help them become "critical consumers" by pointing out the exaggerated claims. Even three-year-olds can answer the question "What are they trying to sell us?"

4. *Express your views.* Call a station that airs a show or commercial you find offensive, or write a letter to the Children's Advertising Review unit of the Better Business Bureau. Action for Children's Television in Cambridge, Massachusetts, has been a leading public interest group for more than 20 years and has valuable suggestions for how adults can influence children's television programming.

Violence and Disaster

The trend of children's increasing exposure to conflict that ends in violence is alarming. What is offered on television and other media, the kinds and choices of toys, and the interpersonal situations in children's homes, neighborhoods, and the world all contribute to an increased awareness of and exposure to violence. Parents report tensions in the relationships between themselves and their children. Increased violence on television along with a rising tide of war toys contribute to a sense of being out of control in limiting or influencing children's behavior. Teachers see similar tensions with children in school and child care and notice changes in children's play. Many teachers report that the weapon and war play in classrooms is so single-purpose and intense that it is difficult to redirect; rule setting and controlling overzealous play take an inordinate amount of teachers' energy.

When a catastrophe happens, children need help making sense of the calamity, then support in recovery. Shock, confusion, fear, anxiety, grief, anger, guilt, helplessness are all common emotional responses to trauma. Whether the event be national—as 9/11 was for the United States—or local, children worry. Figure 1–4 gives suggestions for how to help children in case of a disaster. Teachers work on their own personal feelings and seek out supportive resources. A teacher must prepare for controversy; differences in opinions are common in the daily social interactions of children in a classroom. Recognizing children's need to discuss their feelings, teachers help parents to be a source of information and support for their children.

Diversity

Facing Reality. America as "melting pot," in which all racial and cultural differences are smoothly mixed into one single blend, is a myth. Unfortunately, much of America's history has been characterized as **racist, classist, sexist,** and **ethnocentric** in nature by one group or another. The discrepancy between our ideals of equal opportunity and freedom and the daily reality can be altered only if we recognize the

When a Child Experiences Disaster

For all children . . .

Stop, look, and listen.

Spend time with the child; be aware of actions and feelings.

Be aware of your feelings and reactions.

Ask open-ended questions.

Give reassurance and physical comfort.

Welcome children's talking about it.

Provide structure throughout the day.

Work with parents and significant adults.

Adapt the curriculum:

• Give them more time for relaxing, therapeutic experiences of playing with sand, water, clay, and play dough.

• Allow plenty of time to work out their concerns through dramatic play.

• Spend more time in physical activity for emotional release.

For children under age three . . .

Resume normal routines and favorite rituals.

Give limited exposure to the media and adult conversations about the crisis.

For children under age five . . .

Be reassuring verbally that you and they will be okay.

Make sure they know where you are at all times.

Model peaceful resolution to conflict.

Make opportunities for children to write, dictate stories, and create pictures about their experiences.

Give special time at nap time and bed time (including letting the child sleep with parents).

For school-age children . . .

Give verbal and physical assurance that you and they will be okay.

Help them know where their important adults are at any given time.

Ask what is on their minds and answer their questions honestly.

Make emergency plans so children know safety measures for the future.

Provide guided exposure to the media; try to watch/hear with them.

Begin to explain what motivates people to act in violent ways.

Take action: Send help directly, help them organize relief efforts.

Allow them extra time at bed time (including letting the child sleep with parents).

FIGURE 1-4 A catastrophe such as an earthquake, hurricane, or fire or a disaster such as a war or an act of terrorism is frightening to both adults and children (AACAP, 1997; Davis & Keyser, 2001; Farish, 1995; Greenman, 2001).

problems and then set specific goals for change.

Today's demographics point to a trend of an increasingly diverse society. By the year 2000, Hispanic students were almost as numerous as whites. Forty-six percent of the nation's schoolchildren are children of color (CDF, 2000).

Attitudes have not yet responded to reality. A University of Chicago survey on racial attitudes found that although support for racial equality has grown, "negative images of members of other racial and ethnic groups are widespread among whites, and most groups have at least one prejudice against all the other groups" (Armstrong, 1991). In a comprehensive study titled "A Common Destiny: Black and American Society," the National Research Council (Schmidt, 1989) concluded that despite gains in recent decades, African-Americans still faced formidable barriers on their path to educational parity with whites.

Moreover, we know that children exhibit an awareness of racial and gender differences by age three (Derman-Sparks, 1989) and formulate rudimentary concepts about the meaning of those differences in the preschool years. It is logical to conclude that by the end of the early childhood years, children have consolidated their attitudes about race, ethnicity, gender, and (dis)ability and are far along the path of **attitude crystallization.** Unless the social environment changes, children will re-create the prejudices of the current adult society.

The early childhood education community has been responsive to issues of diversity. For instance, DAP approaches children with the belief in the uniqueness of the individual child. One of the major differences between the first position statement (1986) and its revision (1997) is that the latter recognizes the role of the cultural context in development and learning:

> Group cultural differences are now recognized as separate from individual differences; that is, at the same time individuals develop with personal histories, they also develop within a cultural context that influences behavioral expectations shared within a group. Culture consists of values, rules, and expectations for behavior that are passed on within families and communities, both explicitly and implicitly. . . . [C]hildren and their families form

distinct cultural and linguistic groups that must be recognized with sensitivity and respect by classroom teacher (Gestwicki, 1999).

Multicultural Education. Multicultural education is the system of teaching and learning that includes the contributions of all ethnic and racial groups. In other words, it is a comprehensive educational approach that reflects more minority perspectives, providing all children with a fuller, more balanced truth about themselves, their own history, and culture. This means that we respond to the child's origins, habits at home, and ways of self-expression. When the metaphor of "melting pot" changes to one of "mosaic" or "mixed salad," we encourage a new way of thinking that might be termed cultural pluralism— the idea that "we are all one people, but we do not necessarily divest ourselves of our ethnic origin" (Sobol in Viadero, 1990). The early childhood program that responds most genuinely to diversity is one in which the child is accepted, the child's total personal diversity is respected, and the child's family, language, and cultural traditions are part of the classroom. Teachers will need special training that prepares them to be effective educators, addressing such topics as prejudice reduction training, bicultural expectations, physical and interpersonal environmental factors, varied teaching strategies, inclusive curriculum, and culturally responsible conduct.

Bilingual Education. The goals and purposes of bilingual education are controversial, for there are disagreements over how to define bilingualism, how to determine who needs it, and who is to provide the services. Bilingual education has been part of the American experience since before the Revolutionary War, when school was taught in any one of the more than 18

languages that were spoken by the colonists. Nonetheless, numerous cultures have been suppressed with regularity in the United States. Speaking English is only part of bilingual education: At issue are the civil and educational rights of people who speak limited English, the respect or assimilation of their culture, and their participation and acceptance in society.

Children younger than five are primarily taught in regular classroom settings, usually with little extra instruction, though often with some support from teachers who learn words or phrases in children's home languages. This type of instruction is known as the "English immersion" system. Research shows that children can acquire native-like mastery of a second language if they learn to speak the language before the age of five. There has been some controversy due to the finding that language-minority children in English-speaking schools experience a substantial erosion of their native-language ability and have difficulty communicating with their parents (Fillmore, 1991). Still, the immersion system remains the standard.

For school-age children, the issues of linguistic skill development are different than those for the young child. In elementary school, teachers and children are forced to deal with issues beyond those of receptive and expressive language. Learning graphic language (reading and writing), acquiring concepts in other subject areas through listening, and dealing with the more complex social patterns and interpersonal issues are just a few of these. With a bilingual child, the level of competence in both languages may be low while gaining mastery in the second language.

Bilingual programs in the United States serve primarily Spanish-speaking students, and those states that do not have bilingual programs still need to meet the needs of limited-English-proficient (LEP) students in schools through other means. Since 1968, Title VII programs (the Elementary and Secondary Education Act, also known as the Bilingual Education Act) have addressed the needs of students with limited proficiency in English. State bilingual education laws vary, requiring special instruction for children who lack competence in English. For example, a 1998 California law effectively ended publicly funded bilingual programs, to be replaced by shorter-term, intensive English-immersion programs at the elementary and secondary levels.

Bilingual programs are so varied that it is difficult to assess them. Some work to mainstream children into regular classrooms as quickly as possible; others try to maintain the child's native language. A more recent program, the dual or bilingual immersion method, attempts a blending of language instruction by putting together both English speakers and those with limited English and teaching "two-way" bilingual education. This method also indicates respect for both languages as assets and shows promise as a truly multicultural tool for desegregation. However, without consensus on the effectiveness and goals of bilingual education, educators must press for continuing research and clarity.

Immigrant Children. Another serious challenge for schools is posed by the educational and socioeconomic needs of immigrant children. Attempting to immerse new children into an "American way" and to teach basic skills needed to succeed in the new country have been central functions of schools throughout U.S. history. Nationwide, there are more than 2.5 million school-age immigrants and at least as many children younger than five (CDF, 2000). Immigrant enrollment in schools varies among the states and can reach as high as 95% in some schools.

The language barrier is the most immediate problem, followed by that of acceptance of the immigrants' native culture.

Further, many newcomers arrive from countries racked with war, violence, and poverty. These children and families are under tremendous pressures and need help coping with the overwhelming stress and dislocation. The way schools place and monitor immigrant children—both their educational progress and their general well-being—challenges educators and all American citizens to clarify the responsibilities our society has toward its newcomers.

Inclusive Education. Since the 1970s, recognition of people with disabilities has been paired with public funding for education (see Chapter 3). The most recent legislation, the Americans with Disabilities Act, is designed "to reasonably accommodate individuals with disabilities in order to integrate them into the program to the extent feasible, given each individual's limitations" (Child Care Law Center, 1994). Key principles are:

- Individuality (understand the limitations and needs of each individual)
- Reasonableness (of the accommodation to the program and the person)
- Integration (of the individual with others)

Accommodating a child with special needs is unreasonable only if it puts an undue burden on a program, would fundamentally alter the nature of the program, or poses a threat to the health or safety of the other children and staff. With these guidelines in mind, children with special needs will do best in the *least restrictive environment*, with as much full **inclusion** as possible.

Many programs, including Head Start from its inception, have welcomed children with special needs. Early intervention for children with special needs can minimize the effect of a condition or help such special needs from becoming more serious

problems. Recommended practices now include (Udell, Peters, & Templeton, 1998):

- Intervention focused on specific and measurable child goals
- Services that are family-centered
- Regular monitoring and adjustments of the intervention
- Planning for transitions and changes
- Providing multidisciplinary services

Chapter 3 provides more details. Still, many children have special needs that remain undiagnosed. Many others have difficulty finding appropriate placement, particularly in programs for children younger than age five. Early childhood special education is a relatively new area of our profession, and most educators need support in learning about special needs and what it means to be inclusive of children with special needs without altering program quality for all children or overwhelming and exhausting staff.

Class Differences. By the year 2000, more than one-third of the school population were minority and poor. Although these children enter kindergarten only slightly behind, by third grade the average African-American and Latino student is already six months behind his white classmate. In the 1990s the ethnic gap in academic achievement was either staying the same or widening, depending on grade and subject area. Although no one likes to talk about it, the class differences cause many children, particularly children of poor and minority families, to get less:

- Less in the way of experienced and well-trained teachers
- Less in the way of a rich and well-balanced curriculum
- Less actual instructional time
- Less in the way of well-equipped and well-stocked laboratories and libraries

What is our vision of the future for these children?

✸ Less of what undoubtedly is most important of all—a belief that they can really learn (Haycock, 1991)

We have to deal with the "lesses." We know what makes good schools work, and DAP helps us articulate what makes good teaching and improved educational experiences for all children. We have to join with other community efforts in building support systems so families can thrive and help their children succeed. In speaking out about children's needs and pushing for adequate teaching conditions, we can do our part (see Appendix C).

Equal Play and Gender Issues. There is ample research to confirm the widespread occurrence of gender segregation in childhood (Grossman & Grossman, 1994). Although adults may not always directly contribute to biased development, teachers and parents are indirectly responsible for the inequity between the sexes in their chil-

dren. For instance, in unstructured play situations, children will choose playmates and play situations that are comfortable to them. They will not, typically, choose those activities with which they have had little or no experience, nor will they ordinarily choose cross-sex playmates (particularly as peer pressure increases with age). Further, boys still get more attention than girls at most grade levels and in most subject areas. Sexist treatment in the classroom encourages the formation of patterns of power and dominance that occur very early, though it is inappropriate to our current culture.

Teachers and parents must take an assertive role in recognizing this sexist bias and replacing it with more equitable experiences for all children. Schlank and Metzger (1997) suggest that these guidelines be followed when trying to teach for change:

✸ *Begin with yourself.* Start with self-awareness and reflection on one's own behavior, responses, and attitudes.

- *What you say and do can make a difference.* Be gender inclusive or neutral, acknowledging positive behaviors and milestones by describing what you see and avoiding using gender designations (such as "All boys get your jackets," or "All girls go to the snack tables.")

- *Watch your language.* Avoid descriptions of children such as "pretty/handsome" and treat the class as a group ("friends" rather than "boys and girls"); be careful of word choices that reflect gender bias (such as "He is confident/She is full of herself").

- *Establish rules and conduct for cooperation and gender equity.* Everybody may play everywhere with any toy; blocks are not just for boys and the house corner is not for girls only; no child may be kept from playing because of something she or he cannot change—skin color, disability, or gender.

- *Be ready to intervene and support.* If you hear a "No boys allowed," or "Girls can't do that," be ready to intervene in a supportive way, finding out why children think that, evaluating your thoughts, and pointing out what the class rule is.

- *Think about how to cope with superheroes and Barbie dolls.* Develop strategies for all children, including providing activities that all children may use, that are sex fair and sex affirmative in content, and using strategies such as teacher proximity and structured playtime to involve children in activities they may otherwise avoid.

Sexuality. Although human sexuality is not likely to be among typical early childhood curriculum topics, teachers are likely to encounter issues of homosexuality in the following ways: working with gay or lesbian families or coworkers, dealing with aspects of femininity and masculinity in children's sex role identity, and having multicultural children's books about gay families. Some experts estimate that approximately 10% of the children in our classes will grow up to be gay or lesbian adults (Corbett, 1993). Whether or not the estimates are accurate, the issue is controversial and anxiety-producing for many; often it seems easier to ignore the whole issue.

Friemann et al. (1996) offer steps for teachers similar to those dealing with other forms of bias:

- Examine their own feelings about homosexuality.

- Honestly recognize any biases that children may have about other children who are stigmatized as sissies (or tomboys), and keep those biases out of the classroom.

- Immediately handle any instances of students-to-student abuse and harassment, no matter how slight.

- Challenge negative remarks about gay people and other minority groups.

- Use classroom meetings or informal small groups, starting with a stem phrase for the children to complete, such as "When I am teased it makes me feel. . ." and help children focus on how people feel when they are harassed. No child should feel ashamed about her family, teachers, or self.

Families and educators need to work out how we can work together to teach basic life skills, ethics, culture, traditions, and the important small things that build substance in our children and in our society. This teamwork is possible IF these adults can find a way to honor diversity and still form a cohesive culture with each child's roots. "An ability to reach unity in diversity will be the beauty and test of our civilization," said Mahatma Gandhi. It is our ethical responsibility to articulate our values as educators and to include those of the families we teach.[1]

Professionalism

If you are thinking about working with young children as a career, you may be wondering if early childhood education is a profession worthy of a lifetime commitment. Can a person look forward to a challenging, intellectually stimulating, and rewarding future? To find those answers in today's world, we look at two issues: standards (for children's programs and teacher preparation) and the "trilemma."

Standards

Children's Programs. In Chapter 2, you will read about the rich array of programs offered for children in group care from infancy through age eight. Because they are so diverse, it is often difficult to define and assess the standard of care and education with one set of guidelines. Consider these statistics:

- ✪ Thirty-two states do not require prior training to teach in child care centers, and 39 and the District of Columbia do not require training of family child care providers (CDF, 2001).

- ✪ A study of child/staff ratios (Snow, Teleki, & Reguero-de-Atiles, 1996) found that fewer states met NAEYC-recommended standards for four-year-olds in 1995 than in 1981.

- ✪ Snow and coworkers (1996) also found that only 18 states met the NAEYC recommendations for group size for infants.

The most comprehensive set of standards for quality education and care in early childhood is DAP (Bredekamp, 1997). We need a core set of standards and an assessment system to evaluate them. This will ensure young children receive quality care and will help us to achieve professional status. The National Association for the Education of Young Children reports that more than 9,000 programs are accredited, serving 800,000 children (see Chapter 2).

Teacher Preparation. The quality of care in child development centers is linked to the training and education of the staff. Consequently, it is imperative that we attract and recruit to the field of early childhood education individuals who not only are dedicated to working with young children but also are skilled and competent. Many states are working on developing a career lattice and professional development plan for early childhood staff. Consideration must be given to developing a coordinated system that (1) welcomes peo-

Video   View Point   1-3

"Defining ECE as a Profession: Early childhood teachers and caregivers are part of a large and growing body of professionals."

Competency: Professionalism

Age Group: Preschool

Critical Thinking Questions:

1. Do you see yourself as a professional? Why or why not?

2. How do the characteristics on the videotape compare with the themes in the text?

[1] The early childhood education profession provides the opportunity for one to be an agent for social change—to actually translate the values of democracy into practice.

ple into the field from a variety of points, (2) offers clear career pathways with articulated training and credentialing systems, and (3) provides a variety of incentives to stay in the field. (See Chapter 5 for a description of teacher preparation in the early childhood field.)

Further, teacher preparation institutions are embarking on a cycle of self-study and articulation of coursework and experience that is offered at both the community college and four-year institutions in the United States. NAEYC's Standards for Programs (Hyson, 2003) is leading the charge, as do incentive programs such as California's Mentor Teacher Program. We look to continued efforts to articulate and upgrade the standards of care and education in early childhood programs.

A Trilemma

"The economics of child care continue to create a trilemma—quality for children, affordability for parents, and *adequate compensation for staff*" (Bredekamp et al., 1997). Quality is significantly related to staff: how many adults there are compared with the number of children in a class; whether the salaries and benefits provide incentive for teachers to be retained for a number of years; the level of the staff's education and training and their years of experience. These factors have created a staffing crisis of major proportion in the country today.

- Between 1982 and 1997, wages for all female workers increased by 79% compared with an 11% increase for all child care employees (U.S. Bureau of Labor Statistics, 2000).

- The average annual salary for a child care worker is approximately $15,400 without any benefits (U.S. Bureau of Labor Statistics, 2000).

- The annual turnover rate for child care staff is over 30% (Whitebook et al., 2001).

Important factors in determining program quality are high staff experience and education, little or no staff turnover, small teacher/student ratios, group size, and parent participation. Child care programs are having difficulty recruiting and hiring qualified replacement staff for those who leave. To improve the quality of child care, improved working conditions for teachers, appropriate licensing for early childhood care and education, staff training and preparation, and funding that is commensurate with per-child levels for elementary school children are areas of concern that must be addressed.

The challenge is before all of us—the child care professionals, the parents, the leaders of business and industry, and the legislators on the local, state, and national scene. National efforts called "Worthy Wage Campaign" and "Full Cost of Quality in Early Childhood Education Programs Campaign" are leading the early childhood field to advocacy and in bringing the issues of the child care crisis to national attention. It is a formidable challenge—and a worthy one for all of us as early childhood professionals.

Is this profession a worthwhile one? The early years are a special time of life, and those who work with young children might reflect on the following aspects of professionalism:

- *Sense of identity.* Early childhood education professionals see themselves as caregivers who strive to educate the whole child, taking into consideration the body, the mind, and the heart and soul (see Chapter 3).

- *Purpose to engage in DAP.* Quality care and education calls for blending child development and learning the strengths, interests, and needs of each child, and the social and cultural contexts in which children live (see Chapter 2).

- *Commitment to ethical teaching and to child advocacy.* Being a professional means behaving with a child's best interests in mind, maintaining confidentiality when discussing issues in the classroom and about families, upholding a code of ethics, and taking oneself and one's work seriously (see Chapter 5 and Appendix C).

Participation in the work as a legitimate livelihood. The people who provide care and education to young children deserve wages and working conditions that are worthy of their efforts.

Ours is a profession that is constantly growing, branching out in many directions and ready to meet emerging challenges in flexible, innovative ways. We have professional organizations to guide us. The NAEYC is the largest professional organization. ACEI includes both preschool and elementary school. The CDF lobbies for children in Washington, D.C., particularly addressing the needs of poor and minority children and those with disabilities. Their efforts have resulted in important improvements in the status of children, and they have begun to outline standards and practices for the people who call themselves "early childhood professionals."

KEY TERMS

accreditation
attitude crystallization
bilingual education
child-centered approach
child abuse
child neglect
children's garden
classist
compensatory education
demographics
developmentally appropriate practices (DAP)
early childhood education
ethnocentric
inclusion
integrated curriculum

kindergarten
kinship networks
laboratory schools
literacy
media culture
multicultural education
parent cooperative schools
prepared environment
professionalism
quality
racist
school readiness
self-correcting
sexist
tabula rasa
trilemma

Teaching Applications

1. Look at the list of important names and contributions to the field. Put them in the order that best matches your priorities in early childhood education. Add your reasons.
   Rousseau   children are naturally good
   Montessori   "prepared environment"
   McMillan sisters   "nurture" school
   Froebel   "a child's garden"
   Dewey   "child-centered"
   Malaguzzi   creativity
   Brazelton   reasonable discipline

2. Read the list below of some nontraditional and mainstream perspectives as described in the chapter. After each, trace its original root and put at least one example of how this perspective could be practiced in an early childhood classroom today.

   Perspective   **Harmony**
      Roots
      In Practice Today

   Perspective   **Kinship networks**
      Roots
      In Practice Today

Perspective   **Close ties to nature**
Roots
In Practice Today

Perspective   **Respect for elders**
Roots
In Practice Today

Perspective   **Cooperative work**
Roots
In Practice Today

Perspective   **Expressiveness**
Roots
In Practice Today

3. Maria Montessori made several contributions to education. What are some of her theories, and how did she adapt them for classroom use? How are Montessori materials or teaching methods used in your classroom?

4. Find out when and by whom the school or center in which you are teaching was started. What philosophies are important? Ask to look at any old photos, handbooks, or newspaper clippings. What were some of the social, economic, and political issues of those times? How might they have affected the philosophy of the school?

5. Make a list of the values you think are important to teach children. In an adjoining column, add the ways in which you would help children learn those values. In other words, list the materials and curriculum you would use.

REFERENCES

Armstrong, L. S. (1991, January 16). Racial ethnic prejudice still prevalent, survey finds. *Education Week*.

Biber, B. (1984). *Early Education and Psychological Development*. New Haven, CT: Yale University Press.

Brazelton, T. B., & Greenspan, S.D. (2001, March). The irreducible needs of children. *Young Children,* 6–13.

Bredekamp, S., et al. (1997). Developmentally appropriate practices (Rev. ed.). Washington, DC: NAEYC.

Carlisle, C. (1991). Children of divorce. *Childhood Education*.

Carolina Abecedarian Project. (1999). *The Frank Porter Graham Child Development Institute.* The University of North Carolina at Chapel Hill: Author.

CDC [Centers for Disease Control and Prevention]. (1999). *AIDS surveillance by race/ethnicity.* Atlanta, GA: Author.

Center for Children and Families. (2000b). "Growing Up in Poverty" Project. New York: Teachers College, Columbia University, www.teacherscollege.edu.

Center for Media Literacy. (1993, August). *Beyond blame: Challenging violence in the media: Report from the American Psychological Association's Commission on Violence and Youth in America.* Multimedia presentation. Los Angeles: Author.

Chen, M. (1994). The smart parents' guide to kids' TV. San Francisco: KQED Books.

CDF [Children's Defense Fund]. (2000a). *The state of America's children: Leave no child behind.* Washington, DC: Author.

CDF. (2001). The state of America's children: Leave no child behind. Washington, DC: Author.

Child Care Law Center. (1994, November) "The ADA: a new way of thinking" (brochure). Available through Web site: www.childcarelaw.org.

Clarke-Stewart, K. A. (1989, January). Single-parent families: How bad for the children? *NEA Today.*

Corbett, S. (1993, March). A complicated bias. *Young Children.*

CQCOS [Cost, Quality, and Child Outcomes Study] team. (1995). *Cost, quality, and child outcomes in child care centers public report.* Denver: Economics Department, University of Colorado–Denver.

DeMause, L. (1974). *The history of childhood.* New York: Psychohistory Press.

Derman-Sparks, L., et al. (1989). *Anti-bias curriculum: Tools for empowering young children.* Washington, DC: National Association for the Education of Young Children.

Du Bois, W. E. B. (1903 [1995]). The talented tenth. In F. Schultz (Ed.), *Notable selections in education.* Guilford, CT: Dushkin Publishing Group.

Edelman, M. W. (1998). *The state of America's children.* Washington, DC: Children's Defense Fund.

Fillmore, L. W. (1991, June 19). A question for early-childhood programs: English first or families first? *Education Week.*

Friemann, B. B., O'Hara, H., & Settel, J. (1996, Fall). What heterosexual teachers need to know about homosexuality. *Childhood Education.*

Gestwicki, C. (1999) *Developmentally appropriate practice: Curriculum and development in early education* (2nd ed.). Clifton Park, NY: Thomson Delmar Learning.

Gonzalez-Mena, J. (2001). *Foundations: Early childhood education in a diverse society.* Mountain View, CA: Mayfield Publishing Company.

Grossman, H., & Grossman, S. H. (1994). *Gender issues in education.* Boston: Allyn & Bacon.

Haycock, K. (1991, March). Reaching for the year 2000. *Childhood Education.*

Hilliard, A. G., III. (1997, September). Teacher education from an African American perspective. In J. Irvine (Ed.), *Critical knowledge for diverse teachers and learners.* Washington, DC: American Association of Colleges for Teacher Education (AACTE).

Hymes, J. L., Jr. (1978–79). *Living history interviews* (Books 1–3). Carmel, CA: Hacienda Press.

Hyson, M. (Ed.).(2003) *Preparing early childhood professionals: NAEYC's Standards for Programs.* Washington, DC: NAEYC.

Kagan, S. L., & Neuman, M. J. (1997). Highlights of the Quality 2000 Initiative: Not by chance. *Young Children* 52: 54–62.

Karoly, Lynn A., and Bigelow, James H. (2005). *The Economics of Investing in Universal Preschool Education in California.* Santa Monica, CA: RAND [Research and Development] Corporation.

Malaguzzi, L. (1993). For an education based on relationships. *Young Children* 49: 9–12.

McMillan, R. (Deptford School). www.spartacus.schoolnet.co.uk/WmcmillanR.htm.

NAEYC [National Association for the Education of Young Children]. (1990). *Media violence and children.* Washington, DC: Author.

NEGP [National Education Goals Panel]. (1991). *The national education goals report: Building a nation of learners.* Washington, DC: Author.

Osborn, D. K. (1991). *Early childhood education in historical perspective* (3rd ed.). Athens, GA: Education Associates.

Peisner-Feinberg, E. S., Burchinal, M. R., Clifford, R. M., Culkin, M.L., Howes, C., Kagan, S. L., et al. (2000). *The children of the Cost, Quality, and Outcomes Study go to school:*

Technical report. Chapel Hill: University of North Carolina at Chapel Hill, Frank Porter Graham Child Development Center.

Schmidt, P. (1989). Outlook is bleak for many blacks. *Education Week,* August 2.

Schlank, C. H., & Metzger, B. (1997). *Together and equal.* Boston: Allyn & Bacon.

Snow, C. W., Teleki, J. K., & Reguero-de-Atiles, J. T. (1996, September). Child care center licensing standards in the United States: 1981 to 1995. *Young Children,* 36–41.

Udell, T., Peters, J., and Templeman, T. P. (1998, January/February). From philosophy to practice in inclusive early childhood programs. *Teaching Exceptional Children.*

U.S. Department of Labor. (2000). *1999 National occupational employment and wage estimates.* Washington, DC: Author.

U.S. Census Bureau. (2002). *School enrollment in the United States—social and economic characteristics of students.* Washington, DC: Author.

U.S. Department of Education. (2001). *National household education survey.* Washington, DC: Author.

U.S. Department of Health and Human Services. (2002). *National Child Abuse and Neglect Data System: Summary of key findings from calendar year 2000.* Washington, DC: Author.

Viadero, D. (1990, November 28). Battle over multicultural education rises in intensity. *Education Week.*

Wallerstein, J., in Jacobson, L. (1997, June 11). Emotional damage from divorce found to linger. *Education Week.*

Whitebook, M., Sakai, L., Gerber, E., & Howes, C. (2001). Then and now: changes in child care staffing, 1994–2000. Washington, DC: Center for the Child Care Workforce.

Additional resources for this chapter can be found by visiting the Online Companion™ at www.earlychilded.delmar.com. This supplemental material includes a Study Guide with chapter review questions (and answers), critical thinking questions and activities, and annotated Web sites.

Types of Programs

QUESTIONS FOR THOUGHT

What are the different types of early childhood programs?

What are the indicators of quality in group programs for young children?

What is a developmentally appropriate program?

How does the role of the teacher differ in each of the early childhood settings?

How are programs structured to meet specific needs of children and families?

How can evaluating programs help children and teachers?

DIVERSITY OF PROGRAMS

From the types available, to the numbers of children who attend these schools, the name of the game in early childhood programs is diversity. The range can encompass a morning nursery school for toddlers, a primary school classroom, an infant–parent stimulation program, or a full child care service for three- to six-year-olds. Some programs run for only a half-day; others are open from 6:00 AM until 7:00 PM. Still other programs, such as those in hospitals, accept children on a drop-in basis or for 24-hour care. Child care arrangements can range from informal home-based care to more formal school or center settings. Churches, school districts, community-action groups, parents, governments, private social agencies, and businesses may run schools.

Serving Many Needs

Programs for young children exist to serve a number of needs, which often overlap. Some of these are

- Caring for children while parents work (e.g., family child care homes, child care center)
- Enrichment programs for children (e.g., half-day nursery school, laboratory school)
- Educational programs for parent and child (e.g., parent cooperatives, parent–child public school programs, high school parent classes)
- An activity arena for children (e.g., most early childhood programs)
- Academic instruction (e.g., kindergarten, many early childhood programs)

- Culturally or religiously specific programs (e.g., a school setting with a definitive African-American focus, a **faith-based school** that teaches religious dogma).

Programs generally reflect the needs of society as a whole. With millions of mothers of children under six in the labor force as never before, one of the greatest needs is to provide the kind of programs to meet the demands of today's working mothers. Early childhood settings provide a wide range of services for children from infancy through eight years of age to serve these families.

In the human life cycle, early childhood is a period of maximum dependency. Individual programs reflect this need in a number of ways. The teacher/child ratio varies in relation to the child's age; infants, at the higher end of the dependency scale, require more teachers per child in a classroom than do six-year-olds. The program itself reflects the age group it serves. The size of the group, the length of the program, and the equipment used are related to the enrolled children's capabilities and needs. Even the daily schedule mirrors the dependent relationship between the child and the teacher. Bathrooming and snack and meal routines, as well as clothing needs, call for longer periods of time in a toddler group than in a class of four-year-olds.

Diversity is apparent, too, in the philosophy expressed by the specific program.[1] Some schools, such as Montessori programs, follow a very clear, precise outline based on a philosophical approach developed by Maria Montessori nearly 100

[1]In observing programs for young children, consider the influences on the teachers' philosophy and practice; in many cases it is eclectic, a little bit of this and a little bit of that. It is another indication of how practice is influenced by life in a democratic and multicultural society.

years ago. Other schools are more eclectic; they draw from a number of theories, choosing those methods and ideas that best suit their needs, some of which may be culturally or theologically based (Figure 2–1).

Special Features

Mixed-Age Grouping

One factor that may cut across program considerations is that of placing children of several age levels into the same classroom.

Factors that Determine Types of Early Childhood Education Programs
Many factors determine exactly what type of program will best serve young children. Some of these variables are
1. age of the children served
2. philosophical, theoretical, or theological approach
3. goals of the program
4. purpose for which the program was established
5. requirements of a sponsoring agency
6. quality and training of teaching staff
7. shape, size, and location of physical environment
8. cultural, ethnic, economic, and social makeup of community
9. financial stability

FIGURE 2–1 Programs in early childhood settings are defined by these elements, and each factor has to be taken into consideration regarding its impact on the program. Any given program is a combination of these ingredients.

This practice is often referred to as family grouping or heterogeneous, vertical, or ungraded grouping and, though not a new idea, is emerging as an area of considerable interest to early childhood educators. Montessori schools, one-room schoolhouses, and the Reggio Emilia schools have observed this practice for many years.

The age range among children in **mixed-age groups** is usually larger than one year. Advocates of mixed-age groups point to a number of developmental advantages when children interact with peers above and below their age level:

1. Each child's own developmental level and pace are accommodated, allowing children to advance as they are ready.
2. Age and competition are de-emphasized, as cooperative learning is enhanced.
3. Caring and helping behaviors toward younger children and a sense of responsibility toward one another are fostered.
4. Diverse learning styles and multiple intelligences are appreciated.
5. A variety and number of different models for learning and for friendships are available.
6. Children grow in independence in their work and in socialization.

There are risks associated with mixed-age groupings. The potential for older children to take over and/or overwhelm the younger ones is real, as is the possibility that younger children will pester the older children. This requires monitoring by the teaching staff, and the Reggio Emilia schools offer a good model here. In these Italian programs, older children have the responsibility to work with the younger children, explaining things and helping them find appropriate roles to take in their projects.

The academic and social advantages of mixed-age grouping cannot occur without a variety of activities from which children may freely choose and the opportunity for small groups of children to work together. Teachers must be intentional about encouraging children to work with others who have skills and knowledge they do not yet possess.

It is easy to see how mixed-age groupings reflect the principles of Dewey, Piaget, Gardner, and Vygotsky, whose "zone of proximal development" is made more available through the interactions of peers as well as adults. The practice of mixed-age grouping has much to commend it and must be seriously addressed as an issue in programs for young children.

Looping

The practice of keeping a group of children and their teacher together in the same class for at least two years is called **looping**. Like mixed-age grouping, it is an old idea revisited. The one-room schoolhouse of days gone by and the British Infant Schools used this practice. Today, looping is customary in the Waldorf Schools and Reggio Emilia programs, and it has emerged in other programs for a number of reasons. In the schools in Reggio Emilia, for instance, infants and toddlers are kept in the same class with the same teachers for three years to provide a family-like environment. Looping is often paired with mixed-age

Differences in age can enrich the learning environment.

classrooms, which further extends the natural, family-like atmosphere.

Benefits of looping are (1) stability and emotional security to children, (2) giving teachers a greater opportunity to get to know children and therefore be able to individualize the program for them, (3) fostering better social interactions among children, and (4) enhancing a sense of family and community within the classroom. Critics of looping cite the need for experienced teachers who enjoy teaching across the age levels and who can work with the same children over an extended period of time. Looping does not fit all teachers and all children, and it could be offered as an option for parents and teachers to meet the needs of those who believe its advantages are worthwhile (Bellis, 1999; Chapman, 1999).

INDICATORS OF QUALITY

Early childhood education programs vary greatly in their educational goals and practices, their methods of instruction, and even in the kind of social "mood" or atmosphere they create. Yet, varied as they are, most early childhood programs share some common principles. The quality of these programs is based on three essential factors:

1. the teacher/child ratio, that is, the number of children cared for by each staff member

2. the total size of the group or class

3. the education, experience, and training of the staff

The National Association for the Education of Young Children (NAEYC), the largest professional organization for early childhood educators and caregivers, has established a list of criteria for high-quality early childhood programs, based on a consensus of thousands of early childhood professionals. NAEYC (1998b) defines a **high-quality program** as one that "meets the needs of and promotes the physical, social, emotional, and cognitive development of the children and adults—parents, staff, and administrators—who are involved in the program."

Figure 2–2 indicates the 10 criteria that serve as a standard of excellence for any group program for young children. After each one is a reference to the chapter(s) in this text where the topic is more fully developed.

Developmentally Appropriate Practice

Throughout this text and whenever NAEYC principles are discussed, we use the term **developmentally appropriate practice** (DAP). What exactly is DAP?

In the late 1980s, the NAEYC published a position paper, *Developmentally Appropriate Practice in Early Childhood Programs Serving Children from Birth to Age 8,* which articulated standards for high-quality care and education for young children. The guidelines were issued in response to the need for a set of unified standards for accreditation through NAEYC's newly established National Academy of Early Childhood Programs. The guidelines provided a necessary antidote to the more teacher-directed, academic preparation, and skills-teaching methods that were encroaching on many early childhood programs.

The position paper was revised by NAEYC in 1996, following an extensive review by early childhood professionals over a two-year period. One of the significant changes was to move from DAP being an "either/or" point of view to that of "both/and." In other words, there are many right ways to apply the DAP principles. That position statement, revised again in 2005, cites *three criteria* on which teachers

and caregivers should base their decisions about young children's growth and development:

1. What is known about *child development and learning*—knowledge of age-related human characteristics that permit general predictions within an age range about what activities, materials, interactions, or experiences will be safe, healthy, interesting, achievable, and also challenging to children.

2. What is known about the strengths, interests, and needs of *each individual child* in the group to be able to adapt for and be responsive to inevitable individual variation.

3. Knowledge of *the social and cultural contexts* in which children live—to ensure that learning experiences are meaningful, relevant, and respectful for the participating children and their families (NAEYC, 2005).

What does this mean to an early childhood professional who wants to develop a program and curriculum that is developmentally appropriate? The key element in the DAP philosophy is a solid grounding in child development knowledge. That is the core around which the idea of *developmentally appropriate* is built and provides the base for learning environments in which children's abilities are matched to the developmental tasks they need to learn at any given age. Programs are designed *for* young children based on what is known *about* young children (Bredekamp & Copple, 1997). To that mix we add what we learn about the individual children and their families. This collective knowledge is applied to each decision that is made about the program: What are children like? How do they learn? What should they learn? When should they learn it? How should they be taught? How do we know they are learning? Gestwicki (1999) reminds us that finding a balance between the teacher's

Ten Essentials for High-Quality Programs

1. Interactions between children and staff provide opportunities for children to develop an understanding of self and others and are characterized by warmth, personal respect, individuality, positive support, and responsiveness (Chapters 3, 5, 7, 9).

2. The curriculum encourages children to be actively involved in the learning process, to experience a variety of developmentally appropriate activities and materials, and to pursue their own interests in the context of life in the community and the world. The program is inclusive of all children, including those with identified disabilities and special learning and developmental needs[1] (Chapters 4, 10, 11).

3. Relationships among teachers and families are based on a partnership to ensure high-quality care and education, and parents feel supported and welcomed as observers and contributors to the program (Chapters 5, 8).

4. The program is staffed by adults who are trained in child and family development and who recognize and meet the developmental and learning needs of children and families. They recognize that the quality and competence of the staff are the most important determinants of the quality of an early childhood program (Chapters 3, 5).

5. The quality of the early childhood experience for children is affected by the efficiency and stability of the program's administration. Effective administration includes good communication, positive community relationships, fiscal stability, and attention to the needs and working conditions of staff members (Chapters 1, 2).

6. The staffing structure of the program is organized to ensure that the needs of individual children are met, and it facilitates individualized, responsive care and supports learning. Smaller group size and high staff/child ratios are related to positive outcomes for children (Chapters 3, 5, and 10).

7. The indoor and outdoor physical environments should be designed to promote optimal growth and development through opportunities for exploration and learning. The quality of physical space and materials affects the levels of involvement of the children and the quality of interaction between adults and children (Chapters 9 and 10).

8. The health and safety of children and adults are protected and enhanced. Good programs act to prevent illness and accidents, are prepared to deal with emergencies should they occur, and also educate children concerning safe and healthy practices (Chapter 9).

9. Children are provided with adequate nutrition and are taught good eating habits (Chapter 9).

10. Ongoing and systematic evaluation are essential to improving and maintaining the quality of an early childhood program. Evaluation should focus on the program's effectiveness in meeting the needs of children, families, and staff (Chapters 2, 6, and 8).

[1]Young children with special needs should have opportunities to engage in the normal activities of early childhood.

FIGURE 2–2 These are the 10 essential components on which a program is judged for accreditation through NAEYC's Academy of Early Childhood Programs.

knowledge and understanding of the child and the family's desires and expectations is an important component of DAP. This can be particularly sensitive when cultural values are at stake. The following examples are based on what is developmentally appropriate planning, as is Figure 2–3.

Developmentally appropriate principles are reflected when

* Programs and curriculum respond to the children's interests as well as their needs.

* *Example: While digging in the sandpit, four children uncover water. Others rush to see it. The teacher sees their interest and asks them about building dams, bridges or tunnels. A project in the making: children research, experiment, build, and learn.*

* Children are actively involved in their own learning, choosing from a variety of materials and equipment.

* *Example: Some children search the yard for materials that would bridge the water. Others go inside to find the big book on bridges. Still others dig in other areas of the sandpit to find more water. One child finds a walnut shell and floats it on the water. The teacher encourages and supports each child's involvement.*

* Play is the primary context in which young children learn and grow.

* *Example: Each day, the children rush outside to see their bridges and tunnels. The teacher has helped them find materials that will act as a cover over the bridge. Inside, several children are making dolls from twigs and fabric scraps to use in the project.*

* Teachers apply what they know about each child and use a variety of strategies, materials, and learning experiences to be responsive to individual children.

* *Example: Josephina is drawing a picture of the bridge in the sandpit and is having trouble with the arches. Knowing that Josephina is somewhat shy and uneasy in large groups, the teacher asks Aldo (who is easygoing and loves to draw) to look at Josephina's picture to see if he might help her. The two children focus on the drawing, each making observations that helps Josephina take the next step in her artwork.*

* Teachers consider widely held expectations about each age group and temper that with challenging yet achievable learning goals.

* *Example: In preparation for a field trip to see two bridges that are near the school, the teacher sets out her expectations (walk with a buddy, stay together, stay on the sidewalk, walk, don't run, etc.). Because this is their first field trip of the school year, the teacher rehearses the children for several days prior to the trip. Music and rhythm accompany them as they practice walking with a friend, play number games of "two-by-two" during group times, and so on.*

* Teachers understand that any activity has the potential for different children to realize different learning from the same experience.

* *After the field trip, Josephina draws a different type of arch for her bridges. Selena, Gracie, and Sam take over the block corner to build bridges and tunnels; three others join them. Maddie finds a book on flowers. They look like some of the flowers she saw on the walk to the bridge. Reilly wants to play London Bridge at group time.*

* All aspects of development—physical, social-emotional, cognitive, and language—are integrated in the activities and opportunities of the program.

* *The bridge project promoted physical (walking to the bridge), social-emotional (pairing up two-by-two), cognitive (learning how bridges and tunnels are built, researching in books), and language (construction terms such as piers, spans, suspension).*

The early childhood professional should address all three principles when designing good programs for young children, keeping in mind that each is connected to the other two in significant ways. Figure 2–3 shows what might happen when planning programs for a toddler group and a class of four-year-olds.

Scenario 1

1. *What does child development tell us about toddlers?* **We know that they want to do everything by themselves, usually more than they can actually achieve. They like to feel independent and learn quickly if given a little help and then encouraged to do what they can for themselves.**

2. *What do we know about each individual child in the group?* **Many of these toddlers rely on their parents to do things for them; such as helping them put on coats or shoes, feeding them, or putting their toys away. Others are encouraged to try these activities by themselves, and some of them are being taught at home. Most children come to a teacher for assistance, and a few call for help. On the other hand, one child will stay at a dressing task for nearly five minutes, while another will throw shoes across the floor if they don't slip on easily the first time she tries.**

3. *What do we know about the social and cultural context of their homes?* **Most of the children in this group come from homes in which help is readily available through siblings and extended family members. The dominant cultural values and child-rearing practices reinforce dependence and com-**

Scenario 2

1. *What does child development tell us about four- and five-year-olds?* **We know that they are great talkers; they like to play with language, making up stories, songs, and poems. They love being read to, and they enjoy dictating stories of their experiences and ideas. We know that children this age need experiences in using oral language to connect those experiences with words and letters to understand the use of the written word in their daily lives. We know that children of this age learn to read by spending time reading and writing about what interests them.**

2. *What do we know about each individual child in the group?* **We have observed that a few of the children are creating more elaborate stories, complete with drawings. At the same time, there are several children who rarely participate in any of the art or story activities.**

3. *What do we know about the social and cultural context of their homes?* **We know that all of the parents have expressed interest, if not concern, that their children learn to read to do well when they get to kindergarten. Many of the children come from homes in which reading is highly valued. Many**

FIGURE 2–3 Programs that are developmentally appropriate take many factors into consideration that reflect the children, their families, and the teacher's understanding and knowledge of child development.

Continued

munity, although there is a smaller group of families that want their children to become independent as soon as possible.

By looking at all three criteria in relation to one another, we have some decisions to make about setting goals for the toddlers, which would help them achieve greater independence. Respecting cultural diversity means we begin by talking to parents, perhaps at a parent meeting, in which families are invited to share their child-rearing practices from their cultural viewpoints. Once we have an understanding of what families expect and want, we have an opportunity to work together to find a solution that would be good for the toddler and good for the parents as well. This is what Hyun (1998) refers to as "*negotiable curriculum,* where teachers are no longer the ultimate power holders in any decision-making." According to Hyun, the diverse voices of children and their parents are the "main agent in teacher's appropriate approach," creating a sense of shared power.

come from family backgrounds in which storytelling is a primary method of transmitting culture, history, and values. Most of the children are encouraged by their families to draw "stories" about their experiences.

There appears to be a common interest among the parents about reinforcing the concept of reading. The task becomes one of helping parents understand the meaning of literacy in the early years and developing an activity area that engages the preschoolers in meaningful activities that support the program's goals for literacy development. The daily schedule is adjusted to allow for small group times when the children tell stories to one another or dictate them to a teacher. Areas of the classroom are modified for literacy-rich experiences: Picture books about building are added to the block corner; children are encouraged to write or draw notes to one another; recipes with drawings instead of words are used in cooking activities; paper and crayons are placed in the dramatic play area to encourage the writing of grocery lists and telephone numbers. Long-term projects involving children writing stories together or writing stories of their lives can be integrated into the planning as well.

FIGURE 2–3, continued

According to NAEYC (2005), developmentally appropriate principles are reflected when children

1. construct their own understanding of concepts and benefit from instruction by more competent peers and adults

2. benefit from opportunities to see connections across disciplines through integration of curriculum and from opportunities to engage in in-depth study

3. benefit from predictable structure and routine in the learning environment and from the teacher's flexibility and spontaneity in responding to their emerging ideas, needs, and interests

4. benefit from making meaningful choices about what they will do

5. benefit from situations that challenge them to work at the edge of their capacities and from ample opportunities to practice newly acquired skills

6. benefit from opportunities to collaborate with their peers and acquire a sense of community

7. need to develop a positive sense of their own self-identity and respect for other people, whose perspective and experiences may be different from their own

8. have enormous curiosity and capacities to learn and have recognized age-related limits on their intellectual and linguistic capacity

9. benefit from engaging in self-initiated, spontaneous play and from teacher-planned structured activities, projects, and experiences.

As you observe in classrooms and read further chapters on the teacher's role, behavior, environments, and curriculum, reflect on these developmental principles. Do they match your understanding of early childhood development?

DAP is integrated into many other sections of the text. The Word Pictures in Chapter 3 offer a view of some general characteristics of children at various age levels, which can inform a teacher's decision-making process about developmentally appropriate practices. In Chapter 6, observations that focus on individual children are discussed and related to DAP. Chapter 9 outlines DAP daily schedules and environments for young children. Chapter 3 discusses developmentally appropriate evaluation of children, and, in Chapter 10, curriculum approaches that meet DAP criteria are discussed. A reading

of NAEYC's position paper (see Appendix C) provides a more in-depth rationale for the various components of DAP, its philosophical foundation, and examples of appropriate practice for infants and children through age eight.

Developmentally and Culturally Appropriate Practice

Culturally appropriate practice is the ability to go beyond one's own sociocultural background to ensure equal and fair teaching and learning experiences for all. This concept, developed by Hyun (1998), expands DAP to address cultural influences that emphasize the adult's ability to develop a multiethnic outlook. Preparing teachers and caregivers for multiculturalism is not just about becoming sensitive to race, gender, ethnicity, religion, socioeconomic status, or sexual orientation, according to Hyun. It is also related to an understanding of the way individual histories, families of origin, and ethnic family cultures make us similar to and yet different from others. Through such insights, teachers will be able to respond positively to the individual child's unique expressions of growth, change, learning styles, culture, language, problem-solving skills, feelings, and communication styles (Hyun, 1998).

Hyun stresses the need for "cultural congruency" between a child's home and school experience[1] and suggests using the following questions:

1. What relationships do children see between the activity and work they do in class and the lives they lead outside school?

[1]Children's growth and development can be understood only within their cultural context.

2. Is it possible to incorporate aspects of children's culture into the work of schooling without simply confirming what they already know?

3. Can this incorporation be practiced without devaluing the objects or relationships important to the children?

4. Can this practice succeed without ignoring particular groups of people as "other" within a "dominant" culture? (Hyun, 1998)

A culturally congruent approach to DAP would respect the variances in children's perceiving and understanding, and teaching practices would be based on children's different decision-making styles and social interaction abilities (Hyun, 1998). NAEYC's criteria for respecting cultural diversity (Figure 2–4) provide examples of ways in which to connect a child's sense

of cultural continuity between home and school.

THE CORE PROGRAMS OF EARLY CHILDHOOD EDUCATION

What do programs for the young child look like? How are the similarities and differences expressed in school settings? What marks a program as unique? The answers to these questions can be found by looking at some of the most common programs in early childhood education.

The Traditional Nursery School/Preschool

The **traditional nursery school** (often called preschool) exemplifies a developmental approach to

DAP in Action—Respect for Cultural Diversity
Using NAEYC's criteria for cultural diversity, these examples demonstrate how DAP supports greater consistency between home and school cultures when you:

- Build a sense of the group as a community, bringing each child's home culture and language into the shared culture of the school so each child feels accepted and gains a sense of belonging

- Provide books, materials, images, and experiences that reflect diverse cultures that children may not likely see, as well as those that represent their family life and cultural group

- Initiate discussions and activities to teach respect and appreciation for similarities and differences among people

- Talk positively about each child's physical characteristics, family, and cultural heritage

- Avoid stereotyping of any group through materials, objects, language

- Invite families' participation in all aspects of the program

- Take trips to museums and cultural resources of the community

- Infuse all curriculum topics with diverse cultural perspectives, avoiding a "tourist" approach

FIGURE 2–4 All children and their families deserve to be in programs in which their lives are respected and in which they can be proud of their cultural heritage (NAEYC, 1998).

learning, in which children actively explore materials and in which activity or learning centers are organized to meet the developing skills and interests of the child. Most of these programs serve children from two-and-a-half to five years of age.

The philosophy of these schools is best described by Katherine Read Baker (1955) in her now classic book *The Nursery School: A Human Relationships Laboratory.* First published more than 50 years ago, this book serves as an encyclopedia of the traditional nursery school, its methods, and its philosophy, reflecting the influence of Comenius, Locke, Rousseau, Pestalozzi, Froebel, and Montessori. Baker's philosophy emphasizes the human needs, growth patterns, and relationships in a young child's life. Developmentally, a traditional nursery school focuses on social competence and emotional well-being. The curriculum encourages self-expression through language, creativity, intellectual skill, and physical activity. The basic underlying belief is the importance of interpersonal con-

nections children make with themselves, each other, and adults.

The daily schedule reflects these beliefs (Figure 2–5). Large blocks of time are devoted to free play, a time when children are free to initiate their own activities and become deeply involved without interruptions, emphasizing the importance of play. In this way, children learn to make their own choices, select their own playmates, and work on their interests and issues at their own rate. A dominant belief is that children learn best in an atmosphere free from excessive restraint and direction.[1]

Typically, there is a balance of activities (indoors and out, free choice, and teacher-directed times) and a wide variety of activities (large- and small-muscle games, intellectual choices, creative arts, social play opportunities).

Video View Point 2-1

"A consistent structure for the day helps preschoolers develop a sense of security."

Competency: Program Management

Age Group: Preschool

Critical Thinking Questions:

1. How does the daily schedule reflect a sense of security?

2. What changes would you make in a preschool program where you have observed or worked to enhance a child's feeling of security?

9:00	Children arrive at school
9:00–9:45	Free play (indoors)
9:45	Cleanup
10:00	Singing time (large group)
10:15–10:30	Toileting/snack time (small groups)
10:30–11:30	Free play (outdoors)
11:30	Cleanup
11:45	Story time
12:00	Children leave for home

FIGURE 2–5 A sample schedule for traditional half-day nursery schools is the core of early childhood education programs.

[1]This is not true for all cultures.

The role of the teacher and methods of teaching are important. Nursery schools assume that young children need individual attention and should have personal, warm relationships with important adults. Therefore, the groups of children are generally small, often fewer than 20 in a class. The teacher/child ratio is low, as few as six to 10 children for each teacher. Teachers learn about children's development and needs by observation and direct interaction, rather than from formalized testing, individually and in small groups. They encourage children to express themselves, their feelings, and their thinking. Such rapport between teacher and pupil fosters self-confidence, security, and belonging. Proponents of the traditional nursery school believe that these feelings promote positive self-image, healthy relationships, and an encouraging learning environment.

Universal Preschools

A growing number of school districts provide prekindergarten programs for four-year-olds, although some include three-year-olds as well. Depending on their goal, these programs fall somewhere between traditional nursery schools and not quite full-day care. For some, the focus is on school readiness; others give priority to children at risk for school failure, children who come from families in which English is not spoken, or low-income families. In states in which early education has achieved a level of support, all four-year-olds are eligible for enrollment, regardless of income.

Laboratory Schools

The college and university **laboratory schools** were among the first preschools established in the United States. They focus on teacher training, research, and innovative education. As part of the child study movement, laboratory schools gathered information previously unknown about children and child development. Early ones include Hampton Institute in 1873; the University of Chicago, founded by John Dewey in 1896; Bank Street School in 1919, begun by Harriet Johnson; and the laboratory nursery school at Columbia Teacher's College, started in 1921 by Patty Smith Hill. More recently, community-college campuses have followed the lead of these pioneers. Campus child care centers have begun to combine child care services with the laboratory function of teacher training in one setting. The types and roles of the schools vary, depending on the educational philosophy and needs of the college and its students. Regardless of their specific purposes, laboratory schools enlarge our understanding of children. They are often excellent places for beginning teachers to learn good teaching practices They encourage the joining of psychology, medicine, and other related fields to early education, and they serve as professional models for the public at large for what is good in child care and education.

Parent Cooperatives

Parent cooperative schools are organized and run by parents. This type of early childhood setting offers a unique opportunity for parents to be involved in the education of their child. Faculty wives at the University of Chicago started the very first parent cooperative, the Chicago Co-operative Nursery School, in 1915.

Parent cooperative schools may offer half-day or full-day child care programs and are usually nonprofit organizations. They are similar to other nursery schools, with two notable exceptions. First, parents organize and maintain the school: They hire the teachers, buy supplies and equipment, recruit members, raise funds, influence school philosophy, and manage the budget.

Second, traditionally, parents or their substitutes were required to participate in the classroom on a regular basis. In light of current family work patterns and the unavailability of many parents, this requirement has been modified in most programs. More professional teachers are hired, or other parents who are available are paid to substitute for parents who cannot work at the center.

Cooperative schools work well for many reasons. Popular with young families, they have low operating costs, the appeal of being with parents in similar circumstances, and the mutual support that is generated among members of a co-op. Friendships grow among parents who share child-rearing as participants in their own and in their child's education. But what a co-op does not cost in dollars, it may cost in time. By their very nature, cooperatives can exclude working parents unless another adult is able to substitute for them in classroom participation. Maintenance is very much the parents' responsibility; they must regularly schedule work parties to refurbish the facility.

Depending on the size of the school, parents hire one or more professional teachers. These teachers must be able to work well with adults, have curriculum-building skills, and model good guidance and discipline techniques. Because many parent cooperatives require a weekly or monthly parent meeting, the teaching staff must also be competent in parent education. Child development and child-rearing topics are part of almost any cooperative nursery school discussion and require a practiced teacher to lead. The role of the teacher in this setting, then, is twofold: to provide for a sound educational experience for young children and to guide and direct parents in their own learning.

FULL-DAY CHILD CARE PROGRAMS

Some of the first nursery schools in England operated from 8:00 AM until 4:00 or 5:00 PM. Child care is not a modern phenomenon. By definition, a full-day child care program is a place for children who need care for a greater portion of the day than the traditional nursery school offers. A longer day means that ordinary routines such as meals and naps are part of the schedule. A full-day option is also educational. Much of the curriculum of a good full-day program will echo the quality of the traditional nursery school or preschool. The school schedule, from 6:00 or 7:00 AM to 6 or 7:00 PM, is extended to fit the hours of working parents. Child care centers often serve infants and toddlers, as well as

Parents want individual attention and warm relationships from their child care centers.

the two-and-a-half to five-year-old range. Many offer an after-school option as well. There are many full-day care options.

Child Care Centers

Child care centers serve children from infancy through preschool, and some include kindergarten. More than 25% of parents needing care choose this option (Smith, 2002). They vary in their services and locations. These centers can be found in churches and synagogues, in YWCA/YMCAs, in community and recreational facilities, corporate business buildings, and hospitals. They are private and public. Most of them operate year-round.

Compare the nursery school schedule with the child care schedule. The morning starts slowly, and children arrive early. The center may supply breakfast, midmorning and midafternoon snacks, supplementing a lunch from home. Some centers are funded to supply all of the meals and snacks during the day. A nap period for one to two hours for all the children gives a needed rest and balances their active, social day with quiet, solitary time. The program may also include experiences outside the school—field trips, library story hour, or swimming lessons—because children spend the major portion of their waking hours on-site. As the day draws to a close, children gather together quietly, with less energy and activity.

The staff in a full-day setting is often called on to deal with the parenting side of teaching. Children in full-day care may need more nurturing and clearer consistency in behavioral limits from caring adults. Parents' needs also may be greater and require more of the teachers' time. Teachers should communicate with and support parents effectively. Child care parents may require extra effort; they have full-time jobs as well as child-rearing responsibilities draining their energies. It takes a strong team effort on the part of the teacher and the parent to make sure the lines of communication stay open.

The teaching staff undoubtedly has staggered schedules, perhaps a morning and an afternoon shift. Administration of this type of program is therefore more complex. An effort must be made to ensure that all teachers get together on a regular basis to share the information and details about the children in their care. Both shifts must be aware of what happens when they are not on site to run the program consistently.

7:00–8:30	Arrival/breakfast; limited indoor play
8:30	Large group meeting
9:45	Cleanup/toileting
8:45–9:45	Free play (inside)
10:00	Snack time (small groups)
10:15–11:30	Free play (outside)
11:30	Cleanup/handwashing
12:00	Lunch
12:30	Toothbrushing/toileting
1:00–2:00	Nap time
2:00–3:00	Free play (outside)
3:00	Group time
3:15	Snack time (small groups)
3:30–5:00	Inside and outside free play/library hour
5:00	Cleanup
5:15–5:30	Departure

A typical full-day care schedule. Most child care programs combine education and caring for basic needs.

The most critical issues on child care were noted in Chapter 1. The quality of full-day child care programs is spotty; some are of good quality, with appropriate compensation to maintain staff professionalism and stability; others are low quality with untrained staff and low salaries. As you read in Chapter 1, these factors are related to the quality of the child care experience. It is worth repeating here that high-quality, affordable child care is an issue that will not go away and deserves the attention of early childhood professionals and legislators.

Family Child Care

Family child care is a type of service that cares for children in ways reminiscent of an extended family grouping. The child care provider takes in small numbers of children in the family residence. The group size can range from two to 12, but most homes keep a low adult-child ratio, enrolling fewer than six children. The home setting, sometimes right within the child's own neighborhood, offers a more intimate, flexible, convenient, and possibly less expensive service for working parents. The children in a family child care home can range from infants to school-age children who are cared for after regular school hours.

Because they often care for infants, preschoolers, and after-schoolers, the developmental ranges that family child care providers must meet may span up to 12 years. That poses a challenge to develop experiences and activities for a mixed-age group of children. Family child care providers work and live in the same environment posing logistical problems of storage, space definition, and activity space. Family child care providers are administrators and managers as well as teachers and caregivers, faced with budgets and fee collections.

Family child care has many advantages. It is especially good for children who do well in small groups or whose parents prefer them in a family-style setting. Family child care homes often schedule flexible hours to meet the needs of parents who work. The wide age range can be advantageous as well. Consistency and stability from a single caregiver throughout the child's early years and a family grouping of children provide a homelike atmosphere that is especially appropriate for infants and toddlers.

Family child care has its disadvantages, too. Many homes are unregulated; that is, they are not under any sponsorship or agency that enforces quality care, and many are exempt from state licensing. Many family children care providers lack knowledge of child development and early education, and are not required to take courses. The National Association for Family Child Care, a network of family child care providers, has established a quarterly publication and is making efforts to address the challenges to these programs.

This type of care could be a star in the galaxy of child care options. Small and personalized, it offers parents an appealing choice of home-based care. It is obvious, though, that further regulation of standards, availability of training for providers, and an awareness of the advantages of family child care need to be addressed. For those who need child care, this should be a viable alternative; for those who want to work at home, this type of career should be given serious consideration.

Employer-Sponsored Child Care

Employer-sponsored child care refers to child care facilities on or near the job site and supported by the business or industry. Hospitals, factories, colleges, and military bases often provide this service.

The number of women working outside the home and the increase in single-parent families encourage us to look at the workplace as a logical solution for child care needs. Employers who have implemented child care claim that the benefits are increased employee morale and better recruitment and retention of employees. For parents, there is the added appeal of having their children close by and being part of their educational process.

Government agencies are among the largest employers offering child care options. The federal government has more than 1,000 centers and sponsors nearly 10,000 family child care providers for use by military personnel (Neugebauer, 1998).

Several trends are notable. More companies are hiring child care management organizations to operate their facilities rather than maintaining them themselves. Employers are also insisting on quality, and centers are being accredited through NAEYC. The Cost, Quality, and Child Outcomes Study (CQCOS, 1995) revealed that work-site centers receiving employer subsidies ranked among the highest in quality.

Benefits to employees may include the option for one or more of the following: parental leave, flexible hours, corporate group discounts at local centers or family child care homes, resource and referral services, pretax salary reductions for child care, vouchers to purchase child care, reserved spaces in specific child care settings supported by the company. Companies located near each other may collaborate on the costs of these benefits.

For-Profit Child Care

Sometimes called "proprietary child care," for-profit establishments comprise more than one-third of all child care centers. A number of national chains of child care centers developed rapidly over the last 20 years, with some controlling anywhere from 10 to 1,200 centers. For-profit child care was seen as a good investment opportunity, so businesses flourished and grew. A few very large companies dominate the scene, creating child care chains across the country, primarily as managers of employer-sponsored programs or franchisers of centers.

For-profit centers offer a variety of programs to meet parents' needs. Infant and toddler programs, preschools, kindergartens, before-school and after-school care, and summer sessions accommodate working parents. Many programs are expanding into kindergarten and primary grades, and some are opening charter schools. In the last few years, for-profit organizations experienced a slow growth period due to the economic recession but will continue their pattern of growth as the economy turns upward (Neugebauer, 2003).

Nannies

Nannies are professional in-home child care providers. Originating in England, the nanny movement became popular during the 1980s as a child care option for parents who could afford to have child care in their homes. The International Nanny Association emphasizes training and professionalism and provides training and mentoring programs, publications, and a Nanny Credential examination. Nanny training programs can be found in community colleges and vocational schools where their training may include child development, nutrition, and family relationships. Living arrangements vary; nannies may or may not live in the child's home and they may or may not be responsible for housekeeping or meal preparation. Au pairs differ from nannies in that they are allowed to spend only one year in the United States and do not receive any special training for their child care role.

Programs in Religious Facilities

As one of the largest single providers of child care in the United States, church/

synagogue-based centers provide a variety of programs. Twenty-five percent of all child care centers are housed in a religious facility. Each center is owned or operated by an individual congregation or other recognized religious organization. Many different denominations house a variety of educational and child care programs. A program can be under the jurisdiction of an individual congregation or a nonprofit ministry of the congregation, or be run by tenants in a religious institution.

Religious or spiritual development is not the explicit aim of the majority of programs for preschoolers. For many years, churches have been committed to caring for children of working parents, providing a warm and loving environment to help children develop positive self-esteem (Lindner, Mattis, & Rogers, 1983). The teaching of religious values to children in this age group is not common practice in most child care settings. The policy will vary, however, with each center.

Church/synagogue support of child care programs is primarily in the use of space; they typically offer free or reduced-cost rent and may subsidize utilities, maintenance services, repairs, and some insurance. Common problems that arise in religious facilities include sharing space with the congregation's programs, frequent changes in leadership in the denomination's governing body, unclear policies and procedures regarding decision-making groups within the denomination, and unsuitable governance structures regulating the operation of the early childhood program.

✳ EXTENDING SERVICES TO FAMILIES

To serve the scope of human needs today, some early childhood programs focus on caring for children in a very specific context.

Head Start: A Program with a Message

Beginnings

In 1965, the federal government created the largest publicly funded education program for young children ever. Head Start began as part of this country's social action in the "war on poverty," and the implications of the program were clear: If at-risk, poverty-stricken children could be exposed to a program that enhanced their schooling, their intellectual functions might increase, and these gains would help break the poverty cycle.

Over 40 years, Head Start has served more than 20 million children and their families (DHHS, 2002). The success of Head Start can be attributed to its guiding objectives and principles, most notably expressed through

▸ *Its comprehensive nature.* The child was seen as a whole, requiring medical, dental, and nutritional assessment, as well as intellectual growth. Extensive health, education, and social services were offered to children and their families. Today, Head Start is "the leading health care system for low-income children in the country" (Greenberg, 1990), providing health and medical screening and treatment for thousands of youngsters.

There are similarities among all programs, but the relationship among parents, children, and caregiver is the universal consideration.

✸ *Parent participation and involvement.* Head Start expected parents to serve as active participants and get involved in the pro- gram at all levels: in the classroom as teacher aides, on governing boards making decisions about the program, and as bus drivers and cooks.

✸ *Services to families.* Many of the comprehensive services offered to children were extended to parents as well to assist them in their fight against poverty. Paid jobs in the program, on-the-job training, continuing education and training to prepare for some jobs, and health care are some of the support services families received.

✸ *Community collaboration.* Interest and support from the local community helped Head Start respond to the needs of the children and families it served. Public schools, religious institutions, libraries, service clubs, and local industry and businesses helped to foster responsible attitudes toward society and provided opportunities for the poor to work with members of the community in solving problems.

✸ *Multicultural/multiracial education.* Since its inception, Head Start has sought to provide a curriculum that reflects the culture, language, and values of the children in the program. Head Start efforts in this regard have been the models for other early childhood programs.

✸ *Inclusion of children with special needs.* Since 1972, Head Start has pioneered the inclusion of children with disabili- ties in its classrooms. Head Start has the distinction of being the first and largest federally funded program for children with special needs (Greenberg, 1990).[1]

✸ *Ecology of the family.* Head Start programs have looked at children within the context of the family in which they lived and viewed the family in the context of the neighborhood and community.

The success of Head Start led to the creation of three specific programs that furthered its goals: Parent and Child Centers, which serve infants and toddlers and their families; the Child and Family Resource Programs, which provide family support services; and Follow Through/Child Development Associate credentials, which provide early childhood education training and education for Head Start teachers.

It should be noted that at the beginning, one aim of Head Start was to change the language and behavior patterns of low-income children, many who came from minority groups, and to resocialize them into cultural patterns and values of the mainstream, middle class. This widely held perspective of the 1960s was known as the "cultural disadvantage" model, which suggested that any language, or cognitive or relational style that differed from the Anglo, mainstream, middle-class style was necessarily detrimental to rather than supportive of the educational process. Contrast this view with the more recent, pluralistic perspective, the "cultural difference" model, which affirms that no one way of "behaving and believing" should be required for successful participation in school or society. Current "multicultural policies" of Head Start reflect this pluralistic view.

[1]Early childhood educators should advocate for consistent and quality care and education for all children whether their challenge is economic, social, or physical.

Early Head Start

Early Head Start was established in 1994 as part of the Head Start Reauthorization Act. This program serves low-income families with infants and toddlers and pregnant women and is based on Head Start's four cornerstones: child development, family development, staff development, and community development.

Head Start and Multiculturalism

Head Start program performance standards (Head Start, 1998) reflect a strong commitment to multicultural principles, with explicit references to the importance of respecting cultural diversity, language differences, and cultural backgrounds.

The performance standards define an "environment of respect" as provided by adults who

* demonstrate through actions a genuine respect for each child's family, culture, and lifestyle
* provide an environment that reflects the cultures of all children in the program in an integrated, natural way
* foster children's primary language while supporting the continued development of English
* avoid activities and materials that stereotype or limit children according to their gender, age, disability, race, ethnicity, or family composition
* model respect and help children demonstrate appreciation of others (Head Start, 1998)

Evaluating Head Start's Effectiveness

Two studies have helped highlight Head Start's impact over the years. The most recent, a seven-year national study of Early Head Start conducted by the Department of Health and Human Services (HHS News, 2002) shows positive results for the three-year-old children who completed the program. They (1) performed better in cognitive and language development than did those not participating in the program, (2) may need fewer special learning interventions later on, and (3) developed behavior patterns that prepared them for school success, such as engaging in tasks, paying attention, and showing less aggression. Parents in the program showed more positive parenting behavior and were less likely to use physical punishment, were more likely to read to their children, and were more emotionally supportive.

The High/Scope Perry Preschool Study. This study, though not of a Head Start program, presented the most convincing evidence to date of the effectiveness of early intervention programs for low-income children. Begun in the 1960s, it is the first longitudinal study to measure the effects of preschool education and to track the children from preschool years through age 27.

Children from one randomly assigned group were placed in high-quality early childhood programs at age 3; the other group did not attend preschool. The results showed great differences between the children who had the advantage of a high-quality program and those who did not. Low-income children who had attended preschool significantly outperformed those who had not. The children attending the preschool program were better educated, spent less than half as many years in special education programs, had higher earnings, were less likely to receive welfare, and were five times less likely to be arrested (Schweinhart & Weikart, 1993). Gender differences were also noted: Preschool-program girls had a significantly higher rate of graduation than did the girls who did not attend preschool, whereas, in comparison, preschool-program boys completed slightly less schooling than non-preschool boys (Cohen, 1993b).

Not only does this study underscore the need for high-quality preschool programs for children who live in poverty, but it also demonstrates the potential impact that Head Start has on the country's future. It is the first study of its kind to suggest the economic impact of early intervention. Because most of the children in the high-quality early childhood program required less remedial education, had better earning prospects, and were less costly to the welfare and justice systems, early intervention in education was shown to be cost-effective.

Other Programs

Teen Parent Programs

Many high schools now have on-campus child care programs. Some serve as laboratory facilities to introduce adolescents to child care principles and practices before they become parents. Others are part of a growing trend to provide support services to teenage parents. Young mothers are encouraged to complete their high school education by returning to campus with their young children. In addition to their regular academic classes, parents are required to participate in parent education classes, in which they discuss child-rearing policies and parenting concerns. They also spend time in the children's classroom, applying their skills under the supervision of early childhood professionals. The aim of these programs is to help meet the long-term needs of adolescent parents by providing educational skills necessary to secure a job. At the same time, valuable support and training for parenthood help teenagers deal with the reality of the young children in their lives.

Early Intervention and Special Programs

Programs for children with special needs offer a combination of educational, medical, and therapeutic service.[1] Early childhood special education (ECSE) is a relatively new field and includes programs for early intervention for infants and toddlers through age two, and preschool special education for three- to five-year-old children with disabilities or developmental delays. A team of professionals, including early childhood special educators, social workers, and physical, language, and occupational therapists, work together with parents to enhance each child's progress.

Any inclusive early childhood education program may be an appropriate setting for children with disabilities as long as there is adequate planning and support. Further discussion of children with special needs follows in Chapter 3.

Hospital Settings

Hospitals provide group settings for children who are confined for a period of time. Many hospitals provide on-site child care for their employees as well.

Migrant Children's Programs

Early childhood education programs serve the needs of migrant farm families and rural poor families. Often migrant farm worker mothers are employed to work alongside the early childhood professionals. The focus of these programs is often on improving the child's primary language skills and developing a second language, job training, and access to health care and social services.

[1] In the study of child development one needs to be aware of the full range of development and not focus on only typically developing children. Many programs are attempting to integrate 75% typically developing children along with 25% children who have been recognized as having a special need.

Meeting the Needs of Homeless Children

The plight of homeless children raises questions about program needs for this new and tragic phenomenon. Families with children now represent more than one-third of the homeless population (CDF, 2001). These children attend schools closest to the shelter in which they stay for a brief time, then change schools when their parents move to another shelter. Many times these are children who already experience problems and failures in school. State and federal legislation is now being enacted to ensure full and equal educational opportunities for homeless children. A discussion of children at risk from abuse and neglect is found in Chapter 1. A discussion of children with special needs and programmatic implications follows in Chapter 3.

Home Schooling

The home school movement began in the 1950s as an alternative to public education. In the 1980s, groups of conservative religious groups rallied support for home schooling. Today, approximately 850,000 students are home schooled (Bieleck et al., 2001). The primary reasons parents give for this fast-growing movement have been documented in the first comprehensive study by the federal government (ibid). Nearly half of the parents cite the potential for a better education as their first reason. Thirty-eight percent say that religious philosophy is their motivation, and one-quarter of the parents cite poor learning environments in public schools as their grounds.

The educational philosophies and methods are widely diverse and range from prepackaged curriculum, which parents buy, to "relaxed home schooling" and "unschooling" (Cloud & Morse, 2001), a method that uses real-life projects as teaching opportunities, such as taking care of the farm animals or building a table, tailored to the child's interests and abilities. About 7% of home schoolers use no curriculum plans, and children pursue their own interests in the method called "unschooling" (ibid). If some of this seems familiar, you might want to look back at Chapter 1 and review the various educational philosophies on which early childhood programs are based.

There are a number of concerns expressed by educators regarding home school educational programs, which include: (1) lack of quality control due to varying regulations; (2) lack of socialization opportunities for students; (3) lack of sports opportunities; (4) the extreme time commitment demanded of parents; (5) unstructured curriculum and the lack of **accountability**, regulations, and policies surround this movement; and (6) the loss of revenue for public education.

As this movement progresses it will be interesting to watch how these criticisms are addressed and how more effective educational programs are developed through home schooling.

Out-of-School-Time Care

Before-school and after-school programs are designed for children before they start or after they finish their regular academic day. **Out-of-school-time care** is usually available for children from ages six to 16, with the vast majority (83%) in the kindergarten to third-grade age group (Neugebauer, 1996). More than 2 million children attend programs in child care centers, public and private schools, religious facilities, family child care homes, community centers, work sites, and recreation and youth programs.

Two national organizations, the National School-Age Care Alliance and the School-Age Child Care Project (now called the National Institute on Out-Of-School Time), joined forces in 1996 to create an accreditation system for after-school care. Their goals are to set professional standards, accredit high-quality programs, and support program improvement (NAEYC, 1999).

The essentials of out-of-school care are: flexible hours, reasonable tuition rates, and clear lines of communication to parents. To ensure continual care, scheduling must take into consideration the elementary school calendar. Holidays, conference times, and minimum-day schedules of schools must be considered

Out-of-school care is not intended to be an extension of a regular school day. Ideally, the program should supplement and support the regular school program. The teaching staff is usually different from the regular school faculty and should be specially trained in how to operate extended programs for young children. They must know how to create a homey, relaxed, and accepting atmosphere in an environment that supports large blocks of time for free play, where children can be self-directed and self-paced, where there are many opportunities for creative expression, where cooperation is emphasized and competition is limited, and where children may form small groups or find private spaces and places to play.

Children need the safety, the creative opportunity, and the emotionally supportive relationships that out-of-school care can provide. These programs are natural extensions of responsible child care and are essential services to children and their families.

✸ EXTENDING THE AGE RANGE

Infant/Toddler Programs

The inclusion of group care for infants and toddlers was affected by the rising number of women in the workforce who combine child-rearing and careers and by the increasing number of single-parent families in which the parent must work. Gonzalez-Mena and Eyer (1993) define the infant/toddler age group: Infancy is from babyhood until the child learns to walk. Then he or she is called a toddler until almost three years old.

Infant/toddler centers may be full-day centers or they may be part-time. They may be more educational, with parent involvement programs, than centers for group care. Most are a combination of physical care coupled with intellectual simulation and development.

Parent relationships are an important part of any program for young children, but especially so when babies and toddlers are involved. The general intention of these centers is to provide care that is supplemental to family life and that supports the child's family structure. To do that, the

The need for quality child care has increased as thousands of mothers enter the workforce.

caregiver at an infant/toddler center involves the parents in the everyday decisions about the care of their child, provides them with information about the child's day, and strengthens the child's sense of belonging to that particular family.[1]

Philosophy of Infant/Toddler Care

Through the insights of Piaget and Erikson (see Chapter 4), we have come to view the infant more and more as an involved person, one who experiences a wide range of intellectual and emotional abilities. Although they may appear to be helpless beings, babies are in fact persons with feelings, rights, and an individual nature. The caregiver in a quality infant/toddler center understands that feeding, diapering, and playing are, in fact, the curriculum of this age group. Caregiving routines are at the heart of the infant/toddler program. The challenge is to find ways to use these daily routines to interact, develop trust and security, and provide educational opportunities. In many cases, the caregiver's role extends to helping parents use these same common occurrences to promote the optimal development of their child.[2]

Magda Gerber has been a pioneer in infant care and coined the term **educaring** to describe the relationship between an infant and an adult. Gerber's philosophy is based on a respect for babies and the use of responsive and reciprocal interactions in which baby and caregiver learn about each other. Communicating through caregiving routines (diapering, feeding) in one-to-one intense and focused interactions is a foun-

dation of Gerber's approach to caring for infants and toddlers (Gerber, 1979). Observing, listening, and reading babies' cues are key elements in educaring.

Program Differences

The distinction between programs for infants and those for toddlers is also important to note. Just as a scaled-down version of preschool is not a toddler program, neither is a scaled-down version of a good day for toddlers an appropriate model for infants. The mobility of the toddler, for instance, requires different amounts of space and time in the schedule than are required for infants. Common routines such as diapering create the curriculum as caregivers talk with the babies about what they are doing and what is happening to them.

Routines are also the focus of the toddler's day but in a somewhat different way.

[1]The early childhood educator should respond to the child and parent as individuals in a unique family context and foster healthy family relationships.
[2]The caregiver must be culturally sensitive to the parent's background. There are many cultural differences in caring for infants, such as the amount of vocalizations, how and when babies are held, and sleep routines.

Mealtimes and toileting provide daily opportunities for toddlers to explore and to express their emerging sense of self. Hand washing—even eating—becomes a time to fill, to taste, to dump, to pick up. Again, the curriculum emerges from a developmental need toddlers have of "Me! Mine!" To foster that independence, that wanting to "do it myself," routines that allow for experimentation, mistakes, and messes make a good toddler curriculum.

Good programs for infants and toddlers, then, are distinctly arranged for them and are not simply modified versions of what works well in a program for three-year-olds.

Kindergarten

The **kindergarten** year is one of transition from early childhood programs into a more formal school setting. Whereas some kindergartens extend the "learning through play" philosophy found in developmental preschool programs, others become more focused on the academic skills of 5-year-olds.

Kindergarten programs are universally available throughout the United States. They are found in elementary public and private schools, churches, and as part of preschool child care centers. As of 1999, 93% of all five-year-olds were enrolled in a kindergarten program (NCES, 2002). Every state provides some funding for kindergartens, and 41 of the states require kindergarten programs. Yet only eight states require offering a full-day kindergarten, and only 19 states have a set of standard expectations for kindergarten education.

The length of the kindergarten day is under debate in many states and school districts. Some offer kindergarten programs that operate for half days only while others offer whole day programs. Only a few states fund full-day programs. Too often the arguments regarding the costs of such programs overshadow a more basic question: What are the best and most appropriate kindergarten programs, teaching methods, and curricula, regardless of the length of day? The following should be considered:

- *The purpose of the kindergarten program.* How will the program foster the goals in appropriate programming and adapt to the needs of children? The goal should begin with the child and build the program to fit the child's needs, skills, and developing abilities.

- *The effects of a full day on children.* Many children have already been in a child care setting for up to 10 hours a day and have shown they thrive in programs that are suited to their ages, development styles, and needs. Most children can handle a full-day kindergarten program, providing it is adapted to their age, interests, and abilities.

- *The needs and concerns of parents.* Some parents may want a full-day program because they work and need a safe and nurturing place for their children. Others who do not work outside the home may want to keep their children with them a while longer.[1] Parents need to have a choice about the type of program that best suits their family.

- *The effect on teachers.* A full-day kindergarten means that class is extended for a longer period of time, providing op-

[1]This may or may not be culturally related.

portunities to improve the quality of the program by individualizing the curriculum. Teachers in half-day kindergartens often teach a morning and afternoon class. The negative effects on planning, continuity, parent relationships, and individualizing curriculum are obvious, including teacher burnout.

✲ *The concerns of the administration.* The cost-effectiveness of extending a kindergarten program all day will undoubtedly require more staff, more supplies and equipment, and greater food service costs. The policymakers in any school setting must take these into account along with the other issues; hopefully, they would not be limited by them.

✲ *The nature and quality of the extended-day program.* Often, in programs in which children are in half-day kindergarten, the quality of the extended-care part of their day is not equal to their school experience. In many extended-day programs, the staff is untrained, has a high turnover rate, and does not reflect the same program goals for the kindergartner.

School Entry Age

Every state establishes an arbitrary date (e.g., September) by which children must be a certain age to enter kindergarten. In the United States, compulsory age for kindergarten ranges from five to eight.

what do YOU think?

Do you think that all kindergartens should be full-day? Why? Should half-day kindergartens be retained? Why? Are "transitional" or "developmental" kindergartens useful? How? What do you think about the use of more testing as a way to assess kindergartners' success in school?

Lowering and raising the age for beginning school is debated periodically. In recent years, parents hold children out for one year and enroll them when they are six; teachers retain many children each year in kindergarten; and administrators have created an array of kindergarten-substitute programs called trendy names such as "developmental," "extra-year," or "transitional" kindergartens. By the time they finally reach kindergarten, children are now in class with late-four-year-olds, fives, and sixes—a vast developmental span under one roof. The National Center for Education Statistics (NCES, 2002) notes that approximately 9% of eligible kindergartners are held back each year and that most are males who were born in the months between July and December. White, non-Hispanic children are more than twice as likely as black, non-Hispanic children to be delayed in kindergarten entrance (West, Meek, & Hurst, 2000).

Some of the methods used to create more homogeneous kindergarten classrooms, or to raise expectations for kindergarten admittance, are inappropriate uses of screening and readiness tests; discouragement and/or denial of entrance for eligible children; creation of transitional classes for those who are considered not ready for kindergarten; and an increasing use of retention (NAECS/NAEYC, 2001).

Katz (2000) notes that research does not yet provide a clear direction for retaining children in kindergarten or denying them entrance. Along with NAECS/NAEYC, Katz raises the issue of tailoring programs to fit children rather than requiring that children to fit the prescribed kindergarten format.

Curriculum: Developmental or Academic?

Critical issues such as school entry age and length of school day are deeply related to kindergarten curriculum issues. Kindergarten programs range from relatively traditional classes to highly structured, academically oriented classes. Over the last 20 years, the push to teach separate skills, such as reading, writing, and math, has created more and more academically focused kindergartens. As kindergartens have changed, there is greater pressure on teachers to accelerate children's learning. Hatch (2005) cites three specific changes that have altered the course of kindergarten programs:

1. Children today experience very different childhoods than even a decade ago.

2. Knowledge of how children learn and develop has expanded.

3. The standards-based reform movement has changed expectations for kindergartners by imposing arbitrary standards of performance. This increases the academic expectations on them and the pressure on teachers to comply with regulations.

Hatch (2005) recommends a more balanced approach to kindergarten teaching that would "take the best of traditional approaches, integrate emerging understanding of what children are like and what they need, and meet the challenges of the accountability movement being pushed down into early childhood education." (For further discussion on the negative effects of early academics, see Chapter 3, which includes developmental ranges and Word Pictures for appropriate expectations. In Chapter 6, the related questions of standardized testing and screening are discussed. In Chapters 1 and 10, related issues are explored.)

Primary Grades

Early childhood is defined as children from birth through age eight. Often overlooked as part of a comprehensive view of young children is grades one, two, and three, serving children who range from six to eight years old. Primary grades, in both public and private schools, focus on the basic academic skills of reading, writing, math, science, social studies, art and drama, health and safety, and physical education. They are usually part of a larger school with grades up to six or eight.

As the NAEYC position statement on developmentally appropriate practice states, "too many schools . . . adopt instructional approaches that are incompatible with . . . how young children learn and develop . . . emphasizing rote learning of academic skills rather than active, experiential learning in a meaningful context," with the result that children "are not learning to apply those skills to problems . . . and they are not developing more complex thinking skills" (Bredekamp & Copple, 1997). Fortunately, this seems to be changing in the primary grades. Collaborative learning, an integrated curriculum (see Chapter 10), an emphasis on literacy, and promoting critical thinking skills is now on the agenda of many elementary schools. Bredekamp and Copple further state:

Along with the home, church, and community,[1] primary-grade schools and school-age care programs are among the key settings in which children's character is shaped. Therefore, the primary-grade years are an impor-

[1]This presents a broad, ecological view of the child's socialization in a family and community context.

tant time not only to support children's intellectual development but also to help them develop the ability to work collaboratively with peers; express tolerance, empathy, and caring for other people; function responsibly; and gain positive dispositions toward learning, such as curiosity, initiative, persistence, risk taking, and self-regulation.

EVALUATING FOR QUALITY

Evaluation as a Process

Evaluation involves making decisions, choices, and selections. In its simplest form, evaluation is a process of appraisal. A useful assessment encourages positive change. It is easy to continue the same program, the same teaching techniques, even the same assessment techniques, year after year when a school is operating smoothly. Sometimes it is not clear what—or how—improvements could be made. A regular evaluation keeps a system alive and fresh.

Evaluations help give meaning and perspective to children, teachers, and programs. An assessment that helps clarify

these processes brings renewed dedication and inspiration.

Programs may be evaluated by taking an inventory of a school's curriculum and educational materials. Program evaluation involves analyzing children, teachers, parents, and administration and how they all work together to meet the goals of the program.

Evaluation Essentials

1. *Setting goals.* Without evaluation, goals are meaningless. Evaluation helps shape a goal into a meaningful plan of action. To be useful, an evaluation must include suggestions for improving the performance or behavior. The assessment tool that only describes a situation is an unfinished evaluation; goals for improvement must be established.

2. *Expectations.* In every early childhood setting, more than one set of expectations is at work. The director has job expectations of all the teachers. Teachers have standards of performance for themselves, the children, and parents. Parents have some expectations about what their children will do in school and about the role of the teachers. Children develop expectations regarding themselves, their parents, teachers, and the school.

3. *The degree to which expectations are met.* By evaluating, people check to see if the goals have been realized. A good evaluation tool outlines clearly and specifically how expectations have been met in a system of mutual accountability. It is a way of stating expectations and defining how they are being met. Evaluating is a way to look at where and how improvements can be made, to challenge methods, assumptions, and purposes. Total programs are evaluated to see if they ac-

Program evaluations can ensure that physical development and outdoor play is a part of the daily schedule.

complish their objectives. In fact, evaluations provide information by which to rate performance, define areas of difficulty, look for possible solutions, and plan for the future.

Why Evaluate?

To Gain an Overview

Evaluating a program gives an overview of how all the various components function together. This assessment asks the essential questions, "Is this a good place for children? Would you want your child to be here? What is a high-quality program for young children?"

Looking at children, teachers, and the total environment, a program evaluation reveals the entire environment as an integrated whole. These assessments add an awareness of how one area is related to another and how the parts mesh in a particular setting. Such evaluations, then, are the standards of quality and include:

- children's progress
- teacher performance
- curriculum development
- the financial structure
- family involvement
- the community at large

- the governing organization of the school

In program evaluations, each of these is assessed for how it functions alone and how each works in concert with the others.

To Establish Accountability

A program evaluation establishes accountability. This refers to a program's being answerable to a controlling group or agency—for instance, the school board or the government office or to parents and the community in which you work. These groups want to know how their funds are being spent and how their philosophy is being expressed through the overall program.

To Make Improvements

Program evaluations are an opportunity to take an objective look at how the goals of the school are being met. A good evaluation will support the strengths of the existing program and suggest where changes might improve overall effectiveness. An in-depth assessment increases the likelihood that program goals and visions will be realized. The evaluation helps determine the direction the program may take in the future.

To Acquire Accreditation

Evaluations are a necessary step for schools that wish to be approved for certification or accreditation by various organizations or government agencies. Such groups require that a school meet certain evaluation standards before the necessary permits are issued or membership is granted. Agencies, such as a state department of social services or department of education, often license family child care homes, and private schools may need to follow certain criteria to be affiliated with a larger organization (such as the American Montessori Society).

One system established by early childhood professionals is noteworthy. The National Academy of Early Childhood Programs, a division of NAEYC, has established an accreditation system for improving the quality of life for young children and their families. The Academy established goals around several component areas, which include curriculum goals, adult–child interactions, health, safety, nutrition, relations between the home and program, developmental evaluation of children, and qualifications and ongoing staff development of teachers.

How to Evaluate a Program
Define the Objectives

A program evaluation begins with a definition of the program's objectives. Knowing why a program is to be evaluated indicates how to tailor the procedure to the needs and characteristics of an individual school.

With the objectives defined, the choice of evaluation instrument becomes clear. If, for example, a program objective is to provide a healthy environment for children, the evaluation tool used must address the issues of health, safety, and nutrition.

Choose an Evaluation Instrument

Evaluation instruments vary with the purpose of the program evaluation. NAEYC's accreditation guidelines are suitable, as is the *Early Childhood Environmental Rating Scale-Revised* (ECERS-R) (Harms, Clifford, & Cryer, 1998) for most preschools, kindergartens and child care centers. These instruments will include many, if not all of the areas noted in Figure 2–6, and may be self-administered or used by an outside evaluator.

Implement the Findings

The evaluation process is complete when the results are tabulated and goals are set

The Physical Environment
Are the facilities clean, comfortable, safe?
Are room arrangements orderly and attractive?
Are materials and equipment in good repair and maintained?
Is there a variety of materials, appropriate to age levels?
Are activity areas well defined?
Are cleanup and room restoration a part of the daily schedule?
Are samples of children's work on display?
Is play space adequate, both inside and out?
Is personal space (e.g., cubby) provided for each child?

The Staff
Are there enough teachers for the number of children?
How is this determined?
Are the teachers qualified? What criteria are used?
Is the staff evaluated periodically? By whom and how?
Does the school provide/encourage in-service training and continuing education?
Do the teachers encourage the children to be independent and self-sufficient?
Are the teachers genuinely interested in children?
Are teachers aware of children's individual abilities and limitations?

FIGURE 2–6 Areas of program evaluation.

Continued

What guidance and disciplinary techniques are used?

Do teachers observe, record, and write reports on children's progress?

Are teachers skilled in working with individual children, small groups, and large groups?

Does the teaching staff give the children a feeling of stability and belonging?

Do teachers provide curriculum that is age-appropriate and challenging?

How would you describe the teachers' relationships with other adults in the setting? Who does this include, and how?

Can the teaching staff articulate good early education principles and relate them to their teaching?

Parent Relationships

How does the classroom include parents?

Are parents welcome to observe, discuss policies, make suggestions, help in the class?

Are different needs of parents taken into account?

Where and how do parents have a voice in the school?

Are parent-teacher conferences scheduled?

Does the school attempt to use community resources and social service agencies in meeting parents' needs?

The Organization and Administration

Does the school maintain and keep records?

Are there scholarships or subsidies available?

What socioeconomic, cultural, religious groups does the school serve?

What is the funding agency, and what role does it play?

Is there a school board, and how is it chosen?

Does the school serve children with special needs or handicaps?

Are the classroom groups homogeneous or heterogeneous?

What hours is the school open?

What age range is served?

Are there both full- and part-day options?

Is after-school care available?

Does the school conduct research or train teachers?

What is the teacher-child ratio?

The Overall Program

Does the school have a written, stated educational philosophy?

Are there developmental goals for the children's physical, social, intellectual, and emotional growth?

Are the children evaluated periodically?

Is the program capable of being individualized to fit the needs of all the children?

Does the program include time for a variety of free, spontaneous activities?

Is the curriculum varied to include music, art, science, nature, math, language, social studies, motor skills, etc.?

Are there ample opportunities to learn through a variety of media and types of equipment and materials?

Is there ample outdoor activity?

Is there a daily provision for routines: eating, sleeping, toileting, play?

Is the major emphasis in activities on concrete experiences?

Are the materials and equipment capable of stimulating and sustaining interest?

Are field trips offered?

Do children have a chance to be alone? In small groups? In large groups?

FIGURE 2–6, continued

Cultural Responsiveness

Are multicultural perspectives already incorporated throughout the school, classroom curriculum, and classroom environment?

Do my attitudes (and those of all staff) indicate a willingness to accept and respect cultural diversity? How is this demonstrated?

Do classroom materials recognize the value of cultural diversity, gender, and social class equity?

Do curricular activities and methods provide children opportunities to work and play together cooperatively? In mixed groups of their choice and the teacher direction?

Do schoolwide activities reflect cultural diversity? How is this noticed?

Does the program planning reflect the reality (views and opinions) of families and the community?

Does the curriculum include planning for language diversity? For full inclusion? (Adapted from Baruth & Manning, 1992, and de Melendez & Ostertag, 1997.)

FIGURE 2–6, continued

to meet the recommendations of the evaluation. Program administrators meet with the teaching staff to discuss the challenges highlighted by the evaluation. A process is put in place for addressing the issues, a calendar is established to create a timeline for improvement, the appropriate staff members are assigned the responsibility for making changes, and the process begins anew. Evaluations are only as useful as the implementation plan. It can help identify specific concerns, determine the areas of growth and potential development, and be a blueprint for the future.

KEY TERMS

accountability
child care centers
comprehensive
culturally appropriate practice
developmentally appropriate practice
educaring
employer-sponsored child care
evaluation
faith-based school
family child care

high-quality program
kindergarten
laboratory schools
looping
mixed-age groups
out-of-school-time care
parent cooperative schools
Perry Preschool Study
traditional nursery school

Teaching Applications

1. Visit a family child care home. Look at the home as if you were a prospective parent. What did you like most? Least? Is the home licensed? If so, for how many children? After talking with the family child care provider, what do you think are the disadvantages of this type of program? What do you think are possible solutions to these problems?

2. Research the licensing regulations for child care in your area. Describe the steps necessary in your town to open a nursery school, child care center, and a family child care home.

3. Does your own setting have an evaluation plan? Analyze the goals of your process and note where the implementation meets (or does not meet) the goals.

4. Locate a copy of *Developmentally Appropriate Practices.* (NAEYC's position paper, *Developmentally Appropriate Practices: Early Childhood Programs Serving Children from Birth Through Age 8* [2005], is online at naeyc.org.) Using the categories it outlines, make an informal assessment of the program in which you observe or work. Share your results with another teacher or supervisor.

5. Evaluate an early childhood education setting with the criteria on page 53.

REFERENCES

Baker, K. R. (1955). *The nursery school.* Philadelphia: W. B. Saunders.

Bellis, M. (1999, May). Look before you loop. *Young Children,* 70–72.

Bieleck, S., Chandler, K., and Broughman, S. (2001). Homeschooling in the United States: 1999. *Education Statistics Quarterly* (NCES 2001-033). Washington, DC: DHHS.

Bredekamp, S., and Copple, C. (Eds.). (1997). Developmentally appropriate practice in early childhood programs. Washington DC: National Association for the Education of Young Children.

CDF [Children's Defense Fund]. (2001). *The state of America's children, yearbook 2001.* Washington, DC: Author.

Chapman, J. (1999, May). A looping journey. *Young Children,* 80–83.

Cloud, J., & Morse, J. (2001, August 27). Home sweet school. *Time,* 47–54.

Cohen, D. L. (1993b, April 21). Perry preschool graduates show dramatic new social gains at 27. *Education Week,* 1.

CQCOS [Cost, Quality, and Child Outcomes Study] team (1995). *Cost, quality and child outcomes in child care centers.* Denver: Department of Economics, University of Colorado at Denver, 187–203.

DHHS [U.S. Department of Health and Human Services]. *2002 Head Start Fact Sheet.* Washington, DC: Head Start Bureau, Author.

Gerber, M. (1979). Respecting infants: The Loczy model of infant care. In E. Jones (Ed.), *Supporting the growth of infants, toddlers, and parents.* Pasadena, CA: Pacific Oaks.

Gestwicki, C. (1999). *Developmentally appropriate practice: Curriculum and development in early education* (2nd ed.). Clifton Park, NY: Thomson Delmar Learning.

Gonzalez-Mena, J., & Eyer, D. W. (1989, 1993). *Infants, toddlers, and caregivers.* Mountain View, CA: Mayfield Publishing.

Greenberg, P. (1990, September). Before the beginning: A participant's view. *Young Children,* 41–52.

Harms, T., Clifford, R. M., & Cryer, D. (1998). *Early Childhood Environment Rating Scale* (Rev. ed.). New York: Teachers College Press.

Hatch, J. A. (2005). *Teaching in the new kindergarten.* Clifton Park, NY: Thomson Delmar Learning.

Head Start. (1998). Program performance standards and other regulations. Washington, DC: Head Start Bureau, Administration on Children, Youth and Families, Administration for Children and Families, U.S. DHHS.

HHS News (2002, June). *Study shows positive results from Early Head Start program.* Washington, DC: U.S. DHHS.

Hyun, E. (1998). *Making sense of developmentally and culturally appropriate practice (DCAP) in early childhood education.* New York: Peter Lang Publishing.

Katz, L. (2000, August). *Academic redshirting and young children.* ERIC Digest. EDO-PS-00-13.

Lindner, E., Mattis, M. C., & Rogers, J. (1983). *When churches mind the children.* Ypsilanti, MI: High/Scope Press.

NAEYC [National Association for the Education of Young Children]. (2005). Developmentally appropriate practice in early childhood programs serving children from birth through age 8. In S. Bredekamp and C. Copple (Eds.), *Developmentally appropriate practice in early childhood programs.* Washington, DC: Author.

NAEYC. (1998b). *Accreditation criteria and procedures of the National Academy of Early Childhood Programs.* Washington, DC: Author.

NAEYC. (1999, July). NAEYC position statement on developing and implementing effective public policies to promote early childhood and school-age care program accreditation. *Young Children,* 36–40.

NAECS/NAEYC [National Association of Early Childhood Specialists in State Departments of Education/National Association of Education for Young Children]. (2001, September). Still unacceptable trends in kindergarten entry and placement. *Young Children,* 59–62.

NCES [National Center for Education Statistics]. (2002). *Digest of Education Statistics: 2001.* Washington, DC: U.S. Government Printing Office.

Neugebauer, R. (1996, July). Promising development and new directions in school-age care. *Child Care Information Exchange,* 7–13.

Neugebauer, R. (2003, January). For-profit organizations maintaining status Quo: Sixteenth annual report on for-profit child care. *Child Care Information Exchange,* 65–69.

Neugebauer, R. (1998, January/February). Sesame Street meets Wall Street. Eleventh annual status report on for-profit child care. *Child Care Information Exchange,* 12–16.

Schweinhart, L. J. & Weikart, D. P. (1993, November). Success by empowerment: The High/Scope Perry Preschool Study through age 27. *Young Children,* 54–58.

Smith, K. (2000). Who's minding the kids? Child care arrangements: Fall, 1995. *Current Population Reports Series P 70-70.* Table 14. Washington, DC: U.S. Government Printing Office.

West, J., Meek, A., & Hurst, D. (2000). *Children who enter kindergarten late or repeat kindergarten: Their characteristics and later school performance.* National Center for Education Statistics No. 2000-039. Washington, DC: United States Department of Education.

Additional resources for this chapter can be found by visiting the Online Companion™ at www.earlychilded.delmar.com. This supplemental material includes a Study Guide with chapter review questions (and answers), critical thinking questions and activities, and annotated Web sites.

Section 2

Who Is the
Young Child?

Defining the Young Child

QUESTIONS FOR THOUGHT

What is meant by the "whole child"?

How are age-level characteristic charts (Word Pictures) useful?

What are the implications for teaching children of varying levels of development?

Who are children with special needs?

What is an inclusive classroom?

THE WHOLE CHILD

The concept of **the whole child** is based on the accepted principle that all areas of human growth and development are interrelated. It is only for the purpose of studying one area or another in depth that such categories are created.

Each Child Is Unique

Each child is a sum total of a multitude of parts and, as such, is different from anyone else. The concept of the whole child suggests the uniqueness of the person. Although they are often discussed separately, the areas of development (social-emotional, physical, language, cultural awareness, intellectual, and creativity) cannot be isolated from one another. They each make a valuable contribution to the whole child.

Growth Is Interrelated

One area of development affects the other. A child with a hearing loss is likely to have language delay as well; thus, the physical development affects the language skills. The child who has trouble making friends (social) is likely to exhibit his unhappiness (emotional) in the schoolyard (physical) and in the math period (intellectual). The interdependence of the areas of development has some positive aspects as well. The child who has a good breakfast and starts the school day with parent interest is ready to tackle new puzzles and new relationships. The kindergartner who masters using scissors is ready to try printing: The fine-motor skills enhance the cognitive task of learning the alphabet.

One way to look at this concept of development is to plot the relationships visually. Think of each area of development as a circle. There are five of them: physical-motor, language, intellectual, social-emotional, and creative (Figure 3–1).

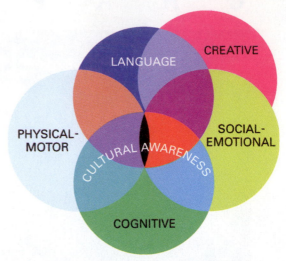

FIGURE 3–1 How areas of growth are interrelated: Each area of growth is affected by and influences every other area of development.

Children: alike, yet different.

Normal development depends on meeting not only the child's physical (adequate nutrition) needs but psychological (nurturing caregivers/parents) and social (adequate play/exploration) needs as well. Social development is aided by the ability to communicate verbally; a well-developed attention span helps the child develop fine-motor skills; relating to others is more successful if intellectual problem-solving skills are already mature. The circularity of the child's growth and development is a key element to understanding the "whole" child.

✿ HOW CHILDREN ARE ALIKE

There are three common characteristics that unite all children.[1] Each child is like every other in that (1) they all have the same basic needs, the most important of which are food, shelter, and care; (2) they all go through the same **developmental stages;** and (3) they all have the same developmental goals, although the timing and the cultural influences will differ (Caldwell, 1993). The similarities of a group of children in a single classroom are striking. Teachers can see wide differences, yet there are shared characteristics within the age group itself. Three toddlers who are fingerpainting exhibit three different personal styles; yet, typically, they all become distracted and leave their work unfinished.

Descriptions of these common characteristics date back to a classic collection of research by Gesell and Ilg. (See both Chapters 1 and 4 for related discussions.) Following are **Word Pictures** depicting these **age-level characteristics** from infancy through age eight. In looking at individual children or a group, these descriptions are helpful in understanding common characteristics. Age alone does not determine a child's capabilities, but it does provide a guideline for establishing appropriate expectations.

Word Pictures

In the following pages some of the classic normative data collected by Gesell are combined with theories of Piaget, Elkind, Erikson, and Vygotsky (see Chapter 4) to demonstrate what children have in common at various ages. Despite the wide range of individual differences at all ages, common behaviors lend a perspective to help teachers prescribe programs, plan activities, and create curricula.

The Value of Word Pictures

In Behavior and Guidance. We base guidance and discipline strategies on an awareness of the expected behaviors common to a given age range. Many so-called problem behaviors are normal behaviors of the age at which they occur. Two-year-olds are easily frustrated as they grow increasingly independent. The wise teacher accepts the child's lack of control and draws on the knowledge that two-year-olds are easily distracted and enjoy a variety of play activities. Once the two-year-old is comforted, play is resumed. (See Chapter 7 for more classroom applications regarding children's behavior.) Word Pictures help teachers know what to expect and when to expect it. By using the charts as a reference, teachers lessen

---

Video ⦿ View Point 3-1

"Many preschoolers still show a wide variety of imaginary fears that relate to their inability to understand the difference between fantasy and reality."

Competency: Emotional Development

Age Group: Preschool

Critical Thinking Questions:

1. What fears do you remember having before the age of five?

2. Watch an episode of *Mr. Rogers' Neighborhood.* How does he deal with the difference between fantasy and reality?

[1]Children are sometimes more alike than they are different.

the risk of expecting too much or too little of children at any given age. If, for instance, four-year-olds typically "tell tall tales," teachers' responses to their stories reflect an awareness of that tendency. The fun of making up a story and the use of imagination are acknowledged, but there is not a concern that the child is lying. Age-level characteristics give a frame of reference with which to handle daily situations and a basis for planning appropriate guidance measures.

In Curricula. Word Pictures can be used to tailor curriculum planning to an individual child or a particular class or group on the basis of known developmental standards. A group cooking experience, for instance, allows children to choose their level of comfort and involvement. As an early reader at age four, Darragh loves to read the recipe to others. Lourdes's favorite activity is to mix the ingredients together, refining her small motor skills. Von, who loves to play with mud and clay, spreads the cookie sheet with oil while Felicity helps the teacher adjust the oven temperature. When planning an activity, the teacher takes into account what she knows about each child's development. Cooking is always a fun activity but serves a greater purpose when planned with individual children in mind. See Figure 3–2 for guidelines on using these tools. (Chapter 10 has more practical applications and examples for planning curriculum.)

Cultural Awareness and Identity. Derman-Sparks and the ABC Task Force (1989) point out that children become aware of and form attitudes about racial and cultural differences at a very early age. Their experiences with their bodies, social environment, and cognitive-developmental stage combine to help them form their own identity and at-

Guidelines for Using Word Pictures

Age-level charts can be misunderstood unless used with discretion. The following suggestions should be kept in mind for the Word Pictures to be a valuable teaching tool:

1. **Balance your impressions of the Word Pictures with classroom experience. Observe children to add a measure of reality as you interpret the phrases.**

   Example: Toddlers are always on the move and seem to prefer standing and squatting to sitting on a chair. Observe a toddler story-time to see how many children are sitting on the floor, how many are standing, and how many are squatting on their haunches. What do they do if the story lasts too long? Are they back on the move again?

2. **Make a profile of the whole child, and resist the tendency to categorize him or her.**

   Example: An unfortunate label, "the terrible two's," has defined this age group for years. Yet seeing two-year-olds at play, you can get another picture of their emerging development: They enjoy singing parts of the songs they know. They are intrigued by sensory activities; they watch and imitate other children and are excited about their own capabilities. When adults interact with them, they enjoy the attention and, with appropriate encouragement, learn to control their impulses.

FIGURE 3–2

3. Get perspective on the range of developmental norms a child exhibits over several of the chronological age groupings.

Example: Look at the Word Pictures for the group just below and just above the age level of the child. Children will exhibit some of the behaviors appropriate to all three groups you check. Darius, who is five, lacks the coordination of most children his age. Yet his interest in using symbols and devising codes is that of a six-year-old and his bossiness echoes that of some four-year-olds. This picture of Darius shows his unique pattern of development across the age spans. Teachers will want to support him in each of these areas of development and respect his pace of growth.

4. Remember that these norms of development refer to average or typical behavior. They cannot be applied too literally.

Example: In a class of seven-year-olds, for instance, maybe half of the children would fit the majority of the description in the Word Picture for that age group. Some would not yet have reached this developmental level, and others would show characteristics common to the next age level. There may even be characteristics that some of the children will never exhibit. Sabina, for instance, seems typically seven. She is feeling her first knowledge of peer pressure and loves jokes and guessing games (as do a lot of seven-year-olds), but she does not limit her friendships to girls, nor does she particularly enjoy solitary activities or value physical skills. Yet Sabina is indeed all of seven years old and needs to be appreciated as the competent child she is.

5. Keep in mind that children go through most of the stages described and in the same sequence, but they will do so at their own rates of growth.

Example: Development follows an orderly, predictable sequence in the early years, even though some individual differences will occur. Teachers need to be aware of the early stages of growth and create programs that allow children the time and space to acquire the abilities and skills they need to succeed in the following stages. Pushing children to read or write when they do not yet have the development skills to do so ignores the key element of developmentally appropriate practices (DAP): applying your knowledge about child development in programs and practices.

6. Focus on what a child can do rather than on what he or she cannot do. Use the characteristics to compare the child with him/herself.

Example: Word Pictures are not meant to compare one child with another, because children develop at their own rates and in their own ways. In observing Dwayne, it is important to know where he is in relation to most three-year-olds, but it is more important where he is six months from now, a year from now, and what he was like a year ago. A clear picture of his rate of growth emerges.

FIGURE 3–2, continued

titudes. As they develop cognitively, children become aware of differences and similarities in people. These cultural milestones are included in the Word Pictures to indicate how as children come to a sense of themselves as individuals, their attitudes and behaviors toward others can be influenced.

Using Word Pictures

Six developmental areas are included in the Word Pictures:

1. *Social-emotional development.* Includes a child's relationship with himself and others, self-concept, self-esteem, and the ability to express feelings.

2. *Language development.* Includes children's utterances, pronunciation, vocabulary, sentence length, and the ability to express ideas, needs, and feelings. It includes receptive and verbal language.

3. *Physical-motor development.* Includes gross motor, fine motor, and perceptual motor.

4. *Cognitive development.* This includes curiosity, the ability to perceive and think, memory, attention span, general knowledge, problem solving, analytical thinking, beginning reading, computing skills, and other cognitive processes.

5. *Cultural identity development.* This suggests the interconnections between developmental stages and a growing awareness of one's attitudes toward others. Various cultural milestones appear in each age group which, when appropriately fostered, can increase a child's sensitivity to differences.[1]

6. *Creative development.* This includes the usual creative activities such as movement, dance, music, and painting, as well as originality, imagination, divergent thinking, and problem solving.

Characteristics listed in the Word Pictures were chosen on the basis of

1. behaviors most common to the age group

2. those that have implications for children in group settings

3. those that suggest guidance and disciplinary measures

4. those that have implications for planning a developmentally appropriate curriculum

5. cultural milestones, which are highlighted to suggest the interaction of children's development and their awareness of attitudes toward race and culture.

Individual development affects the way children learn. Each child is unique in the way she grows.

[1] Very early in the course of normal development, children develop attitudes about differences in people.

CHAPTER 3

WORD PICTURES OF AN INFANT

SOCIAL-EMOTIONAL

0–1 month	Cries to express emotions; bonding begins
4–10 weeks	Social smiles
2 months	Begins social games
3 months	Distinguishes familiar faces*
	Turns head toward human voice
	Smiles in response to a smile
	Kicks, smiles, waves in response
	Cries when left alone
	Recognizes parent
4 months	Genuine laugh
	Smiles when spoken to
	Loves attention
5 months to 1 year	Stranger anxiety*
6 months	Distinguishes between voices
	Smiles, babbles at strangers
	Develops attachment
	Begins to play imitation games
	Plays peek-a-boo
	Sensitive to parental moods
8 months	Laughs out loud
9 months	Screams to get own way

Play is activity only for present moment
Fears unfamiliar: people, places, things*
Beginning sense of separate self*

LANGUAGE

0–1 month	Turns head in response to voices
	Cries to express needs
6–8 weeks	Coos
	Gestures to communicate: pushes objects away, squirms, reaches out to people,* pouts, smacks lips, shrieks, points
2 months	Voluntary vocal sounds
3 months	Babbles
6–12 months	Imitation sound games
	Responds to variety of sounds*
	Makes vowel sounds
	Acquires receptive language*
	Cries to communicate
12 months	First words

PHYSICAL-MOTOR

By 1 year	Grows 10 to 12 inches, triples birth weight, lengthens by 40%, doubles brain size, grows full head of hair
	Bounces in crib
	Uses whole-body motions
4 months	Sees, grasps objects
5 months	Examines fingers
	Sits when propped
6 months	Rolls over
	Discovers feet
	Teething begins
7 months	Crawls
8 months	Sits up unaided
	Pulls to standing position
	Pincer grasp established
9 months	Creeps
10 months	Feeds self with spoon
11 months	Stands alone, cruises
12 months	First steps
Late infancy	Can move hands in rotation to turn knobs

Newborn motor activity mostly reflexes

CREATIVE

Discovers and explores hands and feet
Expresses and discovers emotion
Talks by babbling, cooing, and gurgling
Plays peek-a-boo
Responds to facial expressions

COGNITIVE

0–1 month	Responds to mother's voice: Senses function, especially pain, touch*
10 weeks	Memory is evident*
4 months	Smiles of recognition
7–10 months	Solves simple problems (knocks over box to get toy)
8 months	Begins to believe in permanence of objects
	Follows simple instruction
8–12 months	Intentionality in acts
11 months	Begins trial-error experimentation
12 months	Plays drop/retrieve games, pat-a-cake
	Explores with hands and fingers
	Smiles, vocalizes at image in mirror*

*Key characteristics of cultural awareness or identity.

WORD PICTURES OF A TODDLER

SOCIAL-EMOTIONAL

Almost totally egocentric
Likes to be noticed; loves an audience
Lacks inhibitions
Insists on own way, assertive
Likes doing things by self
Independent, has self-identity*
Adapts easily
Refers to self by name
Laughs loudly at peek-a-boo
Cries when left alone
Curious*
Relates to adults better than to children
Active, eager
Talks mostly to self
Usually friendly
Strong sense of ownership
Mimics adult behavior*
Experiences and shows shame*

LANGUAGE

Some two-word phrases
Enjoys vocalizing to self
Babbles in own jargon
Uses "eh-eh" or "uh-uh" with gestures
Names closest relatives*
Repeats adults' words*
Points to communicate needs, wants
Shakes head "no" to respond*
Responds to directions to fetch, point
Obeys verbal requests
Asks "what's that?" or "whassat?"*
Understands simple phrases
Uses 5 to 50 words

PHYSICAL-MOTOR

Awkward coordination; chubby body
Tottering stance
Creeps when in a hurry
Walks with increasing confidence
Always on the move
Walks with feet wide apart, arms out, head forward
Finds it difficult to turn corners
Goes up and down stairs holding on
Backs into chair to sit down
Can squat for long periods of time
Prefers standing to sitting
Motor-minded: constant motion
Loves to pull/push objects
Runs with stiff, flat gait

Uses whole-arm movements
Carry and dump becomes a favorite activity
Scribbles
Turns pages two or three at a time
Zips/unzips large zipper
Likes holding objects in both hands

CREATIVE

Responds to mood of music
Develops ways to move across space
Freely examines every object
Sings phrases of nursery rhymes
Loves to fingerpaint and explore texture
Stares; takes it all in
"Age of exploration"
Makes up nonsense syllables

COGNITIVE

Points to objects in a book
Matches similar objects
Fits round block in round hole
Loves opposites: up/down, yes/no*
Imitates simple tasks
Interest shifts quickly
Short attention span
Follows one direction
Gives up easily but easily engaged*
Conclusions are important: closes doors, shuts books
Thinks with feet; action-oriented
Builds tower of three or four small blocks

*Key characteristics of cultural awareness or identity.

WORD PICTURES OF A TWO-YEAR-OLD

SOCIAL-EMOTIONAL

Self-centered
Possessive about possessions
Clings to the familiar; resistant to change*
Ritualistic; insists on routines*
Dependent
Likes one adult at a time*
Quits readily; easily frustrated
Goes to extremes
Impulsive; shifts activities suddenly
Easily distracted
Pushes, shoves
Finicky, fussy eater, some food jags
Refers to self by given name*
Treats people as inanimate objects*
Dawdles; slow-geared
Plays parallel
Watches others*
Likes people*
Excited about own capabilities

LANGUAGE

Uses two- or three-word sentences
Telegraphic sentences: "Throw ball"
Has difficulty in pronunciation
"Me," "mine" most prominent pronouns*
Spontaneous language; rhythmic, repetitive
Constant talking; interested in sound
Sings phrases of song, not on pitch
Can't articulate feelings
Frustrated when not understood
May stutter
Asks "whassat?" about pictures*
Can match words with objects
Repeats words and phrases
Uses 50 to 300 words

PHYSICAL-MOTOR

Uses whole-body action
Pushes, pulls, pokes
Climbs into things
Leans forward while running

Climbs stairs one by one
Dependent on adults for dressing
Can help undress
Has reached one-half potential height
Bladder/bowel control begins
Feeds self
Thumb-forefinger opposition complete
Grasps cup with two hands
Awkward with small objects
Lugs, tumbles, topples; unsteady
Alternates hands; preference developing
Can rotate to fit objects
Expresses emotions bodily*
Sensory oriented
Cuts last teeth
Has difficulty relaxing

CREATIVE

Imitates other children
Combines parallel play and fantasy play
Plays with sounds; repeats syllables over and over
Enjoys simple finger plays
Can follow simple melodies
Learns to scribble
Uses art for sensory pleasure

COGNITIVE

Recognizes, explores physical characteristics*
Investigates with touch and taste
Intrigued by water, washing
Likes to fill and empty things
Has limited attention span
Lives in present
Understands familiar concepts*
Can tell difference between black and white*
Needs own name used
Likes simple make-believe
Does one thing at a time
Remembers orders of routines
Recalls where toys are left
Classifies people by gender*
Names familiar objects in books

---

*Key characteristics of cultural awareness or identity.

WORD PICTURES OF A THREE-YEAR-OLD

SOCIAL–EMOTIONAL

Highly imitative of adults*
Wants to please adults; conforms*
Responds to verbal suggestions
Easily prompted, redirected
Can be bargained with, reasoned with
Begins to share, take turns, wait
Avid "me-too"-er*
Exuberant, talkative, humorous
Has imaginary companions
Has nightmares, animal phobias
Plays consciously, cooperatively with others*
Plays spontaneously in groups
Demonstrates fears
Goes after desires; fights for them
Asserts independence often
Often stymied, frustrated, jealous
Sympathizes*
Strong sex-role stereotypes*

LANGUAGE

Talkative with or without a listener
Can listen to learn*
Likes new words*
Increases use of pronouns, prepositions
Uses "s" to indicate plural nouns
Uses "ed" to indicate past tense
Uses sentences of three or more words
Says "Is that all right?" a lot
Talks about nonpresent situations
Puts words into action
Moves and talks at the same time
Substitutes letters in speech: "w" for "r"
Intrigued by whispering
Uses 300 to 1,000 words

PHYSICAL–MOTOR

Has well-balanced body lines
Walks erect; nimble on feet
Gallops in wide, high steps
Alternates feet in stair climbing
Suddenly starts, stops
Turns corners rapidly
Swings arms when walking
Jumps up and down with ease
Uses toilet alone

Loses baby fat
Achieves bladder control
Rides a tricycle
Puts on, takes off wraps with help
Unbuttons buttons
Has some finger control with small objects
Grasps with thumb and index finger
Holds cup in one hand
Pours easily from small pitcher
Washes hands unassisted
Can carry liquids
Has activity with drive and purpose
Can balance on one foot

CREATIVE

Dramatizes play
Enjoys slapstick humor
Laughs at the ridiculous
Experiments with silly language
Imaginary companion may appear
Tricycle becomes many objects in dramatic play
Acts out own version of favorite story
Enjoys simple poems
Learns color concepts

COGNITIVE

Matches people according to physical
    characteristics*
Estimates "how many"
Enjoys making simple choices
Alert, excited, curious
Asks "why?" constantly*
Understands "It's time to . . ."
Understands "Let's pretend . . ."
Enjoys guessing games, riddles
Has lively imagination*
Often overgeneralizes*
Has short attention span
Carries out two to four directions in sequence
Often colors pages one color
Can't combine two activities
Names and matches simple colors
Has number concepts of one and two
Sees vague cause-and-effect relationships*
Can recognize simple melodies
Distinguishes between night and day
Understands size and shape comparisons

*Key characteristics of cultural awareness or identity.

Word Pictures define many common characteristics of the young child. What ones do you see pictured here?

WORD PICTURES OF A FOUR-YEAR-OLD

SOCIAL–EMOTIONAL

Mood changes rapidly
Tries out feelings of power
Dominates; is bossy, boastful, belligerent
Assertive, argumentative
Shows off; is cocky, noisy
Can fight own battles
Hits, grabs, insists on desires
Explosive, destructive
Easily overstimulated, excitable
Impatient in large groups*
Cooperates in groups of two or three*
Develops "special" friends* but shifts loyalties often
In-group develops, excludes others*
Resistant, tests limits
Exaggerates, tells tall tales
Alibis frequently
Teases, outwits; has terrific humor
May have scary dreams
Tattles frequently
Has food jags, food strikes

LANGUAGE

Has more words than knowledge
A great talker, questioner
Likes words, plays with them
Has high interest in poetry
Able to talk to solve conflicts*
Responds to verbal directions
Enjoys taking turns to sing along
Interested in dramatizing songs, stories
Exaggerates, practices words
Uses voice control, pitch, rhythm
Asks "when?" "why?" "how?"*
Joins sentences together
Loves being read to

PHYSICAL–MOTOR

Longer, leaner body build
Vigorous, dynamic, acrobatic
Active until exhausted
"Works": builds, drives, pilots
Can jump own height and land upright
Hops, skips
Throws large ball, kicks accurately
Hops and stands on one foot
Jumps over objects
Walks in a straight line

Races up and down stairs
Turns somersaults
Walks backward toe–heel
Accurate, rash body movements
Copies a cross, square
Can draw a stick figure
Holds paint brush in adult manner, pencil in fisted grasp
Can lace shoes
Dresses self except back buttons, ties
Has sureness and control in finger activities
Alternates feet going down stairs

CREATIVE

Is adventurous
Shows vivid imagination
Displays great interest in violence in imaginary play
Loves anything new
Demonstrates more elaborate dramatic play
Makes up new words, sounds, and stories
Enjoys complexity in book illustrations
Exaggerates and goes to extremes
Likes funny poetry
Tells spontaneous story with artwork
Can put on elaborate plays with puppets
Finds ways to solve problems
Combines words and ideas

COGNITIVE

Does some naming and representative art
Gives art products personal value
Can work for a goal*
Questions constantly*
Interested in how things work
Interested in life–death concepts
Has an extended attention span
Can do two things at once
Dramatic play is closer to reality*
Judges which of two objects is larger
Has concept of three, can name more
Has accurate sense of time
Full of ideas
Begins to generalize; often faulty*
Likes a variety of materials
Calls people names*
Has dynamic intellectual drive*
Has imaginary playmates
Recognizes several printed words

*Key characteristics of cultural awareness or identity.

WORD PICTURES OF A FIVE-YEAR-OLD

SOCIAL-EMOTIONAL

Poised, self-confident, self-contained
Sensitive to ridicule*
Has to be right; persistent
Has sense of self-identity*
May get silly, high, wild
Enjoys pointless riddles, jokes
Enjoys group play, competitive games*
Aware of rules, defines them for others*
Chooses own friends, is sociable*
Gets involved with group decisions*
Insists on fair play*
Likes adult companionship*
Accepts, respects authority*
Asks permission
Remains calm in emergencies

LANGUAGE

Uses big words and complete sentences
Can define some words
Spells out simple words
Takes turn in conversation
Has clear ideas and articulates them*
Uses words to give, receive information
Insists "I already know that"
Asks questions to learn answers*
Makes up songs
Enjoys dictating stories
Uses 1,500 words
Tells a familiar story
Defines simple words
Answers telephone, takes a message
Thinks out loud*

PHYSICAL-MOTOR

Completely coordinated
Has adultlike posture
Has tremendous physical drive
Likes to use fine-motor skills
Learns how to tie bow knot
Has accuracy, skill with simple tools
Draws a recognizable person*

Handedness is evident
Dresses self completely
Cuts on a line with scissors
Begins to color within the lines
Catches ball from 3 feet away
Skips using alternate feet
Enjoys jumping, running, doing stunts
Rides a two-wheeler
Balances on a balance beam
Jumps rope, skips
Runs lightly on toes
Likes to dance, is graceful, rhythmic
Sometimes roughhouses, fights

CREATIVE

Explores variety of art processes
Becomes engrossed in details of painting, blocks
Fantasy is more active, less verbal
Thinks out loud
Likes to copy
Has ideas, loves to talk about them
Can learn simple dance routine
Enjoys making patterns, designs
Puts on simple plays
Has idea of what to draw—wants to make something recognizable

COGNITIVE

Curious about everything*
Wants to know "how?" "why?"*
Likes to display new knowledge, skills
Somewhat conscious of ignorance*
Attention span increases noticeably
Knows tomorrow, yesterday
Can count 10 objects, rote-counts to 20
Sorts objects by single characteristic*
Knows name, address, town
Makes a plan, follows it, centers on task
Sorts objects by color, shape
Concepts of smallest, less than, one-half
May tell time accurately, on the hour
Knows what a calendar is used for
Seldom sees things from another's point of view

*Key characteristics of cultural awareness or identity.

WORD PICTURES OF A SIX- AND SEVEN-YEAR-OLD

SOCIAL-EMOTIONAL
Six-year-old
Likes to work, yet often does so in spurts
Does not show persistence
Tends to be a know-it-all
Free with opinions and advice
Brings home evidence of good schoolwork
Observes family rules*
Gender-role stereotypes are rigid*
Friends easily gained, easily lost*
Tests and measures self against peers*
Makes social connections through play*
Friends are of same sex*
Believes in rules except for self*
Active, outgoing
Charming
Proud of accomplishments
Shows aggression through insults, name-calling*

Seven-year-old
More serious
Sensitive to others' reactions*
Eager for home responsibilities
Complaining, pensive, impatient
Shame is common emotion*
Leaves rather than face criticism, ridicule, disapproval*
Complains of unfair treatment, not being liked*
Shows politeness and consideration for adults*
Enjoys solitary activities
First peer pressure: needs to be "in"*
Wants to be one of the gang*
Relates physical competence to self-concept*
Self-absorbed; self-conscious

LANGUAGE
Six- and seven-year-olds
Enjoy putting language skill to paper
Talk *with* adults rather than *to* them*
Chatter incessantly
Dominate conversations
Speech irregularities still common
Learning to print/write
Acquisition of new words tapers off
Bilingual capacities nearly complete* if English is second language
Ability to learn new language still present*

PHYSICAL-MOTOR
Six- and seven-year-olds
Basic skills develop, need refinement
Like to test limits of own body
Value physical competence*
Work at self-imposed tasks
Need daily legitimate channels for high energy
Learn to ride two-wheel bike, skate, ski
Motor development is tool for socializing
Boisterous, enjoy stunts and roughhousing
Susceptible to fatigue
Visual acuity reaches normal
Hungry at short intervals, like sweets
Chew pencils, fingernails, hair

CREATIVE
Six-year-old
Tries out artistic exploration seriously for the first time
Industrious
Greater interest in process, not product
Eager, curious, enthusiastic
Loves jokes and guessing games
Loves to color, paint
Understands cause and effect
Likes cooperative projects, activities, tasks
Interested in skill and technique

Seven-year-old
Likes to be alone listening to music
Wants work to look good
The age for starting music lessons
Driven by curiosity, desire to discover and invent
Intensely interested in how things work: takes apart, puts back together
Uses symbols in both writing and drawing
Interested in all sorts of codes
Likes to select and sort

COGNITIVE
Six- and seven-year-olds
Work in spurts, not persistent
Letter and word reversal common
Learn to read, beginning math skills
Can consider others' point of view*
Use logic, systematic thinking*
Can plan ahead
Enjoy collecting: sorting, classifying
Can sequence events and retell stories
Concepts of winning and losing are difficult*
Like games with simple rules*
May cheat or change rules*
Want "real" things: watches and cameras that work
Sift and sort information*
Can conceptualize situations*
Enjoy exploring culture of classmates*

*Key characteristics of cultural awareness or identity.

WORD PICTURES OF AN EIGHT-YEAR-OLD

Video View Point 3-3

"Developmentally, school-age children are keen to forge relationships with their peers and with adults. Their curiosity about the world is at its peak."

Competency: Learning Environment

Age Group: School Age

Critical Thinking Questions:

1. What were you most curious about when you were six to nine years old?
2. How would you use your relationship with a seven-year-old to extend her curiosity and learning?

SOCIAL-EMOTIONAL

Outgoing, enthusiastic
Enormously curious about people and things*
Socially expansive*
Judgmental and critical of self and others*
Ambivalent about growing up
Often hostile but attracted to opposite sex
Growing self-confidence
Learns about self through others: peers, parents*
Is aware of and sensitive to differences in other children*
Begins to evaluate self and others through clothing, physical attraction, social status*
Likes to meet new people, go new places*
Has emerging sensitivity to personality traits of others*
Eager for peer approval and acceptance*
Growing sense of moral responsibility
Joins clubs
Chooses same-sex playmates
Struggles with feelings of inferiority
Likes to work cooperatively
Responds to studies of other cultures*
Has growing interest in fairness and justice issues*

LANGUAGE

Talks with adults
Attentive and responsive to adult communication*
Teases members of opposite sex
Talks about "self"*
Talkative, exaggerates
Likes to explain ideas
Imitates language of peers
Enjoys storytelling and writing short stories

PHYSICAL-MOTOR

Beginning to engage in team sports*
Often a growth-spurt year
Speedy, works fast
Restless, energetic, needs physical release
Plays hard, exhausts self
Eye-hand coordination matures, learns cursive handwriting
Enjoys competitive sports*
Hearty appetite, few food dislikes
Repeatedly practices new skills to perfect them

CREATIVE

Has great imagination
Enjoys riddles, limericks, knock-knock jokes
Likes to explain ideas
Visual acuity and fine motor skills come together
Is most productive in groups
Shows interest in process and product

COGNITIVE

Criticizes abilities in all academic areas
Seeks new experiences*
Likes to barter, bargain, trade
Enjoys creating collections of things
Interested in how children from other countries live*
Thinks beyond the here-and-now boundaries of time and space
Enjoys role-playing character parts*
Tests out parents to learn more about them
Needs direction, focus
Enjoys all types of humor
Full of ideas, plans
Gaining competence in basic skills
Concrete operations are solidifying*
Industrious, but overestimates abilities
Interested in process as well as product of schoolwork
Growing interest in logic and the way things work
Takes responsibility seriously*

*Key characteristics of cultural awareness or identity.

Children refine their skills and abilities between the ages of four and eight. Using the Word Pictures, how would you describe their growth?

In Chapter 4, students will come to appreciate the importance of research and significant theories from which these Word Pictures are drawn.

HOW CHILDREN DIFFER

What makes children differ so, especially when they have so many features in common? Megan gives the tire swing a big push. Ariel shrieks with delight, but Hans bursts into tears and screams to get off. There is a wide range of differences in any group of children. Some of the reasons are:

Developmental Differences

1. *Children grow and develop at different rates.* Each child has a timetable. Timetables vary from child to child. This means that each child is ready to learn at a given time, which may or may not coincide with the timing for the rest of the group. This readiness factor must be respected.

2. *Development is predictable and follows a sequence.* The rate of development may vary, but the sequence remains the same for all children, even those who are disabled. Physical development tends to be from the head downward (notice how large a newborn baby's head is in relation to the rest of its body) and from the center outward (a young child gains control over arm movements before mastering finger control).

Other Factors

1. *Genetic makeup.* Each child has a unique combination of genes (nature) that determine eye and hair color, height, body shape, personality traits, and intelligence as well as the presence of certain diseases, such as Tay-Sachs, cystic fibrosis, and sickle cell anemia.

2. *Environment.* The environment (nurture) has great impact throughout development. From conception, an individual child's rate and sequence of development reflects "an ongoing dialogue between the brain, the body, and the physical and social environment" (Berk, 2002).

   The attitudes with which children are raised, their culture, their socioeconomic status, the kinds of caregiving they experience, and their community combine in countless ways to affect growth. In Chapter 1, this subject is more thoroughly discussed as the "ecology of the family." Nutrition, safety, play space, adult relationships, neighborhood, and family stability affect individual development. Whether a child lives in poverty or affluence, environmental factors interact with genes to create a single, individual person.

   The small child who stands at the classroom door is the sum total of the physical, intellectual, social, and emotional factors of home and heredity. What nature provides, the world shapes. Growth and development is a series of complicated interactions between the two.

3. *Gender and race differences.* Girls and boys differ in both the rate and the pattern of growth, especially in adolescence. Ethnic variations in growth are common. African-American and Asian-American children seem to mature faster than do North American white children, who are more mature than European children (Berk, 2002). Growth "norms" should be used with caution and with respect to ethnic differences.

   Using short phrases (called Word Pictures on pp. 91–100) that identify typical behaviors at a given age helps to remind us

In our diverse world, teachers should be sensitive to the influence of sex, race, and individual patterns of development.

to take a long-range view regarding children's growth. (Chapters 4 and 7 will provide further insights.)

Implications for Teaching

Learning Styles

As you observe young children, you will notice that they exhibit a number of different approaches to learning. Some children are quiet, others move around and talk, while others never seem to listen. While on a field trip to the farm, these children demonstrate three common **learning styles:**

1. Lorenzo watches and looks around. He calls to others, "See the goat!" and "Look at that!" Lorenzo is a visual learner.

2. Olivia chatters away to her friends as they enter the barnyard. "Listen to all the noise the sheep are making." "Hear the horses?" Olivia is an auditory learner.

3. As she runs ahead of the other children, Anna calls out, "Get over here so we can touch them." She begs, "Take me closer. I want to feel the sheep." Anna is a tactile learner.

Each of the children responds to the experience in a way that reflects their individual learning style. Lorenzo draws pictures and paints what he saw at the farm. Olivia will repeat stories about the farm over and over as she integrates her experience. Anna will play out her farm experience by making clay animals and dancing a variety of animal dances. (Figure 3–3; see Chapter 10 for further discussion about learning preferences and how to accommodate them when planning curriculum.)

✸ CHILDREN WITH SPECIAL NEEDS

Approximately 15% to 20% of all children in the United States will exhibit some form of atypical development and need special services (Bee, 1999). These are children who did not develop according to normal standards. They exhibit a wide range of

Program Planning for Developmental Differences and Learning Styles[1]

1. Plan individual and group activities according to the age level of the class, considering the behavior patterns and learning styles that exist. Make sure the materials are in a variety of formats so that children can choose the ones that express their style of learning, such as puzzles and manipulatives, writing and drawing materials, dance and movement accessories, building blocks, and storytelling.

2. Plan for the age level with the understanding and appreciation of the variations within a one-year span. An age-level-appropriate gardening project for four-year-olds will provide many opportunities for differences in learning styles. Some children will want to do the digging, others will want to plan out the flower bed with their friends, still others will want to draw pictures to label the various things growing in the garden.

3. Know the individual children, their strengths, and their challenges. Only through observation can a teacher know where each individual in the class is in relation to developmental norms. Families bring further knowledge of each individual child, and that information needs to be added to the mix when assessing children's progress.

4. Plan around the known similarities, the developmental tasks, and age-appropriate behavior common to that group of children, including children with special needs. Planning needs to include the interests, abilities, and unique characteristics of ALL the children in the class, whether or not they have disabilities. Movement and dance appeal to many children and are a staple of early childhood curriculum. Yet Margie gets upset when the music is too loud, Aaron gets too overstimulated, and Carlo, who is in a wheelchair, cannot dance. Each of these children's needs must be accommodated in the planning. Dancing with scarves to softer music might help Margie and Aaron. Asking the children to dance with their hands and arms brings a new experience in movement and accommodates Carlo's disability without making a point about it.

5. Set group and individual goals based on these general characteristics; change goals as needed. As four-year-olds approach kindergarten, one goal that teachers might have is to ensure that the group has good listening skills and can participate in group discussions. Throughout the year the teachers will assess each child's capacity for sitting and listening and plan strategies to help them expand their capacity for these activities. For the children who need more time to develop these skills, teachers may create small group times to allow for differences in development and abilities to concentrate.

6. Incorporate individual differences, selecting activities that allow for a variety of responses from children at different stages of development. A pasting activity encourages creativity in the most adept three-year-old and still allows the less skilled three-year-old to explore the feel of the paste on fingers and hands.

[1]The learning environment can be arranged so that children of every skill level can work and play together.

Figure 3–3

Continued

7. **Modify activities to make them more accessible or appropriate for children with special needs.** Tables can be made higher or lower for wheelchair access, or a teacher may spend extra time in the dramatic play area to help individual children with social skills.

8. **Programs are planned to meet the needs and challenges of the whole group.** Children are more alike than they are different. In an inclusive early childhood education program children with disabilities participate in the same routines and activities as do other children. Planning for any group of children includes a sensitivity to each child's needs and capabilities and the ability to provide the challenges they need to move forward in their development.

Use the Word Pictures (pp. 91–100) for characteristic traits of development.

FIGURE 3–3, continued

atypical disorders ranging from short-term behavior problems to long-term physical, mental, and emotional disabilities.[1]

Two types of children come under the category of **children with special needs.** Children who are disabled and children who are gifted extend the definition of "Who is the child?"

Children Who Are Disabled

The term *special needs* includes a great many conditions that may or may not be noticeable (Figure 3–4). To be designated disabled, a child's normal growth and development is (1) delayed; (2) distorted, atypical, or abnormal; or (3) severely or negatively affected (Allen & Cowdery, 2005). This definition includes the physical, mental, emotional, and social areas of development.

Some disabilities are multihandicapping, affecting several growth areas. A child with a profound hearing loss is often delayed in speech production or language abilities and suffers social isolation due to the inability to hear and speak with peers. Typically, a child with **Down syndrome** may have congenital heart defects, intellectual impairments, eye abnormalities, or poor physical coordination. Children who have cerebral palsy, a central nervous system disorder, often have other disabling conditions such as intellectual delays; epilepsy; and hearing, visual, and speech problems (Kiernan et al., n.d.).

Learning Disabilities

Children with learning disabilities are found in almost every classroom and may have, among other things, poor memory skills; difficulty in following directions; eye–hand coordination problems; and trouble discriminating between letters, numbers, and sounds. These keep them from storing, processing, and producing information. Dyslexia, the most common specific learning disability, occurs when children have diffi-

[1]More and more early care and education programs are reflecting diversity by creating groups of children exhibiting a wide range of developmental abilities.

A Variety of Disabilities Teachers May Encounter

1. *Speech and language:* hearing impairment, stuttering, articulation problems, cleft palate, chronic voice disorders, learning disabilities

2. *Physical-motor:* visual impairment, blindness, perceptual motor deficits, orthopedic disabilities such as cerebral palsy, spina bifida, loss of limbs, muscular dystrophy

3. *Intellectual:* cognitive delays, brain injury, brain dysfunction, dyslexia, learning disabilities

4. *Social-emotional:* self-destructive behavior, severe withdrawal, dangerous aggression toward self and others, noncommunicativeness, moodiness, tantrums, attention-deficit hyperactivity disorder, severe anxiety, depression, phobias, psychosis, autism

5. *Health impairments:* severe asthma, epilepsy, hemophilia, congenital heart defects, severe anemia, malnutrition, diabetes, tuberculosis, cystic fibrosis, Down syndrome, sickle cell anemia, Tay-Sachs disease, AIDS

6. *Specific learning disabilities:* difficulties with language use and acquisition, spoken and written language affected, perceptual handicaps, brain injury, minimal brain dysfunction, dyslexia, developmental aphasia.

These disorders may range from mild to severe, and children will exhibit a wide variety of abilities and needs even if they are diagnosed with the same condition. For further information concerning a specific one, the student will want to consult a special education textbook.

FIGURE 3–4

culty in learning to read. They may reverse letters (such as *d* and *b*) or words (such as *was* and *saw*), although many children who are not dyslexic do this. A child with a learning disability may have a strength in one area, such as math, and yet have a disability in another area, such as language. A learning disability does not mean that a child is intellectually impaired or delayed.[1]

According to Bee (1999), a child with a learning disorder develops normally in other respects and has no obvious brain damage, but the task of reading seems to highlight several areas of difficulty: problems of visual perception, inability to integrate visual and auditory information, impaired memory, problems with language, and difficulty distinguishing the separate sounds in words. This wide range of symptoms, the number of potential causes, and the varying degrees to which children exhibit the symptoms make learning disorders difficult to diagnose.

Allen and Cowdery (2005) caution against early diagnosis of a young child as "learning disabled," because young children differ in their individual rate of growth and many differences and delays are within the range of normal development.

[1]Children with special needs cut across social, economic, and cultural lines.

Attention-Deficit Hyperactivity Disorder

Do you remember a classmate who could never sit still—one who was constantly on the move, talked excessively, and disrupted classroom activities? You may have also seen a preschooler who couldn't finish a puzzle, take a nap, or wait for a turn. These children are typical of those with a condition known as **attention-deficit hyperactivity disorder (ADHD)**, which affects up to 3% to 5% of all school-age children (Berk, 2003). ADHD is more often found in boys than girls and may be hereditary.

Children with ADHD can be difficult to manage, both at home and in the classroom. They are prone to restlessness, anxiety, short attention spans, and impulsiveness. Hyperactive children have difficulty remaining seated, are in constant motion, do not listen well, may talk excessively, are easily distracted, and have difficulty with social relationships. This constellation of behaviors may apply at some level to many children, but teachers must be cautious about labeling the normally active, somewhat disruptive child as hyperactive. The child with ADHD exhibits these behaviors in extreme, usually before age seven.

Medication with a drug (Ritalin®) is a common treatment for children with ADHD, but its effects are short term and its side effects can be serious. The most effective treatment appears to be a combination of medication and individual behavior management strategies (Allen & Cowdery, 2005). There is no easy solution for dealing with children who are hyperactive; further research into the cause and the development of safe effective treatments are clearly needed (Figure 3–5).

Teachers and Families Working Together

Parents are usually the first to notice that their child is not developing according to the norms. They may ask the child's teacher to

Effective Guidance Strategies for Children with ADHD

1. **Maintain regular and consistent routines and rules:** "Remember, Sitara, we always wash hands before snacks."
2. **Have realistic expectations:** "I know it is hard for you to wait a long time. Why don't you go over to the other cabinet and see if the pencils you want are in there?"
3. **Make eye contact when giving directions using clear and simple explanations:** "Look at me, Toby, so I know that you are listening. Good. Now let's go over the assignment together."
4. **Allow time for transition by giving a plan for the next step:** "In three minutes it will be time to get ready to go home. When the other children begin to leave, I want you to get your coat and come back here to sit with us."
5. **Select jobs in which the child can be successful:** "Connie, please pass out the napkins to this table today."
6. **Recognize accomplishments:** "Good work, Connie. You gave everyone a red napkin and then sat down with one for yourself."

FIGURE 3–5

watch for signs of hearing impairments, lack of necessary motor skills, or language imperfections. Because early diagnosis and intervention are important, teachers should assess the child's overall skills.[1] They can then plan appropriate follow-through with the family. This may include a consultation for further developmental screening and testing to identify any problems and secure the services needed. The early childhood education professional is not expert at diagnosing learning disabilities but can be effective in helping families secure proper referrals and treatment.

Public Recognition

Since the mid-1960s there has been significant public recognition and funding for education programs for children with disabilities. Past generations hid adults and children with disabilities in their homes or secluded them in institutions. Public consciousness is now sufficient to understand that not all people with special needs are necessarily mentally impaired and that many can be integrated into ongoing programs in schools and into the mainstream of life. The story over the past 35 years is this:

1. In 1972 Head Start required that a minimum of 10% of its enrollment be reserved for children with disabilities and led the way toward large-scale inclusion.

2. In 1975 **Public Law 94–142,** the Education for All Handicapped Children Act, was passed. This so-called Bill of Rights for the Handicapped guarantees free public education to disabled persons from three to 21 years of age "in the least restrictive" environment. Parents of children with special needs are an integral part of the development of their child's Individualized Education Plan (IEP). This provides a more family-centered approach in which the strengths and needs of the family are taken into consideration. The success of PL 94–142 means that thousands of children who are disabled who would have been denied any educational opportunities are now in school with their nondisabled peers.[1]

3. **Public Law 99–457,** the Education of the Handicapped Amendments Act of 1986, has had an even more profound impact for early childhood educators. Sections of this law provide funding for children who were not included in the previous law: infants, toddlers, and three- to five-year-olds. This law also allows for the inclusion of "developmentally delayed" youngsters and leaves local agencies the opportunity to include the "at-risk" child in that definition. The vague definitions give local agencies the opportunity to define disabling conditions in terms of local needs.

4. In 1990 Congress reauthorized PL 94–142 and renamed it the Individuals with Disabilities Education Act (IDEA) (PL 101–576). Two new categories, autism and traumatic brain injury, were included, and children from birth to age five years were now eligible to receive services.

5. Many programs may be affected by another piece of legislation, Public Law

[1]We need to remember that inclusion refers to abilities and gender as well as race and culture.

101–336, the Americans with Disabilities Act (ADA), which was passed in 1990. This civil rights act makes it unlawful to discriminate against people with disabilities because of their disability and requires that people with disabilities have equal access to public and private services, as well as reasonable accommodations. This law has had an impact on hiring practices in early childhood centers and family child care homes and may require adaptations to facilities and work environments to make them more accessible to individuals with disabilities. Although not specifically an education law, ADA is another step toward respecting the dignity and worth of all individuals.

Inclusion of Children with Special Needs

Allen and Cowdery (2005) differentiate between the terms **inclusion** and *mainstreaming*. In the past, children with special needs were integrated into classrooms only after they had met certain standards and expectations, and they were assigned to separate special education classes. When ready, they were mainstreamed into classrooms with typically developing children. Inclusion means that a child with a disability is a full-time member of a regular classroom, a more natural environment, with children of differing abilities. Inclusion is about belonging, having worth, and having choices. An inclusive classroom is about "accepting and valuing human diversity and providing support so that all children and families can participate in the program of their choice." (Allen & Cowdery, 2005). Teachers are a key factor in the successful integration of children with disabilities. Their attitude is critical; they must be committed to teaching all children, regardless of their intelligence or skill levels, with equal caring and concern.

The inclusive environment fosters children's interactions with one another.

Promoting inclusion means that

1. teachers foster interactions between children who are disabled and children who are not disabled that promote healthy social relationships.

2. teachers recognize that every child with special needs has strengths as well as deficits and build on those strengths.

3. teachers receive training and guidance in working with children who have special needs and are developmentally disabled.

4. teachers work with families to plan and implement the child's IEP.

5. children with disabilities are actively involved and accepted in the total program.

6. children with special needs are helped to take advantage of, to the fullest extent of their capabilities, all the activities the school has to offer.

7. children's individual disabilities are addressed and considered in program planning and that procedures and curriculum are adapted to fit the children with special needs.

In 1993 the National Association for the Education of Young Children (NAEYC) endorsed a Position on Inclusion, written by the Division of Early Childhood of the Council for Exceptional Children. That statement offers guidelines for implementation.

Children Who Are Gifted

Gifted children are those who demonstrate an intellectual and creative potential superior to that of most children in the same age range and may exhibit an exceptional in-depth knowledge or skill of one or more specific areas (Allen & Cowdery, 2005; Bee, 1999; Berk, 2002). Traditionally, children have been identified as gifted if they score between 130 and 150 on standard IQ tests.

More and more programs for gifted children are open to those who exhibit exceptional talent in other areas than just intellectual superiority—children who are gifted in music, art, and physical skills. The current definition of gifted too often limits programs to those children who are intellectually exceptional. There is a need to enlarge the definition to include children, including those with disabilities, who are gifted in other areas of learning.

Children who are gifted come from all social, economic, and cultural groups; however, there is increasing concern that children from low-income populations, children who are ethnically and culturally in the minority, children who have disabilities, and children who are bilingual are underrepresented in the gifted category.[1]

Gifted children have long attention spans, learn rapidly, and have good memories and advanced vocabularies. They ask a lot of questions and are able to express their ideas easily. Independent and imaginative, gifted children may be bored by normal activities. Socially, the gifted child is sought after by peers, yet may be uneasy about relationships with other children. Planning and organizing skills are evident in their artwork and other creative endeavors. The gifted child is content to be alone, spending time in purposeful activity. Their use of humor is more advanced than children the same age; originality is typically characteristic of the gifted.

The Role of the Early Childhood Educator With Children Who Are Gifted

The teacher's role with the gifted child is that of providing challenge and stimula-

[1]This information provides another opportunity to examine the impact of bias in thinking about children (i.e., do the existing instruments for identifying giftedness identify only particular strengths for a particular segment of the population?).

tion. Curriculum areas are developed in more complex ways. The gifted child is ready to learn in greater depth; the teachers provide added materials and activities that will help the children probe the extent of their interests. The nongifted children in the same classroom benefit from this enrichment; each responds according to his or her abilities. Teachers of children who have special gifts and talents can meet their unique needs in a regular school setting at the same time that they provide a rich curriculum for other students.

Parents of the gifted child will need support and encouragement as well as guidance in dealing with their child's exceptionality. Together, teachers and parents can explore what will best suit each individual child so that this giftedness may be nurtured and challenged at home and at school.

Dealing With Bias and Stereotypes

One of the greatest needs a child with disabilities has is to be accepted. Young children are known for their forthrightness in commenting on and asking questions about what confuses and frightens them. They may be anxious about what another child's disability means to them. Although this is a common reaction and age appropriate, we cannot allow an individual to be rejected on the basis of a disability. Derman-Sparks et al. (1989) suggest the following strategies:

1. The rejection must be handled immediately, with support and assurance given to the child who was rejected that this type of behavior will not be permitted.

2. It is important to help children recognize how they are different and how they are alike.

3. Children need to have their fears about disabilities taken seriously and to have adults understand their concerns.

4. Questions must be answered promptly, truthfully, and simply. Use the children's own natural curiosity, and let the child with disabilities answer for him/herself whenever possible.

All children benefit when adults are willing to confront bias and deal with children's prejudice and misconceptions. This example could have been about girls rejecting boys or one child being rejected because of skin color. When we provide opportunities for children to interact with people who look and act differently than they do, we actively foster acceptance and respect for the individual. More gender diversity issues are found in Chapters 4 and 11.

CULTURAL, RACIAL, AND ETHNIC CONSIDERATIONS

The answer to "who is the young child?" takes on a powerful new meaning with the multicultural explosion that has swept across the nation. Early childhood programs are filled with children from many different cultural backgrounds. By 2015, in New York, Texas, New Mexico, Arizona, and California, the school-age population will be more than 50% minority. Nationally, that is likely to happen by 2040 (U.S. Bureau of the Census, 1997).

Nearly 40% of Californians over the age of five speak a language other than English at home; in New Mexico, it is 35%, and in Texas, 32% (Ness, 2001). For a teacher of young children, these statistics have some important implications. There will be more students in the classroom who are culturally and linguistically different. Unless teachers are informed and educated about these differences, they may misinterpret a child's abilities, learning, and needs. Too often, language barriers between a teacher and a child lead to the conclusion that the child is a slow learner or has a disability.

Working with families will become more challenging to a teacher's ingenuity and communication skills. Many parents are unfamiliar with school culture in the United States and the expectations schools have about parent involvement and participation. Some parents are illiterate in their own language. An informed and supportive teacher can help parents help their children succeed under these circumstances (see Chapter 8, "Needs of Immigrant Parents").

A lack of understanding about the culture, history, beliefs, and values of the children is harmful to their self-concept (Derman-Sparks et al., 1989). Interracial marriages have increased in the United States 120% since 1980 (U.S. Bureau of the Census, 1997). The ranks of multiracial children are swelling.

Cultural Sensitivity

Cultural and linguistic sensitivity means that each child's heritage is honored, that it is understood as unique from other cultures, and that it is respected. It means that teachers must become familiar with the cultural norms of the children in their classes and build bridges for children and their families into the more dominant culture.[1]

The culturally sensitive teacher will get to know each of the families as a separate entity and become familiar with their individual expressions of culture and values. Today's teacher will recognize that one family does not represent the totality of the culture (stereotyping) and will be careful

not to overgeneralize. The effective teacher will be called on to integrate these insights into curriculum planning as well as home and school relationships (see also "Attitudes and Biases" in Chapter 5).

KEY TERMS

attention-deficit hyperactivity disorder (ADHD)
age-level characteristics
children with special needs
developmental stages
Down syndrome
gifted children
inclusion
learning styles
Public Law 94–142
Public Law 99–457
the whole child
Word Pictures

Teaching Applications

1. Read the examples of learning styles on page 102. How would you work with each child in a small group that was preparing a cooking experience?

2. Select two children who are approximately the same age. Compare their physical and social development. How are they alike? How are they different? What do you think accounts for these differences?

3. Observe a class of children with special needs in an inclusive classroom. What would you do to foster interactions between the children who are disabled and the children who are not? What verbalizations are used about a child's handicapping condition, and do the nondisabled children seem to under-

[1]Examine your own culturally biased assumptions and note sources of conflict with your cultural influences.

stand how their friends are similar to them as well as different?

4. Using Derman-Sparks's suggestions, create a scenario of how you would deal with a five-year-old child who refused to play with a classmate who wore diapers because of his spina bifida.

5. Create your own posters, materials, and books that show interracial families.

REFERENCES

Allen, K. E., & Cowdery, G. E. (2005). *The exceptional child: Inclusion in early childhood education* (5th ed.). Clifton Park, NY: Thomson Delmar Learning.

Bee, H. (1999). *The developing child.* Menlo Park, CA: Addison-Wesley.

Berk, L. E. (2002). *Infants and children.* Boston: Allyn & Bacon.

Berk, L. E. (2003). *Child development.* Boston: Allyn & Bacon.

Caldwell, B. M. (2004). One world of children. In A. M. Gordon & K. Williams Browne. *Beginnings and beyond* (6th ed.). Clifton Park, NY: Thomson Delmar Learning.

Derman-Sparks, L., & the ABC Task Force. (1989). *Anti-bias curriculum: Tools for empowering young children.* Washington, DC: National Association for the Education of Young Children.

Kiernan, S., et al. (n.d.). *Mainstreaming preschoolers: Children with orthopedic handicaps.* Washington, DC: U.S. Department of Health, Education, and Welfare.

Ness, C. (2001, August 6). 100-year high in California's percentage of foreign-born. *San Francisco Chronicle,* 1.

U.S. Bureau of the Census (1997). *A population projection by age, sex, race, and Hispanic origin for 1995–2025.* Washington, DC: Author.

Additional resources for this chapter can be found by visiting the Online Companion™ at www.earlychilded.delmar.com. This supplemental material includes a Study Guide with chapter review questions (and answers), critical thinking questions and activities, and annotated Web sites.

Developmental and Learning Theories

QUESTIONS FOR THOUGHT

What basic questions do theories and research attempt to answer?

What are the major developmental and learning theories that affect early childhood education?

What are central developmental topics that affect early childhood education?

How can theories be applied to the classroom and work with young children?

✹ INTRODUCTION

While visiting an elementary school, a police officer was asked by a girl of about six years old, "Are you a cop?" "Yes," said the woman. "My mother said if I ever needed help I should ask the police. Is that right?" "Yes, again," replied the officer. "Well, then," the little girl said as she extended her foot forward, "would you please tie my shoe?"

Can you see how the six-year-old took in information from her mother and then applied it to her own life? How do children do that?

While working for an organization that delivers lunches to elderly shut-ins, a mother used to take her preschool son on the afternoon rounds. He was always intrigued by the various appliances there, particularly the canes, walkers, and wheelchairs. One day she saw him staring at a pair of false teeth soaking in a glass. He turned to her and whispered, "The tooth fairy will never believe this!"

Look how this child applied his fantasy world to what he encountered. How do young children make sense of what they see, touch, and experience?

While playing with six-month-old Michiko, her father puts one end of a toy monkey in his mouth and dangles it in front of her. Michiko gazes intently, getting still and wide-eyed, finally reaching up tentatively to touch the doll. Keith's nanny tries the same thing with him. But the nine-month-old acts differently; he smiles, laughs as he grabs it, and tries to shove it back into the nanny's mouth!

Two children respond differently, yet they are only a few months apart in age. Is it because of their gender or ethnic differences? Or has one child played this game before and not the other?

Many remarkable transformations take place in the early years. Development, the orderly set of changes in the life span, occurs as individuals move from conception to death. We want to know the nature of these changes and the reasons why things happen.

- ✹ How do children develop?
- ✹ What do they learn, and in what order?
- ✹ What do people need to be ready to learn?
- ✹ What affects learning?
- ✹ Do all people develop in the same ways?
- ✹ What are the similarities and differences in growth and development?

To begin to answer these questions, we need some way to look for information and then choose and organize the facts so that we can understand what we see. In other words, we need a theory. Theories are especially useful in providing a broad and consistent view of the complexity of human development. They allow us to make educated guesses (called hypotheses) about children's behavior and development. Because these theories are based on experience, their validity can be checked by teachers as they observe children every day.

The Nature of Development

A child is a blend of many parts that interrelate in different ways and change with growth over time. Such complexity and dynamic change is difficult to describe, much less predict. To simplify the study of development, we try to consider separately the aspects that make up the whole of development (Figure 4–1). We can then better understand the major processes of development that parallel these developmental areas.

FIGURE 4-1 We use images, such as this rainbow of developmental areas, to capture the concept of the whole child as a sum of many parts.

- Physical-motor development includes the biological processes that describe changes in the body.
- Intellectual development involves the cognitive processes in thought, intelligence, and language.
- Affective development includes those socioemotional processes that reflect changes in an individual's relationships with self and other people, emotions, personality, creativity, and spirituality.

Major Issues in Development

Is children's development due more to maturation or to experience? The changes we see in children over time may be due to internal or external influences. Some theories claim that children change because of innate, biological, or genetic patterns built into the human being; others claim that they are shaped by the environment and life's experiences (due to parents, learning and play materials, TV, school, and so on). This argument is often referred to as the **nature/nurture** controversy, also known as the problem of heredity versus environment. As you will remember from Chapter 1, Rousseau argued for the "nature" side. He stated that the child is born with natural, or innate, goodness. John Locke, however, asserted that it was "nurture" that mattered. He contended that children entered the world with a clean slate on which all experience and learning was then written. Today, most psychologists and educators agree that the patterns of development and learning are complex and not so simply explained. Modern theories are not set in such black-and-white terms but rather focus on variations that emphasize one or the other (see Figure 4-2).

Is growth smooth and continuous or more stage-like? Some theories emphasize a gradual, cumulative kind of growth, more like "from an acorn, a giant oak will grow." This continuity of development is usually the viewpoint of those theories that emphasize experience (nurture). Others see children growing in stages that are clearly

FIGURE 4–2 Development is a combination of the forces of nature (heredity and parental conditions) and nurture (environmental and life experiences). Every theory focuses on various areas of development and emphasizes a different proportion of these two forces.

marked by distinct changes. This view outlines a sequence of stages in which change is qualitative rather than quantitative. As a caterpillar changes into a butterfly, it does not become more of a caterpillar, but rather turns into a different kind of organism. This viewpoint emphasizes the innate nature of development

What can theory and research do for early childhood educators? Science has opened our eyes to the amazing complexity of the mind and the wondrous path of growth in the body. In previous generations, little scientific information was available. Many beliefs were espoused by adults about children, such as "You'll spoil the baby if you respond to his demands too quickly" or "Children who suffer early neglect will never amount to much." These statements can be powerful, particularly as they are passed on by family

and culture. However, some ideas are rooted in myth rather than reality. Researchers and theorists have accumulated a rich store of knowledge, based on scientific evidence. They can help sort fact from fiction.

Early childhood teachers should know how children develop and how they learn. Developmentally appropriate practices (DAP) are based on this knowledge. For instance, we know that development occurs in a relatively orderly sequence, so that we can plan an environment for two-year-olds with a variety of tactile materials, knowing that their learning is likely to be best suited for sensorimotor input. Figure 4–3 describes the 12 principles distilled from decades of research, theory, and practice.

Knowing how children develop is critical in making the daily decisions about curriculum, the classroom setting, and children. The teacher who is well versed in theory has invaluable tools with which to work with parents, advising them of the range of typical behavior and discussing concerns that go beyond the norms. Therefore, it is important to have a background in both developmental psychology and learning theories.

No one set of principles encompasses all developmental and learning theories. We have chosen eight theories. They are commonly known as (1) **psychodynamic** theory, (2) behaviorist theory, (3) cognitive theory, (4) **sociocultural** theory, (5) ecological theory, (6) **multiple intelligences** theory, (7) maturation theory, and (8) humanist theory.

Basic Principles of Development

1. Domains of children's development—physical, social, emotional, and cognitive—are closely related. Development in one domain influences and is influenced by development in other domains.

2. Development occurs in a relatively orderly sequence, with later abilities, skills, and knowledge building on those already acquired.

3. Development proceeds at varying rates from child to child as well as unevenly within different areas of each child's functioning.

4. Early experiences have both cumulative and delayed effects on individual children's development; optimal periods exist for certain types of development and learning.

5. Development proceeds in predictable directions toward greater complexity, organization, and internalization.

6. Development and learning occur in and are influenced by multiple social and cultural contexts.

7. Children are active learners, drawing on direct physical and social experience as well as culturally transmitted knowledge to construct their own understanding of the world around them.

8. Development and learning result from interaction of biological maturation and the environment, which includes both the physical and the social worlds that children live in.

9. Play is an important vehicle for children's social, emotional, and cognitive development, as well as a reflection of their development.

10. Development advances when children have opportunities to practice newly acquired skills, as well as when they experience a challenge just beyond the level of their present mastery.

11. Children demonstrate different modes of knowing and learning and different ways of representing what they know.

12. Children learn best in the context of a community in which they are safe and valued, their physical needs are met, and they feel psychologically secure.

FIGURE 4–3 Developmentally appropriate practices are based on knowledge of how children develop, which is based on research, theory, and observation (Bredekamp & Copple, 2005).

In addition, there are several special topics for educators in the study of child development. The chapter ends with a discussion of (1) ethnicity and cultural diversity, (2) **attachment,** (3) play, (4) gender identity, (5) moral development, and (6) brain-based research.

The children were playing "school" in the dramatic play area. Noemi insisted on wearing pretend glasses so she could look like her favorite teacher. "No!" cried Venecia. "They will make you mad and crabby!" In fact, that teacher wore the glasses only when she was too tired to wear contact lenses. "Yes, I will," replied Noemi. "She wears them cuz they makes her smarty-pants." Notice the child's mistaken notion about intelligence and eyewear. "You're both wrong," called out Charly. "Everybody knows you have to wear glasses and hoop earrings to be a teacher." As a matter of fact, that teacher did wear both. Everyone looked puzzled, and then the play resumed.

Just like these children, not all the experts agree or even think alike. Because the field of child development is broad, encompassing a wide variety of opinion and fact, there is no one theory that describes everything. Moreover, these theories arose at different time periods, in various countries. Each theory will describe children and their processes in a different way. Teachers put together what has been historically and empirically learned about young children and develop programs that best respond to their needs and assist in their growth. The National Association for the Education of Young Children (NAEYC) recommends DAP that are based on many of these theories. It is up to the educator to decide which ones best describe children and their growth. Read carefully, and then compare your experiences with the theories and con-

cepts you read here. As a teacher, you have a diversity of thought on which to establish a professional philosophy.

PSYCHODYNAMIC THEORY

Psychodynamic theory is about personality development and emotional problems. Psychodynamic, or psychoanalytic, theories look at development in terms of internal drives that are often **unconscious,** or hidden from our awareness. These motives are the underlying forces that influence human thinking and behavior and provide the foundation for universal stages of development. In psychoanalytic terms, children's behavior can be interpreted by knowing their various stages and the tasks within those stages.

Sigmund Freud

Sigmund Freud began his career as a medical doctor and became interested in the irrational side of human behavior as he treated "hysterics." His technique, asking people to recline on a couch and talk about everything that was going on with them, was ridiculed by the medical establishment as the "talking cure." Then, as patients revealed their thoughts, fantasies, and problems, Freud began to see patterns.

Theory of Psychosexual Development

According to Freud, people possess three basic drives: the sexual drive, survival instincts, and a drive for destructiveness. Of the first—childhood sexuality—Freud outlined development in terms of psychosexual stages, each characterized by a particular part of the body (Figure 4–4). In each stage, the sensual satisfaction associated with each body part is linked to major challenges of that age. For instance, think about how some of the issues of toddlers, such as biting or thumb sucking, and the preschool concerns with "doctor play," masturbation, or gender identification in the dress-up cor-

Stage	Age	Description/Major Area
Oral	Birth to 2	Mouth (sucking, biting) source of pleasure Eating and teething
Anal	2–3	Bowel movements source of pleasure Toilet learning
Phallic	3–6	Genitals source of pleasure Sex role identification and conscience development
Latency	6–12	Sexual forces dormant Energy put into schoolwork and sports
Genital	12–18	Genitals source of pleasure Stimulation and satisfaction from relationships

FIGURE 4–4 Freud's psychoanalytic theory of childhood sexuality. Freud's stage theory contends that each stage has its own area of pleasure and crisis between the child and parent or society.

ner might be seen in a psychosexual context. Each stage also has its own conflicts between child and parent, and how the child experiences those conflicts will determine basic personality and behavior patterns (Freud, 1968).

Freud's theory and ideas were expanded by Anna Freud (his daughter), Carl Jung, Karen Horney, and others. Although Freud's interest was in abnormal adult behavior and its causes, his conclusions have had a major effect on our conception of childhood and its place in the life span.

To Freud, the personality was the most important aspect of development, more central to human growth than language, perception, or cognition. Personality was defined by three structures: the id, which is the instinctive part that drives a person to seek satisfaction; the ego, the rational structure that forms a person's sense of self; and the superego, the moral side that informs the person of right and wrong. He thought that the personality developed in a fixed pattern of stages that emerged as the body matured naturally. But even though the sequence of the stages might be firm, how children were treated while going through those stages determined whether they developed healthy or abnormal personalities. In particular, the mother–child relationship was important in each stage. Thus, the interaction between the child's wishes and needs and how these were treated (by the mother or other adults) was a focal point for proper development.

All psychoanalytic explanations of human development emphasize the critical importance of relationships with people and the sequence, or stages, of personality development. The psychoanalyst Erik Erikson also expanded and refined Freud's theory of development.

Erik Erikson

Erik Homberg Erikson is perhaps the most influential psychoanalyst and key figure in the study of children and development. His interests in children and education included a teaching background in progressive and Montessori schools in Europe. After clinical training in psychoanalysis, he remained interested in the connections between psychotherapy and education. Erikson became the first child analyst in the Boston area and worked for years in several universities in the United States.

Theory of Psychosocial Development

To Erikson, life is a series of stages through which each person passes, each stage growing from the previous ones. He proposed eight stages of **psychosocial** development, each representing a critical period for the development of an important strength. Positive growth allowed the individual to integrate his or her physical and biological development with the challenges that the social institutions and culture present. Each stage was characterized by an emotional challenge. Erikson gave us the term *identity crisis* to describe how people struggle with a pair of contrasting issues (Figure 4–5) as they try to answer, "Who am I?" Personality strength needed to be built through balancing a child's wishes with the demands of the environment.

Like Freud, Erikson believed in certain developmental stages. A *stage* is a period during which certain changes occur. What one achieves in each stage is based on the developments of the previous stages, and each stage presents the child with certain kinds of problems to be solved. When children succeed, they go on to attack new problems and grow through solving them.

Erikson differed from Freud in some fundamental ways. First, he emphasized the drive for identity and meaning in a social context rather than in the Freudian context of sexual and aggressive drives. Second, development occurs throughout the life span, in contrast with the notion that personality is shaped only in childhood. Finally, the developmental struggles that occur during one's life can be overcome later. You can go back; while it is true that the first four stages play a key role in developing ego identity, problems of childhood can be dealt with in later stages so the adult can achieve vitality.

Everyone has certain biological, social, and psychological needs that must be satisfied to ensure growth in a healthy manner. Medicine has learned much about physical needs—diet, rest, exercise. Basic intellectual, social, and emotional needs also must be met for an organism to be healthy. Eriksonian theory speaks to these

Stage	Description	Challenge	Strength
Stage One	The newborn	Trust vs. Mistrust	Hope
Stage Two	Toddlers	Autonomy vs. Shame and Doubt	Willpower
Stage Three	Childhood	Initiative vs. Guilt	Purpose
Stage Four	School	Industry (or competence) vs. Inferiority	Competence
Stage Five	Adolescence	Search for Identity vs. Role Confusion	Fidelity
Stage Six	Young adulthood	Intimacy (love and friendship) vs. Isolation (loneliness)	Love
Stage Seven	Grown-ups	Generativity (caring for the next generation) vs. Stagnation	Care
Stage Eight	Old age	Integrity vs. Despair	Wisdom

FIGURE 4–5 Erikson's theory of psychosocial development centers on basic crises that people face from birth to old age. This stage theory of development proposes that these conflicts are part of the life process and that successful handling of these issues can give a person the "ego strength" to face life positively. (Adapted from Hubley and Hubley, 1976.)

needs; whether they are met or unfulfilled will affect development (see Figure 4–5).

The Stages

Stage 1: Trust Versus Mistrust (Birth to One Year).

Erikson's first stage is roughly the first year of life. Attitudes important to development are the capacity to trust—or mistrust—inner and outer experiences. By providing consistent care, parents help an infant develop a basic sense of trust in self and an ability to trust other people. They give affection and emotional security as well as provide for physical needs. Inconsistent or inadequate care creates mistrust. In extreme cases, lack of care can actually lead to infant death. A less extreme case might form isolation or distrust of others. Given a solid base in early trust, the typical infant develops hope.

Babies must learn trust at two levels: At an external level, infants see that significant adults will be present to meet their needs, and at an internal level, they come to believe in their own power to effect changes and cope with a variety of circumstances. As adults engage with infants, they encourage attachment (see the section on Developmental Topics). Developmentally appropriate ways to work with infants at this stage include giving babies an active voice in decisions about their lives. Follow babies' self-demand schedules for feeding, sleeping, and playing. Assume that babies are crying for a reason, so respond by letting the infant know you have received the message. "I know you are hungry, Ty," says Teacher Sara. "I am warming your bottle right now."

Thus, caregivers and families teach in two ways:

- ✲ Holding babies close and having warm physical contact with them while they are being fed
- ✲ Responding right away to their distress when they cry

When working with infants and toddlers, teachers must take special care to provide a predictable environment and consistent caregiving. Babies are totally dependent on adults to meet their needs; they are particularly vulnerable to difficulties because they have few skills for coping with discomfort and stress. It is crucial that they be cared for by warm, positive adults who are sensitive and respond affectionately to their needs as soon as they arise. In this way, the very young develop the trust in the world that will support their growth into the next stage.

Stage 2: Autonomy Versus Shame and Doubt (Two to Three Years).

The second stage corresponds to the second and third years of life. The child learns to manage and control impulses and to use both motor and mental skills. To help a child develop a healthy balance between autonomy and doubt, adults should consider how to handle their toddlers' toilet training and growing curiosity to explore. Restrictive or compulsive parents may give the child a feeling of shame and doubt, causing a sense of insecurity. Successful growth in this stage gives the child strength of will. "This stage, therefore, becomes decisive for the ratio of love and hate, cooperation and willfulness, freedom of self-expression and its suppression. From a sense of self-control without loss of self-esteem comes a lasting sense of good will and pride; from a sense of loss of self-control and of foreign overcontrol comes a lasting propensity for doubt and shame" (Erikson, 1963).

Encouraging a sense of autonomy while teaching limits without shaming is a delicate balance. Adults foster independence in toddlers by:

- ✲ giving children simple choices.
- ✲ not giving false choices.
- ✲ setting clear, consistent, reasonable limits.

✿ accepting children's swings between independence and dependence.

At the same time, adults are careful to keep a child safe, giving important boundaries to keep a toddler from hurting self or others. "You want to play with the bucket now, Patrick, but Sheila has it now," warns Teacher Marks. "When she is finished, you will have a turn. Do you want the scoop while you are waiting?"

Chapter 7 elaborates on how to help guide children using positive discipline.

Budding curiosity means high energy, so the daily schedule should include plenty of time for active movement and flexibility to deal with fluctuating energy and mood. Toileting is a learned behavior just as eating, dressing, painting, and singing are; a relaxed attitude about this area helps the child gain mastery without shame. Allowing for plenty of "two steps forward, one back" acknowledges the child's natural doubts and the balancing that happens in this stage.

Stage 3: Initiative Versus Guilt (Three to Five or Six Years).

The third stage of Eriksonian theory corresponds to the preschool and kindergarten years. The developmental task is to develop a sense of purpose. Out of autonomy comes initiative, and from healthy doubt can come a conscience (Figure 4–6). The child is ready to plan and carry out thoughts and ideas. The teacher can encourage the child's natural curiosity to plan and execute activities that are constructive and cooperative. An overly restrictive adult may raise a child who is easily discouraged and inhibited. On the other hand, offering no restraints gives a child no clear idea of what is socially acceptable and what is not. The key strength that grows out of this stage is purpose.

Teaching children of this age is both exhilarating and exasperating. Many find

FIGURE 4–6 An Eriksonian crisis in a young child's life. The child who has successfully mastered the first of Erikson's psychosocial conflicts will then be able to cope with future challenges. In this instance, the child who takes initiative (grabbing a toy) also can feel guilt (returning it).

this stage easier physically than the previous two but more challenging socially. It is a time when children move in two opposing directions: accomplishment or destruction. "You are so proud you can hit the ball, Emma," says Teacher Ayanna. "But telling Juana she can't do it hurt her feelings. Juana, how did it feel when Emma called you a dummy? You can tell her 'Emma, I don't like it when you call me names.'"

To support children's development of initiative with reasonable expectations, teachers can:

✿ encourage children to be as independent as possible.

✿ focus on gains as children practice new skills, not on the mistakes they make.

✿ set expectations that are in line with children's individual abilities.

✿ focus curriculum on real things and on doing (Mooney, 2000).

Remember, the child who takes initiative is ready to meet the world head-on and wants to do it "all by myself." This may include both putting on a jacket and hitting someone who has said something unkind. An environment that can respond to a child's interests, both in theme and at the moment, will be interesting and successful. At the same time, teachers must be prepared with a small set of logical limits (or "rules") and the means to follow through kindly and firmly when those limits are tested. Socializing at this age is the very point of the emotional states of initiative and guilt; children must have enough freedom to develop their own ways to deal with one another and still develop a sense of fairness and conscience.

Stage 4: Industry Versus Inferiority (Six to 12 Years).

Erikson's fourth stage begins with the primary school years and ends with puberty. The major theme in this stage is mastery of life, primarily by adapting to laws of society (people, laws and rules, relationships) and objects (tools, machines, the physical world). This is the child's most enthusiastic time for learning. This stage is the end of early childhood's period of expansive imagination. The danger in elementary school is the development of a sense of inferiority, of feeling incompetent or unproductive. It is also a time of great adventure. The child begins to think of being big and to identify with people whose work or whose personality he can understand and admire. This means finding a place in one's own school, be it in a classroom, on a soccer field, or at a club meeting. Children are ready to apply themselves to skills and tasks and to receive systematic instruction in the culture. They also need to handle the "tools of the tribe" (Erikson, 1963), which in the United States include pencils, reading and arithmetic books, and computers, as well as balls and bats. Problems arise if the child feels inadequate and inferior to such tasks. For instance, first-grade teacher Wayne looks for opportunities for each child to contribute to the group. Antonio struggles with English, so Wayne has asked him to teach the other children some words in Spanish, because he knows two languages. Now the children see him as someone with mastery, rather than inadequacies.

Overemphasizing mistakes could make children despair of ever learning, for instance, the multiplication tables or cursive handwriting. At the same time, adults must encourage children to work toward mastery. Adults should "mildly but firmly coerce children into the adventure of finding out that one can learn to accomplish things which one would never have thought possible by oneself" (Erikson, 1963). Adults must not let children restrict their own horizons by doing only what they already know. Particularly in social situations, it is essential for children to learn to do things with others, as difficult and unfair as this may sometimes be.

Applications to Teaching

First, Erikson has a clear message about the importance of play. Second, the theory helps shape guidelines for the role of adults in children's lives.

Play is a critical part of children's total development. Most schools for children under age six have periods of time allotted for play called "choice time" or "free play."

Video View Point 4-1

"Development: The interconnections of all processes of development become more evident as the school-age child gets older."

Competency: Cognitive Development

Age Group: School Age

Critical Thinking Questions:

1. How does a teacher of six- to 12-year-olds balance a child's attempts at "Industry" (competence) with the experiences of "Inferiority" (failure)?

2. How do you encourage the positive aspects of peer groups (friendships) while dealing with the difficulties (peer pressure, bullying/teasing)?

Erikson supports these ideas explicitly by stating that autonomy and initiative are developed mainly through social and fantasy play. He suggests that child's play is "the infantile form of the human ability to deal with experiences by creating model situations and to master reality by experiment and planning. . . . To 'play it out' in play is the most natural self-healing measure childhood affords" (Erikson, 1963).

The adult is primarily an emotional base and a social mediator for the child. Teachers become interpreters of feelings, actions, reasons, and solutions. We help children understand situations and motives so that they can solve their own problems. Teachers look at each child's emotional makeup and monitor their progress through developmental crises; each crisis is a turning point of increased vulnerability and also enhanced potential.

In Erikson's theory, the adult serves as a social mediator for the child.

Erikson tells us to encourage a very young child:

> . . . to experience over and over again that he is a person who is permitted to make choices. He has to have the right to choose, for example, whether to sit or whether to stand, whether to approach a visitor or to lean against his mother's knee . . . whether to use the toilet or to wet his pants. At the same time he must learn some of the boundaries of self-determination. He inevitably finds that there are some walls he cannot climb, that there are objects out of reach, that, above all, there are innumerable commands enforced by powerful adults (Erikson, 1963).

In preschool and kindergarten, a teacher allows children to take initiative and does not interfere with the results of those actions. At the same time, teachers and parents provide clear limits so that the children can learn what behaviors are unacceptable to society.

The issues of early childhood, from Erikson's theory, are every person's life issues. While the remnants of these stages stay with us all our lives, teachers who are aware of their own processes can fully appreciate the struggles of children.

BEHAVIORIST THEORY

Behaviorism is the most pragmatic and functional of the modern psychological ideologies. Behaviorist theories describe both development and learning. Developed during the 1920s and continually being modified today, behaviorism is the most distinctively American contribution to psychology. It begins with the notion that a child is essentially a clean slate on which events are written throughout life. The conditions of those events cause all important human behavior. Behaviorists often insist that only what can actually be observed will be accepted as fact. Only behavior can be treated, they say, not feelings or internal states. This contrasts with the psychodynamic approach, which insists that behavior is just an indirect clue to the "real" self, that of inner feelings and thoughts.

The Behaviorists

Ivan Pavlov, a Russian physiologist, was working in a laboratory, studying how animals digest food. He noticed that the dogs in his laboratory would anticipate their meals when they heard or saw their attendants making preparations. Instead of starting to salivate just when food was set in front of them, the dogs would salivate to a number of stimuli associated with food. He identified this simple form of learning as respondent conditioning. The association of involuntary reflexes with other environmental conditions became known as *classical conditioning,* a cornerstone of behaviorist theory.

John B. Watson was an American theorist who studied Pavlov's animal experiments. He then translated those ideas of conditioning into human terms. Watson made sweeping claims about the powers of this classical conditioning, declaring that he could shape a person's entire life by controlling exactly the events of an infant's first year. One of his ideas was to discourage emotional ties between parents and children because they interfered with the child's direct learning from the environment (though he later modified this). Nonetheless, he gave scientific validity to the idea that teachers should set conditions for learning and reward proper responses.

Edward L. Thorndike also studied the conditions of learning. Known as the "godfather of standardized testing," Thorndike helped develop scales to measure student achievement and standardized educational testing (see Chapter 6). He set forth the fa-mous **stimulus–response** technique. A stimulus will recall a response in a person; this forms learned habits. Therefore, it is wise to pay close attention to the consequences of behavior and to the various kinds of reinforcement.

B. F. Skinner took the idea of the "clean slate" one step further to create the doctrine of the "empty organism." That is, a person is like a vessel to be filled by carefully designed experiences. All behavior is under the control of one or more aspects of the environment. Furthermore, Skinner maintained that there is no behavior that cannot be modified. Some people argue that Skinnerian concepts tend to depersonalize the learning process and treat people as puppets. Others say that behaviorist psychology has made us develop new ways to help people learn and cope effectively with the world.

Albert Bandura has developed another type of learning theory, called social learning. As behaviorists began to accept that what people said about their feelings and internal states was valid, they looked at how children became socialized. **Socialization** is the process of learning to conform to social rules. Social-learning theorists watch how children learn these rules and use them in groups. They study the patterns of reinforcement and reward in socially appropriate and unacceptable behavior. According to Bandura, children acquire most of their social concepts from models they observe in the course of daily life. Attachment affects the process, since the most significant and influential people are those to whom the child is emotionally tied. From this arose a new concept known as **modeling.**

Theory of Behaviorism and Learning

Learning occurs when an organism interacts with the environment. Through experience, behavior is modified or changed. In the behaviorist's eyes, three types of learning occur: (1) classical conditioning; (2) operant conditioning; and (3) observational learning, or modeling. The first two are based on the idea that learning is mostly the development of habit. What people learn is a series of associations, forming a connection between a stimulus and response that did not exist before. The third is based on a more social approach. Figure 4–7 summarizes these three types of behaviorist learning processes.

Classical Conditioning

Classical conditioning can be explained by reviewing Pavlov's original experiments. A dog normally salivates at the sight of food but not when he hears a bell. When the sound of a bell is paired with the sight of food, the dog "learns" to salivate when he hears the bell, whether or not food is nearby. Thus, the dog has been conditioned to salivate (give the response) for both the food (unconditioned stimulus) and the bell (conditioned stimulus). Similarly, when the school bell rings in the afternoon, children begin to gather their papers into backpacks to go home. They have been conditioned to the sound of the bell. Classical conditioning can also account for the development of phobias. John Watson used a young boy in

a laboratory to test this theory. He showed the boy a white rat, then sounded a loud noise. After only seven pairings, the boy would cringe at the sight of the rat without the bell sounding at all. Only a few painful visits to a childhood dentist can teach a lifetime fear of dental health professionals.

Operant Conditioning

Operant conditioning is slightly different from classical conditioning in that it focuses on the response rather than the stimulus. In operant conditioning, the process that makes it more likely that a behavior will recur is called **reinforcement.** A stimulus that increases the likelihood of repeated behavior is called a reinforcer. Most people are likely to increase what gives them pleasure (be it food or attention) and decrease what gives them displeasure (such as punishment, pain, or the withdrawal of food or attention). The behaviorist tries to influence the organism by controlling these kinds of reinforcement.

A positive reinforcer is something that the learner views as desirable. These can be "social reinforcers," such as attention, praise, smiles, or hugs, or "nonsocial reinforcers," including tokens, toys, food, stickers, and the like. Teacher Meena wants Claire to begin to use a spoon instead of

	Classical Conditioning	Operant Conditioning	Social Learning
Kind of behavior	Reflexive	Voluntary	Voluntary
Type of learning	Learning through association	Learning through reinforcement	Learning through observation and imitation
Role of learner	Passive	Active or passive	Active

FIGURE 4–7 Behaviorist learning processes. Classical conditioning, operant conditioning, and social learning are three ways to develop learned behavior. Each describes how certain kinds of behavior will be learned and what role the learner will take in the process.

her hands to eat. Before conditioning, she talks to her when she eats. During the conditioning period, she gives Claire attention (a positive reinforcer) each time she picks up a spoon during feeding times and ignores her when she uses her hands. Claire begins to use a spoon, and less often her hands, in response to Meena's reinforcement. This is an example of a positive reinforcer, something that increases the likelihood of the desired response.

A negative reinforcer is removal of an unpleasant stimulus as a result of some particular behavior. For example, circle time is Jimmy's favorite activity at school, yet he has difficulty controlling his behavior and consistently disrupts the group. Before conditioning, he is told that if he talks to his neighbors and shouts responses at the teacher, he will be asked to leave the circle. During the conditioning period, Jimmy is praised whenever he pays attention, sings songs, and does not bother those around him (positive reinforcement). When he begins to shout, he is told to leave and return when he can sing without shouting (negative reinforcement). A negative reinforcer is used to stop children from behaving in a particular way by arranging for them to end a mildly adversive situation immediately (in this case, the boy has to leave the group) by improving their behavior. Jimmy, by controlling his own behavior, could end his isolation from the group.

Punishment is different than negative reinforcement. Punishment is an unpleasant event that makes the behavior less likely to be repeated. Look at the previous examples. If Clare's hands are slapped when she uses them to eat, or if Jimmy were spanked every time he shouted, then her eating with hands and his shouting would be the punished behaviors, and it is likely that she would stop using her hands and he would begin to shout less. Of course, punishment can backfire. Clare

may stop eating altogether, or Jimmy may shun group time entirely, and both may become fearful of or hostile toward their teachers. Whether or not an action is a negative reinforcer or punishment sometimes is, ultimately, in the eyes of the child. A "time-out" chair, for instance, could be viewed as either a punishment or a negative reinforcer. If used as exclusion from the group or a withdrawal of playing privileges, a child would find the time-out as a punishment. On the other hand, if a child could leave the time-out more quickly if she exhibited certain behaviors (instead of the "bad" behavior), it might be seen as a negative reinforcer.

Reinforcement, both positive and negative, is a powerful tool. It is important for adults to realize that it can be misused. An adult may not be gentle with a negative reinforcer when angry with a child's inappropriate behavior, and the child may end up feeling punished. Adults who neglect using positive words or actions (smiles, a high-five) are missing opportunities to shape and improve behavior.

Modeling

The third kind of conditioning is called observational learning, or modeling. This is learning and teaching by example. For instance, children who see their parents smoking will likely smoke themselves. According to Bandura, children acquire most of their social concepts from models they observe in the course of daily life. The models, whether adult, peer, or nonhuman, most likely to be imitated are individuals who are nurturant—warm, rewarding, and affectionate. Attachment also affects the process. The most significant and influential people are those to whom the child is emotionally tied.

Bandura's studies showed that exposure to filmed aggression heightens aggressive reactions in children. "Subjects who viewed the aggressive human and cartoon models on film exhibited nearly twice as much aggression than did subjects in the control group who were not exposed to the aggressive film content" (Bandura, 1986). This work suggests that pictorial mass media—television, video games, and computer activities—serve as important sources of social behavior. Any behavior can be learned by watching it, from language (listening to others talk) to fighting (watching violence on television). Bandura's theory has expanded into a more social-cognitive model of children thinking hard about what they see and feel. Thus personal and cognitive factors influence behavior, as does the environment, and in turn children's behavior can affect the environment around them. Adding the factors of observation and thinking to behaviorist theory links it to Piaget's cognitive theory (next in this chapter).

Applications to Teaching

Behaviorist theories make a strong case for how the environment influences our behavior. A teacher arranges the environment so that positive learning is enhanced by paying close attention to how to arrange furniture, materials, and the daily schedule. Further, how teachers interact with children is critical to shaping their behavior.

Adults are powerful reinforcers and models for children. A learning situation is comprised of many cues; it is up to adults to know what those cues are and how to control them. Teachers who use behavior modification techniques know both what children are to do and how they will be reinforced in their behavior. The ethics of using this kind of control concern everyone. Chapter 7 deals with behavior management and has examples of appropriate behavior modification techniques.

What children learn is shaped by the circumstances surrounding the learning. Experiences that are enjoyable are reinforcing. From the peek-a-boo game with an infant to a seven-year-old's first ride on a skateboard, an experience is more likely to be repeated and learned if it is pleasant. Social learning is particularly powerful in the lives of young children. Any behavior is learnable and can become part of children's behavioral repertoire.

❋ COGNITIVE THEORY

Adult: What does it mean to be alive?
Child: It means you can move about, play—that you can do all kinds of things.
Adult: Is a mountain alive?
Child: Yes, because it has grown by itself.
Adult: Is a cloud alive?
Child: Yes, because it sends water.
Adult: Is wind alive?
Child: Yes, because it pushes things.

How do children learn to think, and what do they think about? Cognitive theory describes the structure and development of human thought processes and how those processes affect the way a person understands and perceives the world. Piaget's theory of cognition forms a cornerstone of early childhood educational concepts about children; others have developed this theory further into a constructivist theory of learning.

Jean Jacques Piaget

Jean Jacques Piaget was one of the most exciting research theorists in child development. A major force in child psychology, he studied both thought processes and how they change with age. He had great influence on child psychology, theories of learning, intellectual development, and even philosophy. He became the foremost expert on the development of knowledge from birth to adulthood.

Born at the turn of the 20th century, Piaget built on his childhood curiosity in science and philosophy by working with Dr. Theodore Simon at the Binet Laboratory in Paris (Simon and Alfred Binet devised the first intelligence test). While recording children's abilities to answer questions correctly, he became fascinated with their incorrect responses. He noticed that children tended to give similar kinds of wrong answers at certain ages.

Piaget then began studying children's thought processes. With his wife, one of his former students, he observed his own children. This launched Piaget into a lifelong study of intelligence. He believed that children think in fundamentally different ways from adults. He noticed how actively children engage in their own development. He also developed a new method for studying thought processes. Rather than using a standardized test, he adapted a method of question and response. Called *le methode clinique,* it is a technique in which the adult asks questions, then adapts teaching and further inquiries based on children's answers. This method of observation and assessment, which focuses on children's natural ways of thinking, is discussed in Chapter 6.

Prolific his entire life, Piaget gave us a complex theory of intelligence and child development. He recorded, in a systematic way, how children learn, when they learn, and what they learn.

Theory of Cognitive Development

While others thought that the development of thinking was either intrinsic (nature) or extrinsic (nurture), Piaget thought that neither position offered a full explanation for these amazing and complex behaviors. His theory relies on both maturational and environmental factors. It is called *maturational* because it sets out a sequence of cognitive (thinking) stages governed by heredity. Heredity affects our learning by (1) how the body and brain are structured biologically and (2) what automatic, or instinctive, behavior we present, such as an infant's sucking at birth. Piaget's theory

is *environmental* because the experiences children have will directly influence how they develop. Thinking and learning compose a process of interaction between a person and the environment. Piaget also believed that all species inherit a basic tendency to organize their lives and adapt to the world around them. Because children are developing and constantly revising their own knowledge, the theory is also called constructivist. Piaget believed that children learn best when they are actually doing the work (or play) themselves, rather than being told or shown. Having studied Montessori methods, Piaget concluded that teachers could prepare a stimulating environment and also interact with the children to enhance their thinking.

Piaget theorized that humans develop **schemas,** or mental concepts, as a general way of thinking about, or interacting with, ideas and objects in the environment. Very young children learn perceptual schemas as they taste and feel; preschool children use language and pretend play to create their understanding; older children develop more abstract schemas, such as morality schemas that help them determine how to act. Throughout, we use three basic processes to think: These are known as the adaptive processes of **assimilation** and **accommodation** and the balancing process of **equilibration.** Figure 4–8 demonstrates how these work.

The Stages

Piaget claimed that thinking develops in a certain general pattern in all human beings. These stages of thinking are the psychological structures that go along with adapting to the environment. Piaget identified four major stages of cognitive development:

Sensorimotor stage   Zero to two years
Preoperational stage   Two to six or seven years

Piaget's Adaptive Process

Assimilation: Taking new information and organizing it in such a way that it fits with what the person already knows.

Example: Juanita sees an airplane while walking outside with her father. She knows that birds fly. So, never having seen this flying thing before, she calls it a "bird (pájaro)." This is what we call *assimilation.* She is taking in this new information and making it into what she already knows. Children assimilate what they are taught into their own worlds when they play. This happens when children play "taking turns," or "school" and "house" with their dolls and toy figures. Another way to see assimilation at work is during carpentry, as children hammer and nail triangles and squares after being shown shape books and puzzles by their teacher.

Accommodation: Taking new information and changing what is already thought to fit the new information.

Example: Aaron is at the grocery store with his mother and newborn baby. He calls the woman in the line ahead of them "pregnant" although she is simply overweight. After being corrected, he asks the next person he sees, "Are you pregnant or just fat?" This is what we call *accommodation.* Having learned that not all people with large bellies are pregnant, he changes his knowledge base to include this new information. Children accommodate to the world as they are taught to use a spoon, the toilet, a computer.

Equilibration: A mental process to achieve a mental balance, whereby a person takes new information and continually attempts to make sense of the experiences and perceptions.

Example: Colby, age seven, gets two glasses from the cupboard for his friend Ajit and himself. After putting apple juice into his short, wide glass he decides he'd rather have milk, so he pours it into Ajit's tall, thin glass. "Look, now I have more than you!" says his friend. This puzzles Colby, who is distressed (in "disequilibrium"): How could it be more when he just poured it out of his glass? He thinks about the inconsistency (and pours the juice several times back and forth) and begins to get the notion that pouring liquid into different containers does not change its amount (the conservation of liquids). "No, it isn't," he says, "it's just a different shape!" Thus, Colby learns to make sense of it in a new way and achieve equilibrium in his thinking. Children do this whenever they get new information that asks them to change the actual schemas, making new ones to fit new experiences.

FIGURE 4–8 In Piagetian theory, the processes of assimilation, accommodation, and equilibration are basic to how all people organize their thoughts and, therefore, to all cognitive development.

Concrete operational   Six to 12 years
stage
Formal operational   12 years to adult-
stage   hood

Each person of normal intelligence will go through these stages in this order, although the rate will change depending on the individual and his or her experiences. Each stage of development has critical lessons for the child to learn to think and make sense of the world. Figure 4–9 illustrates key experiences at each stage of cognitive development in the early years.[1]

A Critique

Piaget's theories revolutionized ideas about children's thinking and challenged psychologists and educators to focus less on what children know than the ways they come to know. But was Piaget right? Researchers have been exploring and debating the ideas of cognitive theory for many years. Their first concern has to do with when the various skills of cognitive development occur. The most obvious criticism of Jean Piaget's cognitive-developmental theory is that he seems to have been wrong about just how early many cognitive skills develop. For example, virtually all the achievements of the concrete operational period are present in at least rudimentary or fragmentary form in the preschool years. This might simply mean that Piaget just had the ages wrong—that the concrete operations stage really begins at age three or four. The fact that younger children demonstrate some types of apparently complex logic if the problems are made simple calls this whole assumption into doubt (Bee, 2000).

Researchers' second concern is about the notion of distinct stages. If children are applying the same broad forms of logic to all their experiences, then the amount of specific experience a child has had with some set of material should not make a lot of difference. A great deal of research now shows that specific knowledge makes a huge difference. Children and adults who know a lot about some subject or some set of materials (dinosaurs, baseball cards, mathematics) not only categorize information in that topic area in more complex and hierarchical ways; they are also better at remembering new information on that topic and at applying more advanced forms of logic to material in that area.

Developmental psychologists now believe that Piaget's theory of distinct stages is not correct, but the idea of a sequence in thinking is. Current research on the brain supports Piagetian theory in that brain maturation seems to follow a sequence that parallels the various thinking stages of development. What we do know is that children progress from one stage to the next, changing their thinking depending on their level of maturation and experience with the environment. Certain physical skills, such as fine motor coordination, determine how much a child is capable of doing. Certain environmental factors, such as the kinds of experiences the world and adults provide, influence the rate of growth. Yet throughout the process, children take in new knowledge and decide how it fits with what they already know. As new information comes in, the child learns and grows.

[1]Piaget's stages have been validated in cross-cultural studies (Dasen, 1977; Mali & Howe, 1980; Voyat, 1983).

As a baby
Sensorimotor Period

Key concept
Object permanence

Definition
—the understanding that objects continue to exist even when they are out of sight.
—essential to understanding the physical world.

Explanation
—birth to four months, infants respond to objects, but stop tracking them if they are covered.
—four to eight months, infants will reach for an object if it is partially covered.
—by eight to twelve months, infants will search for hidden objects randomly, anywhere.
—by 12 to 18 months, toddlers will search for an object where they last saw it.
—by 18 to 24 months, toddlers will search for hidden objects in systematic way.

As a preschooler
Preoperational

Key concept
Symbolic play and language

Definition
—the use of ideas, images, sounds, or symbols to stand for objects and events = symbolic play.
—the use of an abstract, rule-governed system of symbols that can be combined to communicate information = language.
—essential to developing the capacity to think.

Explanation
—from 14 to 19 months, representational ability emerges.
—by 24 months, most can use substitute objects in pretend play.
—nine to twelve months, infants begin to use conventional social gestures.
—around one year, first words emerge.
—18 to 24 months, first sentences appear.

As a primary child
Concrete Operational

Key concept
Reasoning

Definition
—actions can be carried out mentally.
—logical reasoning replaces intuitive thinking in concrete situations.
—classification skills develop.
—essential to ability to think logically.

Explanation
—can coordinate several characteristics rather than a single property.
—reversibility emerges; can see the same problem from several perspectives.
—can divide things into sets and reason about their relationships.
—conservation skills emerge; an amount of liquid remains the same, no matter the container.

FIGURE 4–9 In cognitive theory, children's thinking develops in stages, with critical learning occurring at each stage (see Chapter 11).

Applications to Teaching

Piaget's writings do not apply directly to classroom methods or subject matter per se, and therefore careful interpretation is required. In fact, he never claimed to be an educator. However, Piaget's theories provide a framework, or philosophy, about children's thinking.

Children learn by taking new ideas and integrating them into their existing knowledge base. This is exactly in line with Piaget's processes of assimilation and accommodation. It is indicative of the theory of **constructivism,** "which states that individuals learn through adaptation. What they learn or adapt to is directly influenced by the people, materials and situations with which they come into contact" (Meade-Roberts & Spitz, 1998).

Children need many objects to explore so that they can later incorporate these into their symbolic thinking. Such materials need to be balanced among open-ended ones (such as sand and water activities, basic art and construction materials), guided ones (cooking with recipes, conducting experiments, classification and seriated materials), and self-correcting ones (puzzles and matching games, such as some of the Montessori materials). It is important to remember that young children need to be involved with concrete objects and to explore and use them in their own ways, which include both sensorimotor and beginning symbolic play.

Children need lots of time to explore their own reality, especially through the use of play. A Piagetian classroom would have large periods of time for children to "act out" their own ideas. Also, time should be scheduled for imitation of adult-given ideas (songs, fingerplays, and stories). At Reggio Emilia (see Chapter 2), preschool children create their own material representations of what they understand by using many types of media (drawing, sculpture, stories, puppets, paper). In constructivist kindergarten and school-age classrooms, learning literacy and mathematics is considered a developmental process that the teacher facilitates by providing modeling, authentic experiences, mini-lessons on specific topics, and frequent opportunities for students to consult with and learn from each other. Classrooms work on creating community through rule creating; children have choices and make decisions on significant parts of their learning. There may be more "arguments" about how children are to play and build, with children leading discussions and many participating in solutions. All this takes time and a flexible schedule. "Oh no!" says Michael in the block corner. "That part always falls off." Teacher Karen calls over Joachim, "Can you show Michael how you get it to stay up?" Joachim: "See, you have to put the big block on the side and let it slide down a little ways. Then it sticks."

The teacher's role is to build an environment that is stimulating and conducive to the process of constructing meaning and knowledge. The teacher becomes a facilitator and may do less talking while the learners do more, and provide more guidance and written observations rather than enforce rules and give standardized tests. Although there may still be some direct instruction and demonstration, a constructivist program has fundamental differences about teaching and learning, about how children learn best, who and how they should be taught, and who has the answers.

For instance, children under age five do not understand mental representations very well, so they will have trouble recognizing that another person sees things differently than they do. This **egocentric** viewpoint is both natural and normal but must be factored into the teacher's work. While a seven-year-old may understand the question "How would you feel if someone did that to you?" a preschooler may find the question incomprehensible. For the same reason, the younger child may have trouble distinguishing how things seem or appear from how they really are. "For them, if something seems dangerous (the menacing-looking shadow in their unlit bedroom), it is dangerous, and if it seems nondangerous (the friendly acting stranger) it is nondangerous. We often think of young children as naive, credulous, gullible, trusting, and the like. Their inadequate understanding that things may not be as they appear might be partly responsible for this impression" (Flavell, Green, & Flavell, 1989).

To encourage thinking and learning, teachers should refrain from telling children exactly how to solve a problem. Rather, the teacher should ask questions that encourage children to observe and pay attention to their own ideas. Teachers should:

- use or create situations that are personally meaningful to children.
- provide opportunities for them to make decisions.
- provide opportunities for them to exchange viewpoints with their peers.

Learning is an active process, based on the belief that knowledge is constructed by the learner rather than transferred from the teacher to the child. "Constructivist classrooms may do a better job promoting children's social, cognitive, and moral development than do more teacher-centered programs" (DeVries & Kohlberg, 1990).

Perhaps more important is the awareness on the part of all adults that all children have the capability to reason and be thinkers if they are given appropriate materials for their stage of development. Teachers must remember that young children:

1. think differently from adults.
2. need many materials to explore and describe.
3. think in a concrete manner and often cannot think out things in their heads.
4. come to conclusions and decisions based on what they see, rather than on what is sensible and adult logical.
5. need challenging questions and the time to make their own decisions and find their own answers.

The thoughts and ideas of Piaget are impressive, both in quantity and in quality. His collective works are extremely complex, often difficult to understand. Yet they have given us a valuable blueprint. Clearly, Piaget has provided unique and important insights into the development of intelligence and children.

It is Piaget's genius for empathy with children, together with true intellectual genius, that has made him the outstanding child psychologist in the world today and one destined to stand beside Freud with respect to his contributions to psychology, education, and related disciplines. Just as Freud's discoveries of unconscious motivation, infantile sexuality, and the stages of psychosexual growth changed our ways of thinking about human personality, so Piaget's discoveries of children's implicit philosophies, the construction of reality by the infant, and the stages of mental development have altered our ways of thinking about human intelligence (Elkind, 1977).

SOCIOCULTURAL THEORY

Since the end of the 20th century, many American early educators have turned their attention to another theorist. Because of the interest in the programs at Reggio Emilia, Italy, we now look closer at the works of Vygotsky. His sociocultural theory focuses on the child as a whole and incorporates ideas of culture and values into child development, particularly the areas of language and self-identity.

Lev Vygotsky

Born in 1896 in Byelorussia, Lev Vygotsky was educated in Moscow and worked there at the Institute of Psychology, where he focused on the problems of educational practice, particularly those pertaining to handicapped children. He studied the works of Freud, Piaget, and Montessori. Unfortunately, his career was cut short by tuberculosis; he died in 1934 at age 38. His theory is rooted in experimental psychology and in the work of the American philosopher William James and of his own contemporaries Pavlov and Watson (see the Behavior Theory section of this chapter).

The Theory of Sociocultural Development

Vygotsky's work is called sociocultural because it focuses on how values, beliefs, skills, and traditions are transmitted to the next generation. Like Erikson, Vygotsky believed in the interpersonal connection between the child and other important people. Like Piaget, he asserted that much of children's learning takes place during play. Like Maslow (see later in this chapter), he considered the child as a whole, taking a humanistic, more qualitative approach to studying children. And though he understood the primary behaviorists of his day, he differed from them in that he emphasized family, social interaction, and play as primary influences in children's lives, rather than the stimulus–response and schedules of reinforcement that were becoming so popular in his day.

Vygotsky believed that the child is embedded in the family and culture of his community and that much of a child's development is culturally specific. Rather than moving through certain stages or sequences (as Piaget proposed), children's mastery and interaction differ from culture

to culture.[1] Adults teach children socially valued skills from a very early age; children's learning is considerably influenced by their family's priorities and values.

Sociocultural theory dictates that learning is active and constructed, as does cognitive theory. Vygotsky differs from Piaget, however, in the nature and importance of interaction. Piaget insisted that while children needed to interact with people and objects to learn, the stages of thinking were still bound by maturation. Vygotsky claimed that interaction and direct teaching were critical aspects of a child's cognitive development and that a child's level of thinking could be advanced by just such interaction.

Vygotsky believed that language, even in its earliest forms, was socially based. Rather than egocentric or immature, children's speech and language development during the years of three to seven is seen as tied to what children are thinking. During these transition years, children talk aloud to themselves; after a while, this "self-talk" becomes internalized so that the child can act without saying anything out loud. Vygotsky contended that children speak to themselves for self-guidance and self-direction and that this private speech helps children think about their behavior and plan for action. With age, private (inner) speech (once called "egocentric speech"), which goes from out loud to whispers to lip movement, is critical to a child's self-regulation.

In Vygotsky's view, children's development is more than just a response to personal experience. Rather, children are influenced in fundamental ways by their family, community, and socioeconomic status. Vygotsky also emphasized the deeply

[1]Vygotsky promotes what later became the DAP principle that development and learning occur in and are influenced by multiple social and cultural contexts.

In Vygotsky's sociocultural theory, the child's development is inseparable from social and cultural activities.

meaningful role of culture in learning. This theoretical framework and the ecological theory (see the next section) have shifted mainstream thinking to encompass more than a child's individual experiences.

Because language and development build on each other, the best way to develop competency is through interaction with others in a special way. Children learn through guided participation with others, especially in a kind of apprenticeship, whereby a tutor supports the novice not only by instruction but also by doing. Social interactions between a teacher and a learner not only impart skills but also give the learner the context and the cultural values of that skill, and teach relationship building and language at the same time. Engaging together matters. Yesenia seems hesitant to enter dramatic play, as Pia and Katie are busy feeding babies. Teacher David asks if she'll help him deliver a package. "Special delivery!" he calls out, as Yesenia holds a box with baby blankets in it. The two children readily allow her into the play.

When mentors sense that the learner is ready for a new challenge—or simply want the learner to come along—they draw the novice into a **zone of proximal development** (ZPD), the range of learning that is beyond what novices could learn alone but within their grasp with help. Sergio can ride a tricycle by himself and has hopped onto his sister's two-wheeler. Surely he will fall. But if his uncle runs alongside and helps him get balanced, he can do more. Of course, it will take many attempts, but with assistance, Sergio can increase his ZPD and eventually ride on his own.

Sharing experiences and developing a cooperative dialogue with the child is what is needed in a child's ZPD. Initially, it is the family that plays this role. For instance, a young girl is carried even as a toddler to the open-air market with her mother. There she watches and is guided toward learning how to touch cloth, smell herbs, taste food, and weigh and compare amounts. Is it any wonder that she learns advanced math skills and the language of bargaining early on?

Applications to Teaching

Sociocultural theory has four implications for the classroom teacher. First, teachers work to understand and incorporate a child's family and culture into their teach-

ing.[1] This lends credence to the notion of multicultural education, as noted throughout this text in the "Our Diverse World" ideas, and Appendix C regarding cultural and linguistic diversity. This is also a growing specialty in psychology. Teachers and researchers have observed that children of color in this society are socialized to operate in "two worlds," and thus must achieve a kind of **bicognitive development,** along with bicultural and bilingual skills. Such work led the way for the popular "learning styles" movement of the 1970s and 1980s. Research done with different cultural groups has reinforced the importance of looking at culture as part of the context in which the child lives and learns.

Second, teachers must develop comfortable and cooperative relationships with their children. The teacher and learner adjust to one another; teachers use what they know about children to guide their teaching and plan their curriculum. Sociocultural theory supports both the "emergent curriculum" and the idea of spontaneous, teachable moments such as are advocated by proponents of an anti-bias curriculum (see Chapter 10). Further, this theory supports the power of the individual teacher–child relationship, a cornerstone of this text (see Chapter 5) and of DAP (see Chapter 2). Children need adults to help create curriculum and set an environmental stage for learning. Teachers mediate social relationships and conflicts; they ask questions and analyze the answers to know where a child is headed. Adults help children learn by seeing the challenge, giving assistance when needed, and noticing when the task is mastered and the child is ready for a new challenge.

[1]Racial/ethnic identity development is a growing field; works by B. D. Tatum (1995) and Stacey York (2003) are of interest here.

Third, teachers pay close attention to the psychological "tools" used to learn.[1] These include those of the culture. For example, U.S. children are taught to tie a string around their finger as a memory device, whereas in Russia they tie a knot in their handkerchief. They also include the universal tools of drawing, of language, and of mathematics.

Teachers realize that there is much value in play. It is in play that the child can practice operating the symbols and tools of the culture. Vygotsky (1978) puts it this way:

> Action in the imaginative sphere, in an imaginary situation, the creation of voluntary intentions, the formation of real-life plans and volitional motives—all appear in play and make it the highest level of preschool development. The child moves forward essentially through play activity. Only in this sense can play be considered a leading activity that determines the child's development. For instance, children might build a structure with blocks; the teacher encourages them to draw the building and then map the entire block corner as a village or neighborhood. The adult serves an important role as an intellectual mediator, enlarging the child's ZPD, continually shifting to another set of symbols to give children a different way of looking at the same thing.

Finally, in a Vygotskian classroom there will be activity and an awareness of individual differences. Teacher Valeria plans her kindergarten class with time for older, third-grade "buddies" to read and invites siblings younger and older to join the class at pickup time by asking for songs they know.

Other children—older ones who have more expertise or peers who may have superior skills or simply offer help—can be part of a child's learning. When small groups of peers at varying levels of competence work toward a common goal, more advanced thinking occurs. Other people create a kind of scaffolding, or helpful structure, to support the child's learning. Just as a physical scaffold surrounds a building so that it might be worked on, so the child gets hints, advice, and structure to master a skill or activity. Adults can arouse interest in a task, simplify it—scaffold it—so that it is within the child's ability and teach enthusiasm by helping the task get accomplished.

ECOLOGICAL THEORY

As with sociocultural theory, ecological theory is based on the premise that development is greatly influenced by forces outside the child. Urie Bronfenbrenner applied a general systems theory to human development in the 1970s, as the ecology movement began in America and Europe. Development, in his view, is "a joint function of person and environment (Bronfenbrenner, 2000), and human ecosystems include both physical factors (climate, space, home, and school) and the social environment (family, culture, and the larger society).

[1]Work by Janice Hale (1986) has identified and applied sociocultural theory to the development of the African–American child. Ramirez and Casteneda (1974) have identified particular cognitive and language patterns among young children in selected Hispanic populations. In both cases, these patterns are linked to family and cultural styles of relating and problem solving.

Urie Bronfenbrenner

Urie Bronfenbrenner, a professor at Cornell University, has been pursuing the study of psychology and developmental science since the late 1930s. He played an active role in the design of children's programs in both the public and private sectors, including being one of the founders of Head Start.

Theory of Ecological Development

Bronfenbrenner's model describes four systems that influence human development, nested within each other like a circle of rings. With the child at the center, these four are (1) the settings in which a child spends a significant period of time, (2) the relationships of those settings, (3) the soci-

etal structures, and (4) the larger contexts in which these systems operate. Figure 4–10 illustrates these systems. The influences among and within these systems are critical to acknowledge: Just as in nature, activity in one part will affect all the other parts. A sudden income drop will affect the family in many ways: The parents may be preoccupied and unavailable to the child, who may then need more attention from the caregivers at school, who in turn may ask for more resources from the community for the family.

Applications to Teaching

As seen in Figure 4–10, the values of the community (the *exosystem*) can influence social conditions (the *macrosystem*) and in turn be influenced by the individual family or program (the *microsystem*).

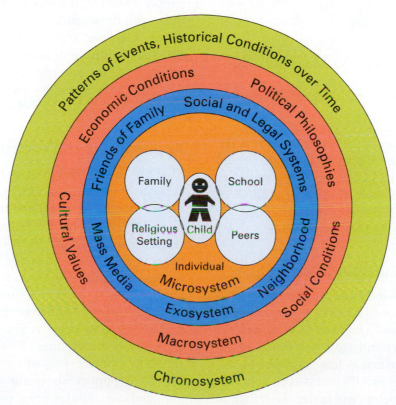

FIGURE 4–10 Ecological theory shows how the many influences in a child's life can affect development.

For example, a neighborhood becomes full of families with young children. The community values shift to incorporate more issues for these families as parents get involved with creating a neighborhood playground. The community starts a parent participation nursery school in a local church, and a retired teacher opens a family child care home in the neighborhood for infants and toddlers. The city council lobbies the state legislature to adopt more "family-friendly" political policies and offers some pre-tax dependent care benefits to its employees.

Teachers can use this theory to build an understanding of the systems that impact the families of the children they serve. The many systems in the child's physical and social world have a profound effect, both directly and indirectly, on the development of the child. This theory underscores the need to have a working partnership between early childhood programs and the families they serve.

MULTIPLE INTELLIGENCES THEORY

Howard Gardner

Howard Gardner, a professor of human development at the Harvard Graduate School of Education, has been very influential in the ongoing debate about the nature of intelligence. His work is influenced by those of Piaget and Jerome Bruner.

Theory of Multiple Intelligences

The theory of multiple intelligences (MI) asserts that there is strong evidence, both from brain-based research (see discussion in this chapter) and from the study of genius, that there are at least eight basic different intelligences (Figure 4–11). "Human cognitive competence is better described in terms of sets of abilities, talents, or mental skills, which we call 'intelligences.' All nor-

mal individuals possess each of these skills to some extent; individuals differ in the degree of skill and the nature of their combination." Intelligence, then, is redefined to mean the ability to solve a problem or to create a product that is in a culture. This is a key point that needs an explanation.

Solving a problem includes the ability to do so in a particular cultural setting or community. The skills needed depend very much on the context in which the child lives. For example, we all know now that certain parts of the brain are designated for perception, bodily movement, language, or spatial processing. Everyone who has a functional brain will be able to demonstrate some skill in these areas. But the child who has special "musical intelligence," for instance, will hear a concert and insist on a violin (as did Yehudi Menuhin). Or a culture that depends on running for its daily living (as do some people of Kenya) is more likely to have children well developed in that area of intelligence. Gardner writes of Anne Sullivan, teacher of blind and deaf Helen Keller, as an example of interpersonal intelligence, for she could understand what Helen needed in a way no one else could.

Applications to Teaching

The MI theory has had a big impact on schools, transforming curricula and teaching methods from preschool to high school. Even the producers of *Sesame Street* have taken to applying the theory to developing programs. Teachers in early childhood use the theory daily as they individualize their environments, curricula, and approaches. The child whose facility with puzzles excels that of his classmates is given a chance to try more complex ones. The children who thrive in dramatic play are offered a time to put on a puppet show for the class. The child whose mind works especially musically, logically, or interpersonally is encouraged to develop those special gifts. Teacher

Area	How Are You Smart? Definition
Musical Intelligence	is the capacity to think in music, to be able to hear patterns, recognize, and then remember them. Certain parts of the brain help in the perception and production of music. Gardner cites as evidence of this as an intelligence the importance of music in cultures worldwide, as well as its role in Stone Age societies.
Bodily-Kinesthetic Intelligence	is the capacity to use parts or all of your body to solve a problem or make something. As bodily movements became specialized over time, it was an obvious advantage to the species. We can see this in a person's ability in sport (to play a game), in dance (to express a feeling, music or rhythm), in acting, or in making a product.
Logical-Mathematical Intelligence 1 - 2 - 3 - 4 - 5	is the capacity to think in a logical, often linear, pattern and to understand principles of a system. Scientists and mathematicians often think this way. Gardner asserts that there are two essential facts of the logical-mathematical intelligence. First, in the gifted individual, the process of problem-solving is often remarkably rapid, and the second is the often nonverbal nature of the intelligence (the familiar *"Aha!"* phenomenon).
Linguistic Intelligence a - b - c - d	is the capacity to use language to express your thoughts, ideas, feelings, and the ability to understand other people and their words. The gift of language is universal, as evidenced by poets and writers as well as speakers and lawyers. The spoken language is constant across cultures, and the development of graphic language is one of the hallmarks of human activity.
Spatial Intelligence 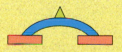	is the capacity to represent the world internally in spatial terms. Spatial problem-solving is required for navigation, in the use of maps, and relying on drawings to build something. Playing games such as chess and all the visual arts—painting, sculpting, drawing—use spatial intelligence, and sciences such as anatomy, architecture, and engineering emphasize this intelligence.
Interpersonal Intelligence	is the capacity to understand other people. Master players in a nursery school notice how others are playing before entering; some children seem to be born leaders; teachers, therapists, religious or political leaders, and many parents seem to have the capacity to notice distinctions among others. This intelligence can focus on contrasts in moods, temperaments, motivations, and intentions.

FIGURE 4–11 In his book *Multiple Intelligences* (1993) and subsequent work, Howard Gardner describes a new way of looking at intelligence that has serious implications for teaching. *Continued*

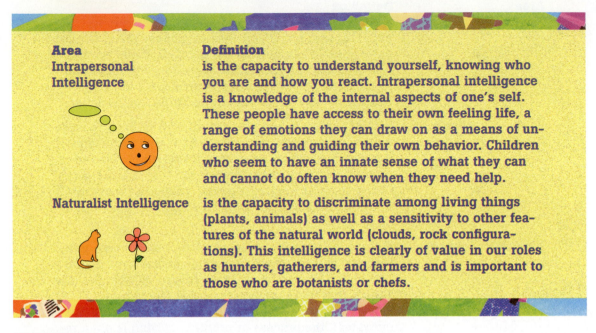

Area	Definition
Intrapersonal Intelligence	is the capacity to understand yourself, knowing who you are and how you react. Intrapersonal intelligence is a knowledge of the internal aspects of one's self. These people have access to their own feeling life, a range of emotions they can draw on as a means of understanding and guiding their own behavior. Children who seem to have an innate sense of what they can and cannot do often know when they need help.
Naturalist Intelligence	is the capacity to discriminate among living things (plants, animals) as well as a sensitivity to other features of the natural world (clouds, rock configurations). This intelligence is clearly of value in our roles as hunters, gatherers, and farmers and is important to those who are botanists or chefs.

FIGURE 4–11, continued

Leena built a Counting Center in her prekindergarten class. There were materials to draw items for counting; Leena worked with children to jump as they counted by twos; music played to encourage counting in rhythm. Chapter 10 will give examples of curriculum development using this theory.

MATURATION THEORY

Arnold Gesell

As noted in Chapter 1, Arnold Gesell was a physician intrigued with the notion that children's internal clocks seemed to govern their growth and behavior. In the 1940s and 1950s, Gesell (1940) established norms for several areas of growth and the behaviors that accompany such development. The Gesell Institute continues to provide guidelines for how children mature from birth to puberty. The Word Pictures in Chapter 3 are an excellent example of the information that maturational theory and research have provided.

Theory of Maturation

Maturation is the process of physical and mental growth that is determined by heredity. The maturation sequence occurs in relatively stable and orderly ways. Maturation theory holds that much growth is genetically determined from conception. This theory differs from behaviorism, which asserts that growth is determined by environmental conditions and experiences, and cognitive theory, which states that growth and behavior are a reflection of both maturation and learning.

Maturation and growth are interrelated and occur together. Maturation describes the quality of growth; that is, while a child grows in inches and pounds, the nature (or quality) of that growth changes. Maturation is qualitative, describing the way a baby moves into walking, rather than simply the age at which the baby took the first step. Growth is what happens; maturation is how it happens.

Studies have established that the maturation sequence is the same for all children, regardless of culture, country of origin, or learning environment. But there are two vital points to remember:

- ❋ Although maturation determines the sequence of development, the precise age is approximate. The sequence of developmental stages may be universal, but the rate at which a child moves through the stages varies tremendously.

- ❋ Growth is uneven. Children grow in spurts. Motor development may be slow in some stages, fast in others. For instance, a baby may gain an ounce a day for two months, then only half a pound in an entire month. Usually there is a growth spurt at puberty, with some children at 13 nearly their adult height, others not yet five feet tall. Unpredictability brings individual variation.

Applications to Teaching

Maturation theory is most useful in describing children's growth and typical behavior. Look at the Word Pictures in Chapter 3. Such charts will help adults understand behavior better and will keep them from expecting too much or too little. Remember that there is great individual variation and uneven growth. Be cautious in overgeneralizing from these normative charts. Gesell's initial data were focused on a narrow portion of the population and were derived from American children only. Further work in the last two decades has adjusted the ranges with succeeding generations of children and an ever-larger and more diverse population. Maturation theory has inspired excellent developmental norms that help parents, teachers, and

physicians alike determine whether a child's growth is within the normal range.

HUMANISTIC THEORY

As the field of psychology began to develop, various schools of thought arose. By the middle of this century, two "camps" dominated American psychological circles. The first, the psychodynamic, included the Freudians and is best known to us through the works of Erik Erikson. The second, behaviorism, began with Watson and Thorndike and was later expanded by Skinner and Bandura. In 1954, Abraham Maslow published a book that articulated another set of ideas. He called it the Third Force (or humanistic psychology), which focused on what motivated people to be well, successful, and mentally healthy.

This humanistic theory has a place in early childhood education because it attempts to explain how people are motivated. Specifically, humanistic theory is centered on people's needs, goals, and successes. This was a change from the study of mental illness, as in psychotherapy, or the study of animal behavior, in the case of much behaviorist research.

The Humanists

The most influential humanist was Dr. Maslow, who studied exceptionally mature and successful people. Others, such as Carl Rogers, Fritz Perls, Alan Watts, and Erich Fromm added to what was known about healthy personalities. The humanists developed a comprehensive theory of human behavior based on mental health.[1]

[1]Maslow's theory of human needs is clearly a "Western" philosophy, although it is often presented as a universal set of ideas. In fact, other cultures would see life differently. An African worldview might see the good of the community as the essential goal of being fully human. Cultures with more of a "collective" orientation, rather than an emphasis on the individual or self, would see the family or group as the ultimate goal of humanity.

Theory of Human Needs

Maslow's theory of **self-actualization** is a set of ideas about what people need to become and stay healthy. He asserts that every human being is motivated by a number of basic needs, regardless of age, gender, race, culture, or geographic location. According to Maslow (1962), a basic need is something:

- ✪ whose absence breeds illness.

- ✪ whose presence prevents illness.

- ✪ whose restoration cures illness.

- ✪ that is preferred by the deprived person over other satisfactions, under certain conditions (such as very complex, free-choice instances).

- ✪ that is found to be inactive, at a low ebb, or functionally absent in the healthy person.

These needs, not to be denied, form a theory of human motivation. The basic needs are sometimes called *deficiency needs* because they are critical for a person's survival, and a deficiency can cause a person to die. Until those are met, no significant growth can take place. *Growth needs* can emerge when the basic needs have been met. *Higher needs* are dependent on those two primary ones. Higher needs are what we strive for to become more satisfied and healthy people.

This theory is described as a hierarchy, or pyramid, because there is a certain way these needs are interrelated, and because the most critical needs form the foundation from which the other needs can be met (Figure 4–12).

Applications to Teaching

How well a teacher knows that a hungry child will ignore a lesson, or simply be unable to concentrate. A tired child often pushes aside learning materials and experiences until rested. The child who is deprived of basic physiologic needs may be able to think of those needs only; in fact, "such a man can fairly be said to live by bread alone" (Maslow, 1962). The humanists would strongly advocate a school breakfast or lunch program and would support regular rest and nap times in programs with long hours.

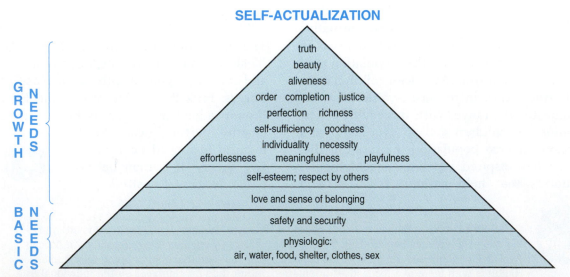

SELF-ACTUALIZATION

GROWTH NEEDS

truth
beauty
aliveness
order   completion   justice
perfection   richness
self-sufficiency   goodness
individuality   necessity
effortlessness   meaningfulness   playfulness

self-esteem; respect by others

love and sense of belonging

BASIC NEEDS

safety and security

physiologic:
air, water, food, shelter, clothes, sex

FIGURE 4–12 Abraham Maslow studied healthy personalities and theorized that what people need for growth is a hierarchy of basic and growth needs. (Adapted from Abraham Maslow, 1954).

Once the physiologic needs are satisfied, the need for safety and security will emerge. Maslow points to insecure or neurotic people as examples of what happens when these needs are left unfulfilled. These people act as if a disaster is about to occur, as if a spanking is on the way. Given an unpredictable home or school, a child cannot find any sense of consistency, and so is preoccupied with worrying and anxiety. Maslow would advise teachers to give freedom within limits, rather than either total neglect or permissiveness.

The growth need for love and belonging is often expressed directly and clearly by the young children in our care. A lack of love and sense of belonging stifles growth. To learn to give love later in life, one has to learn about love by receiving it as a child. This means learning early about the responsibilities of giving as well as receiving love.

The need for esteem can be divided into two categories: self-respect and esteem from others. Self-esteem includes such needs as a desire for confidence, competence, mastery, adequacy, achievement, independence, and freedom. Respect from others includes such concepts as prestige, recognition, acceptance, attention, status, reputation, and appreciation.

Self-actualization is what gives a person satisfaction in life. From the desire to know and understand the world and people around us comes a renewal of self-knowledge. For the early childhood educator, these needs are expressed in the enthusiasm, curiosity, and natural drive to learn and try. In meeting these needs, a person finds meaning in life, an eagerness to live, and a willingness to do so.[1]

Children must have their physical and basic emotional needs met before these requirements of higher cognitive learning can be fulfilled. Moreover, the child who seems stuck in a particular "needs area" will likely stay there until that basic need is satisfied. A hungry, insecure, or hurt child is a poor learner. Teachers must continually advocate better physical and social conditions for all children.

Maslow's theory has important implications for child care. Children's basic needs are teachers' first concern: Teachers must ensure that children are properly clothed, fed, and rested as well as safe and secure. Only then are they ready to address curriculum and skill development.

❀ DEVELOPMENTAL TOPICS

To complete this chapter on developmental and learning theories, we need to expand our knowledge of child development to include several important topics. The teachers well versed in these developmental topics will be able to make better decisions concerning classrooms and curricula. Moreover, they will be able to connect with families around those points and those people most important to them: the children.

Ethnicity and Cultural Diversity

Development can be fully understood only when it is "viewed in the larger cultural context. . . . [Indeed] while culture's important role in shaping child rearing and family interaction is well understood, its effect on education opportunities is not always recognized" (Rodd, 1996). We must know about children in their own setting, their own context, to understand them well enough to teach them. Every child lives "deeply rooted in a cultural milieu" (Hilliard & Vaughn-Scott, 1982), and the

[1]Humanistic psychology can be seen as being at odds with cultures and religions that seek ultimate reliance on a supreme deity, putting "God" rather than "self" at the top of the hierarchy.

ecology of a child's life must be acknowledged and brought into our work. These international examples show the influence of cultural orientation (Rodd, 1996):

> The primary curricular emphasis in England is upon children's social development until age three, after which academic competence is emphasized. Swedish educators focus on developmental issues, particularly socio-emotional development. . . . In Asian countries where children's physical well-being and primary health care have improved to the point where they are no longer issues, the focus is upon academic achievement and excellence. While academic achievement is not stressed in the Czech Republic, young children are taught the value and importance of work and aesthetics, and they participate in cultural programs by the time they are three.

Let us turn to the United States. An important issue for teachers is the fact that "large numbers of children are members of one cultural group while being taught or cared for by members of other cultural groups. Research shows that special problems can arise in many cross-cultural teaching settings" (Hilliard & Vaughn-Scott, 1982). Lightfoot (1978) has documented four problems that tend to develop:

1. There are problems when the language that is spoken by the child is not understood by caregivers from another culture.

2. There are problems when caregivers have low expectations for children based largely on the children's membership in a low-status cultural group, rather than on the actual abilities of the children.

3. There are problems when caregivers are unprepared to deal with children whose general behavioral style is different from that of the caregivers.

4. There are problems when standard testing and assessment techniques are applied to certain cultural groups with insufficient recognition of, or respect for, the cultural patterns of the group.

Historically, ethnic minority children have been ignored in research or viewed as variations from the norm. Often the group studied is given an ethnic label (such as Latino) that assumes the group is homogeneous and glosses over critical differences among the people in the group. Creating a

All children are affected by the socializing experiences they have early in life.

culturally responsive education is the only way we can implement truly developmentally appropriate practices.

In many ways, each child is like every other. Certain universals hold for all children, and knowing them, teachers can apply child development and learning theories. Chapter 3 helps you identify these universals. Try to look beyond any one theory and have principles that are fundamental to good practice, responsive to different values, and inclusive of cultural patterns. This is especially important because there are limits to applying universals in these theories. One limit is the fact that most early theories were based on observations of male or white subjects.[1]

Another limit is that some differences among children exist as a result of cultural commonalities and each child's uniqueness. Caldwell (1983) outlines three areas so teachers can make child development useful without overgeneralizing. First, all children have the same needs and rights, go through the same developmental stages, and have the same developmental goals. Cross-cultural research on Piagetian theory has demonstrated that a sequence of development holds true worldwide, although the ages vary among cultures and individuals.

Second, children are like each other in some ways. While all two-year-olds are in the process of developing language, the actual rate of vocabulary increase will differ according to how important language expression is to the cultural and familial groups. Teachers without appropriate knowledge of their students' cultures run a risk of misapplying developmental theories and norms.

Third, each child is like no other in many respects. What is unique comes from

genetic makeup, temperament, energy level, sensory sensitivity, interests, and motivation, to name several. Child development and learning theories have limits. They can foster a global outlook about children in general, but these theories must be viewed in light of both cultural diversity and a respect for individuality.

A final note: ethnicity and cultural identity clearly play an important role in child development. "In the critical early childhood years, children begin to develop a sense of self as families hand down beliefs, attitudes, and behaviors. Much of what is handed down is unspoken and is acquired through social interactions. In this way adults pass on their culture and shape children's understandings of themselves, their world, and their place in it. As children are forming their identity and self-worth, they often struggle with conflicting messages from home, media, school, and peers about who they are and what they are worth" (Hironaka Cowee, 2001).

Attachment

Attachment is a term used particularly in the works of John Bowlby and Mary Ainsworth and a concept used in Burton White's descriptive work, Magda Gerber's Resources for Infant Educarers (RIE) programs for infants and toddlers, and WestEd/Far West Laboratory's Program for Infant and Toddler Caregivers (PITC). Attachment is emotional connection, an "affectional bond" (Bowlby, 1973) between two people. The child or adult who is attached to another uses that person as a "safe base" from which to venture out into the world, a source of comfort when distressed or stressed, and a support for encouragement. Attachment behaviors are

[1]More recent studies of development include other ethnic populations (Hale, 1986; Hilliard & Vaughn-Scott, 1982; York, 2003).

any that allow a person to get and stay attached, such as smiling, eye contact, talking, touching, even clinging and crying.

Infants are preprogrammed to form attachments to adults, thus ensuring their survival. "It is an essential part of the ground plan of the human species—as well as that of many other species—for an infant to become attached to a mother figure. This figure need not be the natural mother but can be anyone who plays the role of the principal caregiver" (Ainsworth, 1979). Freud believed that infants became attached to those who fed them. Erikson asserted that the first year of life was critical for attachment, in the stage of trust versus mistrust.

The nature of children's attachment has been researched extensively. Research shows that human and animal babies send signals to their mothers very early on. The human infant's early signals include crying and gazing, both of which are powerful to adults, and a kind of rhythmic sucking that appears to keep the mother engaged. Children then develop real mutuality—that is, they learn and practice almost a "dance" between themselves and their favored loved one. For instance, the social smile appears, which is a thrill for parents and a boost in communication skills for the baby.

Although virtually all infants develop attachments, including to multiple caregivers, they differ in how secure they are in those attachments. Attachment can be measured by observing children's response to a stranger both in and out of the parent's presence (Figure 4–13).

Not all developmental psychologists believe that attachment is so important to later competence and identity. Kagan

(1978) believes that infants are resilient and that children can grow positively within wide variations of parenting. Another criticism of attachment theory is that it ignores the context and diversity of how children are socialized, and by whom. There are great cultural variations in attachment. German babies are more likely than American babies to be categorized as avoidant, but this might be because the culture encourages early independence. Japanese babies are more likely to be seen as avoidant, but this could also be a factor of the method used to record it, which calls for children to be left in a room without the mother, a situation that rarely occurs for most Japanese infants.[1]

Researchers have found that a majority of American infants tested in the stranger situation demonstrated secure attachment. Still, when attachment fails, children are placed at tremendous risk. The "dance" requires partners; both infant and parent (or caregiver) must have the skill to connect. Premature infants often lack these skills at first, as their systems are underdeveloped and they often are separated in the first weeks or months, causing parents to report them as quite unresponsive. Failure to attach can come from the parent, too. Some parents of blind infants, who cannot engage in gazing, may wonder if they are being rejected by their babies. Parents who themselves did not have secure attachments as children may not know the needed behaviors. Abusing parents are not doing their part to encourage bonding. Other neglectful conditions, such as depression, abject poverty, and other stresses, increase the likelihood that there

[1]It is interesting to note that European-Americans are most interested in attachment, yet tend to hold babies less than almost any other cultural group in the world. Attachment does not seem to be an issue, much less a concept, in cultures in which children are carried, held, or sleep with their parents for the better part of the first three years (Saxton, 2004).

	Exploratory Behavior Before Separation	Behavior During Separation	Reunion Behavior	Behavior With Stranger
Secure	Separates to explore toys; shares play with mother; friendly toward stranger when mother is present, touches "home base" periodically.	May cry; play is subdued for a while; usually recovers and is able to play.	If distressed during separation, contact ends distress; if not distressed, greets mother warmly; initiates interaction.	Somewhat friendly; may play with stranger after initial distress reaction.
Anxious/ ambivalent (resistant)	Has difficulty separating to explore toys even when mother is present; wary of novel situations and people; stays close to mother and away from stranger.	Very distressed; hysterical crying does not quickly diminish.	Seeks comfort and rejects it; continues to cry or fuss; may be passive—no greeting made.	Wary of stranger; rejects stranger's offers to play.
Anxious/ avoidant	Readily separates to explore toys; does not share play with parent; shows little preference for parent versus stranger.	Does not show distress; continues to play; interacts with the stranger.	Ignores mother— turns or moves away; avoidance is more extreme at the second reunion.	No avoidance of stranger.

SOURCE: Compiled from Ainsworth, M. D. S., & Wittig, B. A. (1969). Attachment and exploratory behavior of one-year-olds in a strange situation. In B. M. Foss (Ed.), *Determinants of infant behavior (Vol. 4).* London: Methuen.

FIGURE 4–13 Patterns of attachment show how important relationships are to young children. (From *Understanding Children* by Judith Schickendanz by permission of Mayfield Publishing Company. Copyright © 1993 by Mayfield Publishing Company.)

will be a failure of attachment. Intervention can help in the form of teaching specific interactive techniques with ongoing supports such as crisis hotlines and personal counseling.

Also, parents and researchers have asked careful questions about full-day child care, particularly for infants, wondering whether such care undermines children's attachment to their parents. The debate has spurred research into both parent–child attachment and child care programs. Whether concerns about infant child care prove valid or not, as of this date we can conclude that children are not at any higher risk in high-quality child care.

Regardless of the setting, all children under three are engaged in the attachment process as part of their development. The Center for Child and Family Studies,

WestEd/Far West Laboratory in San Francisco, has developed an extensive program for infant and toddler caregivers. Under the direction of J. Ronald Lally, the PITC watchword for working with children under three is: "It's all about relationships!"

Play

Play! What a wonderful word! It calls up images from the past, those childhood years when playing was the focus of our waking hours. "Will you play with me?" is one of the most expressive, expectant questions known. It carries with it hope and anticipation about a world of fun and make-believe, a world of adventure and exploration, a world of the young child.

City streets, parks and fields, tenements, huts, empty rooms, and backyards are all settings for play. Play is a way of life for children; it is their natural response. Play is universal to childhood experiences because it is intrinsically motivated and naturally satisfying to children. By definition, play

- ✦ is relatively free of rules except for what children will impose themselves.
- ✦ is controlled and dominated by the children.
- ✦ is carried out as if the activity were real life.
- ✦ focuses on the activity—the doing—rather than on the end result or product.
- ✦ requires the interaction and involvement of the children.

It is what children do and it is serious business to them. Any activity children choose to engage in is play; it is never-ending.

Educators and psychologists have called play a reflection of the child's growth, the essence of the child's life, a window into the child's world. It is a self-satisfying activity through which children gain control and come to understand life.

Play teaches children about themselves; they learn how tall—or short—they are, what words to use to get a turn on the swing, and where to put their hands when climbing a ladder. Through play, children learn about the world: what the color purple is, how to make matzoh balls, and how to be a friend. Play helps children define who they are.

Play takes many forms. Children play when they sing, dig in the mud, build a block tower, or dress up. Play can be purely physical (running, climbing, ball throwing) or highly intellectual (solving an intricate puzzle, remembering the words to a song). Play is creative when crayons, clay, and fingerpaint are used. Its emotional form is expressed when children pretend to be mommies, daddies, or babies. Skipping rope with a friend, playing jacks, and sharing a book are examples of the social side of play.

Types of Play

There is a general sequence to the development of social play (Figure 4–14). Babies and toddlers have a clearly defined social self. Infant play begins with patterns established at birth: Babies gaze, smile, and make sociable sounds in response to the quality and frequency of attention from a parent or caregiver. Socialization of infants occurs through interaction. By the end of their first year, infants smile at and touch one another and vocalize in a sociable effort. Toddlers play well on their own (solitary play) or with adults. They begin solitary pretend play around one year of age. They still watch others (onlooker). As children become more aware of one another, they begin to play side by side, without interacting (parallel play). They are aware of and pleased about, but not directly involved with, the other person. During this stage some form of coordinated play begins, doing something with another child (associative play). The preschool years bring many changes for children in relation to social development. The number and quality of relationships increase. At first, this is accomplished just by a child's presence in a group: playing at the water table with four other children or joining a circle for a story or songs (associative play). Preschoolers begin to join forces with one another in an active way (cooperative play); they verbalize, plan, and carry out play. This becomes the most common type of peer interaction during the preschool and kindergarten years.

Yet developmentally and culturally appropriate practice remind us that our understanding and knowledge about play have been based on Euro-American cultural patterns.[1]

Unoccupied Play
- May stand in one spot
- Looks around the area
- Performs random movements that have no apparent goal

Solitary Play
- Plays alone
- Plays independently of others

Onlooker Play
- May watch while others play
- May talk but does not enter play
- Shows active interest in the play

Parallel Play
- Plays alongside others
- Plays separately from others but with toys or actions that are similar to the others

Associative Play
- Play involves social interaction but little or no organization
- Interested in each other without an agreed-upon plan

Cooperative Play
- Socially interacts in a group with a sense of group identity
- Joins an organized activity, a prototype for games

FIGURE 4–14 Parton's play categories were developed by observing free play in a nursery school.

[1]Children's play is culturally grounded.

The way in which we interpret children's development through play differs from culture to culture. Children's play always portrays their own social values and family ethnic practices (Hyun, 1998), and wise early childhood education practitioners will incorporate this perspective into their work with children.

Most play is unstructured and happens naturally when the curriculum is designed for play. Spontaneous play is the unplanned, self-selected activity in which children freely participate. Children's natural inclinations are toward play materials and experiences that are developmentally appropriate. Therefore, when they are allowed to make choices in a free play situation, children will choose activities that express their individual interests, needs, and readiness levels.

Dramatic play—or imaginative or pretend play—is a common form of sponta-

neous play. Three- and four-year-olds are at the peak of their interest in this type of activity. In dramatic play, children assume the roles of different characters, both animate and inanimate. Children identify themselves with another person or thing, playing out situations that interest or frighten them. Dramatic play reveals children's attitudes and concepts toward people and things in their environment. This is the way children cope with their smallness or lack of strength. Superhero play is appealing because it so readily addresses a child's sense of helplessness and inferiority. Dramatic play provides the means for children to work out their difficulties by themselves. By doing so, they become free to pursue other tasks and more formal learning. For all these reasons, play is invaluable for young children.[1]

Sociodramatic play happens when at least two children cooperate in dramatic play. Both types of play involve two basic elements: imitation and make-believe. It is the most highly developed form of symbolic play. Vygotsky noted that in pretend play, the ZPD allows children to raise themselves to higher levels of behavior. In terms of Piaget's cognitive theory, such play assists the child in creating imaginary situations that are governed by rules. Erikson would remind us that much of play is wishful thinking, pretending great strength and deeds, building hope.

Pretending to be a firefighter, Sherry grabs a piece of rope and runs toward the playhouse, saying "shhshhshshshshsh" while pretending to squirt water on the fire. She shouts to her playmates, "Over here! Come over here! The fire is on this side." Her make-believe scenario and her ability to follow the rules of behavior com-

Video View Point 4-2

"Role of Play in Children's Social Development: Play encourages social interaction, and through this interaction children acquire the social skills that can be learned only through experience."

Competency: Social Development

Age Group: Preschool

Critical Thinking Questions:

1. Observe a group of preschoolers and identify the stages of their play.

2. Find an example of at least six social skills while watching preschoolers engage in pretend play with each other.

[1]Early childhood educators need to be constantly vigilant in noticing their personal gender biases, along with staying current about research in gender differences.

mon to firefighters (grabbing hoses, calling for help) are the two critical factors that support the theory that cognitive skills develop through social interactions. Sherry exemplifies a child moving from concrete to abstract thought because she did not require realistic objects (a hose and water) but imagined them with a rope and her ability to create the sound of water. Knowing how to separate thoughts from actions and objects will stand Sherry in good stead when she studies math concepts. Rules that children follow in make-believe play teach them to make choices, to think and plan about what they will do, and to show willingness toward self-restraint, as children learn to follow the social rules of pretend play. This is important preparation for real-life situations.

Play as a Cornerstone of Learning

For the first half of the 20th century, interest in children's play focused on emotional causes and effects. The main theme was the emotional release that play provided children. Play is a suitable outlet for expressing negative feelings, hostility, and aggression. Clay can be pounded, balls can be kicked and thrown, dolls can be spanked. Young children give free expression to a wide range of emotions, playing them out and releasing tension.

If children are just playing, how will they learn? It turns out that play promotes learning for the whole child as well. A wide range of learning opportunities is inherent in any single play activity. "Each child learns by asking his or her own next questions and trying out the answers. Often both the questions and the answers take the form of actions rather than words. Children learn by doing. In play, children are autonomous; they're independent. They make decisions, solve the problems, deal with the consequences" (Jones, 2000).

A childhood filled with play opportunities should culminate in these three types of learning.

1. Children learn about themselves and develop a positive self-image and a sense of competence. They should know and feel good about themselves as learners. They should develop a sense of independence, a measure of self-discipline, and knowledge based on full use of their sensory skills.

2. Children learn about others and the world around them, developing an awareness of other people. Teachers want children to perfect their communication and social skills so that they will be more sensitive participants in the world in which they live. This means that children learn and appreciate the values of their parents, the community, and society at large. When children become aware of the demands of living in today's society, that awareness can help them become more responsible citizens. The emphasis on social interaction and group relationships in the early childhood setting underscores this goal.

3. To learn to solve problems, children need to be accomplished in observation and investigation. When exploring a puzzle, for example, children need to know how to manipulate it, take it apart, and put it back together, to see how other people solve puzzles, and to know how to get help when the pieces just do not seem to fit together. They should know how to predict and experiment. What will happen, wonders a kindergartner, when a glass is placed over a glowing candle? How will that change if the glass is large or small? What is the effect if the glass is left over the candle for a long time or for a second? Young children also need to learn how to negotiate, discuss, compromise, and stand their ground, par-

ticularly when they encounter and solve problems socially. "I want the red cart and Jackie already has it," thinks preschooler Jamal. "Now what? How can I get it? What if Jackie says no? Will the plan that works with my best friend Yim-Tong work with her? When do I ask for help? Will crying make a difference?" Teacher Lorie should be nearby, watching Jamal's face and body as he works on solving his problem. If he grabs or lashes out at Jackie, she can stop the aggression and give him the words he needs to express himself. The use of DAP involves teachers helping children to become effective problem solvers through experience.

Gender Identity

Are girls and boys different in terms of development and learning? What are these differences, and how do they occur? Which differences are caused by "nature" and which by "nurture"? Should we treat our

girls and boys the same or differently? The realities and the myths surrounding sex differences and their effects on behavior from infancy to adulthood are the subject of interest, controversy, and research.

Gender is the sociocultural dimension of being female or male. There are two aspects of gender development that are particularly important in the early years: gender identity (the sense of being female or male, which most children acquire by three years old) and gender role (the set of expectations that define how a male or female should behave, think, and feel).

Gender has been important to some developmental and learning theories. One of Freud's assumptions was that behavior was directly related to reproductive processes. His stages of psychosexual development reflect the belief that gender and sexual behavior are instinctual. Erikson also claimed that anatomy was destiny: males were more intrusive because of genital structure, and females were more inclusive. He later modified his view, saying

With encouragement, boys can learn to enjoy activities, such as drawing and sewing, that are often associated with girls. (Courtesy of Centro Infantil & de Reabilitacao de A-De-Beja, Lisbon, Portugal.)

that women were overcoming their biological heritage. These identification theories come from the view that the preschool child will find the opposite-sex parent attractive but will steer away from this by identifying with the same-sex parent.

A more social cognitive view (Bandura, Piaget) emphasizes that children learn through observation and imitation and that through reinforcement (rewards and punishment) children learn gender-appropriate behavior. Proponents of this view point to how parents encourage girls and boys to engage in certain activities and types of play. They note that in elementary school, the playground is like a "gender school," with children showing a clear preference for same-sex peers. Certainly the media communicates sexist messages; this theory would claim that such stereotyping influences the development of gender roles. The work of Eleanor Maccoby (1998) has provided both hard data and an open forum for discussions about how people grow and the complex interaction between heredity and environment that makes child development so fascinating.

The child's emerging sense of self has several elements. Children generally acquire the ability to label themselves and others correctly by age two or three; they develop gender stability (the understanding of staying the same sex throughout life) by age four and gender constancy (a person keeps the same gender regardless of appearance) by about five or six.

Young children begin to develop ideas about gender roles, what girls/women and boys/men do. Sex-typed behavior begins to appear at two or three, when children tend to choose same-sex playmates and sex-typed toy preferences. Physically, males grow to be 10 percent taller than females, and girls are less likely to develop physical or mental disorders than boys. Boys are also more active than girls. There are sex differences in the amount of physical aggression; however, there are fewer differences in verbal aggression, though males do show less self-regulation than females. Research indicates that there are no significant differences between girls and boys in intelligence or reasoning behavior. Some cognitive functioning and personality differences do exist, but overall the differences are small and there is no overall pattern.

Because there is controversy about how similar or different the two sexes may be, teachers need to attend to both girls and boys fairly. Children form their ideas about gender from one-and-a-half to three years, and then solidify their ideas in the preschool years. To the extent that these gender roles could become constricting for self and for others, adults who work with children are thus well-advised to pay careful attention to the messages they give children.[1]

In the environments we prepare for them, the materials they use, and the examples we model, children create their own ideas and learn behavior that works for them in the world. Socialization accounts for much of the gender-typed behavior we see in children.

Moral Development

Children's moral development is a complex process, with both a cognitive and an emotional side to it. Several theorists and re-

[1]These characteristics may not be *gender specific* (i.e., "only girls do this and only boys do that"), but may be *gender related* (i.e., "many girls often . . . and some boys may do the same"). What is important to remember in our diverse world is that one way is not necessarily better than another way, just *different*.

searchers have proposed how to think about children's moral development. Jean Piaget, Lawrence Kohlberg, Nancy Eisenberg, and Carol Gilligan are discussed here.

Piaget investigated children's moral reasoning by presenting children with pairs of stories and asking them which child was "naughtier." From this, he discovered that children under age six base their judgment on the amount of damage done, not the child's intentions. We now know that three-year-olds know that a child who deliberately knocks someone off a swing is worse than one who does so by accident. By four or five, children can tell the difference between truthfulness and lying. Stealing an apple is a greater offense to preschoolers than eating ice cream with your fingers (the latter being a culture-bound rule). The connections to children's cognitive stage of development are interesting, and adults might consider that a child's protests over wrongdoing ("I didn't mean to do it!") may very well signal a new

level of reasoning, with the realization that one's intentions do matter.

Lawrence Kohlberg's theory of moral development involves both social growth and intellectual reasoning. People move from stage to stage as a result of their own reasoning power and they see for themselves the contradictions in their own beliefs. As with Erikson and Piaget, Kohlberg's stages are hierarchical—a person moves forward one stage at a time, and no stage can be skipped. On the basis of children's responses to moral dilemmas similar to those of Piaget, Kohlberg (1981) identified three levels of moral development, as illustrated in Figure 4–15. In the early childhood years, preconventional reasoning (stages 1 and 2) is dominant into elementary school.

Kohlberg's theory has been criticized for placing too much emphasis on moral thought and not enough on moral behavior. Many point out that his view is culturally biased; for example, Western moral doctrine emphasizes individual rights, while

I. Preconventional Morality

Stage 1: Punishment and obedience orientation
Might makes right; obey authority to avoid punishment

Stage 2: Individualism and relativist orientation
Look out for number one; be nice to others so they will be nice to you

II. Conventional Morality

Stage 3: Mutual interpersonal expectations
"Good girl, nice boy"; approval more important than any reward

Stage 4: Social system and conscience
"Law and order"; contributing to society's good is important

III. Postconventional Morality

Stage 5: Social contract
Rules are to benefit all, by mutual agreement; may be changed same way; the greatest good for the greatest number

Stage 6: Universal ethical principles
Values established by individual reflection, may contradict other laws

FIGURE 4–15 Kohlberg's stages of moral development.

other cultures focus on a greater respect for traditional codes and practices.

Nancy Eisenberg has explored the kinds of reasoning children use to justify good (prosocial) behavior (Eisenberg, Lenon, & Roth, 1983). She asks children what they would do in situations with a moral dilemma. One of her stories involves a child on the way to a friend's birthday party. The child encounters someone who has fallen and is hurt. What should the child do, help the hurt person and miss cake and ice cream, or leave the person and go on to the party? In the early years, children seem to be engaged in the first level of reasoning, in which the individual's own needs are put first. The child would leave the hurt person and go to the party ("I won't help because I have to go to the party"). As children move through middle childhood, they tend to move to the next level, in which the needs of another begin to be considered and increase in importance. Answers to the story would begin to shift toward including others ("I'd help because they'd help me next time").

Carol Gilligan (1982) challenges Kohlberg's theory as placing too much emphasis on justice and fairness (masculine values) and not enough attention on caring and responsiveness (feminine values). Research seems not to bear out this claim by gender alone but does show clear cultural influences. For example, Chinese children are more likely than Canadian children to judge lying favorably if the intention is modesty, while both groups rate lying about the antisocial act of stealing as "naughty."

One aspect of moral development that has been studied very little is that of children's spirituality and faith. Because of the separation of church and state in American public schools, many educators shy away from discussions of anything that might be considered "religious." In doing so, educational programs also find themselves staying out of anything that helps children understand who they are and the greater questions of life and its meaning. Moreover, since the emergence of multicultural education as an important movement in education, teachers are asked to take into account the influence of religion and spiritual beliefs as part of an individual's cultural identity. "Exploring their spiritual life may enhance our understanding of young children," writes Saxton (2004). "As professional educators, we need to initiate opportunities for sharing ideas and concerns on this complex topic. We, ourselves, come from diverse philosophical backgrounds and faith communities and need to develop a 'common language' for dialogue."

Brain-Based Research

Some of the most exciting research discoveries at the turn of the millennium have been in the area of brain-based research. Neuroscience research has developed sophisticated technologies, such as ultrasound; magnetic resonance imaging (MRI); positron emission tomography (PET); and effective, noninvasive ways to study brain chemistry (such as the steroid hormone cortisol). Brain scans and other technologies have made it possible to investigate the intricate circuitry of the brain.

What have we learned? The brain seems to operate on a "use it or lose it" principle. At birth, one has about 100 billion brain cells and 50 trillion connections among them. With use, these cells grow branches (dendrites) that reach out to make connections with other cells. With impoverishments, you may lose the dendrites. Over the first decade of life, the number of connections begins to decline, and by the teenage years about half have been discarded (this number will remain relatively stable throughout life). As Galinsky (1997) tells us, "The connections that have been reinforced by repeated experience tend to remain while those that are not are dis-

Key Finding

1. "Human development hinges on the interplay between nature and nurture."

2. "Early care has a decisive and long-lasting impact on how people develop, their ability to learn, and their capacity to regulate their own emotions."

3. "The human brain has a remarkable capacity to change, but timing is crucial."

4. "There are times when negative experiences or the absence of appropriate stimulation are more likely to have serious and sustained effects."

5. "Evidence amassed over the last decade points to the wisdom and efficacy of prevention and early intervention."

Implications for Educators

Remember the nature/nurture controversy described in Chapter 1 and this chapter? Think, too, about the contributions of Piaget, the constructivists, and sociocultural theorists in regard to the dynamic interplay between the environment and learning. We now know that the brain is affected by all kinds of environmental and interactive conditions. The impact is both specific and dramatic, influencing both the general direction and the actual circuitry of the brain.

This finding confirms the work on attachment (see this chapter) and underscores the importance of warm and responsive care. It is in the daily interaction with nurturing adults that children develop the network of brain cells that help them learn to regulate and calm themselves, which actually helps the brain turn off a stress-sensitive response quickly and efficiently.

Sound familiar? Montessori's *sensitive* periods and Steiner's belief in a seven-year cycle of growth (see Chapter 1) both stress the notion of timing. Brain research is helping us pinpoint those periods. Experiments have proven that there are certain "windows of opportunity" for the proper development of vision and language, and studies show certain effective times in the learning of music. There are limits to the brain's ability to create itself, and researchers have found that these limitations have some time periods to them that we ought not to ignore.

Consider the impact of trauma and neglect, of maternal depression, of substance abuse, and of poverty. The parts of the brain associated with expression and regulation of emotions seem to show the most effect. Brain activity and children's behavior can improve when some of these problems, such as maternal depression, are treated. However, many of the risk factors occur together.

We know this in our hearts and we know this from the research on Head Start (see Chapters 1 and 2). Now the studies of brain research point to the value of timely, well-designed, and intensive intervention.

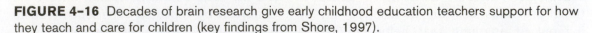

FIGURE 4–16 Decades of brain research give early childhood education teachers support for how they teach and care for children (key findings from Shore, 1997).

carded. Thus, a child's early experiences—both positive and negative—help shape the brain, affecting to some degree how he thinks, feels and relates to others throughout his life." Every environment has opportunities for interaction with a variety of objects, people, and circumstances that can stimulate brain growth. Conversely, any environment can be impoverished. This is less about toys than it is about interactions and the emotional atmosphere. When the brain perceives a threat or stress, the body reacts, and a kind of **downshifting** occurs that can compromise the brain's capabilities (Caine & Caine, 1994). A chronic threat of emotional embarrassment, social disrespect, or simply hurried, restrictive time settings can all trigger this downshifting. (See Chapter 1 for a discussion of childhood stress.) Applying brain research to the early childhood classroom is a challenge (Figure 4–16).

The following framework for action offers some general advice:

- First, do no harm. Let us do everything to help parents and caregivers form strong, secure attachments. At the same time, we need to provide education for parents and information about what helps their children's brains and well-being to grow. Finally, we must educate ourselves so the quality of child care and early education is ensured.

- Second, prevention is best, but when a child needs help, intervene quickly and intensively. The brain is a work in progress, and children can recover from serious stress. But the list of preventable conditions is clear, and it is everyone's job to work toward eliminating the unnecessary traumas.

- Third, promote the healthy development and learning of every child. "Risk is not destiny," reminds Shore (1997). "The medical, psychological, and edu-

cational literatures contain a sufficient number of examples of people who develop or recover significant capacities after critical periods have passed to sustain hope for every individual." Figure 4–17 summarizes key principles for teachers in early childhood classrooms.

 ## USING DEVELOPMENTAL AND LEARNING THEORIES

Applying Theory to Practice

As a teacher, you are responsible for applying theory to practice. No one theory tells us everything. Thoughtful teachers develop their own viewpoints. To integrate theory into your teaching practices, compare the major developmental and learning theories. Figure 4–18 reviews the highlights of each theory.

Most early childhood educators are eclectic in their theoretical biases. That is, they have developed their own philosophies of education based on a little of each theory. Each teacher has an obligation to develop a clear set of ideas of how children grow and learn. We are fortunate to have choices. Most educators agree on some basic tenets, based in part on theories of development and learning.

1. Children's basic physiologic needs and their needs for physical and psychological safety must be met satisfactorily before they can experience and respond to "growth motives." (Humanist, psychodynamic, attachment, and brain-based research)

2. Children develop unevenly and not in a linear fashion as they grow toward psychosocial maturity and psychological well-being. A wide variety of factors in children's lives, as well as the manner in which they interpret their own experiences, will have a bearing on the pattern and rate of progress toward greater

Principles of Brain-Based Learning

1. *Each brain is unique.* It develops on different timetables; normal brains can be as much as 3 years apart in developmental stages. We should not hold each age- or grade-level learner to the same standards.

2. *Stress and threat impact the brain in many ways.* They reduce capacity for understanding, meaning, and memory. They reduce higher order thinking skills. Learners are threatened by loss of approval, helplessness, lack of resources, and unmeetable deadlines.

3. *Emotions run the brain. Bad ones flavor all attempts at learning.* Good ones create an excitement and love of learning. More importantly, we only believe something and give it meaning when we feel strongly about it.

4. *The neocortex is strongly run by patterns, not facts.* We learn best with themes, patterns, and whole experiences. The patterns of information provide the understanding learners seek.

5. *We learn in a multipath, simultaneous style* that is visual, auditory, kinesthetic, conscious, and nonconscious. We do most poorly when we "piecemeal" learning into linear, sequential math facts and other out-of-context information lists.

6. *Our memory is very poor in rote, semantic situations.* It is best in contextual, episodic, event-oriented situations.

7. *All learning is mind–body.* Physiology states, posture, and breathing affect learning. Teachers should learn how to better manage students' states as well as teach students how to manage their own states.

8. *Feed the brain.* Our brains are stimulated by challenge, novelty, and feedback in our learning environments. Creating more of these conditions is critical to brain growth.

9. *Ritual is a way for the reptilian brain to have a productive expression.* More positive and productive rituals can lower perceived stress and threat.

10. *The brain is poorly designed for formal instruction.* It is designed to learn what it needs to learn to survive. It can usually learn what it wants to learn. By focusing on learning, not instruction or teaching, we can allow the brain to learn more.

11. *Cycles and rhythms.* Our brain is designed for ups and downs, not constant attention. The terms "on" or "off task" are irrelevant to the brain.

12. *Assessment.* Most of what is critical to the brain and learning cannot be assessed. The best learning is often the creation of biases, themes, models, and patterns of deep understanding.

FIGURE 4–17 All early childhood education teachers can benefit from the knowledge of the brain and how it works.

social and emotional maturity. (Psychodynamic, sociocultural, behaviorist, maturational, ecological theories)

3. Developmental crises that occur in the normal process of growing up may offer maximum opportunities for psychological growth, but these crises are also full of possibilities for regression or even negative adaptation. (Psychodynamic, attachment, moral, brain-based research)

Theory	Major Theorists	Important Facts
Psychosocial	Erik Erikson	Maturational emphasis Stage theory of social and emotional development Crises at each level Teacher: Emotional base, social mediator
Behaviorist	John Watson Edward Thorndike B. F. Skinner Albert Bandura	Environmental emphasis Stimulus–response Conditioning (classical and operant) Reinforcement (positive and negative) Modeling Teacher: Arranger of environment and reinforcer of behavior
Cognitive	Jean Piaget	Maturational and environmental emphasis Assimilation and accommodation Stage theory of cognitive development Teacher: Provider of materials and time and supporter of children's unique ways of thinking
Sociocultural	Lev Vygotsky	Zone of proximal development Private speech Collaborative/assisted learning
Multiple intelligences	Howard Gardner	Many kinds of intelligence Problem-solving and product-creating
Maturation	Arnold Gesell	Emphasis on heredity Normative data Teacher: Guider of behavior based on what is typical and normal
Humanist	Abraham Maslow	Environmental emphasis Mental health model Hierarchy of human needs Teacher: Provider of basic and growth needs
Others	Mary Ainsworth John Bowlby Nancy Eisenberg Carol Gilligan Lawrence Kohlberg Eleanor Maccoby	Attachment and categories research Attachment theory Expands moral development to prosocial Questions categories of moral development Moral, cognitive, and sex-role development Sex differences research
Brain-based research	Neuroscientists	New insights into early development "Use it or lose it" principle Warm and responsive care matters

FIGURE 4–18 The major theories of and research on development and learning describe children and their growth in different ways.

4. Children strive for mastery of their own private inner worlds as well as of the world outside them. (Erikson, Piaget)

5. The child's interactions with significant persons in his or her life play a major part in his or her development. (Erikson, the behaviorists, Vygotsky, Maslow, ethnicity/culture, gender)

Developmental Research Conclusions

Research, and the information it yields, must serve the needs of the practitioner to be useful. Teachers can combine researchers' with personal observations and experiences. Figure 4–19 consolidates what developmental research has found and how it can be put into practical use with

what do YOU think?

Decision making in teaching can be difficult. Can theory help us?

It is 10 AM at the infant-toddler center. Fifteen-month-olds Kenya and Peter are crying and fussy this morning. Neither has eaten since breakfast. They have been indoors all morning.

Theory: *Maturation theory.* Children's physical developmental needs affect their emotional states.

Plan: Schedule regular times for active movement. Be sure to offer food and watch for signs of hunger.

Mario and Therese, both in wheelchairs, joined the first grade last month, but their parents report that neither wants to come to school. Their academic work is at grade level but they participate very little. They seem familiar with their teacher.

Theory: *Sociocultural theory.* Children need to feel part of the class culture in order to learn well.

Psychosocial theory. The children can identify with the teacher and become successful, but may feel incompetent with unfriendly or indifferent classmates.

Cognitive theory. They can understand other points of view as long as it is in real situations.

Plan: Put each child in a small group to design and build wheel toys for pets. Building on the newcomers' expertise in a cooperative activity gives all the children the scaffolding needed to be successful and helps the new children become accepted into the class.

Preschoolers Jared and Panya have been arguing about who has brought the "best" toy to child care. Others have heard the ruckus and have stopped to watch the two start a fight.

Theory: *Cognitive theory.* Their egocentric thinking prevents them from seeing any view other than their own. Also, they are unable to hold two ideas at the same time, so cannot see that both toys are "good."

Behaviorist theory. The children can learn from watching others and applying other's example to their own behavior.

Plan. The teacher engages the children in a conflict resolution method that gets all children to express their own ideas, both about the problem and for some solutions, so they can practice hearing another's ideas while still holding their own. The teacher models praising each child's positive characteristics in the other's presence, showing other ways to behave appropriately and how the children and their toys can play together.

Developmental Research Tells Us:	Teachers Can:
1. Growth occurs in a sequence.	Think about the steps children will take when planning projects. Know the sequence of growth in their children's age group.
2. Children in any age group will behave similarly in certain ways.	Plan for activities in relation to age range of children. Know the characteristics of their children's age group.
3. Children grow through certain stages.	Know the stages of growth in their class. Identify to family any behavior inconsistent with general stages of development.
4. Growth occurs in four interrelated areas.	Understand that a person's work in one area can help in another. Plan for language growth, while children use their bodies.
5. Intellectual growth: Children learn through their senses. Children learn by doing; adults learn in abstract ways, while children need concrete learning. Cognitive growth occurs in four areas: perception (visual, auditory, etc.)	Have activities in looking, smelling, tasting, hearing, and touching. Realize that talking is abstract; have children touch. Provide materials and activities in matching, finding same/different, putting a picture with a sound, taste, or with a symbol.
language	Provide opportunities to find and label things, talk with grown-ups, friends, tell what it "looks like," "smells like," etc.
memory	Know that by age three, a child can often remember 2 to 3 directions. Know that memory is helped by seeing, holding objects and people.
reasoning	Recognize that it is just beginning, so children judge on what they see rather than what they reason they should see. Be sure adult explanations aid in understanding reasons. Practice finding "answers" to open-ended questions such as "How can you tell when you are tired?"

FIGURE 4–19 Developmental research tests theories of growth and learning to find out about children and childhood.

Continued

6. Social growth:	Expect that children will know their ideas only.
The world is only from the child's viewpoint.	Be aware that the rights of others are minimal to them.
Seeing is believing.	Remember that if they cannot see the situation, they may not be able to talk about it.
Group play is developing.	Provide free-play sessions, with places to play socially.
	Understand that group play in structured situations is difficult, because of "self" orientation.
Independence increases as competence grows.	Know that children test to see how far they can go.
	Realize that children will vary from independent to dependent (both among the group and within one child).
People are born not knowing when it is safe to go on.	Understand that children will need to learn by trial and error.
Adult attention is very important.	Know the children individually.
	Be with the child, not just with the group.
Young children are not born with an internal mechanism that says "slow down."	Move into a situation before children lose control.
7. Emotional growth:	Watch for what each person's self-image is becoming.
Self-image is developing.	Give praise to enhance good feelings about oneself.
	Know that giving children responsibilities helps self-image.
	Talk to children at eye level. Children learn by example.
	Model appropriate behavior by doing yourself what you want the children to do.
8. Physical growth:	Do not expect perfection, in either small- or large-muscle activity.
Muscle development is not complete.	Plan short times for children to sit.
Muscles cannot stay still for long.	Give lots of chances to move about; be gentle with expectations for hand work.
Large muscles are better developed than small ones.	
Hand preference is being established.	Watch to see how children decide their handedness.
	Let children trade hands in their play.
A skill must be done several times before it is internalized.	Have materials available to be used often.
	Plan projects to use the same skill over and over.
Bowel and bladder control is not completely internalized.	Be understanding of "accidents."
	If possible, have toilet facilities available always, and keep them attractive.

FIGURE 4–19, continued

young children. Also, look back to Figure 4–3 for DAP principles based on developmental and learning theories.

There is much information now about children and their development, so keep in mind these cautions (Santrock, 2001):

- Be cautious about what is reported in the popular media.
- Don't assume that group research applies to an individual.
- Don't generalize about a small or clinical sample.
- Don't take a single study as the defining word.
- Don't accept causal conclusions from correlational studies.
- Always consider the source of the information and evaluate its credibility.

Conditions for Learning

Developmental theory helps define conditions that enhance learning and from which positive learning environments are created. Research on all theories extends the knowledge of children and learning. Both theory and research have helped all to recognize that:

1. Learning must be real. We teach about the children's bodies, their families, their neighborhoods, and their school. We start with who children are and expand this to include the world, in their terms. We give them the words, the ideas, the ways to question and figure things out for themselves.

2. Learning must be rewarding. Practice makes better, but only if it is all right to practice, to stumble, and try again. We include the time to do all this, by providing an atmosphere of acceptance and of immediate feedback as to what was accomplished (even what boundary was just overstepped). Also, practice can make a good experience even better, as it reminds children in their terms of what they can do.

3. Learning must build on children's lives. We help connect the family to the child and the teacher. We realize that children learn about culture from family and knowledgeable members of the community, such as teachers, librarians, grocers. We know important family events and help the family support happenings at school. For children, learning goes on wherever they may be, awake and asleep. Parents can learn to value learning and help it happen for their child.

4. Learning needs a good stage. Healthy bodies make for alert minds, so good education means caring for children's health. This includes physical health, and emotional and mental health, too. A teacher who is aware and available helps provide psychological safety and well-being. Mental health is both emotional and intellectual. Teachers have a variety of activities and a flexible schedule, when someone is pursuing an idea, building a project, finishing a disagreement.

As long as we care for children, we will have our hands full. With the theoretical underpinnings presented here, we have the tools with which to make our own way into the world of children and of early childhood education.

KEY TERMS

accommodation
assimilation
attachment
bicognitive development
constructivism
downshifting
egocentric
equilibration
hypotheses
maturation

modeling
multiple intelligences
nature/nurture
prosocial
psychodynamic
psychosocial
reinforcement
schemas
self-actualization
socialization
sociocultural
stimulus–response
theory
unconscious
zone of proximal development

Teaching Applications

1. You are a teacher in a large urban child care center. Your children arrive by 7:00 AM and usually stay until after 5:00 PM each day. What would you do first thing in the morning? Use Maslow's hierarchy of needs to justify your answer.

2. What do you think of the influence of television on children's behavior? Consider the typical cartoons that the children you know are watching. From a social learning perspective, what are they learning? What else would you have them watch?

3. You are a teacher in a middle-class suburban preschool. What do you know about your group's needs and developmental stage? What assumptions, if any, can you make about development and social class? What does their cultural background tell you about what to teach? How will you find out about what each child is ready to learn?

4. Observe teachers as children play. What is the difference in the play when (1) a teacher interacts with children in their play and (2) a teacher intervenes? What happens to the play immediately after teacher contact is made? How long does the play last? What is your conclusion?

5. "Well, it looks nice enough, but don't they just play all day?" Write a defense of play as part of your philosophy and curriculum. How would you adapt the paper for parents? for a student of early childhood education? for teachers?

REFERENCES

Ainsworth, M. (1979, October). Infant-mother attachment. *American Psychologist*, pp. 131–142.

Bandura, A. (1986). *Social foundations of thought and action: A social cognitive theory.* New York: Prentice Hall.

Bee, H. (2000). Criticisms of Piaget's theory. In Gordon and Browne (Eds.), *Beginnings and beyond* (6th ed.). Clifton Park, NY: Thomson Delmar Learning.

Bowlby, J. (1973). *Attachment and loss* (Vol. 2). New York: Basic Books.

Bredekamp, S., & Copple, C. (Eds.). (2005). *Developmentally appropriate practice in early childhood programs* (3rd ed.). Washington, DC: NAEYC.

Bronfenbrenner, U. (2000). Ecological system theory. In A. Kazdin (Ed.), *Encyclopedia of psychology.* Washington, DC: American Psychological Association/Oxford Press.

Caine, G., & Caine, R. (1994). *Making connections: Teaching and the human brain.* New York: Addison-Wesley.

Caldwell, B. (1983). *Child development and cultural diversity.* Geneva, Switzerland: OMEP World Assembly.

DeVries, R., & Kohlberg, L. (1990). *Constructivist early education: An overview and comparison with other programs.* Washington, DC: National Association for Education of Young Children.

Eisenberg, N., Lenon, R., & Roth, K. (1983). Prosocial development in middle childhood: A longitudinal study. *Developmental Psychology, 23,* 712–718.

Elkind, D. (1977). Giant in the nursery school—Jean Piaget. In E. M. Hetherington & R. D. Parke (Eds.), *Contemporary readings in psychology.* New York: McGraw-Hill.

Erikson, E. H. (1963). *Childhood and society* (2nd ed.). New York: Norton.

Flavell, J. H., Green, F. L., & Flavell, E. R. (1989). Young children's ability to differentiate appearance-reality. *Child Development, 60,* 201–213.

Freud, S. (1968). *A general introduction to psychoanalysis.* New York: Washington Square Press.

Galinsky, E. (1997, Winter). *New research on the brain development of young children.* CAEYC Connections.

Gardner, H. (1993). *Multiple intelligences.* New York: Basic Books.

Gesell, A. (1940). *The first five years of life.* New York: Harper & Row.

Gilligan, C. (1982). *In a different voice.* Cambridge, MA: Harvard University Press.

Hale, J. (1986). *Black children: Their roots, culture and learning styles.* Baltimore, MD: Johns Hopkins University Press.

Hilliard, A., & Vaughn-Scott, M. (1982). The quest for the 'minority' child. In S. Moore & C. Cooper (Eds.), *The young child: Review of research* (Vol. 3). Washington, DC: National Association for Education of Young Children.

Hironaka Cowee, M. (2001). *Identity tied to culture.* CAEYC Connections.

Hyun, E. (1998). *Making sense of developmentally and culturally appropriate practice (DCAP) in early childhood education.* New York: Peter Lang Publishing.

Jones, E. (2000). Who Are the Teachers of the Young Child? In A. M. Gordon & K. W. Browne (Eds.), *Beginnings and beyond* (6th ed.). Clifton Park, NY: Thomson Delmar Learning.

Kagan, J. (1978). Perspectives on infancy. In J. D. Godowsky (Ed.), *Handbook on infant development* (2nd ed.). New York: Saxon (2001).

Kohlberg, L. (1981). *The philosophy of moral development.* New York: Harper & Row.

Lightfoot, S. L. (1978). *Worlds apart.* New York: Basic Books.

Maccoby, E. E. (1998). *The two sexes.* Cambridge, MA: Harvard University Press.

Maslow, A. H. (1962). *Towards a psychology of being.* New York: Van Nostrand.

Meade-Roberts, J., & Spitz, G. (1998). "Under construction." Unpublished documents.

Mooney, C. G. (2000). *Theories of childhood.* Beltsville, MD: Redleaf Press.

Ramirez, M., & Casteneda, A. (1974). *Cultural democracy, biocognitive development and education.* New York: Academic Press.

Rodd, J. (1996). Children, culture and education. *Childhood Education, Intenational Focus Issue.*

Santrock, J. W. (2001). *Child development* (9th ed.). Boston: McGraw Hill.

Saxton, R. (2004). A place for faith. In Gordon & Browne (Eds.), *Beginnings and beyond* (6th ed.). Clifton Park, NY: Thomson Delmar Learning.

Schickendanz, J., Hansen, K., & Forsyth, P. (1993). *Understanding children.* Mountain View, CA: Mayfield.

Shore, R. (1997). *Rethinking the brain: New insights into early development.* New York: Families and Work Institute.

Tatum, B. D. (1995, February). *Stages of racial/ethnic identity development in the United States.* Paper presented at the National Association for Multicultural Education, Washington, DC.

Vygotsky, L. S. (1978). *Mind in society: The development of higher psychological processes.* Cambridge, MA: Harvard University Press.

York, S. (2003). *Roots and wings: Affirming culture in early childhood programs.* St. Paul, MN: Redleaf Press.

Additional resources for this chapter can be found by visiting the Online Companion™ at www.earlychilded.delmar.com. This supplemental material includes a Study Guide with chapter review questions (and answers), critical thinking questions and activities, and annotated Web sites.

Section 3

Who Are the Teachers?

Teaching: A Professional Commitment

QUESTIONS FOR THOUGHT

What qualifications does a good teacher possess?

How is my own personal development related to my growth as a teacher?

What is a professional code of ethics, and why should we have one?

What does it mean to be a member of the teaching profession?

How can teachers be culturally competent?

What makes up a good teacher evaluation process?

WHO ARE THE TEACHERS OF THE YOUNG CHILD?

Margarita had always wanted to be an early childhood teacher. Shortly after her first child was born, she became a licensed family child care provider and cares for infants and toddlers in her own home. It is important to Margarita that she feels she is making a contribution to the family's well-being as well as enjoying a satisfying career. She has been taking early childhood education courses at the community college to enlarge her understanding of the young children she cares for.

Paul spent several years teaching in a school for emotionally disturbed children. He has been a lead teacher for four-year-olds at the child care center for two years, gaining experience with children whose developmental patterns are typical. Paul wants to remain a teacher but is concerned about the salary levels and lack of benefits. He has given himself one more year before he will make a decision.

Kendra's four children were in parent cooperative nursery schools, where she enjoyed the companionship of other parents of young children. After a few years of teaching elementary school, she is now director of a parent co-op and teaches children ages two to five. She particularly enjoys leading weekly parent discussion groups.

Elva was the most sought after parent aide in the school after she began helping out when her two boys were ages four and five. This success stimulated her to get a degree in child development and a teaching credential. She is now a kindergarten teacher in a bilingual program.

All of these people had different motivations, yet they all were drawn to the early childhood classroom. They may teach in different settings and have different educational backgrounds and skills, yet they do share common everyday experiences of the teacher of young children. They plan, observe, listen, help, learn, play, console, discipline, confer, comfort, and teach the children and adults who make up their particular world of early childhood. They are professional early childhood teachers and enjoy the unique nature of the early childhood teacher's role.

The nature of teaching the early years is unlike that of teaching other age groups. At first glance, the differences in teaching preschool and older children may outweigh any similarities. There are some common elements, however, that link the two. Early childhood teachers teach what other teachers teach. The curriculum in the early years is rich in math, science, social studies, history, language, art, and geography, as it is in any other grade. Early childhood teachers and their elementary and high school counterparts share many of the frustrations of the teaching profession—long hours, low pay, and a people-intensive workplace. They also share the joy of teaching—the opportunity to influence children's lives and the satisfaction of meeting the daily challenges that teaching children provides. Figure 5–1 highlights the similarities and differences between early childhood teachers and others.

THE TEACHER'S ROLE: PROFESSIONALISM IN ACTION

Phillips (1994) defined *teaching* as those daily "acts of creation" that are built from the teacher's own repertoire of skills, knowledge, and training, added to what he or she observes about children and his or her interactions with their families. What teachers do with children is not all there is to teaching. Some of the work occurs outside the classroom. What are the things a teacher does with children? What are the things a

Elements of Teaching and Learning	Early Childhood Settings	Elementary and High School Settings
How teaching and learning occur	Through teacher-child interactions and concrete use of materials Guides children toward discovery	Through lectures and demonstrations that are often teacher dominated Teaches subject matter
Play opportunities	Primary learning medium is play	Usually just at recess
Opportunity for child to make choices	Many choices throughout the day both inside and out	Few options—all students do same activity most of the day
Classroom environment	Abundant floor space, many activity centers, variety of materials	Rows of desks and tables
Daily schedule	Large blocks of time for unlimited exploration of materials and for play	45-minute to 1-hour periods on subject matter
Small group interactions	Majority of teaching	Much less frequent
Large group interactions	Few times a day	Majority of teaching
Outdoor activity	Teachers involved as intensively as they are in the classroom	Others usually supervise play yard—little direct teacher interaction
Parent relationships	Frequent, if not daily, contact	May see them once a year as child grows older
Working with other adults	Often works with aide, assistant teachers, and parents	Usually teaches alone or with part-time aide
Educational materials	Toys, games, natural materials, blocks	Textbooks and worksheets
Evaluating students	Observational and anecdotal assessments, portfolios Emphasis on growth of whole child	Grades, tests, and report cards Standardized academic assessment
Age range of students	May have 2–2½ year age span or greater	Usually same age
Art, music, and physical education	Available throughout the day as an ongoing part of curriculum	Restricted to a special class, time, or teacher
Teacher training	Strong child development foundation	Emphasis on subject matter

FIGURE 5–1 The nature of teaching in the early years is unlike that of other age groups.

teacher does after the children go home? How does the teacher interact with other adults in the early childhood setting?

In the Classroom

Interacting with Children

Teachers find their greatest satisfaction and challenges in their first role—who and what they are with children. The teacher–child interactions, the spur-of-the-moment crises, the intense activity, the on-the-spot decisions, the loving and nurturing go far in making one "feel" like a real teacher. Helping Rhonda get a good grip on the hammer, soothing Josh and Benno after they bump heads, and talking with Alexa about her science project are at the heart of teaching young children. These encounters are enjoyable, provide opportunities for interactive teaching, and help establish good relationships with the children.[1] It is during these spontaneous, anything-can-happen-and-probably-will times that teachers display their craftsmanship, Phillips's "acts of creation." The art of teaching comes on the floor of the classroom. All teaching skills are called on. Responses are ingrained. Teachers intuitively use their knowledge base, their experience, and their proven techniques. Almost unconsciously, they reach back in their minds for all those things they know about children. Throughout the school day they apply that combination of knowledge and know-how to motivate children's interest and learning.

Managing the Classroom

Being a successful manager is a little like being a successful juggler. Both require the ability to think about and react to more than three things at once. With a simple gesture, a significant look, or merely moving nearby, the teacher maintains the ongoing activity.

Anticipating a clash between Nathan and Julie, Teacher Miriam intervenes, redirects them, and moves away. At the same time, she has kept a watchful eye on Bobby at the bathroom sink. Passing close to Francie, she touches the child's shoulder in brief acknowledgment, smiling down as Francie struggles with the doll's dress. Miguel and Lea run up to her, grab her by the skirt and hand, and pull her toward the science display. They need to ask her something about the snake . . . NOW! Jake, the handyman, has come into the classroom wanting to know exactly which of the climbers needs repair. Sarah, the parent volunteer, waves to her; it is time to check on the cornbread baking in the kitchen. Quickly, the teacher files a mental note of the names of the children who accompany Sarah to the kitchen. As she reaches for a copy of *Ranger Rick* (the one with the great snake pictures in it), she observes

Teachers model learning, listening, and loving.

[1]Teaching about the rich diversity that makes up our world can be an integral and spontaneous response when interacting with children.

Angie and her father entering the room. They both look upset. Telling Miguel and Lea she will return, the teacher walks over to greet the late-comers. As she moves past Doug, the student teacher, she comments on how well his language game is going and suggests he continue for another five minutes. Glancing at the clock, she realizes it is almost cleanup time. Her assistant, LaShanna, watches her. She looks her way, and a nonverbal signal passes between them. Without a word, they both understand that snacks will be a little late today. Angie's father begins to explain their delay as the teacher bends down to invite the child to come and look at the new snake cage with her.

In this setting, the teacher has a major role in supervising a number of people. Aides and volunteers, student teachers, and visitors add to the richness of a program. But it is the teacher who coordinates and supervises their various functions. From the description, it is clear that the teacher's role as a supervisor and manager includes being:

1. caretaker for a safe environment.
2. observer of and listener to children.
3. on-the-spot teacher trainer for aides and volunteers.
4. on-site supervisor for student teachers.
5. a liaison and communicator with parents.

Setting the Tone

The teacher sets the tone, creating an atmosphere in which teachers and children will learn and play. The skill with which it is done can make the critical difference between a classroom that is alive and supportive and one that is chaotic and tense. The teacher establishes what will be the **emotional framework.** This is done with body movements, the tone of voice, facial expressions or lack of them, and nonverbal as well as verbal gestures. This interaction between the atmosphere the teacher creates and the child's behavior sets the tone. Young children are very sensitive to adult moods and attitudes. A teacher who believes that children deserve respect and are intelligent and capable and who exudes confidence, strength, and support will inspire a more relaxed, comfortable atmosphere in which children can learn and grow.

The way teachers handle conflict and react to tears, the words they use, and their tone of voice communicate a direct message to the child. The understanding, the soothing, the warmth, and the acceptance create a climate in which children feel safe and secure. This requires teachers who respect childhood, the individuality of children, their growing patterns, their emerging feelings, and their special capacity to learn. Further, it requires that teachers accept and understand cultural differences, have a working knowledge of the cultural backgrounds of the children in the class, and appreciate that this may be the children's first experience outside their own culture.[1] The end result is that preschoolers will thrive in an atmosphere influenced by teachers who understand this time of tension and growth in their lives.

[1] Emotional support is evident when children see that their family culture is valued.

Planning and Evaluating the Curriculum

As teachers move through the school day interacting with children, managing the classroom, and sensing the tone, they consciously or unconsciously evaluate what is happening:

1. The relay race outdoors produced more tears than cheers; most of the children were interested in participating when the game started but drifted away. Why?

2. The Cuisenaire™ rods were never touched today. How can we make this a more inviting activity?

3. The toddlers are beginning to participate fully in the "Eensy Weensy Spider" fingerplay. What might they like to learn next?

4. Several children have asked why Sasha "talks funny." When would be a good time to talk about his home language and teach the class a few words in Russian?[1]

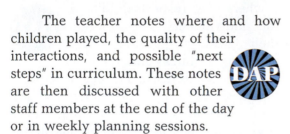

The teacher notes where and how children played, the quality of their interactions, and possible "next steps" in curriculum. These notes are then discussed with other staff members at the end of the day or in weekly planning sessions.

Effective ways to develop curriculum planning are discussed in Chapter 10. It is important to note here that the process has its roots in what the teacher sees happening in the classroom as children play and learn. It is constructivist theory in action: teachers watching and observing children to give meaning and support to their learning. Early childhood education teachers use their observation skills, collect data as they work with children, and build curriculum around their knowledge of actual classroom practice and behavior.

Out-of-Class Responsibilities

A good classroom is often dependent on how teachers spend their time away from the children. Many of the tasks that give added strength and depth to teaching are those that, out of necessity, must be accomplished after-hours.

Keeping Records

Early childhood education professionals keep a variety of records; the type and kind will vary from one setting to another. Although report writing and record keeping are time-consuming, they are essential to any good early childhood education program. Record keeping is based on a number of factors:

1. *The purpose for which the records will be used.* In schools that rely on government funding, record keeping is not optional. The children's progress, the teacher's performance, and the program itself must be monitored on a regular basis to ensure continued funding.

2. *The philosophy of the school.* In laboratory schools and teacher training centers, teachers write periodic progress reports on the children to guide them in planning.

3. *As part of a teacher training process.* Documentation is critical for accreditation of early childhood education programs. Child Development Associate (CDA) candidates submit a written portfolio of their experiences in the classroom as supportive evidence of

[1]A goal of every early childhood education program should be to foster positive attitudes and awareness of cultural differences.

their competency as teachers of young children.

4. *As part of an accreditation process.* The accreditation procedures of the National Association for the Education of Young Children (NAEYC) require extensive documentation of the school's operation, ranging from governance and management issues to teacher effectiveness, space usage, parent involvement, school philosophy, and curriculum.

5. *As a commitment to quality and appropriate child development practices.* Recording children's social and emotional growth provides information from which insights and interpretation can develop. It may be just a brief note taken on the run, an anecdote written at length after class, or a checklist of the child's playmates for one day. All of these give teachers a greater understanding of the role they play in children's development.

6. *As a means of parent information and education.* Recorded observations, notes, and similar data collected over a three-month period may show that Abraham is not participating in any strenuous physical activity and avoids activities that involve balancing and climbing. This information, when shared with parents, could lead to a medical evaluation and diagnosis of possible perceptual problems.[1]

7. *As a means of developing curriculum.* Curriculum plans and learning activities sprout from such reports and records. It wasn't until such data were collected for entry into kindergarten that a teacher realized most of the children in the class were not proficient with scissors. Curriculum was planned around this need, and the class learned a necessary skill.

Attending Meetings

Meetings are probably the most time-consuming of all out-of-class tasks. Figure 5–2 lists the most common.

Organizing and Collecting Materials

A teacher might collect space-shuttle books from the library, add pictures to the bulletin board, buy new books and records, reprint a timely article for parents, or replenish materials and equipment.

In addition to working with children, teachers support parents when they keep in touch. A brief, friendly phone call can make a family feel included in their child's education process.

 [1]Early childhood teachers are in a unique position to support early identification, prevention, and treatment of developmental problems.

Staff Meetings
Held usually once a week for individual teaching items. Purpose is to plan curriculum, set goals, and discuss children's progress. Faculty meetings for all school personnel may be held less frequently.

Parent-Teacher Conferences
May be offered on a scheduled basis or they may be called by either parents or teachers as needed Each school defines its own policy as to the number and frequency of parent contacts.

Parent Education Meetings
Many schools offer evening programs for parents. Teacher attendance may or may not be required.

Professional Meetings
Attendance at workshops, seminars, in-service training. Local, state, and national conferences are sponsored by the National Association for the Education of Young Children, Association for Childhood Education International, and Child Care Coordinating Council.

Student-Teacher Conferences
In schools used as training sites, teachers arrange time with individual students assigned to their classes.

Home Visits
May or may not be optional. Some schools schedule them before opening day. Otherwise teachers must arrange them on their own time.

FIGURE 5–2 Teachers attend many different types of meetings, which help them create better programs, learn more about children, and learn how to become better teachers.

Making Phone Calls and Sending E-mails

A quick and efficient way of keeping in touch is to contact parents to check on children who are sick or absent, or return inquiries from parents and colleagues. For children with special needs, teachers may need to contact doctors, therapists, and other specialists.

Working with Parents

This may include working on multicultural issues, organizing class fairs or school fundraising events, and scheduling a Saturday work party.[1] Further examples can be found in Chapter 8.

These duties are a part of the job of teaching young children but many will be shared with other teachers on the team or at the school. Though time-consuming, these responsibilities add to the creativity and care that teachers express for their classes.

ESSENTIAL QUALITIES: PERSONAL AND PROFESSIONAL

Personal Attributes

Good teachers should have dedication, compassion, insight, flexibility, patience, energy, self-confidence, and the desire to work with

[1]Many parents welcome a teacher's visit. Others may fear criticism or judgment about their home environment or family practices.

children. They should also be able to laugh and use their sense of humor wisely. Teachers need to be fair-minded, showing concern for all the people they meet in their early childhood setting. Their personal qualities should foster the same learning in children: being kind, warm, and loving, yet firm and consistent. Physical and mental well-being are important, as is a demonstrated sense of responsibility and reliability.

Well-rounded teachers, while maintaining a professional commitment, have other interests as well. They are involved with the world outside the walls of the classroom. They want to help children understand some of the real-life issues and concerns and have their interest in the world at large transmit itself to children.

The best teachers are the ones who are struggling to become more than they are, on any given day, and who demonstrate to their students that this quest to learn and to grow, to accept failure and go on to new challenges, is what life is all about (LeShan, 1992).

Self-Awareness

To be the best teacher possible, understanding and accepting oneself is vital. Each teacher must ask, "Who and what and why am I? How does knowing this bring some meaning into my life? How does it affect my commitment to teaching?"

Asking—and then answering—these questions helps teachers gain insights into their own behavior as adults and as professionals who work with children. Pausing to look at their own behavior when faced with a difficult task or in handling a mistake helps teachers remember what children experience each day.

The first step is **self-awareness**; the second step is self-acceptance. Adults who work with children adopt these insights into their relationships with students, parents, and other staff members. When teachers take the time to look at their own style of behavior and how it affects others, they place themselves on a par with children as learning, growing people.

Self-knowledge—examining values and personal qualities—takes courage and a willingness to risk oneself. Accepting oneself is where to begin in accepting children.

Attitudes and Bias

Most adults have opinions, born of their own experiences, of what is "good" behavior. Personal histories are filled with bias. Children they might consider "messy," who have odors, whose clothes are too big or too small, who eat "strange" food, who don't do what girls or boys are supposed to do may bother some teachers. Some of these biases can be resolved, but only if teachers take time to examine their attitudes and feelings.

Personal beliefs concerning race, culture, gender, disabilities, and economic status may negatively affect our teaching in ways of which we are not aware. Facing prejudices about children and parents based on long-held beliefs may be one of the most difficult things for a teacher to do. Most teachers will not have lived through the significant experiences of adapting to a new culture, learning a new language, surviving on food stamps and Aid to Dependent Children, or living in a wheelchair. As a result, they may be uncomfortable with people who live with these issues.

There is a great deal of emphasis today on what is termed the "**anti-bias** approach" to teaching young children (Derman-Sparks, 1989).[1] (See sections in Chapters 9 and 11 for more in-depth discussion.) This

[1]All early childhood education programs should be examined for discrimination, bias, and ethnocentrism so that children can develop a positive self-identity.

important movement promotes the concept that all children are born equal and are worthy of our respect, and it challenges teachers to examine beliefs, attitudes, and actions that might deny any child that unconditional respect.

The anti-bias approach affords teachers a tremendous opportunity to confront their own anxieties and biases and begin to deal with discrimination within themselves and their classrooms. As a way to begin, teachers might ask themselves a few questions:

1. Am I aware of my own identity and its influences on my beliefs and behaviors?

2. Do I truly foster a respect for the values of those who are somehow different from me? How?

3. Do I examine my biases and look at ways I can change my own attitudes? When? How?

4. Do I show a preference for children who most closely fit my own ethnic, cultural, and religious background? When? How?

5. Do I somehow pass along my biases to the children I teach? When? How? With whom?

6. Do I truly enjoy differences in human beings? When? With whom?

Figure 5–3 suggests a number of ways to work with families in which English is not the first language. These ideas reinforce the need for teachers to become more sensitive to their own attitudes and beliefs about cultures other than their own.

EIGHT ESSENTIALS OF PROFESSIONALISM

Knowledge and Skills

There is a body of knowledge, an educational foundation that is assumed of anyone entering the early childhood education profession. Some basic teaching skills also are necessary. These include methods and techniques appropriate for teaching the very young child.

There are professional expectations, starting with having a common background

---

Issues for Teachers When Parents Speak Other Languages

1. **Fluency in the child's language is critical for effective communication and for maximizing the child's learning experience.**

2. **The focus should be on the family's competency and learning to value the family's child-rearing practices.**

3. **Teachers are able to preserve and enhance a family's culture by learning and valuing their own first.**

4. **Multi-age groupings of children go far toward fostering social responsibility.[1]**

5. **Teachers must confront their own personal attitudes and biases.[2]**

[1]This activity may be a developmentally appropriate practice that complements many diverse cultural traditions.
[2]Teachers may need to learn new skills to effectively enhance a child's sense of self.

FIGURE 5–3 Kuster (1994) suggests five critical issues for teachers who work with children and families who speak languages other than English.

with others in the field. This includes studying child development and human behavior, family relations, parent education and development, and curriculum planning. Some practical teaching experience under the guidance of a master teacher is assumed, as is a familiarity with observation and recording techniques. This foundation of knowledge and experience provides the framework for **professional development.** Teachers gradually acquire further skills on the job.

The process of becoming a professional teacher is an orderly progression along a continuum of development. The state you live in may or may not have regulations; some states offer a specialized certification for early childhood educators. Figure 5–4 is one example of a California statewide certification program. This career lattice has a number of levels, each with alternative qualifications for meeting the requirements. Within each level there are varieties of roles available.

Figure 5–5 has some useful descriptions of various roles teachers have in many early childhood education programs. While not a career ladder, this chart shows how the progression from teacher aide to master teacher is matched to increasing responsibilities and education.

A Professional Code of Ethics

These issues are related to ethical conflicts and moral principles. Teachers are, after all, human beings, and that entails genuine conflict about behavior. Doing what is right becomes difficult at times; knowing what is right may be elusive. Even identifying what is right—an ethical conflict—may not be obvious.

Every day, situations arise with parents, other teachers, and administrators that require teachers to make some hard

Child Development Permit Matrix		
Level	**Education Requirement**	**Experience Requirement**
Assistant	6 units of ECE or CD	None
Associate Teacher	12 units ECE/CD, including core courses	50 days of 3+ hr/day within 4 yr
Teacher	24 units ECE/CD, including core courses + 16 GE units	175 days of 3+ hr/day within 4 yr
Master Teacher	24 units ECE/CD, including 16 GE units + 6 specialization units + 2 adult supervision units	350 days of 3+ hr/day within 4 yr
Site Supervisor	AA (or 60 units) with 24 ECE/CD units, including core + 6 units administration + 2 units adult supervision	350 days of 4+ hr/day including at least 100 days of supervising adults
Program Director	BA with 24 ECE/CD units, including core + 6 units administration + 2 units adult supervision	Site supervisor status and one program year of site supervisor experience

FIGURE 5–4 A combination of education and experience works to form a career ladder for early childhood professionals in California who want a child development permit.

General Role Definitions for the Early Childhood Teacher

Title	Description	Minimum Qualifications
Apprentice/ Teacher Aide	Is responsible to teacher for implementing program	Entry level, no previous formal training but enrolled in early childhood education classes
Assistant or associate teacher	Is part of the teaching team under the direction of teacher; may implement curriculum, supervise children, and communicate with parents	Child Development Associate (CDA) credential
Teacher	Is coleader who plans and implements curriculum, works with parents, and evaluates children's progress	Associate degree in early childhood education or related field
Lead Teacher	Creates a model classroom, applies good early childhood education practices, supervises other team members, develops new curriculum, provides leadership to team	Bachelor's degree in early childhood education or related field; supervised teaching experience; additional coursework in family life, assessment, supervision, etc.

FIGURE 5–5 There are many ways to reach the top of a career ladder. Each role has its own job description that will vary with the type of early childhood education setting. The qualifications will also be based on individual programs and their needs. (Adapted from Bloom, P. J. (2005). *Blueprint for action: Achieving center-based change through staff development.* Lake Forest, IL: New Horizons. Reprinted with permission.)

choices. Some cases are clearly ethical dilemmas: suspected child abuse by a parent or teacher, loose talk about children and their families outside school, or the firing of a staff member without due cause. Others may not seem as obvious. Some everyday examples are:

When parents:

1. Ask the director to advance their child into the next class against your advice.

2. Want you to use discipline practices common to their family and culture but at odds with your own sense of what children need.[1]

3. Attempt to gossip with you about another staff member.

When another teacher:

1. Suggests a private staff meeting outside school with a select group of teachers.

2. Refuses to take a turn cleaning out the animal cages.

3. Regularly is absent from staff meetings.

4. Disagrees with the school's educational philosophy and continues to teach in

[1]Teachers will need to become aware of child-rearing practices from many cultures.

ways that differ from the approved methods in that setting.

5. Goes to the school administrator with an inappropriate complaint about a staff team member.

When the administrator:

1. Insists on adding one more child to an already overenrolled class.

2. Makes personnel decisions based on friendship, not performance.

3. Backs a parent who complains about a teacher without hearing the teacher's side of the story.

Teachers may find it helpful to discuss their ethical concerns with colleagues. Some centers provide in-service programs for the staff when these issues are raised. Other schools have a **code of ethics** for their employees to follow.

Just what are ethics? Essentially, they are the moral guidelines by which we govern our own behavior and that of society. "Ethics—in the form of knowledge and skill in making responsible professional decisions—is one of the most fundamental qualities of a competent early childhood educator" (Smith, 1999).

We can strictly define ethics as "the system or code of morals of a particular philosopher, religion, group, or profession." This definition suggests that a personal code of ethics can be supported by a professional code of ethics. A code of ethics is a set of statements that helps us deal with the temptations inherent in our occupations. It helps us act in terms of what is right rather than what is expedient (Katz & Ward, 1991).[1]

Why might the early childhood education profession need such a code? A pri-

mary reason is that a code of ethics provides collective wisdom and advice from a broad base in the profession. It states the principles by which each individual can measure and govern professional behavior. It says that a group or association has recognized the moral dimensions of its work. It provides teachers with a known, defined core of professional values— those basic commitments that any early childhood educator should consider inviolate. This protects teachers and administrators from having to make hard ethical decisions on the spur of the moment, possibly on the basis of personal bias. An established professional code supports the teacher's choice by saying, "It isn't that I won't act this way: No early childhood educator should act this way" (Kipnis, 1987).

NAEYC adopted a revised Code of Ethical Conduct and Statement of Commitment in 2005. The four sections of the code cover ethical responsibilities to (1) children, (2) families, (3) colleagues, and (4) the community and society. The Code of Ethical Conduct and NAEYC's Statement of Commitment may be found in Appendix B at the back of this text.

A basic list of core values has emerged from this work, values "that are deeply rooted in the history of our field" (NAEYC, 2005). Core values form the basis of agreement in the profession about standards of ethical behavior. They are:

1. Appreciating childhood as a unique and valuable stage of the human life cycle.

2. Basing our work with children on knowledge of child development.

3. Appreciating and supporting the close ties between the child and family.

[1]One of the values in NAEYC's Code of Ethical Conduct is the recognition that children are best understood in the context of family, culture, and society.

Ethical questions arise daily. This child has been taught to hit back if anyone hits him. What does the teacher say to him? How should this situation be handled?

4. Recognizing that children are best understood in the context of family, culture, and society.

5. Respecting the dignity, worth, and uniqueness of each individual (child, family member, and colleague).

6. Helping children and adults achieve their full potential in the context of relationships that are based on trust, respect, and positive regard.

Continuing Education and Professional Development

Teachers communicate an authentic appreciation of learning when they have a sense of it in their own lives. A sense of self-awareness heightens the ability to learn: "Do I see myself as a learner? Where does my learning take place? How? What happens to me when something is difficult or when I make a mistake? Do I learn from other teachers? Do I learn from children?" Teachers' recognition of themselves as learning, growing persons gives an added degree of authenticity to teaching. In perceiving themselves as learners, for instance, they might see a similarity between

what do YOU think?

What do you think the Code of Ethics has to say about cultural diversity in early childhood education programs? Which ideals and principles in the code would you use as references in making a decision related to cultural sensitivity and understanding? Look at the situations described on pages 182–183. How do you see the Code of Ethics supporting resolutions to those dilemmas?

their own learning style and that of some of the children in the class.

The professional teacher is a lifelong learner. As such, ongoing education is a part of his or her professional commitment. Opening themselves up to the possibility of learning from students stretches teachers' capacity to grow and have relationships with children based on mutual respect and trust. This is especially important when teachers do not share the same cultural background or have no experience with a particular disability. Opening themselves to learning from other teachers creates a foundation for mutual support, collegiality, professional mind stretching, and deepening of friendships.

Look back at the career lattice in Figure 5–4 and see how many opportunities there are for advancement with the right education and experience. As you achieve each level, there are challenges to be met. A course in group dynamics, cultural sensitivity, or adult assessment portfolios will enhance your chances to move into more satisfying work and enlarge your contribution to those you work with and to the profession as a whole.

Creative and stimulating classes are the product of teachers who continue to learn more about how to teach. After the initial stage of teaching, many teachers begin to seek new ways to improve the quality of their teaching. Usually this search leads to some form of **continuing education,** such as participation in workshops, courses, or seminars. If time to pursue continuing education is not built into a teacher's schedule, there may be other options:

1. In-service training programs may be brought into the school setting. Resource people can be invited to lead the staff in discussions about children's behavior, parent relationships, science curricula, and creating multicultural classrooms.

2. Various members of the teaching staff can develop a program of their own, offering their expertise to fellow faculty at an in-service meeting.

3. A computer specialist, art resource teacher, or multicultural expert can be invited to visit the classrooms, instructing children and providing staff with some useful ideas and plans.

4. A family therapist can be invited to speak at a staff meeting about strategies for supporting families in crisis.

5. A library for teachers, stocked with professional books, journals (such as

Young Children), and newspapers (such as *Education Week*), can provide a teacher with the means to keep up with current trends and practices and to improve teaching skills in the classroom.

6. Parents who are professionals in their fields can be utilized whenever possible to enrich the knowledge and skills of the staff.

Professional Affiliations

Early childhood education professionals may choose to join one of the professional organizations devoted to the field. The NAEYC, one of the largest, has local and state affiliate groups through which one can become a member. It offers a range of services to its members, including conferences and publications such as the journal *Young Children*. The Association for Childhood Education International (ACEI) has a similar function, whereas the Society for Research in Child Development (SRCD) focuses on child psychology, research, and development.

Video View Point 5-1

"Professionals in any field are inspired by conferences, seminars, workshops, courses, and meetings with their professional organization."

Competency: Professionalism

Age Group: Infant-Toddler

Critical Thinking Questions:

1. Why do you think it is important for an early childhood educator to belong to a professional organization?

2. What associations and professional organizations might you consider joining?

There are a number of organizations concerned with young children, teachers, and issues related to the early childhood education profession. Abundant resources (print and Internet) are available from these groups.

Career Options

The need for quality programs for young children has never been greater, and the demand for early childhood education specialists will continue, fostered by national attention to the issues of children and families. If you are considering a career in early childhood education, the options are many and varied. Figure 5–6 lists some of the possibilities that exist in this profession.

Cultural Competency

Throughout this text you will be exposed to cultural awareness and sensitivity in many contexts (in Chapter 1, see Diversity, Immigrant Children, Class Differences; in Chapter 3, Cultural Sensitivity, Family Cultural

Direct Services to Children and Families
Teacher in early childhood program
Director of child care facility, nursery school, Montessori program
Family day care provider
Nanny or au pair
Foster parent
Social worker/adoption agent
Pediatric nurse/school nurse
Family therapist/parent educator
Pediatrician
Parent educator
Early intervention specialist
Recreation leader
Play group leader
Home visitor

Indirect Services to Children and Families
Curriculum specialist
Instructional specialist—computers
Child development researcher
Early childhood education specialist
Program consultant
Consumer advocate
Teacher trainer, 2- and 4-year colleges
Consultant
Resource and referral programs
State and national departments of education and/or human services

Community Involvement
State/local licensing worker
Legislative advocate
Child care law specialist
ECE environmental consultant
Interior designer for children's spaces
Government planning agent on children's issues
Consultant in bilingual education, multiculturalism
Nutrition specialist for children
Child care referral counselor

Other Options
Communications consultant
Script writer/editor
Freelance writer
Children's book author
Children's photographer
Microcomputer specialist/program consultant

FIGURE 5–6 There are many challenges in a variety of careers awaiting the early childhood professional. (Adapted from Eyer, D. (2004). Career Options in Early Childhood Education. In A. M. Gordon & K. Williams Browne, *Beginnings and beyond* (6th ed.). Clifton Park, NY: Thomson Delmar Learning.)

Influences; in Chapter 7, Culturally Appropriate Guidance; and in Chapter 8, The Changing American Family). The culturally competent early childhood professional must be aware of these issues. Population trends within the United States have changed dramatically over the last few decades, and the ability to adapt to a diversified group of families will be the challenge for the teachers of the 21st century.

This requires teachers to have a pluralistic mindset and an ability to communicate across cultures and individual circumstances. As professionals, we must examine our own values and learn about the beliefs held by the parents of the children we teach. We must make our own personal and professional journey through these remarkable times to prepare young children to live in a diverse world. How prepared are you?

Advocacy

Teachers are, by definition, advocates for children, as they are dedicated to providing a better future for them. "You have chosen to enter the nation's most powerful profession," said Jonah Edelman (2002), executive director of the advocacy group Stand for Children. "You will be the caretakers, educators, and teachers of your nation's future: our children." Professionally, there is a next step to take. As teachers, we must increase our power in the political arena of daily life. We must support each other in taking the initiative for our own profession's well-being. With the issues of diversity, distribution of resource money, and educational reform of such immediate concern, teachers need to understand the forces that affect how these issues are resolved.

Teachers will have to educate themselves about the political process. They will need to know the rules and regulations regarding public funding sources. It is impor-
tant to know how moneys are allocated and whom to work with to affect the decisions regarding education. By being acquainted with legislation, teachers can rally support for bills that will help children, families, and schools.

It was just such a coalition and coordinated effort among many people in child advocacy that secured the passage of the Child Care and Development Block Grants in 1990, the first such legislation to pass Congress in 20 years. Large-scale cooperation increased significantly the political success of that bill on behalf of all children. The advocacy group Stand for Children was begun in 1996 by the Children's Defense Fund. Its grassroots membership advocates for children to become a higher priority in our public agencies and in our lives.

Every teacher can become a child advocate. By working for children and children's services, teachers advocate for themselves as well. There are different kinds of advocacy; look at Figure 5–7 and see where you fit in. By finding your voice and keeping focused, you express your commitment and make change for children more likely to be successful.

Video View Point 5-2

"In their role as advocates, teachers demonstrate the vital importance of care and education for young children to their community."

Competency: Professionalism

Age Group: Preschool

Critical Thinking Questions:

1. What can you do to become an advocate for young children?

2. What early childhood education issues in your local community appeal to you as an advocate?

Different Kinds of Child Advocacy

Personal advocacy: Sharing personal views and philosophies with others.

Example: "Maria was concerned about the safety of the neighborhood playground. While pushing her toddler on the swing, she mentioned to the mother next to her that she was frustrated by the litter in the park, including the broken glass in the sandbox. The two women agreed to ask other parents and neighbors to come back the next day with trash bags and gloves to pick up litter while taking turns playing with the children" (Robinson & Stark, 2002).

Public policy advocacy: Influencing public policies and practices so that they are more responsive to children.

Example: Frustrated with changes the state legislature was considering, the local child care planning council sent a letter to state legislators and the chair of the funding committee. They also attended a hearing to offer testimony about how the allocation of preschool funds would affect everyone.

Private-sector advocacy: Changing private policies to better support children, families, and teachers.

Example: A group of teachers approached its local school board about the lack of technology in the schools. They talked to local businesses and the parents of the community, identified a collaborative committee of all three groups, and began volunteering their expertise about children and learning. Within two years, the school had a list of needs and priorities, had received donations of time and technical assistance from parents, and received a grant for computers in all classrooms.

FIGURE 5–7 Early childhood advocacy takes many forms.

In accepting the challenge to become an effective advocate, you can take the following steps:

1. Make a personal commitment to advocacy.
2. Keep informed about legislative issues that affect children and families.
3. Know the process and how to access it.
4. Express your view in appropriate places.
5. Let others know what is at stake.
6. Be visible in your support.
7. Show appreciation for what is being done by others.
8. Watch the implementation and its impact.
9. Build rapport and trust with those on all sides of the issue.
10. Educate your legislators about the needs of children, families, and teachers.

By getting involved, early childhood educators could help society make child-friendly choices. The teacher who works to ensure high-quality programs and services for children and their families also increases the likelihood of achieving the improved working conditions, professional opportunities, and public recognition that early childhood education so deserves.

Becoming a Whole Teacher

At some point teachers emerge with their own point of view about teaching, based on self-knowledge of what calls them to teach, why they teach the way they do, and what they know of the children they teach. This integration of knowledge and training, experience and life, is a reflection of the relationship between how teachers view children and how they see themselves. There is a blending of the emotional, physical, intellectual, and social aspects of each human being, adult or child.

Something happens when this blending occurs. During the first few years in the classroom, teachers consolidate their various official functions—merging their teacher training and experience with their personal style and nature. To discover and define the role of a teacher means to develop a personal teaching style, a voice. This is the sum of one's response to teaching, and it is unique to each teacher. When it happens, a beginning teacher becomes aware of "feeling" like a teacher. The strengths and convictions one has as a person blend with those one has as a teacher; they become inseparable. What teachers do and what teachers are become woven together. And in adding the personal teacher to the professional teacher, the sum becomes greater than the two, allowing the whole teacher the freedom to grow in insight and understanding.

✺ EVALUATING TEACHERS: A KEY TO QUALITY

Teachers are the single most important factor in determining program quality. What makes "the effective teacher" has no one simple answer. Earlier sections in this chapter describe important attributes of the teacher. How these can be assessed is complicated, but assessing them is necessary to ensure the highest quality of teaching. There are ways to evaluate teachers that guide them toward more effective teaching in their work with children, coworkers, parents, and administrators.

Why Evaluate?

It is a professional expectation in many programs that an annual assessment will be made of the teaching staff. Teachers are evaluated for many other reasons:

To Describe Job Responsibilities

It is essential for teachers to understand their job to do it well. A good job descrip-

Evaluating teachers can help set professional growth goals and clarify a teacher's strengths and areas of improvement.

tion outlines what is expected. One purpose of an evaluation is to see how those expectations are being met.

In an infant and toddler center, for example, teachers try to help children learn to separate comfortably from their parents. Evaluation in this setting could focus on the exact skills needed to implement this goal. How does a teacher help a parent separate from a young child? What environmental cues does the teacher prepare? How is the child in distress comforted? What teaching strategies are important?

Evaluation for specifying job responsibilities is a part of one's professional self-definition as well as a clarification of actual duties. Studying ourselves helps us know who we are and what we do. Assessing job responsibilities aids in this process.

To Monitor Job Effectiveness

Once clear guidelines are set for teaching expectations, a method is needed to monitor actual teaching. Most evaluation systems attempt to check teacher effectiveness. It is important to establish a process for analyzing how teachers are doing their jobs.

This process may vary from school to school. In some schools, teaching effectiveness is measured, in part, by child achievement, such as how children score on tests. Other centers may solicit parent opinion. A teacher's coworkers may be part of an assessment team. For the most part, an evaluation for job effectiveness will include an observation of teaching time with children.

To Clarify Strengths and Weaknesses

An evaluation procedure preferred by many teachers is one that identifies specific areas of strength and weakness. Feedback

about actual teaching and other job responsibilities is helpful to all teachers, whether beginners or experienced personnel. An assessment that offers teachers information about how to perform their job better contributes to job competence and satisfaction. By recognizing strengths, teachers receive positive feedback for high-quality work.[1] By identifying weaknesses, they can begin to set realistic goals for improvement.

To Create a Plan for Professional Development

One function of teacher evaluation is to foster professional development. Teachers do not become "good" and then stay that way for life. Regardless of their stage of development, teachers need goals to continually improve.

To be effective, goal setting must be embedded in an ongoing system of professional development. Caruso and Fawcett (1999) note that staff development must also be integrated with the overall goals of the center or program for which a teacher is being evaluated.

Professional development takes into consideration the various stages of expertise and development of the individuals on the staff. A career ladder plan, adopted by NAEYC in 1993, takes into account the diversity of education, training, and experience of early childhood professionals. The ladder sets out steps that individuals can take to assume more responsibility as they become more qualified and prepared. This lattice framework promotes a system of professional development, which can motivate early childhood professionals at all levels toward professional growth (Willer, 1994).

[1]Teacher expectations can have a substantial effect on children's behavior and self-esteem. Check yourself for biases: How you interact with children is key to your effectiveness, and discriminatory interactions must be noted and remedied.

To Determine Employment

An evaluation can also be used to decide whether teachers should be retained, promoted, or released. Assessment procedures are an administrator's most valuable tools in making that decision. A clear and effective evaluation tool enables the administrator to monitor performance and target specific areas for improvement. The administrator then has a fair and equitable way to determine the promotional status of each employee.

To Meet Accreditation Requirements

Many programs seek accreditation by organizations whose standards they embrace. NAEYC is the leading accrediting body for early childhood education programs through its National Academy of Early Childhood Programs. The self-study aspect of the accreditation process includes a teacher's self-assessment, the director's assessment of the teaching staff, and the teacher's assessment of the director. The standards against which these evaluations are made are contained within the criteria in the self-study, providing concrete ways to measure quality.

Issues in Teacher Evaluation

How to evaluate is an important issue in teacher assessment. A system for evaluating employees can be one of trust and mutual respect or of anxiety and tension. The method often determines how successful the entire evaluation will be.

Preliminary Steps

To begin with, a school follows the same guidelines for developing a teacher evaluation as it does for a child assessment (see Chapter 6). The process includes determining a purpose, establishing who will collect the data and how, and clarifying how the evaluation will be used. In the assessment of teachers, the important components are purpose (as described in Chapter 2), evalu-

ators, a systematic process, cultural awareness/sensitivity, and follow-through.

Evaluators

Several models have been developed around the issue of who will assess teacher performance.

Self-Evaluation. Figure 5–8 illustrates one type of systematic self-assessment. Another self-assessment technique, somewhat less formal, is to ask questions about yourself and your job, such as:

1. What aspects of my work give me the greatest sense of satisfaction and achievement?
2. What changes in my work assignment would increase my contribution to the school and my own personal satisfaction?
3. What additional development activities would help me do a more effective job or prepare me for the next step on my career path?
4. What would improve the effectiveness and quality of my relationship with my supervisor? (Young-Holt, Spitz, & Heffron, 1983)

The answers to these few questions can provide a solid base for discussion between teacher and supervisor or assessment team.

One drawback of self-assessment is its subjectivity. We see ourselves too closely and too personally to be able to be entirely objective about our teaching. Therefore, self-assessment must be accompanied by other evaluating feedback.

Supervisory Evaluation

Supervisors, directors, or head teachers are usually part of the evaluation process. Job performance is an administrator's responsibility; therefore, teachers can expect their supervisors to be involved in their evalua-

Sample Self-Evaluation

Rate the following items on the scale below based upon your performance in the classroom. (Note: This form allows for a yes/no response if desired. Supervisors may use this same form to rate the student after the self-evaluation.)

Superior Perf.	Acceptable Perf.	Unacceptable Perf.	Not Applicable
3	2	1	0

Relationship to Children

_____ I am able to understand and accept a child as he/she is and recognize individual needs.

_____ I use knowledge and understanding of child development principles to understand children.

_____ I use information regarding home, family, and sociocultural background to understand children.

_____ I am able to modify situations to forestall negative behavior.

_____ I use positive suggestions and choices to redirect behavior.

_____ I use prescribed limits and follow-through.

_____ I adapt methods of guidance to the individual and adjust guidance measures to fit the situation.

_____ I avoid the use of threats.

_____ I express positive reinforcement when appropriate.

_____ I can verbalize my own feelings in an honest, open, and humane manner when interacting with children.

_____ I avoid using baby talk.

_____ I relate to individual children.

_____ I relate to children in small groups.

_____ I relate to children in large groups.

Developing the Program

_____ I permit the children to explore materials in a variety of ways.

_____ I recognize and use spontaneous happenings to help children's learning.

_____ I make use of child development principles to plan curriculum for children.

_____ I offer a wide range of experiences so children can make choices according to their interests and needs.

_____ I allow for various levels of ability among children.

_____ I utilize a variety of media when developing instructional materials.

_____ I use a note-taking system to assist in planning and evaluating experiences for children.

_____ I maintain equipment and materials in good order and consider health and safety factors.

Relating to Parents

_____ I recognize parents by name.

_____ I converse with parents at appropriate times.

FIGURE 5–8 Self-evaluation can be an insightful and useful process. (Adapted from Young-Holt, C., Spitz, G., & Heffron, M. C. (1983). *A model for staff evaluation, validation, and growth.* Palo Alto, CA: Center for the Study of Self-Esteem.)

_____ I incorporate the cultural backgrounds of families into the program.
_____ I facilitate a free flow of information between staff and parents.
_____ I communicate concerns to parents in both written and verbal forms.
_____ I recognize and appreciate parental values and priorities for their children.
_____ I communicate children's school experiences to parents.

Administration and Professional Development

_____ I recognize and use policies and procedures of the program.
_____ I attend and participate in staff meetings.
_____ I inform the administrative staff correctly of illness, time off, vacation, and so forth.
_____ I am a member of at least one professional organization in the field of early childhood.
_____ I attend meetings conducted by professional groups.
_____ I make use of professional resources and contacts.
_____ I maintain professional confidentiality and discretion.

Working with Other Staff Members

_____ I show positive attitudes toward other staff members.
_____ I give directions carefully.
_____ I take directions from others.
_____ I participate as a team member.
_____ I coordinate my efforts with those of my coworkers.
_____ I share my time, interest, and resources with other staff members.
_____ I listen and hear staff feedback regarding my teaching.
_____ I act on suggestions.
_____ I communicate my perceptions of my teaching in an honest and clear manner.

FIGURE 5–8, continued

tion. Supervisors often use a single form combining a teacher's self-assessment and the supervisor's evaluation. This kind of form simplifies the paperwork and assures both teacher and supervisor that both are using the same criteria for evaluation. There are a number of formats, including observations, conferences, videotapes, reports, portfolios, and storytelling.

An appropriate assessment tool will have a balance in the categories on which a teacher is being evaluated. These usually include some of the following:

1. Knowledge and application of child development principles
2. Planning
3. Behavior management
4. Interactions with children
5. Interactions with adults (other teachers, administrators, and parents)
6. Interpersonal communication
7. Professionalism
8. Dependency
9. Cultural sensitivity
10. Respect for individual differences in adults and children
11. Preparing and maintaining appropriate learning environments
12. Health and safety
13. Personal qualities

Coevaluation

Evaluation by others associated with the teachers is a welcome addition to the evaluation process. Often a system includes more than a teacher's supervisor. Possible combinations are:

1. Teacher (self-evaluation) and supervisor
2. Teacher, supervisor, and parent
3. Teacher, supervisor, and another team member (teacher, aide, student teacher)

A team evaluation is a more collaborative approach, which may be more valid and balanced because a decision about teaching will be made by consensus and discussion rather than individual, perhaps arbitrary, methods. The evaluation will have a wider perspective, evaluating a teacher's job performance from several viewpoints.

Coevaluation does have its disadvantages, however. It is a time-consuming process because more than one person is asked to evaluate a teacher. Feedback may be contradictory; what one evaluator sees as strength, another may view as a shortcoming. The system can be complicated to implement. For instance, how do teachers work in a classroom and evaluate another team member at the same time? Can funds be found to bring in substitutes? Do fellow teachers have the time to devote to evaluating each other? How and when does a parent evaluate a teacher? Clearly, a school must weigh these issues carefully as evaluation systems are devised.

A Systematic Process

Many evaluations are based on observable, specific information about a teacher's activities and responsibilities. This is known as a **performance-based assessment.** Figure 5–9 is an example of a performance-based assessment in regard to a teacher's work with children. When paired with specific goals and expectations, this system is known as **competency-based assessment.**

Competency-based assessments outline exactly what teachers must do to demonstrate their competency, or skill, in their job responsibilities. Criteria are set as a teacher begins working (or a student starts a class or teacher education program). Areas are targeted that pinpoint what knowledge, skills, and behaviors the teacher must acquire.

Portfolio-based assessments are becoming a popular tool for helping teachers make sense of the experiences that help them become better teachers. A portfolio is not an assessment tool in and of itself; it is the display or collection system used to demonstrate evidence of professional growth. Folders, boxes, files, and binders are all used to house the collection of data. It is an intentional compilation of materials and resources, collected over a period of time, that provides evidence for others to review.

A teacher's self-evaluation provides an opportunity to improve her effectiveness with children.

Campbell et al. (1997) define a portfolio as "an organized, goal-driven documentation of your professional growth and achieved competence in the complex act called teaching."

Documentation is systematic and an important part of creating a portfolio. Concrete evidence of how a teacher understands and implements the best teaching practices, translates theory into action, and has a knowledge of the multifaceted nature of teaching should be included.

The portfolio is ever-changing and reflects the individuality of the teacher by virtue of what it contains. As an assessment tool, the portfolio is useful in many ways. It helps teachers clarify their values and keep focused on the goals they have set, provides an avenue for self-reflection, and demonstrates growth. By what is included and what is omitted, a portfolio shows evaluators tangible evidence of a teacher's abilities, provides a framework for setting new goals, and gives a more personal sense of the teacher's commitment and professionalism.

A portfolio may include but not be limited to the following: materials developed by the teacher; a videotape of his or her performance; lesson plans with an evaluation of a specific activity; samples of materials developed for the classroom; articles written for newsletters, parents, colleagues; a journal of experiences; photos of field trips or projects; self-reflective notes on teaching; and professional articles. If a portfolio is required as part of the evaluation process, the individual center will have its own criteria for inclusion.

The evaluation tools or format determine how valid the information gathered will be. Informal techniques may result in unreliable conclusions. A process that is

Teacher Goal	Example
To help each child develop a positive self-concept	I greet each child with a smile and a personal comment.
To help each child develop socially, emotionally, cognitively, and physically	I have goals for each child in each developmental area, Fall and Spring.
To help provide many opportunities for each child to be successful	My parent conference sheets have examples; for instance, Charlie didn't want to come to group time, so I had him pick the story and help me read it—he comes every day now!
To encourage creativity, questioning, and problem-solving	This is my weak point. I tend to talk too much and tell them what to do.
To foster enjoyment for learning in each child	I do great group times and give everyone turns.
To facilitate children's development of a healthy identity and inclusive social skills	I participated in our center's self-study and am taking an anti-bias curriculum class.

FIGURE 5–9 Performance-based assessment ties the goals of the program to a teacher's work. This example asks the teacher to do a self-assessment; a director, parent, or peer could observe and make a second assessment.

formalized and systematic, related to goal setting and professional development, has a greater chance of success. Although it is important to select an appropriate method and assessment tool, keep in mind that it is the process through which the evaluation is conducted that matters most.

Cultural Awareness and Sensitivity

Cultural awareness has an effect on how a teacher relates to children, and this needs to be taken into consideration when assessing a teacher's performance. Insight about a teacher's social and cultural background is particularly useful if the evaluator is a member of the majority population and the teacher is not.

Caruso and Fawcett (1999) define five specific cultural factors that can affect communication, particularly where supervisors and staff members are concerned. They are:

1. *Time sense.* Being on time and doing tasks in a timely fashion are high priorities for many people raised in mainstream American culture. Each culture has its own concept of time, and the teacher who is always late for meetings may be reflecting the cultural context in which he or she was raised.

2. *Space.* How close you get to someone while talking is also a function of cultural context. In some cultures, invading another's personal space (his or her "comfort zone") is considered rude. If a teacher backs away, she may be considered cold and unfriendly. If the teacher is the one getting too close, he may be seen as forward and aggressive. These perceptions may be innocent reactions based on cultural sensibilities and should be viewed in that light.

3. *Verbal and nonverbal communication.* Eye contact is seen in some cultures to be disrespectful if prolonged; to others it may be a sign of interest and attentiveness. Other facial expressions, such as smiling (or not), gestures, and body language, communicate different things from culture to culture. Silence, too, is used in different cultures in a variety of ways with an assortment of meanings. Speaking loudly may be a cultural norm or it may communicate anger and accusations. Teachers and their supervisors need to learn each other's communication styles and be particularly aware of those that are culture bound.

4. *Values.* Our values drive our behavior and responses. If a teacher comes from a background that emphasizes dependency in the early years and the school philosophy is one that encourages early independence, a cultural conflict can erupt and affect a teacher's evaluation adversely. Supervisors and teachers must understand each other's value system and what causes each of them to make certain decisions.

5. *Concepts of authority.* The way people deal with authority is also culture specific. Early childhood education professionals who supervise and evaluate staff members from cultures different than their own need to be aware of what cultural expectations surround the issue of authority. In some instances, authority figures are often male, and females are raised not to question authority. A correct answer may be more culturally appropriate than expressing one's true feelings or ideas. The supervisor can avoid misunderstandings if he or she is aware that the teacher is used to an authoritarian style of leadership from supervisors and thus gears the conversation accordingly.

The evaluator has a rare opportunity to create bridges of understanding between and among many cultures. Jones (1994) notes that by seeing the connection "between their own cultural knowledge and their behavior as professionals in an early childhood setting," they can become "cultural brokers." Within their school community, they can create a two-way interchange about culturally relevant issues with children, parents, and other teachers.

Follow-Through

What happens after evaluation is critical to the overall success of an evaluation system. For instance, after gathering information for an evaluation session, a supervisor and teacher might discuss and evaluate concrete examples and live performance. Together they can establish goals for changing what may be ineffective or problematic.

Follow-through is the final part of the continuous **feedback loop** in a good evaluation system. Data are collected on teacher behavior and given to the teacher in person. Goals are set to improve teaching. A follow-up check is done periodically to see how—and if—goals are being met. Teaching improves as recommendations are put into practice. Follow-through makes the feedback loop complete as information about improvement is communicated. Figure 5–10 illustrates this cycle.

KEY TERMS

anti-bias
code of ethics
competency-based assessment
continuing education
emotional framework
feedback loop
performance-based assessment
professional development
self-awareness

Teaching Applications

1. Draw a picture of the first classroom you remember. Place furniture in it,

FIGURE 5–10 A feedback loop is a continuous cycle in which teacher behavior is observed for a performance evaluation. The evaluation is offered through growth goals, which are set to affect teacher behavior. Thus, the cycle is continuous, with each part helping the next.

and note where your friends sat, where you sat, and where the teacher sat. Down one side of the paper write one-word descriptions of what you felt when you were in that classroom.

2. Survey a classroom where you teach or observe. How many different cultures are represented? How does the teacher respond to the cultural diversity?

3. Have you ever had a teacher who was "different"? Describe the person. What did you like most about that teacher? What did you like least? Would you hire that teacher? Why?

4. Read the ethical situations posed in the section on professional development. Think about how you would solve them. Discuss your answers with a member of your class, a teacher, and a parent.

5. In small groups, discuss the popular images of teachers as reflected in current movies and literature. Is there consensus on the portrait of teachers today? Where

do early childhood education professionals fit into the picture? Are issues raised
about teachers being addressed anywhere? Where? How? By whom? What
would you conclude about your role as a
member of the teaching profession?

REFERENCES

Bloom, P. J. (2005).*Blueprint for action: Achieving center-based change through staff development.* Lake Forest, IL: New Horizons.

Campbell, D. M., Cignetti, P. B., Melenyzer, B. J., Nettles, D. H., & Wyman, R. M. (1997). *How to develop a professional portfolio: A manual for teachers.* Boston: Allyn & Bacon.

Caruso, J. J., & Fawcett, M. T. (1999). *Supervision in early childhood education: A developmental perspective.* New York: Teachers College Press.

Derman-Sparks, L. (1989). *Anti-bias curriculum: Tools for empowering young children.* Washington, DC: National Association for the Education of Young Children.

Eyer, D. (2004). Career options in early childhood education. In A. M. Gordon & K. Williams Browne, *Beginnings and beyond* (6th ed.). Clifton Park, NY: Thomson Delmar Learning.

Gordon, A., & Williams Browne, K. (1996). *Guiding young children in a diverse society.* Boston: Allyn & Bacon.

Jones, E. (1994). Breaking the ice: Confronting status differences among professions. In J. Johnson & J. B. McCracken (Eds.), *The early childhood career lattice: Perspectives on professional development.* Washington, DC: National Association for the Education of Young Children.

Katz, L. G., & Ward, E. H. (1991). *Ethical behavior in early childhood education.* Expanded edition. Washington, DC: National Association for Education of Young Children.

Kipnis, K. (1987, May). How to discuss professional ethics. *Young Children,* pp. 26–30.

Kuster, C. A. (1994). Language and cultural competence. In J. Johnson & J. B. McCracken (Eds.), *Early childhood career lattice: Perspectives on professional development.* Washington, DC: National Association for the Education of Young Children.

LeShan, E. (1992). *When your child drives you crazy.* New York: St. Martin's Press.

NAEYC [National Association for the Education of Young Children]. (2005). *Code of Ethical Conduct.* Washington, DC: Author.

Phillips, C. B. (1994). What every early childhood professional should know. In J. Johnson & J. B. McCracken (Eds.), *The early childhood career lattice: Perspectives on professional development.* Washington, DC: National Association for the Education of Young Children.

Sharpe, C. (2004). What A Wonderful Career It Is! In A. M. Gordon & K. Williams Browne, *Beginnings & Beyond* (6th ed.). Clifton Park, NY: Thomson Delmar Learning.

Smith, M. M. (1999). Foreword. In S. Feeney & N. K. Freeman (Eds.), *Ethics and the early childhood educator using the NAEYC code.* Washington, DC: National Association for the Education of Young Children.

Willer, B. (Ed.). (1994). A conceptual framework for early childhood professional development: NAEYC Position Statement, adopted November 1993. In J. Johnson & J. B. McCracken (Eds.), *The early childhood career lattice: Perspectives on professional development* (pp. 4–21). Washington, DC: National Association for the Education of Young Children.

Young-Holt, C., Spitz, G., & Heffron, M. C. (1983). *A model for staff evaluation, validation, and growth.* Palo Alto, CA: Center for the Study of Self-Esteem.

Additional resources for this chapter can be found by visiting the Online Companion™ at www.earlychilded.delmar.com. This supplemental material includes a Study Guide with chapter review questions (and answers), critical thinking questions and activities, and annotated Web sites.

Observation and Assessment: Learning to Read the Child

QUESTIONS FOR THOUGHT

How do observations help us understand people and their behavior?

What is the difference between fact and inference?

How can we record what we see?

How can young children be assessed appropriately?

What concerns are there about standardized testing and screening?

❊ INTRODUCTION

Children are fascinating. They are charming, needful, busy, creative, unpredictable, and emotional. At school, at home, in the grocery store, and in the park, children demonstrate a variety of behaviors. There is the happy child who toddles toward the swing. The angry, defiant child grabs a book or toy and runs away. The studious child works seriously on a puzzle.

These pictures of children flash through the mind, caught for an instant as if by a camera. Such snapshots of children working, playing, and living together can be very useful to teachers.[1]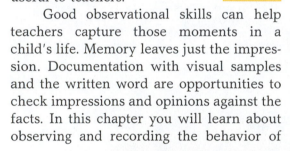

Good observational skills can help teachers capture those moments in a child's life. Memory leaves just the impression. Documentation with visual samples and the written word are opportunities to check impressions and opinions against the facts. In this chapter you will learn about observing and recording the behavior of young children and how to apply these skills to assess them, to collect their work in a way that reflects each of them, and to evaluate their growth.

What Is Observation?

Teachers learn to make mental notes of the important details in each interaction:

> That's the first time I've seen Karen playing with Bryce. They are laughing together as they build with blocks.

> For five minutes now, Teddy has been standing on the fringes of the sand area where the toddler group is playing. He has ignored the children's smiles and refused the teacher's invitation to join in the play.

> Antonio stops climbing each time he reaches the top of the climbing frame. He looks quickly around and if he catches a teacher's eye, he scrambles down and runs away.

What can you see by observing these three children at the puzzle table?

[1] A skilled observer, with an awareness of our diverse world, is reminded of the ways in which all children are the same as well as the characteristics that make each child unique.

Through their behavior, these three children reveal much about their personalities. The teacher's responsibility is to notice all the clues and put them together in meaningful ways. The teacher sees the obvious clues as well as the more subtle ones. The way observations are put together with other pertinent information becomes critical. The first child, Karen, has been looking for a special friend. Now that she has learned some ways to approach other children that don't frighten and overwhelm them, children want to play with her. Teddy's parents divorced two weeks ago. It appears he is just beginning to feel some of that pain and has become withdrawn at school. At home, Antonio is expected to do things right the first time. Because climbing over the top of the frame might be tricky, he does not attempt it at all. At school, he generally attempts only what he knows he can do without making a mistake.

The ability to observe—to "read" the child, understand a group, "see" a situation—is one of the most important and satisfying skills a teacher can have. As Cartwright (1994) tells us:

> Really seeing means sensitive observation, keen listening, and simultaneous note-taking. It's not easy to master and it takes much practice, but the results are remarkable. The very process of learning skilled observation keeps teacher concern primarily with the children (where it should be!).

A consistent practice of observation will help teachers develop a "child-sense—a feeling for how individual children and groups of children are feeling and functioning" (Feeney et al., 2001).

Observation is the basis of so much of a teacher's work. It influences how a teacher sets up the environment and how and when it will be changed. It helps a teacher create the daily schedule, planning appropriate time periods for various activities. It allows the teacher to make sense of and respond well to interpersonal exchanges.

Observing is more than ordinary looking. It takes energy and concentration to become an accurate observer. Teachers must train themselves to record what they see on a regular basis. They need to discipline themselves to distinguish between detail and trivia as well as learn to spot biases that might invalidate observation (see Figure 6–1). Once acquired, objective observation techniques help give a scientific and professional character to the role of early childhood educator.

Seeing Children Through Observation

Play is the work of childhood. It is the way children express themselves and how they show what they are really like. By observing play, teachers can see children as they are and as they see themselves. Much of what children do gives clues to their inner beings. Developing sound observational skills enables teachers to better meet the social, emotional, and intellectual needs of each child.

The stage is set; the action begins as soon as the first child enters the room. Here, teachers can see children in action and watch for important behavior. All that is needed is to be alert to the clues and make note of them:

> Sierra, a toddler, walks up to Brooke. Sierra grabs Brooke's toy, a shape sorter, away from her. Then she begins to place shapes into the sorter. She has difficulty placing the shapes into the container. Sierra then throws the shapes, her face turns red, and she kicks the container away from her.
>
> Nico kneels on the chair placed at the puzzle table, selecting a 10-piece puzzle. He turns the puzzle upside

Poor Observation

A. Julio walked over to the coat rack and dropped his sweater on the floor. He is <u>shy</u> (1) of teachers, so he didn't ask anyone to help him pick it up. He walked over to Cynthia <u>because she's his best friend</u> (2). <u>He wasn't nice</u> (3) to the other children when he started being <u>pushy and bossy</u> (4). He <u>wanted their attention</u> (5), so he <u>nagged</u> (6) them into leaving the table and going to the blocks <u>like four-year-old boys do</u> (7).

Analysis and Comments

(1) Inference of a general characteristic.
(2) Inference of child's emotion.
(3) Observer's opinion.
(4) Inference with no physical evidence stated.
(5) Opinion of child's motivation.
(6) Observer's inference.
(7) Overgeneralization; stereotyping.

Good Observation

B. Emilio pulled out a puzzle from the rack with his right hand, then carried it with both hands to the table nearby. Using both hands, he methodically took each piece out of the frame and set it to his left. Sara, who had been seated across from Emilio with some table toys in front of her, reached out and pushed all the puzzle pieces onto the floor. Emilio's face reddened as he stared directly at Sara with his mouth in a taut line. His hands turned to fists, his brown furrowed, and he yelled at Sara in a forceful tone, "Stop it! I hate you!"

Analysis and Comments

Emilio was clearly *angry* as demonstrated in his facial expressions, hand gestures, and body movements. The way a child speaks is as revealing as what a child says when one wants to determine what a child is feeling. Muscular tension is another clue to the child's emotions. But the physical attitude of the child is not enough; one must also consider the context. Just seeing a child sitting in a chair with a red face, one doesn't know if he is embarrassed, angry, feverish, or overstimulated. We need to know the events that led to this appearance. Then we can correctly assess the entire situation. By being open to what is happening without judging it first, we begin to see children more clearly.

FIGURE 6–1 Two observations. Example A contains numerous biases, which are underlined in the left column and explained in the right column. Example B has clear descriptions and is relatively free of biases.

down, allowing the pieces to fall on the table. He selects one piece at a time with his left hand and successfully puts every piece in the frame the first time. He raises both hands in the air and yells, "I did it!"

What are children telling us about themselves? Which actions are most im-

portant to note? Understanding children is difficult because so many factors influence their behavior. A child's development stage, culture, health, fatigue, and hunger can all make a difference in how he or she behaves. Additionally, environmental factors such as the noise level, congestion, or time of day can add to the complex character of children's actions. Therefore, the teacher must make it a point to observe children at critical moments.

For instance, an alert teacher will notice the way a child begins each morning. Sierra always clings to her blanket after her dad leaves her at school, while David says good-bye to his grandmother, then circles the room, hugging each adult before settling into an activity. Another important behavior to watch is how children use their bodies. The basic routines of eating, napping, toileting, and dressing show how they take care of themselves. How Nico works on puzzles may indicate his skills in other areas that require initiative and self-sufficiency.

Seeing children in relation to other people is a third area to notice. Teachers see whom children choose as playmates and whom they avoid. Noting that Karen plays with Bryce indicates what she looks for in friends. The observant teacher will also make note of the adults in each child's life. Who does the child seek for comfort? Finally, in selecting play materials and equipment, children show what they like to do, how well they use the environment, and what they avoid. Specific observations about the various areas of skill development—physical-motor, intellectual, affective—can be mirrors of growth. Teddy's hesitancy at the sand area shows his tendency toward the familiar rather than the challenges of something new. Observing children at play and at work can tell us how they learn and what methods they use to gain information.

Why Observe?

To Improve Your Teaching

The most effective teachers are those who are thorough in their preparation and systematic in evaluating their own work. It takes a certain level of awareness—of self, of the children, and of the environment—to monitor our own progress. Observing children helps teachers become more objective about the children in their care. When making observational notes, teachers look first at what the child is doing. This is different from looking at how a child ought to be doing something. The teacher becomes like a camera, recording what is seen without immediately judging it. This **objectivity** can balance the intense, personal side of teaching.

Bias is inherent in all our perceptions. We must acknowledge this truth without falling prey to the notion that because our efforts will be flawed, they are worthless. Observing is not a precise or wholly objective act (Figure 6–2). No two people will see something in identical ways. For instance, re-read the segment about Sierra. One teacher sees in Sierra a child demonstrating an age-appropriate response to frustration; another sees someone who is too aggressive; a third focuses on Brooke as a victim, rushing to comfort her and ignores Sierra altogether. Observing can never be totally objective because everything passes through the filter of the observer's beliefs, biases, assumptions, history, understanding, and knowledge.

Teachers are influenced in their work by their own early childhood experiences. They have notions about how children learn, play, grow, or behave because of the way they were raised and trained. Moreover, when teachers are in the thick of activity, they see only a narrow picture. To pull back, take some notes, and make an observation gives the teacher a chance to see the larger scene.

Teams of teachers help each other gain perspective on the class, an individual, a time of the day. Observations can be a means of validating one teacher's point of view. By checking out an opinion or idea through systematic observation, teachers get a sense of direction in their planning. Such an assessment implies self-assessment. A team that looks at what their program is or isn't accomplishing and how the program may be affecting children values the

Check Your Lenses!

What we see is in the eye of the beholder. What do you behold?

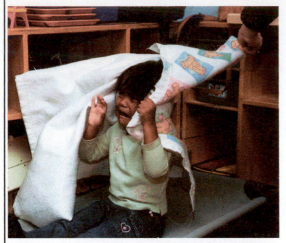

A two-year-old screams "Mine!" and fends off a boy trying to grab the blanket she's holding.

You see: "She's obviously protecting her security blanket; she is standing up for herself."

*Believing in private property.

Or: "Look at that selfish child; she disturbs the group and is unkind."

*Believing in group harmony.

A four-year-old shouts at another, "No; don't knock it down; we just built it ourselves!"

You see: "He's protecting his space; he takes pride in what he creates."

*Believing in self-expression and low frustration tolerance.

Or: "He is rude; he hurts others' feelings and is unfriendly."

*Believing in group affiliation and building community.

Kindergartners are sifting and sorting rice at a sensory table.

You see: "They are learning pre-math concepts through their senses."

*Believing children learn best by doing, by using their hands.

Or: "They are playing with food, and rice is sacred."

*Believing people must take care of food and treat it with respect.

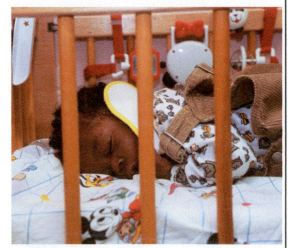

Infants sleeping in cribs in a child care center.

You see: "It is wonderful how the room is set up for quiet napping."

*Believing in children sleeping independently, on their own.

Or: "How sad that the babies are left alone like that."

*Believing in children being held, cared for always.

FIGURE 6–2 Observers watching the same scene, seeing the same behavior, think of it in very different terms. Seeing through a different pair of cultural eyes, each of us is thus affected in our reactions and assessments. (Excerpted from Gonzales-Mena, J., 2000.)

reflective process and professional level of teamwork that goes with it.

Additionally, all teachers develop ideas and impressions about children when they spend time with them. Some children seem shy, some helpful, some affectionate, aggressive, cooperative, stubborn, and so on. These opinions influence the way teachers behave and interact with children.[1]

See Figure 6–2 for some key examples.

Two guidelines come to mind as one begins to observe:

☢ *Practice intensive waiting.* Cultivate an ability to wait and see what is really happening instead of rushing to conclusions about what it means, where such behavior comes from, or what should be done.

☢ *Become part scientist.* A good observer makes a clear distinction between fact and inference, between real behavior and an impression or conclusion drawn from it. See something and wonder why. After developing hunches or intuitions about the problem, generate alternatives and then test the hypothesis. This kind of "action research" is easily adaptable to teaching.

If we teach ourselves to be available and focused on children, we engage in a kind of "slowing down" that serves both children and teacher well. "We emphasize that the most fundamental skill is observation," writes Jones and Reynolds (1992), "in which teachers ask some of these questions:

☢ What is happening for this child in this play?

☢ What is his agenda?

☢ Does he have the skills and materials he needs to accomplish his intent?

To answer these questions, adults need to practice taking the child's perspective, and careful observation of children at play enables one to do just that."

To Construct Theory

Observations are a link between theory and practice. Early childhood education is the one level of teaching that systematically bases its teaching on child development. If we are to develop programs that work for young children—what they can do, how they think and communicate, and what they feel—we need to be able to apply sound child development knowledge to the classroom. Further, we can use what researchers have learned to understand the individual children in our care. For instance, knowing Nico is a preschooler reminds his teacher that concreteness is part of preoperational thinking, so cleanup time will work best for him when he is given a specific task (how about the puzzles, because he's so good at doing them?).

To Build Curriculum

Observation also helps a teaching team record what they do in curriculum, such as the documentation process used in Reggio Emilia programs (see Chapter 2 for program description). *Emergent curriculum* describes the kind of curriculum that develops when the team explores what is interesting, meaningful, and engaging to children. In contrast to traditional planning, which tends to be teacher dominated and planned ahead of time, this kind of curriculum involves observing the children to see their interests, then building activities that evolve from the interaction of the children and adults. In one children's center, a nearby construction site brought keen interest in building activities to the classroom. The discovery center turned into a workshop, a woodworking table became a regular station outdoors, weekly field trips by small groups resulted in stories and drawings that were then put on a documentation panel for parents to see children's learning in action. Imagine the class's excitement when members of the construction crew arrived one day for snack and donated six hardhats to the dramatic play corner! Chapter 10 elaborates on this kind of curriculum model.

To Help Parents

Parents benefit from observations. A collection of notes about an individual child can be used in parent conferences. The teacher shares fresh, meaningful examples that demonstrate the child's growth and abilities and gains perspective when the notes are accumulated and discussed with parents. Problems become clearer, and plans can be made to work together between home and school. Results can be further tested through continuing observation. Authentic assessments such as child portfolios (see the section toward the end of this chapter) are an ideal tool for communication.

To Use as an Assessment Tool

Assessment is a critical part of a teacher's job, and evaluating children includes observing and assessing their behavior and their development. Authentic assessment, done when children are in their natural setting and performing real tasks, fits best with the overall goal of developmentally appropriate practice. Teachers are called on to set specific goals for the children in their classes and for the overall class performance. They document children's progress. In this way teachers are accountable to their clients: the children, the parents, and the public. Learning to assess children's skills and behavior and to document them is becoming increasingly important to the early childhood educator. Assessment techniques such as portfolios and screening are described later in this chapter.

UNDERSTANDING WHAT WE OBSERVE

The goal of observing children is to understand them better. Observational data help adults know children in several significant ways.

Children as Individuals

How do children spend their time at school? What activities are difficult? Who is the child's best friend? By watching individual children, teachers can choose activities and materials to match interests and skills. This is called **individualized curriculum:** tailoring what is taught to

Observing children closely reveals their feelings and needs.

what a child is ready and willing to learn. This kind of curriculum gives children educational experiences that offer **connected knowledge,** that is, a curriculum that is real and relevant to the individual child and is part of developmentally appropriate practices (see Chapters 1, 2, 9, and 10). It is also part of programs for children with special needs; in these cases an individualized education plan (IEP) is developed jointly by teachers, education specialists, and parents to better serve the child.

Observation of a child can be made on three levels (see Figure 6–2):

1. Report exactly what the child does: Note exactly what actions the child takes.

2. Express how the child seems to feel about what happened: Note facial expressions, body language, the quality of the behavior.

3. Include your own interpretations: Add as a last and separate step some of your own personal responses and impressions.

what do YOU think?

Meet Jody, age five.

Observations:

- He uses scissors in a "hedge clippers" fashion.

- He has an awkward grip when using a pencil.

- He finds it difficult to fit puzzle pieces together.

- He does not choose the woodworking table, manipulative table, or cooking project during free choice.

If you were his kindergarten teacher, would you be concerned about his fine motor skills? Does he need intervention?

Assessment: A check with his parents revealed two important facts: Jody had trouble handling table utensils and couldn't button his sweater. They said there was no provision at home for him to pursue any fine motor activities. The teachers used Jody's interest in airplanes to draw him into areas of the curriculum he didn't ordinarily pursue. Small airplanes were added to the block corner, and airplane stencils were placed near the art table. A large mural of an airport was hung on the fence, and children were invited to paint on it. One day children cut airplane pictures out of magazines and used them in a collage. Simple airplane puzzles were placed on the puzzle table. Felt shapes and small plastic airplanes in the water table helped draw Jody toward activities requiring fine motor skills. Jody's parents supplied him with a special art box at home, full of crayons, scissors, pens, watercolors, and stencils. As his fine motor skills increased and refined, Jody became a more confident and happier child. By the end of three months he was a regular participant in all areas of the school and seemed to be enjoying his newfound interest in art materials.

Observing helps a teacher spot a child's strengths and areas of difficulty. Once these are known, teachers plan intervention measures, helping to make the school experience successful for the child.

Children in General

When recording behavior, teachers see growth patterns emerge. Both Piaget and Erikson used observation to learn how children think and develop socially and emotionally. Gesell studied large numbers of children to get developmental **norms** of physical growth.

Observation gives a feeling for group behavior as well as a developmental yardstick to compare individuals within the group. Observing children can provide the answer to these questions:

- ✴ What might you expect when two-year-olds pour juice?

Understanding the child is the goal of observation. Noticing how a child interacts with materials enriches the teacher's knowledge of growth and behavior.

- ✴ How will the second-grade class behave on a field trip?
- ✴ What will children do when left at kindergarten the first day?
- ✴ What is the difference between the attention span at storytime of three-year-olds and fives?

Teachers then determine age-appropriate expectations for their group.

Finally, knowledge of children in general gives teachers a solid foundation on which to base decisions about individuals. For example, experienced teachers of toddlers will not put out watercolor sets, while the second-grade teacher will do so routinely. Teachers learn that it is typical of four- and five-year-olds to exclude others from their play because teachers see it happen countless times. The three-and-a-half-year-old who is sure she is "too little" to use the toilet won't concern the knowledgeable teacher, who knows that this is developmentally appropriate behavior! Decisions about *single* children come from watching and knowing *many* children. This understanding is a valuable asset when talking to parents.[1]

Developmental Relationships

Observing brings about an understanding of the various developmental areas and how they are related. Children's behavior is both a mix of several distinct developmental areas (see Chapter 4) and an integrated whole whose parts influence each other. By "the whole child" we mean a consideration of how development works in unison.

[1]Keen observers of young children come to realize that there is a wide spectrum of ways in which children develop, with numerous ways in which parents support this growth—not good ways and bad ways, but many different ways.

Observing helps teachers see how the pieces fit together. For instance, when given a set of blocks in various sizes, colors, and shapes, four-year-old Piper has no difficulty finding the red ones or square ones but is puzzled when asked to find those that are both red and square. No wonder she has difficulty understanding that Sarda can be *her* best friend and Fadwa's friend *at the same time*.

Practiced observation will show that a child's skills are multiple and varied and have only limited connection to age. Derek has the physical coordination of a four-and-a-half-year-old, the language skills of a six-year-old, and the social skills of a two-year-old—all bound up in a body that just turned three!

Influences on Behavior

Careful observation gives us insight into the influences and dynamics of behavior.

Boaz has separation anxiety when he enters his child care each morning, yet he is competent and says he likes school. Close observation reveals that his favorite areas are climbing outdoor games and the sandbox. Boaz feels least successful in the construction and creative arts areas, the primary choices indoors, where his school day begins.

Mari, on the other hand, starts the day happily but cries frequently throughout the day. Is there a pattern to her outbursts? Watch what happens to Mari when free play is over and group time begins. She falls apart readily when it is time to move outdoors to play, time to have snacks, time to nap, and so on.

The classroom arrangement and daily schedule impact children's behavior because children are highly influenced by

their environment. Boaz feels unsure of himself in those activities that are offered as he starts his day, and he shows his discomfort by crying and clinging to his dad. By adding something he enjoys, such as a sand table indoors, the teacher changes the physical environment to be more appealing and positive. Boaz's difficulties in saying goodbye disappear as he finds he can be successful and comfortable.

The cause of Mari's problem is more difficult to detect. The physical environment seems to interest and appeal to her. On closer observation, her crying and disruptive behavior appear to happen just at the point of change, regardless of the activities before or afterward. It is the time aspect of the environment that causes difficulty for her. The teacher makes a special effort to signal upcoming transitions and to involve her in bringing them about. Telling Mari, "Five more minutes until naptime" or "After you wash your hands, go to the snack table" gives her the clues she needs to anticipate the process of change. Asking her to announce cleanup time to the class lets her be in control of that transition.

Children also influence one another in powerful ways. Anyone who has worked with toddlers knows how attractive a toy becomes to a child once another has it. The second-grader who suddenly dislikes school may be feeling left out of a friendship group. Teachers need to carefully observe the social dynamics of the class as they seek to understand individual children.

Understanding of Self

Observing children can be a key to understanding ourselves. People who become skilled at seeing small but important facets of human personality increase their self-awareness. "It is difficult to be objective about yourself, but as you watch your own behavior and interactions you can learn more about how you feel and respond in various situations and realize the impact of your behavior on others (Feeney et al., 2001). For example, a teacher whose own experience of school authority was problematic may react to a program's "rules" by making frequent exceptions for children. She may not intend to undermine class guidelines, but her inconsistency results in uncooperative behavior. Becoming aware of her own action—and being introspective about its motivation—improves her teaching.

✿ RECORDING WHAT WE SEE

By practicing observing—what it takes to look, to see, to become more sensitive— teachers can learn to record children's behavior fully and vividly, capturing the unique qualities, culture, and personality of each child and the group. Although children are constantly under the teacher's eyes, so much happens so fast that critical events are lost in the daily routine of classrooms. Systematic observations aid in recording events and help teachers make sense of them. In recording what you observe, you need to learn how to look and to learn the language of recording.

✪ *Learning to look.* Although it is true that teachers rarely have the luxury of observing uninterrupted for long periods of time, they can often plan shorter segments. Practice by paying attention to the content of children's play during free periods—theirs and yours. Carry a small notebook in your pocket, and jot down who is playing together whenever you can. At the end of the day, spread out your notes and see what you learned about your group's play partners.

✪ *Language of recording.* Try your hand at jotting down some notes about the play. It is easy to get discouraged, especially if you are unaccustomed to writing, but it gets easier as you practice finding synonyms for common words. For instance, children are active creatures— how many ways do they run? They may gallop, dart, whirl, saunter, skip, hop. Or think of the various ways children talk to you: they shriek, whisper, whine, shout, demand, whimper, lisp, roar.

Be sure to record what you see in the language that comes easiest to you. Once you have mastered a descriptive vocabulary, recording important behavior will become easier (Figure 6–3).

Learning to look takes a level of awareness and willingness to do more than simply watch.

Common Elements of Observations

All types of observations used in recording children's behavior have the key ingredients of defining and describing the behaviors and repeating the observation in terms of several factors such as time, number of children, and activities. All observational systems have certain elements in common:

Focus

- ✸ What do you want to know?
- ✸ Whom/what do you want to observe?

  A child or a group, the teacher or the environment

- ✸ What aspects of behavior do you want to know about?

  Motor skills, social development, problem solving

- ✸ What is your purpose?

  Study the environment, observe the daily schedule

  Evaluate a child's skills, deal with negative behavior

  Confer with parents, assess teachers

System

- ✸ What will you do?

  Define the terms, decide how long you will record

- ✸ How will you record the information you need?

  Level of detail, units of measure

Tools

- ✸ What will you need for your observations?

  Video/audio tape recorder(s), camera, chart, pencil

Environment

- ✸ Where will you watch?

  Classroom, yard, home

- ✸ What restraints are inherent in the setting?

  Other people, interruptions

Using these building blocks of observational systems, teachers choose a method. Four major methods of observing are:

1. Narratives (baby biographies, diary descriptions, running records, specimen descriptions, anecdotal notes, logs/journals)
2. Time sampling
3. Event sampling
4. Modified child study techniques (checklists, rating scales, shadow study, experimental procedures, the clinical method)

Types of Observations

Narratives

At once the most valuable and the most difficult to compile of records, **narratives** are attempts to record nearly everything that happens. In the case of a young child, this means all that the child does, says, gestures, seems to feel, and appears to think about. Narratives maintain a running record of the excitement and tension of the interaction while remaining an accurate, objective account of the events and behavior. Observers put into words what they see, hear, and know about an event or a person (see Figure 6–3).

Narratives are the oldest and often most informative kind of report. Gesell used mothers' **baby biographies** and doctors' narratives to set basic developmental norms. They are a standard technique in anthropology and the biologic sciences, used by Pestalozzi and Darwin. Piaget watched and recorded in minute detail his own children's growth.

Running records are the most common classroom form of narrative. This means describing every action observed

The Child Alone

Unoccupied Behavior. SH slowly walks from the classroom to the outside play area, looking up each time one of the children swishes by. SH stops when reaching the table and benches and begins pulling the string on the sweatshirt. Still standing, SH looks around the yard for a minute, then wanders slowly over to the seesaw. Learning against it, SH touches the seesaw gingerly, then trails both hands over it while looking out into the yard. (*Interpretive comments:* This unoccupied behavior is probably due to two reasons: SH is overweight and has limited language skills compared with the other children. Pulling at the sweatshirt string is something to do to pass the time, since the overweight body is awkward and not especially skillful.)

Onlooker Behavior. J is standing next to the slide watching her classmates using this piece of equipment. She looks up and says, "Hi." Her eyes open wider as she watches the children go down the slide. P calls to J to join them but J shakes her head "no." (*Interpretive comments:* J is interested in the slide but is reluctant to use it. She has a concerned look on her face when the others slide down; it seems too much of a challenge for J.)

Solitary Play. L comes running onto the yard holding two paintbrushes and a bucket filled with water. He stops about three feet away from a group of children playing with cars, trucks, and buses in the sandbox and sits down. He drops the brushes into the bucket and laughs when the water splashes his face. He begins swishing the water around with the brushes and then starts wiggling his fingers in it. (*Interpretive comments:* L is very energetic and seems to thoroughly enjoy his outside playtime with water. He adds creative touches to this pleasurable experience.)

FIGURE 6–3 The narrative form of observation gives a rich sample of children's behavior; even though it risks teacher bias, it still records valuable information.

within a given time period. It might be a five-minute period during free play to watch and record what one child does. Another way to use this type of narrative is to watch an area of the yard or room, then record descriptions of the children there and how they are using the materials.

The procedure is to take on-the-spot notes each day. This task lends itself easily to most early childhood settings. The teachers carry with them a small notebook and pencil, tucked in a pocket. They jot down whatever seems important or noteworthy during the day. These anecdotal notes are the most familiar form of recording observations (Figure 6–4). They often focus on one item at a time:

 A part of the environment—how is the science area being used?

 A particular time of day—what happens right after naps?

 A specific child—how often is Lucy hitting out at other children?

These notes then become a rich source of information for report writing and parent conferences. They are also part of curriculum documentation, as children's behavior and conversations become part of

Journal entry 4-2-99

Today three children spent the entire morning wrapping and unwrapping "presents" for me. All they needed were small objects, tape, scissors, and paper. They took great delight in my surprise as I opened each present and found lovely objects. So what are these three-year-olds thinking as they work so diligently? I listened to them from a distance as they chatted: "This is the best surprise. . . . Susan won't know where we got this pretty necklace for her."

"You're not putting enough tape on that; let me tape it more."

"When we buy presents for my grandma, we find things she likes and doesn't have . . . then we give the store person a plastic card and then we go home and wrap it up for her . . . she cries when she opens presents."

"Susan didn't cry when she opened this. . . . do you think she liked it?"

"Maybe Susan doesn't like to cry at school."

They seem to be thinking about what presents mean and maybe what it means to give someone something they really want. How can I extend their play, go beyond the repetitive activity and explore something that makes them think more deeply?

FIGURE 6–4 Susan's journal entry is a way or processing what she sees happening in her classroom, a way of examining what she sees as the children's interests, and a way of reflecting on where she wants to go with the interests demonstrated. (Excerpted from Barbour, 2000.)

documentation panels alongside photos and artwork.

Diary descriptions are another form of narrative. Just as the term implies, they are, in diary form, consecutive records of everything children do and say and how they do it. In early education, this becomes a **log/journal** (see Figure 6–4). A page is set aside for each child in the class. At some point, teachers write in details about each child. Because this is time consuming and needs to be done without interruption, it helps to write immediately after the program is over. Sometimes teaching teams organize themselves to enable one member of the staff to observe and record in the journal during class time. The important point is that each child's general behavior is recorded either while it is happening or soon afterward.

The challenging part of the narrative is to be able to write enough detail so the reader will be able to picture whole situations later. Whatever notes the teachers use, however brief, need to be both clear and accurate. This includes being aware of the personal biases that can influence observation.[1]

See Figure 6–3 for an example of the narrative type of observation.

There are many advantages to this type of observation. Narratives are rich in information, provide detailed behavioral accounts, and are relatively easy to record.

[1]It is a given that we all have biases. It is not realistic to think that one can be bias free. The goal is to be conscious of the bias we bring to our work and be open to multiple interpretations of observed behavior. In this way we do not let our individual bias dictate our observations and interactions with children from diverse backgrounds.

With a minimum of equipment and training, teachers can learn to take notes on what children do and say. The main disadvantages of narratives are the time they can take, the language and the vocabulary that must be used, and the biases the recorder may have. Even though the narrative remains one of the most widely used and effective methods of observing young children today, many teachers prefer more structured procedures, such as those that follow.

Time Sampling

The **time sampling** method is an observation of what happens within a given period of time. Developed as an observational strategy in laboratory schools in the 1920s, time sampling was used to collect data on large numbers of children and to get a sense of normative behaviors for particular age groups or sexes. It has been used to record autonomy, dependency, task persistence, aggression, play patterns, and nervous habits (nail biting or hair twisting). The definitive study using time sampling is Parten's (1932) observation in the 1930s of children's play. The codes developed in this study have become classic play patterns used throughout this text and in the professional field to describe the interactions of children.

In a time sample, behavior is recorded at regular time intervals. To use this method, one needs to sample what occurs fairly frequently. It makes sense to choose those behaviors that might occur at least once every 10 minutes (Figure 6–5).

Time sampling has its own advantages and disadvantages. The process itself helps teachers define exactly what it is they want to observe and is ideal for collecting information about the group as a whole. Developing a category and coding system reduces the problem of observer bias.

Yet, diminishing this bias also eliminates some of the richness and quality of information. It is difficult to get the whole picture when one divides it into artificial time units and with only a few categories. The key is to decide what it is teachers want to know, then choose the observational method that best suits those needs. When narratives or time samplings won't suffice, perhaps an event sampling will.

Event Sampling

With the **event sampling** method, the observer defines an event, devises a system for describing and coding it, then waits for it to happen. As soon as it does, the recorder moves into action. Thus, the behavior is recorded as it occurs naturally.

Teachers can use event sampling to examine behaviors such as bossiness, avoidance of teacher requests, or withdrawal. Dawes's (1934) classic analysis of preschool children's quarrels used event sampling. Whenever a quarrel began, the observer recorded it. She recorded how long the quarrel lasted, what was happening when it started, what behaviors happened during the quarrel (including what was done and said), what the outcome was,

Video View Point 6-1

"Observing and Assessing Child Development: Organizations that promote high-quality infant and toddler programs, such as ZERO TO THREE and NAEYC, have identified goals and standards of quality that serve infants and toddlers."

Competency: Professionalism

Age Group: Infant-Toddler

Critical Thinking Questions:

1. How can child care providers become aware of their biases when observing young children?

2. Which assessment tool would you prefer to use and why?

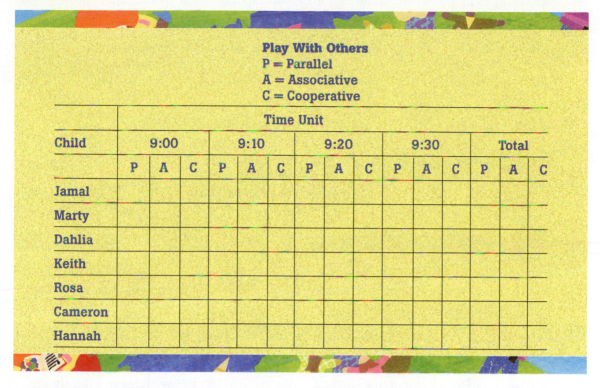

Child	9:00			9:10			9:20			9:30			Total		
	P	A	C	P	A	C	P	A	C	P	A	C	P	A	C
Jamal															
Marty															
Dahlia															
Keith															
Rosa															
Cameron															
Hannah															

Play With Others
P = Parallel
A = Associative
C = Cooperative

Time Unit

FIGURE 6–5 Time sampling of play with others involves defining the behavior and making a coding sheet to tally observations.

and what happened afterward. Her format for recording included duration (x number of seconds), a narrative for the situation, verbal or motor activity, and checklists for the quarrel behavior, outcome, and aftereffects (Irwin & Bushnell, 1980). Like time sampling, event sampling looks at particular behaviors or occurrences (Figure 6–6).

But the unit is the event rather than a prescribed time interval. Event sampling is a favorite of classroom teachers. They can go about the business of teaching children until the event occurs. Then they can record the event quickly and efficiently. Prescribing the context within which the event occurs restores some of the quality often lost in time sampling. The only disadvantage is that the richness of detail of the narrative description is missing.

Modified Child Study Techniques

Because observation is the key method of studying young children in their natural settings, it makes good sense to develop many kinds of observational methods. Each can be tailored to fit the individual child, the particular group, the kind of staff, and the specific problem. Questions arise that need fast answers, and modified child study techniques can define the scope of a problem fairly quickly. Some of the techniques are: checklist systems, rating scales, and shadow studies. Experimental procedures and the clinical technique can study both a group and the individuals in it.

Checklists contain a great deal of information that can be recorded rapidly. A carefully planned checklist can tell a lot about one child or the entire class. The data are collected in a short period of time, usually about a week. Figure 6–7 is an example of an activity checklist. Teachers thus get a broad picture of how children spend their time and what activities interest them. If they want a quicker assessment, teachers might want a yes/no list, such as Figure 6–8.

Event Sampling Guidelines

Behavior to be observed: children's accidents, spills, knock-overs, falls.

Time	Children	Place	Cause	Outcome
8:50	Shelley, Mike	play dough	M steps on S toes	S cries, runs to Tchr
9:33	Tasauna, Yuki	blocks	T runs through, knocks over Y's tower	Y hits T, both cry
9:56	Spencer	yard	S turns trike too sharply, falls off	S cries, wants mom
10:28	Lorena, Shelley	doll corner	L bumps table, spills pitcher S has just set there	S cries, runs to Tchr

Total 8:45–10:30 AM = 4

FIGURE 6–6 Event sampling can be helpful in determining how frequently a specific event takes place. For instance, sampling the number and types of accidents for a given child or time frame helps teachers see what is happening in class.

Observer _____ Date _____ Time _____

Learning Center	Anna	Charlie	Leticia	Hiroko	Max	Josie	Totals
Indoors Science Area					1		1
Dramatic Play	1	1	1			1	4
Art	1		1	1			3
Blocks		1					1
Manipulatives			1	1	1		3
Easels				1			1
Music			1		1		2
Outdoors Water/Sand/Mud		1	1			1	3
Blocks				1	1		2
Wheel Toys		1			1		2
Climbers	1		1			1	3
Woodworking				1			1
Ball Games	1						1
Animal Care	1	1				1	3
Totals	5	5	6	5	5	4	

FIGURE 6–7 An activity checklist. With data collected for a week, teachers have a broad picture of how children spend their time at school and what activities interest them.

Motor Skills Observation (ages 2–4) Child _____ Date _____ Observer _____ Age _____	Yes	No
Eating:		
1. Holds glass with one hand		
2. Pours from pitcher		
3. Spills little from spoon		
4. Selects food with pincer grasp		
Dressing:		
1. Unbuttons		
2. Puts shoes on		
3. Uses both hands together (such as holding jacket with one hand while zipping with the other)		
Fine Motor:		
1. Uses pincer grasp with pencil, brushes		
2. Draws straight line		
3. Copies circles		
4. Cuts at least 2" in line		
5. Makes designs and crude letters		
6. Builds tower of 6–9 blocks		
7. Turns pages singly		
Gross Motor:		
1. Descends/ascends steps with alternate feet		
2. Stands on one foot, unsupported		
3. Hops on two feet		
4. Catches ball, arms straight, elbows in front of body		
5. Operates tricycle		

FIGURE 6–8 A yes/no checklist gives specific information about an individual child's skills.

Checklists can vary in length and complexity depending on their function. To develop one, teachers first determine the purpose of the observation. Next they define what the children will do to demonstrate the behavior being observed. Finally comes the task of designing an actual checklist that is easy to use and simple to set aside when other duties take precedence.

Although they are easy to record, checklists lack the richness of the more descriptive narrative. By looking at the checklist in Figure 6–8, teachers will know which activities children have chosen, but they will not gain a sense of how they played in each area, the time spent there, or whether and with whom they interacted. The ad-

vantages of checklists are that they can tally broad areas of information, and teachers can create one with relative ease. Checklists are often used in **evaluation.**

Rating scales are like checklists, planned in advance to record something specific. They extend checklists by adding some quality to what is observed. They differ from checklists in that they require teachers to make refined decisions. A rating scale may use word phrases ("always," "sometimes," "never") or a numerical key (1 to 5). Figure 6–9 is an example of a rating scale. The advantage is that more information is gathered. A potential problem is added because the observer's opinions are now required and could hamper objectivity.

Never Attends (wiggles, distracts others, wanders away)

Seldom Attends (eyes wander, never follows fingerplays or songs, occasionally watches leader)

Sometimes Attends (can be seen imitating hand gestures, appears to be watching leader about half the time, watches others imitating leader)

Usually Attends (often follows leader, rarely leaves group, rarely needs redirection, occasionally volunteers, usually follows leader's gestures and imitations)

Always Attends (regularly volunteers, enthusiastically enters into each activity, eagerly imitates leader, almost always tries new songs)

FIGURE 6–9 A rating scale measuring attention at group times requires data in terms of frequency, adding depth to the observation.

The **shadow study** is a third type of modified technique. It is similar to the diary description and focuses on one child at a time. An in-depth approach, the shadow study gives a detailed picture. Each teacher attempts to observe and record the behavior of one particular child. Then after a week or so the notes are compared. Although the notes may be random, it is preferable that they have some form and organization (Figure 6–10).

The data in a shadow study are descriptive, so it shares the advantages of narratives. However, it is time consuming; another disadvantage is that teachers may let other matters go while focusing on one child. One interesting side effect often noted is how the behavior of the child being studied improves while the child is being observed. Disruptive behavior seems to diminish or appear less intense. It would appear that in the act of focusing on the child, teacher attention has somehow helped to alter the behavior. Somehow the child feels the impact of all this positive, caring attention and responds to it.

Two additional strategies are used to obtain information about a child. Because they involve some adult intervention, they do not consist strictly of observing and recording naturally occurring behavior. Still, they are very helpful techniques for teachers to understand and use.

Experimental procedures are those in which adult researchers closely control a situation and its variables. Researchers create a situation in which they can:

1. Observe a particular behavior
2. Make a hypothesis, or guess, about that behavior
3. Test the hypothesis by conducting the experiment

For instance, an experimenter might wish to observe fine motor behavior in seven-year-olds to test the hypothesis that these children can significantly improve their fine motor skills in sewing if given specific instructions. Two groups of children are tested. One group is given an embroidery hoop, thread, and needle and asked to make 10 stitches. The other receives a demonstration of how to stitch and is then given the identical task. The embroidery hoops created by both groups are then compared. Some previously agreed-on criteria are used to quantify the fine motor skill demonstrated by the two groups' work.

Few teachers working directly with children will use the stringent criteria needed to undertake a true scientific experiment. However, it is useful to understand

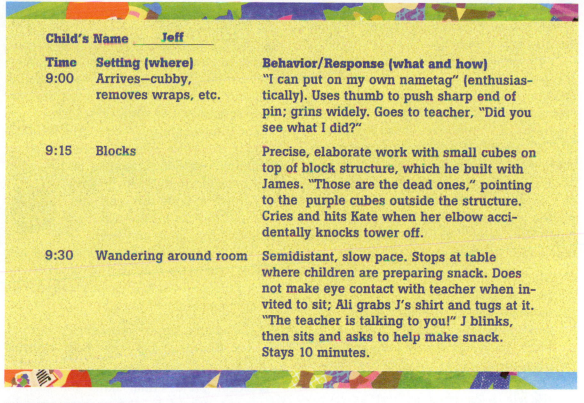

Child's Name ____Jeff____

Time	Setting (where)	Behavior/Response (what and how)
9:00	Arrives—cubby, removes wraps, etc.	"I can put on my own nametag" (enthusiastically). Uses thumb to push sharp end of pin; grins widely. Goes to teacher, "Did you see what I did?"
9:15	Blocks	Precise, elaborate work with small cubes on top of block structure, which he built with James. "Those are the dead ones," pointing to the purple cubes outside the structure. Cries and hits Kate when her elbow accidentally knocks tower off.
9:30	Wandering around room	Semidistant, slow pace. Stops at table where children are preparing snack. Does not make eye contact with teacher when invited to sit; Ali grabs J's shirt and tugs at it. "The teacher is talking to you!" J blinks, then sits and asks to help make snack. Stays 10 minutes.

FIGURE 6–10 A shadow study will profile an individual child in the class. This method is especially useful for children who seem to be having trouble in school.

this process because much basic research conducted to investigate how children think, perceive, and behave utilizes these techniques.

The *clinical* method is the final information-gathering technique that involves the adult directly with the child. This method is used in psychotherapy and in counseling settings, as the therapist asks probing questions. Piaget mastered **le methode clinique** as he observed and questioned or tried out new ideas with children. Two examples of this method are:

✪ Three-month-old Jenna is lying in a crib looking at a mobile. Her hands are waving in the air. Caregiver David wonders whether Jenna will reach out and grasp the mobile if it is moved close to her hands. Or will she bat at the toy or move her hands away? He then tries it to see what will happen.

✪ A group of preschoolers is gathered around a water table. Teacher Miho notices two cups, one deep and narrow, the other broad and shallow, and asks, "I wonder which one holds more, or if they are the same?" The children say what they think and why. Then, one of the children takes the two cups and pours the liquid from one into the other.

In these scenarios, both teachers do more than simply observe and record what happens. With the infant, David questions what Jenna's responses might be and then watches for the answer. With preschoolers, Miho intervenes in the children's natural play to explore a question systematically with them, then listens for and observes the answers. The clinical method is not strictly an observational method, but it is an informative technique that when used carefully, can reveal much about children's abilities and knowledge.

Observation and its various methods are used extensively in early childhood education programs and, increasingly, in elementary education to assess children. Figure 6–11 summarizes these systems. It is safe to say that whenever a teacher encounters a problem—be it a child's behavior, a period of the day, a set of materials, or a puzzling series of events—the first step toward a solution is systematic observation. The following is from a teacher's notebook:

> Matthew has some issues—been here only 3 weeks and I have to shadow most of the day. Today he was knocking down children's block buildings during indoor free play, turning over the chairs at the snack table, pushing William on a tricycle backwards as fast as he could. You should have seen the look of terror on W's face. I talked with his mom after class, just telling her the incidents. She gives him a chair to push around at home, so now I see where some of the pushing comes from. Not only that, she is having him tested next week for sensory processing problems with an occupational therapist. Phew!

By practicing observing—what it takes to look, to see, to become more sensitive—teachers can learn to record children's behavior fully and vividly, capturing the unique qualities, culture, and personality of each child and the group.

ASSESSMENT: EVALUATING CHILDREN

Children are evaluated because teachers and parents want to know what the children are learning. Evaluations set the tone for a child's overall educational experience. Highlighting children's strengths builds a foundation from which to address their limitations or needs. Evaluation processes can help teachers discover who children are, what they can (and cannot) do, and how we can help children grow and learn.[1]

In evaluating children, teachers first decide what it is they want to know about each child, and why. Goals for children stem from program objectives. **Assessment** must:

- Occur in a variety of settings over time, drawing on many sources of information

- Focus on essential skills and dispositions valued by the program and by families and communities

- Have teacher-designed tools and methods that demonstrate the child in action and in a familiar setting

For instance, if the school philosophy is, "Our program is designed to help children grow toward increasing physical, social, and intellectual competencies," an evaluation will measure children's progress in those three areas. One that claims to teach specific language skills will want to assess how speaking and listening are being accomplished.

Evaluations provide teachers with an opportunity to distance themselves from the daily contact with children and look at

[1]The theoretical basis of "testing" is steeped in Western methods of thought. As a result, non-Western thought can easily be misinterpreted as deficient. Hilliard and others caution all teachers to pay close attention to tests in light of cultural diversity.

Method	Observational Interval	Recording Techniques	Advantages	Disadvantages
1. Narratives				
Diary description	Day to day	Using notebook and pencil; can itemize activity or other ongoing behavior; can see growth patterns.	Rich in detail; maintains sequence of events; describes behavior as it occurs.	Open to observer bias; time-consuming.
Specimen descriptions/ running record	Continuous sequences	Same.	Less structured.	Sometimes need follow-up.
Journal	Regular, preferred daily/weekly	Log, usually with space for each child; often a summary.	Same as narratives.	Difficult to find time to do.
"On-the-hoof" anecdotes	Sporadic	Ongoing during class time; using notepad in hand.	Quick and easy to take; short-capture pertinent events/details.	Lack detail; need to be filled later; can detract from teaching responsibilities.
2. Time sampling	Short and uniform time intervals	On-the-spot as time passes; prearranged recording sheets.	Easy to record; easy to analyze; relatively bias free.	Limited behaviors; loss of detail, loss of sequence and ecology of event.
3. Event sampling	For the duration of the event	Same as for time sampling.	Easy to record; easy to analyze; can maintain flow of class activity easily.	Limited behaviors; loss of detail; must wait for behavior to occur.
4. Modifications				
Checklists	Regular or intermittent	Using prepared recording sheets; can be during or after class.	Easy to develop and use.	Lack of detail; tell little of the cause of behaviors.
Rating scales	Continuous behavior	Same as for checklists.	Easy to develop and use; can use for wide range of behaviors.	Ambiguity of terms; high observer bias.
Shadow study	Continuous behavior	Narrative-type recording; uses prepared recording sheets.	Rich in detail; focuses in depth on individual.	Bias problem; can take away too much of a teacher's time and attention.
Experimental procedures	Short and uniform	May be checklists, prearranged recording sheets, audio or video tape.	Simple, clear, pure study, relatively bias free.	Difficult, hard to isolate in the classroom.
Clinical method	Any time	Usually notebook or tape recorder.	Relevant data; can be spontaneous, easy to use.	Adult has changed naturally occurring behavior.

FIGURE 6-11 A summary chart of the major observational techniques that the early childhood professional can use to record children's behavior. (Adapted from Irwin, D. M., and Bushnell, M. M. [1980]. *Observational Strategies for Child Study*. New York: Holt, Rinehart, and Winston.)

them in a more detached, professional way. Teachers can use the results to share their opinions and concerns about children with each other and with parents. Charting individual growth sets the child apart as a unique human being.

For an evaluation to be reliable and valid, multiple sources of information should be used. Observing young children in action is the key to early childhood assessment; most of the child evaluation instruments described in this chapter are based on what children do spontaneously or in their familiar, natural settings. In general, evaluations are made to:

- ✿ Establish a baseline of information about each child

- ✿ Monitor the growth of individual children

- ✿ Have a systematic plan for intervention and guidance

- ✿ Plan the curriculum

- ✿ Provide families with updated information on their child

- ✿ Provide information for making administrative decisions

To Establish a Baseline

One purpose of evaluating children is to establish a starting point of their skills and behavior. It shows where the child is in relation to the program objectives. Baseline data give a realistic picture of a child at that moment in time, but there is a presumption that the picture will change.

A Baseline Tool

The beginning of the school term is an obvious time to start collecting information. Records of a child are established in the context of the child's history and family background. Families frequently submit this information with an application to the school. It is critical to be sensitive about how to ask for personal information and to

A baseline is a picture of a child framed at a particular moment. Children's use of materials, fine muscle control, and task persistence can all be seen in these assessments.

understand family reluctance to share details with adults they have only just met. Teachers can gather the data by visiting the child at home or holding a conference and speaking directly with the family about the child's development. Additionally, more will be revealed as trust and communication build the relationship over time.

An entry-level assessment made during the first few weeks of the program can be informative, particularly when added to the child's family history. The evaluation itself should be done informally, with teachers collecting information as children engage naturally with materials and each other. A few notes jotted during the first month of school can serve as a beginning collection of pertinent data about the child. Or the format can be more structured (Figure 6–12).

Application

Teachers use this information to understand a child and identify any concerns right away. One must remember, however, that the entry assessment is only a first impression. Avoid creating a self-fulfilling prophecy by labeling children so that they become shaped into those beginning patterns. Still, so much happens in the beginning that rich information is gained from documenting this short period of time.

Goals and Plans

Teachers use baseline data to set realistic goals for individual children. They tailor the curriculum to the needs and interests they have observed. For instance, after setting a baseline of Mariko's language ability in English, teachers plan activities to increase her understanding and use of language. Then, they make periodic checks on her increased vocabulary as the school year progresses.

To Monitor Children's Progress

Teachers use evaluations to document children's growth. Data collected provide evidence of children's growth or lack of progress.

Hita has mastered the brushes at the easel. Now we can encourage

her to try the smaller brushes in table painting.

Enrico has been asking how to spell simple words. Let's see that he gets some time away from the blocks to work at the writing center.

All the children seem able to separate from their parents and say good-bye comfortably. How can we celebrate this progress with the group?

A Progress Tool

Figure 6–13 is a sample midyear evaluation. Criteria for each area of development are included to build a profile of the whole child. Teachers note the intervention and guidance steps they plan, where appropriate. Although a general form is outlined here, early childhood education teachers individualize their assessments to specify the skills of their group; an infant and toddler group would have different age-appropriate skills than would a preschool or primary-age class. Such a revised form should include what the child will do to show a suitable level of behavior in each developmental stage.

Application

Information about a child will be used to assess growth and change. How often this happens can vary. Although many changes occur in rapid succession in these early years, it takes time for a child to integrate life experiences and for teachers to see them expressed as a permanent part of behavior. Evaluating too frequently does not reveal sufficient change to make it worthwhile and places an added burden on the teaching staff as well. For centers operating on a year-round basis, an assessment should be done every six months. In programs with a shorter calendar, this would mean establishing a baseline in the fall and checking progress in the winter and/or spring. These need not be time consuming.

Entry-Level Assessment

1. Child's name _____ Teacher _____
   Age _____ Sex _____
   Primary language _____ Fluency in English? _____
   Any previous school experiences? _____
   Siblings/others in household _____
   Family situation (one/two parents, other adults, etc.) _____

2. Separation from parent:
   Smooth ___ Some anxiety ___ Mild difficulty ___ Unable to separate ___
   Did parent have trouble separating? _____
   Comments: _____

3. How does child come to and leave from school?
   Parent _____ Car pool _____ Babysitter _____ Bus _____

4. Physical appearance:
   General health_____
   Expression _____
   Nonrestrictive clothing _____
   Body posture _____

5. Self-care:
   Dressing: Alone _____ Needs assistance _____
   Toileting: By self _____ Needs help _____
   Eating:_____
   Toothbrushing: _____
   Sleeping/resting: _____
   Allergies/other health-related problems: _____

6. Child's Interests:
   Indoors:
   Clay _____ Books _____ Puzzles _____ Water play _____ Easels _____
   Language _____ Table/rug toys _____ Sensory choices _____ Art _____
   Science _____ Blocks _____
   Outdoors:
   Swings _____ Climbers _____ Sandbox _____ Water play _____
   Wheel toys _____ Animals _____ Group games _____ Woodworking _____
   Group times (level of participation):

7. Social-emotional development:
   a. Initiates activities _____ Plays alone _____ Seems happy _____
      Has to be invited _____ Brings security object _____ Seems tense _____
   b. Plays mostly with children of: Same age _____ Younger _____ Older _____
   c. Moves into environment: Easily _____ Hesitantly _____ Not at all _____
      Wanders _____
   d. Special friends: _____
   e. Does the child follow teachers? _____ Anyone in particular? _____

8. Cognitive development:
   Use of language: Follows directions _____ Clear pronunciation _____
   Memory _____ Curiosity _____ Holds conversations _____
   Words/Phrases _____

9. Physical development
   Climbs safely _____ Uses scissors _____ Hand preference _____
   Runs smoothly _____ Uses pens, brushes _____ Foot preference _____
   Handles body well _____

10. Goals/Points to remember: _____
    _____
    _____

FIGURE 6–12 Entry-level assessments collect baseline information. Once teachers and children have had some time together, these first impressions can be documented.

A Tool For Monitoring Children's Progress

Check one of the evaluations below for each skill area; for those that need work, document with specific examples.

Developmental Area	Age Appropriate	Highly Skilled	Needs Work
Self-Management	✔		
Personal care	Can feed, dress, toilet self well		
Making choices	Prefers indoors to outside		
Following routines	Does fine in routines		
Physical/Motor	✔		
1. Fine Motor	Uses easels—brushes good grasp, pens also		
Art materials	Likes blocks, table toys		
Woodworking tools	Hasn't chosen woodworking, but watches often		
Manipulatives			
2. Gross Motor	Very cautious, seems fearful		✔
Ball handling	Won't swing, slide, use climber		
Balancing	Wanders outdoors, sometimes does music		
Jump/hop/skip	Runs away when wheel toys are rolled down hill		
Communication and Language		✔	
Vocabulary	Exceptionally strong		
Articulation	Converses with adults daily		
Comprehension	Responds to children but rarely initiates talk		
English as a second language	Outstanding at group time—lots of ideas		
Converses with children	Talks around fears, but fears seem to keep him from tying		
Converse with adults			
Listens			
Expresses self (needs, ideas, feelings)			
Cognitive Development		✔	✔
Sees cause and effect			
Processes and uses information			
Solves problems with:	Dylan has so much information to share, and lots of		
objects	interest in problem-solving with indoor materials		
peers	and interactions with teachers.		
adults	We wish he could extend these skills into work with		
Premath (sequencing,	children and open up at a bit more.		
measuring, numbers)			
Prereading concepts (size, colors, shapes, letters, position)			
Social-Emotional	✔		
Independence/initiative			
Positive self-concept	Does well on own, gets around		
Recognizes/accepts own feelings	Is comfortable and confident		✔
Deals with frustration	around adults	Seems hesitant/fearful	
Flexibility		outdoors	
Leadership		Is more solitary or on-	
Initiates social contracts		looker; is this self-esteem	
Prosocial behaviors (friendly, sharing, inclusive, cooperative, empathic		or just fear?	
Child–child interactions		Don't know about	
Child–adult interactions		leadership yet;	
		have seen little	
		because of lack	
		of interaction with chil-	
		dren	

OVERALL STRENGTHS: GOALS

FIGURE 6–13 A midyear evaluation is a more detailed description of the child. It highlights areas of concern and progress.

Many evaluations take the form of a checklist and can be accomplished while the class is in session.

Goals and Plans

Goals are established for children as a result of an assessment. These goals are changed as growth takes place. A good assessment tool monitors progress in each developmental area so that plans can be made to challenge the child physically, socially, emotionally, creatively, and intellectually. At the same time, theory reminds us that the child develops as a whole, with each area of growth influencing and being influenced by what changes take place in other areas. Look for the child's collective abilities, as in this example:

Dylan's midyear report shows that he lacks dexterity in running and climbing and that he is exceptionally strong in verbal and listening skills. This influences his development in the following areas:

Emotionally. He appears to lack self-confidence, and his self-esteem deteriorates the longer he feels inept at physical skills. He may even be afraid to master the art of climbing and running for fear he will fail.

Socially. Children tease Dylan because he often cannot keep up with them while playing outside. He often ends up playing alone or watching the other children in more active pursuits.

Intellectually. There is a lack of risk taking in Dylan's whole approach to play. Because of his slow physical development, he seems unlikely to challenge himself in other ways.

Dylan's progress report thus sets a primary goal in physical/motor skills, with the knowledge that such growth can positively affect learning in other areas. Teachers also plan the strategy of helping him talk about what he likes and dislikes about the outdoors and collecting some stories that depict characters persisting to master difficulties (such as *The Little Engine That Could*), using his strength as a springboard for growth.

To Plan for Guidance and Intervention

A third purpose for evaluation is to help teachers determine guidance procedures. When teachers see a problem behavior or

While interacting with children, teachers make careful observations.

are concerned about a child, they plan for further assessment (see Chapter 7). If a developmental screening is done to assess if a child has a learning problem or needs special services, teachers will either refer the family to a proper specialist or agency or administer the screening themselves. Developmental screening tests will be discussed further in this chapter.

A Guidance Tool

Evaluations help in behavior management (see Figure 6–10). Once a need has been pinpointed, the teaching staff decides how to proceed. Individual problems are highlighted when teachers make a point of concentrating on the child's behavior. Used at a team meeting, such a tool can outline the steps to be taken and clarify how to talk to families.

Application

The following case study demonstrates how information from evaluations can be used for guidance and intervention:

> Elizabeth's recent evaluation revealed an increase in the number of toilet accidents she has had. The staff noted a higher incidence during midmorning snacks but came to no conclusion as to the cause. They agreed to continue to treat her behavior in a relaxed manner and have one teacher remind Elizabeth to use the toilet before she washes her hands for snack. At the same time, they made plans to contact the parents for further information and insights. They will confer again afterward and agree on an approach.

Goals and Plans

An evaluation tool helps teachers set goals for children and for adults. Narrowing the focus to include only those behaviors that

concern the staff enables the staff to quickly review the needs of many children.

To Plan Curriculum

Teachers plan the curriculum on the basis of children's evaluations. Translating the assessment to actual classroom practice is an important part of the teacher's role. A thorough evaluation helps teachers plan appropriate activities to meet children's needs.

Planning Tools

All three of the previous evaluation tools can be used to plan curriculum. The entry-level assessment and midyear report are often summarized in a group chart, as in Figure 6–14.

One such chart, made at the end of the first semester of a prekindergarten class, revealed this pattern:

> At least one third of the class was having trouble listening at circle time, as evidenced by the group chart that identified "Group Time" and "Language Listening Skills" as areas for growth for nearly half the children. The staff centered their attention on the group time content. It was concluded that a story made the group times too long; the children were restless throughout most of the reading. It was agreed to move storytime to just before nap and shorten the group time temporarily.

Application

Evaluation results assist teachers in seeing more clearly the strengths and abilities of each child in the class. Curriculum activities are then planned that will continue to enhance the growth of that child. Also, areas of difficulty will be identified. For instance, Jolene has trouble mastering even the simplest puzzle. Provide her with common

Summary of Development/Fall Progress Reports (see forms for details)
Developmental Area: + = fine; - = needs work; ? = don't know

Child	Physical	Language	Cognitive	Social	Emotional	Creative
Greg	-	+	+	+	-	?
Anwar	?	-	+	-	-	+
San-Joo	+	?	?	-	+	+
Reva	+	+	+	+	+	+
Katy	-	+	?	?	?	-

Group Goals for Winter:
• Emphasize social and emotional areas of curriculum.
• Plan physical games (indoor games because of weather).

Individual Goals for Winter:
  Greg: Encourage some creative arts, games. Observe creativity in intellectual activities.
  Anwar: Needs to be helped to feel confident and express himself; don't push too hard on physical risks yet.
  San-Joo: Need assessment of language and cognitive skills; observe use of table toys, receptive language at group time.
  Reva: What is the next step? Is she ready for helping the others? Involve her with 100-piece puzzles and the computer.
  Katy: Need to focus on her overall development; too many unknowns—is she getting enough individual attention?

FIGURE 6–14 A group chart. Teachers can use individual assessment tools to plan for the entire group and for each child in the class.

shapes found in attribute blocks (small plastic shapes of varying color, thickness, size) and do some matching exercises with her.

Goals and Plans

By analyzing both group and individual skills through periodic assessment, teachers maintain a secure and challenging environment. Chapters 10 and 11 expand curriculum planning.

To Communicate with Families

Once a child's needs and capabilities are identified, families are entitled to hear the conclusions. The teaching staff has an obligation to provide a realistic overview of the child's progress and alert families to any pos-sible concerns. See Chapter 8 for details about families and teachers working together.

A Tool with Families

Teachers and families need to talk together, especially when problems are revealed by the evaluation. As knowledge and insights are shared, a fuller picture of the child emerges for both. Each can then assume a role in the resolution of the problem. Evaluation tools can help identify areas in which a child may need special help.

Application

Aside from identifying normal behavior problems, evaluations may raise questions concerning a child's physical development, hearing and visual acuity, or language facility. Potentially serious problems may emerge from the evaluation, and parents can be encouraged to seek further professional guidance.

Goals and Plans

Because evaluation is an ongoing process, reevaluation and goal setting are done regularly. Communicating both progress and new goals is critical for the feedback loop of an evaluation to be effective.

To Make Administrative Decisions

Evaluation results can help a school make administrative decisions. They can lead to changes in the overall program or in the school's philosophy. For example, a child care component might be added to the half-day program after learning that most children are enrolled in another child care situation after nursery school. Or an evaluation might reveal that there is too little emphasis on developing gross-motor skills and coordination, so the administration might decide to remodel the play yard and purchase new equipment.

In the early childhood education setting, both informal and formal methods are used for evaluating children. Informal and homemade methods include observation, note taking, self-assessments, parent interviews and surveys, samples of children's work, and teacher-designed forms. More formal kinds of evaluations may be used, although somewhat less frequently in the early years. These include standardized tests and various "screening" instruments. The yearly tests taken in elementary and secondary school, using a number 2 pencil, are an example of such procedures. Commercially developed, these tests usually compare the individual child's performance with a predetermined norm. There are problems associated with testing and screening of young children (see the section Testing and Screening later in this chapter). It is important to choose assessment tools and techniques that are developmentally appropriate—either for the age of the group or the individual child under consideration.

An Administrative Tool

Many kindergartens and some preschools use various kinds of screening tests before

Parents are excited when presented with in-depth reflections of their child's history and learning.

children begin.[1] These, too, present problems for young children, as they are too often administered to them by strangers and in unfamiliar settings, and the test results are the only criteria used. The usual purpose of these evaluations is to determine readiness, that is, to verify that the child will be able to cope with and succeed in the program. Any tool in an early childhood education program is best when devised to highlight the skills the child has and to identify the areas in which the child may need help in the next step.

Some teachers conclude the year with a summary report. This evaluation serves as an overview of what a child has accomplished, what areas of strength are present, and what future growth might occur. Figure 6–15 shows a homemade summary skills inventory given to the children who were leaving preschool for kindergarten. The activity uses a one-to-one, game-like approach in which a child and a favorite teacher play together in the children's current program.

Application

Making administrative decisions based on evaluation results is a sound idea. Assessments give administrators specific and verifiable information on which to base decisions. A summary of their child's learning experiences is useful for families. Teachers may use such summaries as references should they ever be consulted by another program about the child. Again, it is critical to administer these assessments in a sensitive and accepting manner, to keep the time period as brief as possible, and to communicate the results in the same tone. If this is not done, the child's self-esteem may be damaged and the parents' trust may be lost. The disadvantages of these tools parallel those of standardized tests.

The issue of readiness or placement of children is difficult and complex. The next section describes the potential problems and misapplications of tests in this regard. Whether or not a child is ready to succeed in a program affects families and children personally. Having a good evaluation tool helps in making such decisions equitably and in communicating results in a clear and kind manner.

Goals and Plans

The evaluation tool that gives a specific profile of a child's skills will allow an administrator to share information with a family clearly and honestly. By carefully choosing a tool, administrators give the parents information they can use to plan for the child's development.

Concerns

Assessment is challenging! Of all the functions performed by teachers, probably none calls for more energy, time, and skill than evaluation. Anyone involved in evaluation should avoid:

- *Unfair comparisons.* Evaluations should be used to identify and understand the child involved, not to compare one with another in a competitive manner.

- *Bias.* Evaluations can label unfairly or prematurely the children they are intended to help. Typecasting will not produce a useful assessment. Insufficient data and overemphasis on evaluation-

[1]It must be noted that screening tests can be biased, and their validity especially comes into question if they are developed locally. Additionally, teachers must know whether the purpose of the test is to check for handicapping conditions or to know children's skills; in addition, it might run the risk of simply excluding children.

Skills Inventory

Child _____   Age _____

Teacher _____

Date _____

Task   **Teacher Comments**

Cognitive Skills

1. Can you say the alphabet?

2. Can you tell me what these letters are?

3. Can you count for me?

4. Please point to the number.

5. Can you put these in order from smallest to biggest? Which is the largest? Smallest? First? Last?

6. What color is this? If child cannot name the color, then ask to "point to the red one," etc.

7. What shapes are these? If child cannot name the shape, then ask to "point to the circle," etc.

8. Can you find your shoulders? Elbow? Thumb? Neck? Lips?

9. Name all the animals you can think of.

10. Please put these animals into two groups. One has the animals that live in water, and the other the ones that live on the land.

11. Here are a bear and a cube. Put the cube on top of the bear. Under the bear. Behind the bear. Beside the bear.

12. Here are three pictures. Can you put them in order so that they tell a story?

1. Sequence correct? Yes ___ No ___ Length:

2. Number of letters correct ___ Comment:

3. Note how far: Sequence correct how far? ___

4. 3-1-6-4-8-2-9-7-5 How many correct? ___

5. Three sizes of triangles. Comments:

6. Point to red, blue, yellow, black, green, orange, brown, purple. Comments:

7. Point to circle, square, triangle, rectangle. Comments?

8. Comments:

9. Comments:

10. Giraffe, deer, cat, frog, alligator, shark, goldfish

11. Check correct responses:

12. Tree with green leaves. Tree with orange or red leaves, falling. Bare tree. Comments:

FIGURE 6-15 By creating effective tools for assessment, we are able to evaluate children's developing skills and their readiness for the next educational step.

Continued

Auditory-Perceptual Listening Skills

1. Please repeat these numbers after I say them (Practice with 6-3-1-4):
   5-3-8-2
   2-7-9-3

   1. Sequence correct? Numbers correct?

2. Tell me the sentence in the same order as I say. (Practice with "The dog ran to the park.")
   The mother pointed to the airplane in the sky.

   2. Sequence correct? Words correct?

3. Listen to what I say, and then do what my words tell you. (Practice with "Put your hands on your head.")
   Stand up, go to the door, and walk back to me.

   3. Comments:

Fine-Motor Skills

1. Print your name.

   1. Note grasp, hand preference.

2. Draw a circle, square, triangle, rectangle.

   2. Comments:

3. Write the letters:
   O E P A J

   3. Comments:

4. Write the numbers:
   1 3 7 2 5

   4. Comments:

5. Cut out a circle.

   5. Note scissor grasp, hand preference.

6. Draw the best person that you can. Have you left anything out?

   6. Comments:

Gross-Motor Skills

1. Jump on two feet from A to B.

   1. Note balance.

2. Hop on one foot from B to A.

   2. Note balance.

3. Skip from A to B.

   3. Comments:

4. Walk backward from B to A.

   4. Comments:

5. Stand on one foot while I count to three.

   5. Note balance.

6. Walk across this balance board.

   6. Note balance.

7. Can you jump over these poles with your feet together?

   7. Comments

8. How high can you climb our climber? Go up our slide?

   8. Comments:

9. Now run from the climber to the fence and back to me as fast as you can!

   9. Note gait and balance.

10. Please throw the ball to me. Catch it. Kick it.

    10. Comments:

FIGURE 6–15, continued

tool results are two areas that need close monitoring. Evaluation tools should be free of language or other cultural bias (see Appendix C).[1] For instance, an evaluation of children should not include experiences unfamiliar to the cultural group being assessed.

✵ *Overemphasis on norms.* Most evaluation tools imply some level of normal behavior or performance, acceptable levels of interaction, or quantities of materials and space. People involved in an evaluation must remember to individualize the process rather than try to fit a child into the mold created by the assessment tool.

✵ *Interpretation.* Evaluations evoke a tendency to over-interpret or misinterpret results. It must be clear what is being evaluated and how the information will be used. It is particularly important to be sensitive to the feelings of those being evaluated when communicating the results of the assessment (see Appendix B for the NAEYC Code of Ethics).

✵ *Too narrow a perspective.* An evaluation tool may focus too much on one area and not enough on others. No single occasion or instrument will tell teachers all they need to know about a child's abilities. It is essential that information be gathered in many ways and on several occasions. An imbalanced assessment gives an incomplete picture.

✵ *Too wide a range.* An evaluation should be designed for a single level or age group and not cover too wide a range. It is appropriate to measure a child's ability to print at age six but not at age two. What is expected of the person or task should be taken into account.

✵ *Too little or too much time.* The amount of time necessary to complete an evaluation must be weighed. The evaluation that is too lengthy loses its

Evaluations should avoid unfair comparisons of children, acknowledging individual differences and uniqueness.

[1] As we become aware of those we teach, we must adjust our evaluation systems to avoid bias and to reflect reality accurately.

effectiveness in the time it takes. Time for interpretation and reflection must be included in the overall process.

✦ *"Teaching to the test."* Too much attention on an evaluation can change what happens in the program: Teachers may shape their instruction to match a test's specific focus. "This phenomenon, known as 'measurement-driven instruction,' [creates] a narrowing of the curriculum" (Meisels, 1997).

✹ AUTHENTIC ASSESSMENT: THE PORTFOLIO

The 2001 *Oxford American Dictionary* defines *authentic* as "of undisputed origin, genuine . . . made or done in a way that faithfully resembles an original." For a child assessment to be authentic, it must try to capture who the child is and what that child knows (or doesn't know) and can (or cannot) do.

Many early childhood educators have embraced the idea that a **portfolio** of children's work samples is an excellent way to document children's learning and faithfully capture their development. In light of the concerns you have read in this chapter about the misassessment of young children and the "test mania" that standardized tests in the primary grades have fomented (see the section Testing and Screening in this chapter), many professionals have looked for alternative assessment measures. The "project approach" described in Chapter 10 and the Reggio Emilia program model detailed in Chapter 2 both ascribe to a work-sampling system for assessing children.

Teachers must decide what type of portfolio will give them the information they need. Danielson and Abrutyn (1997) identify three types of portfolios:

1. Display portfolios—scrapbooks that collect items without teacher comments
2. Showcase portfolios—the best pieces of the child's work
3. Working portfolios—include selections of typical work along with teacher documentation to show the child's progress

Collection Plan

Because simple collection of work is not enough, do not try to collect everything. Look for work samples that demonstrate your educational objectives and a child's progress over time on a goal. Be organized when storing work samples—ideas include pocket folders or even pizza boxes.

Make collection a natural extension of your day and what you do with children. Some teachers keep clipboards at activity areas; others use self-sticking notes and cameras at the ready. See Figure 6–16 for an outstanding educator's suggestions about portfolios.

Implementation

Plan your implementation so that you can collect children's work with purpose. Collect pieces of each child's work regularly—some suggest three times a year for documented work in each developmental area. Each child's individual portfolio may have work samples that are completely different from others in the program, but every portfolio will still show growth over time in every developmental area.

Teacher's Evaluation

Finally, teachers add their written comments to the work samples. Teacher commentary becomes a critical source of

Corner #1
Items to include:
- Art samples
- Cutting samples
- Dictated stories
- Invented writing
- Photographs of constructions
- Written samples of children's language and conversations
- Emergent play activities
- Social interactions with peers and adults
- Photographs of children using motor and self-help skills

Corner #2
Use self-sticking notes as a convenient, quick way to capture revealing moments. These notes are easily transferred to individual portfolios. Photographs can also supplement written documentation.

Corner #3
At first, it may look like a scrapbook of professional documentation. Do not despair; teachers who have limited experience in observation and assessment practices can begin with simplicity and convenience. These samples add to the total picture of a child's growth and should not be discredited. All samples and records need names of those involved, time, and date. As you become more proficient, your observation skills become more specific and the samples you choose will not be just the best work of children but those that are indicative of their developmental process.

Corner #4
Use a folding document with separate sections for each developmental domain. Each labeled section has a cascading file of several pages and on each are examples of developmental landmarks or unique attributes of the child. The most historical work is on the bottom page, with each overlap showing the child's progressive development. Then, on the top of each file is a developmental checklist or a summary of growth.

FIGURE 6–16 The portfolio can be an excellent visual "unfolding" of the child, presenting amazing images of each child as a competent learner who actively constructs knowledge within a social and cultural context. (Courtesy of Wiggins-Dowler, 2004.)

information to tell how the child did the samples, what they mean, and how they show growth or lack of it. The commentary enhances the work sample by explaining the process of learning that is going on. A picture may be worth a thousand words, but for assessment purposes, the words are essential, not just the artwork!

Portfolios can provide a "history of learning, a structured record of learner accomplishment . . . as well as a method for assessing progress" (Fenwick & Parsons, 2000). While they take considerable planning—in their organization, storage, and selection of what to collect to show educational goals—they help you collect children's work intentionally. You can evaluate children on their work and play, as they are spontaneously, rather than with standardized tests or unnecessary screening.

Testing and Screening

The practice of testing and screening for readiness and retention has increased dramatically in the last two decades. With the passage of Public Law 94–142 (the Education for All Handicapped Children Act) and the early childhood education amendment to the law (PL 99–457), states now have the responsibility to establish specific procedures and policies to identify, evaluate, and provide services to all children with learning problems. Moreover, testing for admittance to kindergarten or promotion to first grade has become more common. The results are that more children are being denied entrance to a school system, being put into extra-year or pull-out programs or placed in kindergarten twice.

Ironically, standardized tests fail to reflect adequately what children learn. Children know so much more than they are taught, and what is tested may not be the important learning that the children have done. "Over the past several decades the assumptions underlying the current testing edifice have been challenged by develop-

mental, cognitive, and educational studies. There's a considerable body of scientific findings telling us that if we want to understand people's competence or knowledge about something, we should not examine them in an artificial way in an artificial setting" (Gardner, 1988). Moreover, most formal testing engages only two (linguistic and logical mathematical) of the eight intelligences Gardner has identified.

Testing raises both practical and serious philosophical issues, such as the following:

- Young children do not function well in common test situations, nor do the test results necessarily reflect children's true knowledge or skills.

- These practices (often based on inappropriate uses of readiness or screening tests) disregard the potential, documented long-term negative effects of retention on children's self-esteem and the fact that such practices disproportionately affect low-income and minority children (NAEYC, 1988).

- Although the most needed and appropriate tests (teacher-made) are the hardest to create, the standardized ones are frequently misused and misunderstood by teachers and parents (Meisels, 1997).

- Teachers are pressured into running programs that overemphasize the testing situation and test items (Kamii, 1990).

- Most tests focus on cognitive and language skills; such a narrow focus ignores other areas of development.

The practice of standardized testing has caused early childhood education curricula to become increasingly academic. Early childhood educators and parents are alarmed that many kindergartens are now structured and are "watered-down" first grades, emphasizing workbooks and other paper-and-pencil activities that are inappropriate for five-year-olds. The trend further trickles down to preschool and child care programs that feel that their mission is to get children "ready" for kindergarten. Too many school systems, expecting children to conform to an inappropriate curriculum and finding large numbers of "unready" children, react to the problem by raising the entrance age for kindergarten and/or labeling the children as failures.

Teachers and schools can respond to the overuse and inappropriate use of tests. The National Association of Elementary School Principals urges limited use of formal tests and retention. The Texas Board of Education has barred retention before first grade, and in the state of New York a coalition of groups is urging a ban on mass standardized testing of children before grade three.

Does testing have appropriate uses in the early years? Some claim that there are valid screening tests to identify children who, because of the risk of possible learning problems or a handicapping condition, may need more intervention or accommodation. NAEYC has adopted specific guidelines for the use of standardized testing that include using only reliable and valid instruments and interpreting the test results accurately and cautiously to parents and others (NAEYC, 1991; Bredekamp & Rosegrant, 1995).

Perhaps most important is the reminder to all teachers that tests have no special magic. Testing is not a very effective way of evaluating ANY child; but assessment is.

Assessment is not testing; it is so much more than that. The nonstandardized instruments in this chapter can be used to plan programs that respond to the individual children in them, not to categorize or exclude. A standardized test, a homemade tool, or a screening instrument should be only one of several measures used to determine a child's skills, abilities, or readiness. Any result should be part of a multitude of information, such as direct observation, parental report, and children's actual work. Above all, remember this: "Don't pull up the plants to look at them before the roots take hold" (Cryan, 1986).

Video View Point 6-2

"Intelligence: Understanding the concept of intelligence is integral to the school-age child's cognitive development, as much of what the child learns in school is marked by tests that evaluate the child's intelligence."

Competency: Cognitive Development

Age Group: School Age

Critical Thinking Questions:

1. How do traditional intelligence measures contrast with a multiple intelligences notion?

2. What do you think is an appropriate use of testing for school-age children?

❀ HOW TO OBSERVE AND RECORD

"The process of assessment is second nature for those teachers who view children in a holistic manner" (Barbour, 2000), and it includes observation at many levels. Learning how to observe is a serious activity and requires a great deal of concentration. Some preparations can be made beforehand so that full attention is focused on the observation. Thinking through some of the possible problems helps the teacher get the most out of the experience.

Observing While Teaching

To make observing workable in a program, keep in mind that there are many ways to observe and record. Certain times of the day may be easier than others. Many prefer to watch during free play, whereas others find it easier to watch individual children during directed teaching times. Although some teachers keep a pencil and paper handy to write their observations throughout the day, others choose to record what they see after the program is over for the day. The professional team that is committed to observation will find ways to support its implementation.

Finding an opportunity for regular observations is difficult. Centers are rarely staffed so well that one teacher can be free from classroom responsibilities for long periods of time. Some ask for a parent to supervise an activity while a teacher conducts an assessment. In one center the snack was set up ahead of time so a teacher could observe during group time. In another, two teachers teamed up outdoors, one supervising an obstacle course while the other documented the children's skills. Activities that require little supervision allow for more time for observing.

When children know they are being observed, they may feel self-conscious initially, asking pointed questions of the observer and changing their behavior as if they were on stage. Yet when observation is done regularly by familiar adults, children will soon ignore the observer and resume normal activity. Observation helps keep most of the attention child-centered rather than teacher-directed and increases children's and adult's communication. When a teacher begins to write, some of the children will pay immediate attention.

"What are you writing about?" asks four-year-old Nina as I sit down at the edge of the block area. "I'm writing about children playing," I explain. "You're writing about what I'm doing?" Nina asks. "Yes, I am." She's pleased. She goes back to building a careful enclosure with the long blocks (Jones & Carter, 1991).

Teachers can improve their assessment skills outside the classroom as well. Taking an "Observation of Children" class is helpful; so is visiting other programs in pairs and comparing notes afterward. Staff meetings take on added dimension when teachers role-play what they think they've seen and others ask for details.

The teacher who makes notes during class time has other considerations. Be ready to set aside your recording when necessary. Wear clothing with at least one good pocket. This ensures that paper and pencil are available when needed and the children's privacy is protected. Take care not to leave notes out on tables, shelves, or in cupboards for others to see. They should be kept confidential until added to the children's records. Some teachers find the "low-tech" materials of pen, small notebook, or self-sticking notes easiest. Others like a camera, tape recorder, and even a video camcorder, although the expense, storage, and distracting nature of such equipment need to be considered. Regardless of what teachers use, they must organize themselves for success in the following ways:

✸ Gather and prepare the materials ahead of time: This may mean getting everyone aprons with large pockets or a set of cards or labeled spiral notebook.

✸ Consider where you will observe: Set up observation places (chairs, stations); in a well-equipped yard and room, you can plan strategically.

✸ Plan when you will observe: In a well-planned day, teachers can have the freedom to practice observing regularly during play time.

✸ Prepare every adult to be an observer: Give every teacher some regular opportunities to observe and reflect on children's play.

Respect the privacy of the children and their families at all times. Any information gathered as part of an observation is treated with strict confidentiality. Teachers and students are careful not to use children's names in casual conversation. They do not talk about children in front of other children or among themselves. It is the role of the adults to see that children's privacy is maintained. Carrying tales out of school is tempting, but unprofessional.

Beginning to Observe

In some programs, observers are a normal part of the school routine. In colleges where there are laboratory facilities on campus, visitors and student observers are familiar figures. At parent cooperatives, children are used to many adults in their room. It becomes easy to follow established guidelines for making an observation (Figure 6–17).

Many times students are responsible for finding their own places to observe children. If so, the student calls ahead and schedules a time to observe that is convenient, specifying observation needs, the assignment, the ages of children desired, the

---

Guidelines for All Observers and Visitors

1. Please sign in with the front office and obtain a Visitor's badge. **Your badge must be worn and visible at all times while at the center.**

2. Inform the front office when you have completed your visit.

3. **Be unobtrusive.** Please find a spot that doesn't infringe on the children's space.

4. If you are with a small group or another person, **do not observe together;** consciously separate and space yourselves. Do not talk to other visitors during observation, please.

5. Respond to the children, but **please do not initiate conversations with them.**

6. **If a child seems upset that you are near him/her please, remove yourself from the area.** If you receive direct requests from a child to leave, please respond that you realize that he said you are in **HIS** space and will move.

7. **Please do not interfere with the teaching/learning process** during your observation. Save your questions for the end of your observation. Either ask when you check out in the front office or leave a note in the teacher's mailbox requesting a time to meet. Please understand that we welcome questions but cannot interrupt the program to answer them immediately.

8. **Walk around the periphery of the outdoor area or classrooms rather than through them.**

9. **When possible, do not stand. Please do not hover over children.** Sit, squat, or bend down at the knees so you are at the children's level.

10. **Taking photographs is not permitted.** In special cases, permission for photographs may be given by the Dean of Child Development and Education.

Thank you for your help and consideration in making your visit to the center a pleasant one for everyone involved.

FIGURE 6–17 Establishing guidelines for observers and visitors helps remind us of the importance of teaching as watching, not just telling. (Courtesy of K. Burson of De Anza College Child Development Center.)

amount of time needed, and the purpose of the observation.

If you are planning to observe in your own class, several steps are necessary for a professional observation and a believable recording:

- ✤ *Plan the observation.* Have a specific goal in mind, and even put that at the top of your recording sheet. Goals can be general ("Let's see what activities Ajit chooses today") or specific ("Watch for instances of quarreling in the sand area").

- ✤ *Observe and record.* Be as specific and detailed as possible. Write only the behavior—the "raw data"—and save the analysis and your interpretation for later.

- ✤ *Re-read your notes and make some conclusions* (transcribe them into something legible if anyone else might need to read them). Your observation was what happened; the interpretation is the place for your opinions and ideas of why it happened. For instance, you may have found that three of the four quarrels were over holding the hose; this gives you a clear reason for the quarrels.

- ✤ *Use what you found out.* Talk to the teacher, make your report, or plan what you will with your observation. Follow through with your ideas. In our example, a five-pronged hose outlet could be purchased, a waiting list could be started for the "hose-holder job," or the teacher could be in charge of the hose.

Wherever an observation is planned, it is critical to maintain professional **confidentiality**. If observing at another site, call ahead for an appointment. Talk about the purpose and format of your observation with both director and teacher. Check if you need written permission from the family. Finally, in any discussion of the observation, change the names of the children and school to protect those involved.

How to Observe Effectively

The success of the observation depends on how inconspicuous the observer can be. Children are more natural if the observer blends into the scenery. By sitting back, one can observe the whole scene and record what is seen and heard, undisturbed and uninfluenced. This distancing sets up a climate for recording that aids the observer in concentrating on the children.

There are two main reasons for an observer to be unobtrusive. First, it allows for a more accurate recording of the children's activities. Second, it does not interfere with the smooth functioning of the classroom, the children, or the teachers. In the case of teachers observing their own programs, you must plan ahead with colleagues and have materials at hand that can be set aside quickly if necessary.

Learning to observe and record effectively takes time and practice. Remaining unobtrusive and recording quietly allow children to continue their normal behavior without distraction.

KEY TERMS

assessment
baby biographies
bias
checklists
confidentiality
diary descriptions
evaluation
event sampling
individualized curriculum
le methode clinique
log/journal
narratives
norms
objectivity
portfolio
rating scales
shadow study
time sampling

 Teaching Applications

1. Observe one child for 10 minutes. Using language as your paintbrush, make a written picture of that child's physical appearance and movements. Compare the child's size, body build, facial features, and energy level with those of other children in the class. Record as many of the body movements as you can. Be sure to note seemingly useless movements, failures, and partial successes, as well as final achievements.

2. Observe a children's quarrel. How did you feel when you watched it? What does this tell you about your own influences in childhood? How did the teaching staff intervene? How would you? Why?

3. Try a time sample of children's play in your classroom. Observe 10 children for one minute each during free-play times, and record the type(s) of social behavior they show. Using Parten's categories, your chart would look like one at the bottom of the page. Compare your results with the impressions of the other teachers with whom you work. Did you come to any conclusions on how children develop socially?

4. Choose two children, one you think is doing well and one who is having trouble. Observe the adult–child interactions of each. What are the differences from the children's point of view in the quantity and quality of those relationships? What generalizations about the importance of such relationships in the early years can you make?

5. Teachers have noticed that several children consistently interrupt at storytime with seemingly irrelevant questions and constantly grab onto children seated nearby. What's happening—and why? What observational tools would you use to find out? What clues from individual behavior would you look for? How would you look at the group as a whole? What other information would you need?

Special thanks to the following early childhood education students for their observation samples: J. Gallero, C. Grupe, L. Hutton, C. Liner, C. Robinson, M. Saldivar.

Child/ Age	Unoc- cupied	Solitary	Onlooker	Parallel	Associative	Cooperative

Totals

REFERENCES

Barbour, N. (2004). Focus box: Assessment. In A. M. Gordon & K. Williams Browne, *Beginnings and beyond* (6th ed.). Clifton Park, NY: Thomson Delmar Learning.

Bredekamp, S., & Rosegrant, T. (Eds.). (1992, 1995). Reaching potentials (Vols. 1 & 2). Washington, DC: National Association for the Education of Young Children.

Cartwright, S. (1994, September). When we really see the child. *Exchange,* 5–9.

Cryan, J. R. (1986, May/June). Evaluation: Plague or promise? *Childhood Education, 62.*

Danielson, C., & Abrutyn, L. (1997). *An introduction to using portfolios in the classroom.* Alexandria, VA: Association for Supervision and Curriculum Development.

Dawes, H. C. (1934). An analysis of two hundred quarrels of preschool children. *Child Development,* 5, 139–157.

Feeney, S., Christensen, D., & Moravicik, E. (2001). *Who am I in the lives of children?* (6th ed.). Englewood Cliffs, NJ: Prentice-Hall.

Fenwick, T., & Parsons, J. (2000). *The art of evaluation: A handbook for educators and trainers.* Clifton Park, NY: Thomson Delmar Learning.

Gardner, H. (1988, September/October). Alternatives to standardized testing. *Harvard Education Letter.*

Gonzalez-Mena, J.(2004). Focus box: Understanding what we observe: A multicultural perspective. In A. M. Gordon & K. Williams Browne, *Beginnings and beyond* (6th ed.). Clifton Park, NY: Thomson Delmar Learning.

Hilliard, A. (1986). *Black children: Their roots, culture, and learning styles.* Baltimore, MD: The Johns Hopkins University Press.

Irwin, D. M., & Bushnell, M. M. (1980). *Observational strategies for child study.* New York: Holt, Rinehart & Winston.

Jones, E. J., & Carter, M. (1991, January/February). The teacher as observer—Part 1, and Teacher as scribe and broadcaster: Using observation to communicate—Part 2. *Child Care Information Exchange,* 35–38.

Jones, E., & Reynolds, G. (1992). *The play's the thing: Teachers' roles in children's play.* New York: Teachers College Press.

Kamii, C. (Ed.). (1990). *Achievement testing in the early grades: The games grown-ups play.* Washington, DC: National Association for the Education of Young Children.

Meisels, S. J. (1997). Remaking classroom assessment with the Work Sampling System. *Young Children,* 48, 34–40.

NAEYC [National Association for the Education of Young Children]. (1988, March). Position statement on standardized testing of young children 3 through 8 years of age. *Young Children,* 43.

NAEYC [National Association for the Education of Young Children]. (1991). Position statement on guidelines for appropriate curriculum context and assessment. *Young Children,* 46:21–38.

Parten, M. B. (1932). Social participation among preschool children. *Journal of Abnormal and Social Psychology,* 27, 243–269.

Ramsey, P. (1987). *Teaching and learning in a diverse world: Multicultural education for young children.* New York: Teacher College Press.

Wiggins-Dowler, K. (2004). Focus box: The portfolio: An "unfolding" of the child. In A. M. Gordon & K. Williams Browne, *Beginnings and beyond* (6th ed.). Clifton Park, NY: Thomson Delmar Learning.

Additional resources for this chapter can be found by visiting the Online Companion™ at www.earlychilded.delmar.com. This supplemental material includes a Study Guide with chapter review questions (and answers), critical thinking questions and activities, and annotated Web sites.

Guidance Essentials

QUESTIONS FOR THOUGHT

Why do children behave the way they do?

What are some ways in which the classroom environment affects children's behavior?

What is the difference between discipline and punishment?

What are some effective ways to deal with behavior problems?

What should teachers do if school and home guidance techniques differ?

UNDERSTANDING BEHAVIOR

Two-year-olds Shawnsey and Kim are playing in the dress-up area. Kim grabs at one of the many necklaces Shawnsey has draped around her neck. Startled, Shawnsey lets out a cry, grabs Kim's arm, and bites her.

Malcolm, a five-year-old, rushes through the room, heading for the block area. He stands and watches Lorraine balancing blocks on top of one another. With a swift wave of his arm, Malcolm topples the structure.

When a teacher stops at the table to tell the children it is nearly time to clean up, Mac, age six, replies, "Cleaning up is a girl's job and I don't have to do it." He throws the art supplies on the floor and dashes away from the teacher.

(See Figures 7–1 and 7–9 for solutions to these types of situations.)

These are typical scenes in any early childhood education center. No matter how plentiful the materials, how well trained the adults, or how good the program, conflicts are sure to occur. Helping children learn to cope with their anger, fears, frustrations, and desires is one of the most challenging jobs for a teacher.[1]

To guide children's behavior, a teacher must first understand it. This requires a background in child development, skills in observing, and an understanding of why children behave and misbehave. Adults can

For guidance to be successful, a teacher must first understand children's behavior.

help children form new behavior patterns if they understand what is happening to the child. Why do children misbehave? How do children learn appropriate behavior?

FACTORS THAT AFFECT BEHAVIOR

Developmental Factors

Adults who work with children should know developmental theory to understand what type of behavior they might expect at various ages. Developmental theory helps teachers anticipate what children will do and helps them maintain reasonable expectations. To see behavior as predictable and developmentally appropriate helps to guide teachers in solving behavioral problems. (See Chapter 4 for more in-depth discussion of various developmental theories.)

[1]Different cultures have different ways of dealing with emotions. The educator needs an awareness of how he or she deals with particular emotions, as well as how the child's particular family culture deals with emotions.

Environmental Factors

The goals for positive behavior should be reflected in the classroom setting. The physical setting should tell children clearly how to act in that space. This makes it easier for them to know what is expected and how they should behave. Child-size furniture encourages sitting and working; room arrangements avoid spaces that can be used as runways; low, open shelves create an expectation that children will take materials out and put them away after use. Materials, scheduling, and interpersonal relationships are part of the overall environment that can have an impact on children's behavior.

Materials and equipment should be adequate and interesting to the age group. When children are occupied with stimulating, age-appropriate materials, there are fewer opportunities for misbehavior. Adding materials and equipment can help prevent arguments over a favorite toy, create new interests and challenges, and extend children's play ideas.

The *daily schedule and timing* of events indirectly influence classroom behavior. When there are blocks of time in which to choose activities, children can proceed at their own pace without feeling hurried. Schedules that do not allow enough time for cleanup and transitions produce a frantic climate. It is when children are rushed that arguments, accidents, and tears ensue. Uncooperative behavior is sometimes related to time pressures.

The *interpersonal relationships* between and among children and adults have effects and influence children's behavior. An atmosphere of trust and support helps to create good learning environments. Problems that upset adults can make an impression on a child. A family crisis, a new baby, or a recent divorce has an impact that can carry into the classroom. When children sense a feeling of support and acceptance, their behavior can be modified more readily.

Chapter 9 contains a more detailed discussion of the factors that need to be considered when designing spaces for children. Many of these aspects directly influence how children will behave. Use the classroom checklist in Figure 7–1 to evaluate how the environment is related to your guidance philosophy and to children's behavior.

Individual or Personal Factors

Each child in a classroom is unique; each has a personal style that needs to be acknowledged and valued. Teachers of young children soon learn the temperamental characteristics of each child in the class. Hondi works and plays with great intensity; Norman is easily distracted. Tawana fears any change, whereas Enrique thrives on challenges. The consistent patterns of temperament that emerge help define each child's individual style.

Research by Thomas and Chess (1977) has identified three types of temperament in babies: the easy child, the difficult child, and the slow-to-warm-up child. These differences were observed in very young infants and seem to remain consistent as the child grows. Children's temperament also affects the way people deal with them. An easy child is easy to respond to; a slow-to-warm-up child may be harder to reach. Difficult children may tend to be blamed for things they did not do. Identifying such traits can be useful so long as adults are careful not to label children unfairly or prematurely.[1]

[1]Children's individual temperaments are an important consideration in developing an understanding of our diverse world. Differences in temperament may be less immediately obvious than differences in gender or race, but no less significant.

Time

_____ Does the daily schedule provide enough time for unhurried play?

_____ Are those periods that create tension—transitions from one activity to another—given enough time?

_____ Is cleanup a leisurely process built in at the end of each activity, with children participating?

Program Planning and Curriculum

_____ Is there enough to do so that children have choices and alternatives for play?

_____ Is the curriculum challenging enough to prevent boredom and restlessness?

_____ Is the curriculum age appropriate for the children in the class?

_____ Are there activities to help children release tension? Do the activities allow for body movement, exploration, and manipulation of materials?

_____ Are children included in developing the rules and setting guidelines? How is their inclusion demonstrated?

Organization and Order

_____ If children are expected to put things away after use, are the cabinets low, open, and marked in some way?

_____ Are the materials within easy reach of the children, promoting self-selection and independence?

_____ Are there enough materials so that sharing does not become a problem?

_____ Are the areas in which activities take place clearly defined so that children know what happens there?

_____ Does the room arrangement avoid runways and areas with no exits?

_____ Do children have their own private space?

_____ Are children able to use all visible and accessible materials? Are there materials about which children are told, "Don't touch."?

Personnel

_____ Are there enough teachers to give adequate attention to the number of children in the class?

_____ Are the group size and makeup balanced so that children have a variety of playmates?

_____ Are the teachers experienced, and do they seem comfortable in setting limits and guiding children's behavior?

_____ Do teachers use their attention to encourage behavior they want, and do they ignore what they want to discourage?

_____ Do all adults consistently enforce the same rules?

FIGURE 7–1 Classroom checklist. By anticipating children's needs and growth patterns, teachers set up classrooms that foster constructive and purposeful behavior.

Video View Point 7-1

"Children's temperaments shape how they respond to others. Whereas some children are quite responsive and easygoing, other children are more withdrawn, slow to warm up to others, or difficult to please."

Competency: Social Development

Age Group: Infant-Toddler

Critical Thinking Questions:

1. How would you describe your own temperament as a child?

2. What would you do to create a relationship with a toddler who was withdrawn?

Emotional and Social Factors

Some behavior problems stem from the child's attempt to express social and emotional needs. These include the need to feel loved and cared for, the need to be included, the desire to be considered important and valued, the desire to have friends, and the need to feel safe from harm. Young children are still working out ways to express these needs and feelings. Typically, because they are only just learning language and communication skills, it is often through nonverbal or indirect actions that children let us know what is bothering them. It is important to let children know that we recognize they can be angry, jealous, or hurt. The supportive adult will help children find satisfying ways to cope with their social and emotional feelings.

Figure 7-2 describes four categories of misbehavior that seem to stem from the child's social or emotional needs. Because children have something to gain from each type of misbehavior, they are labeled behavior goals. These goals can apply to the child's interactions with adults or with other children. More than one goal may be involved, and the particular reason for misbehavior may not be obvious.

Cultural Factors

Today's children are growing up in a country of unparalleled diversity. Many different cultures are converging and creating a nation of diverse peoples, cultures, languages, and attitudes. Children and their teachers are living in a world of continual cross-cultural interactions. The ability to communicate across cultures is a critical skill to have when guiding children's behavior (see also discussions in Chapters 2, 5, and 8). A review of Erikson and Vygotsky's theories in Chapter 4 and Bronfenbrenner's in Chapter 1 underscores the connection between culture and behavior.

Discipline and guidance are deeply embedded within the values and beliefs of the family. The family's culture shapes how they raise their children, and each family is unique in the way they interpret their cul-

what do YOU think?

Read again the three behavior situations described at the opening of the chapter. What do you think were the goals of Shawnsey, Malcolm, and Mac, and what role do their social and emotional histories play in their behavior?

Teachers are called on to deal with a variety of emotional needs.

Four Goals of Misbehavior

Emotional Need	Child's Behavior
Attention	Child needs to feel accepted and craves attention, either positive or negative.
Power	If they don't gain attention, children will try to gain a sense of control and power over their own life. They like to be "the boss" over others.
Revenge	Children will get revenge for real or perceived hurts by hurting others to gain a sense of importance.
Inadequacy	Children withdraw for fear of failure. They avoid stressful situations, will not try anything new, and feel inadequate to do what is expected of them.

FIGURE 7–2 Because children seem to gain something from each type of behavior, psychiatrist Rudolph Dreikurs calls the behaviors goals. Each goal fulfills a particular social or emotional need for the child. (From Dreikurs, R., & Tolz, V. [1964]. *Children: The challenge.* New York: Hawthorne Books.)

tural values. Child-rearing practices ranging from the timing of toilet training to physical punishment are culturally influenced. The messages children receive about their behavior should be consistent between school and home. Yet conflict may be inevitable because the culturally influenced child-rearing practices of the family[1] may be at odds with a teacher's ideas and expectations (Gordon & Browne, 1996). In some cultures, for instance, children are encouraged to challenge adult opinions, but this would be considered disrespectful in other cultures.

As teachers become familiar with the customs and beliefs of the families in their program, they will gain insights into children's behavior and understand the reasons for the way a child responds. Each child must be valued as part of a family system, and the teacher's role is to support the child's sense of security

and identity within the family. Children reflect the context in which they are being raised: their family, culture, ethnicity, religion, socioeconomic status, neighborhood, and so on. When we are aware of these influences we are better able to match who the child is with the most effective guidance approach (Gordon & Browne, 1996).

In some families, a sense of community is valued over individualism, a concept that can create difficulty in the early childhood classroom unless it is understood and appreciated. Early childhood educators, for the most part, do not force children to share personal possessions before they seem ready to, and they encourage children to become autonomous at an early age. This is at odds with families in which cooperation and sharing are valued concepts. Teachers will need to become culturally sensitive to some of the long-held assumptions of teaching young children. Figure 7–3 shows how different

[1]Culturally sensitive teaching strategies will recognize the parent's perspective and the child's family experiences.

Family Culture	Child's Experience and Behavior	Guidance Strategy
Power Structure Democratic family—members share in decision making	Child is encouraged to negotiate and compromise.	Offer real choices; use problem-solving techniques.
One family member makes all of the decisions	Child is expected to obey, follow commands, and respect adult authority. Child may be unable to choose activities, look adults in the eye, or call them by name.	Don't insist on eye contact. Child may need help in selecting an activity. Work with the family members who make the decisions.
Values Strong, close-knit family	Child learns that the family comes first; the individual sacrifices for the family.	Recognize that family matters may take precedence over school.
Honor, dignity, and pride	Child's behavior reflects family honor; child is disciplined for rudeness and poor manners.	Share achievements with parents; help child learn manners; be sensitive when discussing child's behavior problems.
Expressing feelings is accepted	Child is allowed to cry, scream, throw temper tantrums.	Accept child's crying as you give comfort; stay with child until he is calm.
Issue of Discipline Clear, direct discipline	Child learns to respect authority and does what he is told to do; child may not take positive guidance strategies seriously or ignore them.	Use a sense of humor; make firm statements.
Discipline motivated toward inherent goodness	Child has freedom to explore consequences and is warned of possible embarrassment due to behavior.	Child may be passive if disciplined harshly. Use natural consequences; ask rather than demand.
Discipline motivated from inherent self-interest	Child is scolded, threatened, and controlled by promises.	Model desired behavior; use "if/then" statements: If you finish eating, then you can play. Praise good manners and good behavior.

FIGURE 7–3 Sample of culturally diverse family patterns that affect guidance and discipline. Knowledge of culturally diverse family patterns and guidance strategies to parallel these child-rearing styles can allow you to begin a dialogue with the children you teach. (From *Roots and Wings, Revised Edition*, by Stacey York [Redleaf Press, 2003]. Copyright © 2003 by Stacey York. Adapted with permission from Redleaf Press, St. Paul, Minnesota, www.readleafpress.org. To order, call 800-423-8309.)

family cultural patterns relate to a child's behavior and to an appropriate guidance strategy.

 ## ESSENTIALS FOR GUIDING YOUNG CHILDREN

A Guidance Approach

The children we meet in early childhood education programs are just learning how strong their emotions can be and what impact they have on their own behavior and on others. Behavior is the unspoken language through which children act out feelings and thoughts. Caring adults must help young children learn to behave responsibly and be respectful of others as they explore alternative behaviors, develop social skills, and learn to solve problems.

A large part of an early childhood educator's role is to guide and direct children in learning the inner controls necessary for them to build positive relationships with others. The notion of a *guide* is an important one. A guide is someone who leads, explains, and supports. A guide points out directions, answers questions, and helps you get where you are going. This is what teachers do.

What Are Guidance and Discipline?

The word **discipline** stems from *disciple:* a pupil, a follower, and a learner. This suggests an important concept, that of following an example versus following rules. Adults serve as models for children. How children see adults behave tends to become part of their own behavior. Adults help children learn appropriate behavior by setting good examples. Many people associate discipline with the word **punishment.** Punishment is a penalty for an offense or fault and can be harsh or hurtful. Punishment is generally thought of in negative terms, and to some, the words discipline and punishment are synonymous. But they are not, and Figure 7–4 shows how these terms mean very different things.

The guidance process is something you do *with* children; it is an interaction, not something adults do *to* children. In caring and understanding ways, the effective teacher helps children gain control over their own behavior. To accomplish this, teachers maintain a delicate balance between children's attempts to be independent and their need for outer controls.

Discipline	Punishment
Emphasizes what the child should *do*	Emphasizes what the child should *not* do
Is an ongoing process	Is a one-time occurrence
Sets an example to follow	Insists on obedience
Leads to self-control	Undermines independence
Helps children change	Is an adult release
Is positive	Is negative
Accepts child's need to assert self	*Makes* children behave
Fosters child's ability to think	Thinks *for* the child
Bolsters self-esteem	Defeats self-esteem
Shapes behavior	Condemns misbehavior

FIGURE 7–4 A guidance approach to discipline encourages children's interaction and involvement; punishment is usually something that is done to a child.

One of the goals of a good guidance process is to help children achieve **self-discipline.** This happens only if adults lead in ways that support children's developing ability to control themselves. By gradually handing over to children the opportunity to govern their own actions, adults communicate trust. With added responsibility and trust comes an added dimension of self-respect and self-confidence and a child who feels capable and worthwhile.[1]

A child must taste the freedom that comes with a lessening of adult controls. Only when they have an opportunity to test themselves and make some decisions on their own will children know their capabilities.

Developmentally Appropriate Guidance

To have a developmentally appropriate guidance approach, teachers take their knowledge and understanding of child development principles into consideration as they contemplate how best to respond to a child's behavior.

It is useful to identify the behaviors common to a specific age group, for it provides a context in which to understand the child. Behavior then can be seen as normal and predictable and can be responded to accordingly. Guidance based on a developmental approach would help a teacher to know that

1. first and second graders have an ability to consider others' points of view, so they would choose problem-solving meth-

ods that would ask children to think of how their behavior affected others.

A developmentally appropriate approach also requires that the teacher consider what is known about the individual child as well as what is typical for the age group.

2. Shawnsey (in the opening vignette of this chapter) is an only child of older parents and does not often interact with other children, so the teacher's guidance approach should include suggestions for play dates with others.

3. Toddlers have a strong sense of ownership about their possessions, so teachers should make sure that enough attractive and suitable materials are available so that they do not have to share their favorite toys with others.

These examples ensure that the guidance techniques will match the capabilities of the child and that adult expectations will remain reasonable. (See the section on Cultural Factors in this chapter.)

The Language of Guidance and Discipline

Guidance has a language all its own.[2] The language and communication techniques in guidance are both spoken and unspoken. Adults discover how potent the voice can be, what words will work best and when, and the effectiveness of body language, physical presence, and attitude.

[1]This is a good reminder for teachers to examine their interactions with all the children in their care. Who do they encourage to take risks and assume responsibilities? Are there different assumptions for children of different cultures?
[2]The language of discipline may differ from culture to culture. Gender differences, which may be cultural, may emerge (e.g., boys are encouraged to "hit back," whereas girls are taught a more passive approach to conflicts).

Voice

Talk to children in the same way you talk to other people. Use good speech patterns for children to imitate. Learn to control your loudness volume—to be heard, get close enough to speak in a normal tone. Get down to the child's level. Often, lowering volume and pitch is effective enough to stop the behavior.

Words

The fewer the words, the better. Simple, clear statements, spoken once, will have the greatest impact. The child will be able to focus on the real issues involved. A brief description of what happened, a word or two about what behavior is acceptable and what isn't, and a suggestion for possible solutions are all that is necessary.

Choose words carefully. They should convey to the child exactly what is expected. "Richy, move the block closer to the truck. Then Sarah won't bump into it again" tells Richy in a positive way what he can do to protect his block building. If he had been told, "Richy, watch where you are building," he would not know what action to take to solve the problem. Figure 7–5 has more examples of using positive statements as a guidance measure.

Being Positive

- Tell children what it is you want them to do. Make directions and suggestions in positive statements, not in negative forms. "Walk around the edge of the grass, Hilla, so you won't get hit by the swing" instead of "Don't get hit!"
- Reinforce what children do right, what you like, and what you want to see repeated. This helps build the relationship on positive grounds. "Good job, Sammy. You worked hard on that puzzle."
- Give indirect suggestions or reminders, emphasizing what you want children to do. Help them refocus on the task without nagging or confrontation. "I know you are excited about the field trip, Mickey. Looks like you are almost finished putting on your jacket so we can go" instead of "Hurry and button that jacket so we can go."
- Use positive redirection whenever possible. "Let's get a basket for you to toss those balls in. That way they won't bother other children who are playing nearby."
- Use encouragement appropriately, focusing on helping children achieve success and understanding what it is you want them to learn: "Harry, I notice you are being careful about where you put your feet as you climb that tree. It looks to me like you are finding good places to stand" communicates a supportive attitude and tells the child what he is doing well. Global praise, such as 'Great climbing, Harry. Good for you!" may leave children wondering what exactly it is they have been praised for and omits the learning they can derive from the experience.
- Give reasons for your request. Let children know in simple, straight-forward statements the reasons behind your request. Children are more likely to cooperate when they can understand the reason why. "Tom, if you move those chairs, then you and Dee will have more room to dance" instead of "Move the chairs, Tom."

FIGURE 7–5 Examples of using positive statements as a guidance measure.

Body Language

When working with small children, the teacher must be aware of body height and position. Sit, squat, or kneel—but get down to their level. It is difficult to communicate warmth, caring, and concern from two or three feet above a child's head, or by shouting from across the room.

Making full use of the senses can soften the impact of words. A firm grip on the hand of a child who is hitting out, or a gentle touch on the shoulder, tells children that the adult is there to protect them from themselves and others. Eye contact is essential. Teachers learn to communicate the seriousness of a situation through eye and facial expressions. They also show reassurance, concern, sadness, and affection this way.

Physical presence should convey to the child a message that the teacher is there, available, and interested.

Attitude

This is part of the unspoken language of guiding children. Attitudes are derived from experience. Teachers find it useful to look at the way they were disciplined as youngsters and acknowledge their feelings about it. As they begin to inhibit the behavior of the children in their classes, teachers should be aware of their own attitudes.[1]

Culturally Appropriate Guidance

An emerging issue, as our population becomes more and more diverse, has to do with cultural values and discipline. Parents whose disciplinary practices are contrary to the school's philosophy may challenge teachers.[2] Pressure may be exerted on teachers to apply the same techniques at school that parents use at home. Teachers want to maintain the school's as well as their own standards without communicating to the family that their values are wrong or have children feel that something about their home and family is diminished in the teacher's eyes. Gonzalez-Mena (2001) emphasizes the teacher's responsibility to learn cross-cultural communication when child-rearing practices are in conflict between home and school and suggests the following strategies:

1. Accept that both viewpoints are equally valid; maintain an open attitude that promotes respect and appreciation for each other's view.

2. Resist assigning meaning and values to the behavior of others on the basis of your own culture; remember that your behavior does not necessarily convey your own meaning and values.

3. Educate yourself about the different cultures represented in your classroom. Learn how and what is communicated through facial gestures, touch, eye contact, physical closeness, and time concepts.

4. Observe, ask, and talk about what the differences are; learn from the parents of the children in the classroom what you need to know about their culture.

[1]Attitudes affect expectations. Check to determine whether you have any assumptions on how children behave depending on their race, gender, or culture.
[2]There are *professional codes of guidance* versus *family socialization practices*. Parents and teachers may have the same goals for the child, but the teacher is bound by professional standards and codes of behavior, whereas parental guidance has more latitude because of the strong bond of love, security, authority, and loyalty.

5. Work together to figure out a solution to the situation.

Ethical issues involving culture-based differences are discussed in Chapters 1, 2, 5, 7, and 8. The anti-bias curriculum, as described in Chapters 5 and 9, suggests some strategies as well. Also see discussions of cultural diversity in Chapter 4. The Code of Ethics of the National Association for the Education of Young Children (NAEYC) in Appendix B is a useful resource for ethical concerns about families and culture. (See also Feeney & Freeman, 1999.)

Implications for Teaching

A teacher has both a direct and an indirect influence on children's behavior. Some of the ways teachers deal *directly* with discipline are by what they say and do. *Indirectly,* a teacher's influence is felt just as strongly. Room arrangements and time schedules, attitudes, and behavior can work for or against good guidance practices.

Teachers who are well *grounded in the developmental process* know that problem behaviors are normal and occur in every early childhood setting. They realize that growing children must have a safe, secure place in which to test themselves against the world.

The teacher as a *behavior model* is an important element in guidance. Children pattern their responses after adult behaviors. They are aware of how teachers respond to anger, frustration, and aggression and how they solve problems and conflicts. Adults must be sure to model the desired behavior around the children they teach. To be successful models, teachers should be aware of their emotions and feelings and be careful not to compound a problem by their own reaction.

Being *consistent* is one of the key elements in good guidance practices. If adults want to develop mutual trust, the rules

---

Video View Point 7-2

"Positive guidance emphasizes the importance of the adult as a model of caring and appropriate behavior."

Competency: Guidance

Age group: Preschool

Critical Thinking Questions:

1. What can you do to become a more positive model of caring behavior for young children?

2. What words can you use to communicate a sense of caring as well as concern?

---

must be clear, fair, and enforced consistently and regularly. At the same time, children need to know what will happen if rules are not followed. Consequences, too, should be consistent.

Teachers should have *realistic expectations* for children, neither too high nor too low. Sometimes teachers presume that children have abilities and skills they do not yet possess, and this may cause children to respond in inappropriate ways. It can be helpful to rehearse with children how they are expected to act. Practice sessions are especially useful when introducing a new topic or plan.

Many times children are asked to do jobs that are too complicated for them. The young child who is just learning to put on jackets and pants or to make a bed is a good example; it is helpful if the task is broken down into smaller steps. Straighten the sheet and blanket for Gordon, and then let him pull the spread up over the pillow. Little by little have Gordon assume more of the bed-making job as he becomes capable.

Teachers can learn a great deal about the effects of their discipline and guidance techniques and when to use them if they are *active observers* in their own class-

Plan Ahead

- Allow plenty of time for children to respond. Give them an opportunity to decide their course of action.
- Review limits and rules periodically. Modify them as children's growth and maturation indicate. Change them as circumstances change; be flexible.
- Encourage children to talk things over. Be open to their point of view even if you cannot accept it. Let them know you are willing to listen to all sides of the conflict.
- Become aware of the climate in the room or yard. Anticipate the need for a change of pace or a different activity before children become bored or troublesome.
- Remember, it takes time and numerous opportunities for changes in behavior to occur. By using consistent guidance techniques, you will help children practice new behavior repeatedly.

rooms. When teachers observe, they can time intervention; they do not want to interfere too soon. Observations can be used to show children their actions and the consequences they have for others.

Preventing misbehavior is another part of the teacher's role. Good discipline practices call for teachers to be alert to potential problems and situations before they result in children's inappropriate behavior. Even then, unpredictable situations occur: One of the teachers is called out of the room with a sick child; rain forces an activity to move indoors; or a scheduled event gets postponed. At these trying and typical times, a teacher's full range of abilities is called into play. Ways to help children maintain good behavior patterns in these situations include:

1. Recognize and label the problem or situation. Acknowledge the difficulties it presents to the children. Example: "You seem tired, Gus, and I know you had to

"They won't let me play with them." A sensitive teacher will move in and help redirect a child's behavior before it becomes a problem. What would you do in this situation?

wait a long time for your snack. When you have finished your juice and cracker, put your head down on the table and rest for a minute."

2. Ask children for their help. Get them involved in working out the solutions. Example: "Mr. Gallo had to leave for a while. How can we continue with this cooking project when I need to watch the block area too? Who has an idea? What do you think would work, Henry?"

3. Assign a job or a task to the children who are most likely to react to the crisis. Example: "Lorraine and Paul, will you carry the special drums inside, please, while I help the toddlers put the wagons away before the rain starts."

4. Always be prepared with a story to tell, songs to sing, guessing games to play, or exercises to do. Help children pass the time in an appropriate way by modeling your own ability to cope. Example: "Oh, dear. The fire truck hasn't arrived at school yet; we'll have to wait another five minutes. While we are waiting to go and see it, show me how firefighters climb ladders and slide down poles."

5. Say what you would like to have happen. Admit what you wish you could do to correct the situation. Example: "Oh, Riko, I wish I could bring your mommy back right now but I can't. She has to go to work, but I will hold you until your crying stops."

These disciplinary practices apply equally to infants and toddlers, but there are some special considerations that teachers should remember. Infants cry—sometimes a great deal. It is their only means of communication. When they cry they should not be ignored or chastised, but comforted. It is helpful to talk to the baby, no matter how young, and begin to identify the steps you will take to ease the distress. Toddlers, too, need adults to use words to express problem situations, and the preceding examples readily apply to working with this active and lively age group. One word of caution: Removing infants and toddlers from the group or confining them to a playpen or crib as a means of discipline is not appropriate. Very young children do not understand that kind of isolation. To be effective, guidance should be helpful, not punitive. See the list of reactions to "always avoid" in Figure 7–6.

Always Avoid

- Methods that will shame, frighten, or humiliate children.
- Physical abuse.
- Comparisons among the children. Comparisons foster competitiveness and affect self-esteem.
- Carryovers from the incident. Once it is over, leave it behind; do not keep reminding children about it.
- Consequences that are too long, too punitive, or postponed. Children benefit most from immediate, short consequences.
- Lots of rules. Set only enough to ensure a safe environment for all children.
- Making promises you cannot keep.
- Being overly helpful. Let children do as much as they can by themselves, including solving their own conflicts.
- Threatening children with the loss of your affection.

FIGURE 7–6 Methods that defeat an effective guidance approach.

ESSENTIAL GUIDANCE STRATEGIES

Guidance Techniques

Inductive guidance is one of the most effective guidance methods. There are many examples throughout the chapter. They include such key elements as:

1. Providing appropriate choices (see Figure 7–4)

2. Asking open-ended questions ("What would happen if you . . ." "How do you think he would feel if you . . .")

3. Communicating trust and confidence that children are able solve problems and control their own behavior

4. Modeling guidance as an interactive process and involving children as much as it does adults

5. Holding children increasingly responsible for their actions as they come to understand the impact of their behavior on others

6. Teaching thinking and reasoning skills to help children achieve self-control and the development of a conscience

These principles are based on the theories of Erikson and Piaget but owe particular credit to Vygotsky, who placed the child as a learner in the context of social interactions. The concept of the **zone of proximal distance** (see Chapter 4), for instance, reinforces the reciprocal relationship between adult and child implied in most inductive guidance techniques. Also reflected in these examples is Thomas and Chess's (1977) model of goodness of fit (see the section on Individual or Personal Factors), in which the adult works with the child's unique temperament to determine the best guidance approach to take. Family context as well continues to be a priority when selecting appropriate guidance methods.

At the other end of the guidance spectrum are **power assertive methods,** which rely on children's fear of punishment rather than the use of reason and understanding. Spanking, hitting, calling children names, and otherwise using demeaning punishments exclude the opportunity for teaching and learning to take place or to promote problem solving.

A variety of techniques follow. They range from the least intrusive methods to those that require greater adult involvement, and should be used in that order. They are valuable tools for enlarging the child's capacity to become increasingly self-directed and self-reliant.

Ten Essential Strategies

Ignoring Behavior

When misbehavior is of a less serious nature—for instance, when a child whines constantly—it may be best to ignore it. This kind of behavior, although mildly annoying, is not harmful. To use the technique successfully, the adult chooses not to respond to the child in any way and may even become occupied elsewhere while the behavior persists. This method is based on the learning theory that negative reinforcement (the adult ignoring the child) will eventually cause the child to stop the undesirable behavior. At first there might be an increase in the misbehavior as the child tests to see whether the adult will truly ignore the action. Once the child sees that there is nothing to gain, the behavior disappears.

Active Listening and "I" Messages

Parents and teachers can learn the art of **active listening** to respond to a child's feelings as well as his or her words. The adult listens carefully, trying to understand what the child is saying beyond the words being used. Then the adult, in

"This is our fort and you can't play with us." What are some ways a teacher can handle this situation? What would you do?

his or her own words, reflects back to the child what he or she thinks the child is saying. The child has an opportunity to correct any misinterpretations. Further dialogue helps to clarify what it is the child means. For example:

Rita: I hate school!

Teacher: Sounds as if you are really disappointed you didn't get a turn cooking today.

Rita: I really wanted to help make pancakes.

"I" messages are also an adult's way of reflecting back to children how their actions have affected others.

Parent: When you scream indoors, it really hurts my ears.

Parent: I feel sad when you tell me you don't like me.

"I" messages are honest, nonjudgmental statements that place no blame on the child but state an observation of the behavior and its results (Figure 7–7).

Reinforcement

Behavior modification is based on the premise that behavior is learned through **positive and negative reinforcement,** or rewards. The belief is that children will tend to repeat behavior for which they get the desired results (positive reinforcement) and are likely to avoid doing things that have undesirable consequences (negative reinforcement). Positive reinforcement is used to teach new and different behaviors to a child and to help the child maintain the change. Negative reinforcement may involve ignoring or withdrawing attention when the child acts inappropriately. Initially, the reinforcement (or reward) must be swift and consistently applied, as often as the behavior occurs. If the desired behavior, for instance, is for Janie to always hang her coat on the hook, praise and appreciate the effort each time Janie hangs up her wraps. Once this is a well-established routine, the reinforcement (praise) becomes less intense.

Reinforcers, or rewards, must be individualized to meet the needs of the child and the situation. Social reinforcers, such as smiling, interest and attention, and talking, are powerful tools with young children. Food, tokens, and money are sometimes used as reinforcers in home and school settings. The goal of reinforcement, however, is that inner satisfaction will be-

If This Is the Behavior	Try This	For Example
Whining	Ignoring	Do and say nothing while whining persists. Pay attention to child when whining stops.
Playing cooperatively	Positive reinforcement	"You two are sure working hard on this garden! What a good team you make."
Refusing to cooperate	Provide a choice	"Reva, do you want to pick up the Legos off the floor or help Charlie empty the water table?"
Restlessness, inattentiveness	Change the activity	"This story seems long today; we'll finish it later. Let's play some music and dance now."
Daydreaming	Indirect suggestion	"As soon as you get your coat, Winona, we'll all be ready to go inside."
Arguing over the use of a toy	Active listening	"You really wanted to be the first one to play with the blue truck today, didn't you, Lief?"
Dawdling, late for snacks	Natural consequences	"Sorry, Nate, the snacks have been put away. Maybe tomorrow you'll remember to come inside when the other children leave the yard."
Pushing, crowding, running inside	Change room arrangement	Create larger, more open spaces so children have greater freedom of movement and do not feel crowded together.
Unable to take turns, to wait	Review daily schedule, equipment	Buy duplicates of popular equipment. Allow enough time for free play so children won't feel anxious about getting a turn.
Boisterous play	Positive redirection	"You and Sergio seem to want to wrestle. Let's go set the mats out in the other room. If you wrestle here you disturb the children who are playing quietly."

FIGURE 7–7 Varieties of guidance techniques. The astute teacher selects from the options available and individualizes the responses.

come its own reward regardless of the type of reinforcer one might use initially.

Behavior modification enables adults to invite children to be part of the process, giving them an active part in monitoring their own behavior. Children are capable of keeping a chart of how many times they finished their homework, played cooperatively, or fed the dog. This chart serves as a natural reinforcer.

Redirecting the Activity

Sometimes the adult will want to change the activity in which the child is engaged to one that is more acceptable. If Pia and Elena are throwing books off the reading loft, the teacher will want to redirect them and may suggest throwing soft foam balls into a makeshift basket. **Redirecting** calls for the adult to make an accurate assessment of what the children really want to do. In this case, it appears they enjoy throwing from a height. Now the teacher can consider alternatives that permit the desired activity while changing the expression or form it takes: "It looks as if you two are enjoying dropping things from up there. Let's figure out a way you can do that so that books won't be damaged."

The substitute activity must be a valid one, acceptable to the adults and fulfilling to the children. In most cases children are not being deliberately malicious or destructive. More than likely they are expressing curiosity, imagination, and the need to explore. Positive redirection satisfies these needs in a way that enhances children's self-concept and self-control.

Giving Choices

Give children choices whenever possible. This allows them some control so they do not always feel dominated by adults. Choices help children practice self-reliance, self-direction, and self-discipline. "Yes, Seth, the cooking area is too crowded. Looks like there is plenty of room at the clay table or at the writing table. Where would you like to play?"

You must give a choice only when you mean for children to make the choice, and be prepared to accept their answer when a choice is offered. "Some of the children are going in for music now. Would you like to join them?" This is a reasonable choice if there is another adult to supervise the outside.

Suggest two choices when there is the possibility of resistance. This lets a child know that you expect him or her to comply with the request but allows some decision making on their part. "It is time to go home now. Would you like to get your artwork before or after you put on your jacket?"

The choice must be valid. You need to acknowledge children's growing ability to deal with responsibility and help them practice making reasonable choices. "It's rest time for everyone now. Do you want to pick out some books before or after you brush your teeth?" Children should be aware of the consequences of the choice they are making. "If you choose to use the computer now, you won't have time to finish your rain forest project." Helping children make reasonable choices gives them a foundation for decision making throughout their life.

Setting Limits

Limits are a necessary part of any group or society; they are the boundaries set up to help children know what behavior will or will not be acceptable. Teachers generally have two reasons for setting limits:

1. To prevent children from injuring themselves or others

2. To prevent the destruction of property, materials, or equipment

Limits are like fences; they are protective structures that help children feel secure.

When children know where fences are, and what limits and rules apply, they do not have to continually try to find out if fences are there. Inside the fences, children are free—and safe—to try out many behaviors.[1]

Children may not like fences; they may resist attempts to limit their behavior. Teachers must learn to set and maintain limits with confidence and authority. Children respond to how limits are set as much as to the limits themselves. A good guidance process involves children as active participants; this fosters self-discipline. Children also seem less resistant to following rules when they are a part of the limit-setting procedure. Figure 7–8 illustrates positive ways to set limits when working with young children.

A natural part of growing up is to stretch those limits and push those fences aside. For the child, limits are self-protective. Young children have not yet learned the skills to control themselves in all situations. Their behavior easily goes out of bounds. Children are just beginning to exert that inner pressure (self-control) that will help them monitor their own actions. Until then, they need adults to help them learn when and how to apply self-restraint. Limits keep them from going too far. Children can frighten themselves and others with anger, frustration, and fear. They need adults who care to stop them from doing physical or emotional harm to themselves. Well-considered limits give the child freedom to try out, test, and explore avenues of self-expression in ways that will promote growth and protect budding autonomy.

Active Problem Solving and Conflict Resolution

The principle in **active problem solving** is to actively engage children in confronting their differences and work together to solve their problems. The adult guides children toward solutions but does not solve problems for them. Posing open-ended questions, the adult helps children keep focused so that they can suggest alternative solutions, for example:

"What could you do?"

"How might she feel when . . . ?"

"What might happen if . . . ?"

"How can you . . . ?"

All of the children's suggestions must be acknowledged seriously, even if they seem unreasonable. Young children are likely to start the discussion by suggesting extreme solutions. In the case of Malcolm, for instance (see the second example at the beginning of this chapter), the class might initially suggest a radical alternative: "Don't let Malcolm come to this school anymore." These suggestions will become tempered as other children respond; fair and reasonable solutions will eventually emerge: "Anyone who knocks over the art supplies won't get to use them for the rest of the day."

Teachers can help children think through a number of alternatives, including the consequences of what they suggest: "If we close the writing area, what will happen when you want to KidWrite this afternoon?" By assisting them in anticipating the results of what they suggest, teachers can help children understand how their be-

[1] A good way to prepare children to live successfully and productively is to help them become increasingly responsible for their actions and behavior.

Area of Focus	What You Can Do

Observations

Collect information about the behavior: Identify the components that cause children to lose control. When does Nan throw a temper tantrum? Only before snack time? Just after her mother leaves? What prompts Rudy's resistance? What precedes it? How long does it last? How much attention does Arturo get when he interrupts story time? How many teachers intervene? For how long? How had his attention been sought prior to his disruption? Observe and learn also when these children are behaving appropriately, and record what and how much attention they receive from teachers at that time.

Modify the classroom

Evaluate the classroom on the basis of the observations you made. Is it orderly and free of clutter? Are there legitimate opportunities to move about and use large muscles? Can children select their own activities and make choices about where they will work and play? Is the curriculum challenging and appropriate to the age level? Is there advanced warning when activities will change? Is there an established routine that children can count on? Is there a cleanup time when the children help restore the play areas?

> *Examples:* Materials should be stored in low, open, easy-to-reach shelves that are labeled (scissors, crayons) and placed in containers that children can handle.

> Remove puzzles if they are crowded on a shelf, leaving only a few. Rotate them frequently.

> Display blocks and block accessories (trucks, people, etc.) clearly. Block sizes and shapes on the shelves give children the necessary cues to assist them with cleanup. Provide protected area for block building, away from quieter activities.

> Check to see if the dividers between the activity centers are low enough for ease of supervision.

Teacher attention and language

Give minimum attention to a child during an aggressive episode, taking care of any injured party first. Use short, direct sentences, without judgment and without lecturing. *Look at and speak to the child at eye level.* Do not shame, ridicule, or use physical punishment.

> *Good Example:* "No. I can't let you hurt children."

> *Poor Example:* "It's not nice to hit other children. They don't like you when you are mean. Why can't you play nice like they do? I'm gonna have to tell your momma you were bad when she comes. Can you promise me you won't hit anybody else today? Now tell Tomi you are sorry."

FIGURE 7–8 Managing aggressive, disruptive, high-energy behavior. (Adapted from Allen, K. E. [1992]. *The exceptional child: Mainstreaming in early childhood education.* Clifton Park, NY: Thomson Delmar Learning. Used with permission. Taken from Gordon, A. M., & Williams Browne, K. [1996]. *Guiding young children in a diverse society.* Boston: Allyn & Bacon.)

Pay attention to disruptive, nonattentive, aggressive children *when they are behaving appropriately.* Talk over with them alternatives to their nonappropriate behavior.

> *Examples:* "Next time, tell someone you are angry instead of hitting." "When you are finished playing with the blocks, call me and I will help you find another place to play." "If you don't want to hear the story, what else could you do that wouldn't bother other people who want to listen?"

Follow through. Help the child return to play, giving choices when possible, with activities that require energy (clay, woodworking, climbing) or those that are more calming (water play, painting), depending on what the child seems to need at the time. Support the child's involvement with relevant comments, interest, and suitable challenges.

> *Examples:* "Let's decide where you want to play now, Faisal. There's room for you at the water table or pounding the clay. I'll help you get started." (Later) "You look as if you are having a good time with that clay, Faisal. I bet you can squeeze it so hard it oozes out your fingers! I'll watch while you try."

Interacting with children

Start with a child's known interests. Through observations, determine which activities consistently hold the child's attention so that you can reinforce positive behavior while the child is engaged. This technique also helps to increase attention span.

> *Example:* "You sure have been having fun at the water table, Jessica. Here are some funnels and tubes. What could you do with them?"

Help the child plan where to go next and assist in getting started, if necessary. This is effective if the child's activity is changed before he loses interest or before he loses control.

> *Example:* "Jay, it is nearly cleanup time and I know that sometimes it is a hard time for you when we stop playing. How about your helping me organize the children who want to move the tables. Could you be my assistant today and show everyone where to put the tables?"

Give time for response; take time to teach. Children need adequate time to respond to requests without being nagged and may need assistance in learning a skill or getting started with what was requested. Make the task manageable. If, after a reasonable time has passed and Shaquille still hasn't put his jacket on, the teacher restates the request and offers assistance.

FIGURE 7–8, Continued

Example: "You may go outside as soon as your jacket is on, Shaquille. If you put the jacket down on the floor like this, and slip your arms in here, you can pull it over your head."

Help children focus their attention. Get down to their eye level, call them by name, look at them, and speak directly to them. Give advance warning, clear and simple directions, and choices when possible. Do not overwhelm a child with rules and instructions.

Example: "Coretta, it will soon be time to go home. When you finish writing your story, you may choose to come over to the rug to sing songs or you may find a favorite book and look at it in the book corner."

Point out the consequences of their actions to help them understand others' feelings and become responsible for what they do.

Examples: "Linda is sad because you won't let her play with you." "Other children won't be able to use the paint when you mix the colors in the paint jar."

Remind children of the rules and expectations. Rehearse them in remembering appropriate behavior. Use positive phrases.

Example: "Before you go to the block area, remember how much space you need for the roads you like to build. Look around and see who else is playing and find a safe place for your road."

FIGURE 7–8, continued

havior influences and affects others. This is an early lesson in a lifelong quest to become responsible for one's own behavior.

Conflict resolution should become part of the child's daily life. Teachers can help children solve disagreements nonviolently and explore alternative ways to reach their goals. Figure 7–9 outlines a process for active problem solving and conflict resolution. It is useful for resolving differences through group discussion, as noted earlier, or when one or more children become embroiled in conflict. By following such a process, children learn to respect others' opinions, to express their own feelings in appropriate ways, and to learn tolerance for doing things in a different way.[1] The process also suggests an important principle in developmentally appropriate guidance and discipline: The adult role is to intervene as little as possible, allowing children

[1]Children should regard schools as places large enough and diverse enough to hold a variety of people whose backgrounds and experience are respected and understood.

Children are often able to work out their own solutions to conflict.

the opportunity to come up with an acceptable solution.

When children help create a solution, they come away with a sense of commitment to it. This process also gives children a sense of power and control, a sense of independence, and a feeling of self-worth.

Distraction

Some problems may be avoided when the adult helps to focus the child's attention elsewhere. Very young children, especially infants and toddlers, can easily be distracted from undesirable actions. Consider the example at the beginning of the chapter in which Kim grabs at one of the necklaces Shawnsey has. A fast-thinking teacher could present Kim with another attractive one. This method calls for well-timed intervention.

Natural and Logical Consequences

Natural and logical consequences allow children to see the real-life outcomes of their own actions. For instance:

- If Libby does not eat her breakfast, she can expect to be hungry long before lunch.

- If Kara does not finish her homework, she may not go to the ballgame.

- If Tony grabs the book away from Ben, Ben may hit him.

This method allows adults to define the situation for children without making judgments and lets children know what to expect. The consequences are a natural result of the child's own actions.

Logical consequences, on the other hand, are a function of what adults impose. A logical consequence of disrupting group time is removal from the group. For the adult, this means a commitment to follow through; consequences, once stated, must be enforced. It is important to give children an opportunity to choose a course of action for themselves once they have some understanding of what is likely to happen.

Time Out

Removing a child from the play area is particularly appropriate when, owing to anger, hurt, or frustration, the child is out of control. Taking children away from the scene of intensity and emotion to allow them time to cool off and settle down is sometimes the only way to help them. The teacher is firm and consistent as the child is quietly removed from play. It is important that this discipline technique be used with a positive attitude and approach, not as punishment for misbehavior. Too often, **time out** is punitive: Children are pulled from an activity, pushed into a chair, and told to "watch how the other children are playing nicely," or "sit there until you can

The Six-Step Approach to Problem-Solving

Scenario: Two children run outdoors to get the available wagon. They reach it simultaneously and start pulling on the handle, yelling "Mine!" One child starts shoving the other child out of the way.

Step 1: Approach (Initiate Mediation)
— Approach the conflict, signaling your awareness and availability.
— Get close enough to intervene if necessary; stop aggressive behavior or neutralize the object of conflict by holding it yourself.

Step 2: Make a Statement
— Describe the scene.
— Reflect what the children have said.
— Offer no judgments, values, solutions.
   "It looks as if you both want the wagon."
   "I see you are yelling at each other."

Step 3: Ask Questions (Gather Data, Define the Problem)
— Don't direct questions toward pinpointing blame.
— Draw out details; define problems.
— Help kids communicate versus slugging it out. "How did this happen?" "What do you want to tell her?" "How could you solve this problem?" "How could you use it without fighting?"

Step 4: Generate Alternative Solutions
— Give children the job of thinking and figuring it out.
— Suggestions may be offered by disputants or observers.
— Ask questions: "Who has an idea of how we could solve . . . ?"
   "You could take turns."
   "You could both use it together."
   "You could both do something else."
   "No one could use it."
— Common mistake: rushing this stage; give it the time it deserves.

Step 5: Agree on Solution
— When both children accept a solution, rephrase it. ("So, you both say that she will be the driver?")
— If any solution seems unsafe or grossly unfair, you must tell the children. ("It is too dangerous for you both to stand up and ride downhill together. What is another way you can agree?")

Step 6: Follow Through
— Monitor to make sure agreement is going according to plan. If the decision involves turn-taking, you may need to be a clock-watcher.
— Tell the player and the group: "Looks as if you solved your problem!"
— Use the power of language to:
  • Reinforce the solvability of the problem
  • Note the ability of the players to do so
  • Point out the positive environment to be successful

FIGURE 7-9 Using these guidelines to help children solve problems, teachers can listen more than talk, allow children the time to make mistakes and figure out solutions, and point out that diversity of viewpoints is natural, normal, and workable.

behave." This is an inappropriate use of time out.

The time-out period is very much like that used in athletic events: a brief respite and a chance to stop all activity and re-group. The teacher's role is to help the child talk about the incident and to give the child an opportunity to gain self-control before resuming play. Children can moni-tor themselves and choose when they are ready to return to classroom activity. Noah, who persists in calling children offensive names, might be told, "You may come back to the play when you think you are ready to play without hurting children's feel-ings." Noah can then assume some respon-sibility for how he will behave and when he is ready to return to play.

Use this technique lightly; adults who leave the child with a sense of rejection can misuse it too easily. As with other good dis-ciplinary techniques, it should be appropri-ate to the misbehavior and should help the child toward self-discipline.

Helping children learn new behaviors is a challenging prospect for teachers. Early childhood educators have a unique respon-sibility to support children as they recon-cile their differences in peaceful ways.

Video View Point 7-3

"Children need to feel powerful; it is part of the developmental design of growing up."

Competency: Guidance

Age Group: School Age

Critical Thinking Questions:

1. Why do you think it is important for a child to feel powerful?

2. What are some ways you could help a six-year-old feel powerful, within DAP and appropriate guidance guidelines?

KEY TERMS

active listening
active problem solving
conflict resolution
discipline
inductive guidance
limits
natural and logical consequences
positive and negative reinforcement
power assertive methods
punishment
redirecting
reinforcers
self-discipline
time out
zone of proximal distance

Teaching Applications

1. Write your own definition of discipline.

2. Discuss in small groups the appropriate (or inappropriate) uses of time out with your classmates and a parent of a preschooler. How did these conversa-tions affect your own beliefs?

3. In what ways might the guidance strategies in Figure 7–3 be considered culturally insensitive to a particular family? How would you adapt the chart?

4. Finish this sentence: "When I was four years old, the worst thing I ever did was . . ." How did the adults around you react? What would you do if you were the adult in charge? Discuss and compare responses with a classmate.

5. Observe a group of young children dur-ing play. See whether you can identify a child who might be described as an easy child, a difficult child, and a slow-to-warm-up child. What disciplinary techniques do the teachers use with each type of child? Are they the same? If they are different, describe the dif-ferences. How successful are the disci-

plinary techniques that are being used? What might you do differently?

6. How do you feel about spanking children? Were you spanked when you were a child? If so, what precipitated the spankings? Can you think of any other forms of behavior control that might have worked instead of spanking? Compare your thoughts and insights with those of another member of this class.

REFERENCES

Feeney, S., & Freeman, N. K. (1999). *Ethics and the early childhood educator: Using the NAEYC code.* Washington, DC: National Association for the Education of Young Children.

Gonzalez-Mena, J. (2001). *Multicultural issues in child care.* Menlo Park, CA: Mayfield.

Gordon, A. M., & Williams Browne, K. (1996). *Guiding young children in a diverse society.* Boston: Allyn & Bacon.

Thomas, A., & Chess, S. (1977). *Temperament and development.* New York: Brunner/Mazel.

Additional resources for this chapter can be found by visiting the Online Companion™ at www.earlychilded.delmar.com. This supplemental material includes a Study Guide with chapter review questions (and answers), critical thinking questions and activities, and annotated Web sites.

Families and Teachers: An Essential Partnership

QUESTIONS FOR THOUGHT

What are the benefits of an effective family–school partnership?

What are the ingredients for a good parent program?

What are the components for a successful parent–teacher conference?

What is the teacher's role in providing a supportive atmosphere for families?

What are some major concerns of parents?

How has the American family changed in recent years?

🌀 A HISTORICAL OVERVIEW

Working with families can be one of the teacher's most satisfying responsibilities, or it can be one of the most frustrating. It is usually both. The potential is present for a dynamic partnership between the most important adults in a child's life. The common goal is obvious: the welfare of the child. Each has knowledge, skills, and a sense of caring to bring to that relationship. Each has a need for the other. Partnerships usually begin with such a need. So, families and teachers become coworkers and colleagues in a joint effort to help the child develop fully.

Historical Precedent

There is a historical precedent for the partnership between parents and teachers. Pestalozzi and Froebel, early-18th-century educators, detailed many of their procedures for home use (as noted in Chapter 1). The involvement of the mother in the education of the child was considered important even then. When kindergartens were organized in the United States, classes for parents and mothers' clubs were also started. The National Congress of Mothers evolved from that movement, and today it is the National Parent Teacher Association. This organization is an integral force in promoting a union between school and home, teachers and parents.

Decades of Change

During the 1930s, parent involvement in education was actively discouraged. Teachers were seen as experts who wanted to be left alone to do their job. In many cases, teachers felt that they did little but remedy parental mistakes. That trend ended in the 1940s when the need for parent support and encouragement was recognized. Closer relationships between teachers and parents were established. This view of a need for closer ties between teacher and parents, now over 60 years old, stands today as a commonly accepted principle.

In training, teachers were exposed to curricula that would help them appreciate and use parents as coworkers in the child's development. By the 1960s, Head Start programs required parental involvement and set about developing parent education and parent training programs. Their commitment to children included a commitment to the parents of those children.

Parent involvement and education were largely ignored in the education reform movement of the 1990s. That omission began to be addressed as parents became empowered in the creation of charter schools, a mid-'90s phenomenon that created greater parent involvement in public schools.

Essential Changes

Two particular changes—collaborating with parents and working within the family context—are significant in today's society. Demographic data reinforce the need for families and teachers of preschool children to become full and equal partners and set the stage for future school–family partnerships. Increasingly, ethnic, racial, and cultural diversity will affect relationships between families and schools. Today's early childhood education professional will need to be skilled in ways that will strengthen the family–school bond.

There is general agreement among early childhood teachers that at no other age is such a relationship more important than in the early years of a child's schooling, for children's needs are interwoven with those of their parents. Strong family–school relationships should be a part of the early childhood educators' portfolio. (Note: Throughout this chapter, the terms *parents* and *parenthood* are meant to include mothers and fathers as well as other extended family members who have the responsibility for raising a child.)

A true partnership happens when parents and teachers share their strengths with one another for the benefit of the children they care for and love.

✸ PARTNERS IN EDUCATION

What Families Contribute

Families have a unique contribution to make in the child's schooling. They have different knowledge about the child from what the teacher has. They know the child's history: physical, medical, social, and intellectual. They know the child as a member of a family and the role that child plays in the total family group, the extended family, and the community. Parents bring with them a sense of continuity about the child. They provide the context with which the teacher can view the whole child. As the teacher will soon learn, the parents already know what makes their children happy or sad or how they react to changes in routines. Thus, parents have a wealth of intimate knowledge about their children that the teacher is only just beginning to discover.

How Families Benefit

One of the greatest values of a strong parent program is the opportunity for parents to meet each other. They find that they share similar problems and frustrations and that they can support one another in finding solutions. Friendships based on mutual interests and concerns about their children can help them forge new relationships.

Through close home–school relationships, parents can find ways to become more effective as parents and as teachers of their children. They can observe modeling techniques that teachers find successful in dealing with children and can learn what behaviors are appropriate at certain ages. By observing how their children relate to other adults and children, parents can come to know them better as social beings. They may become more aware of school and community resources that are available to them, and in the person of the teacher they now have access to a consultant who knows and understands their child and can help them when they need it.

Parents are the child's teachers too. They teach by word, by example, by all they do and say. Through closer home–school relationships, parents can be helped to see that their everyday experiences with their children provide teachable moments and opportunities for educating their children. Teachers support parents by keeping them informed about each stage of their child's development, by showing them how to encourage language and thinking skills, by educating them to children's social needs at any given age, and by providing lists of books and toys that encourage children's thinking and creative abilities.[1] Teachers can make sure parents have copies of children's favorite songs, recipes that are popular at school, and information (in a bilingual format as needed) on how to teach health and safety habits at home. Parents need not teach a curriculum; they do need to use common household routines and experiences to encourage children's total growth. The teaching staff has a strong role to play in helping parents learn how to do this. In Figure 8–1 a noted author and family counselor lists 10 of the most important things parents can teach their children.

A **family-centered approach** to parent–school relationships supports the growth of the family as well as the child. When parents have a meaningful partnership with their children's teachers, it raises their sense of importance and diminishes some of the isolation and anxiety of child-rearing. By empowering parents in a critical area of their children's lives, allowing them to participate in decisions affecting their children's education, teachers can help parents see themselves as part of the solution.

Family Cultural Influences

Families today represent a wide range of cultural backgrounds, so it is more important than ever that their contributions be

The Ten Most Important Things Parents Can Teach Their Children

1. To love themselves
2. To read behavior.
3. To communicate with words.
4. To understand the difference between thoughts and actions.
5. To wonder and ask why.
6. To understand that complicated questions do not have simple answers.
7. To risk failure as a necessary part of growing up.
8. To trust grownups.
9. To have a mind of their own.
10. To know when to lean on adults.

FIGURE 8–1 A list of important basics that children can learn at home. (Adapted from LeShan, E. [1992]. *When your child drives you crazy.* New York: St. Martin's Press.)

Video View Point 8-1

"Parents are their children's first and most important teachers."

Competency: Family Interaction, School, and Community

Age Group: Preschool

Critical Thinking Questions:

1. What does this statement mean to you?
2. How would you describe the parent's role as "teacher" and how does that differ from your role as teacher?

[1]It is important to remember that fewer than half of the children under the age of five are being brought up in two–parent, middle-class, English-speaking, stay-at-home-mom households. Do school or center policies reflect changing demographics?

sought out, acknowledged, and used. This is one of the most pressing issues in teaching today. All of the subtle communication styles that exist within various cultures can be blocks to good family–school relationships, or they can be the basis on which teachers and parents connect with each other. All families have knowledge that the teachers need to know. Those whose linguistic and cultural backgrounds are different from the teacher's need to share their perspectives so that issues relating to basic routines such as discipline, eating, and sleeping may be understood in their cultural context.[1] The same is true for parents' expectations about their child's experiences in the classroom. Only through forging a partnership can families of diverse cultural backgrounds become true contributors to their children's education and care (see Figure 8–1).

(See Chapter 10, pages 373–375, for ideas on culturally responsive teaching.)

What Teachers Contribute

Teachers bring to the partnership another point of view. As child development professionals, they see the child in relation to normal milestones and appropriate behaviors. They notice how each child plays with other children in the group—what seems to challenge Mickey and when Ramon is likely to fall apart. Unlike parents, teachers see individual children from a perspective that is balanced by the numerous other children they have taught. They observe how the child behaves with a variety of adults, sensing children's ability to trust other adults through interactions with them at school.

When parents need help for themselves or for their child, teachers become resources. They may work with the parents to find psychologists, hearing and speech specialists, or other educational programs, if warranted.

Take a look at the Code of Ethical Conduct of the National Association for the Education of Young Children (NAEYC) (located in Appendix B in the back of this book), particularly at Section II on ethical responsibilities to families, for further clarification on ethical responsibilities.

The majority of parents today want to learn the best way to raise their children and want to improve their child-rearing skills. There are numerous opportunities for the early childhood teacher to work with parents. Figure 8–2 cites a multitude of ways to begin to fulfill these needs.

How Teachers and Schools Benefit

Active parental involvement benefits the teacher and school, too. Parents are an untapped resource in most schools. The skills and talents in a group of parents multiply the people resources available for children. Some parents will want to work directly in the classroom with children; others may volunteer to help in the office, the schoolyard, or the kitchen. Parents can sometimes arrange to take time off from their jobs to accompany a class on a field trip. Some parents are willing to work at home: sewing, typing, mending, building, or painting; others are available for a variety of fund-raising activities. In an equal partnership, however, the parent level of involvement must go beyond volunteer participation in school activities to parent

---

[1]As one works in our diverse world, it is important to be mindful that many children are being parented by people other than their biologic or adoptive parents (e.g., grandparents, foster parents, aunts and uncles, legal guardians, an adult living with the parent).

A Checklist For Making Your School "Parent Friendly"

❑ Hold an orientation for parents at a convenient time.

❑ Provide a place for parents to gather.

❑ Create a parent bulletin board.

❑ Give annual parent awards for involvement.

❑ Create a parent advisory committee.

❑ Allow parents to help develop school policies and procedures.

❑ Schedule events on evenings and weekends.

❑ Provide child care for meetings.

❑ Establish a book or toy lending library.

❑ Make informal calls to parents, especially to share a child's successes.

❑ Provide transportation for parents who need it.

❑ Provide translators for parents who need them.

❑ Send appropriate duplicate mailings to noncustodial parents.

❑ Survey parents for issues of interest and need.

❑ Develop links to health and social support services.

❑ Provide resource and referral lists.

❑ Publish a school newsletter on regular basis.

❑ Provide multilingual written communications as needed.

❑ Hire teachers with a strong commitment to supporting families and parents.

❑ Provide in-service training for teachers in working with parents.

❑ Hire teachers who are respectful of social, ethnic, and religious backgrounds of parents.

❑ Hire staff that is reflective of the cultural background of students and parents.

❑ Encourage regularly scheduled conferences between parents and teachers.

❑ Offer a variety of family support programs.

❑ Provide many opportunities for parents to volunteer.

❑ Provide frequent opportunities for parents to air their concerns.

❑ Encourage parents to ask questions, to visit, and to call.

❑ Encourage parents to know what goes on in the classroom.

❑ Encourage parents to report back on what works well.

❑ Encourage parents to attend social events.

❑ Encourage teachers to make home visits.

FIGURE 8–2 A checklist for a family-oriented approach to meeting children's needs.

participation in decision-making roles, such as serving on school boards, parent advisory committees, and other groups that advocate for children's educational needs (see Figure 8–2).

Some parents may be unable to participate because of work schedules, small children to care for at home, lack of transportation, or inability to speak English. If a school is serious about strengthening the family, these issues must be addressed and solutions must be found to involve all parents.[1]

What Children Gain

The children whose parents choose to take an active part in the school reap the rewards of such involvement. Decades of research show the positive effects on achievement when children's parents are involved in their education. The family is the primary source from which children develop and grow. It is needed to reinforce their learning, attitudes, and motivation if they are to succeed. Parent visibility is especially important for low-income and minority children; their parents' presence can heighten a sense of belonging. Children gain and parent impact is increased when parents are able to monitor their children's progress and reinforce the mission of the school at home.

✺ TEN ESSENTIALS FOR TEACHER–FAMILY COLLABORATION

The early childhood educator is often one of the first people, outside the home, to whom parents turn for help. Parents come to the center looking for teachers who

Visits and participation in classroom activities are opportunities for parents and teachers to support a family-centered view of the child.

know about children and who will work with them. Helping parents with their child-rearing problems is part of a teacher's role. The way in which teachers define that role and their response to parental concerns should be carefully thought through. The following are guidelines to consider in establishing a supportive atmosphere for parents. You will also want to read Section II, Ethical Responsibilities to Families, in the NAEYC Code of Ethical Conduct found in Appendix B.

1. *Prepare parents* for what they can expect from their child's school experience. School policies and a yearly

[1]It is important to help all parents feel welcome, wanted, and involved.

calendar should be clearly stated and thoroughly reviewed with parents as the child enters school. Then parents will know what their responsibilities are, where the school can be of assistance to them, and what expectations the school has of the parents.

2. *Support all parents,* even those with differing opinions from yours. Find ways to acknowledge them and what they are trying to do. There is a greater chance to discuss differences and affect change if there are areas in which teachers and parents find agreement. Children are sensitive to adult feelings, whether they are spoken or not. Differences of opinions should be discussed out of the child's hearing, and teachers should do nothing that would undermine that parent in the eyes of his or her child.[1]

3. *Respect the values of all families.* Social, cultural, and religious differences and a variety of lifestyles, child-rearing methods, and educational philosophies are reflected in every classroom. It is important that parents feel accepted. Focus on the similarities among parents and develop an anti-bias approach to teaching.

4. *Keep a professional distance.* The temptation to move into a social relationship with some families in your class is one that many teachers face. You are better able to maintain a more realistic, objective picture of the child if there is some detachment. The child and the family will probably benefit most if a close relationship is postponed until the child moves on to another class.

5. *Ask, don't tell.* Collaboration begins with the parents' concerns. A teacher's role is one of helping parents clarify their own goals for their children and identifying the trouble spots. Teachers then encourage and support parents as they work together to solve the problem. Parents will feel overwhelmed and inadequate if they think they must change their whole child-rearing style. The sensitive teacher will observe parents and move toward reasonable solutions.

6. *Contact* parents frequently and on a regular basis. Keep the lines of communication open and flowing between school and home. Be sure to know the parents by name. Take advantage of the daily contact as they bring their child to and from school. Such contact may be brief and breezy, but it is a good way to stay in touch. Be sure to find ways to touch base with those parents who do not come to school every day, by telephone, note, or home visit.

7. *Help parents support each other.* Any group of parents represents a multitude of resources. Each parent has accumulated experiences that might prove helpful to someone else. Parents have common concerns and a lot to share with one another. The teacher can provide an arena in which sharing happens. Introduce two families to each other by suggesting that their children play together outside school. Parent meetings, work parties, and potluck dinners are methods for getting parents

[1]Early childhood education professionals must be willing to enter into a dialogue with parents that exposes cultural assumptions and allows for differing perspectives.

involved with each other. The teacher's role can be one of providing the setting, encouraging introductions, and then letting it happen.

8. *Enhance parents' perception of their children.* Parents want teachers who know their child, enjoy their child, and are an advocate for their child. That means acknowledging the child's strengths and those personality traits that are particularly pleasing. Help parents to recognize the joys of parenthood, rather than focusing on the burdens.

9. *Focus on the parent–child relationship.* Help reinforce parents in terms of their relationship with their child rather than in terms only of the child's development of academic skills. Concentrate on the nature of the parent–child interaction: how they get along with each other and how they interact as a family. These issues are the heart and soul of the parent–child relationship, and teachers have a role to play in enhancing the quality of those interactions.

10. *Listen to parents.* Hear them out. They too have accumulated experiences to share, and their views are valid. Learn to listen to them with a degree of understanding; try to hear it from their point of view. Listen to parents without judging them or jumping to conclusions; this is the basis for open communication.

what do YOU think?

Do you think parents are comfortable and welcome in the school where you work? What are some stumbling blocks parents might experience there? What would you change?

✿ BECOMING FULL AND EQUAL PARTNERS

Families and schools are natural allies; together they claim the primary responsibility in educating and socializing children. They can and should be equal partners in that effort.

Family-Support Movement

Evolving over the past three decades has been the image of early childhood programs as family support systems that function as modern-day versions of the traditional extended family (Powell, 1998).

Early childhood educators have long recognized the importance of providing parents with child-rearing information and support. Today, the task of raising children has become increasingly difficult, and the type of parent education and participation is changing to meet current parents' needs. What is termed a **family-support movement** is evolving, in which the primary goal is to strengthen families to meet the challenges of parenting in the years ahead.

Parent education has often been achieved through lectures on discipline and guidance or age-appropriate characteristics. Parent participation in school activities has been through fund-raising, volunteering to help out in the classroom, and driving vehicles on field trips. Resource and referrals for children's special needs have defined parent support. These are certainly important aspects of building good relationships between parents and schools, but they are no longer enough for today's parents. Parent involvement will change only when parents are given a greater say in school decision making. Empowering parents to be change agents in their children's educational process results in greater parental commitment and involvement.

As Kagan (1991) remarks, "Children influence and are influenced by a social network: family, school, and community." Many programs today offer a more comprehensive approach to the parent–school partnership out of a growing recognition of the **ecology of the family** (see Chapters 1 and 4 for further discussion). Programs with a strong family orientation create parent centers that offer counseling, cultural events, support groups, weekend family activities, and links to health and social service agencies. Factors that increase the need for a more family-centered approach include the rise in the divorce rate, the growing number of single-parent families and families in which both parents work, and increasing numbers of immigrant families (see the section Today's Parent and Chapter 1 as well). Long-held perceptions of what constitutes a family may no longer correspond to the reality of today's definition of a family. Family support takes on new meaning when the differences in family makeup are acknowledged and supported.[1]

Public Recognition

A growing awareness of the need for a family-centered approach to parent education has been recognized by several government agencies. From its beginning in 1965, the federal Head Start program mandated parent involvement as necessary for the health and welfare of many young children. More recently, the Education of the Handicapped Amendments (PL 99-457) in 1986 required early intervention services aimed at the family, not just the child (see Chapter 3). PL 99-457 includes parents as members of a team of professionals who develop an individualized education plan, an IEP, related to the child and family's needs. Two states, Minnesota and Missouri, have developed comprehensive, family-centered early childhood education programs funded through local school districts. Figure 8–3 summarizes the four components of a high-quality parent program.

Reggio Emilia: An Exemplary Partnership

One of the best examples of school–parent partnerships that bears witness to Powell's (1989) criteria for high-quality programs are the schools of Reggio Emilia, Italy (see discussions in Chapters 1, 2, and 10). There is an assumption of strong and active parent involvement at every level of school functioning. This is not surprising, because the schools were originally founded as par-

A good parent information center can inform parents of the need for greater child advocacy.

[1]The more information the school has about the families of the children enrolled (preferred language, work schedules, particular challenges, areas of expertise, and so forth), the higher the likelihood of successful home–school relationships.

Four Components of a High-Quality Parent Program

1. **Collaboration between parents and teachers** is necessary to ensure that the goals, methods, and content of a parent program are responsive to parent needs, and this will vary according to the population the school serves. Parents have many needs in common, but they do not all have the same needs at the same time. An assessment of parent needs is critical, as is parent involvement in planning the program.

2. **Strengthen social services and community support networks** to sustain the interconnectedness of the child, the family, and the community, balancing the needs of the children and of the parents. Keep in mind that the children's best interests are the common goal of a good parent program.

3. **Tailor programs to the needs and characteristics** of the specific parent population, responding to cultural characteristics and values of ethnic populations. Support groups for teenage parents, non–English-speaking parents, and parents who are working on their high school equivalency tests may be developed alongside the usual parenting classes and workshops.[1]

4. **Base the program on mutual respect**, where parents have the freedom to accept what is useful and reject what they cannot in good conscience adopt for themselves.

[1]As American families continue to change, programs for young children will need to create linkages between family and school environments.

FIGURE 8–3 Powell (1989) has defined elements of a high-quality parent program that promote the family's contribution to their children's education and growth as well as a more equal and meaningful partnership.

ent cooperatives; part of the guiding philosophy continues to uphold a model of equal and extended partnership. Malaguzzi (Edwards, Gandini, & Forman, 1993) refers to this balanced responsibility of teachers, parents, and children as a "triad at the center of education," which in turn counts on the rest of the community to provide a cultural context for children's learning.

School-based management fosters meaningful participation of parents. All of the decisions are made by the teachers, parents, cooks, and other staff members within each school setting. No area seems the exclusive property of either parents or teachers. Curriculum planning, for instance, depends on the family's involvement, interest, and contributions.

Parents are the core of the individual school boards, on which their numbers are well represented; they are an integral part of the decision-making process that determines their children's education. Frequent parent meetings are held to inform parents of the school's program and to bring them up to date on what their children are doing. Other meetings may be focused on a topic of interest or an opportunity for parents to explore and debate, or an expert may lecture on a topic regarding their children's development. Smaller groups of parents meet throughout the year with the teachers to talk about their children and the program. Individual parent–teacher conferences, which either can request, are held to deal with specific concerns.

There are opportunities as well to be actively involved in the daily life of the school. Parents, teachers, and town residents build furnishings and maintain materials for the classrooms and the schoolyard and rearrange the space to accommodate program needs. In sessions with teachers and **pedagogistas,** parents learn various educational techniques necessary to the program, such as photography and puppet making, and they use these new skills in the classroom with their children. Using the whole town as a backdrop, parents participate in many of the field trips to city landmarks, or as small groups visiting a child's home. Recording and transcribing children's activities and projects are often a parent's responsibility (see Chapter 10).

The meaning of family is communicated to the children of Reggio Emilia throughout their school environment. In classroom dramatic play areas and in the school's own kitchen there are displays of foods, materials, and utensils common to the region and found in the children's homes. Children are encouraged to bring special objects from home, and these are accorded special and beautifully arranged display space. Photographs of children and families abound. These elements are the vehicles used to ensure a rich flow of communication between the school and the homes of the children of Reggio Emilia.

The schools of Reggio Emilia seem to have a unique reciprocal relationship with the families they serve. Parents have influence and help effect change; in turn, the schools influence and change parents. Each becomes a stronger voice for what is in the best interest of the child.

✳ TODAY'S PARENT

There is little preparation for the job of being a parent, and many parents are pretty much alone as they strike out in unfamiliar territory. There is often no extended family to teach new mothers and fathers some of the traditional, time-honored child-rearing skills. There is no one with whom parents can share their worries, frustrations, and concerns.

An important change has taken place in recent years. Raising children as a shared experience is becoming a commonly accepted way of life. Influenced by changing values and attitudes toward traditional gender roles, men are taking an active part in raising their families. Fathers seem more aware of the critical role they play in the child's life, and child-rearing is no longer just the mother's responsibility.

Stages of Parent Development

The role of parent is not a static one; parents grow and change as their children do. The six identifiable stages of **parent development** are described in a manner similar to the stages of growth that occur as all humans develop (Galinsky, 1987). Because parents may have children of different ages, they may be going through several stages at once. Growth can occur at any time and during any stage (Figure 8–4).

Because half of the women with children younger than age six work outside the home, fathers often bring children to child care.

Six Stages of Parenthood

Stage	Parent Task	Age of Child(ren)
1. Image-making stage	Parents draw on their memories and fantasies of what kind of parent they want to be; they prepare for changes in themselves and with other important adults.	Occurs during gestation
2. Nurturing stage	Parents confront the demands of attachment; they compare their images with their actual experiences.	From birth until child says "No," around 18–24 months
3. Authority stage	Parents define the rules of the family system and their roles in it; they decide what kind of authority to be.	From 18 months to 5 years of age
4. Interpretive stage	Parents decide how to interpret the world to their child and are concerned with how they interpret themselves to their children, how they are developing the children's self-concepts, and what kind of values, knowledge, and skills to promote.	From late pre-school years until the beginning of adolescence
5. Interdependent stage	Parents renegotiate the rules with their teenagers; issues of stage 3 (authority) reappear; parents form a new relationship with their almost-grown children.	The teenage years
6. Departure stage	Parents evaluate their sense of success or failure—whether they have achieved the parent-child relationship they want—and redefine these new relationships.	When children leave home

FIGURE 8–4 The role of a parent changes in various ways as parent and child grow older together. (Adapted from Galinksy, E. [1987]. *Between generations.* Reading, MA: Addison-Wesley.)

As they gain confidence in themselves, as more children are added to the family, and as each family member matures, parents continually change. The issues they face with only one child are altered considerably when a second or third baby is born. As each of the children grows, develops, and progresses through stages, parents are required to adapt. As parents adjust their own ideas about child-rearing to the realities they experience, they grow as parents. Changing their own behavior is a sign of growth. In other words, parents do not have a consistent or permanent pattern of child rearing over the years (Bee, 1999).

Patterns of Child-Rearing

Baumrind (1972) defined three types of parental styles: authoritative, authoritarian, and permissive. **Authoritative parents** are associated with the highest levels of self-esteem, self-reliance, independence, and curiosity in children. They provide a warm, loving atmosphere with clear limits and high expectations. When Baumrind followed up the children of her study when they were eight or nine, she found that her earlier findings on authoritative parental effects persisted.

In contrast, the child-rearing patterns of **authoritarian parents** reflect high control and strict maturity demands combined with relatively low communication and nurturance. Authoritarian parents are dictatorial; they expect and demand obedience, yet lack warmth and affection. **Permissive parents** are essentially the reverse of authoritarian ones. There is a high level of warmth and affection but little control. Clear standards and rules are not set, nor are they reinforced consistently.

This research points out how children are affected by the way their parents raise them. The role of the teacher becomes one of helping parents learn appropriate and effective ways to raise their children.

The Changing American Family

The American family as a whole is experiencing significant alterations. Statistics gathered almost 30 years apart show a dramatic picture of the changing family, as shown in Figures 8–5 and 8–6.

Since the 1970s the United States has experienced a significant demographic

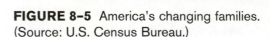

Since 1970, the number of

- **divorced persons has more than tripled.**
- **children living with only one parent has more than doubled.**
- **children living with grandparents has increased 42 percent.**
- **single mothers has more than tripled.**
- **single fathers has increased nearly five times.**
- **births to unmarried teenagers nearly doubled.**

FIGURE 8–5 America's changing families. (Source: U.S. Census Bureau.)

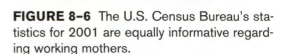

- **78 percent of mothers with children ages six to 13 are in the labor force.**
- **65 percent of mothers with children younger than age six are in the labor force.**
- **59 percent of mothers with infants (younger than age one) are in the labor force.**

FIGURE 8–6 The U.S. Census Bureau's statistics for 2001 are equally informative regarding working mothers.

transformation, with non-European cultural groups playing a more dominant role in American society. A new pluralistic environment of ethnic populations is being created, requiring teachers and caregivers to respond to the cultural needs of children and their families. Data on the ethnic distribution of the school tell the story. These population dynamics will require a multicultural mindset, and educators will lead the way in helping children learn that diversity is not just tolerated, but valued. The challenge for teachers is to be prepared to understand families in their various forms and be part of their family support system. Figure 8–7 shows a recent U.S. Census Bureau breakdown, in percentages, of school enrollment. The Census Bureau projects that in the 21st century, Hispanics will be the fastest-growing population and will surpass African-Americans as the largest minority group in the country. The greatest growth in school enrollment will be among Hispanics, increasing by about 60 percent.

Parents with Unique Needs

Parents are parents the world over and have mutual problems and pleasures as they go about bringing up their young. Their shared experiences create an automatic bond whenever parents meet. Today, there are some families, however, who face additional challenges in child-rearing and who may need added teacher support. These are:

- ✪ parents of children with developmental delays and disabilities
- ✪ single parents

Ethnic Distribution of U.S. School Population, late 1990s	%
White non-Hispanics	65
Hispanics	16
African-Americans	15
Asian/Pacific Islanders	4
Native American/Alaska Natives	1

FIGURE 8–7 The U.S. Census Bureau's statistics regarding the representation of students in elementary and secondary schools in the late 1990s.

- ✪ adoptive and foster parents
- ✪ parents who both work outside the home
- ✪ divorced parents
- ✪ gay/lesbian parents
- ✪ homeless parents
- ✪ teenage parents
- ✪ grandparents raising grandchildren
- ✪ parents who are raising their children in a culture not their own
- ✪ parents who do not speak English and whose child is in a setting in which English is the predominant language
- ✪ multiracial families
- ✪ first-time parents

Many of these family characteristics place parents in situations in which they do not have access to an extended family support system. Any one or combination of these situations can create complex challenges for parents. Teachers should become aware of the forces at work within these families and be sensitive to their needs. Teachers should treat these parents with the same respect as they do any other. It is not necessary to single them out, and, indeed, such an effort may be resented. For the most part, teachers can help these parents by focusing on the many interests and

Video View Point 8-2

"Ethnic pride and cultural pride are important in the identity of school-age children."

Competency: Family Interaction, School, and Community

Age Group: School Age

Critical Thinking Questions:

1. **How does your family express its culture?**
2. **What are the types of family cultures represented in the school where you work or observe? How would you assist children in expressing their culture to others?**

concerns they share with all other parents.[1] In some cases, additional support for these parents may be called for, such as:

- helping parents locate community resources to assist them

- putting them in touch with other parents who have similar parenting circumstances

- assisting them in exploring school settings for the future

- seeing that they are included in all school functions

- learning about their special needs

- seeking their help and advice

- helping them establish contact with other parents who may be willing to assist in translating, transporting, babysitting, and sharing friendship.

Meeting the Needs of Single Parents

Faced with the economic necessity to work, single parents must cope not only with raising children alone, but also with child care arrangements and costs. Particularly hard hit are women who head single-parent households. They are more likely than men to live below the poverty level, to never have married, not to have finished high school, and to be members of a minority population.

To best serve the interests of children, educators must be sensitive to the unique aspects of raising children alone. This means re-examining school policies and attitudes that may overlook the needs of single parents.[2] Overburdened child care profession-

als, some of whom are single parents themselves, need to be flexible in exploring new avenues of home–school collaboration.

Questions you might ask yourself and them are:

1. What kind of involvement in a child's classroom is possible for a working single parent?

2. How can you help parents feel connected even if they are unable to be at the center?

3. What is appropriate support for single parents?

4. How judgmental are you about single parents? about single mothers?

5. How do you help parents and children deal with issues concerning the absent parent?

6. What are some of the best strategies for helping children cope with the transitions when they visit one parent or the other?

These and other similar questions must become part of the agenda at staff meetings, in-service days for teachers, and parent-group meetings.

Needs of Immigrant Families

1970: 4.8 percent of the U.S. population was born outside the United States.
2000: 10.4% of the U.S. population was born outside the United States.

The U.S. Census Bureau (2000) highlights the extensive changes in immigration over the last 30 years. The origin of immigrants has also undergone a significant shift. Over 50 percent of immigrants are from Latin America, 25 percent are from Asia, and 15 percent are from Europe. The

[1]Many of the challenges and joys of parenting young children are universal, crossing the lines of the child's family structure, culture, ability, social class, and so on.
[2]School policies can seem hostile or insensitive to the challenges faced by single–parent families (e.g., policies that require parent conferences during workday hours).

largest individual population of immigrants comes from Mexico (Camarota, 2000). The states with the largest foreign-born populations are California, New York, Florida, Texas, New Jersey, and Illinois. According to the *Harvard Educational Review* (2001), immigrant children are the fastest growing sector of the U.S. population, and one of every five children in the United States is either an immigrant or the child of an immigrant parent.

An immediate effect of this wave of immigrants on schools is that more than 17 percent of children approaching school age are immigrant children (Camarota, 2000). The future school population in the 21st century will be defined by the lack of minority or majority groups. Today, about 65 percent of school-age children are non-Hispanic whites. That is likely to drop to less than 50 percent by 2040. The largest growth will occur among Hispanics, who are expected to reach 25 percent of the school-age population within 20 years (Olson, 2000). These data, added to existing ethnic populations already present in the United States, challenge the early childhood teacher to a multicultural sensitivity not yet realized. They also challenge the profession to aggressively recruit and train early childhood education professionals within these cultures.

A willingness to learn various cultural norms and a knowledge of languages will be helpful for teachers to communicate with children and parents whose primary language is not English. Some studies suggest that teachers' stereotypes of social and racial subgroups influence their attitudes about a parent's ability and competence, so teachers will want to examine their own biases (Powell, 1989). See the appropriate sections in other chapters throughout the text for discussion of teacher bias, anti-bias curricula, and anti-bias environments.

Miscommunication may be a problem when teaching a classroom of diverse children. When cultural perspectives of the family and the school differ markedly, teachers can easily misread a child's attitude and abilities because of different styles of languages and behaviors. Classroom practices may be at odds with a child's cultural norms. For example, in some preschool settings, children are encouraged to call their teachers by their first name. This informal style of addressing authority figures may make some parents uncomfortable. How teachers interact with children, their teaching language, and the strategies they use to guide children's behavior are areas in which immigrant parents can help teachers learn the cultural differences that cause difficulties for children.

✿ COMMUNICATING WITH FAMILIES

Parent Education and Involvement

Almost any contact between the teacher and the parent can be perceived as parent education. Teachers interpret children's behavior to their parents, suggest alternative ways for dealing with problems, show them toys and games that are appropriate, hold workshops on parenting skills, mention books and articles of interest to parents, and reinforce parent interest in and attention to their children's education. All of these activities are considered parent education. Some are planned; some are spontaneous. Parent education happens frequently, whether in a class on positive discipline or in an informal chat about car seat safety.

Parent involvement in children's education has a wide variety of options, as discussed earlier in this chapter. The concept of parent education and involvement in early childhood education programs is broadening to include any number of family support programs based on the needs of parents and their children. Parent education and involvement are at the core of the family–school relationship and go a long way to promote a true partnership between parents and teachers. Again, the NAEYC Code of Ethical Conduct (see Appendix B) can be useful. Sections I and II outline the teacher's professional role regarding children and their families.

Keeping in Touch

There are many ways for teachers to increase their communication with parents.[1] In doing so, teachers demonstrate that they value the role parents play in their children's lives. Five of the most common ways teachers can involve and inform parents are:

- *Classroom newsletters.* They give a general idea of what the children are doing, any special events taking place in class, and personal information about

There are many avenues for parent–teacher communication. This bilingual bulletin board, located just outside the classroom door, holds newsletters, notices, and even children's art.

new babies, vacations, or other important events in the lives of the children. Be sure the newsletter is written in the language of the parents of the children in the class.

- *Bulletin boards.* Posted where parents can see them, these boards contain notices about parent meetings, guest speakers, community resources, child care, babysitting, clothing and furniture exchanges, and library story hours. Information regarding health programs, automobile and toy safety, and immunization clinics are also publicized. Post information on cultural events appropriate to the ethnic makeup of the school community.

- *A parents place.* Providing an area or room at the school set aside for parent use can be an important step in letting parents know they are wanted and needed. Some schools provide space for a parent lounge, complete with a library of resource books on child-rearing. If there is no available space, set up a coffee bar in the office or hall. The smallest amount of space—even a countertop with magazines—is a start.

- *Informal contacts.* These are the easiest and most useful lines of communication with parents. All it takes is a phone call, a brief note, an e-mail, or a brief talk on a daily basis. For parents who have difficulty attending meetings or who do not accompany their child to and from school, teachers can send home a note along with a sample of artwork, a story the child has dictated, or a photograph of the child with friends.

- *Home visits.* Depending on its purpose, a home visit can be used to enhance communications. The visit might be set

[1]Parents can be an invaluable source of information, support, and affirmation to the teacher and the school.

up to focus only on the relationship between the teacher and the child. Or the visit might have a purely social function—a way for teachers to meet the whole family and for the family to get acquainted with the teachers. In any event, the teacher can use this as a bridge to build a pleasant, casual beginning with this family.

Parent–Teacher Conferences

Parent–teacher conferences are the backbone of any good parent–teacher relationship. They provide a way of coming together to focus on the needs of the individual child. Conferencing can be a mutually supportive link established between the adults who are most concerned about an individual child, with the purpose of helping the child reach his or her fullest potential possible.

Conferences between parents and teachers are held for many reasons. The initial conference, when the child first enrolls in school, may focus on the family. It may include a brief overview of the child's development, daily habits, and interests, as well as the parents' view of the child and their expectations. The teacher will want to assure parents that they are free to call at any time if they have questions about the school or their child. Further into the school year, both parents and teachers will want an up-to-date assessment of the child's progress, noting especially the strengths of the child and areas where improvement is needed. (Several formats to help focus the discussion are cited in Chapter 6.)

A conference may be called at any time by either a parent or a teacher if there are concerns to discuss. A written outline listing the goals of the conference will help guide the discussion and direct it to problem areas. Every occasion when parents and teachers get together to talk about a child is a step toward building trusting relationships between home and school.[1] For a conference model that is satisfying and productive to both parties, see Figure 8–8.

Maintaining Privacy and Confidentiality

The more involved parents are in the workings of the school, the more important it is to establish guidelines for protecting the privacy of all the families enrolled. Parents who volunteer in the office, the classroom, or on a field trip must understand they cannot carry tales out of school about any of the children, the teachers, the administration, or other parents. The school must be clear about its expectations for ensuring such privacy and communicate policies to parents. Parents who work on advisory boards, planning committees, or other activities that allow them access to the school office should be sensitive to the confidentiality issue and respect the privacy of every family enrolled in the school.

KEY TERMS

authoritarian parents
authoritative parents
ecology of the family
family-centered approach
family-support movement
parent development
pedagogistas
permissive parents

[1]All parents want their children to do well, yet may feel uncertain when dealing with a language and culture that is not their own.

Building Home and School Relationships Through Effective Parent-Teacher Conferences

1. *Schedule conferences on a regular basis.* Parents and teachers should share some of the positive aspects of child growth and development and not meet only in crisis. This promotes better feelings about one another, not to mention the child, if meetings are at times other than when a problem occurs.

2. *Be prepared.* Discuss with the staff ahead of time any points they want to include. Gather any materials, notes, and samples of the child's work that might illustrate a point.

3. *Select a quiet place, free from interruption.* If necessary, sign up for use of a conference room. Make sure that someone is available to intercept phone calls and other appointments.

4. *Have a clear purpose.* Use a written format as a guide to keep focused on the intent of the conference. This gives a brief reminder of points to be covered and serves to keep parents on the track.

5. *Put parents at ease right away.* Offer them a cup of coffee or share an amusing anecdote that just took place in the classroom. Acknowledge the important part they played in the school fair. These light, positive comments will help relax both teacher and parent.

6. *Use up-to-date information and data.* Cite examples, from teacher's observations, that occurred that morning or a few days ago. Include examples of situations that occurred when they were present. "Timmy is very empathic for a three-year-old, isn't he? That was so clear from the way you two were talking as you came through the door today."

7. *Give them a place to shine.* Tell them what they do well—their success with car-pool crowds or in mediating fights in the yard. If they have a special talent they have shared with the class, comment on its impact on the children.

8. *Ask—don't tell.* Get them talking by asking open-ended questions. "How is that new bedtime arrangement working?" "Tell me more about Katie's eating habits." Teachers will relate these to their own knowledge and experiences with the child and then share what has worked in school, but acknowledge the difference between school and home, teacher and parent. Learn how to listen. Concentrate on what the parents are saying. Don't listen with half an ear while planning an appropriate response or comment.

9. *Avoid blaming parents.* Keep the conversation based on mutual concerns and how to help each other. Look at some alternatives together and make a plan of action. Discuss ways to check in with each other or provide for follow-through at school or home. This way the parent will have a feeling of working together rather than of being blamed.

FIGURE 8–8 One of the most important responsibilities of the teacher is the parent conference. A good parent–teacher conference is focused and strengthens the relationship between home and school.

10. *Know where and how to secure community resources and referrals.* Many parents do not know where to get a child's speech tested, what an IQ test is, or where to secure family therapy. They may be unaware of play groups, gymnastic schools, library story hours, or children's museums. Be sure the school can provide this information for parents who need it.

11. *Take time to write a brief report after the conference.* Make special note of who attended and who requested the conference, what important issues were raised by either the parents or the teacher, what solutions and strategies were discussed, and what time was agreed upon for checking in with each other regarding progress.

12. *Find a good role model.* Ask experienced teachers to share their ingredients for success. When possible, attend a parent conference with one of them. Observe what works for them and learn from their experience. Ask them to critique your own performance after a conference.

FIGURE 8–8, continued

 Teaching Applications

1. What are some of your own myths about parenthood? Make two lists, one headed "Myths Teachers Have about Parents" and the other, "Myths Parents Have about Teachers." Compare the two and then discuss them with both a parent and a teacher.

2. Discuss the following in small groups, then share your responses with the rest of your classmates. Finish the sentences:
   a. "For me, the most difficult part of being a parent today is or would be . . ."
   b. "When I have children, I plan to (work/stay at home/do both) because . . ."
   c. "As a single parent, I will . . ."
   d. "When I have children, I will raise them (just as my parents raised me/the opposite of the way I was raised) because . . ."

3. Look at the Ten Essentials for Teacher–Family Collaboration. Give an example of how you would apply each of these principles in your classroom. Do you see any examples of ways these guidelines are not being met? What would you do to change that?

4. Are there ethnic minorities in your school setting? How are these parents supported or not supported by school practices and policies? What changes would you make?

6. Interview several single parents, both men and women. What do they say are the most critical issues they face? How do they see their children's schools supporting them? Where is there a need for improvement? How will this information influence your work with children and families?

REFERENCES

Baumrind, D. (1972). Socialization and instrumental competence in young children. In W. W. Hartrup (Ed.), *The young child: Review of research* (Vol. 2). Washington, DC: National Association for the Education of Young Children.

Bee, H. (1999). *The developing child.* Menlo Park, CA: Addison-Wesley.

Camarota, S. A. (2001, January). *Immigrants in the United States—2000: A snapshot of America's foreign-born population.* Washington, DC: Center for Immigration Studies.

Edwards, C., Gandini, L., & Forman, G. (1993). *The hundred languages of children: The Reggio Emilia approach to early childhood education.* Norwood, NJ: Albex.

Galinsky, E. (1987). *Between generations.* Reading, MA: Addison-Wesley.

Harvard Educational Review, 71. (2001).

Kagan, S. L. (1991, January 18). Family-support programs and the schools. *Education Week.*

LeShan, E. (1992). *When your child drives you crazy.* New York: St. Martin's Press.

Olson, L. (2000, September 27). Minority groups to emerge as a majority in U.S. schools. *Education Week.*

Powell, D. R. (1989). *Families and early childhood programs.* Washington, DC: National Association for the Education of Young Children.

Powell, D. R. (1998). Research in review: Reweaving parents into the fabric of early childhood programs. *Young Children,* September, 60–67.

U.S. Bureau of the Census. (2000, March). *Current population survey.* Washington, DC: U.S. Government Printing Office.

Additional resources for this chapter can be found by visiting the Online Companion™ at www.earlychilded.delmar.com. This supplemental material includes a Study Guide with chapter review questions (and answers), critical thinking questions and activities, and annotated Web sites.

Section 4

What Is Being Taught?

Creating Environments

QUESTIONS FOR THOUGHT

What criteria are used in creating a developmentally appropriate learning environment?

What health and safety measures are considered when planning the total environment?

What are basic materials for a program?

In planning a temporal environment, what kinds of daily schedules should teachers consider?

In creating an interpersonal environment, how does the teacher create an atmosphere for learning?

✿ CREATING THE ENVIRONMENT

Definition

The **environment** is where children play out the themes of childhood: their interests, triumphs, problems, and concerns. An environment for children, therefore, includes all of the conditions that affect their surroundings and the people in it. It is the sum of the physical and human qualities that combine to create a space in which children and adults work and play together. Environment is the content teachers arrange; it is a schedule they create; it is a feeling they communicate. Environment is the total picture—from the traffic flow to the daily schedule, from the numbers of chairs at a table to the placement of the guinea pig cage. It is a means to an end. The choices teachers make concerning the physical setting (the equipment and materials, the room arrangement, the playground and the facilities available), the **temporal** setting (timing for **transitions, routines,** activities), and the **interpersonal** setting (number and nature of teachers, ages and numbers of children, types and style of interactions among them) combine to support the program goals.

Each environment is unique. There is no such thing as a single model or ideal setting for all children. The environments adults create for children have a powerful effect on their behavior. Children's play is strongly influenced by settings and materials. Social interaction, independence, or imaginary play may all be fostered—or discouraged—by the ways the indoor and outdoor spaces are designed and used. "The environment," say Dodge and Colker (2002), "is the curriculum's textbook." Teachers arrange the environment to promote what they feel is best in children. For instance, in Reggio Emilia the environment is called the "third teacher" (the first is the parents and the second is the teachers). Whether the environment is an adapted church basement, an elementary school classroom, or a space made especially for young children, it will be a powerful force in their lives.

All settings for the care and education of young children have the same basic environmental components and the same basic goals—meeting the needs of children—despite the fact that programs vary widely in the size of the group, age of children, length of day, program focus, and number of staff. For instance, size matters. When a center gets too large, rules and routine guidance are emphasized, outdoor areas often have little variety, and children are often less enthusiastically involved and more often wandering. Figure 9–1 gives recommended standards for group size and adult–child ratios.

Although there are endless variations in planning for children, certain common elements must be considered:

1. The physical plant
2. Available resources
3. Program goals

What do teachers mean when they say they want to create environments for learning?

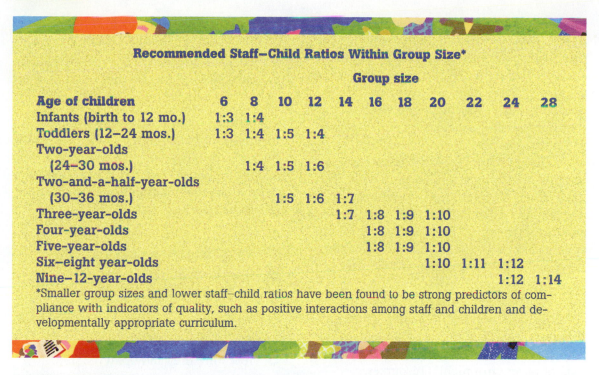

Recommended Staff–Child Ratios Within Group Size*

Age of children	6	8	10	12	14	16	18	20	22	24	28
Infants (birth to 12 mo.)	1:3	1:4									
Toddlers (12–24 mos.)	1:3	1:4	1:5	1:4							
Two-year-olds (24–30 mos.)		1:4	1:5	1:6							
Two-and-a-half-year-olds (30–36 mos.)			1:5	1:6	1:7						
Three-year-olds					1:7	1:8	1:9	1:10			
Four-year-olds						1:8	1:9	1:10			
Five-year-olds						1:8	1:9	1:10			
Six–eight year-olds								1:10	1:11	1:12	
Nine–12-year-olds										1:12	1:14

*Smaller group sizes and lower staff–child ratios have been found to be strong predictors of compliance with indicators of quality, such as positive interactions among staff and children and developmentally appropriate curriculum.

FIGURE 9–1 Group size and staff–child ratio are two aspects of the environment that affect the quality of children's education experience (Bredekamp, 1998).

Physical Plant

Before creating an environment for children, the early childhood education teacher must analyze the physical plant. A building that is inviting and beautiful beckons children to enter; a space with color and light encourages children to play with both. Many settings use space designed for other purposes, such as a family home, a church basement, or an empty elementary school classroom. The size and shape of the designated space determine how to plan for safe and appropriate use. To rescale the space, teachers shift from an adult perspective to a child's scale. Getting on one's knees provides a glimpse of the environment from the child's point of view; child space is measured from the floor and playground up. A child's stature determines what is available to and noticed by that child. For crawling infants, space consists primarily of the floor, whereas school-aged children can use and learn from the space up to about five feet, roughly their own height. It is this perspective that teachers must remember as they plan the physical space for children (see the section Planning for the Environment).

Resources

In planning the environment, the teacher must know what kinds of resources are available. The first is financial assets. Priority should be given to teacher salaries and benefits, equipment and materials, and other related services (maintenance, office help, bus service). By knowing the extent of the fiscal boundaries and budget limits, a teacher can plan a complete environment.

Good environmental principles do not depend on numerous or expensive equipment, materials, or buildings. Some equipment can be made, borrowed, or purchased second-hand. In church-based schools, annual rummage sales provide dress-up clothes, books, toys, and some appliances. Families can provide computer paper, wood scraps, or office supplies for dramatic play kits. Community sources, such as the public-library storyteller or a seniors group, may be available for extended experiences for the children. Effective fund-raising provides an added source of revenue in many schools and centers.

The human resources must also be identified. Adults do their best with children when their abilities, experience, and availability are matched with what is expected of them. A first-year teacher's resources are best expended in the classroom, whereas a master teacher is ready to use her expertise in other ways, such as orienting parents or evaluating curriculum materials. Just as we try to match children's developing skills to the tasks at hand, so too should we consider individual people as part of an environment's resources.

Program Goals

The program must be defined in relationship to the physical space because the goals and objectives of the program are expressed directly in the arrangement of the environment.

The goals of an early childhood education program will vary widely because early childhood settings contain such a wide range of age and experience. Harms, Cryer, and Clifford (2003) name three general goals in designing environments: to plan soft and responsive settings that avoid behavior problems, to set up predictable environments that encourage independence, and to create a stimulating space for active learning. Teachers plan a program in which the goals are reflected in the environment in the following ways:

1. The room and yard are arranged to give maximum exposure to the materials and equipment teachers want children to use.

2. Teachers take care to arrange the daily schedule in ways that provide the time

blocks needed to teach content when and how they want to teach it.

3. Teachers see that a warm relationship exists among the teachers and in their interactions with children.

When children walk into a classroom, the environment should communicate how they are to live and work in that setting. Children should receive clear messages about what they can and cannot do there, as well as cues that tell them:

- Where they are free to move to and where they cannot go
- How they will be treated
- Who will be there with them
- What material and equipment they can use
- How long they may play
- That they are safe there
- What is expected of them

Figure 9–2 describes how teachers use the environment to tell children what is important there.

For instance, when it is time to go outside, the doors are opened. If children need to stay off a piece of equipment, it is marked by dividers or a flag, and a teacher stationed nearby explains the instruction. Children know that they matter when they are welcomed each day, and they know their time is valued when teachers tell them how long they have to complete a project or play sequence and when that time is nearly up.

The teacher is the key element in making a creative environment. It is not the facility alone that counts as much as it is the teacher's understanding of all the environmental factors and how they are related to one another. The indicators of quality in a program, such as the adult–child ratio, the stability, education, and experience of the caregiver, and group size all contribute to an environment that meets its goals for children.

Children Need To . . .	So the Environment Should . . .
Be treated as individuals, with unique strengths and developmental goals.	Ensure that the teacher–child ratio supports one-to-one interactions. Provide private as well as public spaces so children can experience group and solitary play. Ensure that children have ready access to teachers and materials. Be staffed by teachers who will set goals for each child on the basis of observation and assessment. Be equipped with materials that will match the developmental level of the group. Provide a balance of quiet and active times.
See themselves and their family culture represented positively in the environment; be exposed to cultural diversity in meaningful ways.	Include pictures, books, dolls, dramatic play materials, activities, and people that reflect many cultures and life experiences. Staff teachers who understand and value the children's home cultures and family practices. Provide opportunities for various cultural habits, activities and celebrations to occur.
Have an opportunity to make choices and participate in independent learning.	Be arranged to encourage free exploration and a clear view of what is available. Offer a variety of activity centers so children can explore, manipulate, probe. Allow large blocks of time for child-initiated free play so children can make more than one choice. Provide an adequate number of trained teachers to support self-discovery.
Learn to be part of a group.	Be set up for group play with three to five chairs around the tables, easels adjacent to one another, more than one telephone, carriage, wagon. Facilitate regular scheduling of small and large group times, which children are encouraged to attend and participate in. Include trained staff who select developmentally appropriate group activities for the group. Allow children to use each other as resources. Provide activities that will stress cooperation and social interaction.
Become responsible for the setting and take care of the equipment and materials.	Schedule cleanup times as part of the daily routine. Include teachers and children working together to restore order. Allow time for children to be instructed in the proper use of materials and be made aware of their general care.

FIGURE 9–2 The environment mirrors the goals of the program.

| Be aware of the behavioral limits of the school setting. | Ensure that the teachers and the daily schedule reflect the important rules of behavior.
Include teachers who deal with behavior problems in a fair and consistent way.
Allow plenty of time during transitions so that children can move from one activity to another without stress.
Be arranged to avoid runways and dead ends created by furniture. |
| Be with adults who will supervise and facilitate play and encourage learning throughout the day. | Be set up before children arrive so teachers are free to greet them.
Encourage teacher–child interactions through the use of small groups and a time schedule that allows for in-depth interactions. |

FIGURE 9–2, continued

A room is just a room and a yard is just a yard until a teacher makes them environments for learning. The teachers themselves are the most responsive part of the environment; it is they who converse, smile, appreciate, give information, and see the individuality of each child. They are the ones who create the space, the time, and the atmosphere that will engage children's curiosity and involvement.

Developmentally Appropriate Learning Environments

We are all affected by our environment, and for young children this is especially so. Although some children are particularly sensitive to stimulation (noise, light, clutter), all children's behavior is affected by what is in front of them. Therefore, we must pay attention to what is in their environment and what happens during their stay there.

The following are 16 elements of such an environment:

1. Create a high-activity, low-stress, and brain-compatible environment. Positive changes occur in the brain when a child is engaged in a learning experience, and the brain "downshifts" when a threat is perceived. The classroom environment deter-

mines, to some degree, the functioning ability of children's brains (Jensen, 1998; Rushton, 2001). Centers that allow small groups to form and focus on motor, intellectual, or social activity will stimulate learning without pressure or stress to perform or wait. "A developmentally appropriate learning environment is designed for individual children to be messy, noisy and quiet, alone and social, and active and still," says Greenman (2000). "It is designed to accommodate much STUFF— loose parts—the raw materials of discovery for active hands and minds."

2. Build culturally responsive environments. First and foremost, it is important that the environment reflect the cultures of the children in the classroom. Programs that value interdependence may set up the learning environment to encourage children's reliance on adults and each other; a Euro-American cultural value of independence is expressed when emphasizing **self-help** skills. If the teachers don't look like the children, or their spaces don't look like home, it is critical that the interpersonal and temporal aspects of their environment complement their home culture (Figure 9–3.)

Overall Environment

1. In general, is the classroom hospitable?

2. What is hanging on the walls?

   If there is work done by children, does it all look alike? For example, are there bunnies or other animals that you have cut out and the children colored, or is the art *genuinely* done by the children?

   Yes ___   No ___

   Are the pictures of people hanging on walls or bulletin boards representative of a multicultural community?

   Yes ___   No ___

   Even if pictures *do* represent a diverse population, are they stereotypic in any way? For example, is there an alphabet chart that uses "Indian" to symbolize the letter "I" or a calendar that features little girls wearing dresses watching little boys involved in activities? Are there Hawaiians in grass skirts or people from South America sparsely clothed and with spears and painted faces?

   Yes ___   No ___

3. Are all of the pictures for children and the art hung *at children's eye level?*

   Yes ___   No ___

4. Are parents and/or family members involved in creating a hospitable classroom environment?

   Yes ___   No ___

   If yes, how do you include them? How might you make them feel even more a part of their children's school lives?

Blocks

1. Are the accessories in the block area representative of various cultural groups and family configurations?

   Yes ___   No ___

   List them below to be sure that no major cultural group or family configuration is missing.

2. Are the people block accessories stereotypic in terms of sex roles?

   Yes ___   No ___

   If yes, how will you change them?

Social Studies

1. Does the curriculum as a whole help the children increase their understanding and acceptance of attitudes, values, and lifestyles that are unfamiliar to them?

   Yes ___   No ___

   If yes, how?

   If no, what will you do to change your current curriculum so that it reflects a diversity of values?

2. Are materials and games racially or sex-role stereotypic—for example, black people shooting dice or boys playing war games? Are women depicted only as caregivers while men do lots of exciting jobs?

   Yes ___   No ___

   If yes, what will you weed from your current collection? What materials and games can you add that decrease stereotypes?

FIGURE 9–3 A multicultural environment checklist provides questions for teachers to evaluate and monitor progress toward an anti-bias environment for children. (Adapted from Kendall, 1996.)

Dramatic Play

1. Is there a wide variety of clothes, including garments from various cultural groups, in the dramatic-play area?

   Yes ___ No ___

   If yes, what are they?

   If no, what do you need to add?

2. Are the pictures on the walls and the props in the dramatic-play area representative of a diversity of cultures?

   Yes ___ No ___

   If yes, what is included?

   If no, what do you need to add?

3. Are the dolls in the dramatic-play area representative of a broad variety of racial groups?

   Yes ___ No ___

   If no, what do you need to add?

4. Are the dolls of color just white dolls whose skin color has been changed?

   Yes ___ No ___

   If so, which ones need replacing?

Language Arts

1. Does the classroom have a wide variety of age-appropriate and culturally diverse books and language-arts materials?

   Yes ___ No ___

   What are the strengths of the collection in general?

   Where are there gaps?

2. Are there stories about a variety of people from each of the following groups in the book corner?

   ___ Native-American cultures

   ___ Asian-American cultures

   ___ Black cultures

   ___ White ethnic cultures

   ___ Spanish-speaking cultures

   ___ Biracial or multiracial people

   ___ Family configurations, including biracial and multiracial families and gay and lesbian families

3. Are there any books that speak of people of diverse cultures in stereotypical or derogatory terms (e.g., describing Latinos as "lazy" or Japanese as always taking photographs)?

   Yes ___ No ___

   If yes, what are they? What new titles can you replace them with?

Music and Games

1. Do the music experiences in the curriculum reinforce the children's affirmation of cultural diversity?

   Yes ___ No ___

   If so, how?

2. Are fingerplays, games, and songs from various cultural groups used in the classroom?

   Yes ___ No ___

3. Are there many varieties of musical instruments, including ones made by children, in the classroom?

   Yes ___ No ___

Cooking

1. Do the cooking experiences in the classroom encourage the children to experiment with foods other than those with which they are familiar?

   Yes ___ No ___

2. Are the cooking experiences designed to give young children a general notion of the connections between cultural heritage and the process of preparing, cooking, and eating food?

   Yes ___ No ___

   If so, how?

   If not, what can you do differently to help children make those connections?

FIGURE 9–3, continued

3. Be sure that children have access to enough toys and materials. Make sure that supplies are stored in such a way that adults do not have to hand them to children each time they will be used. Equipment placed at a child's height on open, low shelving permits children to proceed at their own pace and to select materials without depending on adults to serve them.

4. Give children an opportunity to make choices. Both indoors and out, children should be given an abundance of materials and a range of activities from which to choose so that they will decide how they spend their time. Choosing where to play helps children practice self-direction. Children should also be able to decide with whom they would like to play and with which teachers they would like to establish close relationships.

5. Consider the developmental level of the child. Recognize that there are many things young children will not be able to do for themselves, but allow them the chance to do all they can. Be developmentally aware—know what children in the class are capable of, where they are now in their development, and what the next step should be. Three-year-old Sophie has only finished zipping her jacket. Soon she will be able to put the zipper in the housing by herself. Teacher Robert recognizes her readiness for taking the next step by squatting down to her level and holding the housing still while she tries to get the zipper going.

6. Give families ways to identify their children's space. Label cubbies with their names, a photo, or a familiar picture so that they can see where to put up their wraps, artwork, and other personal belongings.

7. See that children are responsible for caring for the equipment and materials. Establish a cleanup time in the daily schedule and allow children time to help restore the room and yard. Label shelves and cupboards with pictures or symbols of what is stored there so that children can readily find where things belong. Outlining block cabinets with the specific shape of the blocks that are stored on each shelf will help develop children's self-help skills. Outdoor areas clearly marked for wheel toys or sand play help children function independently.

8. Involve children in the process of planning and setting up the environment. Let the children help decide what they want to learn by developing areas and units around what they bring into class. For instance, Fu-Ning's guinea pig had babies, so Teacher Tanya arranged with his mother to bring the pet family to school for a visit, then sent a newsletter asking for other pets to visit. Small groups took field trips to a pet store, and the dramatic-play corner became a pet shop/animal hospital.

9. Provide children with enough time. One of the ways children learn is to repeat an activity over and over again. They explore, manipulate, experiment, and come to master an 18-piece puzzle, a lump of clay, or how to brush their teeth. Large blocks of time in the daily schedule—especially for routines—let children proceed to learn at an unhurried pace.

10. Allow children to solve their own problems without adult intervention whenever possible. The Montessori method (see Chapter 2) encourages children to find out for themselves what is or is not successful. One mark of a good teacher is a person who can let a child struggle sufficiently with a problem before stepping in to help.

Allowing children to solve their own problems without interference is one principle of successful educational environments.

11. Accept children's efforts. To support children in their quest for independence, the adult must be satisfied with children's efforts. Be ready to accept the way that Tom made his sandwich or that Shelley put her boots on the "wrong feet."

12. Communicate expectations. Let children know what they are expected to do. Tell them in both verbal and nonverbal ways. "You don't have to hurry; we have plenty of time for cleanup" lets children know they can do a job without pressure. Prompt children by giving them clues that indicate how to proceed: "If you pull up your underpants first, it will be easier to get your shorts up," the teachers tells Raymond, who is waiting for an adult to dress him. "Good. You've got the back up. Now reach around the front." By pointing out how Raymond is succeeding, the teacher communicates confidence in his ability to finish the task.

13. Be sure staff expectations are consistent. The teaching team should set common goals for each child and reinforce them consistently. Janice will become confused if one teacher tells her to get her cot ready for nap and another teacher does it for her.

14. Make it safe to make a mistake. We learn from experience. Let children know it is perfectly acceptable, indeed inevitable, that they will make mistakes. Help them deal with the consequences of their actions. Chelo spills her juice, so Dina points to the sponge and mop in the bucket. She watches and assists Chelo clean up the table, reinforcing her efforts by commenting on her scrubbing ability. Soon, the rest of the snack group is helping with napkins and sponges, too.

15. Give credit where it is due. Provide feedback so that children will know when they have been successful. Compliment Chaz on the length of time he took sorting through the nails to find the one he wanted. Tell Ellen she worked hard at opening her own Thermos bottle. Let children take some credit for their own accomplishments.

16. Let children teach one another. Encourage children to share the skills they have mastered with their peers. Actively seek out each child's way of doing things; support a diversity of approaches. Those who can tie shoes enjoy helping their friends with stubborn laces or slippery knots. Whether reading stories to one another or modeling a fast way to put on a jacket, children benefit from helping each other.

A well-planned environment opens up infinite possibilities for children to achieve a feeling of self-satisfaction while they explore the boundaries of their own beings.

✸ USING CORE VALUES IN THE ENVIRONMENT

Among the core values (see Appendix B and Chapter 5) in any good early childhood education program is the recognition of each child as unique, as deserving of respect, and as a part of a family.[1]

Each child has the right to achieve full potential and to develop a positive **self-esteem.** Each family deserves support for the unique role it plays. Part of the commitment of the early childhood teacher is to help children learn to value one another's uniqueness, the differences as well as the similarities. Teachers do this, in part, by expressing such inclusive attitudes.

The Anti-Bias Environment

The **anti-bias** curriculum, developed at Pacific Oaks College, encourages children and adults to:

💠 explore the differences and similarities that make up our individual and group identities, and

💠 develop skills for identifying and countering the hurtful impact of bias on themselves and their peers (Derman-Sparks & the ABC Task Force, 1989).

Because culture consists of the various ways people do similar activities, the physical environment is used to explore the many ways people do the basic human tasks of everyday life. Think of the diverse cultural practices expressed in how babies and objects are transported on foot from place to place in different parts of the world. How many ways do people eat? Cook? Shop for food? If children are especially interested in making things, perhaps the theme "All people live in homes" emerges, with activities that focus on how people build things, what they use the buildings for, and how they work to get something built.

The anti-bias approach to creating environments has its roots in the theories of Erikson, Piaget, Vygotsky, and Maslow (see Chapter 4). Children begin to notice and construct classifications and evaluative categories very early; indeed, two-year-olds begin to notice gender and racial differences and may even notice physical disabilities. Early childhood education programs must develop a child's basic sense of trust and mastery so that children can learn to understand themselves and become tolerant and compassionate toward others.

This approach is different from the "tourist curriculum," which provides only superficial information that is often detached from the child's own life. This approach is usually based on the interests of only the gender, racial, and cultural groups

Video View Point 9-1

"How Children Learn—Some Theories: Scaffolding, or guided participation, is based on the work of Lev Vygotsky."

Competency: Learning Environment

Age Group: School Age

Critical Thinking Questions:

1. How could scaffolding promote an anti-bias environment?

2. How can the multi-age grouping in school-age programs promote learning through guided assistance?

[1]The anti-bias and inclusive environments encourage children to learn tolerance and acceptance of the diversity in our world.

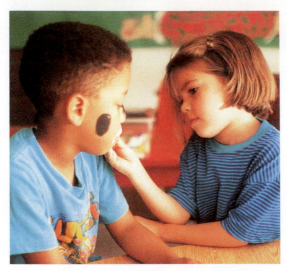

The anti-bias environment encourages girls and boys to play together, respecting differences and including others in new ways.

in the class. The anti-bias environment incorporates the positive aspects of a multicultural curriculum and uses some of the activities that highlight other cultures, but it provides a more inclusive, ongoing approach. A value common to all early childhood education programs is expressed in this anti-bias curriculum (i.e., that every person matters, so diversity is valued and equitable cooperation among all is possible). The environment derives from three sources: the children and their activities, the teachers' awareness of the developmental needs and learning styles of the group, and societal events.

See how arranging the environment can facilitate problem solving of issues that arise naturally: A toddler teacher sets up the water play table for washing babies. Choosing dolls that represent several racial and ethnic groups, she invites the children to soap and rinse them. One two-year-old begins to wash the teacher's arm, then scrubs it hard. "Do you wonder if my color will wash off?" the teacher asks. The child nods, and several others look up. "Does it? Go ahead and try. . . . See, a person's color is her own and stays with her. Try yours, too. That's one way people look different:

We all have skin, and yet we each have our own color" (M. E. Gutierrez, personal communication, 1987). (Refer to Figure 9–3 for a multicultural checklist that can help teachers evaluate the environment.)

The anti-bias approach takes a broad view of a classroom, as a kind of "mini-society" in which children and adults work together to form a just world. The prevalence of stereotyping in society impacts children's development, so teachers try to counteract such bias formation. A kindergarten teacher shows the children a magazine picture entitled "Brides of America." All of the women pictured are white. She asks, "What do you think of this picture?" Sophia responds, "That's a silly picture. My mom was a bride, and she's Mexican" (Derman-Sparks et al., 1989).

In summary, an anti-bias environment fosters:

✿ *Positive* **self-concept.** Curiosity and creativity stem from being able to affect the environment and what is in it. When Jamal says his baby's hair is fuzzy like his, his smile tells how good he feels about it.

✦ *Awareness.* All people have interests and feelings, both about themselves and about others. Yoko notices that her classmate Julie runs and throws her arms around her dad, but she prefers a less demonstrative greeting.

✦ *Respect for diversity.* This stems from the ability to classify similarities and differences and then to appreciate both. Children making self-portraits for their class books choose different colors of paper for drawing faces, but all of them use the same markers to draw in their features.

✦ *Skills in communication and problem-solving.* Learning how to express thoughts and feelings includes being able to hear others and finding peaceful ways to resolve conflicts. Jim and LaNell are quick to tell Eben he can't play, but they find out that telling him he is "too little" does not work. Being three years old is not a good enough reason to leave him out, and they must either try to include him or make a claim for privacy.

The Self-Help Environment

Promoting self-help and independent behavior in children is a widespread practice in early childhood education programs. Self-concept is based on what we know about ourselves, which includes the ability to take care of our own needs. To care for oneself, to feel capable of learning, to solve problems, all are related to feelings of self-esteem. Self-esteem is the value we place on ourselves; how much we like or dislike who we are. Helping children achieve a positive self-concept and self-esteem is the most important part of teaching. The development of a strong sense of self-esteem is a lifelong process; its origins are in the early years.

A self-help environment has as one of its fundamental goals the development of children's own skills—fostering their mastery of basic abilities that will allow them to become responsible for their own personal care, their own learning, their own emotional controls, their own problem solving, and their own choices and decisions. A self-help environment gives children the feeling that they are capable, competent, and successful. It allows children to do for themselves, to meet the challenge of growing up. A self-help environment has its roots in the Euro-American belief that **autonomy** and independence are important.

Nothing renders people more helpless than not being able to maintain their own

On the left, towels are color coded in easily recognizable shapes in a Russian child care center. On the right, toothbrushes and towels are accessible so that children in the Reggio Emilia centers in Italy can help themselves. (Courtesy of the city of Reggio Emilia, Italy.)

needs or to take care of themselves in basic ways. Children need many different kinds of experiences to help them learn the extent of their capabilities. Most of all, they need adults who understand their tremendous drive to become self-reliant, who will encourage their abilities and provide the time for them to practice skills.

In planning a self-help environment, teachers look at self-care skills of dressing, eating, toileting, and resting as cornerstones for self-help. There will be materials for learning fastening and zipping; shelves will be low and well marked, so toys are available and attractively displayed. Children will participate actively in snack time—their teachers sitting with them—and learn to manage some of their own nap things. Figures 9–10 to 9–13 all reflect self-help environments.

The Inclusive Environment

In 1975, the Education for All Handicapped Children Act (PL 94–142) called for an end to segregation of disabled students from kindergarten through high school. In 1986 an amendment made to this bill (PL 99–457) mandated that preschoolers with special needs be placed in the *least restrictive environment*. The practice of placing children with disabilities in the same classroom as children without disabilities is known as **full inclusion** (see Chapters 2 and 3). The Americans with Disabilities Act of 1990 prohibits child care centers from denying admission to a child simply because the child has a disability. Together, these federal laws form part of the rationale for early childhood centers to become more inclusive environments.

Children with disabilities need the same things in their environments as do other children. They need an environment that is safe, secure, and predictable and that provides a balance of the familiar and the novel, so that there are materials and activities that provide for their development.

When a child with disabilities has different developmental needs than other children of the same age, adaptations must be made. These changes may require either adding something to the environment that is not already there or using something in the environment in a different way. Children with motor disabilities need different adaptations than those with hearing or language disabilities or with visual impairments. Physical changes may be necessary, modifications in the schedule may be recommended, or individualizing activities may be best. Parents will be the best source of information about the child, and other reading or specialists can be further guides. Three key concepts are helpful to remember: access, usability, and maximizing learning.

- Can the child get where she needs to be in the classroom to learn something?

- Once the child is in that location, can she use the materials and equipment and participate in the activity as independently as possible to learn something?

- Are the learning activities arranged and scheduled to meet the individual learning needs of the children, including the child with disabilities? (Youcha & Wood, 1997)

Figure 9–4 is an abbreviated checklist for adaptations to create an inclusive environment.

Consider Andrew in Cindy's prekindergarten class (Rogers, 1994). At five years of age, Andrew had a motor/muscle disability with some speech difficulties. His cognitive skills were very strong and his social skills very weak. Andrew's mother talked to everyone during class about Andrew's needs and fears. If he fell down, he had a hard time righting himself. He needed help sitting and standing. He was afraid of getting bumped because he couldn't catch himself before falling very

Text continued on page 310

Checklist For An Inclusive Environment

Physical Environment

Questions to think about:

- How do different children use their bodies or the space around them for learning?
- How can we enhance or adapt the physical environment for children who have difficulty moving (or who move too much)?
- How can we capitalize on the physical environment for children who learn by moving?

Accessing the environment safely:

- ❑ Are doorway widths in compliance with local building codes?
- ❑ Ramps in addition to or instead of stairs?
- ❑ Low, wide stairs where possible (including playground equipment)?
- ❑ Hand rails on *both* sides of stairs?
- ❑ Easy handles on doors, drawers, etc.
- ❑ At least some kids' chairs with armrests?
  - "Cube" chairs are great!
  - Often a footrest and/or seat strap will provide enough stability for a child to do fine-motor activities.
- ❑ When adapting seating, mobility, and/or gross-motor activities for a specific child with physical disabilities, consult a physical therapist.

Learning through the environment:

- ❑ Do the environment and equipment reflect variety?
  - Surfaces, heights (textured, smooth, low, high, etc.).
  - Space for gross-motor activity (open spaces, climbing structures, floor mats).
  - Quiet/comfort spaces (small spaces, carpet, pillows).
  - Social spaces (dramatic play area, groups of chairs or pillows, etc.).
- ❑ Are toys and equipment physically accessible?
  - Glue magnets to backs of puzzle pieces and attribute blocks and use on a steel cookie tray.
  - Attach large knobs or levers to toys with lids, movable parts.
  - Attach tabs to book pages for easier turning.
- ❑ An occupational therapist can provide specific suggestions for adapting materials and activities so a child with physical disabilities can participate.

Visual Environment

Questions to think about:

- How do different children use their vision for learning?
- How can we enhance the visual environment for a child with low or no vision?
- How can we capitalize on the visual environment for children who learn by seeing?

Accessing the environment safely:

- ❑ Are contrasting colors used on edges and when surfaces change (e.g., tile to carpet, beginning of stairs, etc.)?

FIGURE 9–4 When designing an inclusive environment, keep in mind that the environment needs to be safe and to help everyone participate, learn, and communicate. (Adapted from Haugen, 1997.)

Continued

- ❑ Can windows be shaded to avoid high glare?
  - Also consider darker nonglossy floors and tabletops.
  - Some children's behavior and learning may improve dramatically once a strong glare is eliminated.
- ❑ Is visual clutter avoided on walls, shelves, etc.?
  - Visual clutter can interfere with learning, predictability, and safety.
- ❑ Is "spot lighting" (e.g., swing arm lamp) in a dimmer room available?
  - Spot lamps help some children pay attention and work better on table tasks.
- ❑ Orientation and mobility specialists help children with visual impairments learn to navigate the environment.

Learning through the environment:

- ❑ Are objects and places in the environment labeled ("door," "chair," etc.)?
- ❑ Are the size and contrast of pictures and letters adequate for the children with visual impairments in your program?
- ❑ Are visual displays at the children's eye level?
- ❑ Are large-print materials, textured materials, and auditory materials available (e.g., big books, sandpaper letters, books on tape)?
- ❑ Is the daily schedule represented in words and pictures?
  - A Velcro schedule that allows children to post the schedule and then remove items as activities are completed can help children to stay focused and make the transition more easily from one activity to the next.
- ❑ Are children with low vision seated close to the center of activity and away from high glare?
- ❑ Teachers for the visually impaired assist in selecting and adapting materials for children with low vision.
- ❑ Children who are blind may need a "running commentary" of events, places, etc. Pictures in books and food on plates, for example, should be described.

Auditory Environment

Questions to think about:
- How do different children use their hearing for learning?
- How can we enhance the auditory environment for a child who is deaf, hearing impaired, or has poor auditory discrimination skills?
- How can we capitalize on the auditory environment for auditory learners?

Accessing the environment safely:

- ❑ Does background noise (from indoor or outdoor sources) filter into the area?
- ❑ Is there a way to eliminate or dampen background noise (using carpeting, closing windows and doors, etc.)?
  - Spot kids are unable to do the automatic filtering out of background noises.
- ❑ Is "auditory competition" avoided?
  - Raising one's voice to compete with a roomful of noisy children is rarely as effective as using a "silent signal," for example, holding up a peace sign and encouraging children who notice to do the same until the room is full of quiet children holding up peace signs!
- ❑ Are nonauditory signals needed to alert a child with a hearing impairment?
  - Turning the lights on and off is a common strategy.
  - Ask the child's parents what strategies are used at home.

FIGURE 9–4, continued

Learning through the environment:

❑ Are auditory messages paired with visual ones (e.g., simple sign language, flannel boards, picture schedules)?

❑ Are children with hearing impairments seated so they can see others' faces and actions?

❑ Teachers for the hearing impaired can provide strategies for modifying activities for children with hearing impairments.

❑ A child who is deaf and communicates through sign language will need a teacher or aide who uses sign language.

Social Environment

Questions to think about:

• How do different children use social cues for learning?

• How can we adapt the social environment for children with impulsive behavior, attention deficits, or other behavior problems?

• How can we capitalize on the social environment for children who learn by relating to others?

Accessing the environment safely:

❑ Is the schedule predictable? Are children informed of schedule changes?

❑ Does the schedule provide a range of activity levels (e.g., adequate opportunities for physical activity)?

❑ School psychologists and behavior specialists can help analyze misbehavior and modify the environment or schedule to minimize problems for children with attention deficits or behavior problems.

Learning through the environment:

❑ Does the environment have a positive impact on self-esteem?
  • Allows all children to feel safe?
  • Invites all children to participate?
  • Maximizes all children's opportunities for independence?

❑ Do learning materials and toys include representations of all kinds of people, including children and adults with disabilities?
  • People with disabilities should be represented in active and leadership roles, not just as passive observers.

❑ Does the schedule include opportunities for a variety of groupings (pairs, small groups, whole class) as well as quiet time or time alone?
  • Pairing or grouping children with complementary abilities eases the demands on the teacher and enables children to help one another.
  • When given a chance, peers often come up with the most creative ways for children with disabilities to participate.
  • Creative use of staffing may be needed to provide additional support for some children during some activities.

❑ Does the schedule provide both structured and open activity times?
  • Children who have difficulty with a particular type of activity may need extra support at those times.

FIGURE 9–4, continued

hard and then could not get up. The children all agreed to be careful about **roughhousing** around him. The setting for success was being created.

Because Andrew did not have much control of his fine motor skills, Cindy provided him with painting and play dough. She kept up the crafts table; soon he was gluing pictures on paper, with or without order, and was very proud of his accomplishments. He even started using scissors on simple patterns. The physical environment was responding to his needs. He was a wonderful puzzle builder, and the other children asked for his help often when they were stuck. It was wonderful to watch how they included him in many things. They accepted his differences right from the beginning and treated him just like all the rest—except they were careful when running and playing around him. His fear was apparent, and they respected it. Thus the interpersonal environment was emerging.

There was a regular "PE time" each day in a big room the rest of the program shared. Everyone jumped rope, played Simon Says and Red Light, Green Light, and ran obstacle courses. At first Andrew sat on the sidelines and watched. He cheered and looked interested, so Cindy started asking him if he'd be her partner "because I am a little afraid." At first he refused and told her to use someone else. She kept asking but would drop it as soon as he answered; then one day he said, "Okay." Together, Cindy and Andrew ran and jumped over the snake (rope), and all the kids laughed. They hugged, and that was the beginning. When given the time that is needed (the temporal environment), the child triumphs.

✱ PLANNING FOR THE ENVIRONMENT

Many people live and work in the early childhood education environment. Cooks, bus drivers, office personnel, and yard and building maintenance people have jobs that make special demands on the environment. But teachers, parents, and children have the greatest influence.

- Who are the *children* who will use this space and what are their needs?

- The physical, social, emotional, and intellectual requirements of children suggest the type of building, the size of the furniture, the choice of equipment, the size and age range of the group, the number of teachers who lead and supervise, and the budget allocations.

- What has been done to meet the needs of the *teachers*? All teachers need room to create curriculum materials, to evaluate their programs, to review other educational materials, to meet with their peers. Research (Whitebrook, 1996) indicates that the working environment of caregivers contains important predictors—including the general context of the setting, opportunities for professional development, status, and wages—of the quality of care children receive.

- How does the environment welcome *families*? In settings where adults are free to stay, a comfortable place to talk or read is desirable. Those who participate in the class need a place to put their belongings.

- Is the school environment accessible? All adults who come to the site need

The needs of children include key dimensions of softness/hardness so that the environment invites the children in to work and play.

adequate and safe parking facilities. They need to know how to reach teachers and children in emergencies, including how to reach school authorities after-hours. A bulletin board for community notices and for family use is informative, and mail pockets encourage written communication to parents and among families.

✴ In the environment, the health, safety, and well-being of those participating is critical to its success as a place to learn.

Keeping Children Healthy

Regardless of how many children are in the setting or for how long, the first priority is to provide for their health and safety. Health, safety, and nutrition are closely related because the quality of one affects the quality of the others (Marotz, Rush, & Cross, 2005). Therefore, programs for children must establish policies that provide for the protection, service, and education of child health and safety at all times. Government regulations and professional recommendations vary, but all establish some kind of standards to ensure good health and safety practices.

Sanitation

When groups of people live in close quarters, proper sanitary conditions are imper-

Keeping children healthy becomes part of the regular routines of the day.

ative to prevent the spread of disease. For an early childhood center, the physical plant must have adequate washing and toileting facilities for both children and adults. The number and size of toilets and wash basins are usually prescribed by local health or other regulatory agencies. Teachers must engage in the daily practices of preventive health care.

These include handwashing (the number-one way to prevent unnecessary spread of germs) and an approach known as *universal,* or *standard, precautions.* Through gentle reminders and role modeling, teachers help children learn the habit of washing their hands at important times such as before snack and mealtimes. All programs should be equipped with sets of latex gloves and plastic bags to properly handle and dispose of anything with blood or fecal material. Intact skin is a natural barrier against disease, and it may not always be possible to use gloves. However, it is essential that hands be washed immediately after any toileting activity. All areas for eating, diapering, and toileting must be cleaned and sanitized, using a bleach solution after cleaning away visible soiling.

The classrooms require daily cleaning, and equipment that is used regularly should be sanitized on a periodic basis. Nontoxic paint must be used in all circumstances, including outdoor equipment, cribs, and for art activities with children. Classroom dress-up clothing, pillows, nap blankets, and cuddle toys all need regular laundering, either at school or at home.

Temperature, Ventilation, and Lighting

Heating and ventilation should be comfortable for the activity level of the children and should change when weather conditions do. Adequate, nonglare lighting is a necessity. Studies indicate that uniform, fluorescent lighting may not be the best environment for children; therefore, a mixture of lighting such as is in homes is preferable. Rooms should have some means of controlling light (shades, blinds). Cross-ventilation is necessary in all rooms where children eat, sleep, or play. Proper heating and insulation are important.

Communicable Disease

Some people question the advisability of early group care on the grounds that it exposes children to too much illness. Others claim that such exposure at an early age helps children build up resistance, and that they are actually stronger and healthier by the time they enter primary grades. In the largest U.S. study to date on children's health, the Centers for Disease Control and Prevention (1997) concluded that although infants and toddlers face a higher risk of colds and viruses, day care was seen as not increasing children's illnesses at older ages or as a risk overall.

Parents should be notified when normal childhood diseases (such as chickenpox) or common problems (such as head lice) occur in the classroom. Infections of special concern to adults include chickenpox, hepatitis A, and cytomegalovirus (CMV). A description of the symptoms and the dates of exposure and incubation period may be helpful to parents. They can then assist in controlling the spread of the disease. Figure 9–5 summarizes the 10 most common health problems in school, with tips for dealing with them.

Health Assessment and School Policies

Every early childhood center should establish clear health policies and make them known to families. Most schools require, under state or local laws, a doctor's examination and permission to participate in an early childhood education program before a child can enter the program. This includes a record of immunizations and the child's general health. Parents, too, should submit a history of the child, highlighting eating, sleeping, and elimination habits. It is critical to note any dietary restrictions or allergies and then post them in the classrooms for a reminder.

A daily inspection of each child will help adults spot nasal discharge, inflamed eyes, and throat and skin conditions of a questionable nature. This daily check will screen out more serious cases of children too ill to stay. Educating families about the warning signs of illness will encourage sick children to be cared for at home. Every program should have explicit and consistent procedures about what happens when children are refused admittance or become ill during the day. Sick children need a place where they can be isolated from others, kept under supervision, and be made comfortable until they are picked up. Teachers must be sensitive to parents' feelings and situations when sending a sick child home. This situation often produces guilt feelings in parents and work-related stress. Working families may need support in locating alternatives for care of a sick child.

Nutrition

What children eat is also important for proper health. Places where food is prepared and stored must be kept especially clean. The child who has regular, nutritious meals and snacks will likely be healthier and less susceptible to disease. Many children do not have the benefits of healthy meals and snacks. Some do not receive adequate food at home; others are accustomed to sugar-laden treats and "fast foods." Education about nutrition becomes the responsibility of a school that is concerned with children's health and physical development. The need for educating parents regarding child nutrition exists in virtually all early childhood education programs, regardless of social or economic status. Some centers establish food regulations

Condition	Tips
1. Allergies and asthma	Post a list of all children with chronic conditions; check ingredient lists on foods; watch what triggers reactions.
2. Scrapes and cuts	Reassure and sympathize with child; supervise child's washing with soaped pad and caring comments; use packs of ice or frozen peas in towel for swelling.
3. Bumps on the head	Notify parents of any loss of consciousness and watch for signs for two–three days.
4. Sand in eyes	Remind child "Do not rub!"; have child wash hands and cover eye with tissue; normal eye tearing will bring sand to inside corner of eye; remove with clean tissue.
5. Splinters	Clean area with alcohol and remove with tweezers or cover with adhesive strip and let parent remove.
6. Conjunctivitis	"Pinkeye" is highly contagious; watch for excess eye rubbing and red eyes; have child wash hands; isolate with washable toys until parent takes child home and gets treatment.
7. Head lice	Distressing but not dangerous; wash shared clothing, stuffed animals, bedding; vacuum rugs and furniture; remove hats, combs and brushes from dramatic-play area; send notices home and inspect children's hair for two–three weeks.
8. Chickenpox	Isolate child until parents pick up; alert all parents about contagious period; watch for signs on all children for three weeks after exposure.
9. Strep throat	Send home notices; wash all equipment that might carry germs.
10. Lingering coughs	At onset, send child home until evaluated; frequent drinks will soothe; coughs may last up to 2 weeks; if longer, may suggest infection or allergy.

FIGURE 9–5 Teachers need to be trained in first aid and cardiopulmonary resuscitation (CPR); in addition, a working knowledge of common health problems in school helps the teacher care for children. (Adapted from Needlman & Needlman, 1995.)

in an attempt to ensure that nutritionally sound meals are served to children. Most schools attempt to provide a relaxed atmosphere at meal- and snack time. Children are asked to sit and eat, sharing conversation, as well as food. Because lifelong eating patterns are established early in life, teachers of young children have a responsibility to understand the critical role nutrition plays in the child's total development.

Eating is a critical intersection between home culture and school environment.

Clothing

The health and safety of children are affected by the clothing they wear. A simple way to be sure children stay healthy is to encourage them to dress properly for play and for varying weather conditions. Children need clothing in which they can be active—clothing that is not binding and is easy to remove and easy to clean. To promote a self-help environment, parents and teachers should provide clothes the children can manage themselves (elastic waistbands, Velcro ties, large zippers). Pants are a good choice for both boys and girls; long dresses can become a hazard when climbing, running, or going up and down stairs. The safest shoes for active play should have composition or rubber soles. Whenever possible, it helps to keep changes of clothes at school.

Health of the Staff

A responsible early childhood center is one that supports and maintains a healthy staff. Teachers should be in good physical and mental health to be at their best with children. It is wise to check the health regulations and benefits of the individual school when employed there. Many states require annual chest x-rays as a condition of employment. Sick leave policies should be clearly stated in print.

Early childhood education is an intense job involving close interpersonal contact. Most teachers work long hours, often with low wages and few health benefits, and with clients in various stages of health. Such working conditions produce fatigue and stress, which can lead to illness or other stress-related problems.

Guarding Children's Safety

Creating a hazard-free environment that still allows for risk and challenge for children takes careful observation and attention to detail. A quick walk around the room and yard will reveal potential problems:

- Are there any sharp corners at children's height?
- Are rug edges snagged or loose?
- Are absorbent surfaces used wherever there is water? Are mops and towels available for spillage?
- Is hot water out of the reach of children?
- Are children allowed to run inside?
- Are there rules governing the children's use of scissors, hammers, and knives?
- Are safety rules explained to children and upheld by adults?
- Are electrical outlets covered when not in use?
- Do open stairwells have gates?
- Do adults monitor the use of extension cords and appliances?
- Is broken equipment removed promptly?

- Are fences high enough to protect and safe to touch?

- Are there areas where wheel toys can move freely without fear of collision?

- Are swings placed away from traffic areas and set apart by bushes or fences?

- Can a child's foot or ankle be caught on equipment? Under a chain-link fence?

- Does playground traffic flow easily?

- Are the toys safe for children's use?

Figure 9–6 is a safety checklist for the indoor areas; Figure 9-14 shows how to make playgrounds safe.

First Aid

Every school should establish procedures for dealing with children who are injured on the property. First aid instructions should be required of all teachers and made available as part of their in-service training. Teachers should know how to treat bumps and bruises, minor cuts and abrasions, bleeding, splinters, bites and stings, seizures, sprains, broken bones, and minor burns.[1]

Each classroom should be equipped with two first-aid kits. One is for use in the classroom and yard; the other should be suitable for taking on field trips. Each kit should be readily available to adults, but out of children's reach, and supplies should be replenished regularly.

Emergency numbers to be posted near the telephone in each room include those of the ambulance squad, fire department, police, health department, nearest hospital, and a consulting physician (if any). All families enrolled at the school should be aware of school policy regarding injuries at school and should provide the school with emer-gency information for each child: the name of the child's physician, how to locate the parents, and who else might be responsible for the injured child if the parents cannot be reached. The school in turn must make sure they notify parents of any injuries the child has incurred during the school day.

Natural Disaster

Most adults are familiar with the most common disaster preparation, the fire drill. Most local fire regulations require that fire extinguishers be in working order and placed in all classrooms and the kitchen area. Fire exits, fire alarms, and fire escapes should be well marked and functioning properly. Children and teachers should participate in fire drills regularly. Other natural disasters vary by geographical location; helping children prepare for earthquakes, tornadoes, hurricanes, floods, and snowstorms will include participating in drills for those disasters. Proper preparedness will include eliminating potential hazards (e.g., bolting down bookcases), establishing a coordinated response plan (a "Code Blue" emergency plan should involve children, parents, all staff, and local emergency agencies), and drills. These experiences can reinforce the need for similar procedures at home.

Automobile Safety

The use of approved car seats and restraints for children riding in automobiles has received national attention in recent years. Some states have passed legislation requiring the use of specific devices to ensure safer travel for young children. Whether or not they walk to school, children should also be aware of basic rules for crossing streets. There are potential risks when cars and children occupy the same space. Children should not be left unattended in parking lots.

[1]All teachers should receive training in using universal health precautions with all children. Teachers should not make assumptions about who is at risk and who is not for HIV infection or hepatitis.

Safety List For Indoor Environments

_____ Person monitoring children (at entrances, indoors, outdoors)

_____ First aid and emergency

    _____ Materials readily available to adults, out of children's reach, and regularly stocked and updated

    _____ Adults trained in first aid and CPR regularly and familiar with emergency routines

_____ Safety plugs on all outlets

_____ Cords

    _____ Electrical cords out of children's reach; avoid using extension cords

    _____ Curtain and window cords, window pulls and poles out of children's reach

_____ Floormat and carpet tacked down to avoid slippage

_____ Doors

    _____ Made to open and close slowly

    _____ All clear access, marked exits, and not blocked

_____ Cubbies and storage cabinets

    _____ Bolted to walls (or back-to-back together)

    _____ Cabinets equipped with child-proof latches

    _____ Any dangerous materials in locked area

_____ Toys

    _____ In good repair; no splinters or sharp, broken edges

    _____ Check for size with younger children (purchase safety-sizing gadget or estimate to keep at the size of a child's fist)

    _____ Check for peeling paint

_____ Plants and animals

    _____ Nonpoisonous plants _only_

    _____ Check animal cages regularly

    _____ Supervise animal handling carefully

    _____ Store animal food away from children's reach

_____ Adult materials

    _____ Keep adult purses, bags, and so on, away from children

    _____ Avoid having hot beverages around children

    _____ No smoking in children's areas

_____ Kitchen and storage

    _____ Children allowed in _only_ with adult supervision

    _____ Poisonous or hazardous materials stored in a locked area

FIGURE 9–6 Children's safety is of primary importance to teachers and caregivers. Careful evaluation and regular safety checks eliminate dangerous materials and conditions in children's spaces.

Maintaining Children's Well-Being

A final factor in children's care and education is their well-being. Young children are growing up in a world threatened by violence abroad and at home, drug abuse, unresolved conflicts among adults, and constant bombardment of television and other media. Because young children do not easily separate the home and school parts of their lives, they readily talk about family details. Teachers are often at a loss as to what to do, either with information that a child shares or with the child's behavior in the program. Yet a situation does not need to be a crisis to affect a child's well-being. As a rule of thumb, when you feel the child's physical or emotional development is in jeopardy, you have a responsibility to take further action.

Children's well-being can be threatened by a difficult situation at school, such as being bitten, left out, or ridiculed. They are also at risk for the variety of crises from home—problems with family members, separation or divorce, violence, or substance abuse. Although much of our response will be with adults—parents, community resources, professional supports—we are also responsible for trying to provide a psychologically safe and positive environment. By design and by responsiveness, teachers provide an interpersonal environment that soothes and cares for young children.

 CREATING THE ENVIRONMENT

The Physical Environment

Every educational setting is organized fundamentally around physical space. Teachers work with the size and limitations of the facility, both indoors and outdoors. The building itself may be new and designed specifically for young children. More often, however, the space is a converted house or store, a parish hall, or an elementary classroom. A program may share space with an-

other group so that furniture is moved daily or weekly. A family child care program is housed in a private home; therefore, adaptations are made in the space both for the children and for the family that lives there. There may be a large yard or none at all. Some playgrounds are on the roof of the building, or a park across the street may serve as the only available playground.

Weather conditions must be considered when planning programs for children. Outside play—and therefore large-muscle equipment—may be unavailable during the winter, so room for active, vigorous play is needed inside during that time. Hot summer months can make some types of play difficult if there is little or no shade outdoors.

Although the site is generally determined by what is available, at a minimum the setting should provide facilities for:

- ✺ Playing/working
- ✺ Eating
- ✺ Washing/toileting
- ✺ Sleeping/resting
- ✺ Food preparation
- ✺ Storage
- ✺ Office/teacher work space
- ✺ Clothing and wraps

Ideally, the setting should have enough space to house these various activities separately. In practice, however, rooms are multipurpose, and more than one event takes place in the same space. A playroom doubles as an eating area because both require the use of tables and chairs. When a room serves many functions (playing, eating, sleeping), convenient and adequate storage space is a necessity. Harms and colleagues (2003) list important environmental supports for each of these areas as:

1. Space and furnishings
2. Personal care routines

3. Language-reasoning

4. Activities (motor, cognitive, creative)

5. Interaction (social, emotional)

6. Program structure (schedules)

7. Parents and staff (personal and professional needs)

The amount of teacher time needed to prepare the room for each change of activity is part of planning the daily schedule (see the Temporal Environment section).

Organizing Space

There are many different ways to arrange and organize space in an early childhood setting. Most environments are arranged by **interest areas, learning centers,** or activity areas. The amount of space devoted to any one activity says a great deal about its value to the staff. A housekeeping area with plenty of space encourages active use by a number of children. Social play is promoted when two or more items are available. Four telephones, three doll buggies, or two easels can be tools for social interaction. At the same time, the environment must be flexible to respond to the developing needs and interests of the children. A group with great interest in block-building may need to have the indoor and outside block area expanded for several weeks. As interests change, so do the room and yard—someone brings in a hamster and the discovery area blossoms, or family camping brings out tents around the grassy outdoor areas.

The physical environment speaks volumes to children, so room and yard arrangement and choice of materials play an important role in their educational experience. A developmentally appropriate room or yard will invite children in and welcome them at their level. For instance, simplicity is a watchword in a toddler room. Lowman and Ruhmann (1998) suggest:

- A large-motor zone is essential in a toddler room.

- The dramatic-play zone is particularly conducive to pretend play.
- The messy zone is that area of the room where children are encouraged to "mess around" with a variety of fluid materials.
- Every toddler room needs a haven where children can unwind, kick back, chill out, sink in, and just relax. The quiet zone provides such a spot.

Family child care homes present special challenges, in terms of both space and the mixed age ranges of children. Creating retreats, such as allowing children into a cabinet or behind the couch, allows moderate privacy while still ensuring supervision.

A room or yard that is arranged well with enough interesting materials will give children choices and open their eyes to possibilities. Teachers who evaluate their materials so that they reflect all children and adults in nonstereotyped activities are committed to an anti-bias environment. A yard with a sand toy storage box and small brooms with dustpans nearby is committed to self-help at cleanup time. A program that has prop boxes with materials for children with visual or auditory disabilities is one that is making real strides to be an inclusive environment.

The placement of the interest centers is important. Balance the number of noisy and

Even the hallways serve a function in the Reggio Emilia schools in Italy. (Courtesy of the city of Reggio Emilia, Italy.)

quiet activities, both indoors and out. Some activities are noisier than others, so place the noisier centers together and cluster the quieter ones together. Quieter activities, such as puzzles, language games, and storytelling, take place in areas away from blocks, water play, or dramatic play, because the last three tend to kindle animated, active, and sometimes noisy behavior. Outdoors, be sure there is a space for reflection and watching, not just places for running and shouting.

General Requirements

Ground-floor classrooms are preferable for young children to ensure that they can enter and leave with relative ease and safety. For noise reduction, the walls and ceilings should be soundproofed. Carpeting, draperies, and other fireproof fabrics in the room will help absorb sound. Floors must be durable, sanitary, and easily cleaned. They should be free from drafts. Rugs should be vacuumed each day. Room size should be sufficient to allow for freedom of movement and the opportunity to play without interference. Some licensing agencies may suggest minimum room and yard size standards.

Many local and state agencies have regulations regarding the use of space for children in group care settings. The fire and health departments must be consulted and their regulations observed. The National Association for the Education of Young Children (1995) has developed guidelines for indoor and outdoor facilities that promote optimal growth. Besides floor and play space (minimum 35 square feet indoors and 75 square feet outdoors), the guidelines suggest how to arrange activity areas to accommodate children and what kinds of activities and materials are safe, clean, and attractive. The Creative Curriculum (Dodge & Colker, 1999) has been used extensively to help programs organize their environments for free choice and active learning, as well as focus on the learning potential in each area of the room and out-

doors. Environmental rating scales (Harms et al., 2003) have been developed for family child care, infant-toddler, preschool, and school-age centers that detail materials and furnishings throughout the area.

There are several key dimensions to any environment that are helpful to consider. If we are to offer children both balance and variety, these criteria need to be included in developing space both indoors and out. Figure 9–7 outlines these dimensions in detail.

Indoors

Interest Areas. Deciding what interest centers you want and what kind of space you will need is good preparation for making a basic floor plan and sketching in the interest centers. Infant and young toddler centers devote plenty of space to diapering and sleeping, with carpeted areas for crawling and playing. Classrooms for two-through eight-year-olds (in school-age centers) usually have most of these interest areas:

- Art
- Blocks
- Dramatic play/house corner
- Library/literacy center

1. **Softness/Hardness**

   Soft: rugs, pillows, play dough, finger paints, grass, sand, swings
   Hard: tile floor, wooden furniture, asphalt, cement

2. **Open/Closed**

   Open (no one right way to use it): sand and water, dress–up, collage materials, painting
   Closed (manipulated only one way to come out right): puzzles, many board games, most Montessori equipment
   In–between: many manipulatives such as Legos®, TinkerToys®, blocks, balls

3. **Simple/Complex**

   "Play equipment can differ in its holding power; i.e., the capacity to sustain attention. . . . A simple unit has one manipulable aspect; a complex unit has two different kinds of materials combined; and a super unit has three different kinds of materials that go together."
   Simple: swings, climbers, sand pile with no toys
   Complex: dramatic play with only a kitchen
   Super: climbers with slides and ropes, playhouse with kitchen, dress–up clothes, dolls, and/or playdough; sand area with equipment and/or water
   As you add more features to a unit, you increase its complexity and the children's interest in it. To simple playdough, add cookie cutters; then add toothpicks or a garlic press and it becomes a super unit.

4. **Intrusion/Seclusion**

   Intrusion: places where children can enter or go through easily; blocks, housekeeping, even the entire environment are often highly intrusive areas
   Seclusion: places where children can be alone or with only one child or adult; cubbies, a fort, or under a table become secret places

5. **High mobility/Low mobility**

   High: whole–body places and activities; outdoors, climbers, trike lanes, gym mats
   Low: sitting-still places and activities; puzzles and games, story and group times, nap time
   In–between: dramatic play, block corner, woodworking

FIGURE 9–7 Key dimensions when considering an early childhood environment. (From Prescott, 1994.)

 Manipulatives/table toys
 Science-discovery/sand & water
 Music & movement/group times
 Computers

Figure 9–8 shows a preschool child care center, and Figures 9–9 and 9–10 demonstrate school-age and toddler environments.

Bathrooms. Bathrooms should be adjacent to the play and sleeping areas and easily reached from outdoors. Child-sized toilets and wash basins are preferable, but if unavailable, a step or platform may be built. In most early childhood settings, the bathrooms are without doors, for ease of supervision. Toileting facilities for children should be light, airy, attractive, and large

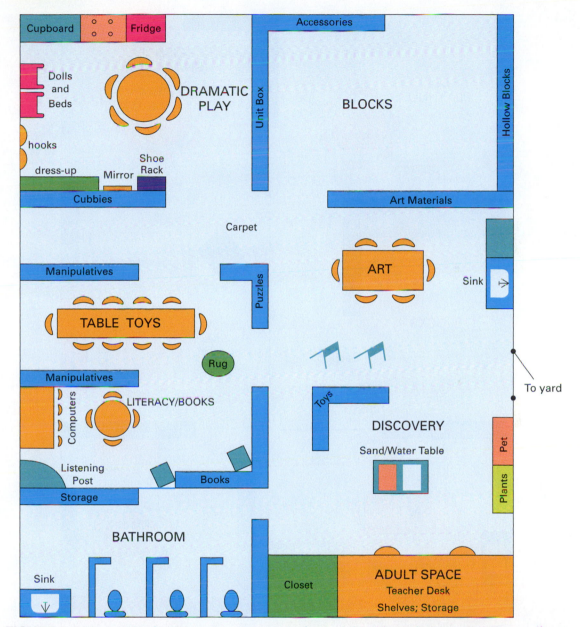

FIGURE 9–8 A preschool child care center needs clearly defined boundaries and obvious pathways to make it easy for children to use this space independently.

enough to serve several children at a time. An exhaust fan is desirable. Paper towel holders should be at child height, and waste baskets placed nearby.

If diapering is part of the program, areas for this purpose should be clearly defined and close to handwashing facilities. Handwashing regulations for the staff should be posted, and an area should be provided for recording children's toileting and elimination patterns. Closed cans and germicidal spray must be used, and diapering materials should be plentiful and handy.

Room to Rest. Schools that provide nap and sleeping facilities require adequate storage space for cots and bedding. Movable screens, low enough for teacher supervision, allow for privacy and help reduce the noise level.

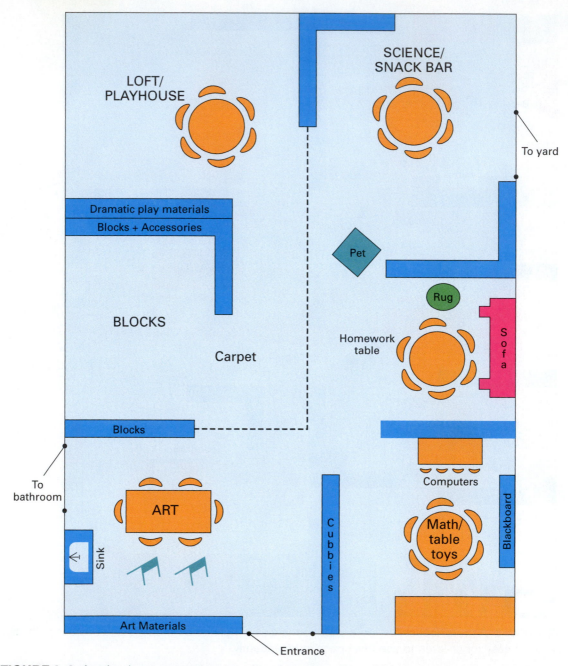

FIGURE 9–9 A school-age center has learning centers to allow children to make clear choices and engage in active learning through play.

Cots or cribs should be labeled with children's names and washed regularly. They should be placed consistently and in such a way that children feel familiar, cozy, and private—not in the center of the room or in rows. Teachers can develop a "nap map" that places children so they can get the rest or sleep they need while still feeling part of the group.

Food Service. "Small children need nutrients for growth and energy. . . . [R]egardless of the guideline selected, the common factor necessary for good nutrition is the

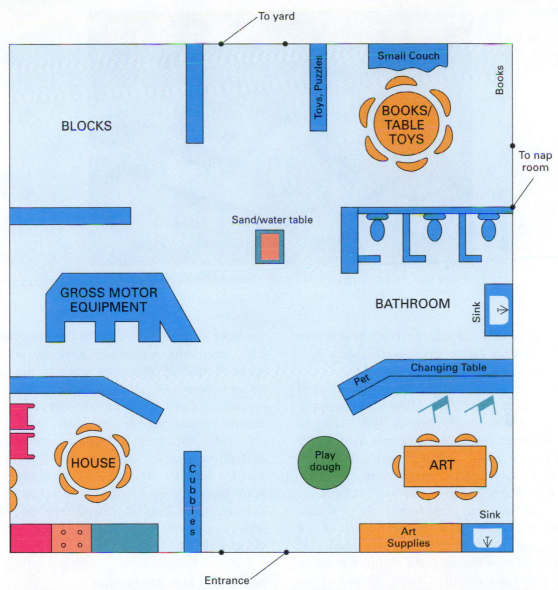

FIGURE 9–10 A toddler environment has safety and accessibility in mind, while helping children to work in small groups so they can be maximally involved, with a minimum of distraction from others.

inclusion of a wide variety of foods" (Marotz, 2005). As early childhood classrooms have become more diverse and multicultural, routines and choices around food, as well as toys and materials, must take into consideration families' cultural practices and preferences.

Each age has its unique food service needs. In an infant program, storing formula and milk is a necessity. As toddlers assert their independence, they begin to make their preferences known. Care must be taken to offer a variety of foods while avoiding a battle of wills over what the child will eat. Preschoolers are influenced by a teacher who sets a good example of eating with balance and variety. School-aged children can understand nutritional concepts better but are more influenced by what their peers are eating.

Whether involved in a light snack or full meal program, the center must adhere

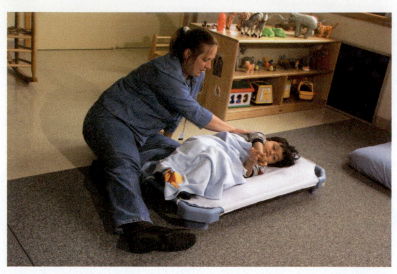

Every routine has a place in an early childhood education program.

to the most rigid standards of health protection and safety provisions. Every precaution must be taken to ensure maximum hygienic food service. Daily cleaning of equipment, counters, floors, and appliances is a necessity. Proper disinfecting of highchairs and tables requires half a cup of bleach to one gallon of water; bottles of this solution can be stored away from children's reach yet be handy for teachers.

Infants will need to be held or seated near an adult. Toddlers should not be fed popcorn, nuts, or raw carrots because of the hazard of choking. All children must be served food on disposable dishes or on dishes cleaned in a dishwasher with a sanitation cycle. Lunches brought from home by school-age and full-day children must be checked for spoilage. Information about eating patterns, proportions, and nutritional needs should be regularly shared with families.

Adult Space. "Oh, for a real 'teacher's desk,'" the early childhood caregiver moans. "I'm lucky if I can find a place to stash my bag!" It is common for early childhood education programs to donate nearly all the available space to child use and materials storage. Yet the personal and professional needs of adults deserve environmental support. Programs sometimes have an adult space or teacher resources space in the director's area. An adult bathroom is also common. However, professionals deserve environmental support for their work. A safe place for their belongings, space for first-aid emergency materials and information for families, and an area for a special adult project goes a long way in respecting the teachers' lives in the classroom. We show our priorities by the space and time we give them.

Materials and Equipment

Selection of materials and equipment is based on a number of criteria. Out of necessity, most budgets have limited money available for such purchases. To make every dollar count, teachers select materials that:

- Are age and developmentally appropriate
- Are related to the school's philosophy and curriculum
- Reflect quality design and workmanship
- Are durable
- Offer **flexibility** and versatility in their uses

- Have safety features (e.g., nontoxic paints, rounded corners)
- Are aesthetically attractive and appealing to children (and adults)
- Are easy to maintain and repair
- Reflect the cultural makeup of the group and the diversity of the culture overall
- Are nonsexist, nonstereotypical, and anti-bias

Materials should be appropriate for a wide range of skills because children within the same age group develop at individual rates. Selecting equipment and toys to support development is important because young children typically will try to play with everything in their environment. Many of the materials can be **open-ended;** that is, they can be used in their most basic form or they can be developed in a variety of ways. Unit blocks, clay, and Legos® are examples of materials that children can use in a simple fashion; as skills develop, these materials can be manipulated in a more complex manner (Figure 9–11).

Try to avoid toys that have limited play value. Teachers Resisting Unhealthy Children's Entertainment (TRUCE, 2002) suggests that we steer away from toys that:

- Make electronic technology the focus of play
- Lure girls into focusing on appearance
- Model violent and sexualized language or behavior
- Are linked to commercial products and advertisements

Toys and materials need to reflect the diversity of the class, the families, and the community.[1] From a developmentally appropriate perspective, materials need to appeal to individual interests and also respond to children's cultural and linguistic strengths. Materials and cultural artifacts help a child feel that the environment is familiar.

With self-help in mind, dressing frames and plenty of workable doll clothes will help children learn those self-care tasks. Children's books that demonstrate social values and attitudes that expand gender roles and family lifestyles show a value for an anti-bias environment. Modifications in the environment that promote inclusiveness might include ramp access for wheelchairs and materials to highlight tactile, auditory, and olfactory experiences for children with visual impairments.

Children are active learners, and their materials should provide them with ways to explore, manipulate, and become involved. Children learn through all their senses, so the materials should be appealing to touch, smell, and so on. Finally, children need opportunities for quiet and privacy. For children in care for long hours or in large group sizes, a cozy corner is essential.

Outdoors

"Children's access to outdoor play has evaporated like water in sunshine. It has happened so fast, along with everything else in this speed-ridden century, that we have not coped with it. . . . Some of our deepest childhood joys—those of field and stream, rocks and vacant lots; of privacy, secrecy, and tiny things that creep across or poke out of the earth's surface" can be experienced out of doors, and nowhere else (Rivkin, 1995). Time for fresh air and open space outdoors is often a child's favorite spot in a program. Indeed, many a

[1]Numerous resources are available to help the teacher select books, dolls, puzzles, and posters that will expose children in a positive way to people who are ethnically different, people with disabilities, and people who have different work and play habits from their own.

Basic Materials in an Early Childhood Classroom

Art Supplies
Easels, paints, watercolors
Plastic dough, clay
Pens, pencils, brushes
Scissors, holepunches
Glue, paste
Collage materials
Assorted paper

Infants/toddlers: Limit materials. Use open shelves with few choices.

School age: Have self-help table and teacher-guided projects.

Discovery and Science
Nature materials
Textured materials
Water/sensory table and materials
Magnifying glasses, mirrors
Scales
Small pets

Infants/toddlers: Simplify, watch for safety. Aquarium.

School age: Display to read, computer.

Dramatic Play
Safety mirrors
Furniture: child-sized, versatile
Clothing: variety, nonstereotyped
Dolls: variety, and accessories
Cooking utensils
Food items
Purses, suitcases, briefcases, backpacks

Infants/toddlers: Limit the choice, add hats or dolls that can get wet.

School age: Varied units such as prehistoric cave, moonscape

Blocks
Unit blocks, hollow blocks (may also be outdoors)
Props: people and animal figures, doll house, transportation toys
Accessories: transportation signage, doll furniture, gas pumps, cloth scraps

Infants/toddlers: Substitute soft blocks and cardboard blocks for unit blocks; limit props and accessories for safety; push-pull toys.

School-age: Include "village" or "castle" blocks; pattern blocks; increase number and types of unit blocks, add paper and pencils for child-made signage; make homemade blocks from milk cartons.

Manipulatives/Table Toys
Puzzles
Construction toys: Legos, Tinkertoys, etc.
Math toys: Unifix cubes, Cuisenaire blocks, attribute blocks, colored cubes, lacing, stringing toys, pegboards
Dressing frames
Montessori materials: pink tower, graduated cylinders, golden cube, etc.; collectibles: buttons, keys, shells, etc. cooperative games: lotto, dominoes, matching games

Infants/toddlers: Provide a few simple puzzles, with knobs, or soft ones; eliminate math toys and replace with large plastic beads, nesting boxes, stacking toys, easy dressing frames for toddlers.

School-age: Emphasize construction, math toys and cooperative games. Add cards, board games.

Language and Books
Books
Flannel board, accessories
Photos
Lotto games
Records, tapes
Writing center: typewriter, pads, and pencils

Infants/toddlers: Cardboard books; use others with adults only.
School age: Readers, listening post

FIGURE 9–11 A sample materials and equipment list for an early childhood program. Although not comprehensive, this lists starts to organize the environment for a variety of play. Note the adjustments that must be made to accommodate different ages. See Figure 9–3 for ideas about culturally diverse materials and Figure 9–4 for how to adapt environments for children with special needs.

preschooler has been able to say good-bye easier when the great outdoors beckon.

General Guidelines. The traditional playgrounds—typically on a flat, barren area with steel structures such as swings, climbers, a slide, perhaps a merry-go-round or seesaws, fixed in concrete and arranged in one row—are poor places for children's play from both safety and developmental perspectives. Children prefer spaces that have a variety of fixed and movable equipment. Raw materials, such as sand, water, tires, spools, sawhorses, bowls, or pans, in combination with larger superstructures or open-air "houses" with some flexible parts, stimulate a wide variety of both social and cognitive play (including constructive, dramatic, and games play). Figure 9–12 is a list of basic outdoor materials.

A wide porch or covered patio is ideal for rainy days or days when the sun is too severe. Many activities can be extended to the outside area with this type of protection. The physical plant should include adequate playground space adjacent to the building. A variety of playground surfaces makes for more interesting play and provides suitable covering for outdoor activities. Tanbark can be used in the swing area,

what do YOU think?

Close your eyes. Think back on the memories of a place you liked to play in when you were young. Was it outdoors? Was it a cozy spot near a loving adult? Did it involve other children? You may want to sketch this place, adding some notes about the feel or the sounds and smells. Can you help the children in your care find such places of delight?

Basic Materials For Outdoor Playground/Yard

Grounds: Various surfaces (grass, asphalt, gravel/sand, tanbark), as much natural habitat as possible.
Equipment: Climbing apparatus with ramps, slide, pole, ladder; swings (various types); house/quiet area
Ramps and supports to build; tires, "loose parts"
Sand/water area and toys
Riding area and various wheel toys
Large building blocks
Dramatic-play props
Balls and game materials
Workbench and woodworking/clay materials
Easel and drying rack
Dancing/parachute/tumbling mat materials
Pet and garden areas
Infant-toddler: Have plenty of simple riding toys, eliminate woodworking, have apparatus correct size and simplicity and/or foam wedges
School-age: Increase game area, may eliminate number or kinds of wheel toys; substitute a stage, mural, boat, creek; increase "loose parts" for child-created forts.

FIGURE 9–12 The possibilities of creating outdoor space are endless; remember that children need space to run and group together, to experience nature first-hand, and to be reflective and alone to watch.

cement for wheel toys, and grass for under climbers. Sand is used for play in a large area and also in a sensory table. No matter what the surface, the yard should be constructed with a good drainage system. Trees, bushes, and other plantings will allow for both sunshine and shade. Fences are *mandatory.* They must be durable and an appropriate height, with no opportunity for a child to gain a foothold.

Because there are no legal standards for the manufacture of play equipment, adults who work with children must assume responsibility for playground design. Teachers can familiarize themselves with the literature, visit high-quality playgrounds, and consult with child development specialists when selecting equipment. Figure 9–13 is a checklist for playground safety.

Playground Designs. Environments must be arranged so that there are enough play spaces for the number of children in the group. When the number of play opportunities is analyzed, areas and activities can be assigned a value (Prescott et al., 1972). A simple area (swings, climbers) counts as one play space, a complex area (housekeeping/dramatic play) counts as four play spaces, and a super area (sand and water play combined) counts as eight play spaces. This generally coincides with the number of children who might be accommodated in that space. By calculating the play space, a teacher can see if there is a place for everyone to play. Clearly defined boundaries and obvious pathways make it easy for children to play. There should be enough space for larger groups to gather together, as well as small groups. Figure 9–14 shows a playground suitable for four- to eight-year-olds.

Outdoors, children develop motor skills of all kinds. In the sand, children dig—a gross motor activity. As they judge how big a hole is or how much water will fill it, they are practicing and improving their perceptual motor skills. Turning on a faucet, planting seeds, and making mudpies are for fine motor development. Wheel toys offer children opportunities in all motor areas. Pushing someone in a wagon develops arm and leg strength—gross motor development. Guiding tricycles and carts on a path and around obstacles requires perceptual motor skill. Trying to "repair" or "paint" a wheel toy with tools or with large brushes, tying wagons together, or weaving streamers through the spokes of a bicycle all use fine motor skills. By looking at the yard with an eye to physical and motor development, teachers can plan activities that support growth in all skill areas.

In summary, the physical environment should be organized for children according to these criteria:

- ✿ *Availability.* Open, low shelving with visual cues for placement of toys, markings for where equipment goes—aids in set up and restoration.

- ✿ *Consistency in organization.* Neat, systematic, in logical order.

- ✿ *Compatibility.* Noisy activities are grouped away from quiet ones; art needs natural light when possible; water play near a bathroom or kitchen; messy projects done on washable floors.

- ✿ *Definition.* Clearly defined boundaries indicating available space and what is to take place; obvious pathways outlined in room and yard; ways to get in and out of an area without disrupting activity in progress; no dead ends or runways.

- ✿ *Spacing.* Interest areas with enough space to hold the children who will play there; one-third to one-half of the surface should remain uncovered; materials stored near space where they

Making Playgrounds Safe

Safety in the yard means:
- Enough room for the number and age of children who will use it.
- Adequate empty space.
- Availability of both hard and soft surfaces.
- Soft surfaces under any equipment from which a child might fall.
- Shady areas alternating with sunny spots.
- No standing water—good drainage.
- No poisonous or thorny plants, or litter or debris.
- Areas of play clearly defined and differentiated from one another.
- Sand area protected at night from animals.
- Fences high enough and in good repair.
- Gates secure with latches out of children's reach.

Equipment is:
- Well maintained—no exposed nails, screws, sharp edges, chipped paint.
- Chosen with children's ages in mind in regard to height and complexity.
- Stable and securely anchored.
- Repaired immediately or removed if damaged.
- Varied to allow for wide range of skills.
- Not crowded.
- Smooth where children's hands are likely to be placed.
- Checked frequently.
- Placed appropriately: slides facing north, swings away from other structures and busy areas.
- Scaled to age level: steps and other openings are 4 inches or less apart *or* 8 to 10 inches apart.
- Modified for age levels: swings have soft seats.

Teachers:
- Reinforce safe practices.
- Wear appropriate outdoor clothing.
- Check frequently *where* children are playing.
- Involve children in safety checks of yard, equipment, and grounds.
- Provide continual, adequate supervision.
- Avoid congregating to talk.
- Get involved with children.
- Provide enough activities and challenges.
- Watch for sun exposure, especially with toddlers.
- Assist children when they want to rearrange movable equipment.

FIGURE 9–13 Before children are allowed to use a playground, teachers should use a checklist such as this to ensure that safety standards are met. A safe playground stimulates physical development, social interaction, and full exploration of the materials and environment.

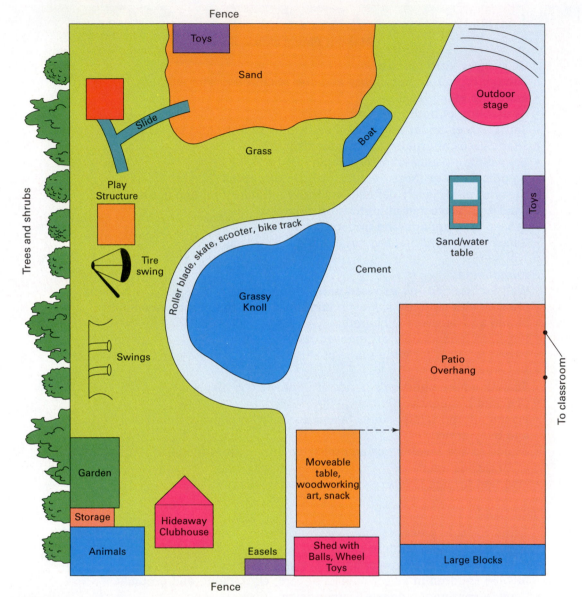

FIGURE 9–14 A playground or yard suitable for ages four and older will give children a sense of security and adventure, providing "contact with nature, opportunities for social play, and freedom of movement and active physical play" (Themes, 1999).

are used; storage and activity spaces have visual cues.

❂ *Communicability.* Tells children what to do instead of relying on adults to monitor activities; communicates to children what behavior is expected; arrangement suggests numbers of children, levels of activity.

 **THE TEMPORAL ENVIRONMENT**

Daily Schedule: Time to Learn

The daily schedule defines the structure of each program. It creates the format for how children will experience the events of the day—in what order and for what length of time. No two schedules are alike because each reflects the program it represents. The amount of time devoted to specific activities communicates clearly what value the school places on them.

In developing a schedule, teachers first decide what is important for children to learn, how that learning should take place, and how much time to allow in the daily program. A children's program must be for children and on their timetable as much as possible. The golden rule for child care is to treat children as we want them to treat us:

1. Build on choices as much of the time as possible, avoiding the expectation that everyone should do the same thing at the same time.

2. Provide a sensitive and flexible settling-in period. Different people cope with change and new experiences in different ways.

3. Avoid meaningless and sometimes mindless activities that simply "fill up the day" or "help pass the time."

4. Balance the need for autonomy, freedom, and independence with the need for rules that help us get along together.

5. Strike a balance between the comfort and reassurance of the familiar and the need for variety and novelty for a change.

Figure 9–15 outlines three daily schedules that demonstrate these guidelines.

The physical plant itself may dictate a portion of the daily schedule. If toilet facilities are not located adjacent to the classroom, then more time must be scheduled to travel to and from the bathrooms. If the yard is shared with other groups, some portion of the schedule may be modified.

Two aspects of the daily schedule are especially important: routines and transitions.

Routines

A routine is a constant; each day, certain events are repeated, providing continuity

---

Video View Point 9-3

"Daily Routines: Much of the daily routine in infant care revolves around arrival and departure times, their eating, sleeping, and diaper-changing schedules, and their independent play."

Competency: Program Management

Age Group: Infant–Toddler

Critical Thinking Questions:

1. How can a team of caregivers establish a flexible routine in an infant center?

2. Why should infants have at least two scheduled outside times?

---

and a sense of order to the schedule. Most routines are personal and individual rituals in children's daily lives. Children bring to school a history firmly established around routines, one that is deeply embedded in their family and culture. They are reassuring to children, who take pride in mastering them; they are also a highly emotional issue for some.

Routines are the pegs on which to hang the daily calendar. When children should eat, sleep, play, or be alone or together is determined by the placement of routines. The rest of the curriculum—art activities, field trips, wood-working—works around them. Routines in an early childhood education setting include:

- Self-care (eating, rest/sleeping, dressing, toileting)
- Transitions between activities
- Group times
- Beginning and ending the day or session
- Making choices
- Task completion
- Room cleanup and yard restoration

The self-care tasks can be difficult issues between adult and child. Everyone can

Half-Day Toddler Program

9:00–9:30	Greet children Inside activities • play dough and arts/easel • home living • blocks and manipulatives • books
9:30	Door to outdoors opens
9:45–10:20	Outdoor play • large motor • social play
10:20	Music/movement outdoors
10:30	Snack/"Here We Are Together" song • washing hands • eating/pouring/cleanup
10:45–11:45	Outside
11:15	"Time to Put Our Toys Away" song • all encouraged to participate in cleanup
11:20	Closure (indoors) • parent–child together • story or flannel board

Full-Day Program for Preschoolers

7:00	Arrival, breakfast
7:30	Inside free play • arts/easels • table toys/games/blocks • dramatic-play center; house, grocery store, etc.
9:00	Cleanup
9:15	Group time: songs/fingerplays and small group choices
9:30	Choice time/small groups • discovery/math lab/science activity • cooking for morning or afternoon snack • language art/prereading choice
10:00	Snack (at outside tables/cloths on warm days) or snack center during free play
10:15	Outside free play • climbing, swinging, sand and water, wheel toys, group games
12:00	Handwash and lunch
12:45	Get ready: toileting, handwashing, toothbrushing, prepare beds
1:15	Bedtime story
1:30	Rest time
2:30	Outdoors for those awake
3:30	Cleanup outdoors and singing time
4:00	Snacktime
4:15	Learning centers; some outdoor/indoor choices, field trips, story teller
5:30	Cleanup and read books until going home

Half-Day Kindergarten Plan

8:15–8:30	Arrival Getting ready to start • checking in library books, lunch money, etc.
8:30	Newstelling • "anything you want to tell for news" • newsletter written weekly
9:00	Work assignment • write a story about your news or • make a page in your book (topic assigned) or • work in math lab
9:30–10:15	Choice of indoors (paints, blocks, computer, table toys) or second-grade tutors read books to children • When finished, play in loft or read books until recess

FIGURE 9–15 Daily schedules reflect the children's needs and ages while meeting the program's goals. The time and timing of the school day show what is valued in the program. *Continued*

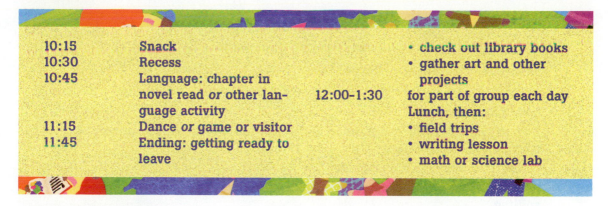

10:15	Snack		• check out library books
10:30	Recess		• gather art and other
10:45	Language: chapter in novel read or other language activity		projects for part of group each day
		12:00–1:30	Lunch, then:
11:15	Dance or game or visitor		• field trips
11:45	Ending: getting ready to leave		• writing lesson
			• math or science lab

FIGURE 9–15, continued

recall vivid memories associated with at least one routine. They seem to become battlegrounds on which children and adults often struggle. Many times this is where children choose to take their first stand on the road to independence (Figure 9–16).

The early childhood teacher must be able to deal with the issue of self-care routines in sensitive and understanding ways. Children adjust to routines when they are regularly scheduled in the daily program and when there are clear expectations. All three environmental factors are influenced by routines:

1. *Physical.* Child-sized bathroom and eating facilities; storage of cots, blankets, and sleeping accessories; equipment for food storage and preparation.

2. *Temporal.* Amount of time in daily schedule for eating, resting, toileting, and cleanup.

3. *Interpersonal.* Attitudes toward body functions; willingness to plan for self-care tasks; interactions during activities and transitions; expectations of staff, parents, and children.

When the time sequence is clear, everyone can go about the business of learning and teaching. Children are more secure in a place that has a consistent schedule; they can begin to anticipate the regularity of what comes next and count on it. They can freely involve themselves

without fear of being interrupted. Adults, too, enjoy the predictability of a daily schedule. By knowing the sequence of events, they are then free to flex the timing when unforeseen circumstances arise.

And it is the unforeseen that often does happen. For instance, Chad unexpectedly decides that he doesn't want Dad to go—just as the teacher was helping Shana onto the toilet for the first time. Or chaos breaks out in the block corner—at the moment a teacher was leaving with a group of children for the kitchen with several cookie sheets full of carefully constructed gingerbread people. A parent is walking in the door with a special grouptime activity—and this time Marisa refuses to clean up her play dough creation. Flexibility to handle these situations comes from creating a humane schedule in the first place.

Transitions

As a species, humans are known for their adaptability. And yet we are resistant to change. For young children, too, change is difficult. Teachers and caregivers can make the necessary changes easier for children if they focus their attention on those times. Rather than trying to rush through quickly to get to the next event, allow for enough transition time. Helping children anticipate, figure out, work through, and successfully manage the changes in their day guides them to maturity (Figure 9–17).

Routines: Learning Opportunities

- **Eating Teaches Health:**

  Introduction to new and different foods, good nutritional habits

- **Eating Teaches Social Skills:**

  How to manage oneself in a group eating situation, focusing on eating and conversing; acceptable mealtime behavior and manners

- **Eating Teaches Fine Motor Skills:**

  Pouring, handling spoons, forks; serving self; drinking, eating without spilling

- **Eating Teaches Independence Skills:**

  Finding and setting one's place, serving self, making choices, cleaning up at snack and lunch times

- **Eating Teaches Individual Differences:**

  Likes and dislikes; choices of food; pace of eating

- **Resting and Sleeping Teach Health:**

  Personal care skills; relaxation habits; internal balance and change of pace; alternating activity to allow body to rest

- **Resting and Sleeping Teach Independence Skills:**

  Preparing own rest place; selecting book or toy; clearing bed things after rest

- **Dressing Teaches Independence Skills:**

  Self-awareness: size of clothes, comparisons between clothes for girls and boys, younger and older, larger and smaller children, and children in and out of diapers or training pants

  Self-esteem: caring for one's own body; choosing one's own clothes

- **Dressing Teaches Fine Motor Skills:**

  How to manage snaps, buttons, zippers; handling all garments; maneuvering in and out of a snowsuit or jacket; matching hands and feet with mittens and boots or shoes

- **Toileting Teaches Emotional Skills:**

  Self-awareness: body functions, learning the names and physical sensations that go with body functions

  Self-identity: comparisons between girls and boys (sit versus stand)

  Self-esteem: caring for one's own body without guilt, fear, shame

  Human sexuality: in a natural setting, promotes healthy attitudes toward the body and its functions, and that adults can be accepting, open, and reassuring about the body and its care

FIGURE 9–16 Every routine can be used as a vehicle for learning within the environment.

Transition Times Made Easier

Questions for Planning
- Who is involved in the transition time (child, parents, teachers, other children, visitors, etc.)?
- What kind of activity has preceded the transition time and what will follow?
- What will the children be asked to do during transition?
- What will the teachers be doing *during* transition?
- How will the children be told or find out what to do during the transition?
- What do you know about child development and this particular child(ren) that can help with these questions?

Teaching Strategies
Arrival
- Greet each child with a smile, and welcome child and parent with what activities are available.
- Make name cards and/or an attendance sheet that child and parent can participate in as a starting point.
- Plan with parents, and alert the child, a simple and clear way for them to say goodbye and for the parents to leave (see Chapter 8 for details).

Cleanup Materials
- Give the children a five-minute" warning" to alert them to upcoming changes.
- Have a consistent and calm signal to start putting away toys.
- Use music as background and/or sing during cleanup.
- Consider having necklaces or cards of specific areas for children, or make teams.
- Construct the environment so that it is clear where things go and children can do the majority of it themselves.
- Occasionally thank the children publicly for cleaning up, noting individual efforts and specific chores done well.

Preparing Children to Attend
- Make a chart that shows the choices available.
- Sing a song or familiar fingerplay to get everyone's attention and participation.
- Ask the children to put on "elephant ears" (rabbit, etc.) or lock their lips and put the key in their pockets.

Ready to Rest/Nap Time
- Prepare the environment ahead of time to be restful—darkened room, soft blanket/cuddlies nearby, quiet music, teachers whispering and available to walk children to their places and stay with them.
- Read a story to the group in one place before they are to lie quietly, or split larger groups into small subgroups with a teacher reading to each.

FIGURE 9–17 Transitions are a regular part of children's routines and should be learning times that are as well planned as other parts of the day.

Continued

Moving to Another Place/Building
- Gather the group and tell them exactly what will be happening.
- Ask for ideas of how to behave ("What will we need to remember? How can we stay safe and have fun together?") and reinforce with a few concrete rules.
- Have the children be a train, with adults as the engine and caboose, or a dragon with head and tail.
- Have the children choose a partner to stay with and hold hands.
- Ask preschoolers and early primary children to remember the "B" words ("beside or behind") in staying near adults.

Waiting for Others to Finish
- Prepare a part of the room for children to move to, such as a book corner or listening post, having an adult in that space with more than two children.
- Make an apron or hanging with several pockets filled with activity cards or small manipulatives for children to use alone.
- Plan a special table with folders or large envelopes with activities.
- Have a "waiting box" with special small items for these times only.

FIGURE 9–17, continued

Good teachers prepare children for upcoming transitions, using a song or strumming of an instrument and the words, "Get ready to clean up soon." And they are also prepared for children's perceptions of time, immediacy, and closure to collide with the schedule. So if Chad doesn't want his Dad to go, perhaps getting Shana on the toilet will have to wait, or Dad can read him another story until Shana's "all done now." The gingerbread sheets can be held momentarily so the quarrel can be resolved, or some of the "fighters" could be invited to be door openers and help march the group to the kitchen. Perhaps Marisa could keep working on her masterpiece while the rest of the class joins the parent on the rug (at least, just this once?).

Developmentally Appropriate Schedules

Just as the arrangement of space should reflect the group of children within, so does the daily schedule allow for appropriate growth at the developmental level of the group. There are common factors to consider for all children in the early years, as well as some developmental distinctions at the various ages.

There are common elements in all schedules, whether they are designed for toddler groups or five-year-olds, all-day programs or half-day nurseries. Sound child development principles provide the framework on which the daily schedule is structured. Individual programs then adapt these requirements to their own philosophy as they work out their daily schedule. All schedules must:

- Be consistent. Consistency brings security and closure, allowing for teacher authority and expertise to assert themselves.

- Provide for flexibility so that children's interests can be maintained and emergencies met. Flexibility invites sensitivity to individuals and respectful agreements to be reached.

✸ Include time for routines as well as time for transitions.

✸ Alternate quiet and active play and work to help children pace themselves.

✸ Provide opportunities for both inside and outside play.

✸ Allow children to participate in structured activities, as well as those of their own choosing. This often includes whole-group times (circle time to begin the day, songtime for announcements, or storytime as closure).

✸ Make it possible for children to work individually, in small groups, or in larger ones.

✸ Gear the time to the age and developmental levels of the group.

✸ Have a beginning and an end. Some provisions must be made for children to be met and greeted when they enter. Allow time for dismissal and transition, bringing the children closure with a review of the day's activities and anticipation of what will come tomorrow.

✸ Involve the adults in daily planning and review; include a regular meeting time for more substantial discussion of children, long-range planning, and evaluation.

✸ Include time for cleanup and room restoration.

✸ Incorporate the teachers' roles/assignments so that they know their responsibilities.

✸ Be posted in an obvious place in the classroom for all to see.

All schedules have a great deal in common, but certain age-related differences can be seen. There are several important differences in schedules for the various age groups:

✸ More choices are available to children as they grow.

Example: Two-year-olds could be overstimulated by the selection of ma-

terials that is appropriate for school-aged children.

✸ Transitions are handled differently in the various age groups.

Example: Older children can move through some transitions as a group, such as changing from one activity area to another or going out with a specialist in pairs or even in a single file. This is difficult for younger children, who would push or wander away. For them, the door to the yard opens quietly, allowing children to go out slowly.

Example: A child care class of three- and four-year-olds is dismissed from songtime to snack by the color of people's shirts, or the first letter of their names, rather than as one whole group. Figure 9–17 gives examples of handling transitions for all ages.

✸ The structure of the day changes with age.

Example: The balance of free-play and teacher-directed activities shifts from relatively few directed activities for younger children to some more for the nursery school and child care ages. The kindergarten schedule provides more structure both in individual work projects and teacher-focused time. A first-grade schedule with some whole-group teacher instruction times is developmentally appropriate for those older children.

✸ The content of group activities changes with age.

Example: In the toddler class, group times are simple: A short fingerplay, story with a flannel board or puppets, or a song to dismiss is adequate. The preschool group times include several songs, a dramatization of a favorite fingerplay, and a short story. In the kindergarten, circle lasts 15 to 20 minutes, with announcement and weather board; children's "newstelling;" longer dramas; and even chapter stories.

Centers are very busy environments for children. So many things, so much learning, so much to do! Kielar (1999) offers these suggestions as an "antidote" to such noisy times:

- ❂ Reserve an area of your school or center for those who want to sit quietly.
- ❂ Make lunchtime a time for peace and quiet.
- ❂ Wake up children from naps a little sooner than is needed to give them time to transition.
- ❂ Don't decorate every window with paintings.
- ❂ Change room displays often.

Thus the temporal environment mirrors the children's age and individual interests. A special note: many programs divide the day into small segments of time in the belief that young children have such short attention spans that they cannot remain at an activity for long. However, we know that children can stay focused for long periods of time on activities of *their* choice or interest. Although they may last only a short time in teacher-planned, structured activities, children need and thrive with more time to get their own creative

juices flowing. Consult Figure 9–15 to see how the temporal environment allots time for successful free-play time.

THE INTERPERSONAL ENVIRONMENT

A child responds to everything in school: the color of the room, the way the furniture is arranged, how much time there is to play, and how people treat one another. The feeling in a room is as real as the blocks or the books. Thus, the interpersonal (social) aspects of an early childhood setting are powerful components of the environment.

Defining the Tone

Children are the most important people in the setting; they should feel safe and comfortable. A warm, interpersonal environment invites children to participate and to learn. When children feel secure with one another and with the setting, they will be able to engage more fully in the total program.

Teachers will be the key ingredient in determining the atmosphere of a group. The first component of the National Academy's criteria for high-quality early child-

The teacher's posture and facial expressions show her respect for children and their learning pace and style.

hood programs is the interactions among the staff and children (see Chapter 2). The human component, the connections among the people in a center or home, makes all the difference to young children, for they are the barometers of interpersonal tension or openness and freedom.

Parents matter in the life of school, especially in the early years. The way people feel about each other and how they express their feelings have an affect on children.

Teachers have to see children within their family and social context, and to do so, they must invite families into the schooling process, as in these situations:

You can't believe it; no matter how many times you tell Kai's Chinese grandfather that school starts at 9 A.M., he continues to bring him between 9:30 and 10 . . . until you find out that in China, old people are often late and the people respect their habits. Now you may need to flex your schedule to allow for this late arrival and support this family custom.

Elena's father is large and speaks with such an accent you can hardly understand him. You'd like to just avoid talking with him, but then you'd connect only when there's a problem . . . and you discover that, in his Central American culture, teachers' ideas are to be solicited for parents to be seen as "good parents." Now you may need to overcome your discomfort and ask him respectfully to repeat what he is saying a bit more slowly.

Every day Maryam brings her lunch, and it is so difficult to manage. These Iranian foods are not the same as the other children's, and there is often teasing that you have to keep redirecting. You wonder if you should

simply tell her auntie to send her with a sandwich . . . only you realize that everyone wants to eat familiar foods, and letting Maryam eat what her parents want her to should also be coupled with having the other children learn some tolerance, too. Now you might use the lunchtime situation to help everyone become curious and interested in new foods.

Learning is enhanced when parents and teachers come to communicate in supportive, nonthreatening ways. Quality in a program is determined by the interactions between children and adults and the relationships that such interactions develop. Researchers have found a pattern of positive relationships between children's sensitive, involved interactions with teachers and children's enhanced development. The effect of these types of interactions is likely to be seen in children's cognitive, socioemotional, and language development (Kontos & Wilcox-Herzog, 1997). Further, the nature of the classroom atmosphere contributes greatly to children's success in learning English as a second language (Elgas et al., 2002). Such research confirms the findings of recent brain-based research and theories of Erikson, Bandura, and Vygotsky (see Chapter 4).

Young children develop best through close, affectionate relationships with people. This is particularly important for children under three and for children whose primary language is not the dominant one spoken in the program. "The interpersonal aspect of environment is the central element affecting the quality of toddler play, more important than elaborateness of physical setting," declares Zeavin (1997). "Toddlers cannot talk about what is going on inside them. It is through their play that they externalize troubling feelings, work out emotional conflicts, and gain control of their world. . . . Every issue is a relationship issue."

Teachers observe and engage children in interactions that include smiling, touching, listening, asking questions, and speaking on eye level. The language and tone of voice used are respectful and friendly, with children treated equally across lines of race, culture, language, ability, and sex.[1]

Staff use positive guidance rather than punitive discipline techniques (see Chapter 7) and develop warm relationships with families (see Chapter 8).

A Quick Check

Questions teachers can ask themselves as they evaluate the quality of the environment are:

- Is there a feeling of mutual respect between children and adults?

- Do teachers pick up on nonverbal and verbal expressions of both girls and boys? Of children with varying abilities? Of children of color?

- How do children treat one another?

- Do teachers model cooperative behavior with other adults and children? Do they show by example how to work through a disagreement or problem?

- Does the physical setup allow the teacher to focus on the children?

- Do housekeeping details keep teachers disconnected from children?

- Do teachers encourage children to use one another as resources?

- Do teachers take time to show children how to accomplish a task by themselves?

- Are girls complimented only on appearance and boys just for achievement? Are all children helped to appreciate similarities and differences?

- Do teachers use reasoning and following-through?

- How and when do teachers interact with children?

- What are the teacher's posture and facial expression when involved in a problem situation?

- If I were a child, would I like to come to school here?

The answers to these questions provide a barometer of how well teachers are maintaining an atmosphere of positive social interaction. The most important thing to remember is that the way people feel about each other and how they express their feelings have an impact on children. Teachers must focus as much attention on the interpersonal part of the environment as they do on buying equipment or arranging the room.

KEY TERMS

anti-bias
autonomy
environment
flexibility
full inclusion
group times
interest areas
interpersonal
learning centers
open-ended
roughhousing
routines
self-concept
self-esteem
self-help
temporal
transitions

[1]The interpersonal connection between families and teachers can bolster what happens to the child if the child's home culture and traditions are respected.

Teaching Applications

1. Hunch down on your knees and look at a classroom from the child's perspective. Describe what you see in terms of the principles of successful environments. Recommend changes that improve the physical environment.

2. Examine a daily schedule from an early childhood center. What do you think are the program goals of the school? How can you tell? Are there times for routines and transitions? For free play and group times? Compare this with a daily schedule of a family child care home. How are they alike? How are they different? Why?

3. Below are listed some common problems that can be remedied by changing the environment. List at least one solution for each problem.
   a. Too many children crowding into one area
   b. Overcrowded shelves
   c. Grabbing or arguments over the same toy
   d. Hoarding of materials
   e. Lack of cooperation during cleanup
   f. Wheel toy collisions
   g. Children crying when others' parents leave

4. Visit a toddler program, a four-year-old program, and a kindergarten. How are the learning centers defined? Name the centers of interest, and indicate which of them are for quiet play and which are for active play and work.

5. Check a classroom for diversity. Using the checklist (de Melendez, 2007), enter a checkmark whenever you find something in the classroom that complies with the element of diversity.

	Ethnicity	Gender	Social class	Disability	Age
Pictures/posters					
Books					
Housekeeping items					
Manipulatives					
Art materials					
Dramatic area					
Music					

Comments:

• Things I need to change:

• Things I need to add:

REFERENCES

Bredekamp, S. (Ed.) (1998). *Accreditation and criteria procedures* (Revised ed.). Washington, DC: National Association for the Education of Young Children.

Centers for Disease Control and Prevention (1997). *The ABCs of safe and healthy child care.* Atlanta, GA: Author.

de Melendez, W. R. (2007). *Teaching children in multicultural classrooms.* Clifton Park, NY: Thomson Delmar Learning

Derman-Sparks, L., & the ABC Task Force. (1989). *Anti-bias curriculum: Tools for empowering young children.* Washington, DC: National Association for the Education of Young Children.

Dodge, D. T., & Colker, L. J. (2002). *The creative curriculum* (4th ed.). Washington, DC: Teaching Strategies.

Elgas, P. M., Prendeville, J., Moomaw, S., & Kretschmer, R. R. (2002). Early childhood classroom setup. *Child Care Information Exchange,* 143, 17–20.

Greenman, J. (2004).What is the setting? Places for childhood. In Gordon A. M., & Williams Browne, K. *Beginnings and beyond* (6th ed.). Clifton Park, NY: Thomson Delmar Learning.

Harms, T., Cryer, D., & Clifford, R. M. (2003). *The Early Childhood (Rev.), Family Day Care, Infant/toddler (Rev.), and School Age Environmental RatingScales.* New York: Teachers College Press.

Haugen, K. (1997, March). Using your senses to adapt environments: Checklist for an accessible environment: Beginnings workshop. *Child Care Information Exchange.*

Jensen, E. (1998). *Teaching with the brain in mind.* Alexandria, VA: Association for Supervision and Curriculum Development.

Kendall, F. (1996). *Diversity in the classroom* (2nd ed.). New York: Teachers College Press.

Kielar, Joann. (1999). An antidote to the noisy nineties. *Young Children,* 54.

Kontos, S., & Wilcox-Herzog. A. (1997, January). Research in review. Teachers' interactions with children: Why are they so important? *Young Children, 52.*

Lowman, Linda H., & Ruhmann, Linda H. (1998, May). Simply sensational spaces: A multi-"S" approach to toddler environments. *Young Children, 53.*

Marotz, L. R., Cross, M. Z., & Rush, J. M. (2005). *Health, safety, and nutrition for the young child* (6th ed.). Clifton Park, NY: Thomson Delmar Learning.

NAEYC [National Association for the Education of Young Children]. (1995). *Keeping healthy: Parents, teachers, and children.* Washington, DC: Author.

Needlman, R., & Needlman, G. (1995, November/December). 10 most common health problems in school. *Scholastic Early Childhood Today.*

Prescott, E. (1994, November). The physical environment—a powerful regulator of experience. *Exchange.*

Prescott, E., Jones, E., & Kritschevsky, S. (1972). *Group care as a child-rearing environment.* Washington, DC: National Association for the Education of Young Children.

Rivkin, Mary S. (1995). *The great outdoors: Restoring children's right to play outdoors.* Washington, DC: National Association for the Education of Young Children.

Rogers, C. (1994, Spring). *Mainstreaming: Special needs—special experiences.* Unpublished paper.

Rushton, Stephen P. (2001). Applying brain research to create developmentally appropriate environments. *Young Children,* 56. Washington, DC: National Association for the Education of Young Children.

Themes, Tracy. (1999). *Let's go outside: Designing the early childhood playground.* Ypsilanti, MI: High/Scope Press.

TRUCE [Teachers Resisting Unhealthy Children's Entertainment]. (2002). Toys and toy trends to avoid. West Somerville, MA: Author.

Whitebrook, M. (1996). NAEYC accreditation as an indicator of quality: What research tells us. In S. Bredekamp & B. Willer (Eds.), *NAEYC accreditation: A decade of learning and the years ahead.* Washington, DC: National Association for the Education of Young Children.

Youcha, V., & Wood, K. (1997, March). Enhancing the environment for ALL children: Beginnings workshop. *Exchange.*

Zeavin, C. (1997, March). Toddlers at play: Environments at work. *Young Children,* 52.

Additional resources for this chapter can be found by visiting the Online Companion™ at www.earlychilded.delmar.com. This supplemental material includes a Study Guide with chapter review questions (and answers), critical thinking questions and activities, and annotated Web sites.

Curriculum Essentials

QUESTIONS FOR THOUGHT

What factors define curriculum in the early childhood setting?

What is developmentally appropriate curriculum? culturally appropriate curriculum?

What is the relationship between play and curriculum?

What is the teacher's role in planning curriculum?

Identify four effective curriculum models.

✿ CURRICULUM BASICS

What Is Curriculum?

In an early childhood education setting, the curriculum consists of the art activity and language game, the impulsive investigation of pouring milk at lunchtime, the song that accompanies digging in the sand, and the teacher's explanation of why the hamster died.

Young children are like sponges; they absorb everything going on about them. They do not discriminate between what is prepared for them to learn and whatever else happens at school. It is all learning. Curriculum includes all of the activities as well as the subject matter, the interactions with people, and all of the experiences of the children's day.

Bredekamp and Rosegrant (1995) provide an all-inclusive definition:

Curriculum happens when child meets materials.

Curriculum is an organized framework that delineates the *content* that children are to learn, the *process* through which children achieve the identified curricular goals, what *teachers* do to help children achieve these goals, and the *context* in which teaching and learning occur.

The key words in their definition can be broken down as follows:

1. The *content* is what is being taught—the subject matter reflects the interests, needs, and experiences of the child and addresses what children should learn.

2. The *process* is how and when learning takes place, the choice of activities or projects and how they are integrated with one another, and the time frame within the daily schedule or yearly calendar. The process enhances children's involvement in their own learning through a hands-on, exploratory approach with a variety of open-ended materials. Play is the medium for the process.

3. *Teachers* create the curriculum, planning and providing for activities and materials in relation to the age range of the group and observing and evaluating children's growth. Teachers are grounded in child development theory, have an understanding of how children learn, and are aware of the need to individualize to meet children's **special needs.**

4. The *context* is why certain projects and activities are chosen and is based on the program's philosophy and goals, the cultural backgrounds of the children, and their family and community values and influences.

The relevance of curriculum is important to note. Head Start classes on Native American reservations in the Southwest will develop curricula that utilize the history and traditions of the various Native American tribes the students represent. Relevant curriculum for a suburban preschool in Seattle may include field trips to the Pike Street Market to see the recent salmon catch, while a transportation unit for inner-city Boston preschoolers may include subway rides.

Developmentally Appropriate Curriculum

Appropriate early childhood curriculum is based on the theory, research, and experience of knowing how young children develop and learn. An infant curriculum meets the basic needs of young babies; a toddler curriculum considers the emerging independence and mobility of toddlers. Four-year-olds require different materials to expand their thinking, and early primary children need to learn skills. Each age level deserves special consideration when curriculum is being planned.

Developmentally appropriate programs, curricula, and practices have been defined by the National Association for the Education of Young Children (NAEYC) (Bredekamp & Copple, 1997) as follows:

1. *Appropriateness.* Programs and practices are based on knowledge of normal child development within a given age span.

2. *Individual appropriateness.* Programs and practices are based on respect for the individual child, the individual rate of growth, and the unique learning style.

3. *Social and cultural appropriateness.* Programs and practices provide meaningful and relevant learning experiences that are respectful of the backgrounds of the children and families in the group.

Developmentally appropriate curriculum takes into account a knowledge of child development theory, research, and practice, including various related disciplines; cultural values; parental desires and concerns; community context; individual children; teachers' knowledge and experience; and it is related to overall program goals.[1] The foundation for **developmentally appropriate practices** and curriculum content is historically rooted in John Dewey's vision that schools prepare students to think and reason to participate in a democratic society (see Chapter 1). Figure 10–1 lists 20 guidelines jointly endorsed by the NAEYC and the National Association of Early Childhood Specialists in state departments of education to ensure developmentally appropriate curriculum.

Video **View** Point 10-1

"Truly, the most fascinating, interactive, developmentally appropriate toys for infants are the adults and children in their lives."

Competency: Learning Environment

Age Group: Infant/Toddler

Critical Thinking Questions

1. What does this statement mean to you?

2. As an infant/toddler caregiver, how would you implement this statement?

[1]DAP is CAC. Developmentally appropriate practices include culturally appropriate curriculum.

Guidelines for Developmentally Appropriate Curriculum

NAEYC and the National Association of Early Childhood Specialists in state Departments of Education jointly developed guidelines to ensure developmentally appropriate curriculum. Each of the guidelines is in the form of a question to which teachers developing curriculum for young children should be able to answer yes.

1. Does it promote interactive learning and encourage the child's construction of knowledge?

2. Does it help achieve social, emotional, physical, and cognitive goals?

3. Does it encourage development of positive feelings and dispositions toward learning while leading to acquisition of knowledge and skills?

4. Is it meaningful for these children? Is it relevant to the children's lives? Can it be made more relevant by relating it to a personal experience children have had, or can they easily gain direct experience with it?

5. Are the expectations realistic and attainable at this time, or could the children more easily and efficiently acquire the knowledge or skills later on?

6. Is it of interest to children and to the teacher?

7. Is it sensitive to and respectful of cultural and linguistic diversity? Does it expect, allow, and appreciate individual differences? Does it promote positive relationships with families?

8. Does it build on and elaborate children's current knowledge and abilities?

9. Does it lead to conceptual understanding by helping children construct their own understanding in meaningful contexts?

10. Does it facilitate integration of content across traditional subject matter areas?

11. Is the information presented accurately and credibly according to the recognized standards of the relevant discipline?

12. Is this content worth knowing? Can it be learned by these children efficiently and effectively now?

13. Does it encourage active learning and allow children to make meaningful choices?

14. Does it foster children's exploration and inquiry, rather than focusing on "right" answers or "right" ways to complete a task?

15. Does it promote the development of higher order abilities such as thinking, reasoning, problem solving, and decision making?

16. Does it promote and encourage social interaction among children and adults?

17. Does it respect children's physiological needs for activity, sensory stimulation, fresh air, rest, and nourishment/elimination?

18. Does it promote feelings of psychological safety, security, and belonging?

19. Does it provide experiences that promote feelings of success, competence, and enjoyment of learning?

20. Does it permit flexibility for children and teachers?

FIGURE 10–1 (Reprinted, with permission, from S. Bredekamp, & T. Rosegrant, "Reaching potentials through transforming curriculum, assessment, and teaching," in *Reaching Potentials: Transforming Early Childhood Curriculum and Assessment*, Vol. 2, eds. S. Bredekamp, & T. Rosegrant. [Washington, DC: National Association for the Education of Young Children (NAEYC), 1995], 16.)

Culturally Appropriate Curriculum

If meaningful learning is derived from a social and cultural context, then a multicultural atmosphere must be created in which awareness and concern for true diversity (including ethnicity, gender, and abilities) permeate the program. Creating a truly multicultural classroom calls into question the familiar ways of doing things and provides new insights and ways of thinking about culture. Multicultural education is about "modifying the total school environment so that students from diverse ethnic and cultural groups will experience equal educational opportunities" (Banks, 1994a). Figure 10–2 highlights the difference by comparing common characteristics of a dominant culture with an approach that would offer more perspectives from other cultures.

Characteristics of a Multicultural Curriculum

Common Practices of Dominant Culture	For a Multicultural Approach
Focuses on isolated aspects of the histories and cultures of ethnic groups	Describes the history and cultures of ethnic groups holistically
Trivializes the histories and cultures of ethnic groups	Describes the cultures of ethnic groups as dynamic wholes
Presents events, issues, and concepts primarily from Anglocentric and mainstream perspectives	Presents events, issues, concepts from the perspectives of diverse racial and ethnic groups
Is Eurocentric—shows the development of the Untied States primarily as an extension of Europe into the Americas	Is multidimensional and geocultural—shows how many peoples and cultures came to the United States from many parts of the world, including Asia and Africa, and the important roles they played in the development of U.S. society
Content about ethnic groups is an appendage to regular curriculum	Content about ethnic groups is an integral part of regular curriculum
Ethnic minority cultures are described as deprived or dysfunctional	Ethnic minority cultures are described as different from mainstream Anglo culture but as rich and functional
Focuses on ethnic heroes, holidays, and factual information	Focuses on concepts, generalizations, and theories
Emphasizes the mastery of knowledge and cognitive outcomes	Emphasizes knowledge formation and decision making
Encourages acceptance of existing ethnic, class, and racial stratification	Focuses on social criticism and social change

FIGURE 10–2 A comparison of two different approaches to multicultural curriculum, one from a Eurocentric point of view, the other from a culturally sensitive perspective. (Reprinted with permission from James A. Banks, CULTURAL DIVERSITY AND EDUCATION: FOUNDATIONS, CURRICULUM, AND TEACHING [5th Edition. Boston: Allyn and Bacon, 2006], page 238.)

Culturally appropriate curriculum is also developmentally appropriate curriculum. The challenge is to develop a curriculum that reflects the plurality of contemporary American society in general and the individual classroom, in particular, and present them in sensitive, relevant ways. This does not necessarily mean creating a whole new curriculum.

Banks (1992) suggests the **infusion** of multicultural content within current practices as a way to begin to develop a multicultural curriculum. Infusion, according to Banks (1994a), allows the teacher to continue using a developmentally appropriate curriculum while incorporating many perspectives, frames of reference, and content from various groups that will extend a child's understanding of today's society.

The infusion approach calls into question the common practice in many early childhood education programs of cooking ethnic foods or celebrating ethnic or cultural holidays as isolated experiences, which often trivialize or stereotype groups of people.[1] Folk tales, songs, food, and dress are symbols and expressions of a culture, not the culture itself. For children to gain any meaningful knowledge, the content must contribute to a fuller understanding of human diversity, not just a special-occasion topic. On the other hand, using music from various cultures for movement and dance activities in the curriculum throughout the year incorporates the perspective of a pluralistic society into the established routines and rituals of the classroom.

Curriculum materials and activities should be evaluated to ensure fair and sensitive portrayals of various cultures. Make sure they are consistent with the phi-

losophy and goals of the school, and it should contribute to the understanding of life in our diverse society. De Melendez and Ostertag (1997) propose the following questions as a way of assessing the choice of a topic for infusion. Does the topic:

1. present, elaborate, and/or expand concepts of diversity?

2. fit logically into the child's learning and experience, giving a sense of real, not unimportant, learning?

3. include the perspectives of how people with diverse cultural views would behave or react to it?

4. reflect issues that are common to the children in the classroom or the community?

5. offer opportunities to present other positions that expose the children to divergent views?

6. serve as a link to discuss emotions and feelings as perceived by the children?

7. facilitate clarification of stereotypes and biases? How?

To gain a greater sense of what multicultural curriculum can be in the early years, keep these questions in mind as you read through the rest of this chapter. Refer to the sections in Chapter 9 on anti-bias environments and inclusive environments and to the multicultural environment checklist (Figure 9–3) as well.

Inclusive Curriculum

Inclusive curricula are those that reflect awareness of and sensitivity to diversity in all areas of a child's life: cultural, social, linguistic, and religious, as well as in terms of gender and capabilities. The inclusion of chil-

[1]This is often referred to as the tourist approach to diversity.

dren with any and all varieties of disabilities and reflecting various cultural backgrounds has been built into all of the chapters of this text.

Cultural sensitivity is described in terms of developmentally appropriate practices in Chapter 2 and in defining the young child later on in that chapter. Chapter 7 includes cultural influences on children's behavior and various patterns of family behavior, and Vygotsky's theory that development and knowledge are culturally specific is discussed in Chapter 4. Chapter 3 describes how a child with disabilities is included within the early childhood education program. In Chapter 9 you will find suggestions for creating inclusive environments, with a checklist in Figure 9–4.

The basic premise in this text is that children with disabilities, children from immigrant families, children from families whose first language is not English, girls and boys, and young children from all cultures need the same things in a learning environment. Quality early childhood education programs and curricula are based on the same principles described throughout this book, no matter what characteristics define the children who attend these programs. Adaptations are made to fit the capacities of each individual child as needed. See Figure 10–3 for ways to enhance diversity and inclusivity through curriculum planning.

The curriculum philosophy becomes a crucial element in an inclusive environment. How can differences in children be accommodated within the curriculum? The curriculum should be flexible and provide a variety of learning activities and opportunities for a wide range of skills and abilities all at one time. It needs to be a curriculum in which children can participate at their developmental level, yet challenging enough to help them learn. It is a curriculum that depends on the differences in children.

FOUR COMPONENTS OF EFFECTIVE CURRICULUM

Effective curriculum consists of any number of factors. Four important features of any curriculum are that it is (1) integrated and (2) emergent, (3) considers the use of **multiple intelligences** (MI), and (4) bears in mind differences in **learning styles.** These components will allow for a more flexible curriculum, based on the children in the classroom.

Integrated Curriculum

Do you remember the discussion in Chapters 3 and 4 about the whole child? The developmental concept that growth consists of interrelationships is a significant point made in Figure 3–1. This drawing shows how one area of development affects and is affected by the others. For instance, social development (which affects a child's ability to relate to others) is connected to language development (the ability to express thoughts and feelings) and to cognitive development (the ability to define and communicate ideas and concepts). As young children learn, the social, emotional, cognitive, creative, and physical areas of development work together to help children find meaning in and mastery of their world.

It is useful to think of **integrated curriculum** in the same way. Integrated curriculum coordinates many subject areas and utilizes a holistic approach to learning. Developmentally appropriately curriculum is integrated curriculum, blending hands-on learning with acquisition of skills. An integrated curriculum weaves across many subject areas throughout the school day and includes skills development activities in the context of other learning. Subject matter is not taught as separate and unique topics, such as math, science, art, and language. Instead, these are all planned components of the curriculum experience. The subject areas cut across the learning activity and re-

Play Materials to Enhance Cultural Diversity and Inclusivity

Curriculum Area	Materials and Equipment
Music	Rainstick (Chile), marimba (Zulu), balaphon (West Africa), ankle bells (Native American), maracas (Latin America), Den-den (Japan), Shakeree (Nigeria), drums (many cultures), ocarina (Peru), songs of many cultures
Literature	Books on family life of many cultures, stories of children from far and near, legends and folktales from many countries, stories with common childhood themes from many lands, favorite books in several languages, wordless books, sign language, Braille books
Blocks and accessories	Variety of accessories depicting many ethnic people, aging people, community workers of both sexes in nonstereotyped roles and with various disabilities; Russian nesting dolls, Pueblo storytellers,[1] animals from around the world
Art	Paints, crayons, markers, and construction paper in variety of skin tone colors, child-size mirrors
Dramatic play	Anatomically correct dolls representing many ethnic groups, doll accessories, including glasses, wheelchairs, crutches, walkers, leg braces, and hearing aids; doll clothes, including cultural costumes and dress-up clothing from many cultures, cooking utensils, such as a wok, tortilla press, cutlery, chopsticks
Games	Language lotto, dreidel game, lotto of faces of people from around the world, Black history playing cards, world globe
Outdoors	Elevated sand and water table and ramps for wheelchair access, lowered basketball hoops, sensory-rich materials.
Classrooms	Carp banners (Japan), paper cuttings from Mexico and China, photographs and magazine pictures of daily life from many cultures, artwork by artists from a variety of ethnic backgrounds, pictures of children from many ethnic backgrounds and cultures

[1]When using artifacts from other cultures, take care to avoid using materials or items that may have sacred or privileged status in that culture.

FIGURE 10-3 A child's family and culture can be brought into the classroom through a variety of curriculum materials; so too can children with disabilities feel included.

inforce concepts in meaningful ways as children engage in their work and play. If this sounds familiar, go back to Chapter 1 and read about John Dewey's philosophy of education. The concept has been used in curriculum development using **themes** and projects for many years. The guidelines for developmentally appropriate curriculum found in Figure 10–1 contain many of the characteristics of an integrated curriculum.

Planning for physical development indoors and outdoors is essential to developmentally appropriate curriculum.

It is easy to see how an integrated curriculum works. Figure 10–4 shows how mathematical principles are fostered as an integral part of the daily curriculum.

Experiencing the usefulness of numbers in a variety of contexts is a natural rather than a contrived way for children to learn.

Emergent Curriculum

Emergent curriculum is just what it says: curriculum that emerges—comes from or slowly evolves—out of the child's experiences and interests. The emphasis is on children's interests, their involvement in their learning, and their ability to make constructive choices. Teachers set up materials and equipment in the room and the yard, sometimes planning a few activities each day that will capture children's attention. For the most part, teachers then watch and evaluate what children do and then support and extend what use children make of their experiences.

Taking Cues from Children

A lively grouptime discussion one day in the three-year-old class involved the construction site for a new hospital near the school. The teachers had noticed that the blocks area had been unused by most

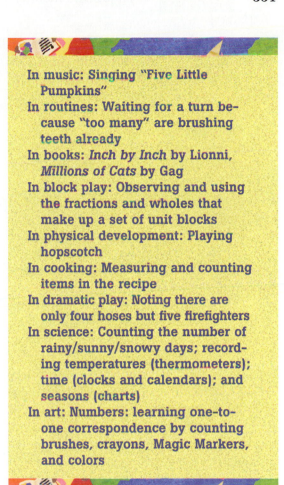

In music: Singing "Five Little Pumpkins"

In routines: Waiting for a turn because "too many" are brushing teeth already

In books: *Inch by Inch* by Lionni, *Millions of Cats* by Gag

In block play: Observing and using the fractions and wholes that make up a set of unit blocks

In physical development: Playing hopscotch

In cooking: Measuring and counting items in the recipe

In dramatic play: Noting there are only four hoses but five firefighters

In science: Counting the number of rainy/sunny/snowy days; recording temperatures (thermometers); time (clocks and calendars); and seasons (charts)

In art: Numbers: learning one-to-one correspondence by counting brushes, crayons, Magic Markers, and colors

FIGURE 10–4 Young children learn best from an integrated approach to curriculum. Mathematical concepts are reflected throughout the classroom in a variety of activities.

of the children during the week, so they added books on buildings, towers, hospitals, paper, crayons, and scissors to the shelves near the blocks and put up pictures of different kinds of community buildings. A variety of buildings were drawn and built and discussions included the purpose of hospitals and who used them. The dramatic play area, filled with medical accessories and uniforms, became a popular activity. The curriculum content in this example is apparent but an end product is not the major focus. It is an example of integrated curriculum as well as emergent curriculum.

The process children go through in creating knowledge will foster new insights, and learning is the key factor. The focus in emergent curriculum is always on the child, not on the activity.

This practice of taking cues from children—noting what they play with, what they avoid, what they change—is one of the components of emergent curriculum and stems from the belief that to be a meaningful learning experience, the curriculum should come out of the daily life in the classroom. Based on the principles of Erikson, Piaget, and Vygotsky, emergent curriculum assumes that children are active, curious, powerful learners, capable of taking the initiative and constructing their knowledge through experience. Children are encouraged to use whatever style of learning is most natural to them (Gardner, 1983), making use of the variety of materials in their own way. A materials-rich environment in which play is valued forms the foundation for the curriculum.

On the part of the teachers, emergent curriculum calls for collaboration and mutual learning with children and other adults; teachers and children both offer suggestions and ideas. For emergent curriculum to be successful, teachers have a responsibility to listen and observe carefully as children play and generate new ideas and then respond to what they hear and see that children have learned. Although emergent curriculum calls for collaboration and negotiation between children and teachers, it is the teacher who knows what is necessary for children's education and development and sets the goals for learning.

Multiple Intelligences

In Chapter 4, you read about Gardner's theory of MI. According to this theory, children are capable of at least eight distinct categories of intelligence. That is, they have many different ways of knowing or of being "smart." Refresh your memory by reviewing Chapter 4, Figure 4–11. The potential for developing the various intelligences is based on the child's experience, culture, and motivation. The following is a summary of this theory (Armstrong, 2000; New City School, 1994). The eight MI categories are:

1. *Linguistic.* Sensitivity to the sounds, structure, meanings, and functions of words and language.

2. *Logical-mathematical.* Sensitivity to, and capacity to discern, logical or numerical patterns; ability to handle long chains of reasoning.

3. *Spatial.* Capacity to perceive the visual-spatial world accurately and to perform transformations on one's initial perceptions.

4. *Bodily-kinesthetic.* Ability to control one's body movements and to handle objects skillfully.

5. *Musical.* Ability to produce and appreciate rhythm, pitch, and timbre; appreciation of the forms of musical expressiveness.

6. *Interpersonal.* Capacity to discern and respond to the moods, temperaments, motivations, and desires of other people.

7. *Intrapersonal.* Access to one's own feelings and the ability to discriminate among one's emotions; knowledge of one's own strengths and weaknesses.

8. *Naturalist.* Expertise in distinguishing among members of a species; recognizing the existence of other, neighboring species; and charting out the relations, formally or informally, among several species.

In a group of preschoolers it is easy to notice these varied approaches children have to learning. Some children excel at puzzles and manipulative games, while others are busy dictating stories, building a

Interpersonal intelligence.

boatyard with blocks, or holding the guinea pig. There are children who cannot be still for very long and need to be actively and physically involved in play and work for much of the day. We all have the capacities for the eight categories of MI, but we are not equally proficient in all of them.

Through a wide variety of meaningful learning experiences, children's strengths (and primary intelligences) can be assessed, and curriculum can be developed that fosters new knowledge thinking. Jmel is strong in spatial intelligence, and that can serve as a context for other learning in different intelligence categories. Her intrapersonal and linguistic intelligences can be encouraged through activities that include her telling or writing stories about something she drew and what it means to her. Bodily-kinesthetic and music abilities can emerge through dancing and moving the body through space in different ways. This allows Jmel to experience and reinforce

her own strengths and increase her strengths in other areas as well.

The relationship of MI-based curriculum to integrated curriculum is fairly clear. If children have different ways of knowing, they should experience a concept, lesson, or subject matter in a variety of ways. As teachers and caregivers expand their own thinking about children's abilities, they can vary what and how they teach and teach to many intelligences instead of just one, many developmental areas, not just one. An integrated MI curriculum makes it possible to involve many intelligences in a wide range of activities and enable more children to succeed by drawing on their own capacities to learn.

Differences in Learning Styles

Some people like going to lectures to learn about a new culture or country. Others prefer to watch a travelogue. Still others get the most out of traveling to that country and living among its people, eating the food, and absorbing the atmosphere. Each of these is a legitimate method of learning and processing information, and each indicates the preferred style of that particular person. In Chapter 3, the discussion about learning styles related to differences in children's behavior. Here, we will focus on how basic learning styles affect curriculum goals.

Sensory Styles

Three basic sensory styles were mentioned in Chapter 3, and they follow here with examples (Schirrmacher, 2002). These are the preferred mode of each child but not the only method by which the child can integrate knowledge.

1. *The visual learner.* These are children who prefer pictures to words; photos, charts, and graphs provide the necessary clues; they like to represent their

learning by reading, writing, drawing; the finished product is important.

2. *The auditory learner.* These are children who listen to others to learn and speak and discuss what they are learning. They are good at following directions in the appropriate sequence from one task to another.

3. *The bodily-kinesthetic learner.* These children are active, full-body learners; they need hands-on activity with tactile materials and learn by doing, not listening or sitting still.

These modalities are the favored ways children learn through the use of their five senses. It seems clear that an integrated, emergent curriculum would be easily adaptable to all three learning modes. In fact, most early childhood education experiences are heavily weighted toward the development of the five senses, which provide many opportunities for children to learn through their preferred style.[1]

✷ CURRICULUM: IT'S CHILD'S PLAY

In Chapter 4 you learned about the value and process of children's play. You may want to review the Types of Play section in that chapter for a clear understanding of why play-based curriculum enhances children's potential for learning. The vast knowledge of human development and behavior comes from researchers who spent countless hours observing and recording children playing. As noted by many (from Froebel to Vygotsky to Gardner), children need active and meaningful materials and activities to learn. They need to be physically as well as mentally and emotionally in-

volved in what and how they learn, and they need to play. Through the use of **activity centers,** a variety of play opportunities are available throughout the school day.

Foundation for Learning

Play is the foundation from which children venture forth to investigate and try out their ideas. Teachers want children to learn about themselves and the world around them and how to solve problems. They plan curriculum that uses play as the medium for learning, as the expression of the curriculum. As they mature, children integrate their play experiences. What started out as play—for the sheer fun of it—is transformed into knowledge. Curiosity about magnets at age five nourishes a scientific attitude for the later years, as well as a foundation for studying gravity, planetary movements, and space. Feeling free to sing out at grouptime at age three can prepare a child to be an active participant in the kindergarten classroom meeting at age six (Figure 10–5).

Play takes many forms and promotes friendship and learning.

[1]Learning styles are also influenced by culture and gender. In some cultures in which cooperation is more important than competition, students experience cultural conflict when the curriculum stresses competition.

COGNITIVE/LANGUAGE

Distinguishes between reality and fantasy
Encourages creative thought and curiosity
Allows for problem-solving
Encourages thinking, planning
Develops memory, perceptual skills, and
   concept formation
Learns to try on other roles
Acquires knowledge and integrates learning
Learns communication skills
Develops listening and oral language skills

CREATIVE

Fosters use of imagination and make-believe
Encourages flexible thinking and
   problem-solving
Provides opportunity to act upon original
   ideas
Supports taking risks
Learns to use senses to explore
Re-creates images in buildings and art
   media
Sharpens observational skills
Provides variety of experiences
Learns to express self in art, music, and
   dance
Develops abilities to create images and use
   symbols
Acquires other perspectives

SOCIAL

Tries on other personalities, roles
Learns cooperation and taking turns
Learns to lead, follow
Builds a repertoire of social language
Learns to verbalize needs
Reflects own culture, heritage, values
Learns society's rules and group responsi-
   bility
Shows respect for other's property, rights
Teaches an awareness of others
Learns how to join a group
Builds awareness of self as member of a
   group
Gives sense of identification
Promotes self-image, self-esteem
Experiences, joy, fun

PHYSICAL

Releases energy
Builds fine and gross motor skills
Grains control over body
Provides challenges
Requires active use of body
Allows for repetition and practice
Refines eye–hand coordination
Develops self-awareness
Encourages health and fitness

EMOTIONAL

Develops self-confidence and self-
   esteem
Learns to take a different viewpoint
Resolves inner fears, conflicts
Builds trust in self and others
Reveals child's personality
Encourages autonomy
Learns to take risks
Acts out anger, hostility, frustration, joy
Gains self-control
Becomes competent in several areas
Takes initiative

FIGURE 10–5 Play is the cornerstone of learning.

The Teacher's Role in Play

Supporting Play

Many adults enjoy playing with the children in their class; others feel more comfortable as active observers. But every teaching situation will demand the teacher's involvement at some level. The hesitant child may need help entering a play situation; children may become too embroiled in an argument to settle it alone; play may become inappropriate, exploitative, or dominated by a particular child.

Vygotsky gives us other reasons to be involved with children as they play, particularly in relation to the interpersonal nature of teaching (see Chapter 4). The belief that learning is interpersonal and collaborative is exemplified by the teachers of Reggio Emilia (see Chapter 5 and later in this chapter), who guide and support children's learning by engaging in play and knowing what strategy will best help an individual child reach the next level of skill (the **zone of proximal development**). The Reggio Emilia approach to curriculum finds an appropriate and appealing blend of Vygotsky's concern for individual exploration and assisted discovery. The teacher's role is a balance between facilitating children's development and taking advantage of those teachable moments in which further learning is enhanced. See Figure 10–6 for guidelines on supporting play.

what do YOU think?

What do you think are the most compelling arguments that play is a necessary part of any early childhood program? How would you respond to a first-grade teacher who thought too much time was be devoted to play? What would you say to a parent who was interested in enrolling a child in your school but wanted to know why so much time was devoted to play?

Guidelines for ways teachers facilitate play. A good teacher:

1. **Guides the play, but does not direct or dominate the situation or overwhelm children by participation.**

2. **Capitalizes on the children's thoughts and ideas; does not enforce a point of view on them.**

3. **Models play when necessary. Shows children how a specific character might act, how to ask for a turn, how to hold a hammer when hammering. Models ways to solve problems that involve children interacting on their own behalf.**

4. **Asks questions; clarifies to children what is happening.**

5. **Helps children start, end, and begin again. Gives them verbal cues to enable them to follow through on an idea.**

6. **Focuses the children's attention on one another. Encourages them to interact with each other.**

7. **Interprets children's behavior aloud, when necessary; helps them verbalize their feelings as they work through conflicts.**

8. **Expands the play potential by making statements and asking questions that lead to discovery and exploration.**

DAP

FIGURE 10–6 Supporting play: helping children learn through play.

Setting the Stage for Play

Structuring the Environment

To structure the environment for play, teachers include uninterrupted time blocks in the daily schedule (at least 45 minutes to an hour) for free-play time. This allows children to explore many avenues of the curriculum free from time restraints. It is frustrating to young children to have their play cut off just as they are getting deeply involved.

Established routines in the schedule add to the framework of a day planned for play. The raw materials of play—toys, games, equipment—are changed periodically so that new ones may be introduced for further challenge.[1]

Materials that are open-ended further enlarge play. These are materials that will expand the children's learning opportunities because they can be used in more than one way. Blocks, a staple of the early childhood curriculum, are a case in point. The youngest child will carry the blocks around, stack them, and put them in wagons and trucks. Older preschoolers will build multistoried structures as part of their dramatic play.

Classroom Activity Centers

The activity centers in most early childhood education programs consist of those noted in Chapter 9. A variety of activity areas and learning centers are set up with specific play and learning materials that provide children with choices for play. There should be enough to do so that each child has a choice between at least two play options.

All of these centers offer activities and materials for children to choose from during free-play time—the greatest portion of their school day. (See typical daily schedules in Chapter 2.) Teachers plan the resources and materials and place them so children readily see the alternatives available to them. Some of these activities might be teacher-directed on occasion: cooking snacks in the housekeeping area, fingerpainting in art, creating castles with blocks. For the most part, however, these activities will be self-initiated and child-directed. At all times, the emphasis will be on providing a child-centered curriculum.

Video View Point 10-2

"Preschool children learn by trial and error, hands-on exploration and experimentation, and self-directed play."

Competency: Learning Environment

Age Group: Preschool

Critical Thinking Questions

1. How do you feel about play as a medium for learning?
2. What do you remember about your childhood and the opportunities to learn by trial and error?

[1]Choosing materials to place in a classroom should be done with an awareness of exposing children to images of diversity (e.g., male nurses, female construction workers, African-American physicians) rather than fostering and reinforcing existing stereotypes. These materials are available to purchase, or you can make your own photo albums and posters.

✿ CONSIDERATIONS FOR CURRICULUM PLANNING

Acquiring Skills

The aim of the curriculum is to help children acquire the skills and behaviors that will promote their optimal growth physically, socially, emotionally, and intellectually. Chapter 11 provides a more in-depth identification of the skills that children learn in all developmental areas. Here the focus is on creating a curriculum to enhance each of the developmental areas.

Planning for a broad range of developmental skills and interests is a key factor in creating a classroom curriculum. Because the abilities of children even of the same age vary, activities must be open-ended and flexible enough to be used by a number of children with varieties of skills. Remember, too, that some children may not be interested in formal or organized art projects or science experiences. These children may learn more easily through self-selected play: by wearing a space helmet and fantasizing a trip to the moon, by building with blocks for long periods, or by running and climbing outdoors.

The developmental Word Pictures of children from birth through age eight found in Chapter 3 can be useful in determining what kinds of activities appeal to young children.

Focus on Developmental Areas

Physical Motor

Children learning physical motor skills need experience; they must learn simple skills before combining them into complex activities and have time to try, refine, and try again. Rehearsal is as important to the young child as it is to the actors in a play. Through play, the child can practice:

Fine motor skills such as:

- ✪ holding a paintbrush, scissors, or rattle
- ✪ tiptoeing to music
- ✪ grasping a bottle, a hand, a toy
- ✪ threading a bead or a wide needle
- ✪ buttoning a coat
- ✪ eating, brushing hair

Gross motor skills such as:

- ✪ pumping on a swing
- ✪ climbing a tree
- ✪ digging a garden
- ✪ balancing on a board on one foot

Any group of young children will have a variety of levels of motor growth and physical development. An individual child may have different abilities and skills in gross, fine, and perceptual motor areas; activities should, therefore, be offered on several developmental levels. Play materials and equipment, such as balls, climbers, and ladders, should accommodate a variety of skill levels, particularly if children with physical disabilities are in the class. Climbing boards put on several levels and puzzles ranging from six to 60 pieces are two examples of how teachers can meet the need for success and challenge.

Video View Point 10-3

"Children need to have good balance between challenge and mastery."

Competency: Learning Environment

Age Group: School age

Critical Thinking Questions

1. What are some of the challenges a school-age child faces?

2. What help would you provide them in mastering one of those skills?

Physical/motor development should play a central role in planning the curriculum. It should be both planned and spontaneous. The greatest portion of the young child's day should be spent in physical activity. Quality early childhood education programs recognize this, providing for a full range of physical and motor experiences. Indoors, children use puzzles, scissors, and sewing frames as they practice fine motor skills. They dance with scarves and streamers to music. **Perceptual motor development**, as with body awareness, occurs when children learn songs and games ("Head and Shoulders, Knees and Toes" or "Mother May I Take Two Giant Steps?") or while finger-painting. Outdoors, gross motor skills are refined by the use of climbers, swings, hopscotch, and ring-toss. Figure 10–7 shows

Type of Motor Skill	Infants Zero to One-and-a-Half Years	Toddlers One-and-a-Half Years to Three Years	Preschoolers Three to Five Years	Early School Years Six to Eight Years
Locomotor: Walking Running Jumping Hopping Skipping Leaping Climbing Galloping Sliding	Safe areas to explore body movements Balls to roll Hanging jumpseats Walkers on wheels Simple obstacle course	Walker wagons Pull/push toys Dancing Wide balance board Toddler gym—stairs and slide "Ring around the Rosey"	Hippity-hop balls Sled Beginning skis Trampoline Roller skates Jump rope Balance beam Climber Dancing	Jump rope Roller skates Ice skates Climbing rope Tumbling mats Hopscotch
Nonlocomotor: Pushing Pulling Bending Balancing Stretching Rolling Turning Twisting	Large, safe areas for exploration Parent/caregiver play: holding, pushing arms, legs, sturdy push toys Soft obstacle course of pillows	Pounding board Simple, low rocking horse Ride-on toys Toddler-type swing Large Legos® Sturdy doll buggy Wagon Fabric tunnels Blocks Cars, trucks to push	Shopping cart/ doll carriage Wheelbarrow Pedal toys, trike Rakes, shovels Slide Swing Punching bag	Scooter Two-wheel bike Sled, toboggan Exercise mat Acrobatics Diving mask for swimming Doorway gym bar
Manipulative: Grasping Throwing Catching Kicking Receiving/ moving objects Bouncing	Mobile attached to crib—kicking feet moves it Rattles, teething rings Crib activity board Soft foam blocks Snap beads Floating bath toys	Variety of balls Stacking, nesting toys Activity box—on floor Shape sorters Large, fat crayons Large pegs and board Water/sand table	Crayons, markers Clay, dough Bowling games Puzzles Woodworking tools Balls Lacing board Water/sand table	Baseball glove/bat Ring toss game Full-size balls Oversize bat Frisbee "Miss Mary Mack"

FIGURE 10–7 Toys and games help develop specific motor skills in young children.

Skill	Teachers Can:

Inquiry	• Ask questions so children make statements about their conversations.
	  Example: "What do you notice about the guinea pig?"
	• Try to be more specific if such questions seem overwhelming or if they elicit little response.
	  Example: "What sounds do you hear? What can you find out by touching her?"
	• Ask how children arrived at their answers.
	  Example: "How did you know that the marble wouldn't roll up the ramp?"
	• Ask questions that expand the process.
	  Example: "Can you tell me anything else about your doll?"

Social Knowledge	• Try not to respond to unstated needs.
	  Example: "Do you want something? Can I help you?"
	• Help children define what they want or need, so that they learn how to ask for it.
	  Example: Marie: I wonder who is going to tie my shoes?
	  Teacher: So do I. When you want someone to tie your shoe, you can say, "Would you tie my shoe?"
	  Marie: Would you tie my shoe?
	  Teacher: I'd be glad to.

Classification	• Ask questions that will help children focus on objects and see differences and details.
	  Example: While cooking, ask
	  Which things on the table do we put in the bowl?
	  Which are made of plastic?
	  Which go in the oven?
	  What on the table is used for measuring? How do you know?
	  Now look carefully—what do you see on the measuring cup?
	  What do those little red lines mean?

Spatial Relationships	• Ask for the precise location of an object the child asks for or is interested in:
	  Examples: "Where did you say you saw the bird's nest?"
	  "You can find another stapler in the cabinet underneath the fish tank."

Concept of Time	• Use accurate time sequences with children.
	  Example: Teacher: Just a minute.
	  Milo: Is this a real minute, or a "wait a minute"?
	  Teacher: You're right. I'm with Phoebe now. I'll help you next.

FIGURE 10–8 Teachers' use of language affects how children develop cognitive skills. The more children are allowed and encouraged to think for themselves, the more their cognitive skills will develop.

a wide range of materials and equipment that enhance physical skills in all ages.

Cognitive Development

The teacher plans activities for all cognitive skills to ensure challenging children's thinking. Figure 10–8 shows how a teacher's thoughtful questioning and response will enhance a child's cognitive development, and Figure 10–9 is an example of how the skill of classification can be developed.

Cognitive Considerations.

When considering children's intellectual development, teachers should keep the following in mind:

1. Education is exploration. By allowing children to interact with the environment, the teacher is a source of information and support rather than one who gives answers or commands. With the **project approach,** children explore a theme or topic (such as shadows, houses, building a table) over a period of weeks.

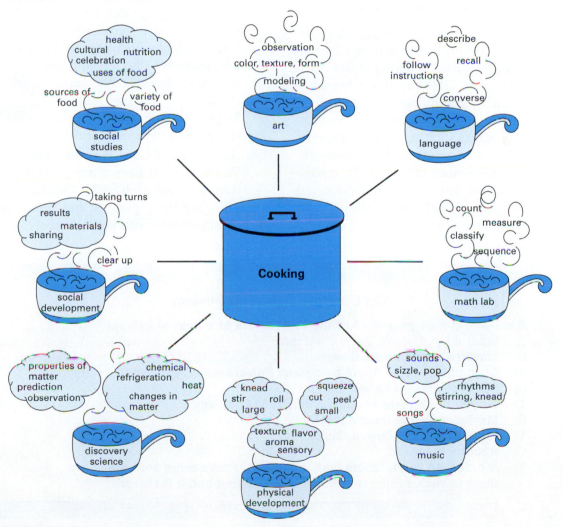

FIGURE 10–9 Each activity, such as cooking, can enhance cognitive development throughout the curriculum. A trip to the market can be an experience in classification and calculation.

2. Children do not think like adults. Children think and perceive in their own ways. They think in sensory and concrete terms and come to conclusions based on what they see and touch.

3. Children's thinking is legitimate and should be valued. Teachers support those processes by asking questions to stimulate further thought and by providing materials for exploration.

4. The language of the teacher should support cognitive development. Throughout their interactions with children, teachers help children use words, terms, and concepts correctly (see the following section on Language Development).

The teacher must consider, include, and plan for children with learning disabilities and other varied learning styles. Each type of learning disability (see Chapter 3) has its own description and treatment. Teachers must develop a wide range of techniques to address such disabilities. After the identification and assessment phases, teachers and families need to work with specialists and devise options (an individualized education plan, or IEP) that include the child and establish reasonable learning goals.

Language Development

To promote language development teachers, should consider the following:

1. *Children need an "envelope of language."* Before we talk about a "print-rich" program, we must provide a *language-rich* environment.

2. *Children must use language in order to learn it.* Adults often spend much of their time with children talking to, at, for, or about them. Yet, to learn language, children must be doing the talking. Figure 10–10 gives a good example.

3. *The most verbal children tend to monopolize language interactions.* Seek out and support language development in those with fewer skills, generally by drawing them out individually through (1) reading the unspoken (body) language that communicates their ideas, needs, and feelings and (2) helping them express verbally those ideas, needs, and feelings.

4. *Adults should know the individual child.* Teachers must have a meaningful relationship with each child. This includes knowing their parents and how they communicate with their child.

The Question: A Teaching Strategy

A six-and-a-half-year-old looking at a picture of a field of flowers

T: What do you see in the photograph?
C: Flowers . . . a buncha flowers.
T: Good observation. About how many flowers would you say there are?
C: I dunno. About a hundred.
T: Do you think there are only a hundred? Look again.
C: Maybe, probably there's more.
T: Well, how many do you think?
C: About a thousand.
T: A thousand is a lot more than a hundred. That's more accurate, since there is such a difference between a hundred and a thousand.

FIGURE 10–10 Questions are the building blocks of teaching. The adept teacher asks questions that stimulate language, thinking, and interacting between a child and teacher and among children.

5. *Home languages are to be invited into the classroom.* "The explanations for home language are several fold," writes Chang (1993). "Language and culture are closely related since the language of an ethnic group is usually the vehicle through which the community transmits to its young its customs and beliefs. . . . The development of a child's primary language skills is integral to helping a child succeed academically and to eventually develop skills in English." See Appendix C for NAEYC's position paper on linguistic and cultural diversity.

6. *Dialect differences expand your speech community.* Dialects are as much a part of children's culture and identity as is their home language

7. *Some children may have speech and language disorders.* Early detection of and intervention for speech and language disorders is possible without the teacher being a speech therapist. (See Chapter 3 for more information.)

8. *The language of the teacher influences the classroom.* What teachers say—and how they say it—is important. To make sure that all children experience the art of conversation, be sure to provide plenty of opportunities for them to converse with adults as well as peers to help them learn the reciprocal nature of communication. Ask them to say what they are doing. Make a statement describing the child's behavior or actions. Figure 10–11 demonstrates some exam-

---

Curriculum Planning for Language Development: The Teacher Talks

Description

- Use nouns for people, places, events: "We are going to visit Grandma now. That means we need to get dressed and walk to her apartment."
- Use modifiers: "That is your uncle's truck outside" or "Can you find your sister's teddy bear?"
- Use relational terms: "You are taller than the chair; the wagon is wider than the bed."
- Try more differentiated words to express differences: Instead of just "big/little," try "fat/thin" and "tall/short."

Narration

- Describe simple relationships of time: "Yesterday you stayed at home. Today is a school day. Tomorrow is Saturday, a stay-home day."
- Clarify a sequence of events: "When you come to school, first you put your things in your cubby, then you make an inside choice."
- Use words to describe repetition, continuation, and completion: "We are going to the store again, to buy food for dinner" or "I see that you and Juana are still playing together today" or "You finished building the box last time; now you are ready to paint it."

Explanation

- Point out similarities and differences: "Both Cathi and I have brown hair, but what is different about us? Yes, she has on shorts and I am wearing overalls."
- Try classifying what you see as well as asking children to do so: "I notice that all these shells have ridges on the outside; what do you see that is different about them?"

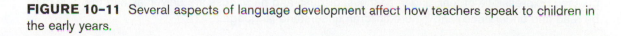

FIGURE 10–11 Several aspects of language development affect how teachers speak to children in the early years.

ples of ways teachers can use language to encourage language development in young children.

Emotional Development

In early childhood, children learn to respond to new situations and to connect with a teacher, both very emotional experiences. Good teachers stimulate a positive emotional response. Creating the right emotional conditions accesses a child's capacity for learning. Young children are not yet limited by social standards of conduct, so they are usually sincere and truthful in their self-expression. The major skills learned in early childhood are the ability to deal with feelings, to handle change, to exercise judg-

ment, and to enjoy oneself and one's power. Some of the feelings children experience and their way of showing them are described in Figure 10–12. An effective teacher can plan curriculum that helps children develop emotional skills. Figure 10–13 is an example of using a curriculum activity focusing on the senses to enhance the emotional growth of the children in the class.

Social Development

A major role for the early childhood teacher is to see that children have enjoyable social contacts and to help motivate children toward a desire to be with others. There are a number of strategies that are useful for developing social skills:

Feeling	Behavioral Definition
1. Fear	Pale face, alert eyes, tense mouth, rigid body.
2. Surprise	Wide eyes, eyebrows uplifted, involuntary cry or scream, quick inhale of breath.
3. Anger	Red face, eyes staring, face taut, fists and jaw clenched, voice harsh or yelling, large gestures.
4. Joy	Smiling face, shining eyes, free and easy body movements, laughing.
5. Pride	Head held high, smiling face, jaunty walk or strut, tendency to announce or point out.
6. Embarrassment	Red face, glazed and downcast eyes, tight mouth, tense body, small and jerky movements, soft voice.
7. Sadness	Unsmiling face, downturned mouth, glazed and teary eyes, crying or rubbing eyes, limp body, slow or small movements, soft and trembly voice.
8. Anxiety	Puckered brow, pale face, tight mouth, whiny voice, jerky movements, lack of or difficulty in concentration.
9. Curiosity	Raised brow, shining eyes, perhaps tense body in absorption of the object of curiosity; often hand movements to touch and pick up object; sometimes mouth agape.

FIGURE 10–12 As we observe children's behavior, we understand how their feelings are expressed. Expressions of fear, anger, sadness, disgust, and happiness are universal, and the face can be read and understood long before children understand language.

Emotional Skill Development

Self-Esteem

1. *Identity:* "Look at what I can do, the noise I can make, the weight I can pick up and move!"

2. *Connectedness:* "I can make the same snakes as you; we can all make cakes."

3. *Uniqueness:* "I'm pouring mine; you're dripping yours; and she is squeezing her stuff out her fingers!"

4. *Power:* "I can make this water go anywhere I want; look out for the tidal waves!"

Deal with Feelings

1. *Identification* (to notice and label): "Does it feel very smooth, slippery, slidy? Is it soft and soothing?"

2. *Mastery* (to accept): "She took your baker's dough and that made you angry. You can tell her you don't like it when she grabs what you are using."

3. *Expressing* (to express appropriately):

   Child: "Tami has all the big pitchers."

   Teacher: "How can you let her know you want one?"

   Child: "And she splashed me two times!"

   Teacher: "If you feel too crowded, you need to tell her so."

4. *Feelings* (to deal with others): "Whee! Yuk! Mmm! Ha!"

Curriculum Activity (Use of Senses)

- Use rocks of various sizes with balances, so that children can touch and hear when they move things around.

- A malleable material such as play dough can be used first alone, then with tools.

- Make "oobleck," a mixture of cornstarch and water, in separate tubs for each child. Children can manipulate it in their own ways.

- Water play offers the child choices: pour into any of several containers, fill or empty the jug, use a funnel or a baster to squirt the water, make waves or splash hands.

- When fingerpainting, the teacher can describe what it appears the child is feeling. Children can identify their feelings as the teacher describes them while they use the materials.

- Whether the sensory material is clay, soapy water, or fine sand, the issues of ownership and use of materials arise. Then, teachers reflect children's feelings and help them take responsibility for their own feelings.

- As children begin to use the sensory materials, they need to communicate to others. Usually the issues are about wanting more material and personal space.

- When children share in a sensory activity, such as a feeling walking through tubs of small pebbles, sand, and soapsuds, they have the delightful experience of enjoying their own feelings with another.

FIGURE 10–13 Sensory materials offer a sensorimotor opportunity to deal with materials in a non-structured way. Because children relax with open-ended activities, they will often share their feelings as they use sensory materials.

✿ *Plan and arrange a social environment.* A coacting environment (Bos, 1978) offers "a way of interacting with others, more often one-on-one than in larger groups, with an emphasis on process rather than product. The placement of two telephones, three wagons, and eight firefighter hats fosters child–child interactions."

✿ *Help children develop trust.* Building trust helps build relationships.

✿ *Facilitate children's interactions and interpret their behavior.* To help young children understand each other and to pave the way for continued cooperation, the teacher reports and reflects on what is happening. In the classroom setting, during an active, free-play period, the teacher might:

Reflect the Action:	Say:
Call attention to the effect one child's behavior is having on another.	"Randy, when you scream like that, other children become frightened and are afraid to play with you."
Show approval to reinforce positive social behavior.	"I like the way you carefully stepped over their block building, Dannetta."
Support a child in asserting her rights.	"Crystal is hanging on to the doll because she isn't finished playing yet, Wilbur."
Support a child's desire to be independent.	"I know you want to help, Keyetta, but Sammy is trying to put his coat on by himself."
Acknowledge and help children establish contact with others.	"Omar would like to play, too. That's why he brought you another bucket of water. Is there a place where he can help?"
Reflect back to a child the depth of his feelings and what form those feelings might take.	"I know George made you very angry when he took your sponge, but I can't let you throw water at him. What can you tell him so he knows you didn't like what he did?"

The teacher's role in creating curriculum that fosters social interactions and growth is to provide the arena and then observe the children's responses. This is a sensitive role, and Figure 10–14 lists a number of do's and don'ts to ensure success.

Cooperation is high on the list of social skills children need to learn in the early years. Figure 10–15 shows ways in which a teacher can foster this throughout the curriculum.

Creativity

Here are some ways to encourage creativity in the curriculum:

1. *Provide continuous availability, abundance, and variety of materials.* An art center (Schirrmacher, 2002) is an artist's studio. It is conveniently located, easily accessible, and well-stocked with developmentally appropriate materials that are orderly and organized. There are at least six basic categories of art materials, including tools for mark making; papers in a variety of shapes/sizes/textures; modeling and molding materials such as play dough/clay; items for cutting, fastening, and attaching such as scissors and string; items for painting; and col-

Social Competence: The Teacher's Role

Do	Don't
• Respect individual timetables and feelings.	• Make implied comparisons.
• Establish authority and credibility.	• Issue empty threats.
• Express expectations simply and directly.	• Hover.
• Redefine children's characters in positive terms.	• Make teacher–child interaction be all about misbehavior.
• Encourage impulse control.	• Motivate children by indirect disapproval.
• Appeal to children's good sense.	• Lose your sense of humor.
• Invoke ground rules.	• Allow a rigid curriculum to narrow possibilities for social interaction.
• Mix it up: Arrange things to get one child next to another.	
• Move it: people, toys, you!	

Question everything you do: Could I open this up for more than one child?

FIGURE 10–14 The do's and don'ts of facilitating social competence. (Adapted from Box, 1990; Katz & McClelland, 1997.)

lage items. Figure 10–16 gives some suggestions for adapting art for children with special needs.

2. *Give children regular creative opportunities to experience and the skill necessary to be creative.* Creativity does not respond well to the clock. Routines, transitions, and groups must be handled so as not to interrupt children too often. Children's own sense of time and their personal rhythms should be considered. Teach the necessary skills, such as tracing and cutting, when children exhibit the need to learn them.

3. *Encourage divergent thinking.* "Children need to please only themselves. . . . Once you've presented the materials, forget how you intended them to be used" (Bos, 1978). Where there are no "right" or "wrong" answers, children are free to create.

4. *Avoid models, making things for children to copy.* It insults children, and can make

them feel inadequate in the face of something you can do so much better.

5. *Help foster conversation:*

Teacher: How do you think we could share the swings?

David: The kids who give me a turn can come to my birthday party.

Sabrina: No. We will have to make a waiting list.

Xenia: Only girls can use the swings. The boys can have all the cars.

Frederico: Buy a new swing set.

6. *Talk with young children about what they create.* Schirrmacher (2002) tells us that rather than approach children's work with compliments, judgments, or even questions:

✿ Allow children to go about their artistic discoveries without your comparing, correct-

LANGUAGE

Plan and perform a favorite story.
Choose a story at the listening post
   together.
Learn "I love you" in sign language.
Copy someone's motions, dance, block
   patterns.
Put on a puppet show.
Develop a "What Can I Share?" chart.
Discuss how new toys, equipment will
   be shared so everyone gets a turn.

SCIENCE

Care for classroom pets.
Have group cooking
   projects.
Plan and plant a garden.

MUSIC

Sing together each day.
Have a rhythm band.
Dance in groups of two
   or three.
Dance with a parachute.

ENVIRONMENT

Schedule cleanup daily.
Have two children share cubbies.
Bring snacks from home to share.
Set tables for two or more children.
Use large bins to store some materials;
   children will need to share contents.

SOCIAL STUDIES

Make a group gift for hospital, rest home.
Create an art display for the local library.
Make cookies to sell at the school fair.
Run errands for teachers, each other.
Develop dramatic play themes of: shoe
   stores, hospital, doctors, ecology.
Collect and sort recycling materials.
Take a field trip to the town dump for re-
   cycling.
Write a "protest letter" about an inferior
   product.

OUTDOORS

Push someone on a swing.
Pull a friend in a wagon.
Make bird feeders.
Set up bowling alley, with bowler and
   pin setters.
Make an obstacle course.
Use seesaws.
Play group jump rope.
Play Follow the Leader.

ART

Trace each other's bodies on paper.
Share paste and collage materials.
Share paints.
Make a mural.
Make litter bags.
Create a wall hanging: fabric, crayons
   and sheets; each child draws part.
Create a class quilt: each child sews a
   square; teacher puts it together.

COOPERATION

GAMES

Play Simon Says.
Play board games:
   Winnie-The-Pooh and Candy Land.
Play Lotto.
Play Bingo.

FIGURE 10–15 The social skill of cooperation can be fostered throughout the curriculum. (How to plan a lesson and build a unit are discussed in Chapter 11.)

ing, or projecting yourself into their art. (You do not need to ask, "What is it?" or say, "I like it.")

✲ Shift from searching for representation in children's art to a focus on the abstract, design qualities. ("I see wiggly lines all down one side.")

✲ Use reflective dialogue. (Yes, there IS a lot of blue there!")

✲ Smile, pause, and say nothing at first.

7. *Allow children to take the lead from start to finish.* Notice how correcting the child's intense language does not sidetrack the teacher:

Child: The monster's gonna get you and eat you up!

Teacher: You made a monster with the wood scraps.

Child: Yes, and it's for my daddy.

Teacher: Let's put it on the counter so it will be dry when he picks you up.

8. *Integrate creativity and learning in the classroom.* Early childhood education theorists such as Dewey, Piaget, and Montessori (see Chapter 1) have advocated multisensory learning through experimentation and discovery.

9. *Teacher timing and attitudes stimulate creativity.* Don't delay; children want to see immediate results and act on their ideas now. "Listen carefully to each child, and try to provide what the child asks for. I try never to say, 'We're not doing that today' (Bos, 1978). Give plenty of time for a dramatic theme to develop, to pursue the props needed, or

---

Adapting Art for Children With Special Needs

_____ **Visual:**
Verbally describe materials and how they might be used.
Provide a tray that outlines the visual boundaries.
Offer bright paint to contrast with paper.
Go slowly and encourage children to manipulate the items as you talk.

_____ **Auditory:**
Model the process, facing the child and using gestures for emphasis.
Use sign language as needed.

_____ **Physical:**
Make sure there is a clear path to the art center.
Provide adaptive art tools such as chunky crayons, large markers.
Provide double ambidextrous scissors so you can help, or a cutting wheel.
Velcro can be attached to marking instruments or paintbrushes.
Use contact paper for collage, or glue sticks instead of bottles.

_____ **Attention-deficit and/or behavioral:**
Provide children with their own materials and workspace, minimizing waiting and crowding.
Offer materials like play dough to express feelings and energy.
Limit children to a few choices rather than overwhelming them with everything in the art center.

FIGURE 10–16 The value of art activities for children with special needs cannot be overemphasized.

to find the players and audience. The early childhood years are "[w]here the initial attitudes are established . . . and school can be a fun place where the individual's contribution is welcome and where changes can be sought and made" (Lowenfeld & Brittain, 1975).

Planning the Curriculum

Planning the curriculum is the process of translating theories of education into practice, based on the children's interests, and tempered by adult awareness of children's needs. The process of developing curriculum begins with setting goals for learning. Teachers base these goals on their knowledge of

Goal setting begins with children's interests and needs.

child development, their knowledge of the individual children in their classrooms, and the educational philosophy of the program. The goals of the program must be reflected in the educational philosophy of the school. Curriculum, materials, and activities should support the goals of the program and result in those goals being accomplished.

Guidelines

The process of developing curriculum begins with understanding what goals are set for learning and then choosing the most pressing ones for attention. Using available resources, teachers plan effective curricula for young children. The following five steps are guidelines to sound curriculum planning.

1. *Set goals.* Decide what it is you want children to learn. What do you want them to know about themselves? about others? about the world? State goals clearly, preferably in behavioral terms so results can be measured.

2. *Establish priorities.* Make a list of three to five goals or objectives you consider most important. State the reasons for your choices; your own values and educational priorities will emerge more clearly.

3. *Know the resources.* A rich, successful, and creative curriculum relies on a vast number of resources. To create a health clinic in the dramatic-play area, for instance, you might need the following resources:

   ✸ Materials: props, such as stethoscopes, x-ray machines, tongue depressors, adhesive strips, medical gowns, and masks.

   ✸ People: parents and/or community people in the health care professions visit the class.[1]

[1]Involving parents in their work or professional role is a supportive and meaningful way to help them become involved in their child's learning.

✪ Community: Field trips to a nearby clinic, hospital, or dentist's office.

4. *Plan ahead.* Set aside a regular time to meet for curriculum planning. This may be on a weekly, monthly, or seasonal basis. Discuss the curriculum activities as well as the daily routines in order to integrate the two. Figure 10–17 shows a weekly planning form.

5. *Evaluate.* Reflect on the outcome of your planning. Consider what worked and why it was successful or not. Look at the part of the experience that did not work as well as you would have liked. How can it be improved? What can you change about it? An evaluation should be immediate, precise, and supportive. Teachers need feedback about their planning and implementing skills. The needs of children are best served when the curriculum is refined and improved. Figure 10–18 is an evaluation form for activities.

Written Plans

In the development of curriculum, written plans are helpful, especially for the beginning teacher. A written plan is an organized agenda, an outline to follow, a framework for the curriculum. It may include a list of activities, goals for children's learning experiences, the process or method of instruction, the teacher's responsibilities, the time of day, and other special notations. A curriculum may be developed for a day, a week, a month, or a specific unit or theme. The framework in Figure 10–19 should be addressed when planning a curriculum activity for young children. Written plans may or may not include all of the other activities normally available in the interest centers. Blocks, manipulatives, and dra-matic play, as well as science, math, and language materials remain available to children, but some teachers include only planned learning experiences and teacher-directed activities in their written plans.

Two important factors in developing curriculum plans are: (1) how much knowledge and understanding children have and (2) what children are interested in. The most effective curriculum grows out of the children's interests and experiences. As they play, children reveal their levels of experience and information as well as their misconceptions and confusions. These provide the clues from which teachers can develop curriculum that is meaningful.[1]

Teacher-Directed Learning

"The visible acts of teaching," according to Schickedanz et al. (1997), "are preceded by thinking about the aims of education and about how children learn." Teacher-directed activities need to be included in the curriculum planning process.

This text promotes teaching through active learning by children who have an active part in creating the curriculum. That does not exclude, however, the need for teacher-planned experiences in order to further the educational goals of the program.

When is it appropriate for teacher-directed learning? Arce (2000) notes that it is a good teaching strategy when materials are complex or the concept is unknown to the children. Teaching certain skills, such as cleaning off the paintbrush before dipping into another color, requires teacher guidance. The continuum that is shown in Figure 10–20 suggests a broad range of teaching behaviors, including opportunities

[1]Adults who are culturally sensitive can use this information to plan activities that deal with racism, sexism, and disabilities bias.

Weekly Planning Form

Target goals/objectives: *To learn about their feelings! To be able to express their feelings in appropriate ways*

Week of: 10/18

Changes to the Environment

Create a reading nook with soft pillows and a hanging book packet so child can sit and look at books.

Add more blocks so several children can build together.

Add doctor props to pretend play area because Eddie has a series of doctor appointments coming up.

Rotate and clean toys.

Special Activities I Plan to Offer This Week

	Monday	Tuesday	Wednesday	Thursday	Friday
Indoor Opportunities to Explore and Discover	*Serve apple butter—children spread it on crackers*	*Make play dough*	*play dough*	*Fingerpainting* *Sing songs about feelings*	*Fingerpainting*
Outdoor Opportunities to explore and Discover	*Paint with water*	*Blow bubbles*	*Blow bubbles*		*Walk to library for Story Time*

Changes to Daily Routines

Make a point of inviting children to help me prepare snacks and lunches and to set the table. See if this helps lunchtime go smoother.

Family Involvement

Talk with the Curtises who are concerned about Valisha hitting other children. Ask them what they do to help Jonisha when her sister hurts her. Share the new article about positive guidance with all families.

To Do

Borrow a set of blocks from provider association's toy lending library. Copy article on guiding behavior for all families.

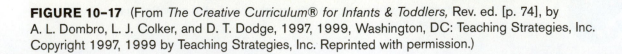

FIGURE 10–17 (From *The Creative Curriculum® for Infants & Toddlers,* Rev. ed. [p. 74], by A. L. Dombro, L. J. Colker, and D. T. Dodge, 1997, 1999, Washington, DC: Teaching Strategies, Inc. Copyright 1997, 1999 by Teaching Strategies, Inc. Reprinted with permission.)

Evaluating Classroom Activity

Activity _____

How many children participated? _____ Did any avoid the activity? _____

How involved did children become? Very ____ Briefly ____ Watched only ____

What were children's reactions? Describe what they said and did. _____

_____

_____

_____

What did you do to attract children? To maintain their interest? _____

_____

_____

How would you rate the success of this activity? Poor ___
Adequate ____ Good ____ Great ____ Why? _____

What skills/abilities were needed? Did the children exhibit the skills? _____

_____

What parts of the activity were most successful? Why? _____

_____

Describe any difficulty you encountered. Give reasons and tell how you would
handle it if it happened again. _____

_____

_____

If you did this activity again, what would you change? _____

_____

In light of your evaluation, what would you plan for a follow-up activity? _____

_____

How did this activity compare with your goals and expectations? _____

_____

FIGURE 10–18 Evaluating daily activities lets teachers use assessment as a curriculum planning tool. Although not every activity will need this scrutiny on a daily basis, careful planning and evaluation create effective classrooms. (Adapted from Vassar College Nursery school.)

for teachers to demonstrate and to be directive in their teaching. All of the methods mentioned are suitable at one time or another for certain children, activities, and situations.

Culturally Responsive Teaching

Positive attitudes toward self and others emerge when children know they are valued for their individuality and appreciated as members of a family and a culture. The

Activity Plan Worksheet

Date of activity: _____

Children's age group: _____

Number of children in this group (large group, small group, or individual activity): _____

Learning center to be used: _____

Name of Activity and Brief Description

Purpose/Objectives of Activity

(Concepts, skills, awareness, or attitudes you have designed the activity to teach or develop. Describe in measurable objectives.)

Space and Materials Needed

Procedure

(Step-by-step description of the activity. Tips for getting started: describe what you will say or do to get the children interested in the activity, and let them know what they will be doing.

Describe the activity in the sequential order you will use with the children. Where will this activity take place? Plan for ending the activity. How will you help the children make a smooth transition to the next activity?)

Guidance

Establish necessary limits for behavior and boundaries of activity. Anticipate problems that may develop during this activity and consider ways to handle them.

Evaluation and Follow-Up

What was the children's response? What worked well? What didn't work? How could this activity be changed to make it effective or more appropriate? List possible activities that would extend or give practice to the objectives of this activity.

FIGURE 10–19 Good planning takes time and thought. This worksheet can help the teacher focus on the important aspects of planning an activity for young children. (From Jackman, H. L. [2005]. *Early education curriculum: A child's connection to the world* (3rd ed.). Clifton Park, NY: Thomson Delmar Learning.)

curriculum process can reflect this in a number of ways. Children with special needs are often able to use most of the curriculum materials typically found in early childhood classrooms. They too need their life mirrored in the school setting with dolls, books, and play accessories that signify acceptance and belonging. Throughout this text, especially in Chapters 2 and 5, cultural sensitivity on the part of teachers is emphasized. Banks (2001) identifies five important characteristics of effective teachers in a multicultural society, which have implications for creating curriculum:

1. They will seek pedagogical knowledge of the characteristics of students from diverse ethnic, racial, cultural, and social-class groups; of prejudice and prejudice reduction theory and research; and of teaching strategies and techniques.

2. They have reflected upon and clarified an understanding of their own cultural heritage, and experience and knowledge of how it relates to and interacts with the experiences of other ethnic and cultural groups.

3. They have reflected on their own attitude toward different racial, ethnic, cultural, and social-class groups.

Nondirective			Mediating				Directive	
Acknowledge	**Model**	**Facilitate**	**Support**	**Scaffold**	**Co-construct**	**Demonstrate**	**Direct**
Give attention and positive encouragement to keep a child engaged in an activity	Display for children a skill or desirable way of behaving in the classroom, through actions only or with cues, prompts, or other forms of coaching	Offer short-term assistance to help a child achieve the next level of functioning (as an adult does in holding the back of a bicycle while a child pedals)	Provide a fixed form of assistance, such as a bicycle's training wheels, to help a child achieve the next level of functioning	Set up challenges or assist children to work "on the edge" of their current competence	Learn or work collaboratively with children on a problem or task, such as building a model or block structure	Actively display a behavior or engage in an activity while children observe the outcome	Provide specific directions for children's behavior within narrowly defined dimensions of error

FIGURE 10–20 A continuum of teaching behavior. (Reprinted, with permission, from S. Bredekamp, & T. Rosegrant, "Reaching potentials through transforming curriculum, assessment, and teaching," in *Reaching Potentials: Transforming Early Childhood Curriculum and Assessment,* Vol. 2, eds. S. Bredekamp, & T. Rosegrant. [Washington, DC: National Association for the Education of Young Children (NAEYC), 1995], 21.)

4. They have the skills to make effective instructional decisions and reduce prejudice and intergroup conflict.

5. They will devise a range of teaching strategies and activities that will facilitate the achievement of students from diverse racial, ethnic, cultural, and social-class groups.

Figure 10–21 shows the complexity of the teacher's role in creating appropriate curriculum for young children.

Themes and Projects

Themes. A traditional method of developing curriculum is to focus on a broad, general topic or theme. Although used interchangeably with units, themes are a smaller part of a unit, allowing for a more specific focus. For example, a unit on the body may have "What can I do with my hands?" as one theme. Life-oriented themes are of great interest to young children: home and family, pets and animals, and so on.

Classroom themes should reflect the children's interests and abilities. An urban child will relate to themes about subways, taxis, and tall buildings. A child living in Houston or central Florida may have more of an interest in space exploration. By choosing themes that coincide with chil-

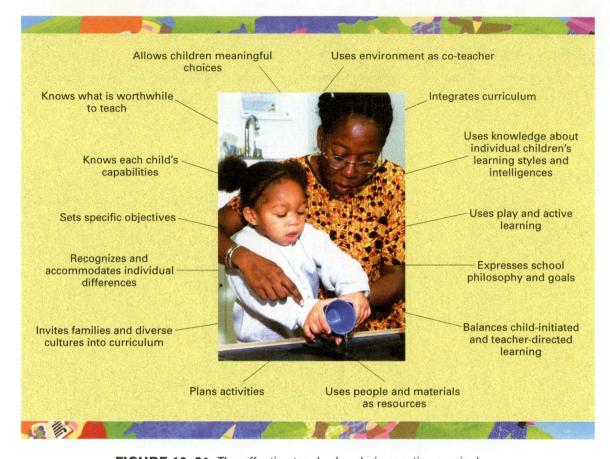

Allows children meaningful choices

Uses environment as co-teacher

Knows what is worthwhile to teach

Integrates curriculum

Knows each child's capabilities

Uses knowledge about individual children's learning styles and intelligences

Sets specific objectives

Uses play and active learning

Recognizes and accommodates individual differences

Expresses school philosophy and goals

Invites families and diverse cultures into curriculum

Balances child-initiated and teacher-directed learning

Plans activities

Uses people and materials as resources

FIGURE 10–21 The effective teacher's role in creating curriculum.

dren's daily lives, teachers promote connected and relevant learning.

Some themes address children's own issues. All young children share similar fears and curiosity about the world they do not yet know. Before Halloween, for example, a theme about masks can be helpful and reassuring. Select headgear that has a function, such as hospital masks, ski masks, clear safety glasses, snorkel masks, and helmets for bicycling, wrestling, or football. Children can try them on and become comfortable with the way their appearance changes. They can laugh with their friends about the way they look and how the mask may change their appearance, but does not change the person.

A thematic approach can utilize many of the attributes of an inclusive, inte-

grated and developmentally appropriate curriculum:

1. Children can help choose and plan themes, thereby constructing their own learning.

2. Activities can be chosen to reflect the curriculum goals—the needs of the students and the teachers.

3. The emphasis is on active learning, and the most appropriate themes are those that have a meaningful connection to children's lives.

4. A thematic approach provides for an in-depth study of a topic, and many subject areas can be integrated into the various activities.

5. A variety of learning styles can be accommodated through different media and teaching techniques.

6. Teacher permitting, a thematic approach can be quite flexible to allow for student response and need.

Figure 10–22 is an example of a developmentally appropriate use of themes when planning curriculum (refer also to Figure 10–3).

Holidays could offer an opportunity to use a thematic approach to creating curriculum. Too often, however, these themes are narrowly defined and isolate the topic. Many holiday themes may not be appropriate to the families represented by the group of students. Some programs choose not to celebrate holidays at all, questioning whether it is a developmentally appropriate practice and how to adequately understand and explain the many holidays observed in the United States. Other programs invite members of the community to educate them about their particular observances. What is critical is to remember that if holidays are celebrated, celebrations beyond the dominant culture should be included.

The Project Approach. Projects are probably the epitome of an integrated, thematic curriculum, embracing all the key characteristics of integrated learning, and they allow for the incorporation of a wide range of subject areas. Katz (1994) defines the "project approach" as

an in-depth investigation of a topic worth learning more about . . . usually undertaken by a small group of children within a class . . . the whole class . . . or even an individual child. The key feature . . . is that it is a research effort deliberately focused on finding answers to

questions about the topic posed by the children . . . or the teacher.

The project approach consists of exploring a theme or topic (such as dinosaurs, shadows, babies, building a table) over a period of days or weeks. Investigation of the theme and preplanning by the children and the teachers is the first step; they observe, question, estimate, experiment, and research items and events related to the topics. Together they make dramatic play and display materials that they need. Children work in small groups throughout the process and have the opportunity to make numerous choices about their level of participation. The teacher often records the activities with photographs. Project work has different levels of complexity so that it meets the needs of children of different ages and abilities. In the Reggio Emilia schools, the project approach is used as the primary vehicle for learning.

Projects emerge from children's own interests, teacher observations of children's needs, and parents' suggestions. The topics reflect the local culture.[1] This approach to teaching and learning easily lends itself to an inclusive classroom and curriculum, responding to diverse points of view as children discuss and agree on their plans.

The planning process is crucial to the success of the project approach, as is the underlying philosophy that children can be co-constructors of their own learning. This approach has much in common with the ideas of Dewey and the Summerhill School. The teacher helps the children explore what they already know about the topic, what they might need to know, and how they can represent that knowledge

 [1]The project approach provides the opportunity to avoid a tourist approach (emphasizing superficial facts on "foreign" customs) and provides children and teachers with an in-depth understanding of a particular culture and its traditions.

CURRICULUM THROUGH PLAY FOR THE ONE-AND-A-HALF-YEAR-OLD

Sensory Stimulation

Objective: To help toddlers begin to explore and understand the five senses.

	Activity	Small-Group Focus	Optional Activities
Monday	Soap painting	Guessing game: textures. Distinguish soft from hard using familiar objects.	Play hide-and-seek with two or three.
Tuesday	Water table play	Guessing game: smells. Identify familiar scents in jars.	Blow bubbles.
Wednesday	Fingerpainting	Guessing game: weights. Distinguish heavy/not heavy using familiar objects such as book or doll.	Take walk to collect collage materials of different textures.
Thursday	Making collages of textures collected day before	Guessing game: shapes. Use puzzles of shapes and shape-sorting boxes.	Have a parade of sounds from many musical instruments.
Friday	Play dough	Food fest of finger foods: Try different textures, sizes, shapes, and flavors.	Make foot or hand prints on large mural paper.

Water play is fun and promotes learning.

FIGURE 10–22 A theme of sensory exploration helps toddlers learn through play.

through various media (dramatic play, art, music). Teachers pose questions for children (What might happen if you do that? How do you think you could you make that work?) that lead them to suggest a hypothesis. This reinforces Vygotsky's theory that interaction and direct teaching are important aspects of intellectual development. (A developmentally appropriate project has been suggested earlier in this chapter in the section Taking Cues from Children, and in Chapter 2 in the section Developmentally Appropriate Practice.)

 ## CURRICULUM MODELS

High/Scope: A Cognitively Oriented Model

The High/Scope curriculum stresses active learning through a variety of learning centers with plenty of materials and developmentally appropriate activities. Active problem solving is encouraged as children plan, with teachers' assistance, what they will do each day, carry out their plan, and review what they have done. Appropriately, this is known as the "plan–do–review" process. Teachers use small groups to encourage, question, support, and extend children's learning while emphasizing their communication skills. There is a balance between child-initiated experiences and teacher-planned instructional activities. Teachers use observational techniques to focus on children and to understand children's play.

Teachers are responsible for planning curriculum organized around key experiences that reinforce and extend the learning activities the children select for themselves. These key experiences are concepts that form the basis of the curriculum and include creative representation, language and literacy, initiative and social relations, movement, music, classifi-

cation, seriation, number, space, and time (Hohmann & Weikart, 1995).

Children with special needs are integrated readily into High/Scope programs; and with a curriculum developed especially for kindergarten to third grade and early adolescents, High/Scope extends its active learning philosophy into further school years.

High/Scope's approach to children's learning is deeply rooted in Piagetian theory and supports Vygotsky's theory of social interaction and cognition: Children learn when interacting with the people and materials in their environment. The schools of Reggio Emilia share core elements of the High/Scope philosophy. Both philosophies stress the importance of children's constructing their knowledge from activities that interest them; team teaching is an important concept, to allow the children access to adult support; and the process of planning, acting, recording, and reassessing is one that both approaches use to foster critical-thinking skills.

To document children's growth using a portfolio system (see Chapter 6), the High/Scope program uses the following categories (Schweinhart, 1993; Brewer, 1995):

1. Initiative: Expressing choices, engaging in complex play

2. Creative representation: Making, building, pretending

3. Social relations: Relating to children and adults, making friends

4. Music and movement: Exhibiting body coordination, following a musical beat

5. Language and literacy: Showing interest in reading, beginning reading, and beginning writing

6. Logic and mathematics: Sorting, counting objects, and describing time sequences

Teachers evaluate these abilities as they observe children's use of key experiences and plan the curriculum accordingly.

Bank Street: A Developmental-Interaction Model

Bank Street was founded by Lucy Sprague Mitchell (see Chapter 1), and its roots reflect the thinking of Freud, Dewey, Erikson, Vygotsky, and Piaget, among others. There is a clear connection between education and psychology in its approach (Mitchell & David, 1992). It is developmental because knowledge of child development principles informs the curriculum planning, and interactive because of the connections made among children, adults, and the greater environment. The interaction between cognitive and socioemotional development is a key element as well, underscoring the connections between thinking and emotions (Mitchell & David, 1992).

Children are seen as active learners who learn by interacting with and transforming the world about them. Play is seen as the primary vehicle for encouraging involvement between and among children, adults, and materials. The teacher's primary role is to observe and respond to activities initiated by the children. Classrooms are organized into learning centers, where children can work individually or in groups.

The Bank Street model exemplifies an integrated curriculum. It is rooted in social studies (Mitchell & David, 1992), so that children learn about the world in which they live through concrete, firsthand experiences. Mitchell and David emphasize that the school is an active community connected to the social world of which it is a part and that "the school shares the responsibility with children's families and with other neighborhood institutions." Units and themes are used to focus the curriculum. There is freedom of movement and choice and easy access to materials (Epstein et al., 1996).

A teacher's knowledge and understanding of child development principles is crucial to this approach. Educational goals are set in terms of developmental processes and include the development of competence, a sense of autonomy and individuality, social relatedness and connectedness, creativity, and an integration of different ways of experiencing the world.

The Schools of Reggio Emilia

Respect for children's investigative powers and for their ability to think, plan, criticize, collaborate, and learn from all they do is the hallmark of the Reggio Emilia approach and is an excellent example of an integrated and emerging approach to learning. This collection of schools in Italy, with separate programs for infants to three-year-olds and for three- to six-year-olds, has commanded worldwide attention for its philosophy and practices. "Nowhere else in the world," states Gardner (Edwards et al., 1993), "is there such a seamless and symbiotic relationship between a school's progressive philosophy and its practices." The curriculum takes the project approach to its highest levels.

Influenced by Dewey's progressive education movement, the philosophies and practices of Reggio Emilia owe a great deal

Reggio Emilia: A materials-rich environment. (Courtesy of St. Louis–Reggio Collaborative. Copyright ©2001.)

as well to Piaget's constructivist theory, Vygotsky's belief in social discourse as a method of learning, and Gardner's own theory of MI (see Chapters 1, 4, and the section earlier in this chapter). Therefore, children are actively engaged in long-term projects that they initiate, design, and carry out with the support of the teacher. Art is the primary medium for learning.

Some of the key components of the Reggio Emilia approach are:

- materials-rich environment that is aesthetically appealing
- community-based attitude involving the entire city
- family support system
- commitment to process

These elements are manifested in the program through astonishingly beautiful school settings, replete with the work of children and evidence of their projects elegantly displayed throughout; by support realized through a large portion of the city's budget; through small groups of children who stay together for a three-year period with the same teacher; and through intentionally bringing the children's culture into school life.[1]

The teacher's role is unique: Two co-equal teachers work with a class of 25 children. There is no head teacher or director of the school. The teachers are supported by a **pedagogista**, a person trained in early childhood pedagogy who meets with the teachers weekly. Also on the staff of every school is an **atelierista**, or workshop/studio teacher, a person trained in the arts who teaches techniques and skills the children learn for their projects.

Process is highly respected as the way to plan and work together. Teachers and children—collaborators—listen to one another, and many points of view are encouraged. Debate and discussion are key elements in the process of deciding what project to do and how to go about it. The attitude that a child is a natural researcher as well as an able learner and communicator has molded the organization and structure of the schools. The schools of Reggio Emilia are worth knowing about just for the strong and powerful view they hold of the child and the concept of teacher and student learning from one another. There are a growing number of American models as well.

Montessori Schools

In Chapter 1, Maria Montessori was discussed in relation to the history of early childhood education. What follows here is an explanation of the Montessori method as a program for young children.

Maria Montessori's approach to learning has had a continuing influence in education since its inception. Of her work, three features stand out: (1) adapting school work to the individual rather than molding the child to fit the curriculum; (2) insisting on freedom for children in selection of materials and choice of activities; and (3) training of the senses and on practical life issues.

A common misunderstanding is that all schools with the Montessori name are the same. They are not. There are many variations and types of Montessori schools throughout the United States, reflecting an infinite variety of interpretations of the Montessori method. Within the Montessori movement itself, there are at least two fac-

[1]For example, common household objects and displays of pasta, fruits, and vegetables representing locally produced foods are often arranged in the lunch area.

tions claiming to be the voice of the true Montessori approach to education.

Although the most common form of Montessori program is one in which three- to five-year-olds are grouped together, there are a growing number of schools for six- to nine-year-olds and even nine- to 12-year-olds. Teacher education programs now prepare Montessori teachers to work with infants and toddlers as well as high schoolers.

The most striking feature of the Montessori classroom is its materials. Many are made of wood and designed to emphasize learning through the senses. Color, texture, and quality of craftsmanship of the materials appeal to the hand as well as the eye; they demand to be touched. "Smooth" and "oval" take on new meaning as a child runs a finger around Montessori-designed puzzle shapes.

Montessori materials have other unique characteristics besides their tactile appeal. They are self-correcting; that is, they fit together or work in only one way so that children will know immediately whether they are successful. The Montessori curriculum presents the materials in a sequence, from simplest to most difficult. Many of the learning tasks have a series of steps and must be learned in a prescribed order. Whether sponging a table clean or using the number rods, the child is taught the precise order in which to use the materials. Montessori developed curriculum materials and tasks that are related to real life. "Practical life" activities range from cleaning tasks (hands, tables) to clothing tasks (lacing, buttoning, or tying garment closures).

In a Montessori classroom, children work by themselves at their own pace. They are free to choose the materials with which they want to "work"—the word used to described their activity. Children must accomplish one task before starting another one, including the replacing of the materials on the shelf for someone else to use. The prepared environment in a Montessori program has child-sized furniture and equipment—one of Froebel's ideas that Montessori used. Materials are set out on low shelves, in an orderly fashion, to encourage children's independent use.

The teacher in the Montessori setting has the prescribed role of observing the children. Teachers become familiar with skills and developmental levels, then match the children to the appropriate material or task. There is little teacher intervention beyond giving clear directions for how to use the materials. Group instruction is not common; learning is an individual experience.

Program Changes

Many changes have taken place in Montessori practices over the years, and today's best Montessori programs are those that are true to philosophical traditions of the Montessori method but make changes and adjustments to fit children's needs. Many Montessori schools are adding curriculum areas of art, dramatic play, gross motor development, and computers. There is also greater teacher flexibility to promote social interaction.

For years, Montessori was separated from the mainstream of American education. That has changed, with over 100 public school districts offering Montessori programs in their elementary schools and with the increased interaction between Montessori advocates and other early childhood professionals.

Maria Montessori's method has found its way into nearly every early childhood education program in existence today. Whether labeled so or not, much of the material and equipment, as well as many of the teaching techniques, in use today originated with this dynamic woman nearly 100 years ago. She is firmly established in early childhood history and its future.

Waldorf Schools

The Waldorf curriculum, shaped by Rudolf Steiner in 1919 (see Chapter 1), emphasizes the development of the whole child through "the head, heart, and hands." Based on the belief that young children learn primarily through observation, imitation, and experience, the curriculum provides a rich environment for children to explore and role models who provide appealing activities. A hallmark of the curriculum is learning through play, and large periods of time are devoted to creative play (Downs, 2003). Other defining features (WECAN, 2005) of a Waldorf curriculum include:

- *Strong rhythmic elements based on the cycles of life and nature.* A daily rhythm of play, work, circle time, and outdoor play, ending with a nature or folk tale, creates a consistent pattern for each session. The weekly rhythm evolves from activities, with one day for baking, another for crafts, another for painting, and so on. Seasonal activities, such as planting bulbs, harvesting produce, or gathering leaves, stress nature's impact on our lives. Seasonal celebrations mark the cyclical changes as well, and often include the families of the children in the class.

- *Environments that nourish the senses.* The walls of the classrooms are usually painted with soft watercolors, curtains may be made from plant-dyed fabrics, and tables and chairs are made of solid wood. The materials used are natural and real; the surroundings are simple and calming.

- *Extensive use of natural materials.* Wood, cotton, and wool are used throughout the classroom. Most of the toys are handcrafted from these natural materials, encouraging children to use their imagination. A piece of wood becomes a ticket to ride the train, which is made from chairs and pieces of wood. It may also become a telephone, a piece of food, or an animal in a barn made of similar materials. The Waldorf philosophy suggests that other, more "finished" toys limit the power of fantasy, imagination, and creativity that is natural in a young child.

- *Play as an imitation of life.* The curriculum fosters skills that imitate the work of adults. Children participate in activities focused on the home: cooking and baking, cleaning, washing and sewing, gardening, and building. Engaging in meaningful life activities is seen as preparation for later academic challenges. Waldorf teachers are good role models in the ways they participate in meaningful work with the children in the hopes that children will imitate good work habits and a sense of responsibility for others.

- *Enhancement of a sense of reverence and wonder.* Children's natural sense of awe and wonder is fostered and deepened, primarily through activities, stories, and festivals that celebrate the cycles of the seasons. In the fall, the classroom may be decorated with corn stalks and sheaves of grain; the seasonal table will be draped with beautiful fabrics in fall colors and hold gourds, pumpkins, acorns, and leaves. When parents join the class for a harvest festival, songs of thankfulness and praise are sung before the feast begins. Each season this is repeated in order to expand the child's sense of reverence for life.

A Waldorf curriculum has much to offer, especially to those who put a premium on the use of imagination and an appreciation for the natural world. There are many elements common to the Montessori method and to the Reggio Emilia approach in particular, as well as to other curriculum models. Can you name them?

KEY TERMS

activity centers
atelierista
culturally appropriate curriculum
developmentally appropriate curriculum
developmentally appropriate practices
emergent curriculum
fine motor skills
gross motor skills
inclusive curricula
integrated curriculum
infusion
learning styles
multiple intelligences
pedagogista
perceptual motor development
project approach
special needs
themes
zone of proximal development

Teaching Applications

1. Observe several early childhood education programs (e.g., a family child care home, a child care center, and an after-school program for primary-age students) for examples of developmentally appropriate curricula.

2. Which curriculum model best represents your own thinking? Why?

3. Observe teachers as children play. What is the difference in the play when (1) a teacher interacts with children in their play and (2) a teacher intervenes? What happens to the play immediately after teacher contact is made? How long does the play last? What is your conclusion?

4. Use the descriptions of multiple intelligences to determine your own style of learning. How has this style affected your abilities as a student? How have teachers responded to this style?

5. What materials do you find in early childhood education classrooms that enhance cultural diversity? What would you add? take away? Why?

REFERENCES

Armstrong, T. (2000). *Multiple intelligences in the classroom.* Alexandria, VA: Association for Supervision and Curriculum Development.

Arce, E. (2000). *Curriculum for young children: An introduction.* Clifton Park, NY: Thomson Delmar Learning.

Banks, J. A. (1992, November/December). Reducing prejudice in children: Guidelines from research. *Social Education,* 3–5.

Banks, J. A. (1994a). *Multiethnic education: Theory and practice.* Boston: Allyn & Bacon.

Banks, J. A. (1994b). *Dominant and desirable characteristics for multiethnic studies* (p. 185). Boston: Allyn & Bacon.

Banks, J. A. (2001). Cultural diversity and education: Foundations, curriculum and teaching. Boston: Allyn & Bacon.

Bos, B. (1978). *Don't move the muffin tins: A hands-off guide to art for the young child.* Carmichael, CA: Burton Gallery

Bredekamp, S., & Copple, C. (1997). *Developmentally appropriate practices in early childhood programs.* Washington, DC: National Association for the Education of Young Children.

Bredekamp, S., & Rosegrant, T. (Eds.). (1995). *Reaching potentials: Transforming early childhood curriculum and assessment* (Vol. 2). Washington, DC: National Association for the Education of Young Children.

Brewer, J. (1995). *Introduction to early childhood education.* Boston: Allyn & Bacon.

Chang, H. (1993). *Affirming children's roots: Cultural and linguistic diversity in early care and education.* Oakland, CA: California Tomorrow.

de Melendez, W. R., & Ostertag, V. (1997). *Teaching young children in multicultural classrooms: Issues, concepts, and strategies.* Clifton Park, NY: Thomson Delmar Learning.

Dombro, A. L., Colker, L., & Dodge, D. T. (1999). *The Creative Curriculum® for infants and toddlers* (rev. ed., p. 74). Washington, DC: Teaching Strategies, Inc.

Downs, M. (2003). The Waldorf preschool curriculum: An engaging path to academic success. *Southern Journal of Teaching and Education.*

Edwards, C., Gandini, L., & Forman, G. (1993). *The hundred languages of children: The Reggio Emilia approach to early childhood education.* Norwood, NJ: Ablex.

Epstein, A. S., Schweinhart, L. J., & McAdoo, L. (1996). *Models of early childhood education.* Ypsilanti, MI: High/Scope Press.

Gardner, H. (1983). *Frames of mind: The theory of multiple intelligences.* New York: Basic Books.

Hohmann, N., and Weikart, D. P. (1995). *Educating young children: Active learning practices for preschool and childcare programs.* Ypsilanti, MI: High/Scope Press.

Jackman, Hilda L. (2005). *Early education curriculum: A child's connection to the world* (3rd ed.). Clifton Park, NY: Thomson Delmar Learning.

Katz, L. (1994). *The project approach.* Champaign, IL: ERIC Clearinghouse on Elementary and Early Childhood Education.

Lowenfeld, V., & Brittain, W. L. (1975). *Creative and mental growth.* New York: Macmillan.

Mitchell, A. & David, J. (Eds.) (1992). *Explorations with young children.* Mt. Ranier, MD: Gryphon House.

New City School (1994). *Celebrating multiple intelligences: Teaching for success.* St. Louis: The New City School.

Schickedanz, J. A., Pergantis, M. L., Kanosky, J., Blaney, A., & Ottinger, J. (1997). *Curriculum in early childhood.* Boston: Allyn & Bacon.

Schirrmacher, R. (2006). *Art and creative development for young children* (4th ed.). Clifton Park, NY: Thomson Delmar Learning.

Schweinhart, L. J. (1993, July). Observing young children in action: The key to early childhood assessment. *Young Children,* 29–33.

WECAN [Waldorf Early Childhood Association of North American] (2005). *The Waldorf kindergarten: The world of the young child.*

Additional resources for this chapter can be found by visiting the Online Companion™ at www.earlychilded.delmar.com. This supplemental material includes a Study Guide with chapter review questions (and answers), critical thinking questions and activities, and annotated Web sites.

Teaching: Taking Development into Action

QUESTIONS FOR THOUGHT

What do children learn in the early years?

What are the physical and motor, cognitive, language, social, emotional, and creative skills that children acquire in an early childhood setting?

How can teachers encourage development?

INTRODUCTION

Our final chapter puts the knowledge about children and child development into action. It is the teacher who translates what we know about how children in general grow into an early childhood program that fosters individual development. In this chapter, we will outline the six major areas of development (see Chapter 4) and the skills that children acquire in the early childhood years.

PHYSICAL GROWTH/MOTOR DEVELOPMENT

Growth and movement are two of the most notable features of young children. Teachers often characterize children through their movements. Pregnant mothers are aware of fetal motions and often assign personality traits to their children by these movements. What is striking about infants is the extent of their full-bodied, random movements and their rapid growth in the first two years. Learning to walk is a major milestone in a child's life. Holding a pencil, cutting with scissors, and tying a shoe are further illustrations of how motor development signifies growth.

Physical Growth

According to Bee (1997), an understanding of physical development is important to teachers and parents for a number of reasons. For example:

✪ New behavior is made possible through physical change; a toddler can be toilet-trained once anal sphincter muscles develop.

✪ Growth determines the child's experiences: Observe the new vistas that open up to the brand new walker.

✪ Growth changes the way people respond to the child: The mobility of crawlers and toddlers leads to more restrictions from parents.

✪ Self-concepts profoundly related to physical development: An obese kindergartner avoids the running and chasing games during recess.

Early childhood is the time of most rapid growth. A child will tend to grow rapidly in infancy and as a toddler, with the growth rate beginning to taper off during preschool and middle childhood years. Although there are individual differences in the rate of maturation among children, growth follows a sequential pattern.

Development seems to follow a directional pattern as well. Large muscles develop before smaller ones—one reason why most preschoolers are more proficient at running than at cutting with scissors. Growth also starts at the center of the body and moves outward. Watch a toddler walk using whole-leg action and compare that with a five-year-old whose knees and ankles are involved in a more developed response. Children also tend to develop in a head-to-toe pattern. Infants move their eyes, head, and hands long before they learn to creep or crawl (see Chapter 3 for developmental norms). It is important to remember, however, that though growth patterns are sequential and directional, they are not smooth and unbroken. While looking at general growth patterns of children, parents and teachers must keep in mind the wide individual differences in the rates at which children grow and in the timing of each change. As a general rule, the pattern within individuals is consistent; that is, a child who is early, average, or late in one aspect of physical development will be so in all aspects. Figure 11–1 shows an overview of these dramatic changes for children up to age eight.

Gender and Cultural Differences

There are gender differences in physical growth patterns. Boys have a larger proportion of muscle tissue than girls, and from the beginning girls have more fat tis-

AGE	WEIGHT	HEIGHT	PROPORTION	TEETH
Newborn	7 lb.	20 in.	Head = 1/4 length	None
Infancy (up to 18 mo.)	Gains 15 lb. (now 20–25 lb.)	Adds 8 in. (now 28–29 in.)	About the same	6
Toddler (18 mo–two-and-a-half years)	Gains 5 lb. (now 28–30 lb.)	Adds another inch or two (now 29–33 in.)	Legs = 34% of body	20
Preschool (two-and-a-half–five years)	About 5 lb./yr. (now 30–40 lb.)	Adds 14–15 in. from birth; at age 2 = half of adult height (now 35–40 in.)	Head growth slows; legs at age five = 44% of body	20
Early-middle childhood (five–eight years)	Doubles before adolescence; (age six = 45–50 lb.)	Adds 9–10 in. (age six = 44–48 in.)	Continues to move slowly toward adult proportions	Begins to lose baby teeth; replaced by permanent teeth (age six = 20–24 teeth)

FIGURE 11–1 An overview of growth shows how rapid physical growth is in childhood.

sue than boys. Each of these differences becomes more obvious in adolescence. In regard to physical development, girls mature earlier than boys, and their growth is more regular and predictable. In motor skills, preschool girls have an edge in fine motor skills, such as writing and drawing, and gross motor skills, such as hopping and skipping. By age five, boys can jump slightly farther, run slightly faster, and throw a ball about five feet farther than girls. These gender differences remain small until adolescence, when girls generally begin puberty two years ahead of boys (Berk, 2002).

There is some indication that physical development differs among ethnic groups.[1] African-

Video View Point 11-1

"Physical development: What physical skills do one- and two-year-old children have?"

Competency: Physical Development

Age Group: Infant-Toddler

Critical Thinking Questions:

1. How would you keep toddlers safe, yet let them explore?
2. Which activities in the video clip could you offer toddlers, and how would this practice improve their fine or gross motor skills?

[1] Be aware of the possibilities in the way children grow, but be careful not to stereotype them.

American infants and toddlers seem to walk earlier and as a group are taller than Euro-Americans. Asian children also seem to develop physically earlier than Euro-American babies but are smaller and shorter overall (Bee, 1997). Some researchers suggest that because African-American children have longer limbs, they have better leverage, which accounts for their superior performance in running and jumping (Berk, 2002). Bee also found that as a group, poor children grow more slowly and are shorter than middle-class children, a finding attributed to diet. Even though the rate of physical development may differ, however, the sequence of development remains the same. This holds true even for children who are physically or mentally disabled.[1]

Including Children with Special Needs

Every classroom is likely to have children who have **special needs** that must be met. Children with physical, cognitive, emotional, or learning disabilities are faced with a variety of challenges, many of which may be met by adapting the environment and planning for activities that help children function within their range of abilities (see Chapters 3 and 9). Gallahue (1996) suggests a number of teaching strategies that can enhance the participation of children with special needs in regular classroom activities:

1. For children with learning disabilities:
   - ✪ Help them gain a better understanding of their body, the space it occupies, and how it can move.
   - ✪ Structure personalized activities that work within the child's present level of abilities.
   - ✪ Progress from simple to more complex activities in small increments.
   - ✪ Make frequent use of rhythmic activities, stressing the rhythmic elements to movement.
2. For children who are visually impaired:
   - ✪ Use many auditory cues to help them gain a sense of space and distance.
   - ✪ Include strenuous, big-muscle activities.
   - ✪ Modify activities that require quick directional changes.
3. For children with cognitive disabilities:
   - ✪ Stress gross motor activities.
   - ✪ Focus on fundamental stability and locomotor and manipulative skills.
   - ✪ Allow children to repeat their successes to enjoy the accomplishment.
   - ✪ Avoid activities in which participants are eliminated from the game.

Including children with special needs takes some careful thought about what kinds of movement experiences and physical development activities are within their abilities (Figure 11–2). Many of the suggestions are appropriate for all children, reminding us that the needs and interests of all children are essentially the same.

Motor Development

Motor development is the process of change in motor behavior based on the interaction of (1) maturation (i.e., the genetically controlled rate of growth), (2) prior experiences, and (3) new motor activities. Like physical growth, motor development is a sequence of stages that is universal but

[1]Variations in growth patterns are influenced by environment and genetic makeup. This holds true for all children.

PLANNING INCLUSIVELY FOR CHILDREN WITH SPECIAL NEEDS

(*Nathan* is a short-statured four-year-old, approximately two-thirds as tall as his peers. His legs are short in proportion to his body size and he loses his balance easily. *Ana's* physical development is normal, but she is quite shy and prefers to watch others rather than participate in activities. A step-by-step process that builds on children's strengths and skills helps teachers plan meaningful activities for each child.)

1. **Ascertain child's strengths**

   Nathan—imaginative, agile, healthy, outgoing, demonstrates positive self-image
   Ana—persevering, patient, compliant, methodical, each small success is evident in her expression

2. **Ascertain child's needs**

   Nathan—to prove that he is as competent as his peers, despite short stature; to improve poor balance due to disproportionately short legs
   Ana—to improve large motor skills; to gain confidence in joining groups

3. **Set goals**

   Nathan—to gain better balance and to be offered the chance to feel tall and big
   Ana—to become a bit more adventurous, more sociable, and more comfortable with her body in space

4. **Brainstorm: What group activities are suitable?**

   Nathan—physical activities that require stretching and balancing
   Ana—noncompetitive experiences that require different kinds of motor planning and that allow her to proceed at her own pace while participating with her peers

5. **Select an activity** (e.g., an outdoor obstacle course)

6. **Plan the activity**

7. **Implement the activity**

8. **Evaluate the activity**

   Nathan—Was he able to stretch sufficiently to climb the rungs and reach across the empty spaces between obstacles? Did he work on his balancing skills?
   Ana—Was she willing and able to work through the course? Did she need a teacher's hand throughout? Did she interact with her peers?
   Both—Did they do the whole course, or did they skip some obstacles? Did they return to a favorite spot? Did they voluntarily repeat the whole course?
   All—Did everybody have fun?

9. **Refine the activity—and try again!**

FIGURE 11–2 Planning inclusively for children with special needs. (Reprinted, with permission, from C.S. Kranowitz, "Obstacle courses are for every body," in *Alike and Different: Exploring Our Humanity with Young Children,* ed. B. Neugebauer [Washington, DC: National Association for the Education of Young Children (NAEYC), 1992], 23.)

still allows for individual differences.[1] Each stage is different from, yet grows out of, the preceding level. Figure 11–3 charts motor development through the early years.

Any discussion of motor development should include reference to bodily-kinesthetic intelligence, part of Gardner's multiple intelligence theory (see Chapters 4 and 10). Bodily-kinesthetic intelligence occurs when children use their bodies to help them process information and communicate their understanding of school. For instance, children who learn best through bodily-kinesthetic intelligence need active

manipulation of materials. Drama, creative movement, dance, manipulatives, games, and exercises, both indoors and outdoors, benefit the bodily-kinesthetic learner.

Basic motor skills develop in the early childhood years and form the foundation for movement and motor proficiency. If children do not develop them during the early years, these skills often remain unlearned. Physical growth and motor development are partly determined by a child's genetic makeup. Equally as important are environmental factors, such as nourishment, health, safety, stimulation, opportunity, practice, encouragement, and instruction. The crucial interplay of hered-

- roller-skating/bicycling (5–8 years)
- running faster (5 years and up)
- skipping (5–6 years)
- hopping on one foot (3–5 years)
- up/downstairs with continuous movement (4 years)
- jumping on two feet (3–5 years)
- running (2–3 years)
- walks up/downstairs alone (3 years)
- toddling (18–24 months)
- standing/walking alone (12–15 months)
- climbing stairs (13 months)
- walking when led (11–12 months)
- creeping/crawling (8–10 months)
- standing holding onto something/someone (8–10 months)
- sitting and supporting self (6–8 months)
- infant on belly, with chest up (2 months)

FIGURE 11–3 Motor development follows a developmental sequence. (Adapted from Allen K.E., & Marotz, L. R. [2003]. *Developmental profiles: Pre-birth through twelve* [4th ed.]. Clifton Park, NY: Thomson Delmar Learning.)

[1]Be aware of the possibilities in the way children grow, but be careful not to stereotype them.

ity and environment guides the child's progress through life. Recent research in brain development underscores the importance of motor skill development in young children (Shore, 1997). Physical growth milestones are reinforced daily by parents and caregivers. This reinforcement strengthens the network of synapses, and they become a permanent part of the brain. By adolescence, the brain is beginning to rid itself of excess synapses. Those that have been activated and experienced most often are the ones that will survive.

Gross Motor Development

Gross motor activity involves movements of the entire body or large parts of the body. Using various large muscle groups, children try to creep, crawl, roll, bounce, throw, or hop. Activities that foster gross motor development include balance, agility, coordination, **flexibility,** strength, speed, and endurance.

Fine Motor Development

Fine motor activity uses the small muscles of the body and its extremities (the hands and feet). Such movement requires dexterity, precision, and manipulative skill. Grasping, reaching, holding, banging, pushing, spinning, and turning are all activities that refine these skills. Weaving, sewing, using tools of all sorts, playing games with toys all help these small muscles to develop.

what do YOU think?

Are you physically active? Do you participate in a sport or exercise on a regular basis? What would you do to create opportunities for all children to be physically active for some part of each school day? List some examples that would be especially appropriate indoors.

Perceptual Motor Development

Perceptual motor development is a process in which the child develops the skill and ability to take in and interpret information from the environment and respond to it with movement. Children obtain data and impressions primarily through their senses. For instance, you have probably often seen babies mimic a parent's or caregiver's mouth movements—taking in visually the various expressions, then physically responding in kind.

In a sense, every movement is perceptual motor activity because the body and mind must work together to complete all motor tasks. The perceptual task is to process information; the motor response activates what is received in a physical way, although perceptual and motor abilities do not necessarily develop at the same time or the same rate. The complex nature of perceptual motor development can be seen when examining the three basic categories of spatial, temporal, and sensory awareness:

Spatial awareness is a sense of the body's relationship to space, as well as knowledge of what the body parts can do. For the toddler, concepts of spatial relationships are developed through motor activity: dropping objects from a highchair or forcing a large stuffed animal into a small box. Their definition of space is related to the action and movement involved in specific activities. A sense of relationship to less immediate things and places (knowing a specific route to school and home, making simple maps) develops in the preschool years. Not until ages six to eight do children develop the more abstract spatial ability of distinguishing left from right on their own bodies and others'. Specifically, directional awareness refers to left and right, up and down, front and behind, over and under. Two-and-a-half-year-old Tamara demonstrates her awareness of spatial relationships as she moves herself up to a table

Developing spatial awareness involves gaining a sense of your body and what it can do.

(without bumping into it), reaches to her left to pick up a ball of clay, and turns around behind her to choose a rolling pin.

Temporal awareness is the child's inner clock, a time structure that lets the child coordinate body parts. Dancing to a rhythmic beat—speeding up and slowing down—develops this kind of skill. It is also a force that helps children predict time. For instance, seven-year-olds Luis and Aref ask if it is time to clean up as they finish their game of soccer. The after-school center has sports time for about an hour before getting ready for snack; the children have an inner sense of time that parallels their knowledge of the daily schedule.

Sensory awareness refers to using the senses to give the mind information. Vision is the dominant sense for young children. Visual awareness is the ability to mimic demonstrated movements and to discriminate faces, emotions, sizes, shapes, and colors. It is the ability in three-month-old babies to recognize their mothers. Auditory awareness includes the ability to understand and carry out verbal directions and to discriminate among a variety of sounds. Auditory skills help children process information about language. From infancy, children seem to be able to combine visual and auditory awareness. Further sensory awareness develops through touch. Babies seem to put everything in their mouths to learn. Looking in on a high-quality infant center, one notices the area under 24 inches offering babies a rich variety of materials to stimulate all the senses. Unbreakable stainless steel mirrors are attached to the baseboards; there is an aquarium with fish and plants, soft carpet and hard linoleum to crawl on, tempting smells from the kitchen in the air, and plenty of rattles, bells, and chimes to provide sensory stimulation.

Physical/Motor Skills in Early Childhood

Types of Movement

Physical/motor skills involve three basic types of movement: locomotor, nonlocomotor, and manipulative abilities.

- ✪ Locomotor abilities involve a change of location of the body and include the skills of walking, running, leaping, jumping, climbing, hopping, skipping, galloping, sliding, and tricycling.

- ✪ Nonlocomotor abilities (sometimes referred to as balancing or stabilizing) are any movements that require some degree of balancing. These skills are turning, twisting, pushing, bending, stretching, pulling, swinging, rolling, dodging, and balancing.

- ✪ Manipulative abilities include the operation and control of limited and precise movements of the small muscles, especially those in the hands and feet. Manipulative skills include throwing, catching, reaching, bouncing, striking, kicking (gross motor manipulation), and holding, grasping, cutting, and sewing (fine motor manipulation).

These three basic movements are necessarily combined when children are active in physical play:

With doll buggy: Holding onto buggy—
            Manipulative
            Pushing buggy—
            Nonlocomotor
            Walking with buggy—
            Locomotor

Playing ball: Bending down for the ball—
            Nonlocomotor
            Throwing the ball—
            Manipulative
            Running to base—Locomotor

Jumping rope: Holding and turning the
            rope—Manipulative
            Jumping—Locomotor
            Balancing self after jump—
            Nonlocomotor

Breaking a piñata: Holding the bat—
            Manipulative
            Swinging the bat—
            Nonlocomotor
            Running to get the
            prize—Locomotor

Learning Motor Skills

Children must use their bodies to learn motor skills. They acquire these skills by making comparisons between their past experience and new actions. Memory plays an important part in learning motor movements because children need to recall what they just did to make corrections or refinements. In the short term, the ball that does

not reach the basket is tossed farther on the next shot. To get the puzzle piece to fit, a child remembers other ways to manipulate the pieces. A long-term memory of movement is one that may go unrehearsed for long periods of time. The experience of swimming, for example, may be recalled only in the summer.

Children modify and improve their motor skills as they receive information about their movements, both **intrinsic** (the paintbrush makes marks when it is pushed across the paper) and **extrinsic** ("I notice that your legs are very far apart as you try to somersault; how about holding them together as you roll next time?"). Feedback helps.[1]

Movement exploration enhances children's ability to:

- ✸ problem-solve
- ✸ exercise **divergent thinking**
- ✸ respond at their own age and developmental level
- ✸ learn to cooperate with others
- ✸ become more aware of others' viewpoints and ideas
- ✸ share, take turns
- ✸ be self-expressive
- ✸ be creative
- ✸ gain confidence
- ✸ develop strong muscles
- ✸ refine motor skills

The traditional nursery school (see Chapter 2) gave children nearly as much time outdoors as inside, assuming a great need for physical activity. However, many outdoor areas contain few challenges, perhaps only a blacktop for bouncing balls and a small metal climber for hanging and climbing. Moreover, American children are ex-

[1]Children with physical limitations can experience many daily activities if the environment is appropriately adapted.

posed to a value system in which physical/motor fitness is not always a high priority. Children are often encouraged toward sedentary activities at an early age, such as watching television or using computers.

Motor skills affect other areas of development. For instance, Tim is reluctant to climb outside. He is easily frightened when he—or anyone else—is up in a tree or on any climber. Because he cannot risk using his body in space, he stops himself from playing with anyone who invites him to try these activities. Thus, Tim's lack of gross motor development is affecting his **social skills.** See Figure 11–4 for a checklist of possible problems.

At the same time, children's motor strengths enhance their development. Samantha loves to draw and cut. She chooses the art area every day she attends the two-year-old class. Not only are her fine motor skills well developed for her age; she takes great pride in her creations. Her motor skills enhance her self-confidence in school. In turn, she receives praise and attention from others as she communicates with both adults and children through her work. Providing a curriculum for acquiring physical and motor skills helps the whole child.

With practice comes a sense of competence. Children can learn to relax as they gain experience in physical activities, and thus reduce the **stress** of anticipating failure. Teachers support positive self-concept through physical and motor development in several ways. They let children discover their own physical limits, rather

CHECK WHETHER CHILD:

☐ 1. **Has trouble holding or maintaining balance**

☐ 2. **Appears to have difficulty balancing and moves awkwardly**

☐ 3. **Cannot carry self well in motion**

☐ 4. **Appears generally awkward in activities requiring coordination**

☐ 5. **Has difficulty making changes in movement**

☐ 6. **Has difficulty performing combinations of simple movements**

☐ 7. **Has difficulty in gauging space with respect to own body; bumps and collides with objects and other children**

☐ 8. **Tends to fall often**

☐ 9. **Has poor eye–hand coordination**

☐ 10. **Has difficulty handling the simple tools of physical activity (beanbags, balls, other objects that require visual–motor coordination)**

FIGURE 11–4 A checklist of possible problems in physical/motor development serves as a guideline when devising a developmentally specific profile for spotting problems.

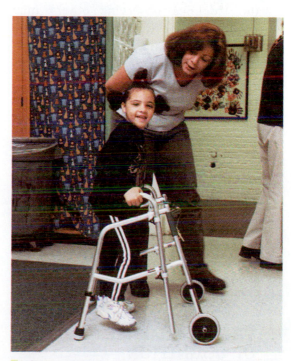

To learn a motor skill, children must combine memory with experience, taking advantage of opportunities to try something new and to practice what has already been learned.

than warning or stopping them from trying out an activity for themselves.

✿ "I'm stuck!" A child shouts across the yard. Rather than rushing to lift the child down, the teacher walks over to the child and replies, "Where can you put your foot next?" "How can you find a way to get across that branch?"

✿ "I'm afraid!" The teacher stands close to the child who is climbing and responds to the fear: "I'll stand close to the climbing ropes so you will feel safe."

✿ "Look what I can do!" Teachers reinforce children who try something new: "Greg, it's good to see you cutting out that pumpkin all by yourself."

✿ "I tried." Teachers congratulate efforts for the achievement they really are: "Your hands reached the top this time, Shannon. I'll bet you are feeling proud of yourself."

✿ "I can't do it." Children who stand on the sidelines observing others may need some encouragement from the teacher to take the first step in mastering the climbing frame or slide: "Here's a good place for you to put your foot, Arturo. I'll hold on to your hand until you get me to let go."

Competence breeds self-confidence and a willingness to try greater challenges. It is important to support the progress of physical skills because one must achieve mastery before moving to the next physical challenge. As children try new activities, they learn more about themselves. And physical activity increases awareness of what fun it is to move—to run through a field or pump a swing just for the sheer joy of it!

✿ THE DEVELOPMENT OF COGNITION

The amount of learning that takes place in early childhood is staggering. How do children manage to absorb the sheer quantity of information and experience they accumulate in their first few years of life? Every child accomplishes this mighty feat by thinking. Cognition is the mental process or faculty that children use to acquire knowledge. To think is to be able to acquire and apply knowledge. By using conscious thought and memory, children think about themselves, the world, and others. Typically, we find out what children think by listening to them talk or asking them to tell us what they know. Yet cognition can occur without the language to express it. For example, an infant's laughter during a game of peek-a-boo indicates the child's knowledge that the hidden face will reappear. Conversely, the use of language can occur without cognition (i.e., without knowing the meaning). A child's counting from 1 to 20 (". . .11, 13, 17, 19, 20!") is a case in point.

Cognitive Growth

Cognition and language generally become more interdependent as development progresses. Children expand their knowledge base through language. They listen, question, tell. The child with good language skills can thus apply them to widen the horizons of knowledge.

Cognition is related not only to the developing mind but also to all areas of the child's growth. Young thinkers are at work no matter what they are doing. For example, physical/motor development is also a cognitive process. Learning to roller-skate involves skinned knees and learning to balance (motor tasks), along with analyzing, predicting, generalizing, evaluating, and practicing the art of locomotion on wheels (cognitive skills). When trying to enter into group play (a social task), children will think of strategies for how to get started (cognitive skill). In trying to enhance cognitive development, early childhood educators draw on developmental and learning theories and their direct experiences with children.[1,2]

By combining theoretical and practical viewpoints, teachers take a blended, or eclectic, perspective on the development of the thinking process. They work with children to encourage their ability to formulate ideas and to think rationally and logically.

Most important, the early childhood professional works toward helping children acquire skills that will lead to the development of:

Concepts: Labeling or naming an idea, moving from the specific to the abstract

"What is a grape?"

Relationships: What is the association between two or more things? How are they similar or different? What are their functions, characteristics?

"How many colors of grapes are there? Do all of them have seeds? Are they different sizes? Do they taste alike?"

Generalizations: Drawing conclusions from relationships and concepts/ideas. This means grouping things into classes and finding common elements.

"Are grapes a fruit or meat? How do grapes grow?"

Piaget's theory is an important part of what we know about children's thinking.

Recent research on information processing and the brain and the theories of Vygotsky and Gardner have broadened our notions of thinking and **intelligence** (see Chapter 4).

A Piagetian Perspective

Piaget's view of cognition is twofold. First, learning is a process of discovery, of finding out what one needs to know to solve a particular problem. Second, knowledge results from active thought, from making mental connections among objects, from constructing a meaningful reality for understanding. Figure 11–5 describes how teachers help children construct reality.

Piaget divided knowledge into three types: physical, logical-mathematical, and social. **Physical knowledge** is what children learn through external sensory experiences. Watching leaves blow in the wind, grabbing a ball, sniffing a fresh slice of bread are all instances of children learning about different physical objects and how they feel, taste, smell, move, and so on. The basic cognitive process involved in the development of physical knowledge is discrimination. For example, by touching magnets to paper clips, puzzles, and paper dolls, children learn firsthand about magnetism. They learn to discriminate between those objects that "stick" to the magnet and those that do not.

Logical-mathematical knowledge derives from coordinating physical actions into some kind of order, or logic. This is not to be confused with formal mathematics; rather it is the kind of mathematical thinking children use in making connections about what they see, such as an infant's lift-

[1]Teachers must blend what they know about theory and concepts with what they learn about individual children and culture; see Chapter 3 for learning styles and Chapter 9 for anti–bias environment discussions.

[2]The role of culture in cognition is one of several major diversity areas in this chapter. Piaget's constructivism informs educators about how they should teach; because children construct knowledge from their own personal experiences, their culture will have a major impact on how they come to know.

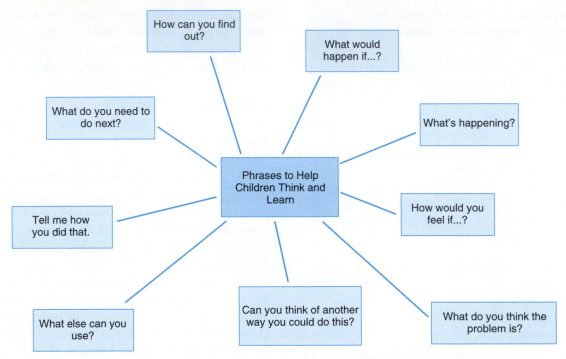

How can you find out?

What would happen if...?

What do you need to do next?

What's happening?

Phrases to Help Children Think and Learn

How would you feel if...?

Tell me how you did that.

What else can you use?

Can you think of another way you could do this?

What do you think the problem is?

FIGURE 11–5 Teachers encourage children's thinking when they ask questions. Posted in the classroom or given to students and parents, this chart serves as a reminder that to TEACH is to ASK more often than to TELL.

ing the blanket to find a hidden toy. The logic of the young child is seen in the coordination of actions to make an inference. Think back to the magnets example. If a child deliberately takes a magnet to the metal drawer pulls and metal climbing bars, we can see the logical knowledge used: The child has made the **inference** that it is the metal things that "stick" on the magnet.

Social knowledge comes from our culture, the rules of the game, the right vocabulary, the moral codes. It includes learning vocabulary and being taught or told things, as well as knowledge about the social aspects of life. Value laden and often arbitrary, social knowledge can rarely be constructed logically but is learned through life. With the aforementioned magnets, social knowledge would need to be used to decide who gets to play with the magnets, or when it is somebody else's turn.

In developing cognitive curriculum, teachers plan experiences that enhance those types of knowledge. They can teach

using different forms of knowledge. **Rote knowledge** is information given with no particular meaning to the learner—that which could be learned meaningfully but is not. A teacher talking about magnets or telling children what attracts or repels gives children rote knowledge. **Meaningful knowledge** is what children learn gradually and within the context of what they already know and want to find out—like the example of letting the children handle the magnets themselves if they choose, and answering their questions as they arise. Both telling (rote) and asking or allowing (meaningful) can be useful; for the children, it is a question of the balance between the two in everyday educational encounters.

Watching cognitive development in action, teachers apply constructivist theory by:

✺ *Offering choices.* Have several interest areas in your room and yard.

✺ *Giving children time to play.* The daily schedule should include at least 45 minutes of free-play indoors and outdoors per half-day.

✺ *Providing activities.* Make available open-ended materials such as clay/play dough, water/sand, and woodworking for experimentation and interaction.

✺ *Being a facilitator instead of "teller."* Ask "What if, I wonder, I notice" questions.

✺ *Developing curriculum from children's interests.* Ask, "What do they love?"

In one child care center, many children rushed to the dress-up area, arguing over the skirts and scarves. This same group thrived on music and dancing. A student teacher was in a local Baile Folklorico group and brought her fellow dancers to the class. Her mother sewed costumes for dramatic play, which stimulated weeks of weaving and sewing activities. A nearby college hosted a special showing of "Riverdance," which developed into more children's participation in creating their own "stomps." As children's interests grew, so the teacher constructed interesting curriculum.

Gardner's Multiple Intelligences

Research in cognition documents that children possess different kinds of minds and therefore understand, learn, remember, and perform in different ways. Most experts agree that intelligence is complex and that traditional tests do not measure the entire host of skills or abilities involved.[1]

Multiple intelligences theory acknowledges that people learn and use

knowledge in different ways. Therefore, we will need to vary both what and how we teach. "Gardner's theory is a dream come true for teachers," says Nelson (1995), "because it means many intelligences can be nurtured. And with that in mind, I [can] reinvent my curriculum and the way I teach it so that it meets the needs of a wider range" (Figure 11–6).

This does not mean that teachers must develop every activity to all eight intelligences. Rather, teachers learn about each individual child and then tailor their curriculum to build on their children's strengths. "Students who need to learn counting, one-to-one correspondence, or math facts can do so, for example, through centers which tap into their spatial talents: students draw items—or group already-drawn images—to capture the math concepts. Students might go to a bodily-kinesthetic center to snap fingers or jump as they count by by two's. Or perhaps students listen to music, clapping hands to catch the rhythm and beat of the numbers" (Hoerr, 2004). The curriculum expands by asking, "How is each child smart?"

Vygotsky, Thinking, and Culture

Sociocultural theory states that much of children's development and knowledge is culturally specific. Because children learn from more knowledgeable members of the community, they come to know what is socially valued. If knowledge is connected to what a culture values, then teachers and parents must have some agreement about what is important to teach children.[2]

Also, the best way of teaching is a kind of assisted learning, which allows for

[1]Considering intelligence beyond standard IQ testing provides the opportunity to consider the diverse forms that individual children's intelligence may take.
[2]Vygotsky's approach to development recognizes the social origins of an individual's thinking functioning: For instance, taking into account children's home language experiences can turn passive learners into lively participants.

MULTIPLE INTELLIGENCES IN ACTION

1. Linguistic
   - Story/words—sort objects that begin with the letter F, make an F chant, with every word starting with F
   - Listening—listen to "Frog Went A Courtin'"
   - Computer—play "Fun on the Farm"
2. Logical-Mathematical
   - Manipulatives—measure by the foot
   - Language—learn about feelings; talk about feeling frustrated
3. Spatial
   - Art—paint fancy feet or do face painting
   - Clay—make the letter F out of play dough
4. Musical
   - Dramatic play—listen to *Fantasia* while you play in the playhouse
   - Music—listen and sing in French; make rhythms with your feet
5. Bodily-Kinesthetic
   - Outdoors—bounce balls around a giant letter F
   - Group time—draw imaginary letters (F) on each other's back
   - Sensory—use funnels
6. Intrapersonal
   - Manipulatives—a "one-only" game with sandpaper letters (F)
   - "Me place"—a beanbag chair for one only
7. Interpersonal
   - "Social table" or "help-yourself" table—F templates with markers and paper; F lacing cards
   - Small-group time—partners find all the F's in a sheet of letters
8. Naturalistic
   - Group time—How many dinosaurs can we think of that start with the letter F?
   - Discovery/science table—start a flora and fauna mural

FIGURE 11–6 The New City School (1995) has developed a curriculum for multiple intelligences, such as these center activities for the letter F.

scaffolding, a natural learning technique known as apprenticeship. Such learning can occur via physical or verbal interaction and as long as both the learner and the teacher are motivated (one to learn and the other to assist). An older child or adult serves as a guide who is responsive to what the child is ready to learn.

This method makes a strong case for mixed-age groupings so that young children can learn from older ones. Indeed, of all the strategies used to deal with reading problems in primary grades (which have devastating effects on children), the most effective for preventing early reading fail-

Scaffolding is a kind of assisted learning that often takes place in mixed-age groups.

ure are approaches incorporating one-to-one tutoring of at-risk first graders. Play is a valuable way for children to work with the symbols and other higher forms of thinking. With other people alongside, the child practices what is to be expected and valued in society. The teacher is both observer and participant. Three-year-old Josh is building with blocks, crying out in frustration. Teacher Louise moves in: "I hear you are upset; what's the problem?" Josh wants to build a ramp for the cars, but the board keeps falling flat. Louise calls over Miguel, a five-year-old who is the class block expert. While he shows Josh how to build it better, Louise sketches Josh's first creation, then draws what the two build together. Seeing the new creation stand tall, Louise gives high-fives to both children, then encourages a joint effort to use measurement tools.

DAP

Brain-Based Research

"The human brain is the most fascinatingly organized three pounds of matter on this planet" (Schiller, 2001). The only unfinished organ at birth, it continues to grow throughout the life cycle. The principal task of the brain in early childhood is the connection of brain cells, as a child's brain is two and a half times as active as an adult's. As noted in Chapter 4, a child is born with a billion cells (neurons) not yet connected in a meaningful way. Over the next few years, the brain forms trillions of networks (synapses), many more than a child will ever need. As they multiply and connect, a sophisticated network of neural pathways is created (Shore, 1997).

Providing quality experiences and relationships will create lasting effects on how the brain gets wired. Children's brains need to be stimulated for the network of connections to grow and be protected from being discarded. "Brain connections that have been reinforced by repeated experience tend to remain while those that are not are discarded" (Galinsky, 1997). Thus, a child's early experiences help to shape the brain and will affect to some extent how one thinks, feels, and behaves. Attention, processing, memory, and retention are all brain functions. Figure 11–7 shows how to translate brain research into curriculum.

Brain-based research reveals development in action. Keep these ideas in mind:

❂ *Birth to age four.* Provide for healthy sensory stimulation. This means all the senses need to be included in a child's exploration of the world. During the

TRANSLATING BRAIN RESEARCH INTO CURRICULUM

Brain research discovery: The brain is strongly run by patterns rather than facts. The key to our intelligence is the recognition of patterns and relationships.

Curriculum translation: Develop meaningful themes for activity planning. Uninteresting or abstract pieces of information (e.g., drilling young children on alphabet letters) will not provide understanding. Plan some kinds of "immersion experiences" that encourage children to go deeply into their play and work.

Brain research discovery: Stress and threat affect the brain in many ways. Emotions run the brain, and bad emotions reduce the capacity for memory and understanding as well as higher-order thinking skills. Good emotions create excitement and love of learning.

Curriculum translation: Make a positive, personal connection with each child. Avoid threats by loss of approval, hurried schedules, or implying that children are helpless or bad. A secure environment counteracts the downshifting that may occur when the stress regulation mechanisms are triggered too often. Good emotions enhance memory.

Brain research discovery: The brain runs better when food intake is steady. Insulin levels stay more even, cortisol levels are lower, and glucose tolerance is better. Diet activates memory.

Curriculum translation: Snacks are good! Regular snack times may lead to better cognitive functioning, fewer discipline problems, and an enhanced sense of well-being. Children need diets rich in proteins (meats, nuts, cheese), omega-3 fatty acids, and selenium and boron (leafy green vegetables). Rest time is critical for a balanced day.

Brain research discovery: All learning is mind–body. A person's physical state, posture, and breathing affect learning. Our brain is designed for cycles and rhythms; sleep helps the brain reorganize itself. Practice makes permanent, and memory is kept more accurate when information is revisited.

Curriculum translation: Plan a daily schedule with both variety and balance. Work in regular routines and productive rituals. Keep track of and teach to children's bodily functions and body states and how long they are expected to sit or nap.

FIGURE 11–7 Key ideas from brain research translate into appropriate curriculum.

first years, children should be living in an enriched environment—visual, auditory, linguistic, and so on—because that lays the foundation for development later in life. Further, there are circuits that are responsible for emotional and social functioning (not just perception and motor action) that come "on line" during the first years of life.

✺ *Age four to eight.* The brain is eagerly searching for stimulation. Kindergarten through third grade must be richly stimulating, with activities that reward the brain's insatiable appetite for meaning. Give children plenty of opportunities to use stories, explore ideas, and master tasks rather than use worksheets or other repetitive tools that kill enthusiasm for learning. In Ms. Gardyn's kindergarten, children are encouraged to write their own stories. Each week, the group brainstorms topics that interest them, and the chart is posted in the "authors corner." When Barbara and Jenny head there after finishing the math lab game, they grab pieces of lined paper and begin: Barbara uses "scribble writing" that she then dictates to the volunteer parent for "publication" in the weekly newsletter, while Jenny draws two children and writes "wr frndz [we are friends]" underneath.

✺ *All ages.* Develop curriculum that emphasizes choices. "Exercise and positive social contacts, such as hugging, music, and the supportive comments of friends, can elevate endorphin levels and thus make us feel good about ourselves and our social environment" (Leventhal in Sylwester, 1995). Create opportunities for "collaboration" and cooperation, both among children and between children and teachers. And remember that the brain can only handle so much; while experiencing a growth spurt in one area, others may be stable.

Cognitive Skills in Early Childhood

The actual skills children acquire as they learn to think are considerable. A basic skill is defined by two fundamental qualities:

1. A skill is basic if it is **transcurricular,** that is, if the child can use it in a variety of situations and activities throughout the school day. For example, children who can express feelings and opinions clearly—who can let adults know when they are having difficulties with a particular task or social situation—have acquired a skill that is useful anywhere.

2. A skill is also basic if it has **dynamic consequences,** that is, if it leads to other worthwhile responses. For instance, children who are articulate tend to elicit more verbal responses from adults. Consequently, they are exposed to more verbal stimulation, which in turn strengthens their verbal abilities, and so on. Thus, having this skill leads to major dynamic consequences in a favorable direction, whereas not having the skill leads to dynamic consequences in an unfavorable direction.

Most skills fall into the nine categories that follow. The teacher plans activities for all cognitive skills to ensure challenging children's thinking. For ideas for curriculum, see Chapter 10.

Skills of Inquiry

Young children are curious, watching the world carefully. Through exploration and examination, they increase their attention span. Inquisitive children begin to organize what they see, analyzing and identifying confusions or obstacles for themselves. The child asks questions, listens, gets ideas, and makes suggestions. This includes interpreting what others communicate. Then children are ready to use resources, seeking assistance from other people and materials.

We develop this skill by helping children build what they already know in order to construct new knowledge. These basic skills of inquiry are the foundation for thinking; as such, they are far more important to develop than are simple pre-reading or number skills.

Knowledge of the Physical World

Children learn about the physical world by spending plenty of time exploring, manipulating, choosing, and using toys and natural materials. Babies search for something to suck; they begin to grasp objects and let them go. Toddlers will pick up and throw things or drop objects from a highchair to see what happens. Children observe reactions, discover relationships, and try to predict what will happen. Six-year-olds with balloons and water explore how to fill, roll, throw, and burst the balloons. As they learn the properties of objects, children gain a better understanding of the concept of cause and effect. Experience with the physical world gives children a base for comparing and contrasting, key skills for mathematical classification and scientific thinking. Participation in an environment filled with interesting sights, sounds, and people enriches a child's schemes of thought and action.

Knowledge of the Social World

Relationships are primary to development, and children's early experiences significantly influence social and emotional brain functions. "Attachment relationships are important in the unfolding of the emotional and social development of the child. . . . [I]t is not a matter of overwhelming enrichment or excessive sensory stimulation that is needed during this time, but one of attunement between adult and child" (Siegel, 1999).

Infants begin by distinguishing friends from strangers. Toddlers learn to use "mine" and then to use others' names as well. The next step is to expand their knowledge of roles to include those of family, school, and the community. Four- and five-year-olds are provided with daily opportunities to cooperate, to help, and to negotiate with others about their needs and wishes. Children are encouraged to notice both similarities and differences in people and then are led to develop tolerance for both. As they seek small groups and moments of private time with a close friend, school-age children can develop conscience and rules for social living.

Classification

Classification is the ability to group like objects in sets by a specific characteristic. Consider how two-year-old Tisa learns to classify.

> What can Tisa do to the stuffed bear and the pet dog? What can she do with one and not the other? Which are her toys? Which are Rover's? Which ones have fur? What is different about them?

Tisa learns the attributes of the objects by exploring, learning the class names of "toy" and "pet." Tisa makes collections, sorting by similarity those that are Rover's toys and those that are her own. She uses class relationships to understand that both animals have fur, but she can tug on only one animal's ears without encountering a problem.

Once they develop language proficiency, children can name their classifications. Gradually, and with help from adults who stimulate describing and manipulating, they learn that objects have more than one attribute and can be classified in more than one class.

Seriation

Seriation is "the ability to put an object or group of objects in a logical series based on a property of those objects" (Geist, 2001). To illustrate its development, look at some

As children learn categories for objects, they become more sophisticated in their classification skills.

of the materials designed by Montessori. These toys were developed to make clear to children exactly what seriation is and how it can be learned. Many of these toys distinguish grades of intensity by size, color, weight, number. Children build pyramid towers, fit nesting blocks together, and use the counting rods. By noting differences, often through trial and error, children learn seriation systematically. For instance, the pyramid tower is ordered from largest piece to smallest as it is built. Boxes are nested, one inside the other, by their graduated size or volume. The counting rods can be put into a staircase array, the units building on each other from one to 10. Children can arrange several things in order and fit one ordered set of objects to another.

Numbers

Understanding the concept of number means learning about quantity: that is, understanding amount, degree, and position. Mathematical knowledge is now being seen as an emergent understanding of concepts. Once infants develop an understanding of object permanence (that an object exists whether or not it can be seen), they are ready to learn about quantity as they compare objects—for example, by stacking

rings on a stick. Toddlers and twos can sort by groups (large vs. small, hard vs. soft) and start noticing what is "more." Children under five need plenty of songs, chants, and fingerplays that include numbers ("One Potato, Two Potato" or "Five Speckled Frogs"). Once children comprehend numbers, they are ready to use mathematical terms and forms of expression. For instance, after singing about the frog that jumped into the pool in the song "Five Speckled Frogs," Chantel can begin to understand that four is one less than five.

Knowing numbers is neither complete nor meaningful unless children have direct experience with materials and objects. Learning about quantity means comparing amounts (as when children work with table toys, blocks, sensory materials, and the like) and arranging two sets of objects in one-to-one correspondence ("Each person needs one and only one napkin for snack, Tyler"). Children can also count objects and begin computation ("Parvin, you have three shovels. Here is one more; now how many do you have?").

Symbols

A symbol stands for something else; to symbolize means learning to use one object to represent something else. "The value of revisiting and re-representing children's symbolic representations for both teachers and children has been well-documented" (Moran & Jarvis, 2001). Make-believe helps in the process of symbolizing (playing dress-up), as does making sounds to represent objects ("Choo-choo" is a train, for example). Using and making two- and three-dimensional models are other ways children symbolize, when they transfer what they see to the easel or to the clay table (see the Reggio Emilia curriculum model in Chapter 10). Description games encourage children to use language as symbols. For example, "It is round and red and you eat it. What is it?" (An apple!) After all these skills have been mastered, children are ready for written symbols, when they can use the written word to label, take dictation, or write notes.

Spatial Relationships

Spatial relationships develop early. Infants visually track what they see, trying to reach and grasp. As they experience one object's position in relation to another, they begin to have a mental picture of spatial relationships. Toddlers learn to steer themselves around tables and seat themselves on the potty. Children learn to fit things together and take them apart. They rearrange and shape objects, seeing things from different spatial viewpoints. This perspective is learned only through experience. What you see from the bottom of the hill is different than what can be seen at the top. Teachers encourage children to represent such spatial relationships in their drawings, with pictures, and in photographs.

Time

Understanding time is a complicated affair because time is composed of at least three dimensions: time as the present, time as a continuum, and time as a sequence of events. Children can learn to stop and start an activity on a signal (when the teacher strikes a chord on the piano for cleanup time). They try to move their bodies at different speeds, indoors and out. Older children begin to observe that clocks and calendars are used to mark the passage of time. Specifically, children come to know the sequencing of events in time: Which comes first, next, last? Having an order of events through a consistent daily schedule helps children learn this aspect of time. They also benefit from anticipating future events and making the appropriate preparations. Planning a course of action and completing that plan give meaning to the idea of time.

 ## THE DEVELOPMENT OF LANGUAGE

Alexis: Laleña, will you help me full this pitcher up?

Laleña: No, because my ponytail is keeping me in bothers.

Veronique: Hey, come here! I dropped some bread and the birds yummed it right up!

Abhi: I know, that's what the tooth fairy did to my tooth.

Marty: I'm going to keep all my baby teeth in a jar and the next time a baby comes along, I'll give him my baby teeth.

Language is the aspect of human behavior that involves the use of sounds in meaningful patterns. This includes the corresponding symbols that are used to form, express, and communicate thoughts and feelings. Language seems to be an innate characteristic of humankind.

Languages worldwide vary remarkably in their sounds, words, and grammatical structure. Any system of signs used for communication is language. For the developing child, language is the ability to express oneself. Language is both receptive—

listening, understanding, and responding—and expressive—articulation, vocabulary, grammar, and graphic language. In other words, as illustrated earlier, language is meaningful, enjoyable communication.

Language Growth

Language and thought are closely related. Thoughts are produced when people internalize what they experience, and language is how they express or describe it. Language shapes the way thoughts are produced and stored. Language is a tool in thinking. The child who comes to the bazaar with her mother learns the language of bargaining better than one who is in a shopping cart in a grocery store. The Inuit of Canada developed language to describe the many kinds of water conditions, entailing a different vocabulary than that used to describe water conditions in tropical Puerto Rico. Language and thought are instruments people use to make sense of and interact with the world.[1]

A baby may not start life with language, yet always communicates. Crying, laughing, smiling, and wiggling are body language to express and transmit information. Some communication is nonsymbolic (gestures or pointing), and some is symbolic (words). A child progresses naturally from nonsymbolic communication (pointing at the window to mean "go outside") to symbolic communication, when the child says "out go" or "me go out." Spoken language is by far the most common form of symbolic language. The growing child learns to use meaningful language to communicate thoughts; thus language and thought are intertwined.

Language is also related to other areas of development. Children learn to offer an idea as well as a prop to get social play started. They use language in developing emotionally, as they learn to label, describe, question, and demand when they tell each other how they feel and what they want. Anyone who has heard a child talk himself down from a tree knows how language can be a great help in using physical skills. See Figure 11–8 for what research tells us about language development.

Stages of Language Development

Children follow a six-step sequence in language development. Except in cases of deafness or trauma, this sequence seems invariable regardless of what language is being learned:

1. *Infant's response to language.* Babies begin by attending to speech, changes in sound, rhythm, and intonation. These are the **precursors** of speech, and young infants are especially sensitive to some sound differences. Infants need to hear speech, and plenty of it, to develop the foundations of sound.

2. *Vocalization.* By three to four months of age, infants begin cooing and babbling. Babbling increases with age and seems to peak around nine to 12 months. This is a matter of physical maturation, not just experience; children who are deaf or hearing impaired do it at the same time as those whose hearing is normal. Furthermore, similar vocalization patterns are seen among different languages.

3. *Word development.* Children begin playing with sounds around 10 to 15 months of age. The child must first sep-

[1]Teachers must be aware of the children they teach and be alert for a diversity of language issues and skills, particularly in the area of bilingualism, speech or language disorders, and dialects (see later in this chapter).

LANGUAGE RESEARCH IN ACTION

Research says. . .	Which means. . .
The language of children is different from adult language.	• Children's language deals with the present. • Children's language is egocentric, taking into account only the child's own knowledge. • By preschool, children show awareness of language structure (for instance, "feets" to mark the plural form). Children under five tend not to know parts of speech.
Language is not learned simply by imitating adult speech.	• Child language is not garbled adult language. • A child's speech is unique to the age and linguistic level. • Children are not just trying to imitate others and making mistakes but are attempting to understand speech patterns. • The use of speech is not merely imitative but productive and creative.
Experiences help build language.	• Vocabulary is built on firsthand experiences. • The size of a child's vocabulary is strongly correlated with how much a child is talked to, cuddled, and interacted with. • At 20 months of age, children who have mothers who frequently talk to them average 131 more words than children of less talkative mothers.

Language experiences during preschool and kindergarten are reflected in later literary success.	• High-quality programs can reduce the degree of delay for high-risk children in communicative skills.
	• Personal interactions in a stimulating environment increase children's communication effectiveness.
	• Three dimensions of children's experiences that relate to later literary success are:
	  a. Exposure to varied vocabulary
	  b. Opportunities to be part of conversations that use extended discourse
	  c. Home and classroom environments that are cognitively and linguistically stimulating
	• Scores that the kindergartners achieved on the measures were highly predictive of their scores on reading comprehension and receptive vocabulary in fourth and in seventh grade.

Language development is a process of experience and maturation.	• Stages of language growth follow a specific sequence. • There are variations in the timing of the sequence.

FIGURE 11–8 Research into language development and expression reveals several interesting characteristics.

arate the noises heard into speech and nonspeech. The speech noises must be further separated into words and the sounds that form them. The end result is planned, controlled speech. From this point, the development of speech is determined as much by control of motor movements as by the ability to match sounds with objects. Most children can understand and respond to a number of words before they can produce any. Their first words include names of objects and events in their world (people, food, toys, animals). Then the child begins to overextend words, perhaps using "doggy" to refer to all animals. Finally, single words can be used as sentences: "Bye-bye" can refer to someone leaving, a meal the child thinks is finished, the child's going away, a door closing.

4. *Sentences.* Children's sentences usually begin with two words, describing an action ("Me go"), a possession ("My ball"), or a location ("Baby outside"). These sentences get expanded by adding adjectives ("My big ball"), changing the verb tense ("Me jumped down"), or using negatives ("No go outside"). Children learn grammar not by being taught the rules, but as they listen to others' speech and put together the regularities they hear. Child language, though not identical to that of adults, does draw on language heard to build a language base. Children incorporate and imitate what they hear to refine their own language structures.

5. **Elaboration.** Vocabulary begins to increase at an amazing rate. Sentences get longer, and communication begins to work into social interaction (see the introductory conversation to this section).

6. *Graphic representation.* By late preschool and kindergarten, reading and writing emerge as children become aware of language as an entity itself and of the written word as a way of documenting what is spoken. Awareness of print and emerging literacy are the outgrowth of this last stage of development.

In fact, alphabet knowledge and **phonemic awareness** are predictors of early reading success (Wasik, 2001). Children who learn to read well and most easily in first grade are those with prior knowledge of the alphabet and the under-

Graphic representation, in the form of learning sign language, is the final stage of language development.

standing of the sounds that letters represent. "Literate thinking" is the hallmark of this last early childhood stage in language development (Salyer, 2000) and is reflected in the early literacy movement in programs for children four to six years of age.

In her toddler program, Teacher Lisa teaches language by responding to Rishi in these ways:

Rishi	Lisa
"Wuh," holding out cup.	"You want more juice?"
"Muh wok"	"I don't know what you mean; show me."
"Aaaah!"	"Yes, it's hard to get on a jacket."
"Daddy cah"	"Your dad drove you to school in the car."
——, holding foot	"Shoes, are those new shoes, Rishi?"

Figure 11–9 has examples of the stages in language development.

Bilingualism

In early childhood terms, **bilingualism** (or multilingualism) is the ability of a person to speak in a language other than his or her native language with a degree of fluency. A bilingual child must learn to comprehend and produce aspects of each language and to develop two systems of communication. This is a "lengthy and complicated process of getting used to a new culture and a new language" before feeling comfortable enough to use it in a classroom" (Tabors, 1998).

Second-language learning occurs in two general ways. **Simultaneous acquisition** happens if a child is exposed to two lan-

STAGE	AGE (APPROX.)	SAMPLE
1. Response	Zero–six months	Smiles, gazes when hearing voices
2. Vocalization	Six–10 months	Babbles all types of sounds, creating babble-sentences Uses vocal signals other than crying to get help
3. Word Development	10–18 months	Mama, Dada, Doggie Bye-bye, No-no
4. Sentences	18 months–three years	Me want chok-quit (I want chocolate) She goed in the gark (She went in the dark)
5. Elaboration	Three to five or six years	You're my best Mommy, you can hold my turtle at bet-bis (breakfast) (Cough) That was just a sneeze in my mouth
6. Graphic Representation	Five plus to eight years	LAWRENCE BR. 12 13 H 516

FIGURE 11–9 Children's language skills develop with both age and experience.

guages from birth. These bilingual children tend to lag behind in vocabulary development in the early years, often mixing sounds or words. By four or five years, however, most children have separated the languages successfully.

The second pattern is known as **successive acquisition.** This occurs as a child with one language now enters the world of a second language, as when children with one home language enter a school that uses another language. A common pattern among immigrants and many children in the United States, this learning seems to favor younger children in their accent and grammar, but there is no evidence that younger children are any more successful with vocabulary and syntax.

Teachers and families need to understand bilingualism better, sorting myth from truth (Figure 11–10).

With more bilingual/bicultural children in early childhood classrooms, it helps to understand the developmental sequence of second-language acquisition:

1. Children may continue to speak their home language with both those who speak it and those who do not.

2. Children begin to understand that others do not understand their language and give up using it, substituting nonverbal behavior that may appear less mature.

3. Children begin to break out of the nonverbal period with a combination of telegraphic and formulaic language. One-word phrases such as "no, yes, mine, hey" all telegraph meaning, as do catch-words such as "okay, lookit, I dunno" that are used as formulas for communicating.

4. Productive use of the new language appears.

The process of learning a second language in childhood depends, in part, on the individual child. Cognitive, social, and linguistic skills are all at work in acquiring a second language. Moreover, the child's culture, unique temperament, and learning style play a part as well. For instance, Tjarko is of Swiss-German ancestry, so is it any wonder he pronounces an English "v" like an "f," as in "Can I haff one of those?" Sachiko, who has moved from Japan within the year, complains, "My neck hurts when I drink," and disagrees that it is a sore throat, since "neck" is the word she knows.

Adults often mistakenly assume that young children learn a new language quickly and easily and that the younger the child, the more quickly a second language is acquired. This is not necessarily the case. Children of linguistically and culturally diverse backgrounds "are caught in what I call the double-bind of second-language learning: To learn a new language, you have to be socially accepted by those who speak the language; but to be socially accepted, you have to be able to speak the new language" (Tabors, 1998). Lack of a mutual language can result in the child being treated as nearly invisible, or like a baby, by other children, or as less intelligent or able by teachers.

Also, children in an English-dominant classroom may isolate themselves from their families. They may refuse to use their home language anymore, as it is difficult to use both, and English may have greater sta-

GUIDELINES FOR SECOND-LANGUAGE LEARNERS

1. *Understand how children learn a second language.* There is a developmental sequence of second-language acquisition.

2. *Make a plan for the use of the two languages.* Try to have bilingual staff, or at least one teacher who specializes in each language.

3. *Accept individual differences.* Motivation to learn, exposure to the dominant language, the age of the child in relationship to the group, and temperament can all affect language acquisition. Don't insist that a child speak, but do invite and try to include the child in classroom activities. Maria Elena just will not come and sit at group time, so allow her to watch from a distance. Believe that she is learning, rather than be worried or irritated that she isn't with the group yet.

4. *Support children's attempts to communicate.* Encourage children's communication bids rather than correcting them. Recognize developmentally equivalent patterns: Kidah may not say the word "car" but can show it to you when you ask.

5. *Maintain an additive philosophy.* Recognize that children are acquiring more and new language skills, not simply replacing their primary linguistic skills. Asking Giau and his family about their words, foods, and customs allows teachers to use a style and content that are familiar to the Vietnamese, thus smoothing the transition and adding to an already rich base of knowledge.

6. *Provide a stimulating, active, and diverse environment.* Attention to classroom organization can help second-language-learning children.

7. *Use informal observations to guide the planning of activities.* Actively watching will help a teacher find special moments to help a child be accepted and join in. Seeing a group of girls building a zoo, a teacher gives a basket of wild animals to Midori. Walking with her to the block corner, she offers to stock the zoo and then helps all the girls make animal signs in Japanese and English.

8. *Find out about the family.* Establish ties between home and school. While making a home visit, Honwyma's teacher and his family talk together about how the Hopi language and culture can be brought into the classroom.

9. *Provide an accepting classroom climate.* Teachers must come to grips with their own cultural ethnocentricity and learn about the languages, dialects, and cultures beyond their own.

FIGURE 11–10 Teachers need guidance in teaching their second-language learners.

tus in the children's eyes. Families sometimes promote this, as they wish their children to learn English. However, if they themselves do not speak English, they become unable to communicate at length with their children. The lack of a mutual language then grows at home, creating problems of family cohesiveness and harmony.

Three aspects of classroom organization can help second-language-learning children:

1. Have a set routine for activities so that children can catch on and get into the flow of events.

2. Provide safe havens in the classroom so that children can spend some time away from communicatively demanding activities.

3. Make special use of story time. Increase the amount of time when you tell or read aloud stories, and remember that second-language learners are often willing to speak when they can use another identity (puppets, masks, costumes).

Moreover, it is crucial that family culture and language be respected and welcomed into the early childhood education setting. Teacher Venecia encourages her preschool families to keep their home culture and language alive by suggesting that they share family stories with their children and showing their children in specific ways their efforts to learn the new language. She sends a letter home in Spanish with a list for the parents: The children want to know how their parents met, how they lived in their home country, what they played as children, and who took care of them. She then asks the children to tell about this in circle time. She sends the catalogue of ESL (English as a Second Language) classes offered at the local adult school and offers a homework session every other Thursday at closing time, an extra half-hour in which the children play outdoors and she moves between the parents indoors and the playground. In addition, she has a regular children's bookbag program that sends easy-to-read picture books in English home for children and parents to read together.

Dialect Differences

Teachers may encounter differences in the way words are pronounced or grammar is used, even among English-speaking children. These differences reflect a **dialect**, or variation of speech patterns within a language. When we travel to New York, for example, our ear is attuned to the unique pronunciation of "goyl" (girl), and when we move north we hear "habah" (harbor). Southern speakers are easy to identify with elongated vowel sounds such as "Haiiiii, yaaw'll!" In addition to regional dialects, there are also social dialects that are shared by people of the same cultural group or social class. Each language and dialect is a legitimate system of speech rules that governs communication in that language. Some dialects, however, are not viewed favorably within the larger society and often carry a social or economic stigma. In the United States the dialect that has received the most attention and controversy is **Ebonics**, or black English. The name Ebonics is made up of the words *ebony* and *phonics*. "It has a West African base with English vocabulary superimposed on top," says Hoover (1997). "It's based on the grammar of West African languages." Elementary schools have traditionally grappled with the dual missions of doing everything within their power to help all students succeed and, at the same time, respect the cultural and linguistic backgrounds of everyone. Often cited in the argument is the concern for how nonstandard speakers will fare in our future high-tech society. Developmentally appropriate practices point to respecting and welcoming children's individual dialects while also addressing any linguistic differences that limit children. The National Head Start Association has spoken out against Ebonics, emphasizing that all children must be taught to use language in ways to increase their power, not to segregate. Then every child would have "language power" (R. R. Saxton, personal communication, July 1998), becoming a comfortable and capable speaker in any situation demanding either "standard" English or the language of his own "speech community."

Language Skills in Early Childhood

Language skills in the early childhood setting include articulation, receptive language, expressive language, graphic language, and enjoyment.

Articulation

Articulation is how children actually say the sounds and words. Children's ability to produce sound is a critical link in their connecting the sounds to form speech. Mispronunciation is common and normal, especially in children under five years of age. The preschool teacher can expect to hear "Thally" for Sally, "wope" for rope, and "buh-sketty" for spaghetti. Children who repeat sounds, syllables, or words in preschool are not stutterers; 85 percent of two- to six-year-olds hesitate and repeat talking. As children talk, teachers listen for their ability to hear and reproduce sounds in daily conversation. Can they hear and produce sounds that differ widely, such as "sit" and "blocks"? Can they produce sounds that differ in small ways, such as in "man" and "mat"?

How adults respond to dysfluencies can help a child through this normal stage of language development. Chesler (2002) suggests:

- ✪ Pay attention to the child when she talks to you. Don't rush her.

- ✪ Don't demand speech when a child is upset or feels stressed.

- ✪ Don't put children on exhibition by asking them to recite or talk when they don't want to.

- ✪ Avoid interrupting a child when she is talking; avoid completing a sentence for her.

- ✪ Statements like "slow down" or "think before you talk" draw attention to speech and usually cues the child that there is something wrong with the way he talks.

- ✪ Do make an example of your speech by talking slowly, smoothly, and distinctly.

Receptive Language

Receptive language is what children acquire when they learn to listen and understand. It is what they hear. With this skill children are able to understand directions, to answer a question, and to follow a sequence of events. They develop some mental pictures as they listen.

Children begin early and can become experts in reacting to words, voice, emphasis, and inflection. How many times does the child understand by the way the words are spoken?

"You finally finished your lunch." (Hooray for you!)

"You finally finished your lunch?" (You slowpoke.)

Children learn to listen for enjoyment, for the way the wind sounds in the trees, the rhythm of storytelling, or the sound of the car as it brings a parent home. Figure 11–11 has strategies to develop receptive language.

Expressive Language

Expressive language in the early years includes words, grammar, and elaboration.

Words. Expressive language is the spoken word. Children's first words are of what is most important to them (ma-ma, da-da). Adults help children extend their knowledge and vocabulary by using the names of objects and words of action (walk, run, jump) and feelings (happy, sad, mad). By describing objects in greater and greater detail, teachers give children new words that increase their skills. Children are then ready to learn that some words have more than one meaning (the word "orange," for example, is both a color and a fruit) and that different words can have the same meaning (such as "ship" and "boat" as similar objects, or *muñeca* and "doll" as the same word in different languages).

STRATEGIES TO DEVELOP RECEPTIVE LANGUAGE

1. *Give clear directions.* "Please go and sit on the rug next to the chairs," instead of "Go sit over there."

2. *Let children ask questions.* Give them acceptable answers. For example, repeat a phrase from the child's last sentence that asks the child to try again: "You want what?" or "You ate what?" Or cast the question back to a child by changing the phrase "Where did you put it?" into "You put it where?"

3. *Give instructions in a sequence.* "Put your lunch on your desk, then wash your hands. Then you are ready to go to lunch." It often helps to ask the children what they think they are to do: "How do you get ready for lunch? What comes first? Next?"

4. *Try to understand what the child means, regardless of the actual language.* Look for the purpose and intent beyond what the child may have said. This is particularly important with toddlers, non-English speakers, and newcomers.

5. *Ask children to state their thoughts out loud.* "Tell me what you think is going to happen to the eggs in the incubator. Why do you think some might hatch and some might not?"

6. *Use literature, poetry, and your own descriptions.* Give children an idea of how words can be used to paint verbal and mental pictures. Ask questions about children's own images and dreams. To older children read aloud from books without pictures.

FIGURE 11–11 Receptive language can be developed by using six strategies.

Grammar. Basic grammatical structure is learned as children generalize what they hear. They listen to adult speech patterns and use these patterns to organize their own language. It helps to hear simple sentences at a young age, with the words in the correct order. Next, children can grasp past tense as well as present, plural nouns along with the singular. Finally, the use of more complex structures is understood (prepositions, comparatives, various conjugations of verbs).

Elaboration of Language. Elaboration of language takes many, many forms. It is the act of expanding the language. Through description, narration, explanation, and communication, adults elaborate their own speech to encourage children to do the same:

 Verbalize a process aloud, showing how language helps work through a problem. "I am trying to get the plant out of its pot, but when I turn it upside-down, it doesn't fall out by itself. Now I'll use this trowel to loosen the dirt from the sides of the pot, and hope that helps."

 Give and follow directions. "It's time to make a choice for cleanup time. You find something to do and I'll watch you."

 Ask and answer questions. "How do you feel when she says she won't play with you? You say you can't do it; what can I say that will help?"

✿ *Stick to the subject to keep communication flowing.* "I know you want to play kickball, but first let's solve this problem between you and Conor about the wagon."

✿ *Use speech to get involved in play yourself.* "What a great house you have built. How do you get inside? Do you need any dishes?"

Graphic Language

"Talk written down" is the essence of graphic language. The child now learns that there is a way to record, copy, and send to another person one's thoughts. Learning to put language into a symbolic form is the gist of the reading and writing process. Children learn about print when they are read to regularly, when they see adults reading and writing, and when they are surrounded with a print-rich environment. Because words and letters are simply "lines and dots and scribbles" to young children, the teacher and parent must demonstrate how meaningful graphic language can be. The translation of talk into print is a cognitive task (see previous section about symbols), so children's intellectual development is at work when learning about the printed word. The process involved in helping children learn graphic language includes these steps:

1. Young children begin the process of literacy development before they enter elementary school.

2. Reading and writing develop concurrently and in an interrelated manner.

3. Literacy develops in everyday activities.

4. Children learn about literacy through interaction with their world.

Literacy emerges as part of the total communication process that includes listening, speaking, reading, and writing. Children's emergent reading skills follow stages, which can overlap each other (Early Childhood Resources, 1995):

Video View Point 11-2

"**Support for Emerging Literacy:** Although it appears that children learn to listen and speak long before they read and write, the foundations for learning to read and write start in infancy as children then expand to both spoken and written language, to books and other reading materials."

Competency: Communication Development

Age Group: Preschool

Critical Thinking Questions:

1. **What written materials and reading was done in your home? How has that affected your attitude about reading or writing?**

2. **What early writing experiences can be provided in a preschool?**

✿ Stage one: Children learn that print is a form of language. They find that books are filled with magic, messages, and mystery (prereading).

✿ Stage two: Children hear stories, poems, chants, and songs many times. They rehearse by chanting, singing, resaying, and "reading along" as we read to them (prereading).

✿ Stage three: Children learn to recognize words. They read and know the text, and they use some phonics to discover which words say what (beginning reading).

✿ Stage four: Children are readers. Now the task is to make them better readers (reading).

Ashton-Warner (1986) describes one technique for introducing printed language to young children. A kindergarten teacher who believed strongly in children's innate creativity and curiosity, Ashton-Warner developed a system of "organic reading" in which the students themselves build a key vocabulary of words they wish to learn to read and write. This method was effective for her classes of native Maori children in New Zealand, for whom the British basal readers held little meaning. Ashton-Warner's personal, culturally relevant teaching works well because it flows naturally from the child's own life and interests.

Enjoyment

To encourage language is to promote enjoyment in using it. Teachers converse with children, parents, and other adults, modeling for children how useful and fun language can be. Knowing the power and pleasures of language gives children the motivation for the harder work of learning to read and write. Creating readers can be a enjoyable process for children if teachers:

- surround themselves with books and other reading materials.
- set up inviting library learning centers.
- establish regular visits to the local library.
- encourage children to share favorite books.
- take time for conversations (Curry-Rodd, 1999).[1]

Children learn to enjoy language by participating in group discussion and being encouraged to ask questions. Listening to stories and poems every day is an essential part of any program, as well as stories children dictate or write themselves. Figure 11–12 offers ideas for early literacy.

There are many ways to know the power and pleasure of language.

[1]Children's literature provides a window and a mirror to our diverse world.

EARLY LITERACY COMES TO THE CLASSROOM

- Have a cozy library corner, giving children lots of time to explore and read all kinds of books.
- Make a writing corner with different kinds of supplies, using this area to develop grouptime activities (children's stories), meaningful themes (post office), and connected learning (writing and sending letters).
- Take field trips, pointing out print as they find it (street signs, store shelves, bumper stickers) and writing about it afterward.
- Use large charts for poems, fingerplays, and songs as well as for listing choices available and for group dictation.
- Plan activities that incorporate print: read recipes for cooking projects, make menus for lunch and snack, follow directions in using a new manipulative toy, write sales tickets for dramatic play units, bring books into science displays.
- Use written notes regularly, sending a regular newspaper home that the children have written or dictated, writing notes to other team teachers that children deliver, encouraging children to send notes to each other.

FIGURE 11–12 Early literacy activities integrate graphic language activities in a natural, meaningful way.

 ## THE DEVELOPMENT OF EMOTIONS AND EMOTIONAL GROWTH

Emotional Growth

The first thing one notices on entering an early childhood classroom is the children—who is playing or watching, whether there is crying or fighting, and how happy or sad the children look. This overview gives an immediate sense of the affective climate in that early childhood setting. Toddler Abier giggles as she runs her hands across the water table, then cries after she splashes soap suds in her eyes and needs to be comforted. Three-year-old Jared is upset with his teacher's refusal to let him go outdoors during story time. "I hate you!" he screams, "and you aren't the boss of me!" Talbot feels rejected and sad when no one greets him as he enters the kindergarten playhouse. He mistakes the children's busyness as an act of exclusion.

Building a self-image helps young children to affirm their identity in positive ways.

Affirming Identity

As children experience messages from others and through their own perceptions, they construct an understanding of race, ethnicity, gender, and ability. This will shape their self-image and, by extension, their relationships to others. Closely related to the child's **self-concept** and **self-esteem**, affective growth takes place in the context of personal identity. "Identity is tied to culture. In the critical early years, children begin to develop a sense of self as families hand down beliefs, attitudes, and behaviors" (Nakahata, 2001). It is primarily through affective experiences that children learn who they are; only then can they see themselves successfully in relation to others.[1]

Building self-image is complex, multidimensional, and ever-changing. It affects everything we do and is affected by everything we do. Crucial to children's self-image is how children interpret the response of the environment to their actions. And much of a self-image is based on the way society views the child. Teachers play an important role as they provide an essential ingredient of self-image: the quality of human interactions.

Curry and Johnson (1990) have identified several key experiences for children in the early years to have in order to develop and consolidate a sense of self. For very young children (zero to two years), the development of the self is embedded in the context of relationships. Thus attachment and affective development occur as children learn to regulate themselves with others and interact with them. As toddlers become aware of themselves, they also develop a curiosity (and opinions) about others.[2]

For preschool children, then, the next step is the testing and evaluating of oneself. They will press authority, while still being very attached to adults and their positive regard for them. They will test their limits in pretend play, and will stretch themselves as they begin to make friends. It becomes important to preschoolers' budding sense of self that they are powerful, in control, good people, and competent.

Being an effective and successful person extends into kindergarten and primary school. "Kindness and hostility go hand in hand as children exercise their growing abilities to understand and affect the feelings of others" (Curry & Johnson, 1990). At the same time, school-age children are looking at themselves in terms of moral worth, wrestling with good/nice and bad/mean.

Self-esteem

To the extent that children feel worthy and capable, they are ready to succeed. If children disapprove of themselves, they may feel like failures and expect to do poorly. There appear to be four components of self-esteem:

1. A sense of one's own identity
2. A sense of belonging (connectedness)
3. A sense of one's uniqueness
4. A sense of self (power)

[1]"As children are forming their identity and self-worth, they often struggle with conflicting messages from home, media, school, and peers about who they are and what they are worth" (Nakahata, 2001). Caregivers help children grow by first attending to their home cultures and languages as they develop curriculum.

[2]One of the things that research shows is that African-American children are highly people-oriented (Burgess, 1993). There tends to be an "object orientation" in European-Americans and a "people orientation" in African-Americans. Such awareness helps teachers to interact with children in ways that coincide with their cultural orientation and to understand individual children's challenges with social interaction.

Early in life, self-esteem is tied to family, friends, and other important people, such as teachers. Planning for children's success builds self-esteem. It includes the following four components, which we call the "Four I's":

- ✸ *I.* When children enter the classroom, the message they receive is "I am important and this is my place." The physical environment, the daily schedule, and the curriculum are designed to give all children permission to express themselves.

- ✸ *Initiative.* Children are encouraged to initiate their own learning, to make contact with others, to take action, and to make choices.

- ✸ *Independence.* Self-management tasks of dressing, eating, and toileting are given an important place in the curriculum. Children are assisted in taking care of their own belongings and in developing independent judgment about events and activities.

- ✸ *Interaction.* Social interaction has a high priority in the program. The room and yard are busy places, with children moving about and talking among themselves and with adults. Conflicts are accepted as a natural consequence of social life. Being in groups can encourage children to interact and foster a consciousness of interdependence.

Teachers Marty and Cathy apply these Four I's consistently in their preschool program. "You look ready to play, Deirdre," says Marty. "We have the play dough out again. I remember you and Dominique liked it. Is she here yet?" Chris and Clemens rush in, making a beeline for the Legos. Cathy is already there; she knows Chris's mom is a working parent and doesn't have time to spend in the classroom, so she moves to the boys, saying, "Mom's off to work, and I thought you two could make something we'll photograph for her to see."

A positive sense of self is critical for young children. Research (Atkinson & Hornby, 2002) shows that low self-image is correlated with poor mental health, poor academic achievement, and delinquency. In contrast, a positive self-concept is correlated with good mental health, academic achievement, and good behavior. Children with a positive self-image are ready to meet life's challenges. They will have the self-confidence to deal with the reality of emotions, the changing nature of social interaction, and the joys of creativity and spirituality.

Emotions are the feelings a person has—joy and sorrow, love and hate, confidence and fear, loneliness and belonging, anger and contentment, frustration and satisfaction. They are responses to events, people, and circumstances. Feelings are an outgrowth of what a person perceives is happening. Emotionally healthy people learn to give expression to their feelings in appropriate ways. They do not allow their feelings to overshadow the rest of their behavior. The optimal time to learn these skills is in the early years.

Emotional Intelligence

Goleman's (1995) work on emotional intelligence incorporates brain research and multiple intelligences theory (see Chapter 4). As he sees it,

> The emotional brain scans everything happening to us from moment to moment to see if something that happened in the past that made us sad or angry is like what is happening now. If so, [it] calls an alarm—to declare an emergency and to mobilize in a split second to act. And it can do so, in brain time, more rapidly than the thinking brain takes to figure out what is going on, which is why people can get into a rage and do something very inappropriate that they wished

they hadn't. It's called an "emotional hijacking."

Young children experience this constantly, and need our help to develop emotional intelligence. For example, infants respond with agitated emotion whether wet, hungry, hurt, or bored. Gradually, the expression of the emotion becomes more refined and varies with the situation. A toddler's cry of distress is different from the cry of discomfort or hunger. As children get older, their emotional expressions change as they gain control over some of their feelings and learn new ways to express them.

Strong external forces are also at work. Parents, family members, teachers, and friends are social influences, helping the young child learn socially acceptable behavior (Figure 11–13). Much of what children learn is by example (see Chapter 4 on modeling). Therefore, children learn

more from adult models than from simply being told how to behave and feel.

Emotional Skills in Early Childhood

Research shows that some emotions—interest, disgust, distress, to name a few—are observable in the newborn, and it is likely that all the basic emotions are present within the first few weeks of life. These include happiness, interest, surprise, fear, anger, sadness, and disgust. The more complex emotions of shame, guilt, envy, and pride emerge later, once children have had the social experiences of observing these emotions in others or have been in situations that might evoke such feelings. These expressions have been observed in a wide range of cultural and ethnic groups.[1]

INSIGHT INTO EMOTIONS

- What causes children in the class to become excited? frightened? calm? loud? How can it help me handle an unplanned event or change in the schedule?
- How do I anticipate children's emotional behavior? How do I follow through?
- What can I do to handle children's emotional outbursts and crises?
- What happens to the rest of the class when one teacher is occupied in an emotional incident with one or more children?
- What do I do when a child shows emotion? How do I feel when a child displays emotion?
- What types of emotions are most common with the young child?
- What do I do when a child expresses emotions I am uncomfortable with?
- Do I run to the rescue too often, overreacting and encouraging "learned helplessness"? Or do I ignore children's distress?

FIGURE 11–13 Asking reflective questions helps teachers gain insight into their own part in the emotional climate of their program.

[1]Because a child's self-image begins with where she belongs—family, community, culture—it is critical that early childhood education programs support a child's home environment—culture, race, language, lifestyle, and values (Wardle, 1993). One is reminded of the universal qualities to be found in each of us in our diverse world. The challenge is to notice and celebrate our similarities and our differences—both are gifts.

As mentioned in Chapter 10, the major skills in early childhood are the ability to deal with feelings, to handle change, to exercise judgment, and to enjoy oneself and one's power.

Ability to Deal with Feelings

Dealing with feelings involves four steps. Each builds on the other so that they follow a developmental sequence; the learning that takes place at one level affects the development of what follows.

To Notice and Label Feelings. As caring adults recognize the cries of hunger, hurt, and fear, they name these feelings. The child can learn to notice what the feeling is and recognize it. Teachers know how to "read" children's faces and body language to give them the words for and ways to express those feelings. Preschoolers are quite verbal and curious about language and ready to learn words that describe a wider range of feelings. They can learn "lonely," "scared," "silly," "sad," and "happy." Labeling what one feels inside is a critical skill to learn. It is a healthy first-grader who can say, "I have tried to cut this string three times and the scissors aren't working. I am frustrated. I need some help!"

To Accept Feelings. Children are capable of strong feelings and can feel overwhelmed by the very strength and intensity of any one of them. By learning to accept feelings, children learn how to handle their depths and not be overpowered by them. And feelings change; it is a comfort to discover that the strong emotion they experience now will pass. Notice how this teacher helps work through strong feelings:

Carlos feels sad as his mother prepares to leave. His teacher walks them to the door, then bends down and puts an arm around him as his mother waves good-bye. Acknowledging that he is sad, the teacher stays with Carlos, reminding him that his mother will return and that the teacher will take care of him while he is at school. Because the child is allowed to feel the sadness that is natural in leave-taking, the tense feelings are over in a few minutes. The teacher smiles and encourages Carlos to find something fun to do. Once he has recovered his composure, the teacher points out that he's "okay now," and Carlos feels proud for having lived through and grown from saying good-bye.

To Express Feelings in an Appropriate Way. Expressing feelings appropriately is a two-part process. First, children must feel free to express their feelings; second, they must learn ways of expression that are suitable to their age and to the situation. Many beginning teachers are uncomfortable because children express themselves so strongly (and often aggressively). Yet the child who is passive and unable to express feelings freely should be of equal concern and should be encouraged in self-expression.

When teachers create a safe emotional climate, they can effectively help children learn to understand and express themselves. Knowing how to handle upsetting feelings or impulses is the root of emotional intelligence. "I can see you are upset about Joaquin taking the toy you had," you might say. "But I can't let you hit him—and I won't let him hit you, either." Figure 11–14 shows how teachers help manage children's anger.

Children acquire the modes of expression that are developmentally appropriate for their age. Babies and toddlers without language cry to express their feelings. Two-year-olds express their displeasure by

THE TEACHER'S ROLE IN CHILDREN'S ANGER MANAGEMENT

1. Create a safe emotional climate . . . by having clear, firm, and flexible boundaries.

2. Model responsible anger management . . . by acknowledging when you are upset.

3. Help children develop self-regulatory skills . . . by giving children age- and skill-appropriate responsibilities and encouraging problem-solving with support.

4. Encourage children to label feelings of anger . . . start with "mad" and expand to include "upset, annoyed, irritated, furious, steamed," etc.

5. Encourage children to talk about anger-arousing interactions . . . by talking about situations when they aren't happening. "I felt mad when . . ." can start a lively conversation; cards with realistic scenarios can do the same, as can puppets.

6. Use appropriate books and stories about anger to help children understand and manage anger.

7. Communicate with parents. . . . Introduce the books or puppets, let them borrow them overnight. Tell them what you do in your program, and ask what they do.

FIGURE 11–14 When children come to grips with their strong feelings, their emotional growth is encouraged. (Categories from Marion, 1997.)

pushes and shoves; four-year-olds use their verbal power and argue. By six or seven, children can learn to tell others—clearly and with reasons—what they are feeling. The ability to express feelings is intact, but the methods of expression change as children grow. Expression of feelings also has a cultural dimension. Some cultures are open in their display of emotions, whereas others are reserved.[1]

To Deal with the Feelings of Others.

Dealing with the feelings of others is the culminating step in the development of emotional skills. Children who can distinguish among different emotions may be better able to see emotions in others. Thus, empathy can happen at a young age. Toddlers may cry or gather near the teacher when a playmate is hurt or sad; preschoolers smile at another's laughter; and kindergartners imagine themselves vividly in another's predicament during a story. Empathy is affected by early experience and needs nurturing to grow. Helping children to tolerate and appreciate how different people express their emotions leads to understanding and cooperation.

Ability to Handle Change

Isn't it remarkable that as one of the most adaptable species on the planet, we humans resist change so much? Even as our brains are programmed to find pattern and sameness, it is change that is inevitable.

The very act of being born is a change, marking the beginning of a life in which stress is part of the act of developmental achievement. Witness the toddler's numerous falls toward walking, the separation of parent and child at the nursery-school doorway, the concentration and frustrations of the seven-year-old on roller blades. A measure of positive stress encourages a child to strive and achieve, to find out and discover.

Dealing with stress and coping with new information are part of the ability to handle change.

Stress. Stress can arise from several factors, both internal (severe colic) and external (moving to a new home). Some stresses are acute in a child's life, such as a hospitalization, whereas others are chronic, such as living in an alcoholic household. Many variables are associated with different kinds of stress in children's lives. For instance, age, intellectual capacity, and gender can influence a child's response to a stressful situation; research seems to indicate that male children are more vulnerable than female children. Inadequate housing, poverty, and war are ecological stressors. Family changes—the birth of a sibling, death or loss of a close family member, marriage problems and divorce—are sources of stress on a personal level.[2]

Inept parenting practices that neglect or abuse children are especially troublesome, as they hurt children and provide them with poor role models for learning how to cope with stress.

[1]Being encouraged to act out every emotion is not appropriate, for instance, for African-American children. "Living under oppressive conditions mandates learning . . . where to express feelings and who it is safe to let know your feelings," says Cooper (2004). "Their reluctance to engage should be respected, not viewed as a challenge."

[2]Simply living in American society is stressful for many children. For instance, the Native American child lives in "a conflict of cultures. She must 'make it' in the white world to survive, and she must recognize her Indian heritage to affirm her own identity. A teacher must accept the total child and help her function effectively in both worlds" (Reese, 1996).

Coping Skills. The capacity to cope effectively with adversity and bounce back is a combination of the individual's personality and behavior, family attributes, and the social environment. Resilient children have hope and self-esteem. Both of these are under the influence of the teacher and curriculum. Helping children find a haven and creative interests also help develop a protective buffer against difficulties in school or home. Perhaps the single most important intervention is you, the teacher, who is a confidant or a positive role model. Figure 11–15 lists the stages of stress and how to help children manage it.

STAGE	BEHAVIOR	THE TEACHER HELPS
Alarm	Arousal and fear Confusion Swift mood changes	Notices when child is stressed (sees changes in behavior). Listens. Offers words for child's feelings. Offers age-appropriate explanations. Is accepting of unpredictable behavior. Reassures child of teacher's constant availability. Alerts parents and others of child's state. Takes preventive actions to lessen other stressful events.
Appraisal	Attempts to understand the problem	Listens. Offers age-appropriate explanations. Helps child see situation more positively. May make a simple list of the problem. Reassures that the problem *will* be solved. Alerts other adults to the importance of the child's work.
Search	Looks for coping strategy Selects from what is at hand	Listens. Asks for the child's ideas. Helps child list possible solutions. Tells parents and others of child's solutions. Demonstrates self-control and coping skills her/himself. Encourages and enhances child's self-esteem.
Implementation	Tries out a coping strategy Applies a solution to the problem	Listens. Observes child's implementing a solution. Gives supportive feedback about relative success or failure of the plan. Helps child refine or revise strategy as needed. Encourages child's efforts.

FIGURE 11–15 Stages of and strategies for coping with stress: The teacher is observant of the child throughout, makes regular time to talk individually, and encourages the child to use art, books, and class members as supports.

Teachers can help children accept change in several ways. Anticipating changes that are likely to occur and identifying the process for children are very important. "Junko, your mother will be leaving soon. We'll go looking for that favorite puzzle after you say good-bye to her." If the daily routine is altered, children should be notified. "We won't be having snacks inside today; let's use the patio table instead." When children are informed that change is anticipated, accepted, and not necessarily disrupting, they become more relaxed about handling the unpredictable.

Ability to Exercise Judgment

The ability to exercise judgment is an important skill, for it helps children to make decisions and figure out what to do in new situations. On entering school, a child faces many decisions: Where shall I play? Whom shall I play with? What if my friend wants to do something I know is wrong? Whom will I turn to for help when I need it? Judgment is selecting what to do, when to do it, with whom to do it, and when to stop.

Making choices is an essential part of decision making. Children are bombarded with choices in America—too many choices, some people say. Some children must decide about issues that in other times only adults handled. But children "have difficulty discriminating between big choices and little choices. Every choice is a big one for most children" (Simon, 1994). Learning to make good choices takes thought, guidance, and lots of practice.

There is no easy way to teach children how to make decisions because each situation must be dealt with on an individual basis. The judgment a child exercises in choosing a friend to play with today may have other factors to consider tomorrow. Instead, teachers help children base their decisions on the best judgment they are capable of in each instance. One way to encourage decision making is to provide opportunities for choice.

The teacher can encourage this process by serving as a Vygotsky-like mediator, making children participants in their own learning (thinking), and by supporting children's focus on self-competence (emotional).

Enjoying One's Self and One's Power

Teachers want children to feel powerful—to know that they can master their lives and feel confident in their own abilities. This feeling of power is particularly important in the early years, when so much of what a child can see is out of reach, both literally and figuratively.

Responsibility and limits, however, go hand in hand with power. The child who is strong enough to hit someone has to learn not to use that strength unnecessarily. The child who shouts with glee also finds out that noise is unacceptable indoors. By holding children responsible for their own actions, teachers can help children enjoy their power and accept its limitations.

One kind of fantasy play most teachers encounter is that of the **superhero.** Common to children as young as two, superhero play is exciting, rowdy, usually active and loud play-acting of heroic roles that give children powers they lack in everyday life. It is the embodiment of control and strength, even wisdom, and the parts to be played are clear for everyone involved. Children's natural struggles for mastery and the attraction of rough-and-tumble play collide with teachers' concerns about fighting, aggression, and letting the play get out of hand. Figure 11–16 offers suggestions for managing superhero play.

In addition, teachers and parents are rightfully concerned with children's aggression and with their exposure to war and violence, both from the media and at home. **Roughhousing** and aggression have distinctly different patterns of behavior and should be recognized as such. Children need guidance to learn how to express themselves appropriately and exercise their growing powers responsibly.

SUPERHERO PLAY

- Help children recognize humane characteristics of superheroes.
- Discuss real heroes and heroines.
- Talk about the pretend world of acting.
- Limit the place and time for superhero play.
- Explore related concepts.
- Help children de-escalate rough-and-tumble play.
- Make it clear that aggression is unacceptable.
- Give children control over their lives.
- Praise children's attempts at mastery.

FIGURE 11-16 Kostelnik et al. (1986) offer suggestions for managing this special type of dramatic play.

Teachers can help children learn to appreciate and enjoy themselves. Each time a child is acknowledged, a teacher fosters that sense of uniqueness: "Carrie, you have a great sense of humor!" "Freddie, I love the way you sing so clearly." Saying it aloud reinforces in children the feeling that they are enjoyable to themselves and to others.

SOCIAL GROWTH AND DEVELOPMENT

Preschooler Danny wants his favorite red wagon, so Pat, the student teacher, helps him negotiate a turn with Christa. Five-year-old Karena is having trouble letting her best friend Luther play with anyone else; she cannot understand that Luther can be her friend and Dana's at the same time. The toddlers at the water table keep splashing even though one is crying and a teacher is coming close. Every moment of every day, social development happens!

Social Growth

Social development is the process through which children learn what behavior is acceptable and expected. A set of standards is imposed on the child at birth that reflects the values of the family and the society in which the child lives. Young children are influenced from birth by a deliberate attempt on the part of adults to guide them in ways that society expects. Parents attempt to transmit behavior patterns that are characteristic of their culture, religion, gender, educational, and ethnic backgrounds.[1] Children imitate what they see; they adapt social expectations to their own personality. The family, caregivers, teachers, peers, and the community all contribute to children's social world and to the values and attitudes that are developed.[2]

[1]As you gather cultural information, be careful not to stereotype. "Cultural information only provides clues, not concrete data, about particular people; and so, even though you have information about a specific culture or ethnic group, it won't necessarily apply to all the people in that group" (Kendall, 1996).

[2]To feel they belong, children need to have their culture and some of their family rituals and traditions incorporated into their program. For instance, "the rituals of mealtimes, the greetings and good-byes, are all distinctly Hispanic. . . . Ask children how to acknowledge persons who come to the door, especially older persons. Children should always greet each other's parents and each other" (Barrera in Garcia & Baker, 1995).

"Cooperation, generosity, loyalty, and honesty are not inborn. They must be passed on to the child by older people, whether they are parents, other adults, or older youngsters" (Bronfenbrenner in Kostelnik et al., 2006). There are cultural variations in how people relate to each other, what feelings are to be expressed, how and who to touch, and how to respond to personal events. It is critical for programs to inquire about family culture, language, and priorities for each child.

Socialization

The process of social development is called socialization and includes learning appropriate behavior in different settings. Children learn very early to discriminate between the expectations in different environments. At school, free exploration of play materials is encouraged, but in a church pew it is not. Children's understanding of others is critical for their social growth. Showing awareness of what other people feel, infants pay special attention to adults' facial and emotional expressions. Toddlers can ascertain whether someone is happy, sad, or angry and can try to comfort someone in distress. Three-year-olds know that if someone gets what he wants, he will be happy, and if not, he will be sad. During this time of their lives, children work out a separate set of relationships with adults other than their parents. They also establish different relationships with adults than they do with other children, and, most important, they learn to interact with other children. Children also learn social attitudes at an early age. Through socialization, the customary roles that boys and girls play are transmitted. Children come to understand how teachers, mommies, daddies, grandparents, males, and females are expected to act.[1] They learn to enjoy being with people and participating in social activities.

Young children are active social learners, discovering firsthand what happens when they try something.

[1]Early childhood professionals need to be aware of the difference between a child's developing a gender identity and a child's sex role development. One needs to be able to communicate the difference to parents and to be aware of how different cultures may have differing notions about sex role development.

Bias

At the same time, young children can also develop attitudes of bias, and it is in these early years that prejudicial behavior often begins. Promptly responding to negative comments, unfair acts, or exclusivity based on race, gender, or ability is crucial in combating this kind of socialization. A program's emotional climate and teacher's behavior contribute not only to children's sense of personal safety and belonging but also to the development of a sense of community. Favorable attitudes toward people and a strong desire to be part of the social world are established in the early years.

Social Competence

Social competence involves the skills and personal knowledge children develop to deal with the challenges and opportunities they face in life with others. Socially competent children are happier than their less competent peers. Children's social relations have been linked to academic achievement. Lack of social competence has been linked to rejection by peers, poor self-esteem, and poor academic performance. "Indeed, the single best childhood predictor of adult adaptation is not IQ nor school grades, but rather the adequacy with which a child gets along with others" (Hartup, 1992). The components of social competence are:

- ✿ *Emotional regulation.* The ability to regulate emotions
- ✿ *Social knowledge and understanding.* Knowledge of enough language and norms to interact successfully; understanding others' reactions and their feelings (empathy)
- ✿ *Social skills.* Social approach patterns, attention to others, exchange of information, handling aggression
- ✿ *Social dispositions.* Habits or characteristic ways of responding to experiences.

The elements of social competence are illustrated in Figure 11–17.

All areas of children's development play a part in learning social skills:

- ✿ Having the confidence to try joining a group calls on emotional skills.
- ✿ Remembering children's names or how a game works is a cognitive task.
- ✿ "Using your words" to express an idea or feeling requires language.
- ✿ Being able to play chase or to walk in high heels for a dress-up game requires certain physical dexterity.

Social Cognition

Social cognition is the application of thinking to personal and social behavior; it is giving meaning to social experience. Notice the thinking that is going on in these situations:

- ✿ Nadia wants to play with Paul, a very popular four-year-old. She remembers Paul's interest in the rope swing, so she dares him to swing higher than she can. Paul pulls himself away from his buddies, turning toward her for the challenge.
- ✿ Everyone knows that "Bruno can't share." Sandy wants to play with the fire truck he is using. She decides to offer him the ambulance, another of his favorites. He makes the trade and she has what she wants.

Social cognition requires children to interpret events and make decisions, to consider the impact of their behavior on others, and to consider the cause as well as the consequence of an action.

Building on Gardner's social intelligence and Goleman's emotional intelligence, teachers can help children handle their emotions **(self-regulation)** and learn to "read" other people's feelings by their body language or tone of voice (empathy), then lead children to gain social skills. In the

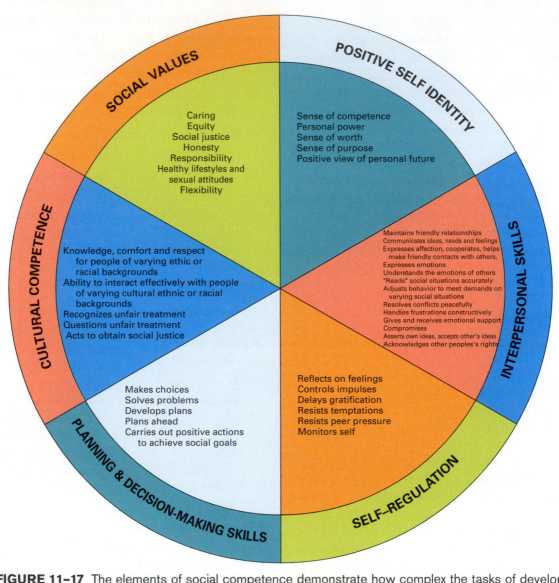

FIGURE 11–17 The elements of social competence demonstrate how complex the tasks of developing socially are for young children. (Courtesy of Kostelnik et al., 2006.)

early years, children mature socially in discernible developmental stages. From birth to age three, children's interest in others begins with a mutual gazing and social smile in the early months (birth through eight months), continues with an exploration of others as well as some anxious behavior around strangers in the crawler and walker stages (eight to 18 months), and develops into an enjoyment of peers and adults along with an awareness of others' rights and feelings as a toddler and two-year-old (18 months to three years).

In the preschool years, children learn to control their aggressive impulses, think about others besides themselves, and resist doing what they shouldn't. This learning translates into four basic expectations. They will:

1. Show interest in others
2. Learn right from wrong
3. Learn to get along with others
4. Learn a role for themselves that takes into consideration their own unique self—gender, race, ethnicity, and abilities.

Children of the primary years (five to eight years) show an increased interest in peers and social competence, and group rules become important. The development of a social conscience and of fairness rounds out the primary-grade developmental milestones. Figure 11–18 shows a social development timetable.

Children learn social skills in several predictable ways:

✪ *The brain is wired to look for patterns.* When an infant smiles and is met with a smile, a pattern of responsiveness and attachment is begun. The preschooler who grabs for toys and usually gets to keep them at home will be surprised

SOCIAL DEVELOPMENT TIMELINE

Infant-Toddler	Preschooler	Primary Child
Response to Other's Distress		
Reacts emotionally by experiencing what the other seems to feel	Begins to make adjustments that reflect the realization that the other person is different and separate from self	Takes other's personality into account and shows concern for other's general condition
Peer Interaction		
• First encounters mutual inspection • First social contacts • (18 months) growth in sensitivity to peer play • (Two years) able to direct social acts to two children at once (beginning of social interaction)	• Adjustment in behavior to fit age and behavior of other • (More than three years) friendship as momentary • (Three to five years) beginning of friendship as constant	• Friend as someone who will do what you want • Beginning of friend as one who embodies admirable, constant characteristics
Social Roles		
• (10–20 days) imitation of adults • (Three months) gurgle in response to others • (Six months) social games based on imitation • (18 months) differentiation between reality and pretend play • (Two years) make doll do something as if it were alive	• (Three years) make a doll carry out several roles or activities • (Four to five years) act out a social role in dramatic play and integrate that role with others (mom and baby)	• (Six years) integrate one role with two complementary roles: doctor, nurse, and sick person • (Eight years) growing understanding that roles can influence behavior (doctor whose daughter is a patient)

FIGURE 11–18 A timetable of social development of the ages of infancy through the primary years. (Special thanks to Gay Spitz.)

(and unhappy) when the pattern is broken at the center and the toy is returned to the one who was using it. Then, a new pattern of asking or trading can begin.

✪ *Children form ideas about how the social world works from their direct experiences.* They are active learners, asserted Piaget and others, who will observe and experiment, learning firsthand what happens when they try something. In-the-moment, on-the-spot lessons will greatly help children learn socially. Sarda wants to play in the block corner, but stands hesitantly as four boys shout and vroom the cars around. "Do you want to play here?" inquires the observant teacher. When she nods, the teacher helps her move in and the two begin building. Soon, the boys notice and come to see a garage being built, so they drive their cars over. The teacher slowly steps aside. Sarda has experienced one way to get started.

✪ *Children have multiple ways of learning.* Because teachers often do not know each child's ways of learning, it is best to try a variety of approaches when teaching social skills. Talking helps some (linguistic), others learn better by seeing patterns (logical-mathematical), and many learn by your model. Rehearsing how to do or say the words helps the bodily-kinesthetic learner.

✪ *Children learn much of their social repertoire through play.* Dramatizations, role playing, and dramatic play provide opportunities to act out many roles and help children deal with some of the demands placed on them. In play, the child experiments with options: finding out what it feels like to behave in ways that might otherwise be unacceptable. Carla was the oldest of three children and had many "big girl" expectations placed on her within the family setting. In child care, Carla enjoyed being the baby, acting out a helpless infant role whenever she could. Under the guise of play, children rehearse for life without suffering the real-life consequences.

Children experience a range of social difficulties (see Chapters 3 and 7). Toddlers develop many forms of testing behavior, including saying no to adult rules and other restraints. Grabbing, biting, and hitting are common forms of aggression and self-expression. Some of this occurs in preschoolers, as do other forms of self-determination. There are problems children encounter when responding to emotions, both theirs and those of others. In primary school, peer status and friendship loom large, where loneliness, exclusion, teasing, and bullying all occur.

The social challenge of peer relationships includes the steady movement away from the **egocentric** position of self (and parents) as central points toward a more **sociocentric** viewpoint that involves others—both adults and, especially, children. During the early years, the child learns to socialize outside the family; social contacts outside the home reinforce the enjoyment of social activities and prepare the child for future group activity.

Through peer interactions, children can identify with models who are like themselves and can learn from each other's behavior. Friends provide models for imitation, for comparison, and for confirmation of themselves, and they are a source of support.

Playing with other children begins with solitary parallel play at around two years of age, in which two or more children are in the same area with each other but do not initiate social interaction. By the ages of three and four, more interaction takes place: There are conversation and conflict as well as cooperation in playing together (see Chapter 10 on how to help children make friends). There are stages in children's friendships:

- **Undifferentiated.** A friend is of the moment, who is next to you.
- **Unilateral.** A friend does what you want.
- **Reciprocal.** A friend engages in give-and-take and in two-way cooperation.

Children move through these stages in observable ways. First, they become more sensitive to their play partners. Second, they begin to use language more effectively in their interactions. Finally, cooperative play increases as parallel play decreases. Children pass through three stages of social understanding in the early years: (1) they shift from a preoccupation with self to an awareness of the thoughts and feelings of another; (2) they shift from the observable, physical qualities of the play partner to an awareness of their friend's less obvious characteristics; and (3) they begin to perceive the friendship as long-lasting. Listen to these four-year-old children working on their friendship:

> Chris: I'll be the teacher; you be the kid.
>
> Suzanne: NO! I want to be the teacher, too.
>
> Chris: No! No! You can't be the teacher, too, 'cause then there'd be no kids.
>
> Suzanne: Okay. Next time, I get to be the teacher.
>
> Chris: Maybe! Okay, everybody go wash your hands for snack time. Suzanne, you can pass out your very nutritious snack to everybody.
>
> Suzanne: Superfasmic, I'm the boss of snack.

Video View Point 11-3

"Peer Acceptance: Popularity and rejection are part of the social experience."

Competency: Social Development

Age Group: School Age

Critical Thinking Questions:

1. What was your social status in elementary school? How has that affected you as a person, and as a teacher?
2. How can a teacher help children acquire social competence?

A peer group is important for a number of reasons. Social development is enhanced because a child learns to conform to established social standards outside of his home setting. The expectations of the larger society are reinforced. To become autonomous, the child must also learn to achieve independence from the family, especially parents. Young children must also come to understand themselves as part of society. Their self-concepts are enlarged by a group of peers as they see how others respond to them and treat them.[1]

Social Skills in Early Childhood

Social skills are strategies children learn that enable them to behave appropriately in many environments. They help children learn to initiate or manage social interaction in a variety of settings and with a

[1]Developing friendships is more than teaching general interpersonal skills and is especially important for children with special needs (Lowenthal, 1996). Facilitating friendship development in inclusive classrooms requires teacher awareness and interaction as well as careful environmental and schedule planning.

number of people. Adults work throughout the early years to teach the "Four Hows":

1. *How to approach.* Getting and being included

2. *How to interact.* Sharing and cooperating

3. *How to deal with difference.* Including others, helping, and teasing

4. *How to manage conflict.* Handling aggression and problem solving

There is a skill set learned in every kind of interaction.

Skills Learned with Adults

In their relationships with adults, children learn:

Peer relationships are a source of pleasure and support. As social understanding develops, children shift from a preoccupation with themselves to an awareness of the thoughts and feelings of others.

- They can stay at school without parents.

- They can enjoy adults other than parents and respond to new adults.

- Adults will help in times of trouble or need.

- Adults will help them learn social protocol.

- Adults will keep children from being hurt and from hurting others.

- Adults will help children learn about ethnic differences and similarities, disabilities, gender identity, and language diversity.

- Adults will resist bias and stereotyping and teach children to actively do the same.

- Adults will not always take a side or solve the problem.

- Adults will work with them to solve problems.

- Adults believe that every child has a right to a satisfying social group experience.

Skills Learned with Peers

In their relationships with other children, children learn:

- Different approaches to others, some of which work, others of which don't

- Interactive skills, and how to sustain a relationship

- How to solve conflicts in ways other than retreat or force

- How to share materials, equipment, other children, friends, teachers, and ideas

- How to achieve mutually satisfying play

- Self-defense, and how to assert their rights in socially acceptable ways

- How to take turns and communicate desires

- Negotiating skills

- ✴ How to be helpful to peers with tasks and information or by modeling behavior
- ✴ To anticipate and avoid problems
- ✴ Realistic expectations of how other children behave and respond toward them
- ✴ Ways to deal with socially awkward and/or difficult situations
- ✴ How to make, be, share, and lose a friend

Skills Learned in a Group

In groups, children learn:

- ✴ How to take part as a member and not as an individual
- ✴ That there are activities that promote group association (stories, music)
- ✴ A group identity (Jackie's house, Ms. T's group, the homework club)
- ✴ To follow a daily schedule and pattern
- ✴ To adapt to school routines
- ✴ School rules and expectations
- ✴ Interaction and participatory skills; how to enter and exit from play
- ✴ To respect the rights, feelings, and property of others
- ✴ To become socially active, especially in the face of unfair behavior and situations
- ✴ How to work together as a group (during cleanup time, on a field trip, at story time)
- ✴ How to delay gratification; how to wait

Skills Learned as an Individual

As individuals, children learn:

- ✴ To take responsibility for self-help and self-care
- ✴ To initiate their own activities and to make choices
- ✴ To work alone close to other children

- ✴ To notice unfairness and injustice and learn how to handle them
- ✴ To negotiate
- ✴ To cope with rejection, hurt feelings, disappointment
- ✴ To communicate in verbal and nonverbal ways; when to talk and listen
- ✴ To test limits other people set
- ✴ Their own personal style of peer interaction; degree, intensity, frequency, quality
- ✴ To express strong feelings in socially acceptable ways
- ✴ To manage social freedom

Specific skills within these four areas include the social and moral aspects of nurturance, kindness, and sharing. As children get older, these skills become more specific: telling the truth, taking turns, keeping promises, respecting others' rights, having tolerance, and following rules. In an antibias curriculum (see Chapter 9), children can learn how to take **social action** to make unfair things fair. Discovering that their adhesive strips are labeled "flesh-colored" but match the skin of only a few children, the class takes photos and sends them to the company (Derman-Sparks, 1989).

THE DEVELOPMENT OF CREATIVITY

It's OK to try something you don't know.

It's OK to make mistakes.

It's OK to take your time.

It's OK to find your own pace.

It's OK to bungle—so next time you are free to succeed.

It's OK to risk looking foolish.

It's OK to be original and different.

It's OK to wait until you are ready.

It's OK to experiment (safely).

It's OK to question "shoulds."

It is special to be you. You are unique.

It is necessary to make a mess (which you need to be willing to clean up!).

"Permissions," by Christina Lopez-Morgan (2002)

Traditionally, early childhood educators have concerned themselves with children's creative expression, knowing that in the early years the foundations must be laid for children to understand themselves and others:

- ✳ Kindergartners Fabio, Erika, and Benjy work steadily to build a tall, intricate block structure. When it is finished, the three children stand back and marvel at their creation.

- ✳ Two-year-old Andrea, whose physical skills do not yet include balancing objects, plays with blocks by piling them on top of one another, filling her wagon, and lugging them from place to place, each step her own creation.

- ✳ The family child care group makes a daily trek to the henhouse as soon as outside time begins. They first gasp as they discover a raccoon has pried open the wire and killed their pet. Ellie speaks up, "I want to make a picture for Henny-Penny to take with her." The group paints a multicolored mural, for which each child dictates ideas. "I am sad you died," says Ellie. "But don't worry, you will rise again!" A child's spiritual notions are allowed to express themselves in creative ways.

Creative Growth

Creativity is the ability to have new ideas, to be original and imaginative, and to make new adaptations on old ideas. Inventors, composers, and designers are creative people, as are those who paint and dance, write speeches, or create curriculum for children.[1] Thinking in a different way and changing a way of learning or seeing something are both creative acts.

Creativity is a process; as such, it is hard to define. As one becomes involved in creative activity, the process and the product merge.

> It is probably best to think of creativity as a continual process for which the best preparation is creativity itself. . . . There is real joy in discovery—which not only is its own reward, but provides the urge for continuing exploration and discovery (Lowenfeld & Brittain, 1975).

Creativity engages certain parts of the brain. The left hemisphere controls the right side of the body and such operations as concrete thinking, systematic planning, and language and mathematical skills—what we might call the more rational and cognitive parts of thinking. It is the right hemisphere of the brain that engages in more spontaneous ideas and thinks in nonverbal, intuitive ways. The right side is the creative information processor that helps us engage in divergent thinking ("thinking outside the box").

Infants' creativity is seen in their efforts to touch and move. Toddlers begin to scribble, build, and move for the pure

[1]Introduce children to a diverse range of creative adults—men and women from a variety of cultural backgrounds. When we become too concerned with molding children to "fit," we miss the fact that accepting and developing the differences among children enhances creativity.

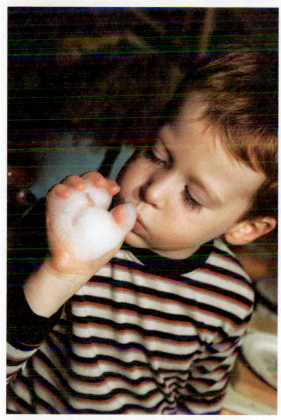

Creative people seem to be sensitive to the world around them, using their senses to experience the world deeply.

physical sensation of movement. Young preschoolers create as they try for more control, such as scribbling with purpose or bobbing and jumping to music. Older preschoolers enjoy their budding mastery. Their drawings take on some basic forms, and they repeat movements deliberately while making a dance. With advanced motor control and hand–eye coordination, school-age children do drawings that are more representational and pictorial, and their dramatic play is more cohesive. Figure 11–19 describes the stages of children's art as they use their creative imaginations.

Creative Skills in Early Childhood

There are characteristics common to creative people. For the teacher interested in fostering creative growth in children, there are special skills they should help children learn.

Of special note is the Reggio Emilia approach, emphasizing children's creative and cognitive expressions (see Chapter 10). They have a special teacher (an *atelierista*, or "workshop specialist," from the French root word *atelier*, meaning workshop or studio) who operates an art studio within the school. The studio is stocked with art materials, and children work alongside this teacher. Most programs will not have a special studio, but the idea of bringing in those with developed talent in all areas is advisable.

Flexibility and Fluency

Flexibility and fluency are dual skills that allow for creative responses. Flexibility is the capacity to shift from one idea to another; fluency is the ability to produce many ideas. "How many ways can you move from one side of the room to another?" is a question likely to produce many different ideas, one example of fluency. Children who must think of another way to share the wagons when taking turns doesn't work learn flexibility.[1]

When Howard Gardner began his studies of intelligence (see Chapter 4), he became intrigued with artistic capacity. Project Zero was the implementation of this interest. A program to study intelligence, the arts, and education for the past 30 years, the project has helped identify some key ideas about art education:

1. In the early childhood years, production of art ought to be central. Chil-

STAGES OF CHILDREN'S ART

Rhoda Kellogg (1969) described the developmental stages of art after having analyzed millions of pieces of children's art from around the world over a 20-year period. Briefly, they are:

- *Placement stage.* Scribble, ages two-three
- *Shape stage.* Vague shapes, ages two-four; actual shapes, ages three-five
- *Design stage.* Combined shapes, ages three-five; mandalas and suns, ages three-five
- *Pictorial stage.* People, ages four-five; beginning recognizable art, ages four-six; later recognizable art, ages five-seven

1. Scribbling:

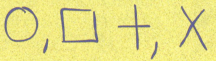

2. Drawing a single shape:

3. Combining single shapes into designs:

4. Drawing mandalas, mandaloids, and sun figures:

5. Drawing a human figure with limbs and torso:

FIGURE 11–19 Children's art follows a sequence of stages. (Courtesy of Robert Schirrmacher, 2006.)

dren need to work directly with the materials.

2. The visual arts ought to be introduced by someone who can think visually or spatially. An early childhood education team ought to be diverse enough to have someone with this intelligence on board.

3. Whenever possible, artistic learning should be organized around meaningful projects. Both the project approach and emergent curriculum address this (see Chapter 10).

4. Artistic learning must entail emotional reflection and personal discovery along with a set of skills. Integration of development is encouraged.

Taken together, these observations help teachers create developmentally appropriate art activities. If you work with infants or toddlers, be sure to help children explore materials and places with all their senses, and expect scribbling by 15 to 20 months. Young preschoolers will work in manipulating tools and materials, discovering what can be done and needing lots of repetition. Do not expect much concern about the final product. By four to six years, children's art becomes more symbolic and planned; more detailed work with forms and shapes may be seen. Children become interested in what they are doing and how it turns out.

Sensitivity

Being creative involves a high degree of sensitivity to one's self and one's mental images. Creative people, from an early age, seem to be aware of the world around them; how things smell, feel, and taste. They are sensitive to mood, texture, and how they feel about someone or something. Creative people notice details; how a

pine cone is attached to the branch is a detail the creative person does not overlook.

A special aspect of this skill is sensitivity to beauty. Also known as **aesthetics,** this sensitivity to what is beautiful is emphasized in some programs (such as Reggio Emilia) and some cultures (such as *tokonoma,* an alcove dedicated to display in Japanese homes).[1] 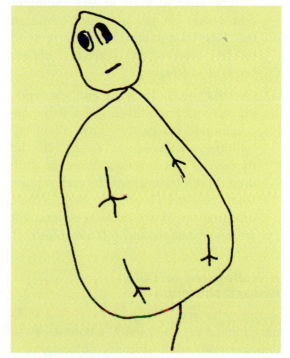 Children have an awareness of the value of their natural environment and what is aesthetically pleasing.

Creative children take delight and satisfaction in making images come to life. Their creative response is in the way they paint a picture, dance with streamers, or find a solution to a problem. Figure 11–20

FIGURE 11–20 Sensitivity to one's own mental images, such as perceiving direction and movement, are part of creativity in the young child. A five-and-a-half-year-old sketched how a pet rat looked from below after picking it up often and watching it run on its exercise wheel.

[1]Teachers can ask the families of children in their care about special places, objects, and rituals that celebrate beauty and help children acquire an aesthetic interest in their environment.

shows how a five-and-a-half-year-old's sensitivity to perspective and detail comes out through a drawing.

Use of Imagination/Originality

Imagination is a natural part of the creative process. Children use their imagination to develop their creativity in several ways:

✹ *Role playing.* In taking on another role, children combine their knowledge of the real world with their internal images. The child becomes a new character, and that role comes to life.

✹ *Image making.* When children create a rainbow with a spraying garden hose or with paints, they are adding something of their own to their understanding of that visual image. In dance, children use their imagination as they pretend to be objects or feelings, images brought to life.

✹ *Constructing.* In building and constructing activities, children seem to be re-creating an image they have about tall buildings, garages, or farms. In the process of construction, however, children do not intend that the end product resemble the building itself. Their imagination allows them to experiment with size, shape, and relationships.

A Willingness to Take Risks/Elaboration

People who are willing to break the ordinary mental set and push the boundaries in defining and using ordinary objects, materials, and ideas are creative people. They take risks. Being open to thinking differently or seeing things differently is essential to creativity. Figure 11–21 shows one group's creation at Reggio Emilia.

When children create, they are revealing themselves. Art, for instance is a form of cultural communication, one of the basic language skills children need to participate in a multicultural democracy. Increasing

FIGURE 11–21 Creativity is the ability to be original and imaginative, to soar above the commonplace. (Courtesy of the city of Reggio Emilia, Italy.)

opportunities for creative expression allows for nonverbal response and success without directions. It encourages children (and families) to share themselves in enjoyable ways. It is, therefore, a good way to teach about cultures and learn about each other in a relaxed, accepting atmosphere.

Self-esteem is a factor in risk taking because people who are tied to what others think of them are more likely to conform rather than follow their own intuitive and creative impulses. People usually do not like to make mistakes or be ridiculed; therefore, they avoid taking risks.

A teacher concerned about creative growth in children realizes that it will surface if allowed and encouraged. When a child is relaxed and not anxious about being judged by others, creativity will more likely be expressed. With support, children can be encouraged to risk themselves.

Using Self as a Resource

Creative people who are aware of themselves and confident in their abilities draw on their own perceptions, questions, and feelings. They know that they are their own richest source of inspiration. Those who excel in creative productivity have a great deal of respect for themselves and they use the self as a resource.

The process of making a creation follows a predictable four-step pattern, although there are many variations on the theme:

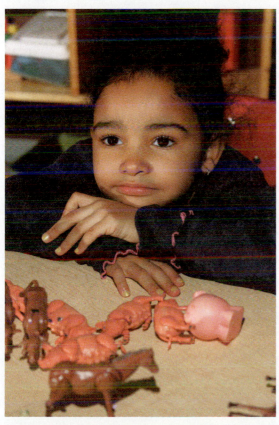

The process of creating art often includes an incubation step that sometimes creates a "spaced out" look.

1. *Preparation.* Gathering materials and ideas to begin
2. *Incubation.* Letting ideas "cook" and develop
3. *Illumination.* The "a-ha" moment when everything gels; the "light bulb"
4. *Verification.* When exhilaration has passed and only time will confirm the effort (Nabors & Edwards, 1994)

Experience

Children need experience to gain skills in using materials creatively. They must learn how to hold a paintbrush before they can paint a picture; once they know how to paint, they can be creative in what they paint. Teachers of young children sometimes overlook the fact that children need competence with the tools to be creative with them. A little sensitive, individual demonstration on the proper use of a watercolor brush, sandpaper, or ink roller can expand a child's ability to create and eliminate needless frustration and disappointment. The teachers of Reggio Emilia demonstrate how to use the tools so that the children can then make outstanding creations; teachers and older children scaffold learning for young children. Anecdotes from highly accomplished people in creative endeavors (pianists, mathematicians, Olympic swimmers) highlight the value of long-term systematic instruction in a sort of apprenticeship with inspiring teachers as well as parents who are committed to assist. When the skill of the medium is mastered, the child is ready to create. Figure 11–22 shows the stages of musical development and the many ways children are aided in their creative experience.[1,2]

 [1]Sharing music and dance from home is an ideal way to incorporate children's individual cultures into the classroom. Translate a simple song into another language; teach the children the song, working in the language that is "home base" for most of the children, then re-teach it. Words and phrases made familiar by melody are remembered and made valuable.
[2]Improvised music and lyrics can sustain sociodramatic play between children with developmental delays and their nondelayed peers (Gunsberg, 1988).

STAGE OF MUSICAL DEVELOPMENT	APPROPRIATE MUSIC/ MOVEMENT ACTIVITY
Two-year-olds	
Use their bodies in response to music	Bounce to music with different tempos
Can learn short, simple songs	Repetitive songs like "Itsy-Bitsy Spider" or "If You're Happy and You Know It"
Enjoy experimenting with sounds	Pound on milk cartons, oatmeal boxes
	Make shakers with gravel in shampoo bottles
Three-year-olds	
Can recognize and sing parts of tunes	Select songs that include their names, such as "Do You Know the Muffin Man?"
Walk, run, jump to music	Use Ella Jenkins recordings, or try "Going on a Bear Hunt"
Make up their own songs	Start "Old MacDonald" and let them make their own additions; dance with scarves or use shakers to sing along with a child.
Four-year-olds	
Can grasp basic musical concepts like tempo, volume, pitch	Be a flying car, trees swaying in the wind; sing "Big, Bigger, Biggest" with variations
Love silly songs	Change "Where Is Thumbkin" to "Where is Fi-fo" and improvise with their ideas
Prefer "active" listening	Accompany music with instruments; "Green Grass Grew All Around" with action
Five- and six-year-olds	
Enjoy singing and moving with a group	Use a parachute to music
Enjoy call-and-response songs	Try "Did You Feed My Cow?"
Have fairly established musical preferences	Be sure to ask the group and use them in selecting music activities.
Seven- and eight-year-olds	
Are learning to read lyrics	Use large word charts
Enjoy musical duets with friends	Do partner games
	Children pick instruments in pairs

FIGURE 11–22 Creative experiences in music and movement engage the whole child and offer children integrated experiences throughout the curriculum. (Adapted from Schirrmacher, 2006.)

Teachers affect the creative process for children in several distinct ways:

- 💠 By how they set up the environment
- 💠 By the choices and kinds of activities they provide
- 💠 By the types of interactions they have with the children during creative activities (Lopez-Morgan, 2002)

Chapter 10 elaborates on how curriculum and the teacher can encourage creativity.

KEY TERMS

aesthetics
bilingualism
continuum
dialect
divergent thinking
dynamic consequences
Ebonics
egocentric
elaboration
extrinsic
flexibility
fluency
inference
intelligence
intrinsic
logical-mathematical knowledge
meaningful knowledge
phonemic awareness
physical knowledge
precursors
receptive
reciprocal
rote knowledge
roughhousing
scaffolding
self-concept
self-esteem
self-regulation
sensory awareness
seriation
simultaneous acquisition

social action
social cognition
social knowledge
social skills
sociocentric
spatial awareness
special needs
stress
successive acquisition
superhero
temporal awareness
transcurricular
undifferentiated
unilateral

Teaching Applications

1. Map the classroom in which you are currently working. List at least one activity in each area that develops physical motor skills. Add one more activity of your own that widens such development.

2. In what ways does a school program you know reinforce sex role stereotyping in motor activities? What could be done to change this?

3. Try to develop the theme of "at the beach" or "camping" in your setting in such a way that physical/motor skills are used. Be sure to include gross motor, fine motor, and perceptual motor activities. List at least six other themes around which you could build a similar curriculum.

4. Make a list of the classroom areas. Beside each, name one activity that would foster cognitive development.

5. Look at the list of cognitive skills and trace how they are developed in each time period of your daily schedule.

6. One theme often used in early childhood education programs is that of the changing season in the fall. How can that theme develop thinking skills in preschoolers?

7. Observe the children in your care. Identify the stages of language development of three children. Give concrete examples that validate your assessment.

8. Choose a child in your care whose primary language is not English. How is that child processing language? What are you doing to foster the child's emerging English skills? How is that child's first language being supported in your program? What can you do to involve the family?

9. Teaching reading readiness involves trying to develop oral language and listening skills. What could a teacher of toddlers plan for each? a kindergarten teacher?

10. How does your center promote positive self-concept? What else could be done?

11. Make behavioral definitions of emotions you think you will see in the children you teach. Observe the children, then check the accuracy of your definitions.

12. Observe a group of four-year-olds at play. How do they decide what roles each one takes? Are they clear in their expectations of what sex roles are appropriate for boys and girls? Is there sex role stereotyping?

13. Taking turns and sharing equipment and materials are difficult for young children. Cite three examples you have seen where children used their social skills to negotiate a turn. Was teacher intervention necessary?

14. Name five people you consider creative. Match their skills with those we have identified in early childhood. Where are they similar? different?

15. Give three examples of children in your center trying to "break the mental set." In what area of the classroom did it occur? What were the adults' responses?

16. How do teachers in your setting plan for creativity? What place does such expression take in the priority of the school philosophy?

REFERENCES

Allen, K. E., & Marotz, L. R. (2003) *Development profiles: Pre-birth through twelve* (4th ed.). Clifton Park, NY: Thomson Delmar Learning.

Ashton-Warner, S. (1986) *Teacher* (5th ed.). New York: Touchstone Books.

Atkinson, M., and Hornby, G. (2002) *Mental health handbook for schools.* New York: Routledge Falmer.

Bee, H. (1997). *The developing child.* Menlo Park, CA: Addison-Wesley.

Berk, L. E. (2002). *Child development.* Boston: Allyn & Bacon.

Burgess, B. (1993). *Kids count: African American children.* Baltimore, MD: Annie E. Casey Foundation.

Chesler, P. (2002). *Bilingualism: Literacy development and activities for the young child.* Unpublished, De Anza College, Cupertino, CA.

Cooper, E. (Ed). (2004). *Teaching all the children.* New York: The Guilford Press.

Curry, N. E., & Johnson, C. N. (1990). *Beyond self-esteem: Developing a genuine sense of human value.* Washington, DC: National Association for the Education of Young Children..

Curry-Rodd, L. (1999, September/October). Creating readers. *Child Care Information Exchange,* 129.

Derman-Sparks, L. (1989). *The anti-bias curriculum.* Washington, DC: National Association for the Education of Young Children.

Early Childhood Resources. (1995). *Implementing developmentally appropriate practice: Kindergarten through third grade.* Corte Madera, CA: Author.

Galinsky, E. (1997, Winter). New research on the brain development of young children. *CAEYC Connections.*

Gallahue, D. L. (1996). *Developmental physical education for today's children.* Madison, WI: Brown and Benchmark.

Garcia, O., and Baker, C. (Eds.). (1995). *Policy and practice in bilingual education.* Bristol, PA:WBC Limited.

Geist, E. (2001, 4 July). Children are born mathematicians: Promoting the construction of early mathematical concepts in children under five. *Young Children,* 56.

Goleman, D. (1995). *Emotional intelligence.* New York: Bantam Books.

Gunsberg, A. (1988). Improvised musical play. *Journal of Music Therapy, 28*(3).

Hartup, W. W. (1992). *Having friends, making friends and keeping friends: Relationships as educational contexts.* ERIC Digest. Urbana, IL: ERIC Clearinghouse on Elementary and Early Childhood Education.

Hoerr, T. (2004) MI: A way for all students to succeed. In Gordon, A. M., & Williams Browne, K. (2004). *Beginnings and beyond* (6th ed). Clifton Park, NY: Thomson Delmar Learning.

Hoover, M. (1997, March/April). Ebonics insider. *Stanford Magazine.*

Kellogg, R. (1969). *Analyzing children's art.* Palo Alto, CA: Mayfield Publishing.

Kendall, F. (1996). *Diversity in the classroom.* New York: Teachers College Press.

Kostelnik, M., Whiren, A. P., & Stein, L. G. (1986, May). Living with He-Man: Managing superhero fantasy play. *Young Children, 41.*

Kostelnik, M. J., Stein, L. C., Whiren, A. P., & Soderman, A. K. (2006). *Guiding children's social development* (5th ed.). Clifton Park, NY: Thomson Delmar Learning.

Kranowitz, C. S. (1992). Obstacle courses are for every body. In B. Neugebauer (Ed.), *Alike and different: Exploring our humanity with young children.* Washington, DC: National Association for the Education of Young Children.

Lopez-Morgan, C. (2002). *Creative arts for the young child.* Cupertino, CA: De Anza College.

Lowenfeld, V., & Brittain, W. L. (1975). *Creative and mental growth.* New York: Macmillan.

Lowenthal, B. (1996, Spring). Teaching social skills to preschoolers with special needs. *Childhood Education.*

Marion, M. (1997, November). Research in review: Guiding young children's understanding and management of anger. *Young Children, 52.*

Moran, M. J., & Jarvis, J. (2001, September 5). Helping young children develop higher order thinking. *Young Children, 56.*

Nabors, M. L., & Edwards, L. C. (1994, Fall) Creativity and the child's social development. *Dimensions in Early Childhood.*

Nakahata, A. (2001, Fall). Identity is tied to culture. Interview by Marion Hironaka. *Cowee in Connections: California AEYC Newsletter.*

Nelson, K. (1995, July/August). Nurturing kids: Seven ways of being smart. *Instructor.*

New City School Faculty. (1995). *Multiple intelligences: Teaching for success.* St. Louis: The New City School.

Reese, D. (1996, May). Teaching young children about Native Americans. Chicago, IL: Clearinghouse on Early Education and Parenting (EDO-PS-963).

Salyer, D. M. (2000, July). "I disagree!" said a second-grader: Butterflies, conflict, and literate thinking. *Young Children, 55.*

Schiller, Pam. (2001, July). Brain research and its implications for early childhood programs. *Child Care Information Exchange, 140.*

Schirrmacher, R. (2006). *Art and creative development for young children* (4th ed). Clifton Park, NY: Thomson Delmar Learning.

Shore, R. (1997). *Rethinking the brain: New insights into early development.* New York: Families and Work Institute.

Siegel, D. L. (1999, November). Relationships and the developing mind. *Child Care Information Exchange* (130).

Simon, T. (1994, September). Helping children make choices. *The Creative Classroom.*

Sylwester, R (1995). *A celebration of neurons: An educator's guide to the human brain.* Alexandria, VA: Association for Supervision and Curriculum Development.

Tabors, P. O. (1998, November). What early childhood educators need to know: Developing effective programs for linguistically and culturally diverse children and families. *Young Children, 53.*

Wardle, F. (1993, March). How young children build images of themselves. *Exchange.*

Wasik, Barbara A. (2001, January). Teaching the alphabet to young children. *Young Children, 56.*

Additional resources for this chapter can be found by visiting the Online Companion™ at www.earlychilded.delmar.com. This supplemental material includes a Study Guide with chapter review questions (and answers), critical thinking questions and activities, and annotated Web sites.

Glossary

A

Accommodation. A concept in Piaget's cognitive theory as one of two processes people use to learn and incorporate new information.

Accountability. The quality or state of being answerable to someone or of being responsible for explaining exact conditions; schools often must give specific account of their actions to a funding agency to assure the group that the funds and operation of the school are being handled properly.

Accreditation. A system of voluntary evaluation for early childhood centers. The goal is to improve the quality of care and education provided for young children. Accreditation is administered by the National Academy, a branch of the National Association for the Education of Young Children.

Active Listening. A child guidance technique of reflecting back to the speaker what the listener thinks has been said.

Active Problem Solving. A principle in which adults actively engage children in confronting their differences and working together to solve their problems. The adult guides children toward solutions but does not solve problems for them. Posing open-ended questions, the adult helps children keep focused so that they can suggest alternative solutions.

Activity Centers. Similar to learning centers and interest areas; areas in a classroom or yard that are designed and arranged for various activities to take place. An early childhood setting will offer several centers, or stations, that are based on both children's interests and what the staff hopes for them to learn in class.

ADHD. A medical condition also known as attention-deficit hyperactivity disorder. It affects up to 3% to 5% of all school-age children. Children with ADHD can be difficult to manage, both at home and in the classroom. They are prone to restlessness, anxiety, short attention spans, and impulsiveness. Medication with a drug (Ritalin®) is a common treatment, but the most effective treatment appears to be a combination of medication and individual behavior management strategies.

Aesthetics. Sensitivity to what is beautiful; the study of beauty.

Age-Level Characteristics. Those features of children's development and behavior that are most common among a given age group.

Anti-bias. A phrase describing the development of curriculum that emphasizes an inclusive look at people and problems, extending the tenets of multicultural education and pluralism.

Assessment. An evaluation or determination of the importance, disposition, or state of something or someone, such as in evaluating a child's skills, a classroom environment, or a teacher's effectiveness.

Assimilation. A concept in Piaget's cognitive theory as one of two processes people use to learn and incorporate new information; the person takes new information and puts it together with what is already known in order to "assimilate" the new information intellectually, such as when a toddler shakes a toy magnet first, as with all other toys, in order to get to know this new object. Children usually first try to put new experiences into the "schema," or categories, they already know and use.

Atelierista. A person trained in the arts who acts as a resource and teaches techniques and skills to children in the schools of Reggio Emilia, Italy.

Attachment/Attachment Behaviors. The relational bond that connects a child to another important person; feelings and behaviors of devotion or positive connection.

Attitude Crystallization. To assume a definite, concrete form in one's attitudes; refers to the formation of a firm set of attitudes and behaviors about others' race, ethnicity, gender, and ability that may be prejudicial and difficult to change.

Authoritarian Parents. Parents whose child-rearing patterns reflect high control and strict maturity demands combined with relatively low communication and nurturance. Authoritarian parents are dictatorial; they expect and demand obedience, yet lack warmth and affection.

Authoritative Parents. Parents whose child-rearing patterns are associated with the highest levels of self-esteem, self-reliance, independence, and curiosity in children. They provide a warm, loving atmosphere with clear limits and high expectations.

Autonomy. The state of being able to exist and operate independently, of being self-sufficient rather than dependent on others.

B

Baby Biographies. One of the first methods of child study, these narratives were written accounts by parents of what their babies did and said, usually in the form of a diary or log.

Bias. A personal and sometimes unreasoned judgment inherent in all our perceptions.

Bicognitive Development. A term coined by Ramirez and Casteneda (see Chapter 4) to describe a set of experiences and environments that promote children's ability to use more than one mode of thinking or linguistic system. Each of us grows up with a preferred cognitive style, such as global or analytic, field dependent or field independent, seeing the parts vs. seeing the whole, as well as a linguistic style. For true cultural democracy to take place, we need to develop a flexibility to switch learning styles or cognitive modes (i.e., develop bicognitive abilities) and have an awareness of and respect for differing cognitive styles.

Bilingual Education. Varied and difficult to assess, it is a system of teaching and learning in which children who speak limited English are taught in English-speaking classrooms.

Bilingualism. The acquisition of two languages during the first years of life; using or being able to use two languages.

C

Checklist. A modified child study technique that uses a list of items for comparison, such as a "yes/no" checklist for the demonstration of a task.

Child Abuse. Violence in the form of physical maltreatment, abusive language, and sexual harassment or misuse of children.

Child Care Center. A place for care of children for a large portion of their waking day; includes basic caretaking activities of eating, dressing, resting, toileting, as well as playing and learning time.

Child-Centered Approach. The manner of establishing educational experiences that takes into consideration children's ways of perceiving and learning; manner of organizing a classroom, schedule, and teaching methods with an eye toward the child's viewpoint.

Child Neglect. The act or situation of parents' or other adults' inattention to a child's basic health needs of adequate food, clothing, shelter, and health care; child neglect may also include not noticing a child or not paying enough attention in general.

Children with Special Needs. Children whose development and/or behavior require help or intervention beyond the scope of the ordinary classroom or adult interactions.

Classist. A biased or discriminating attitude based on distinctions made between social or economic classes.

Code of Ethics. A code of ethics is a set of statements that helps an educator deal with the temptations inherent in that occupation. It helps her or him act in terms of what is right rather than what is expedient.

Compensatory Education. Education designed to supply what is thought to be lacking or missing in children's experiences or ordinary environments.

Competency-Based Assessment. Evaluation in which a teacher is judged or rated in comparison with a predetermined set of skills, or competencies, related to the job.

Comprehensive. Inclusive, covering completely, such as a program for children that concerns itself with the physical, intellectual, social, emotional, creative, and health needs of the children.

Confidentiality. Spoken, written, or acted on in strict privacy, such as keeping the names of children or schools in confidence when discussing observations.

Conflict Resolution. Helping children solve disagreements nonviolently and explore alternative ways to reach their goals. By following such a process, children learn to respect others' opinions, to express their own feelings in appropriate ways, and to learn tolerance for doing things in a different way.

Constructivism. A theory of learning, developed from the principles of children's thinking by Piaget and implemented in programs as those in Reggio Emilia, Italy, which states that individuals learn through adaptation. The "constructivist" model of learning posits that children are not passive receptacles into which knowledge is poured but rather are active at making meaning, testing out theories, and trying to make sense of the world and themselves. Knowledge is subjective as each person creates personal meaning out of experiences and integrates new ideas into existing knowledge structures.

Continuing Education. The commitment of teachers to learning new approaches and ideas and to continuing to challenge themselves to higher levels of learning and competence.

Continuum. Something that is continuous; an uninterrupted, ordered sequence.

Culturally Appropriate Curriculum. Curriculum that helps children understand the way individual histories, families of origins, and ethnic family cultures make us similar to and yet different from others.

Culturally Appropriate Practice. The ability to go beyond one's own sociocultural background to ensure equal and fair teaching and learning experiences for all.

D

Demographics. The statistical graphics of a population, especially showing average age, income, etc.

Developmentally Appropriate Curriculum. A curriculum that takes into account a knowledge of child development theory, research, and practice, including various related disciplines; cultural values; parental desires and concerns; community context; individual children; teachers' knowledge and experience; and it is related to overall program goals.

Developmentally Appropriate Practice (DAP). That which is suitable or fitting to the development of the child; refers to those teaching practices that are based on the observation and responsiveness to children as learners with developing abilities who differ from one another by rate of growth and individual differences, rather than of differing amounts of abilities. It also refers to learning experiences that are relevant to and respectful of the social and cultural aspects of the children and their families.

Developmental Stages. Phases in a child's development.

Dialect. A variation of a language, sufficiently different from the original to become a separate entity but not different enough to be considered as a separate language.

Diary Descriptions. A form of observation technique that involves making a comprehensive narrative record of behavior, in diary form.

Discipline. Ability to follow an example or to follow rules; the development of self-control or control in general, such as by imposing order on a group. In early childhood terms, discipline means everything adults do and say to influence children's behavior.

Divergent Thinking. The processes of thought and perception that involve taking a line of thought or action different from what is the norm or common; finding ideas that branch out rather than converge and center on one answer.

Downshifting. A process by which the brain reacts to perceived threat. The brain/mind learns optimally when appropriately challenged; however, should the person sense a threat or danger (either physical or emotional), the brain will become less flexible and revert to primitive attitudes and procedures (downshift).

Down Syndrome. A genetic abnormality that results in mongolism, one of the most common and easily identified forms of mental retardation.

Dynamic Consequences. Leading to other worthwhile responses.

E

Early Childhood Education. Education in the early years of life; the field of study that deals mainly with the learning and experiences of children from infancy through the primary years (up to approximately eight years of age).

Ebonics. Term used to describe "black English" and the center of a controversy in the late 1990s over whether such language is a dialect of standard English or a separate language altogether.

Ecology of the Family. The concept of viewing the child in the context of his or her impact on the family and the family's impact on the child; stresses the interrelationship of the various family members with one another.

Educaring. A concept of teaching as both educating and care giving; coined by Magda Gerber in referring to people working with infants and toddlers.

Egocentric. Self-centered; regarding the self as the center of all things; in Piaget's theory, young children think using themselves as the center of the universe or as the entire universe.

Elaboration. The act of expanding language; developing language by building complex structures from simple ones and adding details.

Emergent Curriculum. A process for curriculum planning that draws on teachers' observations and children's interests. Plans emerge from daily life interests and issues. This approach takes advantage of children's spontaneity and teachers' planning.

Emotional Framework. The basic "feeling" structure of a classroom that determines the tone and underlying sensibilities that affect how people feel and behave while in class.

Employer-Sponsored Child Care. Child care supported in some way by the parents' employers. Support may be financial (as an employee benefit or subsidy) or physical (offering on-site care).

Environment. All those conditions that affect children's surroundings and the people in them; the physical, interpersonal, and temporal aspects of an early childhood setting.

Equilibration. To balance equally; in Piaget's theory, the thinking process by which a person "makes sense" and puts into balance new information with what is already known.

Ethnocentric. Having one's race as a central interest, or regarding one's race or cultural group as superior to others.

Evaluation. A study to determine or set significance or quality.

Event Sampling. An observation technique that involves defining the event to be observed and coding the event to record what is important to remember about it.

Extrinsic. Originating from or on the outside; external, not derived from one's essential nature.

F

Faith-Based School. A school that teaches religious dogma.

Family-Centered Approach. An approach to parent–school relationships that supports the growth of the family as well as the child.

Family Child Care. Care for children in a small, homelike setting; usually six or fewer children in a family residence.

Family-Support Movement. An early childhood education movement in which the primary goal is to strengthen families to meet the challenges of parenting in the years ahead.

Feedback Loop. In terms of evaluation, *feedback loop* is used to describe the process whereby an evaluator gives information to a teacher, who in turn uses this information to improve teaching skills.

Fine Motor Skills. Having to do with the smaller muscles of the body and the extremities, such as those in the fingers, toes, and face.

Flexibility. Capable of modification or change; willing or easily moved from one idea to another.

Fluency. The ability to produce many ideas; an easy and ready flow of ideas.

Full Inclusion. Providing the "least restrictive environment" for children with physical limitations.

G

Gifted Children. Children who have unusually high intelligence, as characterized by: learning to read spontaneously; being able to solve problems and communicate at a level far advanced from their chronological age; excellent memory; extensive vocabulary; and unusual approaches to ideas, tasks, people.

Gross Motor Skills. Having to do with the entire body or the large muscles of the body, such as the legs, arms, and trunk.

Group Times. Those parts of the program in which the whole class or group is together during one activity, such as music, movement, fingerplays, or stories.

H

High-Quality Program. A program defined by the NAEYC as one that meets the needs of and promotes the physical, social, emotional, and cognitive development of the children and adults who are involved in the program.

Hypothesis. A tentative theory or assumption made to draw inferences or test conclusions; an interpretation of a practical situation that is then taken as the ground for action.

I

Inclusion. When a child with a disability is a full-time member of a regular classroom with children who are developing normally as well as with children with special needs.

Inclusive Curriculum. A curriculum that reflects awareness of and sensitivity to a person's culture, language, religion, gender, and abilities.

Individualized Curriculum. A course of study developed and tailored to meet the needs and interests of an individual, rather than those of a group without regard for the individual child.

Inductive Guidance. A guidance process in which children are held accountable for their actions and are called on to think about the impact of their behavior on others. Reasoning and problem-solving skills are stressed.

Inference. A conclusion reached by reasoning from evidence or after gathering information, whether direct or indirect.

Infusion. The integration of multicultural awareness into the current learning environment. It allows for the integration of many diverse perspectives while maintaining the existing curriculum.

Integrated Curriculum. A set of courses designed to form a whole; coordination of the various areas of study, making for continuous and harmonious learning.

Intelligence. The cluster of capabilities that involves thinking (see Chapter 13 for details.)

Interest Areas. Similar to learning centers and activity areas; one way to design physical space in a classroom or yard, dividing the space into separate centers among which children move about, rather than assigning them desks.

Interpersonal. Relating to, or involving relationships with, other people; those parts of the environment that have to do with the people in a school setting.

Intrinsic. Belonging to the essential nature of or originating from within a person or body, such as intrinsic motivation, whereby one needs no external reward in order to do something.

K

Kindergarten (Children's Garden). A school or class for children four to six years old; in the United States, kindergarten is either the first year of formal, public school or the year of schooling before first grade.

Kinship Networks. Groups formed when people bond together and pool resources for the common good.

L

Laboratory Schools. Educational settings whose purposes include experimental study; schools for testing and analysis of educational and/or psychological theory and practice, with an opportunity for experimentation, observation, and practice.

Learning Centers. Similar to interest areas and activity areas; hubs or areas in a classroom designed to promote learning; the classroom is arranged in discrete areas for activity, and children move from one area to another rather than stay at an assigned desk or seat.

Learning Styles. A child's preferred method of integrating knowledge and experiences.

Le Methode Clinique. A kind of information-gathering technique, first used extensively by Jean Piaget, that involves observing children and asking questions as the situation unfolds. The purpose of this technique is to elicit information about how children are thinking as they behave naturally.

Limits. The boundaries of acceptable behavior beyond which actions are considered misbehavior and unacceptable conduct; the absolute controls an adult puts on children's behavior.

Literacy. The quality or state of being able to read and write.

Logical Mathematical Knowledge. One of three types of knowledge in Piagetian theory; the component of intelligence that uses thinking derived from logic.

Log/Journal. A form of observation technique that involves making a page of notes about children's behavior in a cumulative journal.

Logical Consequences. Consequences that adults impose upon a child's actions.

Looping. The practice of keeping a teacher and a group of children in a class together for two or more years.

M

Maturation. The process of growth whereby a body matures regardless of, and relatively independent of, intervention such as exercise, experience, or environment.

Meaningful Knowledge. The form of knowing that is learned within the context of what is already known; that knowledge that has meaning because it has particular significance of value to an individual.

Media Culture. The state of American society today in which ninety-eight percent of the homes have televisions and the average set is on for more than six hours each day, replacing the adult supervision of the past.

Mixed-Age Groups. The practice of placing children of several levels, generally one year apart, into the same classroom. Also referred to as family grouping, heterogeneous grouping, multiage grouping, vertical grouping, and ungraded classes.

Multicultural Education. The system of teaching and learning that includes the contributions of all ethnic and racial groups.

Multiple Intelligences. A theory of intelligence, proposed by Howard Gardner, that outlines several different kinds of intelligence, rather than the notion of intelligence as measured by standardized testing, such as the IQ.

N

Narratives. A major observation technique that involves attempting to record nearly everything that happens, in as much detail as possible, as it happens. Narratives include several subtypes such as baby biographies, specimen descriptions, diary descriptions, and logs or journals.

Natural Consequences. The real-life outcomes of a child's own actions.

Nature/Nurture. The argument regarding human development that centers around two opposing viewpoints; *nature* refers to the belief that it is a person's genetic, inherent character that determines development; *nurture* applies to the notion that it is the sum total of experiences and the environment that determine development.

Negative Reinforcement. Response to a behavior that decreases the likelihood that the behavior will recur; for instance, a teacher's glare might stop a child from whispering at group time, and from then on, the anticipation of such an angry look could reinforce not whispering in the future.

Norm. An average or general standard of development or achievement, usually derived from the average or median of a large group; a pattern or trait taken to be typical of the behavior, skills, or interests of a group.

O

Objectivity. The quality or state of being able to see what is real and realistic, as distinguished from subjective and personal opinion or bias.

Open-Ended. Activities or statements that allow a variety of responses, as opposed to those that allow only one response; anything organized to allow for variation.

Out-of-School Time Care. Programs for school-age children that take place before and after their regular school day.

P

Parent Cooperative Schools. An educational setting organized by parents for their young children, often with parental control and/or support in the operation of the program itself.

Parent Development. The six stages of growth a parent goes through in the process of raising a child.

Pedagogista. A person trained in early childhood education who meets weekly with the teachers in the schools of Reggio Emilia, Italy.

Perceptual Motor Development. The growth of a person's ability to move (motor) and perceive (perceptual) together; perceptual-motor activity involves the body and the mind together, to co-ordinate movement.

Performance-Based Assessment. Evaluation based on observable, specific information on what a teacher actually does (performance while on the job).

Perry Preschool Study. Begun in the 1960s, it was the first longitudinal study to measure the effects of preschool education and to track the children from preschool years through age 27. It presented the most convincing evidence to date of the effectiveness of early intervention programs for low income children.

Permissive Parents. A child-rearing pattern that is essentially the reverse of authoritarian parents. There is a high level of warmth and affection but little control. Clear standards and rules are not set, nor are they reinforced consistently.

Phonemic Awareness. Having knowledge or perception of the distinct units of sounds that distinguish one word from another; in English this would include buh [b], puh [p], and sss [s], among others.

Physical Knowledge. One of three types of knowledge in Piagetian theory; that knowledge that is learned through external, sensory experiences.

Portfolio. An assessment method that tracks children's growth and development.

Positive Reinforcement. A response to a behavior that increases the likelihood that the behavior will be repeated or increased; for instance, if a child gets attention and praise for crawling, it is likely that the crawling will increase—thus, the attention and praise were positive reinforcers for crawling.

Power Assertive Methods. Harsh, punitive discipline methods that rely on children's fear of punishment rather than on the use of reason and understanding. Hitting and spanking are examples of power assertion.

Precursor. What precedes and indicates the approach of another; predecessor or forerunner.

Prepared Environment. The physical and interpersonal surroundings of an educational setting that are planned and arranged in advance with the group of children in mind.

Professional Development. The process of gaining the body of knowledge and educational foundation that will help in career progression and acquiring further skills on the job.

Professionalism. The competence or skill expected of a professional; in early childhood education, this includes a sense of identity, purpose to engage in developmentally appropriate practices, a commitment to ethical teaching and to child advocacy, and participation in the work as a legitimate livelihood.

Project Approach. An in-depth study of a particular subject or theme by one or more children. Exploration of themes and topics over a period of days or weeks. Working in small groups, children are able to accommodate various levels of complexity and understanding to meet the needs of all the children working on the project.

Prosocial. Behaviors that are considered positive and social in nature, such as sharing, inviting, including, and offering help or friendship.

Psychodynamic Theory. The psychological theory of Dr. Sigmund Freud and others; it asserts that the individual develops a basic personality core in childhood and that responses stem from personality organization and emotional problems as a result of environmental experiences.

Psychosocial. Those psychological issues that deal with how people relate to others and the problems that arise on a social level; a modification by Erikson of the psychodynamic theories of Freud with attention to social and environmental problems of life.

Public Law 94–142. The Education for All Handicapped Children Act. This so-called Bill of Rights for the Handicapped guarantees free public education to disabled persons from three to 21 years of age "in the least restrictive" environment. In 1990 Congress reauthorized PL 94-142 and renamed it the Individuals with Disabilities Education Act (IDEA) (PL 101-576). Two new categories, autism and traumatic brain injury, were included, and children from birth to age five years were now eligible to receive services.

Public Law 99–457. The Education of the Handicapped Amendments Act of 1986. Sections of this law provide funding for children who were not included in the previous law: infants, toddlers, and three- to five-year-olds. This law also allows for the inclusion of "developmentally delayed" youngsters and leaves local agencies the opportunity to include the "at-risk" child in that definition.

Punishment. The act of inflicting a penalty for an offense or behavior.

Q

Quality. A function of group size, low teacher-child ratios, trained and experienced staff, adequate compensation, and safe and stimulating environments.

R

Racist. Attitudes, behavior, or policies that imply either a hatred or intolerance of other race(s) or involving the idea that one's own race is superior and has the right to rule or dominate others.

Rating Scale. A modified child study technique similar to a checklist that classifies behavior according to grade or rank, such as using the descriptors "always, sometimes, never" to describe the frequency of a certain behavior.

Receptive. Those aspects of language development and skill that deal with the ability to receive messages: listening, understanding, and responding.

Reciprocal. The stage of children's friendship in which friendship is given or felt by each toward the other; a kind of give-and-take or two-way relationship, this is the stage most often seen in the latter part of the early childhood years.

Redirecting. Calls for the adult to make an accurate assessment of what the children really want to do, then consider alternatives that permit the desired activity while changing the expression or form it takes.

Reinforcement. A procedure, such as reward or punishment, that changes a response to a stimulus; the act of encouraging a behavior to increase in frequency.

Reinforcers. Rewards in response to a specific behavior, thus increasing the likelihood that behavior will recur; reinforcers may be either social (praise) or nonsocial (food) in nature and may or may not be deliberately controlled.

Rote Knowledge. A form of knowing that is learned by routine or habit and without thought of the meaning.

Roughhousing. Rough and disorderly, but playful, behavior.

Routines. Regular procedures; habitual, repeated or regular parts of the school day; in early childhood programs, routines are those parts of the program schedule that remain constant, such as indoor time followed by cleanup and snack, regardless of what activities are being offered within those time slots.

S

Scaffolding. A useful structure to support a child in learning. A child who gets advice or hints to help master an activity is said to have scaffolding learning, a term Vygotsky used.

Schemas. A plan, scheme, or framework that helps make an organizational pattern from which to operate; in Piaget's theory, cognitive schemas are used for thinking.

School Readiness. Children should be allowed to learn at their own pace, and teachers should work with children's own inclinations. This idea was first proposed by Comenius, but was later reflected in Montessori and Piaget's developmental theories.

Self-Actualization. The set of principles set forth by Abraham Maslow for a person's wellness or ability to be the most that a person can be; the state of being that results from having met all the basic and growth needs.

Self-Awareness. An awareness of one's own personality or individuality; in teaching terms, an ability to understand one's self and assess personal strengths and weaknesses.

Self-Concept. A person's view and opinion of self; in young children, the concept of self develops as they interact with the environment (objects, people, etc.); self-concept can be inferred in how children carry themselves, approach situations, use expressive materials such as art, etc.

Self-Correcting. Materials or experiences that are built or arranged so that the person using them can act automatically to correct errors, without needing another person to check or point out mistakes.

Self-Discipline. Gaining control over one's own behavior.

Self-Esteem. The value we place on ourselves; how much we like or dislike who we are; self-respect.

Self-Help. The act of helping or providing for oneself without dependence on others; in early childhood terms, activities that a child can do alone, without adult assistance.

Self-Regulation. The term used to describe a child's capacity to plan and guide the self. A disposition or part of the personality (rather than a skill or behavior such as self-control), self-regulation is a way of monitoring one's own activity flexibly over changing circumstances.

Sensory Awareness. Having to do with the senses or sensation, as in an awareness of the world as it looks, sounds, feels, smells, tastes.

Seriation. The process of sequencing from beginning to end or in a particular series or succession.

Sexist. Attitudes or behavior based on the traditional stereotype of sexual roles that includes a devaluation or discrimination based on a person's sex.

Shadow Study. A modified child study technique that profiles an individual at a given moment in time; similar to diary description, the shadow study is a narrative recorded as the behavior happens.

Simultaneous/Successive Acquisition. The two major ways second-language learning occurs. Simultaneous acquisition happens if a child is exposed to two languages from birth. Successive acquisition occurs as a child with one language begins to learn another language.

Social Action. Individual or group behavior that involves interaction with other individuals or groups, especially organized action toward social reform.

Social Cognition. The application of thinking to personal and social behavior; giving meaning to social experience.

Social Knowledge. One of three types of knowledge in Piagetian theory; that knowledge that is learned about and from people, such as family and ethnic culture, group behavior, social mores, etc.

Social Skills. Strategies children learn to enable them to respond appropriately in many environments.

Sociocentric. Oriented toward or focused on one's social group rather than on oneself.

Sociocultural. Aspects of theory or development that refer to the social and cultural issues; key descriptor of Vygotsky's theory of development.

Spatial Awareness. Having to do with the nature of space, as in the awareness of the space around a person's body.

Stress. The physical and emotional reactions and behaviors that come from having to cope with difficult situations beyond one's capabilities.

Superhero. Those characters who embody a higher nature and powers beyond ordinary human abilities, such as Superman, Wonder Woman, etc.

T

Tabula Rasa. A mind not affected yet by experiences, sensations, and the like. In John Locke's theory, a child was born with this "clean slate" upon which all experiences were written.

Temporal Awareness. Having to do with time and time sequence; in the early childhood setting, refers to scheduling and how time is sequenced and spent, both at home and in school.

Themes. Broad, general topics used to develop curriculum.

Theory. A group of general principles, ideas, or proposed explanations for explaining some kind of phenomenon; in this case, child development.

Time Out. Removing a child from the play area when, owing to anger, hurt, or frustration, the child is out of control. It is a brief respite and a chance to stop all activity and regroup.

Time Sampling. An observation technique that involves observing certain behavior and settings within a prescribed time frame.

Traditional Nursery School. The core of early childhood educational theory and practice; program designed for children aged two-and-a-half to five years of age, which may be a part- or an all-day program.

Transcurricular. Able to be used or applied in a variety of situations or activities.

Transition. A change from one state or activity to another; in early childhood terms, transitions are those times of change in the daily schedule (whether planned or not), such as from being with a parent to being alone in school, from playing with one toy to choosing another, from being outside to being inside, etc.

Trilemma. A child care issue involving quality for children, affordability for parents, and adequate compensation for staff.

U

Unconscious. Not conscious, without awareness, occurring below the level of conscious thought.

Undifferentiated. The stage of children's friendships in which children do not distinguish between "friend" and "person I'm playing with," considered the first stage, usually from infancy into the preschool years.

Unilateral. The stage of children's friendships in which children think of friendship as involving one side only; that is, a one-way situation in that a "friend" is "someone who does what I want him to do," usually spanning the preschool years and into early primary.

W

The Whole Child. Based on the accepted principle that all areas of human growth and development are interrelated. The concept of the whole child suggests the uniqueness of the person. Although they are often discussed separately, the areas of development (social-emotional, physical, language, cultural awareness, intellectual, and creativity) cannot be isolated from one another.

Word Pictures. Descriptions of children that depict, in words, norms of development; in this text, these are age-level charts that describe common behaviors and characteristics, particularly those that have implications for teaching children (in groups, for curriculum planning, with discipline and guidance).

Z

Zone of Proximal Development. The term in Vygotsky's sociocultural theory that defines which children can learn. Interpersonal and dynamic, the zone refers to the area a child can master (skill, information, etc.) with the assistance of another skilled person; below that, children can learn on their own; above the limit are areas beyond the child's capacity to learn, even with help.

Appendix A

Timeline for Early Childhood Education

Authors' Note: A debt of gratitude is owed to D. Keith Osborn for his outstanding historical research and to James L. Hymes, Jr., for his generous time and perspective.

<u>5th–3rd centuries BC to AD 1400s</u> Few records exist concerning child-rearing practices; the development of cities gives rise to schooling on a larger scale.

<u>1423 & 1439</u> The invention of printing and movable type allows knowledge to spread rapidly; ideas and techniques become available to large numbers of people; printing is credited with bringing about the end of the Middle Ages and the beginning of the Renaissance.

<u>1592–1670</u> Johann Amos Comenius

<u>1657</u> *Orbis Pictus,* by Comenius, is the first children's book with pictures.

<u>1632–1714</u> John Locke
English philosopher, considered the founder of educational philosophy, who postulated that children are born with a *tabula rasa,* or clean slate, on which all experiences are written.

<u>1712–1788</u> Jean Jacques Rousseau

<u>1762</u> *Emile,* by Rousseau, proclaims the child's natural goodness.

<u>1746–1826</u> Johann Heinrich Pestalozzi

<u>1801</u> *How Gertrude Teaches Her Children,* by Pestalozzi, emphasizes home education.

<u>1740–1860s</u> Sabbath Schools and Clandestine Schools are established as facilities to educate African Americans in the United States.

<u>1782–1852</u> Friedrich Wilhelm Froebel

<u>1826</u> *Education of Man,* by Froebel, describes the first system of kindergarten education as a "child's garden," with activities known as "gifts from God."

<u>1837</u> Froebel opens the first kindergarten in Blankenburgh, Germany.

<u>1861</u> Robert Owen sets up infant school in New Lanark, England, as an instrument of social reform for children of parent workers in his mills.

<u>1873</u> The Butler School at Hampton Institute is opened as a free school for black children, including kindergarten curriculum for five-year-olds.

<u>1837</u> Horace Mann, known as the "Father of the Common Schools" because of his contributions in setting up the U.S. elementary school system, becomes Secretary of Massachusetts State Board of Education.

<u>1856</u> Margarethe Schurz opens the first American kindergarten, a German-speaking class in her home in Watertown, Wisconsin.

<u>1804–1894</u> Elizabeth Peabody

<u>1860</u> Elizabeth Peabody opens the first English-speaking kindergarten in Boston.

<u>1843–1916</u> Susan Blow

<u>1873</u> First public school kindergarten, supported by Superintendent William Harris, is directed by Susan Blow in St. Louis, Missouri, who becomes the leading proponent of Froebel in America. The first public kindergarten in North America opens in 1871 in Ontario, Canada.

1856–1939 Sigmund Freud (see Chapter 4)

1892   Freud cites the importance of early experiences to later mental illness, ushering in the beginning of psychoanalysis and the emphasis on the importance of the first five years.

1858–1952 John Dewey

1896   John Dewey establishes a laboratory school at the University of Chicago and develops a pragmatic approach to education, becoming the father of the Progressive Movement in American education.

1897   *My Pedagogic Creed* is published, detailing the opposition to rote learning and the philosophy of educating "the whole child."

1860–1931 Margaret McMillan

1911   Deptford School, an open-air school in the slums of London, is opened by Margaret McMillan. The school emphasizes health and play, thus coining the phrase "nursery school."

1868–1946 Patty Smith Hill

1893   Patty Smith Hill becomes director of the Louisville Free Kindergarten Society, augmenting her original Froebelian training with her work in scientific psychology (G. Stanley Hall) and progressive education (John Dewey). She goes on to found the National Association of Nursery Education (now known as NAEYC) in 1926.

1870–1952 Maria Montessori (see Chapters 1 and 2)

1907   Casa di Bambini (Children's House) is opened by Maria Montessori in a slum district in Rome, Italy. She later develops an educational philosophy and program to guide children's growth through the senses and practical life experiences.

1874–1949 Edward Thorndike, behavioral psychologist (see Chapter 4)

1878–1958 John B. Watson, behavioral psychologist (see Chapter 4)

1878–1967 Lucy Sprague Mitchell

1916   The Bureau of Educational Experiments, which becomes Bank Street College of Education (and laboratory school) in 1922, is founded by L. S. Mitchell, who is a leading proponent of progressive education at the early childhood level.

1879   The first psychological laboratory is established in Germany to train psychologists in the systematic study of human beings.

1880   First teacher-training program for kindergartners, Oshkosh Normal School, Pennsylvania.

1880–1961 Arnold Gesell (see Chapter 4)

1923   Gesell, originally a student of G. Stanley Hall, publishes *The Preschool Child,* which emphasizes the importance of the early years.

1926   Gesell establishes the Clinic of Child Development at Yale University and studies norms of child growth and behavior, founding the maturation theory of development (see Chapters 1 and 4).

1885–1948 Susan Isaacs

1929   Susan Isaacs publishes *The Nursery Years,* which contradicts the more scientific psychological view of behavior shaping and emphasizes the child's viewpoint and the value of play.

1892–1992 Abigail Eliot

1922   Dr. Eliot opens Ruggles Street Nursery School and Training Center.

1892   International Kindergarten Union founded.

1895   G. Stanley Hall runs a child development seminar with kindergarten teachers, explaining the "scientific/new psychology" approach to education. While most leave, Anny Bryan and Patty Smith Hill go on to incorporate such techniques and to see early childhood education as a more multidisciplinary effort.

1896–1980 Jean Jacques Piaget (see Chapter 4)

1926   *The Language and Thought of the Child,* one of a multitude of writings on the development of children's thought, is published by Jean Piaget, who becomes one of the largest forces in child development in the twentieth century.

1952   Piaget's *Origins of Intelligence in Children* is published in English.

1896–1934 Lev Vygotsky (see Chapter 4).

1978   *Mind in Society: The Development of Higher Psychological Processes,* the seminal work of Vygotsky's sociocultural theory, is first published in English.

1897–1905 Alfred Binet develops a test for the French government to determine feeble-mindedness in children. Known as the Binet-Simon test (and tested by Jean Piaget, among others), it is now known as the Stanford-Binet IQ test.

1902–1994 Erik Erikson (see Chapter 4)

1950   *Childhood and Society,* which details Erikson's Eight Stages of Man, is published, thus adding a psychoanalytic influence to early childhood education.

1903–1998 Benjamin Spock

1946 Dr. Spock's *Baby and Child Care* is published. It advocates a more permissive attitude toward children's behavior and encourages exploratory behavior.

1903 The Committee of Nineteen, a splinter group of the International Kindergarten Union, forms to report various philosophical concepts. Members include Patty Smith Hill, Lucy Wheelock, and Susan Blow.

1904–1988 B. F. Skinner (see Chapter 4)

1938 *The Behavior of Organisms,* by B. F. Skinner, is published, advocating the concepts of "radical behaviorism" in psychology.

1906 Josephine Yates publishes an article in the *Colored American Magazine,* which advocates play in the kindergarten and helps translate Froebel's concepts into Black kindergartens of the day.

1908–1984 Sylvia Ashton Warner

1963 *Teacher,* published by this New Zealand kindergarten teacher, develops the concepts of "organic vocabulary" and "key vocabulary."

1909 First White House Conference on Children is held by Theodore Roosevelt, leading to the establishment of the Children's Bureau in 1912.

1915 First U.S. Montessori school opens in New York City.

1916 First Cooperative Nursery School opens at the University of Chicago.

1918 First public nursery schools are opened in England.

1918– T. Berry Brazelton

1969 *Infants and Mothers,* along with several other books and numerous articles, is published by this pediatrician, advocating a sensible and intimate relationship between parents and children.

1980s Dr. Brazelton is one of the founders of "Parent Action," a federal lobby to advocate for the needs of parents and children, particularly for a national policy granting parental leave from work to care for newborns or newly adopted children.

1919 Harriet Johnson starts the Nursery School of the Bureau of Educational Experiments, which later becomes Bank Street School.

1920–1994 Loris Malaguzzi theorizes about good programs and relationships for children, emphasizing the child's individual creative expression; starts school of Reggio Emilia, Italy, in 1946.

1921 Patty Smith Hill opens Columbia Teacher's College Laboratory School.

1921 A. S. Neill founds Summerhill school in England, which becomes a model for the "free school" movement (the book entitled *Summerhill* is published in 1960).

1922 Edna Nobel White directs the Merrill-Palmer School of Motherhood and Home Training, which later becomes the Merrill-Palmer Institute Nursery School.

1925–1926 The National Committee on Nursery Schools is founded by Patty Smith Hill; it becomes NANE and eventually NAEYC.

1925– Albert Bandura, psychologist in social learning theory (see Chapter 4)

1926–1927 Research facilities are founded at several American universities and colleges (e.g., Smith College, Vassar College, Yale University, Mills College).

1927 Dorothy Howard establishes the first Black Nursery School in Washington, DC, and operates it for over 50 years.

1928 John B. Watson publishes *Psychological Care of Infant and Child,* applying his theories of conditioning to child-rearing (see Chapter 4).

1929 Lois Meeks Stolz (1891–1984) becomes the first President of the National Association for Nursery Education (later to become National Association for the Education of Young Children) and joins the Teachers College (Columbia University) faculty to start the laboratory school and Child Development Institute. Stolz later becomes the Director of the Kaiser Child Service Centers during World War II.

1929–1931 Hampton Institute, Spellman College, and Bennett College open Black laboratory nursery schools, emphasizing child development principles as in other lab schools and serving as training centers.

1930 International Kindergarten Union, founded in 1892, becomes the Association for Childhood Education, increasing its scope to include elementary education.

1933 WPA (Works Projects Association) opens emergency nurseries for Depression relief of unemployed teachers. Enrolling over 4000 teachers in 3000 schools, they also help children of unemployed parents and operate under the guidance of people such as Edna Noble White, Abigail Eliot, and Lois Meeks Stolz until World War II.

1935   First toy lending library, Toy Loan, begins in Los Angeles.

1936   The first commercial telecast is shown in New York City, starring Felix the Cat. The pervasiveness of television sets and children's viewing habits become a source of concern for educators and parents in the latter half of the twentieth century.

1943–1945 Kaiser Shipyard Child Care Center, run by Lois Meeks Stolz, James Hymes, and Edith Dowley, operates 24-hour care in Portland, Oregon.

1944   *Young Children* is first published.

1946   Stanford University laboratory school is founded by Edith Dowley.

1948   USNC OMEP, the United States National Committee of the World Organization for Early Childhood Education, is founded to promote the education of children internationally and begins to consult with UNICEF and UNESCO in the United Nations. It starts publishing a journal, *The International Journal of Early Childhood,* in 1969.

1956   La Leche League is established to provide mothers with information on breast-feeding, childbirth, infants, and child care.

1957   *Sputnik,* a Soviet satellite, is successfully launched, sparking a renewed interest in—and criticism of—American education.

1960   Katherine Whiteside Taylor founds the American Council of Parent Cooperatives, which later becomes the Parent Cooperative Pre-schools International.

1960   Nancy McCormick Rambusch (1927–1994) founds the American Montessori movement, splitting from her European counterparts to try to shape Montessori education as a viable American public school alternative and to establish teacher taining programs at both early childhood and elementary levels.

1962   Perry Preschool Project, directed by David Weikart, opens in Ypsilanti, Michigan, and conducts longitudinal study to measure the effects of preschool education on later school and life (see Chapter 2).

1963 & 1966 Lawrence Kohlberg publishes child development works on the development of gender and sex roles and on moral development (see Chapter 4).

1964–1965 The Economic Opportunity Act of 1964 passes, becoming the foundation of Head Start Programs in the United States, as part of a federal "War on Poverty."

1966   The Bureau of Education for the Handicapped is established.

1966   NANE becomes National Association for the Education of Young Children (NAEYC).

1967   Plowden Report from England details the British Infant School system.
The Follow Through Program extends Head Start into the primary grades of the elementary system.

1969   John Bowlby publishes the first of his major works on *Attachment* (see Chapter 4).
The Ford Foundation, Carnegie Corporation, and Department of Health, Education, and Welfare subsidize the Children's Television Workshop, which develops *Sesame Street.*

1971   Stride-Rite Corporation of Boston opens a children's program on site, becoming a vanguard for employer-supported child care.

1972   The Child Development Associate Consortium, headed by Dr. Edward Ziegler, is established to develop a professional training program. Now known as CDA, its administration moves to NAEYC in 1985.

1974   Eleanor Maccoby publishes *The Development of Sex Differences* (see Chapter 4).

1975   P.L. 94-142, the Education for All Handicapped Children bill, passes, mandating appropriate education for special needs children in the "least restrictive environment" possible, thus defining the concepts of "mainstreaming" and "full inclusion."

1975   Mary Ainsworth publishes developmental research on mother–child interaction and follows up with work on patterns of attachment.

1979   Nancy Eisenberg publishes the theory of the development of prosocial development in children (see Chapter 4).
The United Nations declares an International Year of the Child.

1980 The Department of Health, Education, and Welfare is changed to that of Health and Human Services, and a separate Department of Education is established.

1982 Carol Gilligan publishes *In a Different Voice,* challenging accepted psychological theory on moral development (see Chapter 4).

1982– Marion Wright Edelman establishes the Children's Defense Fund, a Washington-based lobby on behalf of children, and particularly children of poverty and color.

1983 Howard Gardner publishes *Frames of Mind,* which outlines the concept of multiple intelligences (see Chapters 4 and 13).

1984 NAEYC publishes a report entitled "Developmentally Appropriate Practices," which outlines what is meant by "quality" work with young children from infancy through age eight.

1985 NAEYC establishes a National Academy and a voluntary accreditation system for centers, in an effort to improve the quality of children's lives, and confers its first accreditation the next year.

1986 U.S. Department of Education declares the Year of the Elementary School. P.L. 99-457, amending 94-142, establishes a national policy on early intervention for children as young as infants.

1988–1990 The Alliance for Better Child Care, a coalition of groups advocating on behalf of young children, sponsors the ABC bill in an effort to get federal support for children and families. It fails to be signed in 1989, but is passed in 1990 and establishes the Child Care Development Block Grant to improve the quality, availability, and affordability of child care programs.

1988 The National Association of State Boards of Education issues *Right from the Start,* a report that calls for a new vision of early childhood education with the establishment of separate public school early childhood units.

1988 The National Education Goals are adopted by President Bush and the nation's governors. Goal One states that all children will come to school ready to learn.

1990 U.N. Children's World Summit includes the following goals to be reached by the year 2000: (1) to reduce child mortality below age five by one third; (2) to provide universal access to basic education; and (3) to protect children in dangerous situations.

1990 The Americans with Disabilities Act (ADA) is passed, requiring programs of all sizes to care for and accommodate the needs of children with disabilities whenever they are reasonably able to do so.

1991 "Ready to Learn/America 2000," part of the U.S. government's educational strategy for reforming American public schools, is published.

1991 The first Worthy Wage Day, organized by the Child Care Employee Project, is held on April 9, drawing attention to the inadequate compensation of early childhood workers and how this affects the retention of a skilled and stable work force.

1993 The Family and Medical Leave Act (FMLA) is passed, providing new parents with 12 weeks of unpaid, job-protected leave.

1996 The first "Stand For Children" demonstration is held in Washington, DC, drawing 200,000 participants. *Rethinking the Brain,* published by the Family and Work Institute, summarizes the new research on children's brain development, shows the decisive impact of early experiences, and considers policy and program implications of these findings.

1997 The Child Development Permit Matrix is adopted by the California Commission on Teacher Credentialing, introducing the career ladder concept into early childhood public education.

1998 The 100,000th CDA Credential is awarded by Carol Brunson Phillips, Executive Director of the Council for Early Childhood Professional Recognition, at NAEYC Annual Conference in Toronto, Ontario, Canada.

2000 In California and other states, public elementary and secondary school systems implement stringent academic and performance standards, with substantial assessment requirements.

2002 In the U.S., the "Leave No Child Behind" legislation is passed.

2003 Universal preschool is considered as a next step in providing equal access to quality early educational experiences for all children under five years of age.

2005 "Preschool for All" initiatives have been passed in several states, making a preschool experience a reality for four-year-olds.

Code of Ethical Conduct and Statement of Commitment

A position statement of the National Association for the Education of Young Children (NAEYC) Revised April 2005

🌀 PREAMBLE

NAEYC recognizes that those who work with young children face many daily decisions that have moral and ethical implications. The NAEYC Code of Ethical Conduct offers guidelines for responsible behavior and sets forth a common basis for resolving the principal ethical dilemmas encountered in early childhood care and education. The Statement of Commitment is not part of the Code but is a personal acknowledgment of an individual's willingness to embrace the distinctive values and moral obligations of the field of early childhood care and education. The primary focus of the Code is on daily practice with children and their families in programs for children from birth through 8 years of age, such as infant/toddler programs, preschool and prekindergarten programs, child care centers, hospital and child life settings, family child care homes, kindergartens, and primary classrooms. When the issues involve young children, then these provisions also apply to specialists who do not work directly with children, including program administrators, parent educators, early childhood adult educators, and officials with responsibility for program monitoring and licensing. (Note: See also the "Code of Ethical Conduct: Supplement for Early Childhood Adult Educators.")

🌀 CORE VALUES

Standards of ethical behavior in early childhood care and education are based on commitment to the following core values that are deeply rooted in the history of the field of early childhood care and education. We have made a commitment to:

- Appreciate childhood as a unique and valuable stage of the human life cycle

- Base our work on knowledge of how children develop and learn

- Appreciate and support the bond between the child and family

- ✺ Recognize that children are best understood and supported in the context of family, culture,* community, and society

- ✺ Respect the dignity, worth, and uniqueness of each individual (child, family member, and colleague)

- ✺ Respect diversity in children, families, and colleagues

- ✺ Recognize that children and adults achieve their full potential in the context of relationships that are based on trust and respect

✺ CONCEPTUAL FRAMEWORK

The Code sets forth a framework of professional responsibilities in four sections. Each section addresses an area of professional relationships: (1) with children, (2) with families, (3) among colleagues, and (4) with the community and society. Each section includes an introduction to the primary responsibilities of the early childhood practitioner in that context. The introduction is followed by (1) a set of ideals that reflect exemplary professional practice and (2) a set of principles describing practices that are required, prohibited, or permitted.

The **ideals** reflect the aspirations of practitioners. The **principles** guide conduct and assist practitioners in resolving ethical dilemmas.† Both ideals and principles are intended to direct practitioners to those questions which, when responsibly answered, can provide the basis for conscientious decision making. While the Code provides specific direction for addressing some ethical dilemmas, many others will require the practitioner to combine the guidance of

the Code with professional judgment. The ideals and principles in this Code present a shared framework of professional responsibility that affirms our commitment to the core values of our field. The Code publicly acknowledges the responsibilities that we in the field have assumed and in so doing supports ethical behavior in our work. Practitioners who face situations with ethical dimensions are urged to seek guidance in the applicable parts of this Code and in the spirit that informs the whole. Often, "the right answer"—the best ethical course of action to take—is not obvious. There may be no readily apparent, positive way to handle a situation. When one important value contradicts another, we face an ethical dilemma. When we face a dilemma, it is our professional responsibility to consult the Code and all relevant parties to find the most ethical resolution.

✺ SECTION I: ETHICAL RESPONSIBILITIES TO CHILDREN

Childhood is a unique and valuable stage in the human life cycle. Our paramount responsibility is to provide care and education in settings that are safe, healthy, nurturing, and responsive for each child. We are committed to supporting children's development and learning; respecting individual differences; and helping children learn to live, play, and work cooperatively. We are also committed to promoting children's self-awareness, competence, self-worth, resiliency, and physical well-being.

Ideals

I-1.1—To be familiar with the knowledge base of early childhood care and education

*Culture includes ethnicity, racial identity, economic level, family structure, language, and religious and political beliefs, which profoundly influence each child's development and relationship to the world.

†There is not a corresponding principle for each ideal.

and to stay informed through continuing education and training.

I-1.2—To base program practices upon current knowledge and research in the field of early childhood education, child development, and related disciplines, as well as on particular knowledge of each child.

I-1.3—To recognize and respect the unique qualities, abilities, and potential of each child.

I-1.4—To appreciate the vulnerability of children and their dependence on adults.

I-1.5—To create and maintain safe and healthy settings that foster children's social, emotional, cognitive, and physical development and that respect their dignity and their contributions.

I-1.6—To use assessment instruments and strategies that are appropriate for the children to be assessed, that are used only for the purposes for which they were designed, and that have the potential to benefit children.

I-1.7—To use assessment information to understand and support children's development and learning, to support instruction, and to identify children who may need additional services.

I-1.8—To support the right of each child to play and learn in an inclusive environment that meets the needs of children with and without disabilities.

I-1.9—To advocate for and ensure that all children, including those with special needs, have access to the support services needed to be successful.

I-1.10—To ensure that each child's culture, language, ethnicity, and family structure are recognized and valued in the program.

I-1.11—To provide all children with experiences in a language that they know, as well as support children in maintaining the use of their home language and in learning English.

I-1.12—To work with families to provide a safe and smooth transition as children and families move from one program to the next.

Principles

P-1.1—**Above all, we shall not harm children. We shall not participate in practices that are emotionally damaging, physically harmful, disrespectful, degrading, dangerous, exploitative, or intimidating to children.** *This principle has precedence over all others in this Code.*

P-1.2—We shall care for and educate children in positive emotional and social environments that are cognitively stimulating and that support each child's culture, language, ethnicity, and family structure.

P-1.3—We shall not participate in practices that discriminate against children by denying benefits, giving special advantages, or excluding them from programs or activities on the basis of their sex, race, national origin, religious beliefs, medical condition, disability, or the marital status/ family structure, sexual orientation, or religious beliefs or other affiliations of their families. (Aspects of this principle do not apply in programs that have a lawful mandate to provide services to a particular population of children.)

P-1.4—We shall involve all those with relevant knowledge (including families and staff) in decisions concerning a child, as appropriate, ensuring confidentiality of sensitive information.

P-1.5—We shall use appropriate assessment systems, which include multiple sources of information, to provide information on children's learning and development.

P-1.6—We shall strive to ensure that decisions such as those related to enrollment, retention, or assignment to special education services, will be based on multiple sources of information and will never be based on a single assessment, such as a test score or a single observation.

P-1.7—We shall strive to build individual relationships with each child; make individualized adaptations in teaching strategies, learning environments, and curricula; and consult with the family so that each child benefits from the program. If after such efforts have been exhausted, the current placement does not meet a child's needs, or the child is seriously jeopardizing the ability of other children to benefit from the program, we shall collaborate with the child's family and appropriate specialists to determine the additional services needed and/or the placement option(s) most likely to ensure the child's success. (Aspects of this principle may not apply in programs that have a lawful mandate to provide services to a particular population of children.)

P-1.8—We shall be familiar with the risk factors for and symptoms of child abuse and neglect, including physical, sexual, verbal, and emotional abuse and physical, emotional, educational, and medical neglect. We shall know and follow state laws and community procedures that protect children against abuse and neglect.

P-1.9—When we have reasonable cause to suspect child abuse or neglect, we shall report it to the appropriate community agency and follow up to ensure that appropriate action has been taken. When appropriate, parents or guardians will be informed that the referral will be or has been made.

P-1.10—When another person tells us of his or her suspicion that a child is being abused or neglected, we shall assist that person in taking appropriate action in order to protect the child.

P-1.11—When we become aware of a practice or situation that endangers the health, safety, or well-being of children, we have an ethical responsibility to protect children or inform parents and/or others who can.

SECTION II: ETHICAL RESPONSIBILITIES TO FAMILIES

Families* are of primary importance in children's development. Because the family and the early childhood practitioner have a common interest in the child's well-being, we acknowledge a primary responsibility to bring about communication, cooperation, and collaboration between the home and early childhood program in ways that enhance the child's development.

Ideals

I-2.1—To be familiar with the knowledge base related to working effectively with families and to stay informed through continuing education and training.

I-2.2—To develop relationships of mutual trust and create partnerships with the families we serve.

I-2.3—To welcome all family members and encourage them to participate in the program.

I-2.4—To listen to families, acknowledge and build upon their strengths and competencies, and learn from families as we support them in their task of nurturing children.

*The term *family* may include those adults, besides parents, with the responsibility of being involved in educating, nurturing, and advocating for the child.

I-2.5—To respect the dignity and preferences of each family and to make an effort to learn about its structure, culture, language, customs, and beliefs.

I-2.6—To acknowledge families' childrearing values and their right to make decisions for their children.

I-2.7—To share information about each child's education and development with families and to help them understand and appreciate the current knowledge base of the early childhood profession.

I-2.8—To help family members enhance their understanding of their children and support the continuing development of their skills as parents.

I-2.9—To participate in building support networks for families by providing them with opportunities to interact with program staff, other families, community resources, and professional services.

Principles

P-2.1—We shall not deny family members access to their child's classroom or program setting unless access is denied by court order or other legal restriction.

P-2.2—We shall inform families of program philosophy, policies, curriculum, assessment system, and personnel qualifications, and explain why we teach as we do—which should be in accordance with our ethical responsibilities to children (see Section I).

P-2.3—We shall inform families of and, when appropriate, involve them in policy decisions.

P-2.4—We shall involve the family in significant decisions affecting their child.

P-2.5—We shall make every effort to communicate effectively with all families in a language that they understand. We shall use community resources for translation and interpretation when we do not have sufficient resources in our own programs.

P-2.6—As families share information with us about their children and families, we shall consider this information to plan and implement the program.

P-2.7—We shall inform families about the nature and purpose of the program's child assessments and how data about their child will be used.

P-2.8—We shall treat child assessment information confidentially and share this information only when there is a legitimate need for it.

P-2.9—We shall inform the family of injuries and incidents involving their child, of risks such as exposures to communicable diseases that might result in infection, and of occurrences that might result in emotional stress.

P-2.10—Families shall be fully informed of any proposed research projects involving their children and shall have the opportunity to give or withhold consent without penalty. We shall not permit or participate in research that could in any way hinder the education, development, or well-being of children.

P-2.11—We shall not engage in or support exploitation of families. We shall not use our relationship with a family for private advantage or personal gain, or enter into relationships with family members that might impair our effectiveness working with their children.

P-2.12—We shall develop written policies for the protection of confidentiality and the disclosure of children's records. These policy documents shall be made available to all program personnel and families. Disclosure of children's records beyond family members, program personnel, and consultants having an obligation of confidentiality shall require familial consent (except in cases of abuse or neglect).

P-2.13—We shall maintain confidentiality and shall respect the family's right to privacy, refraining from disclosure of confidential information and intrusion into family life. However, when we have reason to believe that a child's welfare is at risk, it is permissible to share confidential information with agencies, as well as with individuals who have legal responsibility for intervening in the child's interest.

P-2.14—In cases where family members are in conflict with one another, we shall work openly, sharing our observations of the child, to help all parties involved make informed decisions. We shall refrain from becoming an advocate for one party.

P-2.15—We shall be familiar with and appropriately refer families to community resources and professional support services. After a referral has been made, we shall follow up to ensure that services have been appropriately provided.

SECTION III: ETHICAL RESPONSIBILITIES TO COLLEAGUES

In a caring, cooperative workplace, human dignity is respected, professional satisfaction is promoted, and positive relationships are developed and sustained. Based upon our core values, our primary responsibility to colleagues is to establish and maintain settings and relationships that support productive work and meet professional needs. The same ideals that apply to children also apply as we interact with adults in the workplace.

A—Responsibilities to co-workers
Ideals

I-3A.1—To establish and maintain relationships of respect, trust, confidentiality, collaboration, and cooperation with co-workers.

I-3A.2—To share resources with co-workers, collaborating to ensure that the best possible early childhood care and education program is provided.

I-3A.3—To support co-workers in meeting their professional needs and in their professional development.

I-3A.4—To accord co-workers due recognition of professional achievement.

Principles

P-3A.1—We shall recognize the contributions of colleagues to our program and not participate in practices that diminish their reputations or impair their effectiveness in working with children and families.

P-3A.2—When we have concerns about the professional behavior of a co-worker, we shall first let that person know of our concern in a way that shows respect for personal dignity and for the diversity to be found among staff members, and then attempt to resolve the matter collegially and in a confidential manner.

P-3A.3—We shall exercise care in expressing views regarding the personal attributes or professional conduct of co-workers. Statements should be based on firsthand knowledge, not hearsay, and relevant to the interests of children and programs.

P-3A.4—We shall not participate in practices that discriminate against a co-worker because of sex, race, national origin, religious beliefs or other affiliations, age, marital status/family structure, disability, or sexual orientation.

B—Responsibilities to employers
Ideals

I-3B.1—To assist the program in providing the highest quality of service.

I-3B.2—To do nothing that diminishes the reputation of the program in which we work unless it is violating laws and regulations designed to protect children or is violating the provisions of this Code.

Principles

P-3B.1—We shall follow all program policies. When we do not agree with program policies, we shall attempt to effect change through constructive action within the organization.

P-3B.2—We shall speak or act on behalf of an organization only when authorized. We shall take care to acknowledge when we are speaking for the organization and when we are expressing a personal judgment.

P-3B.3—We shall not violate laws or regulations designed to protect children and shall take appropriate action consistent with this Code when aware of such violations.

P-3B.4—If we have concerns about a colleague's behavior, and children's well-being is not at risk, we may address the concern with that individual. If children are at risk or the situation does not improve after it has been brought to the colleague's attention, we shall report the colleague's unethical or incompetent behavior to an appropriate authority.

P-3B.5—When we have a concern about circumstances or conditions that impact the quality of care and education within the program, we shall inform the program's administration or, when necessary, other appropriate authorities.

C—Responsibilities to employees
Ideals

I-3C.1—To promote safe and healthy working conditions and policies that foster mutual respect, cooperation, collaboration, competence, well-being, confidentiality, and self-esteem in staff members.

I-3C.2—To create and maintain a climate of trust and candor that will enable staff to speak and act in the best interests of children, families, and the field of early childhood care and education.

I-3C.3—To strive to secure adequate and equitable compensation (salary and benefits) for those who work with or on behalf of young children.

I-3C.4—To encourage and support continual development of employees in becoming more skilled and knowledgeable practitioners.

Principles

P-3C.1—In decisions concerning children and programs, we shall draw upon the education, training, experience, and expertise of staff members.

P-3C.2—We shall provide staff members with safe and supportive working conditions that honor confidences and permit them to carry out their responsibilities through fair performance evaluation, written grievance procedures, constructive feedback, and opportunities for continuing professional development and advancement.

P-3C.3—We shall develop and maintain comprehensive written personnel policies that define program standards. These policies shall be given to new staff members and shall be available and easily accessible for review by all staff members.

P-3C.4—We shall inform employees whose performance does not meet program expectations of areas of concern and, when possible, assist in improving their performance.

P-3C.5—We shall conduct employee dismissals for just cause, in accordance with all applicable laws and regulations. We shall inform employees who are dismissed of the reasons for their termination. When a dismissal is for cause, justification must be based on evidence of inadequate or inappropriate behavior that is accurately documented, current, and available for the employee to review.

P-3C.6—In making evaluations and recommendations, we shall make judgments based on fact and relevant to the interests of children and programs.

P-3C.7—We shall make hiring, retention, termination, and promotion decisions based solely on a person's competence, record of accomplishment, ability to carry out the responsibilities of the position, and professional preparation specific to the developmental levels of children in his/her care.

P-3C.8—We shall not make hiring, retention, termination, and promotion decisions based on an individual's sex, race, national origin, religious beliefs or other affiliations, age, marital status/family structure, disability, or sexual orientation. We shall be familiar with and observe laws and regulations that pertain to employment discrimination. (Aspects of this principle do not apply to programs that have a lawful mandate to determine eligibility based on one or more of the criteria identified above.)

P-3C.9—We shall maintain confidentiality in dealing with issues related to an employee's job performance and shall respect an employee's right to privacy regarding personal issues.

✳ SECTION IV: ETHICAL RESPONSIBILITIES TO COMMUNITY AND SOCIETY

Early childhood programs operate within the context of their immediate community made up of families and other institutions concerned with children's welfare. Our responsibilities to the community are to provide programs that meet the diverse needs of families, to cooperate with agencies and professions that share the responsibility for children, to assist families in gaining access to those agencies and allied professionals, and to assist in the development of community programs that are needed but not currently available.

As individuals, we acknowledge our responsibility to provide the best possible programs of care and education for children and to conduct ourselves with honesty and integrity. Because of our specialized expertise in early childhood development and education and because the larger society shares responsibility for the welfare and protection of young children, we acknowledge a collective obligation to advocate for the best interests of children within early childhood programs and in the larger community and to serve as a voice for young children everywhere.

The ideals and principles in this section are presented to distinguish between those that pertain to the work of the individual early childhood educator and those that more typically are engaged in collectively on behalf of the best interests of children—with the understanding that individual early childhood educators have a shared responsibility for addressing the ideals and principles that are identified as "collective."

Ideal (Individual)

1-4.1—To provide the community with high-quality early childhood care and education programs and services.

Ideals (Collective)

I-4.2—To promote cooperation among professionals and agencies and interdisciplinary collaboration among professions concerned with addressing issues in the health, education, and well-being of young children, their families, and their early childhood educators.

I-4.3—To work through education, research, and advocacy toward an environmentally safe world in which all children receive health care, food, and shelter; are nurtured; and live free from violence in their home and their communities.

I-4.4—To work through education, research, and advocacy toward a society in which all young children have access to high-quality early care and education programs.

I-4.5—To work to ensure that appropriate assessment systems, which include multiple sources of information, are used for purposes that benefit children.

I-4.6—To promote knowledge and understanding of young children and their needs. To work toward greater societal acknowledgment of children's rights and greater social acceptance of responsibility for the well-being of all children.

I-4.7—To support policies and laws that promote the well-being of children and families, and to work to change those that impair their well-being. To participate in developing policies and laws that are needed, and to cooperate with other individuals and groups in these efforts.

I-4.8—To further the professional development of the field of early childhood care and education and to strengthen its commitment to realizing its core values as reflected in this Code.

Principles (Individual)

P-4.1—We shall communicate openly and truthfully about the nature and extent of services that we provide.

P-4.2—We shall apply for, accept, and work in positions for which we are personally well-suited and professionally qualified. We shall not offer services that we do not have the competence, qualifications, or resources to provide.

P-4.3—We shall carefully check references and shall not hire or recommend for employment any person whose competence, qualifications, or character makes him or her unsuited for the position.

P-4.4—We shall be objective and accurate in reporting the knowledge upon which we base our program practices.

P-4.5—We shall be knowledgeable about the appropriate use of assessment strategies and instruments and interpret results accurately to families.

P-4.6—We shall be familiar with laws and regulations that serve to protect the children in our programs and be vigilant in ensuring that these laws and regulations are followed.

P-4.7—When we become aware of a practice or situation that endangers the health, safety, or well-being of children, we have an ethical responsibility to protect children or inform parents and/or others who can.

P-4.8—We shall not participate in practices that are in violation of laws and regulations that protect the children in our programs.

P-4.9—When we have evidence that an early childhood program is violating laws or regulations protecting children, we shall report the violation to appropriate authorities who can be expected to remedy the situation.

P-4.10—When a program violates or requires its employees to violate this Code, it is permissible, after fair assessment of the evidence, to disclose the identity of that program.

Principles (Collective)

P-4.11—When policies are enacted for purposes that do not benefit children, we have a collective responsibility to work to change these practices.

P-4.12—When we have evidence that an agency that provides services intended to ensure children's well-being is failing to meet its obligations, we acknowledge a collective ethical responsibility to report the problem to appropriate authorities or to the public. We shall be vigilant in our follow-up until the situation is resolved.

P-4.13—When a child protection agency fails to provide adequate protection for abused or neglected children, we acknowledge a collective ethical responsibility to work toward the improvement of these services.

STATEMENT OF COMMITMENT*

As an individual who works with young children, I commit myself to furthering the values of early childhood education as they are reflected in the ideals and principles of the NAEYC Code of Ethical Conduct. To the best of my ability I will

- Never harm children.

- Ensure that programs for young children are based on current knowledge and research of child development and early childhood education.

- Respect and support families in their task of nurturing children.

- Respect colleagues in early childhood care and education and support them in maintaining the NAEYC Code of Ethical Conduct.

- Serve as an advocate for children, their families, and their teachers in community and society.

- Stay informed of and maintain high standards of professional conduct.

- Engage in an ongoing process of self-reflection, realizing that personal characteristics, biases, and beliefs have an impact on children and families.

- Be open to new ideas and be willing to learn from the suggestions of others.

- Continue to learn, grow, and contribute as a professional.

- Honor the ideals and principles of the NAEYC Code of Ethical Conduct.

*This Statement of Commitment is not part of the Code but is a personal acknowledgment of the individual's willingness to embrace the distinctive values and moral obligations of the field of early childhood care and education. It is recognition of the moral obligations that lead to an individual becoming part of the profession.

Reprinted, with permission, from the National Association for the Education of Young Children.

NAEYC Position Statement: Responding to Linguistic and Cultural Diversity—Recommendations for Effective Early Childhood Education

This is a summary of the Position Statement adopted by NAEYC; it is recommended that the Statement be read in its entirety. It can be accessed on the website http://www.naeyc.org.

❋ INTRODUCTION

The children and families in early childhood programs reflect the ethnic, cultural, and linguistic diversity of the nation. The nation's children all deserve an early childhood education that is responsive to their families, communities, and racial, ethnic, and cultural backgrounds. For young children to develop and learn optimally, the early childhood professional must be prepared to meet their diverse developmental, cultural, linguistic, and educational needs. Early childhood educators face the challenge of how best to respond to those needs. . . .

Linguistic and culturally diverse is an educational term used by the U.S. Department of Education to define children enrolled in educational programs who are either non-English-proficient (NEP) or limited-English-proficient (LEP). Educators use this phrase, linguistically and culturally diverse, to identify children from homes and communities where English is not the primary language of communication. For the purposes of this statement, the phrase will be used in a similar manner. . . .

NAEYC's position. NAEYC's goal is to build support for equal access to high-quality educational programs that recognize and promote all aspects of children's development and learning, establish all children to become competent, successful, and socially responsible adults. . . . For the optimal development and learning of all children, educators must accept the legitimacy of children's home language, respect (hold in high regard) and value (esteem, appreciate) the home culture, and promote and encourage the active involvement and support of all families, including extended and nontraditional family units. . . .

The challenges. Historically, our nation has tended to regard differences, especially language differences, as cultural handicaps rather than cultural resources. "Although most Americans are reluctant to say it publicly, many are anxious about the changing racial and ethnic composition of the country." As the early childhood profession transforms its thinking,

The challenge for early childhood educators is to become more knowledgeable about how to relate to children and families whose linguistic or cultural background is different from their own.

RECOMMENDATIONS FOR A RESPONSIVE LEARNING ENVIRONMENT

The issue of home language and its importance to young children is also relevant for children who speak English but come from different cultural backgrounds, for example, speakers of English who have dialects, such as people from Appalachia or other regions having distinct patterns of speech, speakers of Black English, or second- and third-generation speakers of English who maintain the dominant accent of their heritage language. Although this position statement basically responds to children who are from homes in which English is not the dominant language, the recommendations provided may be helpful when working with children who come from diverse cultural backgrounds, even when they speak only English. The overall goal for early childhood professionals, however, is to provide every child, including children who are linguistically and culturally diverse, with a responsive learning environment. The following recommendations help achieve this goal:

A. Recommendations for working with children

- Recognize that all children are cognitively, linguistically, and emotionally connected to the language and culture of their home.

- Acknowledge that children can demonstrate their knowledge and capabilities in many ways.

- Understand that without comprehensive input, second-language learning can be difficult.

B. Recommendations for working with families

- Actively involve parents and families in the early learning program and setting.

- Encourage and assist all parents in becoming knowledgeable about the cognitive value for children of knowing more than one language, and provide them with strategies to support, maintain, and preserve home-language learning.

- Recognize that parents and families must rely on caregivers and educators to honor and support their children in the cultural values and norms of the home.

C. Recommendations for professional preparation

- Provide early childhood educators with professional preparation and development in the areas of culture, language, and diversity.

- Recruit and support early childhood educators who are trained in languages other than English.

D. Recommendations for programs and practice

- Recognize that children can and will acquire the use of English even when their home language is used and respected.

- Support and preserve home language usage.

- Develop and provide alternative and creative strategies for young children's learning.

✿ SUMMARY

Early childhood educators can best help linguistic and culturally diverse children and their families by acknowledging and responding to the importance of the child's home language and culture. Administrative support for bilingualism as a goal is necessary within the educational setting. Educational practices should focus on "school culture" while preserving and respecting the diversity of the home language and culture that each child brings to the early learning setting. Early childhood professionals and families must work together to achieve high-quality care and education for *all* children.

index

D